War

Patterns of Conflict

The MIT Press   Cambridge, Massachusetts, and London, England

War

Patterns of Conflict

Richard E. Barringer

with the collaboration
of Robert K. Ramers

and a foreword
by Quincy Wright

Library of Congress Cataloging in Publication Data

Barringer, Richard E
  War: patterns of conflict.
  "An earlier version . . . [entitled The conditions of conflict: a configural
analysis] was submitted as a doctoral dissertation to the Department
of Political Science at M.I.T."
  Bibliography: p.
  1. War I. Ramers, Robert K. II. Title.
U21.2.B36 1972   301.6'334   78-123249
ISBN 0-262-02-068-8

Contents

Tables

Figures

List of the Established Conditions of Conflict

		Critical Factor Pattern	Complete Factor Pattern
Conflict (Prehostilities)			
Composite scenario	"stakes not yet worth the candle to all (un)concerned"	102	
Type C1	"an insurgent order in search of a sponsor"	105	211
Type C2	"great-power interests do not yet prevail"	106	213
Type C3	"moderation prevails till accommodation fails"	106	214
Type C4	"the prospect of compromise not yet foreclosed"	106	215
Type C5	"present commitments bid fair an acceptable outcome"	107	216
Type C6	"reason and stability precede the intrusion of ideology"	107	218
Type C7	"no threat to survival is yet discerned"	107	219
Hostilities			
Composite scenario	"accommodation falters on the prospect of sponsorship"	104	
Type H1	"commitment hardens as accommodation fails"	108	227
Type H2	"revolt of the dispossessed in a 'moderate' system"	109	229
Type H3	"taking advantage of the moment"	109	230
Type H4	"exploratory probe in a continuing confrontation"	109	231
Type H5	"my big brother can lick yours; or, what are guns for, anyway?"	110	232
Type H6	"a new conductor, a new arrangement"	110	233
Type H7	"grist for the great-power mill"	110	234
Type H8	"the injection of ideology"	110	235
Escalation			
Composite scenario	"commitments too great to turn back now"	113	
Type E1	"acting with the presumption of immunity"	117	241
Type E2	"diplomacy fails amid unacceptable losses"	117	241
Type E3	"toward a foregone conclusion in proxy conflict"	117	242
Type E4	"reacting to the manifest: expedition and aversion"	118	243

Foreword

In this book Richard Barringer has made a contribution to the study of international conflict by devising a new method of classifying empirical data to characterize conflict and its stages of development, with results of considerable predictive value.

Historians have long applied experienced judgments to appraise the relative importance of factors — quantitative and qualitative, objective and subjective — thought to contribute to the initiation and escalation of international conflicts and to their termination and settlement. Social scientists have sought to make such judgments more objective by correlating statistical series or by formulating equations indicating the relations of variables sufficiently objective to be tested by available data.

The technique of "agreement analysis" developed in this study differs significantly, however, from the common correlational techniques such as factor analysis. It starts from the author's premise that events, particularly human events, cannot usually be attributed to single causes, nor does a single cause usually contribute an ascertainable degree of probability that the event will occur. Rather, an event is the consequence of a particular conjunction of many factors. Agreement analysis establishes types of events manifesting the conjunction of many factors, as does a species of animals. These types or species may be further grouped into genera, families, orders, and classes having successively fewer factors or traits in common.

This technique is applied to a model that formalizes the normal course of conflict from a dispute in which the use of force is not contemplated by either of the parties involved, to a conflict in which diplomacy or discussion seems to be stalemated and one party — or both — considers the alternative of force and prepares to use it, and then to hostilities during which force is employed. Hostilities may escalate or de-escalate until terminated and perhaps a settlement of the dispute is achieved. The model assumes that the transition from one of these stages to another is marked by a definite threshold indicating a change in the "rules of the game." Agreement analysis is applied to define the conditions accounting for the onset of each of these thresholds.

Barringer has defined 300 factors, some geographic or demographic and some economic, political, or military, reflecting the state of relations between the parties and their perceptions of those relations. By elaborate mathematical computations, conjunctures of 50 to 100 of these factors are found to establish species types conditioning the threshold of prehostilities conflict in eighteen selected conflict situations. Most of these cases

Author's note: Quincy Wright died in October 1970 and did not see the final, edited version of this foreword. It is presented here with minor editorial changes from his original manuscript with the kind permission of Mrs. Louise Wright.

occurred after World War II. They include eight international conflicts in three of which a great power was a party, four colonial conflicts in one of which a great power was the metropole, and six initially civil conflicts in three of which a great power intervened. In the same way, types of conjuncture conditioning the thresholds of hostilities, escalation, de-escalation, termination, and settlement are determined. (No attempt was made to determine the conjuncture of factors conditioning the earliest initiation of a dispute.) Seven types of conjuncture are identified that conditioned conflicts in the eighteen cases studied; eight conditioned hostilities, four escalation, four de-escalation, seven termination, and three settlement. Genera, families, orders, and classes of factors conditioning these thresholds are also established, with more generality, fewer factors, and less reliability.

Each species is characterized by two or more of the eighteen cases that exhibited all of the factors establishing the type. It is not easy, however, to characterize these types in simple terms. The author characterizes hostilities, Type 1, exemplified by the Cyprus insurgency of 1955 and the Malayan insurgency of 1948, as "commitment hardens as accommodation fails"; and hostilities, Type 4, exemplified by the Chinese invasion of India in 1962 and the Iranian invasion of Azerbaidzhan in 1946, as an "exploratory probe in a continuing confrontation."

To test the predictive value of his method the author applied it to the Vietnam situation on March 15, 1967, treating the Saigon government and the National Liberation Front (Viet Cong) as the principal parties, with North Vietnam and the United States, and to a lesser extent China and the Soviet Union, as interveners. At this date the Vietnam situation corresponded 92 percent to the escalation "composite scenario" characterized as "commitments too great to turn back now"; 63 percent to the de-escalation "composite scenario" characterized as "retreat while one may for a better day"; 24 percent to the termination "composite scenario" characterized as "accommodating to the fact of a stabilized imbalance"; and not at all to the settlement scenario characterized as "being left alone to realize the inevitable." The expectation, therefore, was escalation for a time. Change of a few factors might bring about a de-escalation, and of more factors a termination, of hostilities; but permanent settlement seemed highly remote. These conclusions seem reasonable, but it is clear that no method can make precise predictions, and some skeptics may question whether the complicated data manipulations of agreement analysis add much to what an experienced observer of the Vietnam situation might have concluded. However, the result undoubtedly fortifies a subjective conclusion.

Application of the method suggests that both escalation and de-escalation may "best be viewed as alternative reactions to the considerable costs and enormous risks of hostilities. Escalation is an attempt on the one hand to expedite and on the other to avert what is rapidly becoming, if it has not already become, an obvious outcome of the conflict. De-escalation, alternatively, follows when at least one of the antagonists feels that he may, without irreversibly jeopardizing his position, alter his objectives, reduce the level of activity in pursuit of his continuing objectives, or broaden the political framework within which hostilities are conducted, for example, by introducing negotiations."

Similarly, the results suggest that the development of local disputes, whether internal or international, into conflicts and hostilities is in large measure due to the influence or the intervention of great powers, whether ostensibly for humanitarian purposes or in pursuit of economic or political interests. Furthermore, this intervention increases the danger of escalation of conflicts into major, even nuclear, hostilities. It appears that if the great powers observed their obligations under international law and the United Nations Charter to refrain from the use or threat of force in international relations and from unilateral intervention in the domestic affairs of other states (Article 2, paragraphs 4 and 7), the lesser nations would usually be able to solve their internal and external problems without serious hostilities, and mankind would enjoy a more peaceful and less dangerous world. There is also evidence that United Nations action, which is permissible only if the dispute or situation "is likely to endanger the maintenance of international peace and security" (Articles 33 and 34) is usually too late to have a moderating effect. Little attention is given here, however, to the conditions that have frequently made a United Nations cease-fire effective at least for a time, in contrast to the lesser frequency of United Nations success in bringing about a permanent settlement of the dispute.

The method developed in this study is complicated, and whether it can produce more reliable predictions than other methods using fewer factors and more subjective judgments can only be determined after it has been applied to a larger number of cases. As the method recognizes, however, it seems probable that the major factors initiating and escalating disputes, conflicts, and hostilities are not so much objective circumstances or capabilities as subjective perceptions by the parties of the importance of the interests involved; of relative capabilities and costs, immediate and potential; of the probable action of allies and of international organizations reflecting world opinion; and of the probable outcome of alternative actions. Such perceptions may differ greatly between the parties and may have little relation to objective facts as seen by an impartial observer or as determined by mathematical models.

"Wars are made in the minds of men," as declared in the UNESCO Constitution. It is the perception not only of future probabilities but of the present situation in the minds of leaders and peoples, not the situation itself, that is the source of action. No mathematical manipulation of numerous, purely objective factors can accurately disclose these unstable perceptions. They are affected by imperfect information, distorting prejudices, wishful thinking, and various personality attributes. Even less can pat formulas accurately predict the response of persons or governments to their perception of the situation. While often automatic, determined by habit, the response may be influenced by capricious impulse, personality bias, or rational consideration of consequences. As L. F. Richardson pointed out, his formulas for predicting the course of arms races would be valid only if people behaved automatically and "did not stop to think" (*Statistics of Deadly Quarrels*, ed. Quincy Wright and C. C. Lienau [Pittsburgh, Pa.: Boxwood Press, 1960], p. 11).

Scientific method is not likely to gain the triumphs in human affairs that it has in less complicated orders of nature, but it undoubtedly can advance understanding, even of that most complicated order: international relations. Mr. Barringer's monumental effort to reduce the course of international conflicts to systematic terms deserves study and comparison with other methods.

Quincy Wright

Norwich, Vermont
July 1970

Preface

Many friends and colleagues have played a part in the production of this book. Let me beg the reader's momentary indulgence to mention just a few to whom my especial thanks are due.

This is a first book. And as it may not come again, I must take this opportunity to acknowledge the two great teachers with whom I have been blessed, Sister Mary Ulicia O'Brien, O.P., and Henry J. Landau: she, for suggesting the scholarly discipline and he, the sheer joy, of learning.

The book is a report on original research. As the reader will soon learn, it is not one whose understanding comes easily. Nor did its conception. The ideas and techniques upon which it builds required lengthy and constant consideration, discussion, criticism, and revision before reaching their present form and use. Throughout the technique-building stage of the research, Robert K. Ramers labored with extraordinary competence and devotion as its sounding board, critic, and collaborator. As the reader will recognize, his assistance in the development of agreement analysis and in the preparation of the computer programs was especially indispensable.

The computer programs and instructions for their use, together with the revised edition of the conflict data codebook that resulted from the research, are contained in a separate technical manual for this book issued simultaneously by the M.I.T. Press. The programs were written by Mr. Ramers for use on the equipment of the M.I.T. Computation Center, although they are by no means restricted to it. I am pleased to acknowledge the assistance of the Center's personnel and the contribution of their facilities to this study.

The empirical data for the research were gathered and prepared with the assistance of Robert Bates, Ralph Brown, Priscilla Clapp, R. Lucas Fischer, Janet Fraser, Edward C. Gude, Stanley Heginbotham, Jane K. Holland, Amelia C. Leiss, Richard H. Moore, Robert K. Ramers, Philip Raup, and Barton S. Whaley. Theirs was an extraordinarily difficult but indispensable task, well performed. And if I may, I would like to single out Colonel Brown, Lucas Fischer, Janet Fraser, Barton Whaley, and Colonel Moore and his staff at the Center for Research on Social Systems, The American University, for contributions and commitments that far exceeded any reasonable expectation. May they prosper!

The book is based in part upon research prepared under a contract from the United States Arms Control and Disarmament Agency. (Of course, the judgments expressed here are my own and do not necessarily reflect the views of any department or agency of the United States government.) The contract was to the Arms Control Project directed by Lincoln P. Bloomfield at the

Center for International Studies, M.I.T. I am grateful to Professor Bloomfield for his faithful support of that research, for his assistance in its execution, and for his advice on an earlier version of this manuscript, which was submitted as a doctoral dissertation to the Department of Political Science at M.I.T. The book was completed while the author was a research fellow of the Institute of Politics in the Kennedy School of Government, Harvard University. I am deeply obliged to Richard E. Neustadt, Director of the Institute, for affording me the time, resources, and freedom that were required to translate an exotic research document to a book worthy of a public.

That translation, in fact, quite defied the author's abilities for well over a year until the patience, discipline, and skill of Mrs. Jean P. S. Clark were mercifully applied to the manuscript. If I am the parent of this book, she surely is its midwife. Ulrike Hochreiter Bigelow typed the original manuscript and made contributions to its style and content in ways that raised the medium of clerical assistance to an expressive art form. Sally von Rumohr and Christina O'Bryan, each in her own way, carried that tradition on through the translation stage, and I am in their debt.

So, too, am I responsible for all the sins — of commission and omission alike — that follow the title. It is Colum Murphy's.

Richard Barringer

Cambridge, Massachusetts
May 1971

for Walter and Helen and for Sandy
for making the best of it

Friar Giovanni,
1604

"No peace lies in the future which is not hidden in this present
instant. Take Peace! . . . We are pilgrims together, wending
through unknown country, home."

War

Patterns of Conflict

1　Causation and Conflict

In its accepted legal sense as recognized by international law under the United Nations Charter, there has been no war among men since September 2, 1945, the date of the articles of Imperial Japanese surrender ending World War II. As one deliberate, if crude, means by which political factions, organizations, and governments seek their established ends, however, war has scarcely ceased to exist. Rather, as with all man-made institutions, its conceptualization and codification in the law have simply lagged behind its evolution in fact. In point of fact, if not of law, war has assumed new forms more appropriate to the present era and its predominant features and conditions.

In another era, when the industrial revolution was as yet in embryo, the great German military theorist Karl von Clausewitz observed that

each age has had its own peculiar forms of war, its own restrictive conditions, and its own prejudices. Each, therefore, would also keep its own theory of war, even if everywhere, in early times as well as in later, there had been an inclination to work it out on philosophical principles. The events in each age must, therefore, be judged with due regard to the peculiarities of the time, and only he who, less by anxious study of minute details than by a shrewd glance at the main features can place himself in each particular age, is able to understand and appreciate its generals.[1]

The industrial revolution has now come to maturity, having itself given birth to a new age containing, in almost absurdly Hegelian fashion, the seeds not only of its own dialectical destruction but even of its cataclysmic extermination. And it contains these in increasing numbers.

This is the central, extraordinary fact of this age, setting human history forevermore apart, in a quantum sense, from what has gone before. One might well expect nuclear weapons, then, to be central to the forms of war peculiar to the present and to the prejudices and restrictive conditions that have and will come to apply to warfare in the last decades of the twentieth century. Indeed, their development has shaped and reshaped national policies, both foreign and domestic. It has forged alliances and undermined them. It has directed and redirected unparalleled resources into research and development of the weapons systems and combat capabilities that follow from the prevailing estimates of the implications of nuclear capability.

Thus, somewhat in the fashion of a strategic reaction formation, the development of Soviet nuclear and hydrogen warfare capabilities was followed by a vast literature on the tactical and strategic problems of limited Soviet–United States military confrontations, especially in Western Europe;[2] on the conditions for their

[1]Karl von Clausewitz, *On War*, trans. O. J. Matthijs Jolles (Washington, D.C.: Infantry Journal Press, 1950), p. 584.
[2]See Morton H. Halperin, *Limited War in the Nuclear Age* (New York: John Wiley & Sons, 1963), Annotated Bibliography, pp. 133–184.

escalation to general nuclear war;[3] and on both the defense measures and the arms control concepts therefore relevant to the United States position in the prevailing international setting.[4] For what could have been more reasonable than to expect that, if these two avowed ideological antagonists were to become involved in a general war, the clash would occur in Central Europe where their continuing armed confrontation was most immediate.

Events in the past decade have made it abundantly clear, however, that general war is far less likely to result from abrasive action in areas of direct confrontation between the great powers than from a series of limited and seemingly rational intensifications of a local conflict in an area of peripheral great-power influence. Such are the conditions of this age that, as increasing détente has been achieved in Europe amid economic prosperity and the nuclear stalemate, events in the "underdeveloped" or "third" world have increasingly embroiled the great powers directly and indirectly in proxy wars for spheres of influence. The war in what was Indochina, for example, has tended steadily and relentlessly, as do all protracted wars, toward its total and absolute expression within existing technological limits.[5] That conflict in particular bears witness to the fact that the present age has spawned its own peculiar form of warfare, one as different from the great interstate conflicts of this century as these were from their own pre-Napoleonic forebears.

In an evolutionary sense, the world wars of this century represent the ultimate, mature expression of their genre: the general war between discrete, legally definable combatants, fought in a specified geographic arena until the outcome was fixed by the relative capacities of the combatants for mobilization, production, and administration of their resources. Now, the postindustrial era "overkill" capabilities have produced a mode of warfare in which, as often as not, the combat zone itself, the sources and avenues of supply, the center of administrative and policy decision, the identity and allegiance of both civilian and military personnel, and the nature and substance of victory defy precise specification and definition. The efficacy of this form of warfare, even in the face of superpower opposition, is now being attested in Vietnam, where the irrelevance and inadequacy of many assumptions deriving from the traditional interstate conflict have long since been demonstrated by U.S. forces.

In a study undertaken in the early 1950s of the conditions per-

---

[3]See Herman Kahn, *On Escalation: Metaphors and Scenarios* (New York: Hudson Institute, 1965).
[4]See Ernest W. Lefever, ed., *Arms and Arms Control: A Symposium* (New York: Frederick A. Praeger, 1962), Bibliography, pp. 313–331.
[5]See Quincy Wright, "The Nature of Conflict," *Western Political Quarterly*, vol. 4, no. 2 (June 1951), pp. 202–203, for a general discussion of this point.

taining in both world wars, Klaus Knorr found "the determinants of potential military power" to be divisible into three broad categories: the will to fight (that is, motivation or morale), administrative competence, and economic capacity. "The margin of combat superiority which accounts for victory," Knorr suggests, may be provided by any, or any combination, of the constituents of military strength, qualitative or quantitative. Yet . . . no net superiority in qualitative attributes can in the longer run make up for a substantial inferiority in the quantity of military manpower and equipment, provided the theater of war permits these to be put to efficient use.[6]

In contemporary and future conflicts that conform more or less to the traditional interstate pattern, it is likely that such statements will remain accurate: numbers and their effective administration will be decisive in any prolonged engagement. The accuracy and hence utility of this easy paradigm is increasingly less clear, however, in a combat situation in which the time, place, and terms of confrontation are not at the discretion of both combatants. If these are always determined by one combatant, his will to survive may well outweigh and outlast any numerical and logistic superiority of his adversary. But even this situation is likely to occur only under certain conditions; that is, will or morale in and of itself is obviously inadequate in the face of superpower logistic capabilities. Clearly, there are certain enabling conditions under which this factor is likely to be of decisive importance in achieving victory, and others in which it may well be of little relevance to the eventual outcome of hostilities.

This study is founded upon precisely this kind of reasoning— that under different conditions the very same act or the very same fact may produce quite a different result. It proceeds from that proposition in the belief that the analysis and understanding of warfare in a new age demand new concepts and new techniques if any extrapolations are to be made from past experience to future situations and events.

A New Direction for Analysis It is especially ironic, given a scientific and technological establishment capable of producing our present means of war, that the study of war itself—at other than the tactical level—has remained a largely subjective, impressionistic, and unscientific affair. Over a decade ago, this century's preeminent student of war, surveying the requirements for a systematic and continuing program of research on war as an instrument of policy, cited the overriding need,

first, to develop an analysis which appears to be comprehensive and fundamental, and then to select for detailed study conflict situations concerning which there is data on all the factors which the analysis considers relevant. Comparison of the cases thus analyzed should throw light on the classification of various types

[6]Klaus Knorr, *The War Potential of Nations* (Princeton: Princeton University Press, 1956), pp. 3, 31.

of conflict situations, on the probable course of development of each of these types, and on the stages in the course of the conflict situations studied at which different actions might have changed the course of development. Reciprocally, the study of a considerable number of conflict situations of varied types should throw light on the analysis, indicating relevant factors which have been omitted, and facilitating its continuous improvement.[7]

In a time of revolutionary developments in the technology of warfare, this was a plea for the establishment of the basis for a rigorous, scientific approach to the study of war, the conditions from which it is likely to emerge, the directions it is likely to follow, and the likely agents of its aggravation and amelioration. It was a declaration that the time had arrived for a mode of inquiry free from the preconceptions and assumptions that had traditionally dominated these pursuits, for a temporary injunction in scholarship against the deductive method. It was a plea for the development and application of inductive techniques that might start from concrete reality to identify the significant features of war and so make it more intelligible, if not more predictable. It was, in effect, a call for a radical departure in one of civilized man's oldest and most persistent preoccupations—the study of war.

The aim of this study is to undertake and to establish just such a departure; to bring the methods of science and the hardware of its technology to bear in meaningful and revealing ways upon the structure and substance of conflicts harboring the potential for war. Its hopeful purpose is to construct an objective, systematic, and partially automated program of research to determine the patterns of factors that condition the origin, development, and termination of those conflicts; to explore the contexts within which individual factors operate with specified effects upon their development; to specify the resulting "types" of conflicts that occur in real life; and so perhaps better to understand and deal with their causes and effects as generic phenomena rather than as random, idiosyncratic events.

To this end an analytic system comprised of an integrated and novel set of assumptions, concepts, and techniques has been developed around the requirements and objectives of the "comprehensive and fundamental analysis" called for by Wright. However, where Wright sought a precise statement of the points in the development of conflicts at which policy measures might be taken to alter their development, as well as of the specific policy measures that might achieve this effect, my aim is more modest. Indeed, it is my contention, like that of Clausewitz, that a theory need not be a body of positive rules; that is to say, it need not be a guide to action. Whenever an activity has, for the most part, continually to do with the same things, with the same ends

[7]Quincy Wright, "Memorandum on Interstate Conflicts," paper prepared for the Carnegie Endowment for International Peace, New York, December 1955.

and means, although with small differences and a corresponding variety of combinations, these things must be capable of becoming an object of observation by reason. . . . If principles and rules result of themselves from the observations that theory institutes, if the truth of itself crystallizes into these forms, then these principles and rules serve more to determine in the reflecting mind the leading outlines of its accustomed movements than, like signposts, to point the way for it to take in execution.[8]

Rather than a concise policy maker's guide to action in every conflict situation, then, the object here has been to elaborate what might at the most practical level become an "early warning system" for conflict at each significant stage of its development. That goal was pursued by extracting sets of predictive factor patterns from a limited number of historical conflicts through the medium of an analytic system designed specifically for application to today's forms of warfare. At the same time, this effort was experimental and proceeded on the basis of a very limited number of case studies. The analytic system employed was accordingly designed specifically to accommodate the increased number of case studies required to give increased statistical comprehensiveness, precision, and confidence to its results. In this sense, the set of assumptions, concepts, and techniques presented may be regarded as both experimental and expandable.

Before they are elaborated, we may well observe with a prominent student of the subject that among the many theories of conflict "a main dividing line is between those that treat conflict as a pathological state and seek its causes and treatment, and those that take conflict for granted and study the behavior associated with it."[9] With a few notable — and generally maligned — exceptions, the former has traditionally been the more prevalent mode of analysis. As a result, the existing literature on causation and, therefore, on appropriate treatment far outnumbers the rest. In this regard, it is perhaps no longer possible either to discover or to hypothesize a specific cause or underlying source of war that has not previously been cataloged.

Most social scientists have long since accepted the principle of multiple causation, from which it follows that any explanation of armed conflict in terms of a single factor — economic competition, lebensraum, or externalization of internal frustrations — represents a gross oversimplification that is likely to lead to ill-conceived policy action. Indeed, this charge may be leveled at any theory that is comprised of even a few such factors and therefore relegates all the other conditions surrounding the conflict event or outcome to a large and residual category of "other factors." These elements in the causal equation are regarded as both too numerous and too complex to be dealt with explicitly by the theory and are, accordingly, assumed to remain constant

[8]Clausewitz, *On War*, pp. 76–77.
[9]Thomas C. Schelling, *The Strategy of Conflict* (Cambridge, Mass.: Harvard University Press, 1963), p. 3.

for purposes of the main theoretical analysis. Their policy implications in any particular real-life case are left to the intuition and judgment of the analyst. In real life, however, "other things" rarely remain constant. Rather, they are in a constant state of flux with respect to the relationships they bear both to each other and to the factors explicitly accounted for in the theory. Thus they impose rigorous limitations upon specific, concrete generalizations from theory and overwhelming risks upon policy conclusions or practical applications.

All of the classical theories of politics—from Plato to Machiavelli, Marx, and Pareto—may be cited as examples in this regard. All are founded upon essentially deterministic models comprised of a very few variables that are cited as causes. All other factors are regarded as too numerous and too complex in their effects to be dealt with explicitly in the theory, but also as too important to be completely disregarded. While their existence and potential for effect upon the output of the causal model are recognized, their influence as individuals and as a whole is left undefined. This, it may be said, is the equivalent of establishing a logical tree with only its trunk and principal branches defined; the fine and delicate network of secondary and tertiary branches that lend beauty, body, and form to a tree—and, in the case of a theory, practical applicability—are left out. Their existence is recognized; their precise effect is ignored.

Wright observed this fact and established as the "basic conception" of his monumental study of the origins of war the notion that peace is a condition of equilibrium among numerous factors: military, legal, social, political, economic, technological, and psychic.[10] In this view, war is both the result of serious disturbances in this equilibrium and a means for restoring it. After examining the massive body of evidence in support of this conception, he concluded that

wars arise because of the changing relations of numerous variables—technological, psychic, social, and intellectual. There is no single cause of war. Peace is an equilibrium among many forces. Change in any one particular force, trend, movement, or policy may at one time make for war but under other conditions a similar change may make for peace. . . . To estimate the probability of war at any time, therefore, involves an appraisal of the effect of current changes upon the complex of intergroup relationships throughout the world.[11]

While an equally strong case might be made for the argument that war is not such an aberrational[12] state of affairs but is itself a differing (albeit more infrequent) equilibrium among the same network of factors, Wright's conception of the complex, structural nature of events is illuminating. Having strived to avoid the

[10]Quincy Wright, *A Study of War*, 2nd ed. (Chicago: University of Chicago Press, 1964), pp. 68–69.
[11]Ibid., p. 1284.
[12]Ibid., p. 12. Wright himself uses the term "abnormal" in this connection.

pitfalls of oversimplification of an enormously complex phenomenon, however, he was forced to recognize the fact that non-impressionistic techniques adequate for the systematic manipulation of the number of variables he knew to be operating were not available. He thus confronted what another leading student of international politics and processes has more recently termed the dilemma of social science analysis: "While single-cause analysis is invalid, multiple causation is valid but too complex for scientific treatment, since it is not possible to follow in all their meanderings the *interrelations* among a large number of factors."[13]

The central problem in the development of an empirical theory adequate for the full richness of reality, then, is to determine the particular interconnected and mutually reinforcing combinations, constellations, patterns, or configurations of factors that result in the analytic preconditions of an event or outcome. In short, the effect of the recognition of multiple causality is that the important questions for analysis become the determination not of the influence of particular factors but of the way in which mutual reinforcement operates to create an effectual or enabling pattern. Similarly, the overriding question for policy becomes the determination of the critical or strategic factors that will alter the existing pattern to produce a desired or preferred outcome. For, given a determinate set of factors that define the system in which an event occurs, the difference between an existing and a desired outcome is the difference between the factor patterns that condition their occurrence as distinct (if not independent) events.

This conception of the relationship between multiple causation and patterns of factors constituting the systematic and enabling preconditions of an event is the methodological touchstone of this study. Moreover, it is assumed that, although conflict may be the ordained order of things, conflict of such a magnitude as to involve the possibility of war is not a random (or even frequent) phenomenon and is conditioned in its development by various configurations of particular values of a determinate set of variables. The causes of such conflict are, in effect, both multiple and systematic.

It is my central hypothesis, therefore, that certain precise patterns of factors exist that variously condition the origin, development, and termination of conflict harboring the potential for war; that the factors comprising these conditions are not purely military in nature but are at once social, political, economic, technological, military, and psychological; and, finally, that these conditions may be systematically observed and usefully isolated by objective analytic techniques. It is hypothesized, in effect, that the world in which peace and war occur is not only a complex but also a

[13]Stanley Hoffmann, *The State of War* (New York: Frederick A. Praeger, 1965), p. 273; emphasis added.

comprehensible system of structural parts or variables, and that changes in the state of that system are occasioned by observable shifts in the structural interconnections among the variables. In this view, both peace and war may be regarded as differing equilibria among various values and combinations of the same variables that define the system in which peace and war occur equally, if with differing frequency.

The question remains, however, how such propositions may be analyzed and tested, especially in light of the traditionally frustrating problem of establishing the significant networks of structural patterns that reside among a large set of variables. To that end, a provisional and eclectic theory of conflict, a descriptive model of its significant stages, a technique of data collection, and a method of data manipulation, analysis, and presentation have been developed. Each proceeded hand in hand with the others, imposing in its turn various assumptions, demands, and limitations upon the others, even while itself being selected and refined specifically to complement and accommodate the others. The result, it is felt, is a set of concepts, assumptions, and techniques so integrated and complementary in terms of the analytic objective as to constitute a whole. For purposes of clarity of presentation, I shall make brief note here of the research strategy followed and of the purpose and requirements of each analytic element before it is presented separately and in detail.

Assumptions and Assertions

In the formulation of both the strategy and the tactics of this study, the dominant consideration has been that war and the potential for war simply *are* and, so long as the means for war exist, will be. No amount of institutional safeguards will alter this fact; these devices are merely its evidence. Whenever policy makers feel both constrained with respect to alternative policy options and convinced of its cost effectiveness with respect to established goals, war may reasonably be expected to ensue. Man's capacity for rationalization in the face of any amount of contradictory evidence is such that, once the objective is determined to be worth the candle, sufficient justification will always be found for war.

The increasing urgency of the problem of war in this nuclear age, however, derives from the profound fact that it is

not a delicate instrument for achieving precise political ends. It is a crude instrument of coercion and persuasion. The violence and destruction of war set off a chain of consequences that can be neither perfectly controlled nor perfectly anticipated, and that may therefore contravene the best laid plans for achieving specific configurations of power and particular political relations among nations.[14]

Regardless of one's purpose, then, the only viable and proper

[14]Robert E. Osgood, *Limited War: The Challenge to American Strategy* (Chicago: University of Chicago Press, 1957), p. 22.

focus for the empirical study of war as an instrument of policy is the effective control of the entire conflict process from which war proceeds. It may be argued in this regard that the determination of the means whereby control is achieved leaves open the larger "value" question of the ends to which knowledge is put.

If, as Quincy Wright suggests, the conditions of war are the absence of the conditions of peace,[15] then it is likely that knowledge of the conditions occasioning conflict at least implies knowledge of both the conditions and the means of its suppression. Of course, the suppression of conflict cannot be said to be always and everywhere a desirable effect. On the other hand, reality is seldom so simple as to admit of direct extrapolation from theoretical knowledge to practical effect. Knowledge implies neither the means nor the will for its own implementation, though it always entails the risk of its own misuse by man. Moreover, it is one thing to establish a conscious policy of conflict suppression and quite another to effect its enduring conditions. Indeed, as Robin Williams has observed in this connection,

there is a definite possibility that the factors that are most important in producing hostility and conflict are by no means the same as those which are most important for control purposes. Thus, the roots of intergroup hostility may be in the early socialization of children in the home. But this process is so inaccessible to direct external control that other, even seemingly far removed, approaches may be much more promising for immediate action.[16]

The same may be said of the factors most important in producing peace or nonviolent relations. In one context or framework, a specific act or set of actions may produce one effect and, in another, yet a different effect. In the short run, the restriction of civil liberties can provide an enabling environment for suppressing violence; in the long run, such a policy in and of itself can go a long way toward breeding even greater violence. In one context, the assassination of a dictator might effect a peaceful, stable change of government; in another, it might produce civil war. And so on. Only a full appreciation of both the policy implications and the structural interconnectedness of the entire set of conditions of any event can fully convey the dangers of extrapolating directly from conditioning factors to effective control measures. The conditions of peace may well be the absence of the conditions of war; but there is certainly no easy or facile inverse correspondence between them.

This same central purpose of controlling the course of conflict and war guided Wright's proposal of the requirements for a "comprehensive and fundamental" analysis that might provide an effective focus and framework for a continuing program of policy-relevant research. Like that proposal, this study proceeded

[15]Wright, *Study of War*, p. 16.
[16]Robin M. Williams, Jr., *The Reduction of Intergroup Tensions* (New York: Social Science Research Council, 1947), pp. 41–42.

from the assumption that it is possible to define, in terms of a comprehensive list of descriptive characteristics and operating variables, the system within which occur those conflicts involving the possibility and fact of war. Such a list of factors would in itself constitute a provisional and eclectic theory of conflict to be modified and refined through application to actual conflict situations. Indeed, one requirement of any method of data analysis employed in combination with such a theory is that it be capable of facilitating the theory's continued improvement by obviating its sins of both omission and inclusion.

The elaboration of a list of factors found or hypothesized by previous analysts to be influential in determining the course of conflict is no great problem. The literature abounds with such lists. In addition to the traditional historical analyses of war, in the past decade a significant trend has developed toward the empirical analysis of armed conflict and its associated activities and behaviors both within and between nations. Various and increasingly complex statistical techniques have been employed to define various types of conflict behavior and their social, economic, and political indicators.[17] Significant progress has been made in defining meaningful and fruitful dimensions in terms of which to compare such conflicts and the parties to them.[18]

Listing purportedly influential factors is thus no problem: the causes of conflict are virtually infinite. Rather, difficulty is encountered in determining the analytic level at which the causes of conflict will be examined. Just where does one look for the causes of war? The UNESCO Constitution suggests in "the minds of men." Quincy Wright, on the other hand, suggests that such an analysis should be

emancipated from the preconceptions of international law, organization, and politics, and reach back to the basic psychological, sociological, geographic, demographic, technological, and ethical conditions and variables functioning, not only in the immediate situation or dispute, but also inside the conflicting states and governments, and in the entire field of international relations at the time.[19]

In somewhat less pretentious fashion, and with no claim to exhaustiveness, it is the latter approach that has been attempted here. Recognition has been accorded the fact that a virtually unlimited number of factors or pressures is at all times operating

[17]See, for example, Lewis F. Richardson, *Arms and Insecurity*, ed. N. Rashevsky and E. Trucco (Pittsburgh, Pa.: Boxwood Press, 1960); Rudolph J. Rummel, "Dimensions of Conflict Behavior within and between Nations," *General Systems Yearbook*, 1963 ed.; and Ivo K. and Rosalind L. Feierabend, "Aggressive Behavior within Polities, 1948–62: A Cross-National Study," *Journal of Conflict Resolution*, vol. 10, no. 3 (September 1966).
[18]See, for example, Bruce Russett et al., *World Handbook of Political and Social Indicators* (New Haven: Yale University Press, 1964), and Arthur S. Banks and Robert B. Textor, *A Cross-Polity Survey* (Cambridge, Mass.: The M.I.T. Press, 1963).
[19]Wright, "Memorandum on Interstate Conflicts," p. 2.

on any conflict, pushing it in various directions. It is also recognized that every conflict at any particular instant in time is, as a particular configuration of these factors, a unique phenomenon. Yet it is asserted that it is possible, building upon established concepts and theories, to define a comprehensive (and tentative) conflict "system" within which all conflicts may be said to originate and variously to develop. Within that system, each conflict is, as a particular configuration of factors, unique; but comparisons between it and other conflicts are facilitated by the common dimensionality of the variables used to define them all. A basis is thereby established for determining not only such commonality as exists between conflicts at comparable points in their development but also the types of cases that occur within the system and their usual courses of development under both normal and specified conditions.

Given this comprehensive approach to causation, however, there remains the question of the inclusiveness of the list of variables or factors that define the conflict system and are used in its analysis. Criteria are required if indiscriminate choice is to be avoided. Robin Williams has suggested three such criteria for use in the study of conflict, which have been adopted for the selection of factors included in this study: (1) those of most promise, by means of their focus, for guiding empirical research; (2) those of most probable validity, as adjudged by the consensus among previous and existing researches; and (3) those of most relevance for application to concrete policy problems and activities.[20]

Still there are the difficulties of selecting the specific factors and of precisely formulating them in terms so that the resulting test instrument is equally applicable to all forms of conflict involving the potential for war. For there is no reason to assume that the traditional internal-interstate-colonial, limited-general-total, or other distinctions that have long dominated both conventional and scholarly thought are meaningful, viable, or practical with respect to the policy issue of controlling conflict.

Once formally elaborated, the list of conditioning factors constitutes a test instrument that may be applied to selected cases of past and present conflict at comparable points in their development, thereby establishing a systematic base for analysis of their comparabilities. Two problems remain, however: at what points in their life cycles should this instrument be applied to the conflicts selected for study, and what criteria should be applied in the selection of conflicts for analysis?

To resolve the first problem, a conceptual model was elaborated, founded on the notion that a regular and specifiable framework of stages exists through which all conflicts pass in their life cycles,

[20]Williams, *Reduction of Intergroup Tensions*, p. 50.

the end of each stage being marked by the threshold of the next. The application of the test instrument to each conflict studied at each threshold through which it passed therefore established the basis for determining the patterns of factors, or the conditions, that apply at those critical turning points in the development of conflicts.

This model also served as the basic frame of reference for the selection of specific conflicts to serve as a data base for analysis. A range of cases was selected that would illustrate the various possible modes of passage through the conflict model. A further consideration in this regard was that the conflicts selected for study should include representatives from each of the traditional types of internal, interstate, and colonial conflict noted earlier, so that the viability of these distinctions might be examined. The final major consideration in selecting the conflicts was that those included should represent varying degrees of local rather than general conflicts. The latter flow only from the former and, if the model of conflict employed is appropriate, should be but exceptional, expanded cases of the localized conflicts that afford the analyst greater ease of definition with respect to the geographic boundaries applying, the interests at variance, the issues involved, and so on.

Finally, there remains the problem of determining the significant and meaningful patterns of factors residing in the data base so established, of effectively coming to grips with the dilemma of multiple causation itself. Philosophers of science since David Hume have recognized that what the scientific analyst observes is not causation but repeated coincidence or association between events. The standard statistical means used by social scientists for measuring such association has long been correlation. It has previously been demonstrated, however, that two or more test items can individually or severally have a zero correlation with a criterion, outcome, or event and yet jointly be perfectly correlated with it.[21] This is the essential shortcoming of all correlational techniques in dealing with problems of multiple causation: their operation requires certain highly restrictive assumptions about the manner in which the data describing an event may relate to one another, thereby invoking the serious risk of ignoring meaningful relationships among the data and misinterpreting the structure of the event itself or of the system of which it is part.

To circumvent this problem of assuming linearity in a generally nonlinear world, a noncorrelational method of data manipulation and analysis has for the first time been fully developed and programmed for automated use in this study. It is a method capable

[21]See P. E. Meehl, "Configural Scoring," *Journal of Consulting Psychology*, vol. 14, no. 3 (June 1950), pp. 165–171.

of extracting from any body of systematic data on a given set of variables for a defined population (1) the significant patterns of variable values (or individual characteristics) residing in the data base and (2) the objective types of individuals existing in the population defined by that data base. We shall see, moreover, that this method establishes patterns of characteristics in such a way as to yield an objective and comprehensive classification of the events, individuals, or phenomena under examination into a hierarchical structure or series of types. It thereby roughly replicates the process and the results of the system of taxonomic classification developed over centuries in biological studies.

As A. J. Cain has observed, biological species are differently defined on the basis of a comparatively large number of characteristics, some smaller subset of which is used to define genus, and still smaller subsets to define the higher levels of classification.[22] Because only the precise, objective pattern or configuration of characteristics is significant, any given characteristic or factor may contribute to the definition of more than one class at each level. On the other hand, no given individual, event, or phenomenon may be classified into more than one class at any level: while it may be characterized by certain features that contribute to the definition of more than one class, an individual can, as a complete network of features, be fully characteristic of only one. Both man and the gorilla, for example, are characterized by their opposable thumbs. At the first level of taxonomic classification, however, man and the gorilla are members of different species, the characteristic patterns of which are defined in part by the single fact of opposable thumbs. It is only at a more restrictive and abstracted level, the descriptive pattern of which contains fewer characteristics (one being opposable thumbs), that they are placed in the same class for various heuristic purposes.

In combination with the data base established, this mathematical method yields a hierarchy of conflict types at each point that is presumed to be critical in its development. These types derive directly from the empirical patterns of conditioning factors that apply to the individual conflicts examined at those turning points. It may be well, then, to reiterate that the conditioning factors or patterns of factors that are most important in producing conflict are by no means necessarily the same as those that are most important for control purposes. It is unlikely, however, that the two are unrelated. For example, Seymour Deitchman has found that certain configurations of climatological and topographical conditions conspire to the distinct advantage of unconventional forces in time of war.[23] This knowledge may hardly be considered

[22]A. J. Cain, *Animal Species and Their Evolution* (London: Hutchinson House, 1954).
[23]See Seymour J. Deitchman, *Limited War and American Defense Policy* (Cambridge, Mass.: The M.I.T. Press, 1964), chap. 6, "Where They Fight: The Environment."

an advantage in controlling a particular conflict once armed hostilities have commenced. Before that time, however, and in the context of an established network of enabling factors, it could well be of critical importance in estimating both the likely course of a conflict and the likely effects of various policy measures upon it.

Summary

In summary, what has been attempted in this study is the establishment of a systematic, reliable, and automated technique for the purposeful and simultaneous manipulation of an extremely large number of variables. It has been estimated that man himself is capable of manipulating at most one hundred variables at any one time. Indeed, most often his deliberations proceed in terms of a vastly smaller number. Public discussions in the United States of the desirability and effectiveness of bombing North Vietnam, for example, generally proceeded in terms of very few factors: the increasing loss of American lives, the continuing flow of troops and supplies from North to South Vietnam, the effectiveness of aerial bombing in slowing German ball-bearing production in World War II, and its failure to produce British capitulation in the Battle of Britain.

Certainly, a far greater number of factors is involved in this, or any, policy problem. But the mind of man is limited. In the face of complex events, he falls back on assumptions, images, and types that may facilitate decision making but are always of questionable validity. Clearly, his analytic capabilities and therefore his policy decisions are likely to gain in precision and efficacy if these vague notions are tested against objective realities and reformulated in light of the established or customary workings of a larger number of operative variables.

This study has attempted to formulate and construct an integrated program of policy-relevant research that will ultimately permit the simultaneous manipulation of a theoretically unlimited but increasingly incisive set of variables affecting the course and outcome of violent conflict. The ultimate result, hopefully, will be a less impressionistic basis for prediction and a more reliable and effective basis for policy action with respect to conflict than presently exist.

2   The Conflict Process

Antecedents

Social scientists have collected an enormous amount of data on the operational sources and phenomenal characteristics of conflict and warfare. From observation of the coincidences and associations among them, they have abstracted an equally assorted number and variety of hypotheses concerning the nature of conflict. With respect to wars of the internal variety as traditionally defined, Harry Eckstein has cataloged a vast number of hypotheses concerning only their origin, much less their development and termination, and classified them into five basic categories that emphasize intellectual factors, economic factors, social-structural factors, political factors, and, finally, no particular aspect of societies themselves but general characteristics of the social process.[1] With regard to wars of the interstate variety, Quincy Wright has cataloged the following distinct approaches to their analysis and consideration: moralistic, literary, historical, political, legalistic, technological, ideological, sociological, psychological, and biological.[2] In methodological terms, the influential variables cited in these lists may be described variously as environmental and organismic, quantitative and qualitative, observable and inferred, complex and simple, independent and dependent, and so on.

It is obvious, then, that to seek an understanding of conflict calls for setting up a model, an abstracted and conceptual analog that will both illumine the development process through which conflict proceeds and serve as a basis for winnowing the relevant elements of its structure from the irrelevant or inconsequential. What we seek is a model that will fit the known facts, facilitate the prediction and control of events, and suggest new questions that will in turn lead to further knowledge. The model should be sufficiently structured to give meaningful direction and sensitivity to the investigation of conflict, yet sufficiently flexible to promote both the discovery of unexpected relations among the data of conflict and the refinement of its own structure.

This and the two following chapters will, first, present a structural or "processual" model of conflict that not only provides a framework of common definitions for this study but also facilitates

Author's note: The processual model of conflict presented in this chapter is an elaboration of a similar model developed by Lincoln P. Bloomfield, Amelia C. Leiss, and the present author. See Lincoln P. Bloomfield, Amelia C. Leiss, et al., "The Control of Local Conflict: A Design Study" (Cambridge, Mass.: M.I.T., Center for International Studies, June 1967). In particular, the phase scheme presented here was originally suggested as a static model in another form by Miss Leiss, and the notion of pressures or factors operating to effect movement from one phase to another was suggested by Professor Bloomfield. It is from these two concepts that the dynamic model presented here proceeds.
[1] Harry Eckstein, "Internal War: The Problem of Anticipation," in Ithiel de Sola Pool et al., *Social Science Research and National Security* (Washington, D.C.: Smithsonian Institution, 1963), pp. 116–117.
[2] Quincy Wright, *A Study of War*, 2nd ed. (Chicago: University of Chicago Press, 1964), Appendix 3.

comparisons between various conflict cases at equivalent, critical points in their development. Second, a "substantive" model of conflict will be developed, a statement in terms of 300 variables of the system within which conflict is postulated to occur. It is the state of this conflict system at any given moment — in terms of the actual values of those variables — that defines a coded conflict at any point in its development. A conflict may thus be defined at that point as a particular configuration of 300 variable values or factors. It may then be compared to other conflicts (similarly defined) for significant commonalities, similarities, and dissimilarities.

Finally, in Chapter 4, a technique of data manipulation and analysis will be developed for the first time in its complete form. Through a series of manipulations upon the factor patterns characterizing the conflict cases coded at the various thresholds of the conflict model, this technique is capable of eliciting the various predominant sets of conditions under which changes in the state of the conflict system occur, or under which movement is effected from one phase or stage of conflict to another. The technique thus establishes rules for movement through the processual model of conflict and thereby furnishes its credentials as a dynamic rather than a static model.

The Conflict Model

The usual manner in which a complex developmental process is reduced to manageable analytic proportions is to translate it into a series of distinct stages or phases that are at once theoretically meaningful and practically relevant. The present study of the conflict process is no exception. If, as Clausewitz has argued, warfare is regarded as but one of many alternative instruments of policy, as a continuation of policy "with other means," then its existence as a distinct phase in the developmental process of policy is already established. In this view, war occurs only when one of at least two parties capable of waging it opts for a military solution to an ongoing conflict between them.

War does not, however, occur in a vacuum. The decision to wage it can be and generally is made neither lightly nor spontaneously. Before war may be undertaken as an instrument of policy, at least one party capable of waging it must have introduced the military option into its policy considerations of an ongoing dispute and must subsequently have realized some degree of military mobilization and preparedness. These actions are, in effect, the necessary though not sufficient conditions or antecedents of war. While some nonviolent mode of settlement may yet be found for the dispute, its nature has been changed fundamentally by introducing the military option.

War may therefore be viewed as one possible mode of policy activity aimed at effectively and favorably resolving an ongoing conflict of interests. In this sense, war is but one of numerous conflict procedures, others being negotiation, conciliation, mediation, arbitration, and adjudication. It is merely a particular subset of the larger set of all conflict modes, encompassing all the socially (if not legally) recognized situations in which armed hostilities of considerable magnitude are conducted on a systematic and continuing basis by the armed forces of two or more political factions, organizations, nations, governments, or states. Because the term war carries legal implications and connotations that no political body cares any longer to suffer or risk publicly, the de facto situation of war will be referred to as hostilities.

Similarly, conflict may usefully be regarded as the subset of all disputes between parties capable of waging war in which the military option has been introduced, and at least one party perceives the issues at stake in partially, if not wholly, military terms.

For purposes of the present analysis, it is postulated that the most significant points in the development of hostilities are those at which (1) a dispute arises between parties capable of waging war; (2) at least one of the parties begins to conceive of the conflict at hand as an actual or potential military issue and takes steps to prepare for that contingency; and (3) other options have been exhausted or abandoned for the while in favor of the military, and organized hostilities occur. Graphically, these three concepts stand in logical relation to each other as follows:

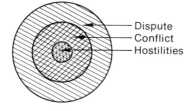

The most inclusive concept is that of dispute, subsuming as it does all conflicts, both those that eventuate in hostilities and those that do not. In analytic terms, a dispute arises between parties capable of waging war when at least one party becomes aware of an incompatibility of perceived interests, objectives, or future positions. The essence of a dispute is a felt grievance by a party capable of waging war that, in its eyes, demands some more tolerable accommodation with another party than presently exists. If the grievance is of such a magnitude as to warrant action by this party (and most, happily, are not), a multiplicity of political mechanisms and institutions exists for achieving accommodation.

In some instances, however, one party will introduce the military option to the dispute. It will see the issue at hand as either so threatening or so central to its interests as to warrant introducing military considerations and activities into what had previously been a purely nonmilitary issue. A dispute thus becomes a conflict. On the relatively rare occasions when organized, systematic, and continued violence is undertaken by any party to a dispute in pursuit of its objectives, the conflict evolves into hostilities.

Within this hostilities phase, moreover, significant changes may occur in the nature of the relations between the belligerents. It has been noted elsewhere that all war is cooperative, at least to the extent necessary to permit communication between belligerents and administration of mutually advantageous rules.[3] Even World War II, usually regarded as a virtually total conflict, was limited in this respect. Herman Kahn has observed that

actually, the war was in many ways limited, and a great deal of implicit and some explicit bargaining and negotiation went on during its course. The limitations existed despite the fact that the intention of both sides was to devote all possible resources to the effort.[4]

Thus it may be argued that, from the moment hostilities break out in any conflict, limitations are set upon their conduct by tacit or explicit bargaining between the belligerents. The extent of these limitations is determined by considerations of mutual advantage, and their effect is to establish a set of "rules of the game"[5] within which the hostilities are to be conducted. Max Singer has observed this process of accommodation and has coined the term "agreed battle" to emphasize that in a conflict situation

in which both sides are accepting limitations, there is in effect an "agreement", whether or not it is explicit or even well understood. Thus, the term does not have any connotation of a completely shared understanding, an intention of continuing indefinitely with the limitations, or even a conscious *quid pro quo* arrangement.[6]

The ambiguity of the rules of the game, which derives from their generally being tacitly rather than explicitly defined, and the correspondingly greater latitude of action it allows the belligerents within their limits, can have both functional and dysfunctional consequences for the belligerents. On the one hand, the use of actions (rather than explicit correspondence) to convey implicit messages can backfire if the adversary interprets a given action in a way quite different from that intended. An act intended to moderate hostilities can have the direct and immediate effect of intensifying them if misperceived by the adversary. Inevitably in times of war, there is careful concern for and attention to the substance and implications of signals or significant acts that might relate to the established rules of the game. On the other hand, the very ambiguity of the rules and their predominantly

[3]See O. Klineberg, *Tensions Affecting International Understanding* (New York: Social Science Research Council, 1950), p. 17.
[4]Herman Kahn, *On Escalation: Metaphors and Scenarios* (New York: Hudson Institute, 1965), p. 26. See also George Quester, "Bargaining and Bombing during World War II in Europe," *World Politics*, vol. 15, no. 3 (April 1963).
[5]The author would like to express his gratitude to Professor William Kaufmann of M.I.T. for suggesting this concept.
[6]In Kahn, *On Escalation*, p. 4n.

tacit character do permit the belligerents a certain freedom to realize with impunity minor changes in the rules that are to their advantage. That freedom would not exist if the rules were more explicitly formulated. Only a change of some considerable magnitude in the rules may be taken as firm indication of a change in the nature of the relations between the parties to the hostilities.

There may then occur what we shall term escalations or de-escalations of the ongoing hostilities, such occurrences being constituted by a gross change effected (regardless of intent) in the existing rules of the game (tacit or explicit) governing the conduct and limitations of hostilities. Indeed, it appears that in the absence of this notion of rules of the game the concepts of escalation and de-escalation can hardly be effectively and reliably operationalized. No quantitative index has been found adequate to the task: increased or decreased numbers of men or matériel may represent nothing more than a logical extension of existing or prior commitments, and may not constitute a meaningful change in the nature of hostilities. Numbers alone have thus been found incapable of fully and fruitfully expressing these concepts.

The problem with quantitative measures is their insufficiency. Escalation or de-escalation of hostilities is at times a simple matter of numbers. More often, however, it is a symbolic or qualitative matter having little or nothing to do with numbers. The acceptance of previously rejected demands concerning the conditions or issues of negotiation, the introduction in small numbers of a new or previously withheld weapon, the intervention of a small but symbolically important third party—each could, under certain conditions and regardless of intention, qualify as an escalation or de-escalation of ongoing hostilities, depending upon its immediate effect on their conduct and on the terms under which they are being conducted.

Finally, hostilities may end with or without a settlement of the underlying dispute as it is presently defined (which may and often does vary considerably from its original formulation). If a total military victory has been achieved, both the conflict and the dispute at hand may be said to have ended. More often, however, hostilities up to that point have involved costs unacceptable to all belligerents concerned and are therefore simply terminated pending further political developments that will define the future course of the conflict. The conflict as now defined may be demilitarized by agreement of the parties thereto and so revert to the status of a dispute. Likewise, the underlying dispute between the parties may be settled by many possible means (including the passage of time or the emergence of more salient issues) and so cease to exist. Alternatively, such a conflict may persist indefinitely, always threatening the renewal of hostilities.

Definitions and Concepts

To provide a framework of common definitions for this study and to facilitate systematic comparisons between specific conflicts at comparable points in their development, it is postulated that all conflicts, in their life cycles, pass variously through the following phase scheme:

P–I Dispute (nonmilitary) phase, in which a grievance among parties capable of waging war is perceived by all parties thereto in non-military terms.

P–II Conflict (prehostilities) phase, in which a dispute is perceived by at least one party thereto in active or abnormal military policy terms (for example, through arms buildup, troop mobilization, or force deployment), and any violence occurs only on a random or accidental basis.

P–III Hostilities phase, in which organized and systematic violence is undertaken by the armed forces of any party to the dispute as a purposeful instrument of policy. Within this phase, there may occur subphases, indicated by a gross change in the existing rules of the game governing the conduct and limitation of hostilities. These are designated escalation (E) or de-escalation (D) in terms of the actual rather than the intended effect of such actions.

P–IV Termination (posthostilities) phase, in which organized hostilities are terminated by all parties to the dispute, although the dispute is as yet unresolved and is perceived in military terms by at least one party and could generate renewed hostilities either immediately or after a prolonged period of cease-fire and renewed preparations for combat.

S Settlement, the point (rather than phase) at which the underlying dispute between the parties, as presently defined, is itself resolved or disposed of by some form of accommodation between the parties, annihilation of one or more of them, loss of saliency, or other means.

The processual model of conflict deriving from these concepts and definitions is depicted graphically in Figure 2.1. (The arrows indicate all possible paths that any given conflict may follow from one phase or subphase to another.)

In addition to these definitions, the following rules were established to govern movement within the conflict model and to aid in determining the precise path of any particular conflict through it:

Rule 1 Any phase or subphase may, in theory and in practice, be of indefinite duration in time.

Rule 2 P–I may advance only to P–II or to S; that is, a dispute may only become a conflict or, alternatively, be settled.

Rule 3 P–II may advance to either P–III or S or revert to P–I; that is, a conflict may eventuate in hostilities, with the outbreak of violence; end with a settlement of the underlying dispute; or, with the de-

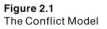

Figure 2.1
The Conflict Model

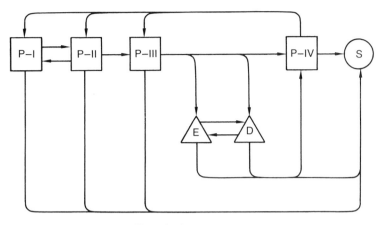

P–I   Dispute (nonmilitary) phase
P–II   Conflict (prehostilities) phase
P–III Hostilities phase
  E   Escalation
  D   De-escalation
P–IV   Termination (posthostilities) phase
S   Settlement

cision of the parties involved to demilitarize the issue, revert to a dispute.

Rule 4   P–III may advance either to P–IV or to S; that is, organized hostilities may terminate with or without a settlement or final disposition of the underlying dispute as presently defined. This rule applies equally to subphases E and D of P–III.

Rule 5   P–IV may either advance to S or revert to P–III, P–II, or P–I; that is, a conflict in which hostilities have once terminated may subsequently proceed directly to a settlement by resolution of the underlying dispute, in which case the advance is to S; alternatively, it may revert to hostilities (P–III) without further ado. On the other hand, if P–IV is prolonged and the level of military commitment of the parties to the conflict becomes normalized, a sudden change in the military posture of one may abnormalize the military situation, precipitating a reversion to P–II and active preparation for renewed hostilities. Finally, by agreement of the parties to the conflict, the issue may be demilitarized altogether, now that hostilities have ceased, and so revert to the status of a dispute. (P–I).

There is, then, no set or established path for any conflict to follow through the model. Each may in its development involve movement forward, backward, or in a loop, thus establishing its own idiosyncratic definition in terms of its path through the model. Any particular case can therefore be expected to follow its own peculiar path through the model, deviating as it will from the basic

sequential phase structure, and may subsequently be characterized in terms of that path.*

Finally, two assumptions were made in the elaboration of the
model to facilitate its application to specific conflicts in real life.
First, *symmetry* was assumed with respect to the location within
the model of all parties to a given conflict at any given moment in
its life cycle; that is, all parties are assumed always to be in the
same phase or suphase of the model. However, since movement
of the conflict from one phase to another may be initiated by only
one party, the conflict may be in a given phase without full knowledge of all the parties involved. I should argue that this assumption does not distort reality so long as attention is focused on the
conflict process itself rather than on the activities of the parties
to the conflict. For instance, a dispute has certainly undergone a
fundamental change (from P–I to P–II in our terms) if just one
party actively prepares to do battle while the other does not but
prefers still to regard the issue as essentially nonmilitary in
nature.

Second, it is assumed that all decisions to take action that will
move a conflict from one phase or subphase to another are *reversible* up to the point of the action itself. Thus it is the action marking movement in terms of the model, rather than the decision to
take it, that constitutes the beginning moment of the phase or subphase at hand. This assumption of the reversibility of decisions is
at times a distortion of reality. It is necessitated in the great majority of conflicts by the difficulty of determining the precise moment at which a particular decision was taken by a party to a conflict. It is probably safe, however, to suggest that many, if not most,
decisions to alter the state of a conflict are in fact reversible up to,
or very close to, the moment of execution. To avoid the problems
of resolving interpretive contradictions concerning the actual date
of these decisions and the extent of their reversibility, it has been
assumed that actions rather than decisions are the meaningful
indicators of movement within the model.

Indeed, it if often quite difficult to pinpoint the precise date of a
historical action or event, much less the moment of decision to
undertake it, if in fact the decision was deliberate. As Quincy
Wright found in his study, for example, it is often impossible even
to determine when war begins or ends.[7] It is seldom separated
from peace by a clearly marked line or point in time; formal
declarations of war are rare, and more often than not they follow
active hostilities by a considerable period. As his commencement
date for wars, therefore, Wright chose the date of the first "impor-

---

*The characteristic definition of each conflict examined in the present
study, in terms of its own path through the model, is presented in Appendix A.
[7]Wright, *Study of War*, Appendix 20.

tant'' hostilities. Likewise, for a termination date he chose that of the signing of a peace treaty or of its going into effect, or, lacking that, the date of the armistice, capitulation, or cessation of active hostilities.

As opposed to the more general concept of war, active hostilities were found in this study to admit of reasonably precise specification in terms of the date of both their outbreak (P–III) and their termination (P–IV). Of the three remaining critical dates applying in the model — that is, the beginning of Phases I and II and the point of settlement — the most difficult to establish for real conflicts was found to be that for P–I, marking the origin of the dispute itself. In well-documented cases, it was generally possible to specify with adequate precision the approximate date on which military considerations were introduced into the relations between the parties to the dispute, thereby establishing a state of conflict between them, as well as the approximate date on which settlement was achieved and the dispute eliminated as a consideration in the relations between the parties to it. For P–I, however, too often the origins of the dispute from which the conflict derived were hidden in the recesses of both temporally and analytically remote history.

This study was therefore restricted to the consideration of the various conditions under which movement occurred into P–II, P–III (and its subphases), P–IV, and S. What could be undertaken, accordingly, was a statement of the various conditions of conflict (P–II), hostilities (P–III), escalation (E), de-escalation (D), termination (P–IV), and settlement (S).

Theory of the Conflict System   The basic premise from which this analysis proceeds is that each stage or event occurs under the conditions of a variety of particular pressures operating in various combinations on the parties to disputes. Morton Halperin has observed within a more limited context that

just as the stabilization of a local war results from a variety of pressures on both sides, so the termination of a local war situation will not be the result of any single pressure. There is nothing inherent within the logic of local war which determines the time or conditions of war termination. It is rather the broader political-effects objectives of the major powers as filtered through decision-makers' image of the world and their domestic political goals which determine when a war is brought to a halt.[8]

It is the contention of this study that various sets of pressures operate on the parties to disputes at *each* significant stage in their development, as postulated in the conflict model. These pressures derive essentially from four sources that condition the origin and development of all disputes:

1. the total existing state of relations between the parties to the dispute, of which it may be merely a part;

[8]Morton H. Halperin, *Limited War in the Nuclear Age* (New York: John Wiley & Sons, 1963), p. 32.

2. the internal policy, structure, and resources of each;
3. the processes and procedures available to and utilized by them for adjustment of the dispute; and
4. the nature and structure of the environment, both physical and strategic, in which the conflict is conducted.[9]

These pressures, moreover, are always operating to a greater or lesser extent, conditioning in various combinations or configurations any and all developments in the life cycle of conflict, any and all movements through the conflict model. They therefore operate continuously throughout each phase. As a conceptual device to facilitate the coding of the conflicts in terms of these pressures, it was assumed that the end of each phase is marked by a threshold at which all the of the pressures operating in that phase realize a particular configuration and achieve a critical mass to move the conflict to its next stage. Thus, for example, the threshold at the end of P–II (prehostilities) may represent, in a given case, the threshold of dispute (P–I), hostilities (P–III), or settlement (S), depending upon the subsequent course of the conflict.

I have argued, however, that the thresholds for each phase (and for all phases and subphases) are characterized by distinct and isolable sets of pressures or factors. Thus various, differentiable patterns of factors characterize the thresholds of conflict, hostilities, escalation, de-escalation, termination, and settlement. It is these factor patterns that constitute the enabling conditions of each phase of conflict. If, then, it is possible to define in terms of such factors the system within which all conflicts occur, the characterization of any particular conflict at any threshold of the model may be said to constitute one distinct set of conditions of the ensuing phase. The real state of that system for a particular conflict at, say, the threshold of hostilities (P–III) constitutes one set of the conditions of hostilities. It is also true, however, that many particular sets of conditions will be found to exist for any given threshold, one set for each case examined. There is no one analytic or practical set of preconditions, circumstances, or pressures under which a particular phase occurs. Only once we have established the significant commonalities among the various conditions that pertain empirically at any given threshold will we arrive at an effective statement of the general preconditions of that phase.

It may, moreover, be assumed that under the various sets of pressures that produce its conditions, any real case of hostilities, termination, or other stage tends itself to develop into an example of several different theoretical types of this event, although one such type may be dominant at a given moment. In any complex

[9]See Quincy Wright, "Memorandum on Interstate Conflicts," paper prepared for the Carnegie Endowment for International Peace, New York, December 1955, p. 6.

event, contradictory and complementary pressures operate simultaneously to obscure the effects of one another and so to confound analysis of its pure characteristics. For example, real life offers many different types of hostilities (P–III), each of which has a combination of conditioning factors (or attributes) that are interrelated in a unique fashion and so are uniquely characteristic of that type. These types exist as pure, distinct entities only in theory. In reality, the existence and interaction of the multiple sets of pressures conditioning hostilities tend to obscure the embodied pure types. Individual instances of hostilities are thus imperfect representatives of the pure types of hostilities. However, the characteristics of the pure types may be approached, even though never fully realized, by classifying reality's imperfect types into internally consistent categories and determining their common characteristics. The validity of a particular representation of a pure type may then be expected to increase as the number of imperfect types or individual cases representing it increases.*

Here, then, is the methodological foundation for establishing not only the enabling conditions of the various significant stages of conflict but, equally, the various *types* of stages that occur in real life. Thus a basis exists in theory for establishing the various conditions and types of conflict, hostilities, escalation, de-escalation, termination, and settlement.

Finally, it is suggested that, once these conditions have been established, any individual conflict may be characterized in terms of the resulting types to the extent that it conforms to the particular configurations of factors unique to those types. That is, once types of events have been established, it is possible, by comparing an individual case with the factor patterns uniquely characteristic of the various types of events, to establish its identity both as a particular event and as a specific type of that event. For if the factor patterns characteristic of the various types of, say, escalation and de-escalation are truly unique, then predictive comparisons of individual conflicts of unknown outcome may usefully be made to them — in terms of both what is likely to eventuate (as it conforms to the established types) and how it is likely to happen (as the cases yielding the types did in fact develop).

The particular mathematical technique by which classification is effected is itself, however, only one part of a classificatory system. The remaining part comprises its substantive content. In this study, this is the list of variables or factors that is assembled in the coding instrument (Appendix B) and postulated to define the conflict system within which all conflicts variously develop. Obviously, this particular list of factors is not inclusive or even represen-

*This is the theoretical foundation for the technique of hierarchical case classification and pattern determination presented in chap. 4.

tative of all factors that might conceivably influence the course of a particular conflict. It is intended in this regard to be theoretically adequate rather than a practically exhaustive listing. Since any given conflict may belong to one type of event in one universe of attributes and to quite another type in another universe, the types deriving from the present conflict system are representative of those pertaining in reality only to the extent that this conflict system meaningfully synthesizes reality and adequately expresses the causal forces operating in it.

Before presenting the derivation and construction of the test instrument or codebook in detail, two further assumptions of the conflict model should be noted. They were necessitated by the aim of achieving a reliable technique of analysis that would be applicable to all forms and levels of conflict.

Some Further Assumptions

First, it was assumed that conflict is an essentially *bilateral* phenomenon; that is, at any given moment in the life cycle of a conflict, only two principal parties, antagonists, or adversaries are involved. All other direct and indirect participants in the conflict are involved third parties, regardless of their effect upon the eventual development or outcome. An antagonist, furthermore, is defined as the sum of the ruling regime (government or effective elite) of the principal party, plus whatever general or civil population is currently within its political jurisdiction or its effective control. These distinctions, it will be seen, are adhered to throughout the conflict codebook, and specific items (or questions) are phrased in terms of each. Indeed, the structure of the codebook itself, and especially the section on the nature and extent of third-party involvement in the conflict, was designed specifically to accommodate to and compensate for these assumptions.

It was found, however, that the assumptions can be made with neither gross distortion of reality nor great difficulty of application to specific conflicts at any point in their development. With respect to the definition of each antagonist, there is some legitimate question about who may be taken to represent a party capable of waging war: the whole population or only the officials or decision makers who act in their behalf. Indeed, what might simplistically be termed a school of analysis has developed from the conviction that it is the latter, that policy is ultimately a practical matter of elite decision making and thus an analytic matter most profitably regarded from that viewpoint.[10] Clearly, however, some of the factors conditioning the development of conflict relate to the population of each antagonist as a whole, while others relate to the characteristics of its decision makers and its decision-making apparatus. Inevitably, certain characteristics of the general

[10]See "Decision-Making as an Approach to the Study of International Politics," in *Foreign Policy Decision-Making*, ed. Richard C. Snyder, H. W. Bruck, and Burton Sapin (Glencoe, Ill.: Free Press, 1962).

population are among the important perceptual inputs to the decision-making apparatus. To regard the definition of the antagonist as an either-or proposition in terms of general populace versus policy makers is, then, futile. Specific items in the codebook have been formulated in terms of both, as appropriate and necessary.

At the same time, application of the assumption that conflict may be regarded as a bilateral phenomenon not only presented no insuperable problems but even afforded an extraordinary degree of flexibility in defining conflicts in terms that allowed relevant and immediately meaningful comparisons to be made among them. It has, moreover, been found previously that there is everywhere "a persistent tendency to reduce multi-party conflict to two-party conflict via coalitions and blocs. . . . The tendency to reduce the number of parties to conflict," report Raymond Mack and Richard Snyder, "is obviously due to the need to make power more effective and to arrive at a clear-cut definition of power relations which is somewhat stable. *Diffuse power relations are notoriously unstable.*"[11]

Besides reflecting the general tendency of all social conflict, then, this assumption provided a flexibility in defining the conflicts that is analytically desirable. For example, the antagonists in the Sinai campaign of 1955–1956 (one of the conflict cases examined here) were defined as Israel and Egypt, with Great Britain and France becoming involved at a given point as third parties acting on behalf of Israel. Had the focus of our attention in this case been the Suez crisis of 1956, these definitions might well and could readily have been different. Again, in the Bay of Pigs invasion or the USSR–Iran dispute of 1941–1947, it may at one time suit the analyst's purpose to define them as internal conflicts between the respective government and an externally supported insurgent organization, and at another time as proxy interstate conflicts between the great-power nations involved.

One special case of defining the principal parties to a conflict arises with a revolution, rebellion, uprising, or resistance movement against a colonial government. In these conflicts, the colonial administration and the rebel or revolutionary organization were considered to be the principal parties, and the metropole to be a third party with which the colonial administration had formal security and economic arrangements. This decision was prompted both by the facts of colonial rule and by the purposes of this study. From the rebel or insurgent organization's viewpoint, on the one hand, what are important besides the very fact of the colonial situation are the characteristics of the colonial administration and of the colony itself. The frame of reference for the

[11]Raymond W. Mack and Richard C. Snyder, "The Analysis of Social Conflict—Toward an Overview and Synthesis," *Journal of Conflict Resolution*, vol. 1, no. 1 (March 1957), p. 231; emphasis added.

insurgents' decision is the colonial situation and the colonial administration as an arm of the metropole. On the other hand, there are the great variety of relationships between metropoles and their colonial administrations, as well as the great variety of governmental and administrative structures established and fostered by the metropoles in their colonies — structures differing not only from each other but surely from the metropole itself.

By definition, however, two characteristics of all metropoles are their willingness to exact tribute from their colonies and to infuse force as colonial circumstances require and more or less scarce metropolitan resources allow. It is this last fact of competing and conflicting demands upon metropolitan resources that made it practically unrealistic and theoretically unproductive to pit the totality of metropolitan resources and capabilities against those of an isolated insurgent organization. Indeed, the very extent of the metropole's commitments generally makes it impossible for it to commit more than a fraction of its resources to any colonial locale. Either to increase the tribute extracted from or to reduce the resources committed to any such locale in order to reinforce one is to invite rebellion in another. The problem for the metropole is essentially one of effectively allocating resources in the face of inevitably conflicting demands, of balancing trade-offs between varying capabilities and ordered commitments.

To account for these relevant perceptions and effective capabilities in this analysis, then, it was determined that colonial conflicts might most fruitfully be regarded as essentially internal conflicts with one party (the colonial administration) receiving varying forms of support from an allied third party to the conflict, the metropole. Again, little difficulty was encountered in defining in these terms the examples of colonial conflict included in the study. And, again, the attempt was made to accommodate the structure and substance of the codebook to this assumption.

Finally, it was assumed for purposes of this study that conflict is a relative, or *relational*, phenomenon; that is, that the significant patterns of factors for our purposes inhere in the relationship between the parties to the conflict rather than in the isolated or absolute characteristics of the parties themselves. This assumption was postulated to reflect the nature of the resources — physical, moral, political, and otherwise — that can be brought to bear in a conflict. Clearly, whatever its component elements (and there is a surprising unanimity among analysts concerning this point), power is a relational concept. Thus it is both the nature and the relative distribution of power between the parties to a conflict that are significant in determining its course and outcome.[12]

[12]See ibid., p. 241, for a discussion of this point.

As will be seen, the codebook constructed and employed to establish the data base for this study was designed specifically to accommodate this assumption. Each item was coded for each principal party to each conflict at each threshold of the conflict model through which it passed. The entire data base established thereby is of a compound nature, each data bit comprising the relationship between two independent and discrete pieces of information. And the enabling conditions of each stage of conflict consist of the ratios formed by the coded values on each variable for each of the two principal antagonists.

The mathematical technique of pattern analysis developed in this study was therefore broadened in scope to operate upon a data base of compound elements and to extract from it the empirical patterns inhering in the relationship between the two data units—the parties to each conflict. To be sure, since the codebook was completed for both principal parties to the conflict, the data base could equally have been analyzed in any or all of three fashions. First, it might have been assessed in terms of the empirical factor patterns in the data for the individual parties to conflict. Such an analysis might be informative of the attributes of parties that become involved in conflict, that initiate conflict, that seek negotiated rather than violent settlement, and so on. Similarly, this approach might yield critical thresholds of weapons capabilities by any party to a conflict that tend to inhibit violence, to promote prolonged violence, and so on. Alternatively, the data might have been analyzed in terms of the empirical patterns existing between the parties to conflict in terms of the same set of variables. It is this approach that was followed in this study. Finally, and perhaps ideally, the analysis might have proceeded in terms of both of these approaches, putting both absolute and relative values into the analytic hopper before determining the enabling factor patterns. This would have the effect of isolating the patterns that existed both for and between the parties to conflict at the several critical thresholds of the conflict model. These three modes of analysis, however, increase in order of sophistication and difficulty in terms of the sheer data manipulation capabilities required of the pattern-analytic technique. Consistent as it is with the present conception of conflict as an essentially relational phenomenon, the second of these three possible modes was selected for exclusive attention in the present study.

Finally, this relational assumption to some extent facilitated data gathering, especially in respect to data on military manpower and hardware capabilities, for which ratios are often available when absolute figures for the individual parties are not.

The Generalizability of the Model

The foregoing set of definitions, concepts, and assumptions constitutes, as a whole, the conflict model employed in this study.

The values of the model would seem to be fourfold. First, despite appearances, it is descriptively and logically simple. Its entire operation is accounted for by three definitions (dispute, conflict, and hostilities); by a concept of thresholds separating these states and of factor patterns conditioning their occurrence; and by four assumptions (symmetry of party position, reversibility of decisions, bilaterality, and relationality). Second, the assumptions were found to be neither excessively unrealistic nor unduly simplifying of the conflict process. Third, the model was found to be equally applicable to all forms of conflict between parties capable of war — internal, interstate, or colonial, unconventional, conventional, or nuclear, and so on. Fourth, the model proved to be extraordinarily flexible in that it may be entered, and the principal parties redefined, at any point to reflect both the purposes of the analyst and the nature of the conflict. In addition to providing a framework for structuring conflicts in a fashion that allows meaningful comparisons to be drawn between them, the model affords the analyst wide latitude for precisely defining any given conflict in terms of both its content and its duration. Thus, for various purposes, it may suit his needs to define a specific conflict in terms of different principal parties and, within that framework, in terms of different phase durations or even paths through the model. Again, the Suez crisis–Sinai campaign of 1956 is an example in point.

Finally, it is as yet an open question whether this analytic model might fruitfully be applied to all forms of human conflict or social interaction in which violent exchange is one available policy option. There is evidence to suggest that such might well be the case. For example, in the highly formalized sixteenth-century Italian duel,[13] a dispute (P–I) arose with the insult, challenge, and acceptance of the challenge. This was followed (in P–II) by a more or less prolonged period of preparation for hostilities (in the unlikely event that they might occur) and of efforts to bluff, terrorize, placate, size up, and shatter the nerves of the enemy and to induce a peaceful settlement (S). The violence of the duel itself, in the unlikely event that it did take place, occurred (in P–III) only after one party was convinced that no other means existed to preserve his honor or prestige. The duel, of course, might itself dispose of the dispute at hand. More often, however, hostilities terminated quickly and inconclusively, in which case the conflict could remain in P–IV indefinitely, pending new provocation; return after a brief respite to violent exchange (P–III); return after a prolonged period of maneuvering to active preparations for renewed hostilities (in P–II); or proceed to some form of accommodated settlement (S), both parties content with having upheld their honor and demonstrated their courage.

[13]See Wright, *Study of War*, Appendix 31, "Illustrations of the Duel."

The extreme formalization of the Italian duel was a product of the most unheroic impulse to substitute argument for fighting, to save face and honor while retaining life and limb. The ultimate historical outcome of this impulse was the substitution of the law court for the duel. Formalization of the duel was thus a step in the direction of that substitution, which eventually eliminated the duel from Italian life by providing a handy and face-saving vehicle for expediting the passage of interpersonal conflict directly from P–I or P–II to settlement, namely, the law court.

Similar examples of the applicability of the model might well be drawn from boyhood fighting,[14] a seemingly informal institution to the untrained or inexperienced observer, or even from professional prizefighting, with all its customs, rituals, norms, and forms.

It may then be that the model presented here is generalizable to include all forms of social conflict and to provide a useful and coherent logical framework in terms of which to examine the relevance and adequacy of various mechanisms of conflict control, moderation, and termination throughout society.

[14]See, for example, the account of Tom Sawyer's encounter with "the stranger" in Mark Twain, *The Adventures of Tom Sawyer* (New York: Harper, 1904), pp. 7–11.

3

The Conflict System

Considerations of Choice

Any significant stage in the life cycle of a conflict can be triggered by an almost infinite variety of specific events or actions. Indeed, it is possible, as we have noted, that under different conditions the very same act may bring war or peace, hostilities or settlement.

In mathematical terms, this is to say that the nature of the conditions under which the events occur in the conflict model is curvilinear and conjunctive rather than linear or compensatory. In conflict, as in gunpowder, the result of joining its component elements is something qualitatively different from what one would infer from considering those elements independently and in isolation. The whole is greater than and different from the sum of its parts. Clausewitz has suggested, for example, that the power of resistance of an opponent in time of conflict is "a product of two inseparable factors: the extent of the means at his disposal and the strength of his will."[1] He does not suggest that the power of resistance is simply the sum of these factors, so that any deficit of one may be compensated for by a surplus of the other. Rather, he suggests that the logical relation between the two is conjunctive: no amount of one can compensate for the absence of the other. For resistance to occur, the presence in some degree of both of these "inseparable" factors is required. Similarly, in another regard, Charles Wrigley has observed that

political history indicates that neither a female nor Negro may at present be elected to the American presidency, no matter how talented the person may be in other respects. There is no overcoming the single biological disability. . . . (Political configurations change. There was a time when a Catholic was also automatically excluded from Presidential consideration.)[2]

The logic is conjunctive rather than compensatory.

It is precisely this logic that characterizes the conception of conflict employed in this study and the notion of the conditions under which the significant stages occur in its development. I have suggested earlier that the causes of conflict are both multiple and systematic. If that is so, the multiple sets of conditions under which conflict originates and develops constitute some manner of system or nonrandom event. It is my contention that that system or event is conjunctive, that various configurations of a determinate set of factors occasion the origin and development of conflict, and that only particular configurations of these factors occasion particular developments in the life cycle of conflict.

Before these configurations may be established, however, the system within which conflict is held to originate and develop must be formulated in terms of a comprehensive list of opera-

[1] Karl von Clausewitz, *On War*, trans. O. J. Matthijs Jolles (Washington, D.C.: Infantry Journal Press, 1950), pp. 5–6.
[2] Charles Wrigley, "The University Computing Center," in *Computer Applications in the Behavioral Sciences*, ed. Harold Borko (Englewood Cliffs, N.J.: Prentice-Hall, 1962), p. 161.

tional indicators, attributes, or factors. Once such a list is established, a set of conflict cases may be selected for analysis and coded in terms of these factors at the threshold of each stage of conflict. A data base is thereby established from which to derive, by means of an appropriate pattern-analytic technique, the configurations of factors systematically attending those thresholds — that is, the systematic conditions of the critical stages of conflict.

Clearly, no finite list of factors can be inclusive of all those that might conceivably influence the course or outcome of any conflict. From this it follows, first, that no exclusive claim of causation can be made for any particular configuration of any finite set of factors found to pertain, at any particular threshold of the model, to any number of cases of historical conflict. Rather, these factors may be said only to precondition the event to the extent that the set of factors postulated to define the conflict system is analytically expressive of the intricate causal networks of reality. Second, some set of criteria of relevance and priority is required to achieve an operational definition of this conflict system.

Several sets of these criteria guided the search for this set of factors, starting with the existing literature on theoretical and empirical investigations of conflict. First, a set of substantive criteria suggested by Quincy Wright[3] for the study of interstate conflicts was broadened in scope to suit the present, more inclusive purposes. Thus it was postulated that all conflict arises from, and is generally conditioned in its development, by
1. the total state of relations existing between the parties to conflict, of which this particular conflict may be merely one part;
2. the internal policy, structure, and resources of each;
3. the processes and procedures available to and utilized by each for adjustment of the underlying dispute; and
4. the nature and structure of the environment, both physical and strategic, in which it is conducted.
Only an effective, operational expression of each of these sets of conditions, it was felt, could ensure the adequacy of the resulting "conflict system" as a reasonable expression of reality. So the search for relevant factors proceeded with the objective of finding the minimum set that would adequately express these four major components of the conflict system.

There remained, however, the problem of selection from among what would seem to be roughly comparable or even quite dissimilar indicators of major variables. As a further screening device among possible indicators, then, Robin Williams's suggested criteria for the selection of causal factors were applied:[4] first,

[3]See Quincy Wright, "Memorandum on Interstate Conflicts," paper prepared for the Carnegie Endowment for International Peace, New York, December 1955, p. 6.
[4]See Robin M. Williams, Jr., *The Reduction of Intergroup Tensions* (New York: Social Science Research Council, 1947), p. 50.

those of most promise, by means of their focus, for guiding empirical research; second, those of most probable validity, as adjudged by the consensus among previous researches; and, third, those of most relevance for application to concrete policy problems and activities.

Finally, these factors had to be chosen to complement the tight framework of the concepts, assumptions, and definitions of the conflict model presented in Chapter 2 and then formulated as an effective, operational test instrument for coding the conflicts to be examined. The major objectives in the design of this instrument or codebook and the final considerations applied in the precise formulation of the test items it contained were, then,
1. that the codebook as a whole complement and compensate for the assumptions of the conflict model employed;
2. that it be equally applicable to all forms of conflict as traditionally defined (for example, internal, interstate, and colonial or conventional, unconventional, and nuclear).
3. that it be comprised of factors assumed to operate continuously (if variously) throughout the life cycle of conflict; and, therefore, that it be equally applicable as an expression of the conflict system at any point or stage in that life cycle;
4. that it be as inclusive as possible of the factors found by previous theorists and investigators to be, either alone or in some combination, influential in determining the course of conflict; and
5. that it be of neither such size nor complexity of format as to detract from its reliability as an instrument of social research.

The result of this effort is the codebook presented in Appendix B, a test instrument postulated as a whole to define the system within which conflict originates and variously develops. The codebook, in effect, constitutes an operational extension and substantive elaboration of the conflict model described in Chapter 2. It may thus be considered an integral part of that model. Without the model and its assumptions, and especially those concerning the bilaterality and relationality of conflict, the codebook would have no theoretical focus, no integrative meaning. Similarly, without the codebook the conflict model would lack operational expression, the very means of transforming it from a formalistic depiction of a complex process to an effective statement of its dynamic function and substance.

Especially notable for their substantive influence in the elaboration of the codebook, as throughout the entirety of this study, are the writings of Clausewitz and Wright.[5] It seems worth the men-

[5]See Clausewitz, *On War*, passim, and Quincy Wright, *A Study of War*, 2nd ed. (Chicago: University of Chicago Press, 1964); "Memorandum on Interstate Conflicts"; "The Escalation of International Conflicts," *Journal of Conflict Resolution*, vol. 9, no. 4 (December 1965), pp. 434–439; and "Criteria for Judging the Relevance of Researches on the Problems of Peace," in Quincy Wright et al., *Research for Peace* (Oslo: Institute for Social Research, 1954).

tion that a survey of the literature on conflict and warfare reveals not only the enormous intellectual debt of all students of conflict to these two men but especially the remarkable extent to which a thorough reading of the magnum opus of each can acquaint one, albeit at times in obscure or oblique passages, with the overwhelming part of man's empirical knowledge and theoretical considerations of large-scale conflict.[6] A most poignant and timely example in this regard is the four-page précis of contemporary writings on wars of national liberation or "people's wars," as he called them, that Clausewitz composed almost a century and a half ago.[7] A reading of these paragraphs is more than sufficient to convince the reader acquainted with the writings of Mao[8] that the translation of Clausewitz into Chinese was one element in a complex causal pattern that changed China and the world.

The Conflict Codebook

The codebook itself comprises 300 items or questions that are grouped into nine more or less functionally coherent sections to facilitate their coding for individual conflicts. The nine sections are
1. "Some Characteristics of the Dispute," including general information on the conflict itself and on the relations between (rather than independent characteristics of) the principal parties or antagonists. These items measure the nature, duration, location, and physical environment of the dispute, as well as the stakes involved in terms of population and land area.
2. "Demographic Characteristics of the Antagonist," including various indices of the general population of each principal party and of its own stake in the dispute.
3. "Economic and Transportation Resources of the Antagonist," including the economic resources, policies, dependencies, vulnerabilities, and capabilities of each principal party.
4. "Political System and Governmental Structure of the Antagonist," characterizing the political system and style of each principal party, as well as the bases of their support and their general policy orientations.
5. "Perceptions and Policies of the Antagonist with Respect to the Dispute," which establishes the interests, objectives, perceptions, policies, commitments, and expectations of each principal party in its efforts to reach an acceptable accommodation with the adversary. Included here is a statement of the procedures employed or initiated by each for dealing with the dispute.
6. "Foreign or External Relations of the Antagonist and Involvement by Third Parties in the Dispute." Here are characterized the political and military relations of each principal party with its

[6]This should not, however, be taken to imply that theirs are the only significant contributions to this codebook. A listing of some of the more important sources employed in the substantive elaboration of this instrument is presented in the Bibliography, Part 1, "Substantive and Methodological Sources."
[7]Clausewitz, *On War*, pp. 457–461.
[8]See Mao Tse-tung, *Guerrilla Warfare*, trans. Samuel B. Griffith (New York: Frederick A. Praeger, 1961).

strategic environment, the extent of support or opposition of each from third parties, and the nature and extent of third-party involvement in the dispute on behalf of each, for whatever purpose.

7. "Military Capabilities of the Antagonist," including the military capabilities (and dependencies) of each principal party, present and anticipated; its capacity for making use of them in the dispute; its military commitments; and the nature and extent of third-party military assistance, if any.

8. "Status and Performance of the Antagonist's Military Capabilities," defining the characteristics, capabilities, operations, and performance of the military forces committed on each side in the conflict, including the antagonist's own plus whatever third-party forces might be involved.

9. "Losses Due to the Dispute for the Antagonist," comprising a statement of the material and human costs of the conflict to both sides (including involved third parties) in several of the alternative forms in which these costs may be expressed.

The codebook was designed to be completed for *both* principal parties to any conflict at each threshold of the conflict model examined. Coding a single conflict at one threshold therefore produces a data base of 600 discrete data bits — 300 for each principal party — or 300 compound data bits.

The first question that comes to mind in the face of a coding instrument of this size is, why so many items? Quincy Wright recently formulated a model in six variables for predicting escalation of international conflict.[9] Similarly, Clark C. Abt has established a model in seven variables of the termination of general war.[10] In both these cases and in others like them, however, the variables chosen are highly aggregative or abstract in nature, far removed from an operational statement in terms of meaningful, reliable indicators. When such variables are translated into operational terms, the number of factors involved as indicators inevitably burgeons. Rather than formulate the conflict system at a high level of generality, then, I decided to cast the net far and wide, to define the conflict system in as many operational dimensions as seemed required to express its own complexity and to capture the full variety of the diverse events it subsumes within its phase structure.

Some attempts have recently been made to apply the mathematical techniques of factor analysis to reduce the acknowledged multidimensionality of conflict to more manageable proportions.[11]

[9]Wright, "Escalation of International Conflicts."
[10]See Clark C. Abt, "The Termination of General War," Ph.D. dissertation, Massachusetts Institute of Technology, Department of Political Science, 1965.
[11]See, for example, R. J. Rummel, "Dimensions of Conflict Behavior within Nations, 1946–59," *Journal of Conflict Resolution*, vol. 10, no. 1 (March 1966), and Raymond Tanter, "Dimensions of Conflict Behavior within and between Nations, 1958–60," ibid.

The results of these efforts have thus far been generally descriptive rather than analytic, and logically aggregative rather than predictive. The problem with factor analysis in this connection has been the problem of all correlational techniques for our purposes. The operation of one variable (or factor) may be found to account for the great majority of statistical variance in another, less abstracted variable or in an entire set of such variables. For example, the rate of urbanization (the percentage of population living in cities of a specified size) may account for 75 percent of the variation in the literacy rate; if the rate of urbanization in a population is known, therefore, one may extrapolate from this figure to its literacy rate, by means of an established equation, with 75 percent accuracy. (The amount of variation accounted for by correlation techniques seldom exceeds 75 percent.) One may then ask why figures on both urbanization and literacy should be included in any test instrument for a given event when one is known to account for most of the variation in the other. The answer in the context of the present study, as Wright has suggested, is that war is in some sense not a normal state of affairs.[12] It may well be that the conditions under which war develops are precisely those in which such variables as urbanization and literacy stand in an abnormal relation to one another. If it is known that urbanization and literacy generally vary directly, it may well be just the set of abnormal conditions that emerges when urbanization is high and literacy is low that produces internal conflict and hostilities.

Some Reliability Checks

Of the 300 items deemed necessary to an adequate definition of the conflict system, 210 have prescaled or closed responses (that is, coding them for any conflict is simply a matter of checking the appropriate prelisted response alternative for each threshold coded). The great majority of these questions are qualitative in nature, and, whenever possible, previously established and tested scales were used to structure the response alternatives. For example, in characterizing the political system, structure, and style of each of the principal parties, extensive use was made of the Banks and Textor formalization[13] of Almond and Coleman's structural-functional model[14] of the political system. Similarly, in most of the quantitative questions that were prescaled for coding (for example, literacy rate and urbanization), the response alternatives represent the figures for the four quartiles of the nations of the world as of 1960, as determined by the Yale Political Data Program.[15]

[12]Wright, *Study of War*, p. 12.
[13]Arthur S. Banks and Robert B. Textor, *A Cross-Polity Survey* (Cambridge, Mass.: The M.I.T. Press, 1963).
[14]Gabriel A. Almond and James S. Coleman, eds., *The Politics of the Developing Areas* (Princeton: Princeton University Press, 1960), especially Introduction and Conclusion.
[15]See Bruce Russett et al., *World Handbook of Political and Social Indicators* (New Haven: Yale University Press, 1964).

Because so many judgmental questions were used in the codebook, however, some procedures and checks were required to
ensure its reliability as an instrument of social research. Several
were introduced. First, a preliminary draft version of the codebook was prepared and given a trial run on six cases of internal,
interstate, and colonial conflict. As with the final draft instrument, the preliminary codebook was completed for both principal
parties to each conflict at each of its phase thresholds. The conceptual and definitional difficulties encountered by the coders,
as well as their comments on the adequacy of the instrument as
an expression of the full richness (though not necessarily of the
precise detail) of each conflict were noted and accorded full consideration in the construction and formulation of the final coding
instrument.

Second, the final test instrument was applied to each of the
eighteen conflicts selected for analysis* by an individual highly knowledgeable, indeed expert, in that subject. This coder
knowledgeability proved indispensable as it meant, first, that
an accurate, apt definition of each conflict in terms of its path
through the conflict model could be achieved by combining the
coder's familiarity with the facts of the case and the author's
familiarity with the terms and concepts of the model. Such an
accurate definition of each case is essential if meaningful comparisons are to be drawn between cases at points in their development that are analytically equivalent. Second, the use of expert
individuals as coders meant that at least the most competent and
reliable, if not all, data sources were employed in completing the
codebook for each conflict. In the study of conflict, concerning
which so much information is erroneous, withheld, classified, or
simply unavailable, such competence is perhaps the most that
can be hoped for.

Finally, as a statistical check on the reliability of the final coding
instrument, one conflict, the Malayan insurgency of 1948–1960,
was coded separately by two coders, each operating independently and using his own data sources. A reliability test was performed on the data provided by the two coders at two separate
thresholds in the conflict: at the outbreak of hostilities (P–III)
in June 1948, when the two principal parties were the Malayan
Communist party (MCP) and the combined U.K.-Malay administration in Malaya, and at the termination of hostilities (P–IV) in
July 1960, when the newly independent Malayan government
declared its "state of emergency" terminated.

This particular case was chosen as a reliability study because it
is an example of an internal conflict with significant external,
or third-party, involvement and with a change in the identity of

*See the final section of this chapter.

the principal parties between the two thresholds examined. The coders of the draft version of the codebook had indicated that the difficulty of coding was increased considerably by each of these considerations, as opposed to the simplest case of interstate conflict between invariant principals with little or no third-party involvement. If intercoder reliability was high in this instance, then, some considerable degree of confidence might be placed in the reliability of the test instrument.

Of the 210 prescaled or judgmental items, it was found that at the threshold of hostilities (P–III) the two coders agreed precisely in their coded responses to 176 items for the MCP and 174 items for the U.K.-Malay administration; at the threshold of termination (P–IV) they agreed precisely in their responses to 182 items for the MCP and 174 items for the administration. Table 3.1 shows the results in graphic, summary form, the percentiles indicating inter- coder agreement.

Of the entire 420 judgmental items coded at hostilities, the coders agreed precisely on 83.3 percent; at termination, 84.8 percent; for the MCP the agreement was 85.2 percent, and for the U.K.- Malay administration, 82.9 percent. Of the total 840 items coded and examined, then, the independent coders adjudged exactly the same prescaled response as appropriate 706 times, or 84.0 percent of the time.

The intercoder reliability score of 84.0 percent was especially encouraging, inasmuch as this conflict was chosen specifically for its conceptual and structural difficulty. The single largest group of items on which the coders disagreed in their responses concerned the precise time when third-party intervention com- menced on behalf of the Malayan Communist party. The coders agreed, however, on the identity of the third party and on the nature of its intervention. If the matter of its timing could have been resolved, perhaps by discussion between the independent coders, there is little doubt that intercoder reliability would have exceeded 90 percent, an extraordinary standard of reliability. In light of this finding, special care was taken, in collaboration with the coder of each case, to establish as precisely as possible the

Table 3.1
Intercoder Agreement in Codebook
Reliability Test

	Hostilities	Termination	Total
MCP	$\frac{176}{210} = 83.8\%$	$\frac{182}{210} = 86.7\%$	$\frac{358}{420} = 85.2\%$
U.K.-Malay	$\frac{174}{210} = 82.9\%$	$\frac{174}{210} = 82.9\%$	$\frac{348}{420} = 82.9\%$
Total	$\frac{350}{420} = 83.3\%$	$\frac{356}{420} = 84.8\%$	$\frac{706}{840} = 84.0\%$

date of the events critical to the operation of the conceptual model of conflict, and therefore to the coding of the conflicts themselves.

The Nature of the Data Base

At the same time that the codebook was being elaborated, a search proceeded for a method of data analysis adequate for establishing the empirical patterns of item responses in the compound data base resulting from the application of the test instrument to the conflicts at their critical turning points. Since it was known that the vast majority of the items contained in the instrument were prescaled with fixed-response alternatives, a technique of analysis was specifically chosen and developed that is incapable of manipulating continuous data, and so is restricted in its applicability to what is called ordinal data. (Of course, some reflexive or mutual causation operated in these decisions. Once the technique of agreement analysis presented in Chapter 4 was chosen for development and its potential range of application, despite its limitations, began to emerge, the decision to use prescaled items in the codebook was reinforced.) The decision to employ this technique and to accept its limitations required selecting or developing some form of scaling technique for the 90 items not prescaled in the codebook. Otherwise, they simply could not have been handled by agreement analysis and included in the determination of the factor patterns. The 90 items in question were quantitative. They could not be prescaled, in general, because no meaningful and adequate means exists for prescaling such data (for example, gross national product, troop commitments, and military hardware capabilities) for conflicts spanning more than half a century marked by revolutionary political, technological, and military change.

The problems involved in the construction of scales for such data are essentially twofold. First, the traditional unreliability of hard data on historical events and the difficulty of obtaining reliable quantitative data are, in the case of conflict, compounded severely by its own frenetic nature. For qualitative or judgmental data, established procedures of historical research may be employed to determine their reliability. For quantitative information on specific conflicts, however, even when independent reference sources are in precise agreement there is the real possibility and frequent certainty that all are incorrect. Moreover, in gathering data on several cases for comparative purposes, one often finds that differing and irreconcilable criteria have been used in different sources to determine seemingly comparable data. Comparisons among these cases are thereby rendered difficult or, at best, questionable. One requirement for a scaling technique adequate to our purposes was that it provide or incorporate some means of correcting or compensating for this imprecision and inaccuracy in historical data.

The second problem of scalar construction arose from the assumption that conflict is essentially a relational phenomenon. The scaling device had to be able to express quantitative data in the relational or compound form of party ratios, even while preserving the significant distinctions inhering in such a data base and facilitating meaningful comparisons between cases.

To meet both these problems an original scaling technique was developed. Before we proceed to a presentation of this device, it should be observed that 3 of these 90 unscaled items concern the nature of the conflict itself rather than the relations between the conflicting parties and so are not compound in nature. These items, designed to establish the duration of the dispute and the size of the area and the population at stake, are discrete or absolute rather than relational in character.* For example, if a dispute had persisted for two years before a particular coding threshold, it would be self-defeating to take the identical values coded for both parties, form a ratio (always 1 to 1), and recode the parties accordingly for analysis. Rather, the absolute value should be retained and, after being imbedded in some scalar interval, attributed to both parties in the recoding.

After several coding techniques for these 3 items had been tried, a simple quartile technique was employed in scaling them for analysis. The entire set of nonzero responses to each item (there being one response to each item for every threshold coded in the study) was ordered by increasing magnitude and divided into four scalar intervals so that each contained an equal number of meaningful responses. Starting from the zero point, these intervals were numbered, respectively, from one to four; each individual response was then recoded for analysis in terms of them.† A basis was thereby established for comparing the conflicts in terms, for example, of very short, short, long, and very long duration with respect to the total data base established in this study.‡

A Logarithmic Scaling Technique for Compound Data

Each of the remaining 87 items included in the analysis was scaled by means of an original logarithmic aggregating device developed specifically to meet the requirements of both the structure and the nature of the quantitative data base established in this study.

In general, however, it may be said that the effect of this logarithmic scaling technique is to establish an objective and flexible means of maintaining the significant distinctions that reside in

*Items 1–6, 1–9, and 1–10 in Appendix B.
†In accordance with the procedure employed throughout this study, zero responses were themselves recoded 8 for purposes of analysis.
‡The scalar intervals resulting from the application of this technique to Items 1–6, 1–9, and 1–10 may be found in Appendix B.

any compound data base, even while facilitating meaningful comparisons between the individual cases from which the data base derives. The resulting scalar intervals proceed exclusively from that (expandable) data base itself and express the relationships residing in that universe in terms that allow significant comparabilities to be established between the individual cases. Moreover, by aggregating as it does, this scaling technique provides a convenient, built-in error-reducing mechanism for the inevitable inaccuracies and imprecisions of hard data on historical events, obscuring anything other than inaccuracies or discrepancies of a gross order of magnitude.

Compound data, it will be recalled, consist of two discrete and independent data bits (in this study, one for each antagonist). The simplest, most direct means of expressing the mathematical relationship between discrete data bits is their ratio. Unless such ratios are somehow aggregated into comparable intervals, however, comparisons between individual cases in terms of a specific item are impossible except where the ratios are precisely equal. Moreover, in the analysis of compound data, it is of paramount importance that fine distinctions be made between ratios around the 1 to 1 or party-parity level, while increasingly aggregative discriminations may reasonably be made as one moves away from that level. In comparing arms ratios, for example, it is essential that fine distinctions be made between interparty ratios around the 1 to 1 level, while little seems to be lost in aggregating ratios between, say, 10 to 1 and 15 to 1 or 50 to 1 and 100 to 1.

It is clear, then, that to effect such discriminations mathematically, some highly exponential function is required. One such function is the logarithm, both natural and common. Its employment in some form as the basis for establishing scalar intervals should allow very fine distinctions to be made about the whole number one (that is, the parity ratio), while increasing aggregation of the independent variables (the ratios) is achieved as one moves by equal intervals away from that point.

After a series of experiments with various forms of both the natural (base *e*) and common (base *10*) logarithms on the data base established in this study, the common log log was chosen because it was found that neither the common nor the natural log function provided satisfactory discrimination about the 1 to 1 level. With these simple functions, for example, 1 to 1 relationships were too often included in the same scalar interval as 2 to 1 and 3 to 1. Use of the highly exponential log log function eliminated this problem, producing generally fine distinctions around the 1 to 1 level.

The common function was chosen, rather than its natural counterpart, because the log log of one (that is, the parity ratio) to either the base *10* or the base *e* is minus infinity, an unwieldy figure for purposes of manipulation. Since it is easier both by hand and by computer to multiply by ten than by e, and since multiplication by ten does not involve the possibly complicating consideration of decimal cutoff points, the common function was selected for use. Thus each compound data bit, before being subjected to the log function, was multiplied by a factor of ten. The result, once the log log operation had been performed, was that one linear power of ten was sacrificed to achieve a functional reduction equal to an exponential power of ten. The problem of manipulating a negative infinity was thus effectively eliminated.

All this is by way of demonstrating the extraordinary flexibility of this scaling technique and its adaptability through experiment to the precise structure of the compound data base and to the specific analytic purposes for which the data are employed. As programmed for use in this study,* the logarithmic scaling technique proceeded for each item as follows:

Rule 1 *All* of the data gathered for each coded item was assembled in ratio form (since it was always gathered at each coding point for two parties), the larger integer being placed in the numerator. Note:
a. In any instance where the value for either party could not be determined or was unknown, the relationship between the parties for this item was indeterminate or unknown, and both were accordingly coded "unknown" (DK) for purposes of analysis.
b. Similarly, if the item was coded "not applicable" (NA) to both parties, no relationship existed between them with respect to that item, and both were coded "not applicable" (NA) for purposes of analysis.
c. Finally, if coded values for both parties were identical, either could be placed in the numerator.

Rule 2 The ratios so derived were converted to their decimal equivalents. Note:
a. If the coded value was zero for both parties, the relationship between them with respect to this item was one of parity, or 1 to 1, which converted to 1.00.
b. Similarly, where the coded value of one party on an item was found to be zero while that for the other party was not applicable, the relationship between them was one of parity, and the decimal conversion was set to 1.00.
c. Finally, if the coded value for one party was either zero or NA while that for the other was some number greater than zero, the latter number itself was taken to define their relationship for this item when the former party was coded zero or NA for analysis, and so was retained unchanged in this step. In the very exceptional case that this (nonzero) number was less than one, its log log

*This program (written in FORTRAN IV, G-level) and instructions for its use on the IBM System/360 (Model 65) may be found in the technical manual accompanying this volume.

translation (in rule 4) was set equal to zero. This, again, avoided the problem of manipulating a negative infinity.

Rule 3   The decimal values so derived were ordered by increasing magnitude and multiplied by a factor of ten.

Rule 4   The common log log values of the resulting numbers were determined.

Rule 5   The four largest differentials between these successive log log values were then determined, establishing cutoff points for five prescalar intervals.
Note:
In the case of ties, the differential nearest the top of the list — that is, the parity ratio — was selected, thus maximizing discrimination about that point.

Rule 6   Starting from the top of the list (the parity ratio), the *first* and *third* differentials were chosen as boundary points between the three scalar intervals to be applied in the final coding of the item for analysis. The boundary values for these three scalar intervals were, respectively, the first ratio value in the ordered listing and the last before the first selected log log differential; the next ratio value and the last before the third selected log log differential; and the next ratio value and the last one in order.

Rule 7   Final coding of the data for purposes of analysis was done in accordance with the empirical relationship between the two parties coded on the item, the scalar intervals so established, and the notations listed.

An example of the operation of this technique will hopefully serve both to clarify these procedures and to illumine the nature of the resulting scales. Suppose, for a particular hypothetical factor in the present study, that the following values have been established for the two principal parties to ten conflicts. (Each case, we shall assume, had crossed only one threshold of the conflict model, and so was coded only once.)

Conflict	1	2	3	4	5	6	7	8	9	10
Party A	12	2	3	10	0	100	15	2	5	DK
Party B	3	4	2	NA	0	4	0	12	5	3

The total data base for the item consists of twenty discrete or ten compound data bits.* From this data base we proceed through

*It will be recalled that the data base for each item so scaled in the present study consisted of one data bit for each antagonist for every threshold coded in each conflict. From the 87 thresholds coded in this study, there resulted 174 discrete or 87 compound data bits for every item.

the application of the rules as follows:

Conflict									
1	2	3	4	5	6	7	8	9	10

	1	2	3	4	5	6	7	8	9	10
Rule 1	$\frac{12}{3}$	$\frac{4}{2}$	$\frac{3}{2}$	$\frac{10}{NA}$	$\frac{0}{0}$	$\frac{100}{4}$	$\frac{15}{0}$	$\frac{12}{2}$	$\frac{5}{5}$	$\frac{DK}{DK}$
Rule 2	4.0	2.0	1.5	10.0	1.0	25.0	15.0	6.0	1.0	DK

Next, the order of the cases is rearranged so that the decimal values are listed in ascending order when multiplied by ten, thus:

Conflict									
5	9	3	2	1	8	4	7	6	10

	5	9	3	2	1	8	4	7	6	10
Rule 3	10	10	15	20	40	60	100	150	250	—

Rule 4   the common log log of

Differentials

$$10 = 0.0000$$
$$\overline{} \quad 0.0000$$
$$10 = 0.0000$$
$$\overline{} \quad 0.0705 \text{—(1)}$$
$$15 = 0.0705$$
$$\overline{} \quad 0.0438$$
$$20 = 0.1143$$
$$\overline{} \quad 0.0904 \text{—(2)}$$
$$40 = 0.2047$$
$$\overline{} \quad 0.0453 \text{—(3)}$$
$$60 = 0.2500$$
$$\overline{} \quad 0.0510 \text{—(4)}$$
$$100 = 0.3010$$
$$\overline{} \quad 0.0367$$
$$150 = 0.3377$$
$$\overline{} \quad 0.0421$$
$$250 = 0.0421$$

Rule 5   the four largest differentials between successive log log values are found to be those between the log logs of 10 and 15, 20 and 40, 40 and 60, and 60 and 100. Given these four cutoff points,

Rule 6   the scalar intervals established for this particular item are 1.0 through 1.0 (up to the first cutoff), 1.5 through 4.0 (between the first and third cutoffs), and 6.0 through 25.0 (from the third cutoff on);

Rule 7   the scale derived for this item is then*

1. 1.0– 1.0
2. 1.5– 4.0
3. 6.0–25.0
8. 0 or NA
9. DK

Accordingly, on the basis of the relationships between them in the original empirical data and the scale thus derived, the parties under examination are coded for analysis as follows:

*Codes 8 and 9 were used throughout this study to indicate 0 or NA (not applicable) and DK (don't know), respectively.

Conflict	1	2	3	4	5	6	7	8	9	10
Party A	2	1	2	3	1	3	3	1	1	9
Party B	1	2	1	8	1	1	8	3	1	9

An examination of these coding results shows that the effect of this scaling device—for this particular item—is to set equal the relationships between the parties to cases 1, 2, and 3, all coded 2/1; cases 4 and 7, coded 3/8; cases 5 and 9, coded 1/1; and cases 6 and 8, coded 3/1. In case 10, since insufficient data existed to specify the relationship between the parties, both were coded "unknown" for purposes of analysis. The effect of this scaling technique as applied to this particular item, then, is to distinguish between response relationships of 1.0 to 1, 1.5 to 1 through 4.0 to 1, and 6.0 to 1 through 25.0 to 1 as the meaningful bases for comparing cases in terms of that item.*

In general, the number of scalar intervals or alternatives established by this technique for an item is determined by the number of differentials selected between successive logarithmic values: $n = d - 1$, where n equals the number of scalar intervals and d equals the number of differentials selected. The number of differentials can therefore be varied to achieve the desired degree of discrimination for a specific item in terms of its derived response structure. The greater the number of differentials selected, the greater the number of response alternatives in coding for analysis and the greater the degree of discrimination achieved with respect to both the response structure of the item and any comparisons made between individual cases in terms of that item.

In the present study, however, special considerations led to the decision to reduce the five intervals that result from selecting four differentials to only three intervals for final scaling purposes. Initially, it was intended that five scalar intervals would be employed in the analysis of the eighteen conflicts. With five scalar intervals plus NA and DK, however, the result is a total of twenty response possibilities for each test item when both parties are coded:

Response
Possibilities

		Party B					
		1	2	3	4	5	0/NA
	1	x	x	x	x	x	x
	2	x					x
Party A	3	x					x
	4	x					x
	5	x					x
	0/NA	x	x	x	x	x	x

*The scales derived for each of the 87 items to which this technique was applied may be found in Appendix B.

With so large a number of possible response alternatives, little chance exists for precise agreement on any specific item among two or more of only eighteen conflicts. Indeed, little agreement was in fact found under this condition.

It was therefore decided that the number of scalar intervals would be reduced from five to three and the total number of meaningful response possibilities thereby reduced from twenty to twelve:

Response
Possibilities

		Party B			
		1	2	3	0/NA
	1	x	x	x	x
Party A	2	x			x
	3	x			x
	0/NA	x	x	x	x

This reduction could be achieved either by selecting alternative scalar intervals or by aggregating the original ones. In the first instance, the number of logarithmic differentials selected as scalar boundary markers could be reduced from four to two. For many of the items in this study, however, it was found that the elimination of these two differentials resulted in scalar intervals that provided insufficient or unsatisfactory discrimination around the parity ratio. In general, for the data base established in this study, four boundary-marking differentials were found to be necessary to achieve satisfactory discrimination.

The reduction to three scalar intervals could be realized, then, only by reducing the original five intervals. The first interval was left intact to retain its established discrimination with respect to 1 to 1 relationships; the second and third intervals and the fourth and fifth intervals following from the four differentials were reduced, respectively, to the second and third intervals for final scaling for analysis.

In the example just given, the five prescalar intervals that resulted from the selection of four log log differentials were reduced to three scalar intervals:

1. 1.0– 1.0   1. 1.0– 1.0
2. 1.5– 2.0 ⎫
3. 4.0– 4.0 ⎭ 2. 1.5– 4.0
4. 6.0– 6.0 ⎫
5. 10.0–25.0 ⎭ 3. 6.0–25.0

This reduction, then, did not alter the discrimination of the resulting scale around the critical parity ratio; it merely retained the degree already achieved at the same time that it facilitated comparisons between cases in terms of the more disproportionate ratios.

However, in 6 of the 87 items scaled in this manner it was found that insufficient or unsatisfactory discrimination was achieved around the parity relationship level; that is, the first pre-scalar interval established for each of these items was greater than 2.0 to 1.* Experimentation with the scaling technique on these items led to the decision to eliminate the *two* greatest log log differentials in the determination of the five prescalar intervals. Thus the third through the sixth largest such differentials were chosen as boundary markers for scaling these items. The result was that some enormously disparate ratios tailing way out at the end of the ordered listing (as 500 and 1000 to 1) were pushed back together (by the exponentiation process) into the fifth prescalar interval, and increased discrimination was achieved about the top of the list or the parity ratio. Comparisons in terms of the items so treated became both more meaningful and more apt.

It should be noted, again, that this entire series of procedures was developed specifically to cope with the structure of the data base established in this study and with the requirements of the technique of analysis (that is, agreement analysis) to which it was subjected. In other studies deriving from compound data structures, other specific requirements might arise, calling for other modifications and adaptations of this basic procedure. Only experimentation with these highly flexible procedures will illumine the precise manner in which they are best employed to effect the desired result.

Finally, I would say a word about interpretation of the results of this scaling technique. The six coded party-party relationships resulting from its application, together with their effective meanings, are
1 to 1:   parity ratio
2 to 1:   moderate disparity between parties
3 to 1:   gross disparity between parties
1 to 0 or NA: little or slight disparity, one party having none
2 to 0 or NA: some or moderate disparity, one party having none
3 to 0 or NA: great or gross disparity, one party having none.
Each interpretation is of course meaningful only in terms of the data base established in the study for the item in question.

This last point is of central importance both in understanding the operation of the scaling technique and in interpreting its results. For, unlike some scaling devices, this technique was designed purposefully for operation on an established (and possibly expandable) data base. The resulting scales are therefore specific to the data base employed and to the universe, or "reality," defined by it. That data base for any item is, in effect, regarded as being expressive of reality, and the relationships residing in that data base as expressive of all those pertaining in reality. Mean-

*See Items 3–5, 7–1, 7–14, 7–22, 7–25, and 9–6 in Appendix B.

while, the possibility remains of refining that reality or expanding that universe by the subsequent addition of other cases, each one further confirming or modifying the scalar intervals developed.

Selection of the Conflicts

Our considerations thus far have resulted in the formulation of, first, a conceptual model of the conflict process, of the significant stages in its development, of the critical turning points or thresholds separating these stages; and, second, a codebook or test instrument designed to express the empirical system within which, and under various states of which, significant transformations occur in the course of conflict. The codebook provides a 300-dimensional profile, as it were, of the structure, resources, capabilities, objectives, and performances of each principal party to a conflict, and of the relationship between them at each point in time when that conflict was on the threshold of some significant change in the course of its development.

Our objective, it will be recalled, is to determine the various sets of conditions under which these changes systematically and regularly occur, to establish the various sets of conditions of the several significant stages of conflict. To achieve this goal, the state of the conflict system must first be established at a number of comparable thresholds in real conflicts; the codebook must be applied to each such threshold in a number of real-life cases. In keeping with the experimental spirit of this study, a data base was established from 87 coded thresholds in eighteen real-life conflicts. While for most statistical purposes eighteen cases is a wholly inadequate number, the technique of data analysis developed here was chosen, among other reasons, for its ability to operate effectively on any number of cases, however small. Moreover, it is believed that eighteen coded cases of conflict are sufficient to demonstrate not only the validity of the set of concepts and techniques developed in this study but also their utility and potential in both theoretical and policy terms.

The conflicts included in this study and coded for analysis are
1. Algeria-Morocco conflict, 1962–1963
2. Angolan insurgency, 1961
3. Cuba: "little" war of August 1906
4. Cuba: Bay of Pigs, 1961
5. Cyprus: war of independence, 1952–1960
6. Cyprus: internal conflict, 1959–1964
7. Ethiopian resistance, 1937–1941
8. Ethiopia-Somalia conflict, 1960–1964
9. Greek insurgency, 1944–1949
10. India-China conflict, 1962
11. Indonesia: war of independence, 1945–1949
12. Indonesia-Malaysia conflict, 1963–1965
13. Israel-Egypt conflict, 1956
14. Kashmir conflict, 1947–1965
15. Malayan insurgency, 1948–1960

16. Spanish civil war, 1936–1939
17. USSR-Iran conflict, 1941–1947
18. Venezuelan insurgency, 1959–1963

As a whole, this set of eighteen cases fulfills the criteria established in Chapter 2 for the cases necessary to the present analysis.*

First and foremost in their selection were considerations of the availability of the data necessary to effect coding. It was expected at the outset that in no case would it be possible to obtain reliable information on all 300 items in the codebook for every applicable threshold.† A preliminary check of the literature on each conflict coded, however, indicated that an overwhelming proportion of this information was readily obtainable.

Second, each is a case of what might loosely be termed local rather than general conflict, thus facilitating, as we have noted, its precise definition and specification in terms of the assumptions and definitions of the conflict model. At the same time, this set of conflicts affords wide variations in the degree of geographic and strategic localization, limitation of the hostilities that occurred (in terms of scale and scope), third-party involvement (subnational, national, and international) and great-power involvement and partisanship, and mode of termination of hostilities or settlement of the dispute. Within the large framework of local conflict, then, the bases for many phenomenological types of conflict were included in the selected conflicts. In addition, they are broadly inclusive and representative of many of the traditionally defined types of conflict and warfare, including examples of the internal, interstate, and colonial, conventional and unconventional, and proxy and authentic varieties.

Finally, the eighteen conflicts afford great variety in terms of alternative paths through the conflict model, thus affording ample opportunity for examination of its richness and utility as a conceptual device. Figure 3.1 depicts graphically the path of each conflict, as defined in this study, through the conflict model and indicates the thresholds at which each was coded. (The dates and events marking the start of each phase or subphase of each conflict, as well as the principal parties established for coding purposes, may be found in Appendix A.)

The application of the codebook to these eighteen conflicts yields a total data base of better than 50,000 pieces of information, that is, 300 data bits for each principal party at each of 87 conflict

*The more important reference sources employed in the coding of each conflict, together with a list of the general references employed throughout, may be found in the Bibliography, Part 2, "Data Sources."
†It will be seen that the technique of data analysis employed was adapted specifically to handle the problem of gaps in the data base and to operate effectively on the data supplied to it.

Figure 3.1
The Conflicts as Defined and
Coded within the Terms of the
Conflict Model

Note: The asterisks (*) indicate the characteristic definition of each conflict in terms of its path through the conflict model. Circled asterisks ⊛ indicate that the conflict was coded for analysis at the threshold of that phase or subphase. The actual events marking the start of each phase and subphase in each case may be found in Appendix A (coding being effected in terms of the events and conditions pertaining up to, but not including, that event). Indicated at the end is the number of instances of each stage of conflict coded from the number of conflicts in which that stage actually occurred one or more times, the course of many conflicts having taken them through a given stage more than once. An arbitrary coding limit of 7 thresholds was placed on each conflict; in the Indonesian independence case, for example, this meant that only the most marked or significant examples of P–III, D, and P–IV were coded.

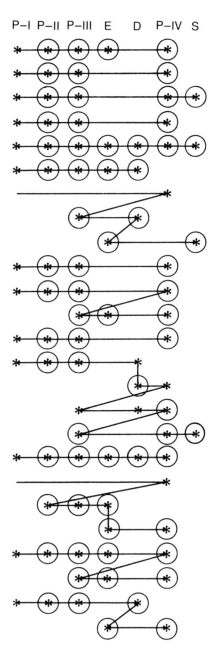

	P–I	P–II	P–III	E	D	P–IV	S

Algeria-Morocco
Angolan insurrection
Cuba: war of 1906
Cuba: Bay of Pigs
Cyprus: independence
Cyprus: internal
Ethiopian resistance
Ethiopia-Somalia
Greek insurgency
India-China
Indonesia: independence
Indonesia-Malaysia
Israel-Egypt
Kashmir
Malayan insurgency

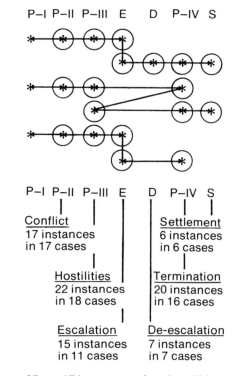

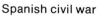

thresholds. Included in these 87 are 17 instances of prehostilities conflict (P–II) in seventeen different conflicts; 22 instances of hostilities (P–III) in eighteen conflicts; 15 instances of escalation (E) in eleven conflicts; 7 instances of de-escalation (D) in seven conflicts; 20 instances of termination (P–IV) in sixteen conflicts; and, finally, 6 instances of settlement (S) in six conflicts.

The result is 87 different depictions or descriptions of the state of the conflict system when these significant changes occurred in the life cycle of particular conflicts. A data base was thus established for determining the various patterns of factors that apply at their thresholds and the various sets of conditions under which those changes occurred. We shall turn now to a discussion and description of the technique developed for deriving the factor patterns from the coded data base.

4

Agreement Analysis

The State of the Art

Concurrently with the development of the data base for this study, a search proceeded for a technique of data manipulation, analysis, and presentation that might productively operate on a relatively large number of variables and a small number of cases even while imposing the minimum number of assumptions and limitations on the objective structure of the data.

As we have seen, both the number and the nomenclature of the variables that have been found relevant to the study of conflict and warfare are nearly overwhelming to the human mind. A modern Linnaeus is required to establish a meaningful hierarchy of conflict-relevant variables. It is perhaps reasonable, if unwise, to suggest that such is the case throughout all the social sciences today, where the number and variety of variously established, behavior-relevant variables are proliferating at an exhausting rate. Short of finding a genius, however, we now have at our disposal the limited but powerful capabilities of the electronic computer to assist in discovering the underlying dimensionality of the behavioral universe. In addition, powerful statistical techniques are being developed and suggested. In combination with the computer's enormous facility at routine, iterative operations, these techniques offer the promise of significant reductions in the analytic dimensionality of behavioral events. Such a method is agreement analysis, which has been developed and programmed here for the first time in its most general and useful form.

Agreement analysis is a technique of data manipulation, analysis, and presentation most excellently suited to the problems of utmost significance to the clinician, that is, behavior or attribute patterns. Through a series of iterative, noncorrelational procedures, it is capable of simultaneously determining the empirical patterns residing in a data base of response (for example, person, case, or object) characteristics while the respondents themselves are being classified for predictive purposes into a series of hierarchical types.

As originally formulated by Louis L. McQuitty,[1] agreement analysis proceeds in its theoretical foundations from a statistically comprehensive definition of types:

a type is a member of a category within some kind of classification system. This person, case, object, etc. and other members of his type have a combination of attributes which is uniquely characteristic of them; furthermore, the attributes of these persons are interrelated in a unique fashion. This set of attributes is not necessarily representative of all attributes; a person may belong to one type in one universe of attributes, and to quite another type in another universe of attributes.[2]

[1]Louis L. McQuitty, "Agreement Analysis: Classifying Persons by Predominant Patterns of Responses," *British Journal of Statistical Psychology*, vol. 9, no. 1 (May 1956), pp. 5–16.
[2]Louis L. McQuitty, "A Mutual Development of Some Typological Theories and Pattern-Analytic Methods," *Educational and Psychological Measurement*, vol. 27, no. 1 (Spring 1967), p. 22.

In the most rigorous and restrictive statistical terms, then, a type is a category of persons or objects wherein

everyone in the category is more like every other person in the category than he is like any person in any other category. This definition is comprehensive in the statistical operations it requires; in order to isolate a type, every person must be compared with every other person.[3]

It is the latter requirement — that classification of persons and aggregation of responses proceed from some complete interperson comparison matrix — that establishes the relationship between agreement analysis and one particular form of a more familiar mode of data reduction, the Q (or inverted) factor analysis.

The most widely used form of factor analysis, the R technique, undertakes to identify basic or underlying sources of covariation among a larger number of observed variables. The correlation established between variables is based on the covariation of individual differences in the several variables across many individuals. The factor or underlying variable generated to account for this covariation is said to be common across persons or cases; aggregation is effected in terms of variables, through the maximization of covariation, across cases.

The Q technique, on the other hand, is designed to identify groups of cases having scores or responses to a set of variables so similar as to justify treating them as a common type of person or case. Aggregation is effected in terms of cases across a number of variables. In application, the Q technique proceeds from an index of association (r, tau, coefficient of profile similarity, and so on) calculated for all possible pairs of individual cases. The resulting matrix of coefficients is analyzed for natural clusters, families, or types of cases. Because individuals or cases, rather than variables or attributes, are clustered by this particular technique, it is referred to as inverse or obverse factor analysis.

The strength of the Q technique lies in the fact that through correlational measures it derives maximum informational content from the data base used to establish case types and their attribute patterns. The correlation coefficient is, however, essentially an index of linear association. Like most traditional multivariate techniques of analysis, the Q technique is very exacting in specifying a linear or compensatory model to which the data are required to conform, within certain specified limits. This linear model is hypothesized as isomorphic to the force, phenomenon, or whatever that lends to the data the form or structure they are found to possess. Variables are thus assumed to be additive or compensatory for purposes of both predicting some variable outcome (as in multiple regression or correlation)[4] and determining relative

---

[3]Ibid., p. 23.
[4]See, for example, Everett M. Rogers, *Diffusion of Innovations* (New York: Free Press, 1962), concerning the use of multiple correlation analysis for predictive purposes.

standing in terms of either some aggregative factor (as in factor analysis)[5] or a latent class (as in latent structure analysis).[6] A deficit in any given variable in the correlative (or predictive) equation may be compensated for by a surplus in another.

It has, however, been found that much information may be lost in restricting data to linear continua. Meehl has demonstrated that it is theoretically possible for responses to items when treated in nonlinear (for example, multiplicative) combination to have a predictive value that they lack when treated separately or in linear combinations alone.[7] In demonstrating this he has, in fact, established himself in perpetuity as author of the Meehl paradox: two or more test items can each have a zero correlation with a criterion and yet jointly be perfectly correlated with it. This possibility arises from the definition of statistical independence itself: two or more items are independent if, and only if, each has a zero correlation with every other item when taken separately and with every possible combination of them.[8]

Since nonlinearities have been found in abundance in the physical sciences, which, it can be argued, deal with a general system far less complex in its structure and operation than do the social sciences, there would seem to be every reason to expect them to exist in abundance in bodies of social and political data. It is, accordingly, preferable that the pattern-analytic methods used to examine and structure data do not themselves specify the kinds of relationships to be reflected by the data, either linear or nonlinear.

Only within recent years have linear methods been sufficiently analyzed and understood to make some investigators feel that data patterns should be examined as nonlinear or configural effects of objective, measurable phenomena. The practical difficulty encountered in isolating those phenomena is the considerable number of empirical patterns that reside in any large body of empirical data, which may be caused by nothing more than random chance. The larger the sample of items in a test of a population, the smaller the probability of finding any two cases with identical patterns of responses to the set of items. In terms of the present study, this means that the chances of finding two identical definitions of the conflict system in real life — as defined by the

[5]See, for example, L. L. Thurstone, *Multiple Factor Analysis* (Chicago: University of Chicago Press, 1947).
[6]See, for example, Daniel Lerner, *The Passing of Traditional Society: Modernizing the Middle East* (Glencoe, Ill.: Free Press, 1958), Appendix C, concerning the use of latent structure analysis in this regard.
[7]See P. E. Meehl, "Configural Scoring," *Journal of Consulting Psychology*, vol. 14, no. 3 (June 1950), pp. 165–171.
[8]In mathematical terms the property b_i is said to be completely independent of every property $b_1, b_2, \ldots, b_n$ if and only if b_i is both independent of every property $b_1, b_2, \ldots, b_n$ taken separately, and independent of the logical product of every group of properties selected out of $b_1, b_2, \ldots, b_n$.

300 items in the eighteen cases — are virtually nil. On the other hand, every conflict may be said to develop through the various operations of multiple sets of common pressures. Within the conflict system the same set of factors is always more or less at work upon any given conflict, operating in various degrees and combinations toward various developmental outcomes. Every conflict may thus be expected to become at once a more or less complete representative of several overlapping and intersecting types, each of which is defined by the particular combination of pressures peculiar to it.

Within the framework of these assumptions, the focus for pattern analysis is shifted to the isolation of the multiple types inhering in individual conflicts and to the determination of the character-istic (or item-response) patterns that define them empirically. A significant advance in this regard was introduced by McQuitty. He suggested that attention be shifted to correspondences of partial patterns of response characteristics and that cases be classified in terms of predominant patterns of nonunique charac-teristics. Specifically, he suggested the technique of agreement analysis that might
1. establish an objective method of data classification based on responses to items and their frequencies across cases, with no reference to correlation or to any specific external criteria;
2. identify configurations or patterns of responses to items in which existing nonlinear as well as linear relations between the items may be identified; and
3. classify cases into a series of hierarchical types based upon the total set of item responses, at the same time that it is assembling the latter into patterns.[9]
The freedom of this technique from dependence upon any exter-nal criterion means that the item-response patterns derived by it are those dominant in the natural structure of the total data base itself. It can therefore be assumed that these patterns, and the types of cases defined by them, are indicative of some inferred phenomenon or construct — a typological differentia, to use Mc-Quitty's term — that causes these specific patterns of item re-sponses to occur.*

In the very simplest terms, the method proceeds by first grouping all individuals or cases at a first level of classification so that each has more nonrandom characteristics (or item responses) in com-mon with the other members of its class or type than with any other type. This grouping process occurs in such a fashion that once all cases have been classified each is classified with the

[9]McQuitty, "Agreement Analysis: Classifying Persons," p. 10.
*It should be noted, however, that the effective operation of this tech-nique does not preclude the use of external criteria for defining the data base to which it is applied or for analyzing its results; rather, such criteria are simply not necessary to its effective operation.

other case(s) with which it has the most characteristics in common. Each resulting grouping of cases is then defined in terms of the characteristics common to all of its member cases and is itself treated as a new case for classification at the next higher level. The second level of commonality among the individual cases is then determined by grouping these new "cases" together in the same manner as at the first level. This hierarchical procedure is repeated indefinitely until that level is reached where no characteristics are common to the newly defined cases or until one case is derived that contains all the characteristics common to all the original cases included in the analysis.

The result is a hierarchical series of patterns that defines at each level of classification the predominant configural characteristics residing in the data base. The types derived at each hierarchical level represent progressive steps between the individual cases or the imperfect types existing in reality and the perfect or pure types existing only in theory. The characteristics of the pure types are therefore approached — though never fully realized — through a series of successively higher-order abstractions from reality by classifying imperfect types into internally consistent categories and determining their common characteristics.

The theory, as McQuitty has suggested, is that "various sets of pressures may be assumed to act on individuals, institutions, and other objects as they develop. Consequently, each object tends to develop more than one type, and a sample of objects reflects more than one typology."[10] The complex interaction of multiple types in any individual case thus obscures each one of those types from direct observation. The individual case may itself, however, be viewed as an imperfect expression of a multiplicity of pure types: "first, an individual type, and then types analogous to a species, a genus, a family, etc. As more and more individual types are classified together to represent higher and higher orders of hierarchical types, the successive categories become better representatives of pure types, which exist only in theory."[11]

Thus a hierarchical organization of the data and a classification of cases may be composed that are analogous to the Linnaean formula for the classification of plants and animals, as illustrated in Figure 4.1. This hierarchical classification of individual cases, proceeding at successive levels of abstraction from reality on the basis of shared characteristics, affords the analyst the opportunity to determine the level of the hierarchy and the least number of characteristics or items that minimize errors in behavioral prediction.   Any type resulting from this scheme may, then, be defined as a set of cases sufficiently similar so that the behavior

[10]McQuitty, "Mutual Development of Some Typological Theories," p. 44.
[11]Ibid., p. 45.

Figure 4.1
A Simple Linnaean Chart

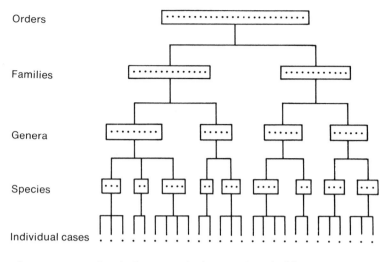

Orders

Families

Genera

Species

Individual cases

of any one member is the expected or most probable response of any other member.

Some Methodological Comparabilities

Before we turn to a more complete presentation of the manner in which agreement analysis operates on the data to obtain these results, it may be worthwhile to consider briefly some further trade-offs involved in its use, compared with other techniques.

The most severe shortcoming of this method, as it was developed and used in this study, is its inability to handle continuous or un-scaled data; that is, it has no generality beyond qualitative or ordinal data. Its use in this study, for example, necessitated the development of a logarithmic scaling technique that could give expression to both the conceptual demands of this method and the empirical demands of the data instrument. On the other hand, agreement analysis was developed in this study to permit its effective operation regardless of either the number of possible response alternatives to any given item in the test instrument or the number of items in the instrument coded for any case. For example, the instrument may at once include both dichotomous and multichotomous items. And if no two respondents to a survey respond either to the same number of items or even to all the same items, the technique is nonetheless maximally effective in terms of its use of the available data base.

Progress has been made elsewhere in extending the applicability of agreement analysis to continuous variables through a similarity index derived from correlations or other indices of associa-tion.[12] As has been noted, however, such indices necessitate

[12]See Louis L. McQuitty, "A Method of Pattern Analysis for Isolating Typo-logical and Dimensional Constructs," Research Report, AFP TRC–TN–55–62 (San Antonio, Tex.: USAFPTRC, December 1955). See also, by the same author, "Similarity Analysis by Reciprocal Pairs for Discrete and Continuous Data," *Educational and Psychological Measurement*, vol. 26, no. 4 (Winter 1966), pp. 825–831.

assumptions about the way in which the data relate and the variables cluster that are themselves undesirable or offensive. To the degree that such assumptions are in error when combining cases, items, or variables, the pure form of agreement analysis seems the more powerful method within its own limits. C. F. Wrigley has presented a study that allows some operational comparisons to be drawn between similarity analysis and factor analysis.[13] His conclusions appear to be equally applicable to a comparison of agreement analysis and factor analysis. Briefly, Wrigley reported that similarity analysis is more quickly effected, is more objective, and has an immediate appeal to the uninitiated in the comparative simplicity of its operation; factor analysis, on the other hand, uses more information, and so probably yields more stable results.

It may be observed, however, that increasing dissatisfaction with factor analysis has followed from both its lack of objective operation and the obscurity of meaning in its results. Dependent as it is on the informed judgments and sensitivities—and therefore prejudices and susceptibilities—of the analyst at both the input and the output ends, factor analysis has not achieved anything like the widespread popularity and use among social scientists anticipated for it in this age of electronic computers. In performing its aggregative operations on any data base, the correlation-based technique of factor analysis undoubtedly does in some sense use more of the total information available than does agreement analysis. The criterion for aggregation by agreement analysis, that is, perfect matching on item responses between all cases classified together, is very strict. As a result, item responses common to some, but not all, of the cases classified in a pattern are not found in the factor patterns produced by agreement analysis. Some information in the data base is thus lost as the analysis proceeds through its various levels of operation. This is, in effect, the price paid for the freedom of this technique from the assumptions imposed by correlation and upon which factor analysis is based. It is perfectly feasible, however, though it was not attempted in this study, to recover the residual data discarded in the classification by agreement analysis and to reanalyze it to determine a second order or subdominant set of factor patterns and case types in the data base.

In terms of comparable substantive output from the two methods of factor and agreement analysis, H. E. Watson has reported a study in which the two were applied to the same data base.[14] His results were virtually the same for both techniques, especially at

[13]C. F. Wrigley, "Cluster Analysis or Factor Analysis: The Divisional Structure of the American Psychological Association," *Psychological Reports*, vol. 3 (1957), pp. 497–506.
[14]H. E. Watson, "Agreement Analysis: A Note on Professor McQuitty's Article," *British Journal of Statistical Psychology*, vol. 9, no. 1 (May 1956), pp. 17–20.

the higher levels of classification or abstraction from reality. But, he adds, ''certain additional points have emerged with the newer method that remained undetected with the factorial procedure. Conversely, the factorial procedure has brought to light other features in the data that were not elicited by the agreement analysis.'' The main difference between them, and what appears to account for the difference in the results, is that

agreement analysis begins with the narrowest classes first, and then proceeds to the broader, whereas the factorial method starts by determining the widest class first of all, and then deals with the narrow classes in descending order, on the ground that it is wisest to begin with those components that account for the greatest amount of variance and therefore possess the greatest statistical significance.[15]

However, the significance to which Watson refers is meaningful only within the restrictive assumptions imposed on the data and therefore only to the extent that the data and those assumptions complement each other in fact. If pure types exist only at some higher level of abstraction from their imperfect expressions in reality, there is at least some philosophical merit to grounding their determination in reality and effecting their reduction with a minimum of assumptions.

In practice, therefore, it is perhaps impossible to say more than that factor analysis and agreement analysis represent two alternative and somewhat similar modes of data manipulation and analysis, the decision among which in any particular case can be made only by a knowledgeable and competent analyst in light of both the presumed structure of the data and the specific analytic purposes at hand. To the extent that the assumption of linearity is valid in a particular case, one may expect their respective results — especially at the higher levels of case classification and pattern determination — to be similar in meaning if not in substance. At lower levels of classification, the results of agreement analysis appear to be both more comprehensive and less concise, and therefore less manageable, than those of factor analysis. In addition, and simply because it is a noncorrelational technique requiring no statistical index of association for its effective operation, agreement analysis is especially well suited to the manipulation of a small number of cases and a large number of variables. This was one major reason for its selection for use in the present study, with eighteen conflict cases and 300 test items. In general, correlational operations on case-item matrices of this modest proportion are far from reliable and possess a predictive value only as great as the courage, rather than knowledge, of the analyst.

Finally, as will be shown, agreement analysis appears to be uniquely adaptable to a base of compound data consisting of the relationship between two independent, discrete pieces of data.

[15]Ibid., p. 20.

Such data present a particularly difficult problem in analyzing attribute patterns or configurations, inasmuch as it is the total pattern of item responses that constitutes the unit of classification. Consistency of juxtaposition of these independent bits must therefore be maintained and controlled throughout the operations required to classify the cases at each level. With two independent data bits to each item, there are two possible juxtapositions of the item itself as a data bit. And the pattern of which it is part has two possible forms, one for each juxtaposition of all its items together. Because the effective unit for the operation of agreement analysis is the total pattern of individual item responses rather than the individual responses themselves, manipulation of a compound data base is achieved by simply doubling its every procedure of normal operation, once for each possible expression of the total response pattern.

In its ready ability to manipulate compound data, agreement analysis may prove to be an especially useful and productive technique for analyzing behavior or significant attribute patterns in institutions or phenomena that are relational or bilateral in their very nature. Likely subjects for this technique are, then, marriage, defined as a husband-wife relationship; acquaintance-ship networks, defined in terms of mutual recognitions; or, as in the present study, conflict, defined as a relational state between two independently characterized parties.

Except for a difference in the order of complexity, agreement analysis operates in essentially the same manner upon either compound data or data consisting of but one independent bit. A discussion of the assumptions by which and of the manner in which agreement analysis operates on the standard or simple data base will now be presented, followed by a statement of the modifications required to perform compound agreement analysis.

Assumptions and Definitions

If the operation of agreement analysis is to be both meaningful and valid, some definitions and assumptions are required.

First, we shall define a "pattern" of responses as a complete set of responses to any given set of specified stimuli, for example, the items or questions in a codebook. The pattern of responses for one individual person, case, or other object is referred to as an "individual pattern." Agreement analysis first classifies individual patterns into categories called species, the item responses common to all individual patterns of a species constituting a species pattern. Only after all individual patterns have been so classified are the species patterns themselves classified at the second level of classification into broader categories called genera. The item responses common to all species patterns classified in any genus constitute the genus pattern. At the next level, the genera are similarly classified into families if it is found that the genus patterns have item responses in common. The families, in turn, are classified into orders, orders into classes, and so on, the category patterns of each being determined by the common item responses among the patterns from which they derive.

Second, it is assumed that the individual patterns of responses to the items of a test instrument are indicative of an indeterminate number of category patterns, the exact number to be determined only by analysis of the data. Furthermore, each response to each item is either relevant or irrelevant to each category, being relevant only if it is included in each pattern of the category. If an item has a response that is relevant to a category, the item is also relevant. The category pattern is the responses to the relevant items contained in the patterns classified in the category; all these patterns have the same response for each relevant item. Finally, responses to irrelevant items are due to chance; that is, they result from influences other than the forces or the typological differentia yielding the categories into which the patterns are classified. These other influences are, we shall assume, random with respect to the patterns of classification.[16]

The statistical touchstone from which agreement analysis proceeds is Zubin's "raw agreement score."[17] A raw agreement score based on two or more individuals' responses to a test is simply the number of items in the instrument to which they respond in exactly the same way. For example, if two individuals respond "yes" to the same ten items of a test and "no" to four, their raw agreement score is fourteen.

It is expected, however, that in any pattern of responses a certain number will be due to random chance and will therefore be irrelevant for classification purposes. Thus, with two possible response alternatives (yes or no) to each item in a 100-item test, it may be expected that any two responding individuals (or cases) could have identical responses to 50 items simply by random chance. No statistical significance may be accorded to such a finding. For any three individuals or cases, the corresponding number is 33.3. It is clear that the statistical significance of any pattern derived from observable data, compared with any other pattern, may be determined only by correcting the raw agreement score by an amount equal to the expected value of random or chance agreement in the pattern.

Thus the raw agreement score when corrected by an amount equal to the expected value of chance agreement on irrelevant responses is defined as the "corrected agreement score." It is

[16]See McQuitty, "Agreement Analysis: Classifying Persons," p. 6.
[17]J. Zubin, "A Technique for Measuring Like-Mindedness," *Journal of Abnormal and Social Psychology*, vol. 33, no. 4 (October 1938), pp. 508–516.

derived as follows:

Let

$r =$ the total number of items in the test,

$i =$ any pattern at any level of classification,

$j =$ any other pattern at any level,

$p =$ the number of individual patterns classified in the category that yields pattern i,

$q =$ the number of individual patterns classified in the category that yields pattern j,

$k_z =$ the number of possible response alternatives to any item in the test (variable; any item may have dichotomous or multichotomous response alternatives),

$Z =$ the number of items in the test having k_z response alternatives,

$n_{ij} =$ the raw agreement score for patterns i and j (the number of items for which the pattern i has the exact same response as the pattern j), and

$n'_{ij} =$ the corrected agreement score for patterns i and j (that is, n_{ij} minus the number of items on which they agree by chance).

It follows from these definitions that

$k_z{}^{p+q} =$ the total number of possible response patterns resulting from $(p+q)$ individual patterns and k_z response alternatives.

$\dfrac{1}{k_z{}^{p+q}} =$ the random probability of obtaining any given response pattern across $(p+q)$ cases for an item with k_z response alternatives.

$\left[\dfrac{Z}{r}\right]\left[\dfrac{1}{k_z{}^{p+q}}\right] =$ the random probability of selecting any one of k_z response alternatives, if Z items in a test of r items have k_z response alternatives.

$\dfrac{1}{r}\displaystyle\sum_{Z,z}\dfrac{Z}{k_z{}^{p+q}} =$ the random probability of selecting any one response alternative from the entire test (that is, the expected value of random variable k_z).

$k_z =$ the total possible number of relevant response patterns among Z items with k_z response alternatives.

$\displaystyle\sum_{Z,z}\left[\dfrac{Z}{r}\right]\left[\dfrac{k_z}{k_z{}^{p+q}}\right] =$ the random probability of selecting (or obtaining) any relevant response pattern across $(p+q)$ cases on a test of r items, with Z items of k_z response alternatives.

$\displaystyle\sum_{Z,z}\left[\dfrac{Z}{r}\right]\left[\dfrac{k_z{}^{p+q}-k_z}{k_z{}^{p+q}}\right] =$ the random probability of selecting any irrelevant response pattern.

$$\frac{r - n_{ij}}{\sum\limits_{Z,z} [(Z/r)][(k_z^{p+q} - k_z)/k_z^{p+q}]} = \text{the total number of irrelevant}$$

= the total number of irrelevant items in the test (items in disagreement plus those agreeing by chance), given $r - n_{ij}$ items found to disagree.

$$\sum\limits_{Z,z} \left[\frac{Z}{r}\right]\left[\frac{1}{k_z^{p+q-1}}\right] \cdot \frac{r - n_{ij}}{\sum\limits_{Z,z} [(Z/r)][(k_z^{p+q} - k_z)/k_z^{p+q}]} = \text{the probability of}$$

= the probability of random or chance agreement on irrelevant items (that is, the probability of random or chance agreement on items found to agree).

Therefore, the corrected agreement score is

$$n'_{ij} = n_{ij} - (r - n_{ij})\left[\frac{\sum\limits_{Z,z}(Z/k_z^{p+q-1})}{\sum\limits_{Z,z}(Z[k_z^{p+q-1} - 1]/k_z^{p+q-1})}\right].$$

This formula represents the generalized expression of McQuitty's fundamental equation for an invariant number of response alternatives to every item in the test instrument.[18] Thus for k constant this equation reduces to the form

$$n'_{ij} = n_{ij} - \frac{r - n_{ij}}{k^{p+q-1} - 1}.$$

The generalized expression was derived to permit the simultaneous treatment of items of varying numbers of response alternatives in the same test instrument or codebook. This elaboration of the correction formula was necessitated by the fact that, due to the manner in which agreement analysis manipulates data, one is not permitted to reduce multichotomous items to dichotomous items (as may be done with other techniques); that is, the items must retain the same degree of independence attributed to them in structuring the test instrument or codebook. It may be argued, however, that this is a strength of the technique, compared with other pattern-analytic methods requiring the tedious dichotomization of multichotomous items for effective manipulation.

Steps in Simple Agreement Analysis

At each level of classification it is assumed that the best initial indication of a category pattern is the two patterns from the preceding level having the highest corrected agreement score. Thus the best initial indication of a species pattern is assumed to be the two individual patterns with the highest corrected agreement score.

[18]McQuitty, "Agreement Analysis: Classifying Persons," p. 9.

To determine which two individual patterns have the highest corrected agreement score, a triangular corrected agreement score matrix is first constructed, containing the scores for every possible pair of individual patterns in the data base. (For N cases, there are $N(N-1)/2$ such scores.) The two individual patterns with the highest corrected agreement score are selected as the basis for the first tentative species, its species pattern consisting of the responses to the items on which the two selected individual patterns match perfectly. The corrected agreement score matrix is then augmented by the corrected agreement scores between the tentative species pattern and all remaining unclassified individual patterns.

Next, the highest corrected score between either two unclassified individual patterns or the tentative species pattern and an unclassified individual pattern is determined. If the score is between two unclassified individual patterns, a new tentative species and species pattern have been isolated, and the selection matrix is simply augmented again as before, with the addition of the scores between the two existing tentative species patterns. If, however, the score is between the tentative species and an unclassified individual pattern, a basis has been established for expanding the tentative category. Before this expansion may be effected, however, several tests must be made.

First, because the correction factor applied to raw agreement scores varies with the number of individual patterns combined in a higher-order pattern (that is, $p+q$), it may be that the individual pattern to be classified has a higher corrected agreement score with another individual pattern when they are combined into a tentative species than with the tentative species presently being considered for expansion. If this is the case, the two individual patterns in question are combined to form a new tentative species, and the selection matrix is augmented as before. If this is not the case, the problem still remains that the addition of this individual pattern to the tentative species may have changed the species pattern so much that some of the original individual patterns classified in it now have a higher corrected agreement score with a pattern not included in the expanded tentative species. If testing proves this not to be the case and each individual pattern classifies best with the new tentative pattern, then the expansion is effected, a new tentative species has been defined, and the selection matrix is again augmented as before.

If, however, an individual pattern now classifies better with a pattern not in the new tentative pattern, an "inconsistency" of classification has been found. A test must now be performed to determine which of the two individual patterns, the new one about to be classified or the old one previously classified, has a higher agreement score with the remainder of the tentative species pattern. If it is the new one, the old individual pattern is redesignated an unclassified individual pattern, and the new one and the remainder of the tentative species pattern are combined to form a new tentative species. If it is the old individual pattern, the original tentative species is retained intact, and the new one is designated an "adjunct" of the tentative species pattern.

The individual pattern designated an adjunct is now considered classified, since it cannot be classified with the existing pattern with which it best agrees without causing an inconsistency of classification elsewhere. As an adjunct, it may subsequently be merged at this level only with the derivatives of the tentative species to which it is adjuncted, and this may be done when it can become part of that pattern without causing an inconsistency. If this adjunct is never merged in this way, the pattern is finally treated as a species containing but a single case, and it may usually be expected to merge quickly with the pattern to which it is adjuncted at the next higher level of classification. If, however, the tentative species to which it is adjuncted is dissolved before finalization of the species patterns (through a subsequent application of the test of consistency), this adjunct reverts to the status of an unclassified individual pattern.

Once a second tentative species pattern has been formed, it is possible that the highest corrected agreement score to be found in the triangular data matrix will be between two tentative species patterns. If so, a consistency test is again performed to ensure that all individual patterns in the two tentative species have higher agreement scores with the new expanded tentative species pattern than with any other existing pattern not in this new species. If no inconsistency is found, the new tentative species is formed, its factor pattern consisting of the item responses on which all the individual patterns it contains agree precisely. If an inconsistency is found, the tentative species patterns are designated adjuncts of each other, and the attempt is made to combine the two whenever either is modified by the addition of another individual or tentative species pattern.

This process continues at the species level until every individual pattern has been classified as a member or an adjunct of a species pattern. The result is a finite number (a maximum of $N/2$ for N cases) of patterns peculiar to a single class or category of cases. Thus while any given item, or any given response to any given item, may appear in more than one pattern at any level of classification, each case may appear in only one pattern.

Next the species patterns are classified into genera in the same fashion as the individual patterns were classified into species. Genera are then classified into families, and so on until there is but one top-level category consisting of all the item responses common to all the cases under analysis or until all raw agreement scores greater than zero between established category patterns have been exhausted.*

It can be demonstrated that this process of classification occurs at every level in such a fashion as to maximize the number of characteristic responses in the category patterns derived, subject to the conditions that (1) each pattern or case is classified with at least one other at that level (unless this produces an inconsistency) and (2) each pattern classified in a category has all the characteristics of the category pattern. If we let i and j have their customary meanings except that they are for patterns at the same level as j', we may set

a = any pattern classified in the category with category pattern i,
b = any pattern classified in the category with category pattern j,
j' = the category pattern for any combination of patterns that did not occur in the final classification but includes pattern b, and
j'' = any one of patterns j and j'.

It follows from the method of classification that

$$n'_{ai} \geq n'_{aj'} \quad \text{and} \quad n'_{ai} \geq n'_{ab};$$

otherwise an inconsistency of classification would exist. But it is known that

$$n'_{ab} < n_{ab} \quad \text{and} \quad n_{ab} \geq n_{aj'};$$

therefore,

$$n_{ai} \geq n_{aj'} \quad \text{and} \quad n_{ai} \geq n_{aj''}.$$

This last inequality means that each pattern has a raw agreement score with the pattern of the category in which it is classified that is at least as great as it could have in any other category that might arise from any combination of patterns at the same level of classification. Operationally, this means that there have been elicited from the data the largest case-item matrices characterized by perfect agreement on item response that are to be found once all individual cases have been classified. Cases are classified in terms of those patterns that include the greatest possible number of responses for each case, and each pattern derived is peculiar to a single class or type of cases. In a mathematical sense, the categories derived are what may be termed both predominant and pure.[19]

The logic involved is that items on which these cases disagree, or agree only by random chance, cannot be essential to the typal patterns characterized by the cases. What emerges is a hierarchy of the statistically most significant types to be found in the uni-

---

*The complete logical flow diagram for agreement analysis, developed for the first time for use in this study, is presented in Appendix C.
[19]See ibid., p. 14.

verse defined by the data base, stripped of their idiosyncratic characteristics as imperfectly typed individual cases so that their credentials as members of higher-order classes may be determined.

Accordingly, the pattern of responses for each higher-order category derived may, as McQuitty suggests, be

assumed to indicate an inferred construct, called a typological differentia, which causes the pattern of answers to occur. Hence, each typological differentia may be described in terms of its pattern of response. In developing these descriptions, the investigator attempts to decide what unitary characteristic would be indicated by each pattern. His description of any one differentia is not merely a combination of single characteristics, i.e., one for each response of the pattern; he has to keep in mind the possibility that many other responses might also have patterned with those used, had other items been included in the test.[20]

It may therefore be possible to gain additional insight into the nature and significance of the differentiating force by further investigation, by any means or method considered appropriate, of the cases classified by the operation of that force.

Compound Agreement Analysis

In practice, compound agreement analysis differs from the simple form in that the data upon which it operates are compound or relational; that is, for every item in a particular test instrument, the response data consist of two separate and independent pieces of information. In the present study, for instance, the specific response to a particular item for a given case of conflict involving party A and party B might be yes/no, or 3/1, and similarly for every response to every item in every conflict coded.

To define or describe each conflict (or other phenomenon) in terms of such a data base, it is essential that party A and party B maintain the same relative position with respect to each other over the entire set (or pattern) of item responses included in the analysis; that is, party A's responses must always be on top or always on the bottom of the ratio formed by the response combination, with the other position reserved similarly for party B. When comparing two individual patterns in terms of their agreement score, then, there are two ways in which they may be compared, with a correspondingly different agreement score for each. For example, to determine the manner in which individual pattern A/B best agrees with pattern C/D, A/B as a whole must be compared with both C/D as a whole and D/C as a whole. Only by calculating agreement scores in both these fashions and selecting the higher agreement score as the basis for case classification can one be sure, first, that consistency is maintained in the definition of the conflict in terms of the responses of parties A and B to the items of the test instrument and, second, that the patterns in which each conflict is finally classified are the largest possible patterns in which they might have been classified.

[20]Ibid.

In terms of the initial calculations of the corrected agreement scores, this means that the original matrix will contain $N(N-1)$ elements for N individual patterns, rather than $N(N-1)/2$ as in simple agreement analysis. While the largest corrected agreement score is still chosen as the initial indication of a tentative species pattern, any given individual pattern is chosen in that form in which it demonstrates higher agreement with another pattern (that is, as A/B or as B/A). Throughout the operation of the technique, then, every comparison or manipulation made upon an individual pattern is made in terms of *both* of its alternative forms of presentation. For example, if a pattern once classified in a particular form becomes unclassified, it then becomes eligible for reclassification in both of its forms (A/B and B/A). Similarly, once species patterns have been formed and classification of genera has commenced, the species patterns derived from the individual patterns are considered for classification in terms of both of their forms. Thus any particular individual pattern may achieve classification in one form at the species level and in its alternative form at a higher level.

Some Further Refinements

The computer program developed for use in this study is fully adaptable to either the simple or the compound form of agreement analysis.* Several further refinements of the technique were developed and incorporated in that program, which I might note here.

First, it was anticipated that for no conflict in the present study would it be possible to obtain reliable information on all items in the codebook for both parties. Further, several "filter" questions were included in the codebook, one possible response to which eliminated several subsequent items from consideration for one party to the conflict or even made those subsequent items "not applicable" to both parties. It was therefore essential that, to be adequate to the demands of the data structure, the method of data analysis should be capable not only of manipulating varying numbers of response alternatives to various items but also of classifying individual patterns despite slightly varying numbers of coded items among them.

Because of the specific manner in which agreement analysis classifies individual patterns and determines precedence for their classification by an expected-value correction factor, this problem was resolved by manipulating the corrected agreement score to adjust for missing items in the data base and to achieve classification on the basis of the information available. It will be remembered that the corrected agreement score equals the raw agreement score (the number of responses to items on which two pat-

*This computer program and instructions for its use on the IBM System/ 360 (Model 65) may be found in the technical manual accompanying this volume.

terns agree precisely) minus the number of items on which they agree by chance. Now, in calculating the corrected agreement score between any two patterns of unequal size (in terms of the number of item responses contained), r and k_z, the total number of relevant items in the test and the number of possible response alternatives to each, are determined by the *smaller* pattern. For example, if the individual pattern for one case contains 90 item responses, while that for another case contains 100, their corrected agreement score is calculated on the basis of a 90-item test ($r = 90$), since this is both the maximum number of items on which they agree and the appropriate mathematical basis for determining the expected value of agreement by random chance.

The second further refinement was prompted by the fact that the response patterns established by agreement analysis consist of nonunique characteristics. It is thus possible that an individual pattern classified in one category pattern at a given level of classification may correspond with another category pattern at the same level to an extent that is of theoretical or practical interest. Similarly, it may be of interest to the analyst to know the extent to which some individual pattern not included in the agreement analysis agrees with the category patterns resulting from that analysis. Indeed, as will be seen in Chapter 6, it is through precisely this comparative approach that the total set of concepts and techniques developed in this study admit of rapid predictive calculations concerning the likely subsequent course of any real or hypothetical conflict at any point in its development. A subroutine was therefore written into the computer program that facilitates a simple expression of these interpattern comparisons.

In the case of simple agreement analysis, the comparison between an individual and a category pattern of interest is effected by determining the number of item responses on which they match exactly and dividing this by the number of items in the category pattern itself. The result is a percentile statement of the extent to which the individual pattern incorporates the item responses constituting the category pattern. In the case of compound agreement analysis, the calculation of this percentile proceeds in exactly the same fashion, except that it is first necessary to determine the form in which the individual pattern better matches the category pattern. That is, with two parties (A and B) making up the individual pattern, it may assume two forms for classification: A/B or B/A. The form in which it better incorporates the category pattern is used as the basis for determining its percentile incorporation of the category pattern. The result in both instances is a percentile statement that facilitates rapid if simple examination of the category patterns in terms of extraneous characteristics of the individual patterns from which they derive. Alternatively, it is a measure of the extent to which an individual pattern not included in the analysis matches any or all of the hierarchical types yielded by the analysis.

In another regard, it was observed earlier that, especially at the top level of classification by agreement analysis, the process of aggregation at times occurs more quickly than the analyst might wish. For example, if only three category patterns have been established at the genus level, it is very likely that these three will quickly combine into one final family pattern: the two genus patterns with the highest corrected agreement score will first be combined to form a tentative family pattern, and the remaining genus pattern will then be combined with the only thing left to combine with — that tentative family pattern — to form a finalized family pattern.

It may at times be of some interest to the analyst to retard this process, as it were, so that the tentative category pattern formed by the first two genus patterns to combine may be examined. This would provide a closer look both at the manner in which the final aggregation of individual cases was effected and at the substantive, informational content of the factor pattern deriving from them.

It was precisely these considerations that prompted the development and use in this study of a concept of "artificial" category patterns. The printout format of the programmed agreement analysis was thus designed to afford the analyst the option of establishing intermediary levels of classification that are not "natural" products of the operation of agreement analysis on the data base but are nevertheless of some special interest to him. In the foregoing example, the initial tentative family pattern might have been designated an artificial family pattern at the discretion of the analyst and printed out in that form. Accordingly, what would naturally have been the family pattern deriving from the three original genus patterns would now become an order pattern. While these artificial patterns do not possess the same methodological significance or validity as their natural counterparts, their usefulness to the analyst may be sufficient justification for the violation of the natural aggregation process of agreement analysis. Nothing is lost in the process.

As will be seen in Appendix D, which contains the factor patterns established in this study, extensive use was made of this notion of artificial category patterns.

Finally, let me repeat that the technique presented and employed here is but one specific form of agreement analysis, a form that may loosely be compared to Q-technique factor analysis for handling a large number of variables and a small number of cases. An alternative form of agreement analysis was developed and programmed for the MISTIC computer at Michigan State University by Peter Wing Hemingway.[21] This adaptation of the basic

[21]Peter Wing Hemingway, "Multiple Agreement Analysis," Ph.D. dissertation, Michigan State University, Department of Psychology, 1961.

method produces a nonhierarchical classification of cases by imposing an information-maximizing criterion on its operation. The result is a considerably foreshortened technique. At the same time, it assumes some rather severe constraints in its capacity to extract in their entirety the various empirical patterns inhering in the available data base. Also, Kern Dickman of the University of Illinois has programmed several foreshortened versions of agreement analysis for the ILLIAC series of computers.

At least in theory, a corresponding form of agreement analysis exists for every type of factor analysis, although relatively little effort has as yet been invested in exploring the parallels, comparabilities, and dissimilarities between agreement analysis and the various forms of factor, latent structure, and multiple-regression or correlation analysis. To the extent that agreement analysis presently represents a technique still in the process of development, much remains to be done in establishing its comparative utility, validity, potential, and range of applicability.

5

The Logic of Abstraction

Before we proceed to a statement of how the various analytic elements of the argument developed to now interact, it may be advisable briefly to review the logic that has brought us to this point and will yet produce the final conceptual device necessary to our purposes.

This study, it will be remembered, derives from an understanding of the enabling conditions of an event not as a specific category or set of causal factors, but simply as a way of viewing the co-ordinated impact of the many elements contributing to its occurrence. This conception was suggested with specific reference to analytically distinct stages in the origin, development, and termination of conflict between parties capable of waging war upon one another. This is not to say that there is something peculiar to the nature of these stages or events that delimits the applicability of the methodological considerations in this study to the present context. Indeed, if they may be validly and reliably applied to the present subject matter, they ought to be equally applicable to the consideration of any event, state, condition, action, or entity whose causes are recognized as at once multiple and systematic. Any such event may be viewed profitably as the end-product of various configurations of its analytic dimensions, be they measured in terms of attributes, characteristics, symptoms, or other correlates.

My principal methodological purpose has therefore been to establish the conceptual framework and technical apparatus necessary to operationalize a novel way of rigorously looking at things or events—as the result of the patterned interconnections and configural interactions of dimensions that define the analytically dominant features of the object of inquiry. That object in this instance is the conflict process.

At one level of comprehension and explanation, surely, every conflict is, like every human personality, an irreducible, unique cluster of characteristics and attributes developed and acquired over the course of its lifetime.[1] No two are identical. This is not to say, however, that no two are at all alike either in terms of the developmental process from which they emerge in mature form or in terms of the individual characteristics that define them. Personality theorists have found a most fruitful construct in the idea of distinct epigenetic stages through which all personalities develop, the developmental impact of the forces operating in each stage being conditioned by and comprehensible only in terms of what has gone before.[2] Similarly, it has long since been

[1]The classic presentation of personality theory in these terms is to be found in Gordon W. Allport, *Personality: A Psychological Interpretation* (New York: Henry Holt & Co., 1937).
[2]See, for example, Erik Erikson's elaboration of Freud's stages of personality development in *Childhood and Society*, 2nd ed. (New York: W. W. Norton, 1963), chap. 7, "Eight Stages of Man."

recognized that the individual personality is unique only as a total configuration of nonunique characteristics or attributes. At some level of analysis, then, it is both possible and legitimate to establish significant comparabilities between and typological classifications of individual personalities on the basis of their common or shared characteristics. Individual personality thus may be shorn of its idiosyncratic characteristics and an empirical statement made of its implications for general personality theory. Finally, some kind of weighting device may be applied to extract from generalized propositions the specific personality dimensions that are fruitful in the analysis of each postulated stage of personality development.

It is precisely this logic that is applied in this study to another processual, developmental realm: conflict. It was accordingly postulated that all conflicts pass variously through a series of stages or phases in the course of their duration or life cycle, each phase being immediately preceded by a threshold at which various, particular configurations of factors come to bear to precondition the succeeding phase. Since transition from one phase to another within this model by definition indicates some significant change in the nature of the conflict itself, it may be assumed that such a transition is occasioned only by some significant change in the configuration of factors applying previously.

Furthermore, since it is possible in terms of this model to establish analytic comparability between the significant events in different conflicts, it may be assumed that examination of the conditions under which distinct but analytically comparable events occur will yield some systematic statements of the various sets of factors that occasion or condition that event. For example, the outbreak of hostilities (P–III) in two distinct cases of conflict constitutes two distinct events. But if the significant conditions under which the two empirical events occurred are precisely codified in terms of some standard set of analytic dimensions, a foundation is established for specifying the conditions under which the generic, analytic event hostilities occurs.

This is not to say that there is any one set of conditions under which hostilities or any other phase in the conflict model occur. It is a fundamental assumption of this analysis that there are many, or at least several, such sets of conditions. In fact, various but particular combinations of mutually reinforcing causal factors will result in the analytic preconditions of any complex event. Once this view of causality is accepted, the most important questions for inquiry become, first, how to establish a common analytic dimensionality in terms of which to express the richness of conditions from which behavioral events emerge. Second, and only after a number of real-life instances of these analytically comparable events have been expressed in terms of those dimensions, is the matter of how to establish the most meaningful comparabilities between such instances and to extract the most significant sets of various preconditions of this event. Third, once these conditions have been established, is the question of how to isolate the strategic or critical conditions that distinguish one type of event from another and so constitute the blueprint for altering an event to produce an alternative outcome.

As of the present time, no one has managed in any but a limited way to express the full analytic dimensionality of conflict. Many cuts have been made into the carcass, but none has satisfied the requirements of all interested academic and operational parties. In this study we cast our net far and wide across previous investigations to construct an eclectic test instrument of some 300 items of established credentials in conflict analysis. This is not to claim that conflict is necessarily a 300-dimensional phenomenon. It is only to postulate, pending analysis, that the full dimensionality of conflict can be adequately expressed in terms of these 300 test items with fruitful results for theory and practice. It is to argue that the systematic interactions and interconnections of this set of items, when applied to real instances of conflict, are sufficiently expressive of its dominant features to allow meaningful theoretical and policy insights into conflict.

The test instrument, or codebook, of 300 items is therefore intended as a whole to be an adequate analytic expression of the conflict system — that is, of the system within which all conflicts may be said variously to originate, develop, and terminate. The result of its application at the threshold of any phase of any conflict is a 300-dimensional, empirical statement of the conditions under which the transition to that phase occurred in that particular case. Its application at many such thresholds of the same analytic event (or conflict phase) provides a systematic data base for establishing the various sets of analytic preconditions of that event.

The use of a common set of test items to define the preconditions of each live instance of each analytic stage of conflict is, moreover, intended to reflect the contention that the same fact, factor, or event may in different contexts condition quite different results. For example, a particular factor may in one context effect a de-escalation of ongoing hostilities, while in another its result may be escalation. To define the preconditions of each instance of these distinct stages in terms of common dimensions is, then, only to reflect a realistic assessment of the relations that causal factors bear to one another in reality.

Having established the reliability of the codebook as an instrument of social research and applied it at the thresholds of some 87 analytic stages in eighteen real-life conflicts, we proceeded to develop a technique of data manipulation and analysis that, in combination with the data base of nonunique characteristics, is at once fully expressive of our two causal concepts. First, the very same analytic event, for example, hostilities (P–III), may be conditioned by various configurations of factors, there being no one set of factors or conditions under which it occurs. Second, the very same factor may, under various conditions or as an element in various configurations of factors, condition quite different empirical events or practical results. This technique of agreement analysis is what might aptly be termed a rigorous, stepwise bridge between two more traditional modes of analytic statement: the one, that every historical event is in all its complexity unique unto itself and, therefore, no two or more events are at all comparable; and, at the other extreme, the more or less standard statistical statement that the only important indicators or sources of an analytic event are those that have been found with some given degree of statistical regularity to be common to all instances of the empirical event that typifies it.

To bridge this gap, agreement analysis accepts as raw input systematic data on any number of individual cases and yields the various patterns of characteristics predominant in the data at each of several hierarchical levels corresponding to the inclusion of those characteristics among increasing numbers of cases. Individual cases are thus classified into a series of hierarchical types defined by the statistically dominant commonalities among their characteristics. At any given level of classification, the same characteristic may be included in more than one typal pattern and so contribute to the definition of more than one type. Indeed, it is only the nonuniqueness of the factors defining the patterns at any level that allows the establishment of successive levels of classification. If we therefore regard the 300-dimensional statement of an individual case as its own individual factor pattern, each of the various species patterns resulting from an agreement analysis of a number of cases consists of all the characteristics common to all the individual patterns from which it derives.

Each genus pattern, in turn, consists of those characteristics common to all the species patterns from which it derives and consequently to all the individual patterns involved. And so the classification goes until at the highest level are found only those characteristics common to all the individual patterns with which the analysis originally began. At each level of classification the statistical mechanisms of agreement analysis thus isolate and identify the "biggest" (in terms of number of items) and "best" (in terms of significance) possible arrangements of all the cases submitted for classification. Isolated and retained at each level are the most significant sets of commonalities existing among the cases presented; shorn away are both the idiosyncracies of particular cases (which are, in any event, irrelevant to the determination of analytic types) and the less significant commonalities among them. What remains are what may be termed the dominant patterns of characteristics or factors residing in the data base, and the dominant analytic types extant in the universe defined by it.

Because this data reduction is effected at several hierarchical levels (the precise number depending in general upon the number of individual cases submitted for analysis), the analyst is afforded the freedom of selecting the results of that level of classification that best meets the requirements of the subject matter and analytic objectives at hand. The trade-off involved, at the extremes, is one between generalization and discrimination, between alternative statements of that which unites individual cases in a common membership and that which characterizes them as more specific examples of a generic phenomenon. Whatever the analytic requirements, it is most important to bear in mind that the hierarchical factor patterns derived by an agreement analysis of individual patterns or cases are not in themselves individual cases or instances of an empirical event. Rather, they are types, abstractions from two or more instances of empirical reality, and incomplete in themselves as events. But as types they are in one sense something more than the actual cases from which they derive: they represent significant movement away from the distracting trivia and idiosyncracies that inevitably accompany any complex phenomenon, event, or process and toward a statement of its analytic essence or systematic generator. No type is empirical actuality; it is abstracted essence. Any comparison of actual cases to types should thus be made only in terms that account for this central fact and understanding.

How, then, we may ask, does the technique of agreement analysis interact with the compound data base established for this study of the various conditions of conflict, and with what effect?

The Complete Factor Patterns

The compound data base, it will be recalled, consists of 87 independent specifications of the state of a 300-item conflict system at the threshold of some significant analytic event or stage in the conflict process. Specifically, the 87 statements of the conflict system were recorded at the thresholds of
1. 17 instances of prehostilities conflict (P–II),
2. 22 instances of hostilities (P–III),
3. 15 instances of escalation (subphase E),
4. 7 instances of de-escalation (subphase D),
5. 20 instances of posthostilities termination (P–IV), and
6. 6 instances of settlement (S)
in eighteen cases of conflict. A run of compound agreement analysis on any set of instances may therefore be expected to classify them into a hierarchical series of types, and the resulting item-compound response patterns to express the various dominant states of the conflict system applying at the threshold of that analytic phase or subphase of the conflict process.

This last point is most important. It will be recalled that the coding (at the thresholds) of each instance of the successive analytic phases was carried out in terms of the very same set of 300 items. For any particular conflict coded at, say, the thresholds of conflict (P–II) and hostilities (P–III), the set of characteristics common to both of its thresholds is therefore not isolable *specifically* as the preconditions of either. Some further weighting device or "filter" is needed to isolate the set of factors that specifically conditions the occurrence of each distinct phase of the conflict. This is also true for the various types of events derived by the agreement analysis and defined by the characteristics common to the two or more individual patterns they contain. Only by applying some weighting device to these characteristic patterns to strip them of what might be termed their nonspecific members may a statement be made of the conditions specific to the analytic event they define.

When one is measuring in terms of 300 test items, any two conflicts may have much in common at the threshold of, say, hostilities (P–III), if only on the basis of random chance. But what is not specifically common to them at the threshold of hostilities is not isolable as part of the specific conditions of hostilities. If, then, the set of their common characteristics at this stage is diminished by those found to be previously or otherwise common to them as mere individual patterns rather than as a dominant type of this particular event, what remains is the set of factors specifically conditioning the occurrence of the analytic event (P–III) defined by the conflicts.

Before the weighting device that performs this final data reduction is applied at any stage, then, it is necessary first to classify the conflict and to determine the factor patterns dominant among them in terms of the full dimensions of the conflict system. We must satisfy the demands of our substantive model of conflict before turning to the filtration problem arising from its interaction with the processual model. Each stage of the conflict must be allowed to establish its own full and various characterizations in terms of the conflict system, and only then be forced back within the logical confines of the stage model and shorn of the characteristics not specific to each stage.

Six compound agreement analysis "runs" were performed in the present study. The results are presented in Appendix D. The various sets of dominant item-compound response patterns established in these runs are what might aptly be termed the complete factor patterns inasmuch as they derive from the operation of agreement analysis upon more or less complete (300-item) definitions of the state of the conflict system at the threshold of each instance of each conflict stage examined. These, then, are the various dominant states of the conflict system applying at the thresholds of (1) prehostilities conflict (P–II), (2) hostilities (P–III), (3) escalation (E), (4) de-escalation (D), (5) posthostilities termination (P–IV), and (6) settlement (S).

The results of the six runs are presented in separate sections in Appendix D, with five sets of information for each. Subsections (a) indicate the conflicts included in the analysis, together with a statement of the event marking the start of the phase (or subphase) in question. (The coding of each event submitted to the analysis, it will be recalled, was done at the threshold of that event in terms of the conditions pertaining up to, but not including, the event itself.) As was shown in Figure 3.1, several of the conflicts coded contain more than one example or instance of three stages of the conflict model — hostilities (P–III), escalation (E), and termination (P–IV). In general, in any conflict where this applies, all instances of the stage in question were coded in terms of the conflict system. This raises the question, in determining the input for an agreement analysis of the dominant states of that system at the threshold of that stage of conflict, of whether to include all instances of the stage from the same conflict or only one, and, if the latter, which one.

To examine this question, an agreement analysis test run was performed on the 22 instances of hostilities (P–III) in the eighteen conflicts. It was expected that, if the two instances of hostilities in the four cases twice represented in the analysis were each classified together at the first (or species) level of classification, it could then be inferred that they resembled each other more as empirical cases of conflict than as representatives of the analytic phenomenon hostilities (P–III). For what would tend to be retained in the response pattern defining such a species would be the enduring characteristics of the conflict itself, as defined within the conflict system. Tending to obscurity at the same time would be the characteristics peculiar to the occurrence of each particular instance of hostilities (P–III) in that conflict. If, on the other hand, it was found that the two instances of hostilities were classified with other, distinct cases in one or two of the four conflicts, then it could be assumed that identity as a particular instance of hostilities within the conflict system is dominant over the enduring empirical characterization of a conflict in terms of the system.

As shown in Figure 5.1, in each of the four conflicts from which two instances of hostilities were submitted to analysis (USSR-Iran, Indonesia: independence, Greek insurgency, and Kashmir), the two were classified together by agreement analysis in the very same species (that is, species 1, 2, 3, and 6, respectively). Moreover, three of these four conflicts yielded the very first three

Figure 5.1
Classification of All Instances of
Hostilities (P–III) by Agreement
Analysis Test Run

Note: Of the 22 individual cases of hostilities (P–III) included in this analysis, 8 derive from the first (1) and second (2) outbreaks in four conflicts. The remaining 14 represent the only instance of hostilities in each conflict.

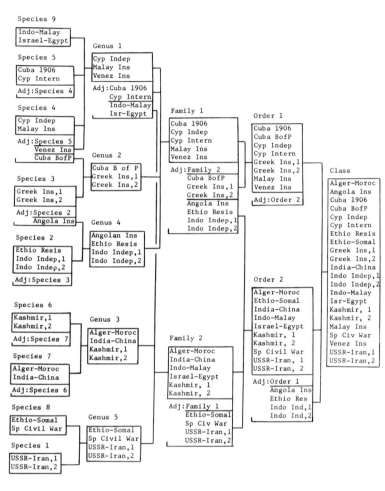

species categories established, thus demonstrating their unusual dominance in terms of the number of factors common to them among the nine species established in the run.

The implications of this finding are, it would seem, twofold. First, it is apparent that, of the 300 characteristics defining each instance of hostilities (P–III), those specifically conditioning that stage rather than generally characterizing the ongoing conflict in terms of the conflict system are relatively few in number. In no instance are the numbers of stage-specific characteristics great enough to offset the sheer numerical weight of the continuing characteristics, and so to effect classification of a hostilities (P–III) event with any instance other than that from the very same conflict. Second, it is apparent that if each of the various dominant states of the conflict system established by an agreement analysis run are to yield characteristics specific to the stage involved, no two instances of that stage from the same conflict should be included in the run.

From each of the four cases in question in the hostilities (P–III) run, the second outbreak was therefore selected for inclusion in the present analysis so that the patterns derived might be equally expressive of the conditions of renewed as well as of initial outbreaks of hostilities. In the few multiple-instance cases involved in the escalation (E) run, that instance was chosen that seemed to be the better example of the escalation genre by having effected a more clear-cut or telling change in the "rules of the game." Finally, in the termination (P–IV) run, the instances chosen from the four cases in question represented the more definitive, conclusive, or final cessation of ongoing hostilities. In each of these three runs, then, all but four coded instances of the stage involved were included in the analysis; in each of the other three runs, every such instance was included. The result is that, of the 87 definitions of the state of the conflict system effected in the coding of the conflicts, 75 were used in the present analysis.

Before proceeding, it should be noted that the question of the dominance of the enduring empirical characteristics of a conflict over its specific characteristics as an instance of an analytic event raises one further question. If the enduring, nondiscriminating elements of the conflict system are dominant in any given conflict, and if conflicts are combined by agreement analysis on the basis of the characteristics dominant among them, is it not likely that precisely the same classification of conflicts will be yielded by any run of agreement analysis regardless of the stage of conflict at which it is executed? Is it not likely that the processual changes in the nature of conflict postulated in the conflict model will be obscured by combining a data base the size of that required to define our conflict system and a technique of analysis that operates in terms of predominant qualities rather than of, say, idiosyncracies? In fact, it was expected that this would occur either if the individual items making up the conflict system were not discriminating or literally critical with respect to the developmental stages of conflict or, alternatively, if the postulated stages of conflict were not themselves empirically distinct and differentiable in terms of some set of conditioning factors.

What I am asking here is whether or not the conflict model and the data base deriving from the notion of a conflict system can be brought together by the technique of agreement analysis to produce significant and discriminating statements about the conflict process. To answer this question, we must examine the manner in which agreement analysis in fact classified the various instances of the various conflict stages in the conflicts submitted to the analysis. Table 5.1 presents the results of the first-level classifications by agreement analysis of the eighteen conflicts at their several analytic stages.

As noted, six agreement analysis runs were performed for this study, there being anywhere from six, in the case of settlement (S), to eighteen, in that of hostilities (P–III), instances of the relevant conflict stage included in each run. In all, the six runs were performed upon a total of 75 such instances, each of which was thereby classified with one or more other like instances to form a first-level type or species. Successive levels of classification by agreement analysis are effected only in terms of what has gone before, and the various categories or types established are never subsequently broken up once they are finalized at a given level. The first level of classification for any individual pattern therefore establishes a basic identity or partnership for it that is expressive of a dominant empirical type in the data base and is never subsequently dissolved.

Table 5.1 shows the other instance in each of the six runs with which each conflict was classified to establish the finalized species patterns for that run. Beside each run in which it participated is indicated the other case not to which it is necessarily most alike in terms of the conflict system but with which it best combined under the aegis of agreement analysis to express a dominant empirical response pattern and analytic type in the data base. In terms of the single most important classification of the conflicts realized, these pairings are the encapsulated classificatory results of the six agreement analysis runs.

Of the eighteen conflicts, it will be seen, four were included in three different runs, nine in four runs, three in five runs, and two in all six runs, these having yielded an instance of each phase included in this analysis. The six runs produced a total of some 75 first-level conflict classifications from the eighteen conflicts. In the six runs, none of the eighteen conflicts was classified with the

Table 5.1
First Classification of Conflicts by
Agreement Analysis

Note: The first column lists the eighteen conflicts included in the analysis, and the second column indicates which of the six agreement analysis runs included each. The third column gives the other conflict with which each was first classified to effect the finalized species (or first-level) patterns derived in the analysis; the dates and specific events involved are given in Appendix A. Since classification at each level of agreement analysis proceeds only in terms of the patterns established at the preceding level, its first classification into a species establishes for any conflict something of a permanent identity with the other member(s) of that species. It should be remembered, however, that classification of an individual conflict in a species does not necessarily mean that it has more in common with the other member(s) of that species than it has with any other conflict included in the analysis. Rather, its final classification in that pattern yields only the biggest and best possible classification of all conflicts once all have been classified (see Chapter 4).

Conflict	Agreement Analysis Run	Final Species-Level Classification
Algeria-Morocco	Conflict	Ethiopia-Somalia
	Hostilities	Spanish civil war
	Escalation	Israel-Egypt
	Termination	Israel-Egypt
Angolan insurgency	Conflict	(Adjunct of Cyprus: independence and Malayan insurgency)
	Hostilities	(Adjunct of Cyprus: independence and Malayan insurgency)
	Termination	Indonesia: independence
Cuba: war of 1906	Conflict	Cuba: Bay of Pigs
	Hostilities	Cyprus: internal
	Termination	(Adjunct of Malayan insurgency and Venezuelan insurgency)
	Settlement	Cyprus: independence
Cuba: Bay of Pigs	Conflict	Cuba: war of 1906
	Hostilities	Greek insurgency
	Termination	Greek insurgency
Cyprus: war of independence	Conflict	Malayan insurgency
	Hostilities	Malayan insurgency
	Escalation	Cyprus: internal
	De-escalation	Malayan insurgency
	Termination	(Adjunct of Malayan insurgency and Venezuelan insurgency)
	Settlement	Cuba: war of 1906
Cyprus: internal	Conflict	Indonesia: independence
	Hostilities	Cuba: war of 1906
	Escalation	Cyprus: independence
	De-escalation	(Adjunct of Cyprus: independence and Malayan insurgency)
Ethiopian resistance	Hostilities	Indonesia: independence
	Escalation	(Adjunct of Greek insurgency and Spanish civil war)
	De-escalation	Spanish civil war
	Settlement	Indonesia: independence

Table 5.1 (*continued*)

Conflict	Agreement Analysis Run	Final Species-Level Classification
Ethiopia-Somalia	Conflict	Algeria-Morocco
	Hostilities	Kashmir
	Termination	Kashmir
Greek insurgency	Conflict	(Adjunct of Cyprus: independence and Malayan Insurgency)
	Hostilities	Cuba: Bay of Pigs
	Escalation	Spanish civil war
	Termination	Cuba: Bay of Pigs
India-China	Conflict	Indonesia-Malaysia
	Hostilities	USSR-Iran
	Termination	USSR-Iran
Indonesia: war of independence	Conflict	Cyprus: internal
	Hostilities	Ethiopian resistance
	De-escalation	Indonesia-Malaysia
	Termination	Angolan insurgency
	Settlement	Ethiopian resistance
Indonesia-Malaysia	Conflict	India-China
	Hostilities	Israel-Egypt
	Escalation	Kashmir
	De-escalation	Indonesia: independence
	Termination	Spanish civil war
Israel-Egypt	Conflict	(Adjunct of India-China and Indonesia-Malaysia)
	Hostilities	Indonesia-Malaysia
	Escalation	Algeria-Morocco
	Termination	Algeria-Morocco
Kashmir	Conflict	USSR-Iran
	Hostilities	Ethiopia-Somalia
	Escalation	Indonesia-Malaysia
	Termination	Ethiopia-Somalia
Malayan insurgency	Conflict	Cyprus: independence
	Hostilities	Cyprus: independence
	Escalation	Venezuelan insurgency
	De-escalation	Cyprus: independence
	Termination	Venezuelan insurgency
Spanish civil war	Conflict	Venezuelan insurgency
	Hostilities	Algeria-Morocco
	Escalation	Greek insurgency
	De-escalation	Ethiopian resistance
	Termination	Indonesia-Malaysia
	Settlement	USSR-Iran

Table 5.1 (*continued*)

Conflict	Agreement Analysis Run	Final Species-Level Classification
USSR-Iran	Conflict	Kashmir
	Hostilities	India-China
	Termination	India-China
	Settlement	Spanish civil war
Venezuelan insurgency	Conflict	Spanish civil war
	Hostilities	(Adjunct of Cyprus: independence and Malayan insurgency)
	Escalation	Malayan insurgency
	Termination	Malayan insurgency

same conflict to form a species more than three times. The only combination that resulted that many times derived from Cyprus: war of independence, and Malayan insurgency. These two conflicts were classified together three times in what might be termed one original and two repeat classifications. Of their combined total of eleven (six and five, respectively) case classifications, then, four are repeats on the basis of this particular repeated classification.

More common is the conflict that was classified twice with another one. Indeed, this occurred in thirteen of the eighteen cases (if repeats among adjunct designations are included), each yielding one original and one repeat classification.* Finally, in four of the eighteen cases—Cuba: war of 1906, Cyprus: internal, Indonesia-Malaysia, and Spanish civil war—there are no repeat classifications whatsoever, each being classified with a different case in each run in which it is represented.

Of the entire set of 75 independent, first-level case classifications yielded by the six agreement analysis runs, 58 were original or distinct classifications, and only 17 were repeats. There is, then, less than one repeat classification for every conflict in the analysis and for each four case classifications effected. On the average, scarcely one of its more than four species-level classifications was repetitive for each conflict. More than three-fourths of all the case classifications were original, distinct, and nonrepetitive.

The implication of this finding, I would maintain, is that the conflict model and the conflict system may indeed be successfully merged with discrimination and sensitivity by the medium of agreement analysis. For, in the main, classification of the same set of conflicts at the thresholds of the different conflict stages yielded dissimilar classification schemes. In less than one-fourth

*The Malayan insurgency is again included in this group, as both of its two remaining classifications are achieved with the Venezuelan insurgency.

of all the case classifications at the various stages did a particular classification at one stage replicate that established at another. And even in the relatively few occurrences of replication it is not to be inferred that the response patterns defining the two resulting species were identical. Since classification of conflicts by agreement analysis proceeds on the basis of sheer numerical comparisons without substantive reference to specific items, the comparability of the factor patterns involved may be determined only by their direct comparison. If these response patterns are indeed identical, it may be inferred that the application of agreement analysis to the data base generated by the conflict system was sensitive only to those characteristics lastingly common to the conflicts classified together, not to those signaling a significant change in the conflict process or a transition from one significant stage of conflict to another. If, on the other hand, the response patterns in question do not generally duplicate one another, it may be said that the classification of the same conflicts together at two different stages merely reflected their continuing great similarity and substantive dominance among the conflicts analyzed. Furthermore, while all the factors common to the two item-response patterns are not discriminating between the stages involved, those factors that can be isolated as specific to each response pattern at that particular stage are indeed so discriminating.

The isolation of those factors specific or peculiar to each of the complete factor patterns at the various distinct stages of conflict is, it will be recalled, the task of the weighting device or filter suggested earlier. A final judgment on the complementarity of the model, the data base, and agreement analysis must therefore wait upon the development of the specific weighting device employed in this study and its production of meaningful results in application to all the complete factor patterns. The former three analytic devices are, in effect, incomplete in themselves, requiring the weighting device to establish and demonstrate their methodological wholeness. The products of the first three, the complete factor patterns, cannot in themselves be termed precisely discriminating statements of the various dominant conditions of the specific stages of conflict. Only a filter built upon the processual scheme of the conflict model itself can isolate those conditions and, in doing so, establish the full complementarity and discrimination of the several component elements of this analysis. As will be seen, the application of this device to the complete factor patterns defined by the 75 case classifications does indeed yield from each pattern a set of factors operating specifically at the threshold of the conflict stage in question and so establishes the discrimination and sensitivity of the various analytic devices when employed in concerted unison.

Again, however, before proceeding to the development of this weighting device, we must return briefly to the results of the agreement analysis runs and the complete factor patterns. The second product of each run is a graphic illustration, analogous to that presented in Figure 5.1, of the precise manner in which the individual conflicts included in each run were combined by compound agreement analysis into hierarchical categories or types. It is presented in subsections (b) of Appendix D. The factor pattern for each type comprises all the item-compound responses common to all the individual conflicts classified therein. The numbers designating each type at each level of classification indicate, moreover, the order of statistical dominance among them after all the individual conflicts have been classified at that level. The charts indicate, first, the number of hierarchical levels of classification found by agreement analysis among the several states of the conflict system applying at the threshold in question; second, the number of conflicts in and the precise case composition of the various dominant states of that system found at each level; and, finally, the order of predominance among the dominant hierarchical states or complete factor patterns.

For each agreement analysis run Appendix D also contains a table, in subsections (c), giving percentile statements of the extent to which each conflict maximally incorporates each complete factor pattern established in that run.* That is, once the dominant patterns existing among them had been established, all the individual instances of that stage originally submitted to the run were compared to each of those dominant patterns. One would expect each individual pattern to incorporate all, or 100 percent, of the pattern of any category in which it was itself classified. Beyond this, however, this simple manipulation affords the opportunity to examine the extent to which each pattern incorporates each of the patterns in which it was *not* classified. It thus offers a chance to examine both the secondary typal dominances residing in any individual pattern and the degree of commonality of the various dominant patterns among the individual patterns yielding them. It may be that the secondary typal dominance in an individual case is important to its full understanding and analysis. Similarly, it is especially worth noting that in none of the six agreement analysis runs performed was a single typological category established that was not at least partially incorporated by every conflict included in that run. Thus each conflict included in every run incorporated at least some portion of every complete factor pattern established in that run.

The fourth, final, and by far the largest content of each section of Appendix D is the complete factor patterns themselves presented

*Recall that an individual category pattern defined in terms of a compound data base has two alternative empirical forms or juxtapositions: A/B and B/A, where A and B are the two independent elements making up the individual category. When any pattern is compared with another, it may be compared in either or both forms, and the form in which it more favorably or closely compares with another is termed its maximal form or juxtaposition.

in subsections (d) and (e). These are listings of the particular item-compound response combinations that define the various dominant states of the conflict system established at the threshold of each of the six conflict stages examined.

Several things should be noted about these listings. First, of course, there is one factor pattern for each category indicated in the graphic presentation of that run's classificatory results. The pattern defining each category consists of all the item-compound responses common to all the individual patterns classified in it, and in that juxtaposition of the principal parties in which the maximal classification was achieved. That particular party juxtaposition is indicated beside each factor pattern, where the conflicts from which the pattern derives are cited. The individual response patterns are listed in the same relative positions as are the antagonists or principal parties to each conflict. The combination of these two parties' responses, then, comprises the compound response for each item listed.

Second, for reasons of economy of presentation, both the items and their responses have been abbreviated in these listings from their full form, which may be found through use of the item identification number in Appendix B, the codebook.* The interested reader will note that the abbreviations used are standardized throughout and are readily mastered. In many cases, however, the precise phrasing of an item or response and the several response possibilities available to it are quite important to their specific meaning and interpretation. The reader may then wish to refer to the item's full statement in the codebook. The items in each pattern are, moreover, divided into groups corresponding to the nine topical sections of the codebook and are bound together by their common substantive focus.

These item-compound response combinations define what we have called the factors operating at the various thresholds of the conflict process to generate movement from one stage to another. Accordingly, the item-compound response patterns in their entirety constitute the complete factor patterns applying at the threshold in question in each of the six agreement analysis runs. It is these configural patterns of factors, abstracted by agreement analysis from a number of complete definitions of the state of the conflict system at a given threshold of the conflict model, that constitute the various dominant and hierarchical states of the conflict system at that stage.

*The listings were effected by applying a translation program and a dictionary of the abbreviated items and responses to the numerical output of the agreement analysis runs. The factor pattern listings in Appendix D are themselves, then, the actual computer printouts from the agreement analysis runs as translated into concise language. The translation dictionary, computer program, and instructions for their use are contained in the technical manual accompanying this volume.

If we therefore regard each individual instance or expression of the state of the conflict system at any threshold as but one specific configuration of the conflict system at that point, the complete factor patterns emerge as the several systematic configurations of that system regularly applying when the transition to each conflict stage occurs. The next step is to examine the various higher-order states of the conflict system at every significant stage of conflict, and to separate the factors that are lastingly common to the individual conflicts classified together from those specifically operating in the type they make up at this particular threshold. What remains, then, is to establish the hierarchical level of the complete factor patterns that affords the greatest discrimination among the various stages of conflict, and to isolate within the category patterns those unique configurations of factors that apply specifically at the threshold of each stage. Only these may be termed the specific conditions of each of the several postulated stages of conflict.

The Critical Factor Patterns

Let us consider an example. A single instance of, say, hostilities (P–III) as submitted to an agreement analysis run comprises an individual pattern of some 300 factors — its particular definition of the state of the conflict system at that threshold of that conflict. Yet it has not up to now been established that the items and their responses making up the conflict system are capable of discriminating in any real-life conflict between this threshold of hostilities (P–III) and the threshold of, say, the preceding phase (P–II). Is there, in other words, any significant difference between the states of the conflict system established in this particular conflict at the several thresholds through which it passed? If not, then the conflict system devised is not sufficiently sensitive to the dynamics of the conflict process to differentiate between the various stages of the conflict being examined. If, on the other hand, the coding of the conflict in question does indeed produce two significantly different statements of the conflict system, then a basis has been established for isolating the factors that distinguish one stage from the other and so are critical in effecting the change from one state of the system to the other.

Now, what of the situation when two (or more) instances of hostilities (P–III) have been combined to form a category defined by the factors specifically common to them? As indicated, the very act of so combining individual patterns strips them of the idiosyncratic factors that fully characterized them as individual conflicts. Does what remains after these idiosyncrasies are gone contain some configuration of factors that applies specifically at the threshold of hostilities (P–III) and so expresses a specific set of preconditions of hostilities? Or is the remnant of this combinatorial process simply the characteristics lastingly common to the individual instances throughout the developmental process of conflict, and so exclusive of any statement of the critical factors specifically attending the significant transition from one stage of conflict to another?

To examine these questions with reference to this particular phase (P–III), we may construct what might be termed a pseudotype deriving from the two conflicts in question and defined by all the item-response combinations common to them at the threshold of the preceding phase, conflict (P–II), care being taken to retain the juxtaposition of the principal parties in which the individual patterns were combined at hostilities (P–III). The factor pattern of this pseudotype may then be compared to that of the category pattern established at hostilities (P–III), and all the factors common to the two eliminated as specific preconditions of hostilities. The factors so eliminated have thus been filtered out of the hostilities typal pattern in question by superimposing upon it both the dynamics of the conflict process and the substance of the conflict system as they interact in this particular conflict.

The theory involved in this manipulation is that, by comparing a dominant category to its pseudotype, the category pattern may be stripped of its pseudomembers, or of those factors not specifically associated with the threshold in question and so not specifically preconditioning transition to the stage of conflict at hand. What remains is that which is different about the category pattern at this particular point in the conflict process, or that which has produced a change in an existing but noncritical set of analytic relations and so has conditioned a specific and significant change in the nature of conflict. It is in this mathematical sense of being the difference between one significant stage of development and another, of being the specific conditions of that change and so a critical mass, that the configuration of factors remaining after the application of this weighting procedure is termed the critical factor pattern.

This is not to suggest that the factors eliminated by this process are necessarily unimportant in the development of the category pattern in question. It says only that they do not, as a set, uniquely characterize that category pattern and so are not isolable as the specific and critical conditions of the conflict stage in question. It should be remembered, however, that the factors eliminated by one filter from a given category pattern might not necessarily be eliminated by another. For example, if the pseudotype used to filter the hostilities pattern just cited had consisted of the individual patterns applying at termination (P–IV) rather than at prehostilities conflict (P–II), the result would be a statement of the critical factors differentiating the outbreak of hostilities from its termination. One would expect these to differ considerably from the previously obtained results.

The precise filter that one would use at any particular threshold follows, therefore, from the focus of one's interest and inquiry. The central focus of the present study, as noted at the start, is the overriding objective of exerting some systematic control over the origin, development, and termination of local conflict. While it is recognized that the factors preconditioning the various significant stages of that process are not necessarily the same ones that might best achieve its control, it has been argued that the isolation of those preconditions and of the configurations in which they operate to various ends is the necessary first step toward the formulation of adequate and effective control measures. To guide the choice of pseudotype filters and effect the final data reduction necessary to the present purposes, then, we return to the logical structure of the developmental process in the conflict model itself.

The three basic concepts of that model, it will be recalled, are dispute, which, it is postulated, gives rise under certain specifiable conditions to conflict, which in turn gives rise similarly to hostilities. Each of the last two concepts was, moreover, further elaborated: conflict into prehostilities and posthostilities phases, and hostilities into escalatory and de-escalatory subphases. Finally, the concept of settlement of the dispute was added to allow exit from the model at any point where the underlying issue at hand is resolved. In graphic terms, these basic concepts, the phases of the conflict model, and the six agreement analysis runs stand in relation to each other as shown in Figure 5.2.

We have observed that settlement (S) may be effected from any phase or subphase of an ongoing dispute. Therefore, the proper filter to determine the conditions specific to any settlement category is the pseudotype defined by the factors common to the individual patterns involved at the threshold of the stage that immediately preceded the settlement. It is the pseudotype apply-

Figure 5.2
Correspondence of the Conflict Model and Agreement Analysis Runs

			Phases of the Model		Relevant Agreement Analysis Run
Dispute			P–I	Nonmilitary dispute	
Dispute	Conflict		P–II	Prehostilities conflict	Conflict
Dispute	Conflict	Hostilities	P–III	Hostilities	Hostilities
Dispute	Conflict	Hostilities	E	Escalation	Escalation
Dispute	Conflict	Hostilities	D	De-escalation	De-escalation
Dispute	Conflict		P–IV	Posthostilities conflict	Termination
			S	Settlement	Settlement

ing at the threshold of that stage in each case that gave rise to S. Similarly, since posthostilities termination (P–IV) may follow only from hostilities (P–III), the appropriate filter for each termination category is the pseudotype deriving from those particular phases or subphases (E or D) of hostilities preceding termination. Since both escalation and de-escalation develop only out of ongoing hostilities, the appropriate filters for both are the pseudotypes deriving from the specific instances of hostilities (P–III) involved in the conflicts at hand. Again, the hostilities phase develops only out of conflict, either prehostilities (P–II) or posthostilities (P–IV). The hostilities categories, then, are properly filtered through the pseudotype deriving from the specific instances of conflict (P–II) or termination (P–IV) immediately preceding the outbreak of P–III. Finally, prehostilities conflict in general develops out of dispute (P–I). As has been noted, however, the thresholds of dispute are difficult to pinpoint in time, and they were in any case not coded in the present study. Alternatively, if one cannot ascertain the specific conditions that distinguish the processual development of conflict from dispute, one may maintain focus on the concept of control by establishing the critical factors that distinguish prehostilities from hostilities. Thus the filter employed for the conflict categories is the pseudotype deriving from the specific instances of hostilities that subsequently ensued in each of the conflicts examined.

The result of this data reduction in each of the conflict (P–II) category patterns is a statement of the conditions of conflict that specifically differentiate it from hostilities (P–III). In each of the succeeding five runs, what was produced by this weighting scheme was a statement of the various, specific preconditions of the stage that set it apart in the natural developmental process of conflict. In brief, for each of the six agreement analysis runs performed, the pseudotypes created to reduce the complete factor patterns to their critical elements were formed as shown in Table 5.2.

To determine the set of critical elements in the dominant category patterns established at the first level in each of the agreement analysis runs, I first determined the conflict cases (usually two) from which each species pattern derived. The pseudotype of that species was then established, comprising all the factors common to the individual patterns at the appropriate threshold indicated for the run in question, care being taken to retain the same juxtaposition of the principal parties as that in which the species itself was formed. The factor patterns defining the species and its pseudotype were then compared, and all factors common to both were eliminated from the species pattern. What remains in the species pattern is that configuration of factors peculiar to this particular combination of cases when it emerged as a dominant typal pattern.

Once this procedure had been followed for every species pattern

Table 5.2
Formation and Effect of
Pseudotypes

Agreement Analysis Run	Pseudotypes Formed at Threshold of	Critical Factor Pattern
Conflict (P–II)	Ensuing hostilities (P–III)	Differentiates between P–II and the state of hostilities that ensued
Hostilities (P–III)	Preceding state of pre- or posthostilities conflict (P–II or P–IV)	Differentiates between P–III and preceding state of conflict (P–II or P–IV)
Escalation (E)	Ongoing hostilities (P–III) from which E developed	Differentiates between E and the ongoing hostilities (P–III)
De-escalation (D)	Ongoing hostilities (P–III) from which D developed	Differentiates between D and the ongoing hostilities (P–III)
Termination (P–IV)	State of hostilities (P–III, E, or D) from which P–IV ensued	Differentiates between P–IV and the ongoing state of hostilities (P–III)
Settlement (S)	Phase or subphase from which S ensued	Differentiates between S and the ongoing state of the dispute

in the six sets of complete factor patterns, it became apparent, given the number of conflict cases from which the present analysis derives, that the species level best accommodated the present purposes of analysis and prediction. For while the 32 species-level complete factor patterns established in the six runs contain anywhere from a minimum of 44 to a maximum of 143 factors, the critical factor patterns derived from them contain an average of only 14.2 factors. As opposed to the complete factor patterns, then, their weighted counterparts afforded the advantage of being small enough in size to be comprehensible at a glance, even while making a comprehensive, discriminating statement of the analytic conditions specific to each significant stage of conflict.

Of the 14.2 factors in the average species-level critical factor pattern, however, 3.1 were found to define the higher levels of classification (genus or above) achieved by the complete species patterns of which they were parts. Because of the precise manner in which the weighting scheme operates, any factor that is critical in a species pattern and is retained in the pattern deriving from that species is likewise a critical member of that higher-order pattern.* Since the average genus pattern derives from two spe-

*Two alternative and equivalent ways of expressing this are that (1) any factor in a complete genus pattern that is critical in any of the species patterns from which it derives is also critical in that genus pattern; or (2) critical in any complete genus pattern are those of its factors that are critical in any of the species patterns from which it derives. Similar considerations, moreover, apply at succeeding levels of classification: any factor that is once critical remains forever critical in all subsequent classifications of the category pattern in which it is contained.

cies patterns, we should therefore expect that the total number of critical patterns residing in the data base might be reduced at the genus level to approximately 16, and that the average genus-level critical pattern would contain something on the order of 7 factors. In simple arithmetic terms, it would seem that their determination at the genus level should afford a more concise, essential statement of the critical factor patterns than that realized at the species level.

In point of fact, however, what is gained at that level in terms of economy of presentation is lost in terms of precision and discrimination. Of the 32 critical factor patterns established at the species level of classification, 6 contained no factors that reached the genus level of classification, 9 contained but 1 factor that achieved the genus level, and 4 more contained just 2 factors. Of the 32 species-level critical patterns, 19 were thus virtually, if not totally, wiped out at the genus level by the dominance of the complete (and not necessarily critical) patterns of the remaining 13. The rich yet comprehensible configural statements of these critical species patterns were lost to the more generalized and therefore less discriminating critical factor patterns existing at the genus level.

Moreover, it was only in the relatively uncommon instance when a species and an adjunct were combined to form a genus that it was possible for a critical factor that was not contained in the critical species pattern to persist at the genus level. In all other instances of genus formation, the critical pattern at that level comprised the configuration of all factors at once critical to any of the several species patterns involved and common to all. If it is known (and shown) which factors in each critical species pattern actually attained the higher levels of classification, then, the analyst is at once afforded (1) the most complete statement existing in the data base of the various analytic conditions of each stage of conflict and (2) an indication of the factors in each configuration that define the still higher-order critical factor patterns and so are most critical among that specific set of conditions.

Finally, it turned out that many of the critical factors in the complete genus patterns were common to all the critical patterns of the species from which they derived. This means that the average number of unique critical factors in the complete species patterns to reach the ensuing genus pattern was significantly less than 3.0; a good part of the average of 3.1 species-level critical factors to reach the ensuing genus level were nonunique or repetitive. The result is that, for the average agreement analysis run, only 13.3 distinct species-level critical factors were found in the definition of the complete, and therefore the critical, factor pattern of the genus into which its species were classified. Given the coincidence between the number of critical factors per run achieving genus-level classifications or higher and the average number of factors (14.1) in the critical factor patterns established at the species level in all runs, a natural break was seen to occur between the species and genus levels of pattern determination among the specific, limited number of cases employed in this experimental effort.

Having settled upon the species as the appropriate level of abstraction for the present purposes, the configuration of factors that specifically and uniquely characterized the threshold of the conflict stage at hand was elicited from each complete factor pattern. In terms of the data base established in this study, these critical factor patterns are the various dominant and isolable sets of conditions under which the significant stages of conflict occur. They are the dominant configurations of factors that specifically precondition the occurrence of each stage. They are, in effect, the rules that define the various conditions of specific transition within the model and so establish the various dynamics of an otherwise static model of conflict.

With respect to five of the six stages of conflict, hostilities (P–III) through settlement (S), the critical factor patterns may be viewed as the various sets of specific preconditions setting each apart in the developmental process of conflict. In the remaining phase, prehostilities (P–II), the critical factor patterns are the various sets of conditions that differentiate conflict from (and therefore keep it from becoming) hostilities (P–III), that distinguish non-violent from violent conflict. Moreover, since they specify both the various and the dominant conditions of these stages, the critical factor patterns may be said to define the dominant analytic types of these stages in the conflict process and in terms of the conflict system.

The Composite Scenarios

Finally, what of the 13.3 factors in the average set of critical preconditions that were found to define the still higher levels of classification, genus and above? By definition, the fact that they attained these higher levels of classification means that their inclusiveness, in terms of the number of individual conflicts that they characterize, is greater than that of the rest of the factors in the critical factor patterns. This establishes them, in fact, as the dominant factors in the dominant states of the conflict system from which the critical factors derive. They are, then, the predominant factors in the critical factor patterns themselves.

As we have seen, not all of the critical factor patterns contain factors that appear in the higher levels of classification, genus or above. Where they are present, however, these factors may be regarded as the dominant or central factors in the configuration effecting the particular conditions of the conflict stage at hand. And the more such higher levels of classification a given factor attains, the more critical or central is its effect in establishing that particular set of conditions. For it is about these factors that the more generalizable sets of preconditions would be developed if a sufficient number of conflicts were included to allow effective genus- or even family-level determination of the critical factor patterns.

Presently, however, it is at least possible to assemble all of the central factors in each set of critical patterns into what might aptly be termed a composite scenario of the most critical conditions of each stage of conflict. Inasmuch as the set of factors defining this scenario derives directly from the several critical factor patterns in question rather than from the action of agreement analysis upon them, the scenario is logically not the same as these patterns. For the critical factor pattern derives from two or more individual conflicts and constitutes a specific configuration of item-response combinations that applies equally and exactly in each relevant conflict at the threshold involved. It is what might be termed a direct, first-order abstraction from specific conflicts, the configural expression of a specific, significant commonality among them. The critical factor pattern is contained as a complete entity in each and every individual pattern (or conflict) from which it derives. This is not the case, on the other hand, with the composite scenario, which is best seen as a second-order abstraction derived not directly and as a whole from individual conflicts but piecemeal from the several types formed by a set of conflicts. Thus no individual pattern (or real instance of the conflict stage in question) incorporates the composite scenario as a whole. Each individual pattern contributes only a bit, if anything, to it; but that bit is the factor or set of factors most central or critical in establishing the analytic preconditions for the occurrence of the conflict stage involved.

The composite scenario does not, then, correspond to reality in the same way as do the critical factor patterns. It has, in terms of any one or more of the conflicts from which it derives, no direct and complete expression in reality. But it does express, in terms of all the conflicts analyzed, a summary statement of the essential conditions under which its particular stage of conflict occurs. The scenario has been composed from the several critical factor patterns established at each threshold, from the several specific sets of conditions of each stage of conflict. It comprises all (and only) the factors that are at once so critical and sufficiently inclusive (in terms of the number of conflicts they characterize) as to have achieved genus-level classification with the complete species patterns to which they are critical. It comprises all (and only) the factors that are thus doubly critical among the entire set of the various conditions of that stage of conflict.

These, then, are the final data manipulations and reductions that were performed with the aim of abstracting analytic preconditions from empirical characteristics, of determining the various configurations of factors that condition the several significant stages of conflict, and of catching a sectional view of the dynamic processes that impel conflict through those junctures most critical in its development.

The set of concepts and techniques developed and employed to that end are, I should argue, most conservative in nature. The criterion of admission to the hierarchical category patterns established by agreement analysis is, it will be recalled, complete agreement among all the individual patterns classified in a category on all the factors that define it — not some percentage less than one hundred but only one hundred percent itself. Moreover, the assumption of the relationality of conflict holds that the factors conditioning the development of conflict derive not from the individual characteristics, capabilities, and resources of the parties involved but from the relationship between them along those dimensions. The compound data base that follows from this assumption in its turn makes even less promising the probability of finding significant commonalities among conflicts at their various stages of development.

What follows from this logically systematic and technically conservative approach, it is felt, is a degree of confidence in the results of this study that would not otherwise apply. It is to the presentation of those results that we now turn.

The Conditions of Conflict

The basic contention of this study is that each of the several significant stages of conflict may proceed only from certain precise and isolable sets of conditions. We have noted, for example, that organized, systematic, and continuing violence between parties capable of such relations is a relatively rare occurrence. The relations between most parties are most often at least tolerable, if not downright desirable, at levels of policy activity short of violence. The risks involved are too great and the ensuing chain of events too uncontrollable for hostilities to be embarked upon except under extreme circumstances and very specific sets of conditions.

I have argued, moreover, that this logic applies at each significant or critical stage of conflict, that is, when a basic change in the nature of the relations between the parties involved signals a basic change in the nature of the conflict itself. A set of assumptions, concepts, and techniques was therefore developed to elicit from eighteen real-life conflicts a precise statement of the various conditions under which these basic changes occurred in the relations between the parties or, accordingly, of the various sets of analytic preconditions of each significant stage of conflict.

Two things follow. First, because the statements of these preconditions derive from but eighteen conflicts, they are not intended, nor are they to be taken, as final, conclusive, or definitive formulations of the various conditions of each stage of conflict. Rather, their presentation is intended merely to represent the best possible statement of the conditions that may be elicited from a limited number of cases, while demonstrating the validity, sensitivity, and potential of the concepts and techniques employed. The addition of other conflicts to this analysis may be expected to modify the results by altering the case classifications realized at each stage of conflict. The complete factor patterns that define the various dominant states of the conflict system applying at each stage will therefore be affected, as well as the critical factor patterns that define the various configurations of factors specifically conditioning each stage. Because of the manner in which the techniques operate, these modifications are likely to involve both the elimination of factors in the critical patterns that do not achieve successively higher levels of classification and the addition of factors that better define the precise effects of the factors that do achieve higher levels.

This, in turn, suggests that what we have called the composite scenario of the conditions of each stage will alter only slightly and slowly as other conflicts are added to the analysis. The individual factors making up the composite scenario define the more inclusive commonalities among the conflicts involved and so may be expected to be persistent in their analytic dominance. As an eclectic entity, however, the scenario does not correspond to reality in the same total and direct manner as do the critical factor patterns. The scenarios do not specify either the precise configurations in which their individual factors have effect or the various sets of complementary environmental conditions within which these most central factors operate empirically. It is these enabling configurations that we should expect to be modified in the direction of greater precision and discrimination by the addition of other cases. The composite scenarios, then, are statements of the more enduring individual factors specifically evoking the conditions of each stage of conflict; the critical factor patterns are statements of the various significant configurations within which these individual factors have operated to condition each stage in the conflicts examined. The former comprise the most stable individual conditions of the various stages of conflict, while the latter may be said to define the various critical contexts within which they have operated empirically to these ends in the conflicts analyzed.

Moreover, it follows from our conception of causation that the preconditions expressed in the critical factor patterns may not be reduced without at the same time doing some violence to our basic assumptions. If different configurations of the same variables may effect the same result, and if the same factor in different contexts may effect different results, then only the various sets of conditions of each conflict stage may speak fully for themselves. The critical factors are the several precise configurations of factors found specifically to condition the development of each stage, and any abbreviated expression of them is also an inadequate expression of them.

The various sets of critical factors isolated for each conflict stage are presented in the tables in this chapter, together with the composite scenario, or summary statement, of the essential conditions of each stage. Each critical factor pattern represents a distinct analytic type of the conflict stage in question and is characterized by a unique descriptive title. The common format in which each type is presented includes several elements. The first column, on the left, lists the descriptive title of the factor pattern and the several conflicts from which it derives. The factor pattern shown in the next two columns is precisely common as a whole to all those conflicts at the thresholds of the events indicated. The second and third columns, then, indicate the specific configuration of factors that define the preconditions of the conflict stage at hand. (See Table 6.3.)

These item-compound response combinations are here presented in the same abbreviated forms used in the complete factor patterns in Appendix D. The complete statement of all these items and responses may be found in Appendix B, the codebook, by means of the item identification numbers at the left. The reader will notice that the items in the critical factor patterns do not necessarily follow consecutively by identification number. They were, in fact, rearranged manually into groups and sequences that better reflect common focus or substance than do the identification numbers themselves. The reader should also make especial note of the numerical ratios that express the responses to the items scaled by means of the logarithmic technique developed in Chapter 3. These scalar ratios, it will be recalled, are meaningful only in terms of the data base employed in this study. The reality to which they correspond is that defined by the totality of these conflicts, and each element of the ratios represents the coded response for each antagonist in terms of the dominant response clusters for that item in this reality.

Finally, in parentheses at the far right of the item-compound response combination that makes up each factor in these patterns there is another response set. This is the compound response to the item in the pseudotype of the relevant complete pattern that caused the item to be weighted or filtered into the critical pattern. Thus it was the change from the indicated compound response in the parenthesized pseudotype to the form actually applying at the threshold in question that made each factor "critical" in this type, at this stage of conflict. It will be recalled, however, that the listed compound response to the pseudotype is not necessarily common to every conflict contributing to the type. For some factors in the critical pattern, the pseudotype column may contain more than one compound response, up to a maximum of one for each conflict involved, and all differing from the critical compound response listed. As in the composite scenario, the compound responses listed for the pseudotype do not have the same configural correspondence to all the conflicts involved as do the critical patterns; they are eclectic, some of the elements coming from only one of the conflicts and some common to all. In listing them, however, consistency of juxtaposition of the compound responses (that is, of the two principal parties) was maintained both between compound responses in the pseudotype (vertically) and between those in the pseudotype and those in the critical pattern (horizontally). As a set, then, the compound responses to the items in the pseudotype have no independent identity or real existence of their own; they are but the base from which one may observe the specific changes in item response or factor arrangement that yielded the critical factor pattern.

Asterisks have been used in the critical patterns to indicate the factors that, under the aegis of agreement analysis, achieved still higher orders of classification (genus or above) with the complete pattern from which they derive. These, as we have seen, are statistically the most critical or essential factors in the critical patterns of which they are a part. The number of asterisks attaching to any factor indicates the number of successive levels of classification attained by it. The more asterisks attaching to a factor, the more critical it is to the establishment of that type, or to the establishment of the specific set of conditions of the conflict stage in question.

These asterisked factors, when brought together from the several sets of preconditions of a conflict stage, comprise what I have called the composite scenario of its most critical or essential preconditions. The important thing to note in their presentation is that there is no listing of a specific set of conflict cases from which this set of factors derives as a configural whole. Rather, the set was manufactured piecemeal from all the conflict cases included in the analysis of the conflict stage in question. The precise juxtaposition of the principal parties in which each factor in each scenario is listed was determined by comparing the several critical patterns involved and fixing upon the juxtaposition that afforded the maximum consistency among the entire set of critical patterns. The individual factors in the scenarios have therefore been arranged to achieve maximum consistency of their juxtaposition among the conflicts involved and to express their maximum correspondence, as a pattern, to reality.

Again, for each factor in the composite scenarios there is indicated in the right-hand column the compound response that characterized the pseudotype from which it emerged, and change from which to its present form signaled its emergence as a critical factor. Here, then, are the most essential individual preconditions of the several stages of conflict, together with the form from which they each emerged to realize their effect.

Conflict and Hostilities

It will be recalled that all the localized conflict cases included in the present analysis resulted in hostilities. Therefore, all the instances of conflict (P–II) established in this analysis were, specifically and literally, instances of prehostilities conflict. We have likewise noted that in real life it is the relatively rare case of conflict that eventuates in hostilities. Most are disposed of by other means, if at all, or otherwise tolerated until their saliency subsides. To make a full and adequate statement of the various conditions of prehostilities conflict, then, the analysis would have to include instances that did *not* result in hostilities.

Of necessity, the weighting device used to isolate the critical elements in the patterns resulting from agreement analysis of these prehostilities conflicts comprised the pseudotypes applying at the threshold of the ensuing hostilities. The result of this first agreement analysis run is a statement of the conditions of each of the seven types of prehostilities conflict (P–II) that specifically differentiate and distinguish it from hostilities (P–III). In the case of hostilities and each subsequent conflict stage, on the other hand, the weighting device reflects the process out of which, rather than into which, the typal patterns developed. Thus the conditions of hostilities (P–III) isolated are the various configurations of factors that specifically preconditioned the outbreak of hostilities in the conflicts examined. They represent the various sets of analytic preconditions of hostilities. The central, individual factors that tend to distinguish instances of nonviolent conflict from violent hostilities, and therefore tend to keep the former from developing into the latter, may be found in the composite scenario of conflict (Table 6.1); and the factors that precondition or tend to promote violent hostilities may be found in the composite scenario of hostilities (Table 6.2).

Among the factors that tend in themselves to distinguish (and keep) conflict (P–II) from hostilities (P–III), several things stand out in Table 6.1. The first is the absence in P–II of an avowed or perceived threat to the continued existence of the regimes involved, and their perception that there is still room for diplomatic maneuvering within the terms of the present nonviolent relations. War is an enormously costly and risky proposition, even more so

Table 6.1
The Conditions of Prehostilities Conflict (P–II): A Composite Scenario ("stakes not yet worth the candle to all [un]concerned")

Note: This composite factor pattern derives from an examination of seventeen instances of conflict (P–II). It consists exclusively of item-response combinations found to define the higher-order classifications (genus or above) isolated by agreement analysis of the conflict patterns. It is therefore what may be termed a second level of abstraction from the real conflicts from which it proceeds.

Item		Relationship Between Antagonists at Threshold of Conflict (P–II)	Subsequent Relationship (That Pertaining at Threshold of Succeeding P–III)
5-21	Likely outcome is now obvious	No/No	(No/Yes)
5-2	Regime seeks overthrow of adv.	No/No	(No/Yes or Yes/No)
5-12	Interest involved–cont'd exis.	No/No	(Yes/No)
8-29	Intell. in adv's policy organs	Ineffective/Ineffective	(Ineffective/Occasional)
5-29	Credibility of communications	High/High	(Low/Low)
6-30	Some 3Pty offered to arbitrate	No/No	(Yes/Yes)
1-11	Dispute has been to reg'l orgn	No	(Yes)
6-32	Regl orgn offered to arbitrate	No/No	(Yes/Yes)
5-32	Brought dispute to int'l orgn	No/No	(Yes/No)
6-11	Has asked an int'l. org'n. in	No/No	(Yes/No)
6-31	Intl orgn offered to arbitrate	No/No	(Yes/Yes)
6-6	A GP is openly partial to ant.	No/No	(Yes/Yes or No)
6-5	Is aided by GP hostile to adv.	No/No	(Yes/Yes)
6-15	A G.P. is inv. on this side	No/No	(Yes/Yes)
6-18	A 3Pty is providing pol. aid	No/No	(Yes/No)
6-19	A 3Pty is providing econ. aid	Yes/Yes	(Yes/No)
5-37	Esc likely bring GP aid to adv	No/No	(Yes/No)
7-14	Total manpower committed	1/1	(0/1 or 2)
7-5	No. of own troops committed	1/1	(0/1 or 2)
7-4	Mobilization of reserves	None/None	(None/Slight)
7-17	Guerrilla manpower committed	1/1	(0/1 or 2)
9-11	Attrition rate for own forces	1/1	(1/2)
2-13	Popn under effective control	3/0	(3/1)
9-1	Pc of industrial capacity lost	1/1	(3/0)
9-2	Pc of civilian population lost	1/1	(1 or 2/0)
9-3	Total no. civn population lost	1/1	(3/0)
4-37	Pop. support for regim's pols.	High/High	(Low/High)
4-38	Att. of intellectuals to regim	Favorable/Favorable	(Unfavorable/Favorable)

for the relatively poor and often unstable antagonists in localized, "third-world" conflicts than for the more prosperous and viable great powers. It is therefore not likely to be resorted to except when very vital interests are seen to be at stake and all nonviolent modes of policy activity promise an unacceptable outcome. This proposition is also reflected in the data concerning losses due to the dispute, where conflict (P–II) is seen tending to persist so long as civilian and industrial casualties do not become excessive and grossly disproportionate for one party. It is when such circumstances do apply that popular support for the policies of one side slips away, the intellectual community becomes disaffected, the regime's popular base becomes imperiled, and hostilities are resorted to.

The second notable feature of the prehostilities conflict mode is the singular absence of any offer from a disinterested third party to arbitrate the dispute or otherwise to effect conciliation. No regional and international organizations are in any way involved in the dispute at this point. As may be seen in the complete factor patterns, only once the dispute has become militarized, only once the flexibility and moderation that had earlier characterized the parties' approaches to the issue have vanished is activity generally forthcoming from these directions. Thus, while it cannot quite be said that the activities of regional and international organizations tend themselves to mark the imminence of hostilities, it may be said that they generally come only too late to be effective as instruments of accommodation.

Finally, and most important, is the significant absence at this early conflict stage of great-power involvement, partiality, or support and the lack of any prospect of great-power aid to either of the adversaries if hostilities occur. The absence of great-power involvement is, however, tempered by economic assistance to both principal parties, the presence of which is seen to moderate the level of conflict. Indeed, examination in their entirety of the critical factor patterns of conflict (P–II) indicates that the absence of great-power and other third-party partiality and partisan involvement is the single characteristic that most effectively differentiates nonviolent conflict from overt hostilities. Again, the costs and risks of war are generally too great to be suffered by the parties who fight and bear the burden of these local conflicts; but the prospect and, better yet, the actuality of great-power assistance in all its possible forms makes the prospect of war itself another matter. Client relationships in great-power politics thus tend to become breeding grounds for cynical exploitation by the great power in pursuit of its perceived local interests and for political blackmail by the client government in pursuit of its own, the two perceptions never quite coinciding.

If we examine the composite scenario of hostilities (P–III) in

Table 6.2
The Conditions of Hostilities
(P–III):
A Composite Scenario
("accommodation falters on the
prospect of sponsorship")

Note: This composite factor pattern derives from an examination of eighteen instances of hostilities (P–III). It consists exclusively of item-response
combinations found to define the higher-order classifications (genus or
above) isolated by agreement analysis of the hostilities patterns. It is
therefore what may be termed a second level of abstraction from the real
conflicts from which it proceeds.

Item	Relationship Between Antagonists at Threshold of Hostilities (P–III)	Previous Relationship (That Pertaining at Threshold of P–II or P–IV Preceding P–III)
4-32 Recent leadership crisis	No/No	(Yes/No)
4-33 Recent change in leadership	No/No	(Yes/No)
5-33 Indicated disput is negotiable	Yes/No	(Yes or No/Yes)
4-25 Const'al status of pol parties	Competitive/NA	(Part compet./NA)
4-18 Pol. integration of genl popn	Moderate/NA	(Low/NA)
1-7 Ideological diff. betw parties	Extreme	Mild
5-4 Interest involved-commitments	Yes/Yes	(No/Yes)
7-11 Total troops given by 3rd Pty	1/1	(3/1)
6-24 Att. of 3Pty public to inv'mnt	Favorable/Favorable	(Unfavorable/Favorable)
7-13 3Pty troop aid seen likely to	Stay same/Stay same	(Decrease/Stay same)
7-5 No. of own troops committed	1/2	(2/0)
7-14 Total manpower committed	1/1	(1/0)

Table 6.2, we find that the most critical preconditions or genera-
tors of hostilities itself are, first, a relative equality of the total
manpower committed from all sources to the conflict and of total
troop support provided the antagonists by third parties. In both
regards, a considerable disproportion had existed previously.
Second, the attitudes among the general publics of both third
parties are generally favorable toward their current involvement
in the conflict; consequently, the regimes of both third parties
expect that their own popular bases of support will not be eroded
by that involvement. Third, both principal parties enjoy the
prospect of receiving continued troop support from third parties,
at least at its present level. Fourth, both principal parties perceive
that some public commitment that it has made is now vitally at
stake in the conflict. And, fifth, the ideological differences between the antagonists are now extreme, whereas they had for-
merly been mild. These, then, are the especially critical ingredi-
ents promoting the outbreak of hostilities in nonviolent conflict
situations.

Another pair of conditions in this scenario would seem to be
rather curious preconditions of hostilities: the establishment of a
fully competitive political party system where previously such
competition had been limited, and an increase in the level of
political integration in the system from low to moderate. As the
latter item (4–18) was defined, however, moderate integration
indicates that some significant minority remains in opposition
to, or not assimilated into, the ongoing political system. Although
a fully competitive political party system may have been estab-

lished, that minority remains outside its pale, ''the dispossessed in a 'moderate' system'' (see Table 6.4, Type H2). This is an indication that establishment of the formal institutions of democracy does not ensure their operation to inhibit or ameliorate conflict. If the government itself does not effectively channel and redress their grievances, the dispossessed will revolt even, and perhaps most surely, in the climate of rising expectations created by a nonoppressive, politically ''moderate'' system.

The hostilities scenario also indicates that interstate conflict tends to erupt into hostilities during the period of attempted stabilization after a crisis and a change in the leadership of one of the antagonists. There is always the temptation at this time of instability for the regime involved to solidify its domestic position by entering upon foreign hostilities and for its adversary to take advantage of the fluid situation and make whatever opportunistic gains it can through violence.

The final factor that stands out in the hostilities scenario is that at least one party no longer feels the issue at hand to be negotiable or subject to political accommodation. The reasonable alternatives are being foreclosed; flexibility and moderation have been abandoned.

These, then, are the most critical individual factors generating the conditions of conflict (P–II) and hostilities (P–III). The precise configurations in which they operate to effect those conditions — that is, to keep conflict from entering the hostilities phase and to promote the latter — are contained in the typal patterns shown in Tables 6.3 and 6.4.

Table 6.3
Conflict (P–II):
The Critical Factor Patterns

Note: Asterisk (*) indicates the factors found to define the higher-order classifications (genus or above) derived by agreement analysis of the conflict (P–II) patterns; the number of asterisks indicates the number of higher orders achieved by that particular item-response combination.

Item	Relationship Between Antagonists at Threshold of Conflict (P–II)	Subsequent Relationship (That Pertaining at Threshold of Succeeding P–III)
*2-13 Popn under effective control	3/0	(3/1)
*7-5 No. of own troops committed	1/1	(0/1 or 2)
7-4 Mobilization of reserves	None/None	(None/Slight or Total)
*7-17 Guerrilla manpower committed	1/1	(0/1 or 2)
6-21 A 3Pty is providing mil hdwre.	Yes/No	(Yes/Yes)
7-13 3Pty troop aid seen likely to	Stay same/Stay same	(Increase/Stay same)
1-12 Dispute has been to int'l orgn	No	Yes

Type C1
(''an insurgent order in search of a sponsor'')

The pattern derives from

Cyprus: independence (Enosists establish a military planning committee — 7/52)

Malayan insurgency (Calcutta conference, Fourth Plenum — 2/48)

Table 6.3 (*continued*)

Item		Relationship Between Antagonists at Threshold of Conflict (P–II)	Subsequent Relationship (That Pertaining at Threshold of Succeeding P–III)

The adjuncts are

Angolan insurgency (Leopoldville riots in Congo; Portugal strengthens Angolan garrison — 1/59)

Greek insurgency (formation of rival government in Greece — 3/44)

Type C2
("great-power interests do not yet prevail")

The pattern derives from

Cuba: "little" war of 1906 (Liberal party withdraws from national elections — 12/05)

Cuba: Bay of Pigs (U.S. president authorizes an exile organization — 3/60)

4-32	Recent leadership crisis	No/No	(Yes/No)
5-13	Commitment to stated goals	Flexible/Total	(Total/Total)
4-26	Effective pol. party system	NA/One pty dom	(NA/One party)
4-8	Status of judiciary	NA/Part. effect.	(NA/Ineffective)
4-9	Character of bureaucracy	NA/Transitional	(NA/Traditional)
4-40	Effect on popular cohesion	NA/Little change	(NA/Grt decrease)
*5-32	Brought dispute to int'l orgn	No/No	(No/Yes)
6-28	Experience with IO peace mach	None/None	(None/Frustrating)
6-29	I.O. peace machinery is seen	Irrelevant/Irrelevant	(Irrelevant/Relevant)
**6-11	Has asked an int'l. org'n. in	No/No	(No/Yes)
5-33	Indicated dispute is negotiable	Yes/No	(No/No)
*6-30	Some 3Pty offered to arbitrate	No/No	(Yes/Yes)
*6-31	Intl orgn offered to arbitrate	No/No	(Yes/Yes)
4-14	International policy of regime	None/Moderate	(None/Leftist)
*6-6	A GP is openly partial to ant.	No/No	(Yes/Yes)
*6-5	Is aided by GP hostile to adv.	No/No	(Yes/No)
6-12	Some 3Pty is inv. on this side	No/No	(Yes/Yes)
*6-15	A G.P. is inv. on this side	No/No	(Yes/Yes)
6-21	A 3Pty is providing mil hdwre.	No/No	(Yes/Yes)
6-20	A 3Pty is providing mil advice	No/No	(Yes/Yes)
5-25	Adversary appears to ant to be	Aut + indep./Aut + indep.	(Aut but dep/A puppet)
8-13	Overall military org'n balance	Unfavorable/Favorable	(Favorable/Unfavorable)
*7-17	Guerrilla manpower committed	1/1	(2/0)
***9-2	Pc of civilian population lost	1/1	(NA/1)
*9-3	Total no. civn population lost	1/1	(NA/3)
*5-37	Esc likely bring GP aid to adv	No/No	(No/Yes)

Type C3
("moderation prevails till accommodation fails")

The pattern derives from

Spanish civil war (Nationalist terror and political assassination — 2/36)

Venezuelan insurgency (MIR/CPV formed — 4/60)

4-23	Interest artic'n by inst'al gp	Pol signif/NA	(Pol insignif/NA)
5-19	Present outlook wrt dispute	Moderate/Moderate	(Moderate/Die-hard)
*9-11	Attrition rate for own forces	1/1	(1/2)

Type C4
("the prospect of compromise not yet foreclosed")

The pattern derives from

Cyprus: internal (London Agreement on Cypriot independence — 2/59)

Indonesia: independence (both sides demonstrate a will to use force — 8/45)

5-34	Has sought a negot. settlement	No/No	(Yes/No)
5-35	Has offered bi-lateral negotns	No/No	(Yes/No)
6-21	A 3Pty is providing mil hdwre.	No/Yes	(Yes/Yes)
7-42	Dep. for battlefield armaments	None/Exclusive	(Somewhat/Exclusive)
7-51	Spare parts and ammunition aid	NA/Adequate	(Adequate/Adequate)
7-53	Pc total costs coming fm 3Pty	0/3	(1/3)

Table 6.3 (*continued*)

Item		Relationship Between Antagonists at Threshold of Conflict (P–II)	Subsequent Relationship (That Pertaining at Threshold of Succeeding P–III)
** 4-37	Pop. support for regim's pol.	High/High	(Low/High)
** 4-38	Att. of intellectuals to regim	Favorable/Favorable	(Unfavorable/Favorable)
* 5-21	Likely outcome is now obvious	No/No	(No/Yes)
* 6-30	Some 3Pty offered to arbitrate	No/No	(Yes/Yes)
5-37	Esc likely bring GP aid to adv	No/No	(No/Yes)
6-21	A 3Pty is providing mil hdwre.	Yes/Yes	(Yes/No)
7-51	Spare parts and ammunition aid	Adequate/Adequate	(Adequate/NA)
7-50	Overtness of 3Pty hardware aid	Gen'ly overt/Gen'ly overt	(Gen'ly overt/NA)
* 6-19	A 3Pty is providing econ. aid	Yes/Yes	(Yes/No)
6-24a	Type of government of 3rd Pty.	Pol. democ./Total olig	(Pol. democ./NA)
6-24c	Internal policies of 3Pty govt	Conservative/Conservative	(Conservative/NA)
6-27	Pc ant's exports cons. by 3Pty	16-33 Pc/0-4 Pc	(16-33 Pc/NA)
6-25	Aid to ant hurts 3Pty economy	No/No	(No/NA)
6-24	Att. of 3Pty public to inv'mnt	Favorable/Favorable	(Favorable/NA)
* 7-14	Total manpower committed	1/1	(0/1)
* 7-4	Mobilization of reserves	None/None	(None/Slight)
7-6	No. troops comm as Pc tot frcs	1/1	(1/2 or 0/1)
** 7-17	Guerrilla manpower committed	1/1	(0/2)
1-7	Ideological diff. betw parties	Mild	(Extreme)
5-19	Present outlook wrt dispute	Moderate/Moderate	(Die-hard/Die-hard)
5-13	Commitment to stated goals	Flexible/Flexible	(Flexible/Total)
*5-2	Regime seeks overthrow of adv.	No/No	(No/Yes)
*5-12	Interest involved-cont'd exis.	No/No	(No/Yes)
5-16	Pc of avail mil frcs committed	0-10 Pc/0-10 Pc	(25-49 Pc/0-10 Pc)
5-42	Martial law is in effect	No/No	(No/Yes or Yes/No)
5-28	Reliability of communications	High/High	(Low/Low)
*5-29	Credibility of communications	High/High	(Low/Low)
6-30	Some 3Pty offered to arbitrate	Yes/Yes	(No/No)
*1-11	Dispute has been to reg'l orgn	No	Yes
***6-32	Regl orgn offered to arbitrate	No/No	(Yes/Yes)
6-10	Has asked a regional org'n in	No/No	(Yes/Yes)
6-17	A aut org is inv. on this side	No/No	(Yes/No)
*6-18	A 3Pty is providing pol. aid	No/No	(No/Yes)
7-43	Battle arms supply likely to	Stay same/Stay same	(Increase/Stay same)
7-32	No. jet aircraft available	1/2	(1/1)
7-47	Air armament supply likely to	Stay same/Stay same	(St sme or Inc/Increase)
7-49	Transp. cap. supply likely to	Stay same/Stay same	(Decrease/Increase or Increase/Stay same)
5-13	Commitment to stated goals	Flexible/Slight	(Flexible/Flexible)
*5-2	Regime seeks overthrow of adv.	No/No	(No/Yes)
4-16	Leadership charisma	Pronounced/Pronounced	(Negligible/Pronounced)
*5-12	Interest involved-cont'd exis.	No/No	(Yes/No)
6-29	I.O. peace machinery is seen	Irrelevant/Irrelevant	(Relevant/Irrelevant)
*5-37	Esc likely bring GP aid to adv	No/No	(Yes/No)
*6-6	A GP is openly partial to ant.	No/No	(Yes/No)
*6-18	A 3Pty is providing pol. aid	No/No	(Yes/No)
3-10	Total foreign aid received	1/1	(1/0)
3-11	Foreign economic aid received	1/1	(1/0)
3-12	For aid as Pc of GNP + for aid	1/1	(1/0)
8-4	Unity within military command	Unified/Unified	(Factional/Unified)
8-20	Use of terror by this ant. is	Absent/Absent	(Widespread/Absent or Absent/Limited)
8-28	Intell. among pop in conf area	Occasional/Ineffective	(Ineffective/Effective)
*8-29	Intell. in adv's policy organs	Ineffective/Ineffective	(Ineffective/Occasional)
**7-14	Total manpower committed	1/1	(2/0 or 0/2)
7-16	Conventional manpower committed	1/1	(0/3)
**7-17	Guerrilla manpower committed	1/1	(2/0 or 0/2)
***9-1	Pc of industrial capacity lost	1/1	(3/0)
***9-2	Pc of civilian population lost	1/1	(2/0)
9-7	Total cas'ties to all forces	1/1	(2/1)

Type C5
("present commitments bid fair an acceptable outcome")

The pattern derives from

India-China (Chinese violate Indian border — 6/54)

Indonesia-Malaysia (Brunei revolt; Indonesia arms "volunteers" — 2/63)

The adjunct is

Israel-Egypt (Czech-Egyptian arms agreement — 9/55)

Type C6
("reason and stability precede the intrusion of ideology")

The pattern derives from

Algeria-Morocco (Algerian independence referendum — 7/62)

Ethiopia-Somalia (Somali independence — 7/60)

Type C7
("no threat to survival is yet discerned")

The pattern derives from

Kashmir (raiding tribesmen enter Kashmir from Pakistan — 10/47)

USSR-Iran (USSR and Britain occupy Iran — 8/41)

Each conflict type in Table 6.3 presents a particular configuration of factors distinguishing conflict (P–II) from hostilities (P–III), together with the form that each factor assumed when hostilities subsequently occurred. The distinctive characteristics of the several types are as follows:

Type C1: the combined effects, in an internal conflict, of the rebels' lack of a popular base and of hardware support from outside sources.

Type C2: the absence of great-power involvement, while no offer to arbitrate has been made despite the continuing flexibility of one of the antagonists.

Type C3: the erosion of moderation attends the elimination of a political power base and the increase in casualties from random violence.

Type C4: here the issue of military assistance arises with the acquisition of arms from outside sources accompanying the frustration of attempts at a negotiated settlement.

Type C5: once it has been established, however, the withdrawal of military and economic aid from one party may contribute to instability, especially when the prospect of an unacceptable outcome confronts that party at its current level of policy activity.

Type C6: moderation, flexibility, and credibility prevail prior to the intrusion of extreme ideological differences and a rearrangement of expectations concerning arms capabilities. Here an early third-party offer of arbitration fails to avert hostilities, demonstrating that, even if the offer comes in time, only under specific conditions will it be immediately pacific or restraining in effect.

Type C7: finally, the absence of any threat to the continued existence of the regimes involved, the absence of open great-power partiality in the conflict, and the absence of terror tactics by the antagonists and of significant losses to them combine to maintain a flexible, fluid, and nonviolent situation — until the situation reverses itself.

Table 6.4
Hostilities: (P–III):
The Critical Factor Patterns

Note: Asterisk (*) indicates the factors found to define the higher-order classifications (genus or above) derived by agreement analysis of the hostilities (P–III) patterns; the number of asterisks indicates the number of higher orders achieved by that particular item-response combination.

Item	Relationship Between Antagonists at Threshold of Hostilities (P–III)	Previous Relationship (That Pertaining at Threshold of P–II or P–IV Preceding P–III)
Type H1 ("commitment hardens as accommodation fails")		
4-19 Freedom of the press allowed	Intermittent/NA	(Complete/NA)
**4-33 Recent change in leadership	No/No	(Yes/No)
5-19 Present outlook wrt dispute	Moderate/Die-hard	(Moderate/Moderate)

Table 6.4 (continued)

	Item	Relationship Between Antagonists at Threshold of Hostilities (P–III)	Previous Relationship (That Pertaining at Threshold of P–II or P–IV Preceding P–III)
The pattern derives from			
Cyprus: independence (insurrection becomes widespread — 4/55)			
Malayan insurgency (state of emergency declared by U.K.-Malay administration — 6/48)			
The adjuncts are			
Angolan insurgency (African insurgents riot in Luanda — 2/61)			
Venezuelan insurgency (attempted "leftist" rebellion — 6/61)			

Type H2
("revolt of the dispossessed in a 'moderate' system")

The pattern derives from

Cuba: "little" war of 1906 (insurgents and government forces clash — 8/06)

Cyprus: internal (Greek and Turkish Cypriots clash — 12/63)

Item		Relationship	Previous
**4-32	Recent leadership crisis	No/No	(No/Yes)
**4-33	Recent change in leadership	No/No	(No/Yes)
4-10	Regime came to power const'ly	NA/Yes	(NA/No)
4-11	Recruitment to pol leadership	Moderate/Moderate	(Moderate/Elitist)
4-6	Status of executive	NA/Strong	(NA/Dominant)
4-7	Status of legislature	NA/Full effect.	(NA/None)
*4-25	Const'al status of pol parties	NA/ Competitive	(NA/Part compet.)
4-19	Freedom of the press allowed	NA/Complete	(NA/Intermittent)
*4-18	Pol. integration of genl popn	NA/Moderate	(NA/Low)
4-28	Pc of popn voting in elections	NA/3	(NA/NA)
4-29	Pc of vote rec'd by this regim	NA/3	(NA/NA)
4-14	International policy of regime	None/Moderate	(None/None)
6-2	Is sec'ty ally of non-G.P.	No/No	(No/Yes)
7-14	Total manpower committed	1/1	(3/1)
7-21	No. rifles available	1/1	(1/2)

Type H3
("taking advantage of the moment")

The pattern derives from

Ethiopia-Somalia (Ethiopia violates Somali borders — 2/64)

Kashmir (Pakistanis infiltrate Kashmir border — 8/65)

Item		Relationship	Previous
4-10	Regime came to power const'ly	No/Yes	(Yes/Yes)
4-17	Mobilizational style of regime	Limited/Full	(Limited/Limited)
4-24	Interest artic'n by pol partys	Pol insignif/Pol signif	(Pol signif/Pol signif)
4-15	Communist orient'n of regime	Non-com./Non-com.	(Anti-com./Non-com.)
4-14	International policy of regime	Moderate/Moderate	(Moderate/Leftist)
*5-4	Interest involved-commitments	Yes/Yes	(No/Yes)
5-10	Interest involved-independence	No/No	(Yes/No)
5-13	Commitments to stated goals	Flexible/Flexible	(Flexible/Slight)
5-19	Present outlook wrt dispute	Moderate/Moderate	(Die-hard/Moderate)
*5-33	Indicated disput is negotiable	Yes/No	(No/Yes)
1-14	Basis of intro. to int'l orgn	Aggression	(Self-determ.)
6-28	Experience with IO peace mach	Frustrating/Frustrating	(Gratifying/Frustrating)
6-2	Is Sec'ty ally of non-G.P.	Yes/No	(No/No)
1-11	Dispute has been to reg'l orgn	Yes	(No)
6-18	A 3Pty is providing pol. aid	Yes/No	(No/Yes or No)
6-26	Pc ant's economy owned by 3Pty	0-4 Pc/NA	(NA/NA)
6-27	Pc Ant's exports cons. by 3Pty	0-4 Pc/NA	(NA/NA)
6-25	Aid to ant. hurts 3Pty economy	No/NA	(NA/NA)
6-24	Att. of 3Pty public to inv'mnt	Favorable/NA	(NA/NA)
7-50	Overtness of 3Pty hardware aid	Gen'ly overt/Gen'ly overt	(NA/NA)
7-51	Spare parts and ammunititon aid	Adequate/Adequate	(NA/NA or Inadequate/Adequate)
*7-11	Total troops given by 3rd Pty	1/1	(3/1)
**7-13	3Pty troop aid seen likely to	Stay same/Stay same	(Decrease/Stay same)
5-20	Perceived balance of will	Even/Even	(Even/Favorable)
8-16	Overall mil. hardware balance	Favorable/Unfavorable	(Unfavorable/Favorable)
7-8	Other signif internal threat	No/No	(Yes/Yes)
8-33	Civn security v. guerr attack	Moderate/Moderate	(Low/Moderate)
7-1	No. of own active mil. troops	1/1	(2/1)
**7-5	No. of own troops committed	1/2	(2/0)
**7-14	Total manpower committed	1/1	(1/0)
7-17	Guerrilla manpower committed	1/1	(2/0)

Type H4
("exploratory probe in a continuing confrontation")

The pattern derives from

India-China (Chinese attack Indian outposts — 9/62)

USSR-Iran (Iranian forces enter Azerbaidzhan — 12/46)

Item		Relationship	Previous
1-6	Duration of dispute	Very long	Long
2-17	Pc of involved area in control	1/1	(2/1 or 0/3)
4-6	Status of executive	Strong/Dominant	(Weak/Dominant)
8-4	Unity within military command	Unified/Unified	(Factional/Unified)
7-40	Has a nuclear capability	No/In dev'ment	(No/No)
4-39	Post-dispute expect'n of popn	Pessimistic/Optimistic	(Optimistic/Optimistic)
5-34	Has sought a negot. settlement	Yes/Yes	(Yes/No)
5-35	Has offered bi-lateral negotns	Yes/Yes	(Yes/No)
5-36	Has attended bi-lat'l negot'ns	Yes/Yes	(NA/NA)
5-26	Treaty experience with adv.	Unsatisf'ory/Satisfactory	(NA/NA)
6-5	Is aided by GP hostile to adv.	Yes/No	(No/No)
6-15	A G.P. is inv. on this side	Yes/No	(No/No)

Table 6.4 (*continued*)

Item	Relationship Between Antagonists at Threshold of Hostilities (P–III)	Previous Relationship (That Pertaining at Threshold of P–II or P–IV Preceding P–III)
7-41 Aiding 3Pty has nuclear cap'ty	Yes/No	(No/Yes or No)
7-50 Overtness of 3Pty hardware aid	Gen'ly overt/NA	(Gen'ly overt/Gen'ly overt)
6-24a Type of government of 3rd pty.	Pol. democ./NA	(Pol. democ./Total olig) or (NA/NA)
6-26 Pc ant's economy owned by 3Pty	5-15 Pc/NA	(0-4/5-15Pc or NA/NA)
6-24 Att. of 3Pty public to inv'mnt	Favorable/NA	(Fav./Fav. or NA/NA)

Type H5
("my big brother can lick yours; or, what are guns for, anyway?")

The pattern derives from

Indonesia-Malaysia (Indonesian attack in Sarawak—4/63)

Israel-Egypt (Israeli attack on Sinai—10/56)

Item	Relationship Between Antagonists at Threshold of Hostilities (P–III)	Previous Relationship (That Pertaining at Threshold of P–II or P–IV Preceding P–III)
6-6 A GP is openly partial to ant.	Yes/Yes	(No/Yes)
6-5 Is aided by GP hostile to adv.	Yes/Yes	(No/Yes)
6-1 Is sec'ty ally of great power	Yes/No	(No/No)
6-12 Some 3Pty is inv. on this side	Yes/Yes	(No/Yes)
6-15 A G.P. is inv. on this side	Yes/Yes	(No/Yes)
7-41 Aiding 3Pty has nuclear cap'ty	Yes/Yes	(No/Yes)
6-21 A 3Pty is providing mil hdwre.	Yes/Yes	(No/Yes)
6-24a Type of government of 3rd pty	Pol. democ./Total olig	(NA/Total olig)
6-24b Recent change in 3rd pty govt.	No/No	(NA/No)
6-25 Aid to ant. hurts 3Pty economy	No/No	(NA/No)
6-24 Att. of 3Pty public to inv'mnt	Favorable/Favorable	(NA/Favorable)
7-43 Battle arms supply likely to	Stay same/Stay same	(Decrease/Increase)
7-52 Training for weapons in aid	Adequate/Selective	(NA/Inadequate)
7-49 Transp. cap. supply likely to	Stay same/Stay same	(Decrease/Stay same)
7-3 No. reserve troops available	1/1	(2/1)

Type H6
("a new conductor, a new arrangement")

The pattern derives from

Ethiopian resistance (attempted assassination of Italian viceroy—2/37)

Indonesia: independence (second large-scale Dutch attack—12/48)

Item	Relationship Between Antagonists at Threshold of Hostilities (P–III)	Previous Relationship (That Pertaining at Threshold of P–II or P–IV Preceding P–III)
6-24b Recent change in 3rd pty govt.	Yes/No	(No/No)
7-4 Mobilization of reserves	Total/Total	(Total/Major)

Type H7
("grist for the great-power mill")

The pattern derives from

Cuba: Bay of Pigs (Bay of Pigs invasion by Cuban exiles—4/61)

Greek insurgency (widespread guerrilla warfare resumed—1/46)

Item	Relationship Between Antagonists at Threshold of Hostilities (P–III)	Previous Relationship (That Pertaining at Threshold of P–II or P–IV Preceding P–III)
5-13 Commitment to stated goals	Total/Total	(Total/Flexible)
5-31 Offered to resolve const'ally	No/No	(No/Yes)
1-12 Dispute has been to int'l orgn	Yes	(No)
1-14 Basis of Intro. to int'l orgn	Aggression	(NA)
**1-7 Ideological diff. betw parties	Extreme	(Mild)
4-12 Ideol. orientation of regime	Left-wing/Moderate	(Moderate/Right wing)
4-15 Communist orient'n of regime	Soviet/Anti-com.	(Non-com./Anti-com.)
4-34 Forn res are mainstay of regim	Yes/Yes	(No/No)
6-6 A GP is openly partial to ant.	Yes/Yes	(No/No)
6-12 Some 3Pty is inv. on this side	Yes/Yes	(No/No)
6-15 A G.P. is inv. on this side	Yes/Yes	(No/No)
6-20 A 3Pty is providing mil advice	Yes/Yes	(No/No)
6-21 A 3Pty is providing mil hdwre.	Yes/Yes	(No/No)
7-42 Dep. for battlefield armaments	Exclusive/Exclusive	(None/Exclusive)
6-22 A 3Pty is providing conv force	No/No	(No/Yes)
7-11 Total troops given by 3rd Pty	1/1	(0/1)
**6-24 Att. of 3Pty public to inv'mnt	Favorable/Favorable	(Favorable/Unfavorable)
8-20 Use of terror by this ant. is	Limited/Absent	(Widespread/Absent)

Type H8
("the injection of ideology")

The pattern derives from

Algeria-Morocco (Algerian attack on Tindouf—10/63)

Spanish civil war (military rising in Morocco by senior officers—7/36)

Item	Relationship Between Antagonists at Threshold of Hostilities (P–III)	Previous Relationship (That Pertaining at Threshold of P–II or P–IV Preceding P–III)
1-7 Ideological diff. betw parties	Extreme	(Mild)
* 5-33 Indicated disput is negotiable	Yes/No	(Yes/Yes)

Inspection of the several hostilities (P–III) types in Table 6.4 reveals both the various sets of its specific preconditions and the forms out of which the critical factors emerged. The distinctive characteristics of each set are as follows:

Type H1: the hardening of an insurgent party's position accompanies increased governmental restrictions, to the point of failure of accommodation.

Type H2: illustrating the failure of democratic institutions to mollify or placate a disenfranchised or dispossessed minority.

Type H3: despite a continuing moderation of approach to the ongoing conflict by both parties, each supplied with outside arms aid, a recent change in the overall military hardware balance is seized upon to gain immediate advantage. Operating here are pressures deriving from established commitments and from frustration with the machinery of international peacekeeping.

Type H4: negotiations fail to avert hostilities as one side appears to have little to lose by intensifying the level of protracted conflict.

Type H5: the prototypical case of local appropriation of great-power facilities and auspices to achieve local objectives; comparable great-power involvement and support on both sides are matched in the clients' minds by expectations of their indefinite continuance.

Type H6: a succinct statement of the potential effect of change in the character of the regime of the third party that is providing aid to one of the adversaries.

Type H7: in essence, the proxy war, conducted by local powers at the vicarious behest and with the unabashed and unlimited support of the great powers, as the latter vie for spheres of influence and local strategic advantage. Here, clearly, it is the intrusion of great-power considerations into the local context that effects the preconditions of hostilities.

Type H8: whereas the parties to the conflict had previously viewed its disposition as negotiable, ideological considerations intrude to create a volatile situation.

Several outstanding impressions remain from these considerations of the various conditions of prehostilities conflict and hostilities. First, it is apparent that impartial third-party conciliation attempts in general come too late, if at all, in local conflicts. While the possibility of accommodation is in each case open at the threshold of conflict, it is often—though not always—foreclosed by the time hostilities break out. Second, it is apparent from both sets of patterns, critical and composite, that equal rather than unequal arms and troop capabilities promote the outbreak of hostilities. Third, the extent to which the outbreak of hostilities in local conflict is preconditioned by the availability of third-party hardware sources can hardly be overemphasized.

The conclusion is therefore inescapable that the single most influential factor in conditioning the outbreak of hostilities in the eighteen local conflicts examined was great-power activity, partiality, involvement, and support. It is an irony that while it is perhaps only through the progressive expansion of local conflict that the great powers are likely to come to confront each other directly, it is they who must be held largely responsible for the course of development of those conflicts. In the pursuit of spheres of influence and in the name of righteous principles, the great powers have generally supplied the public support and the military hardware that are the very fuel of local conflict, even while withholding or failing to furnish the agencies of impartial accommodation.

There seems, then, to be something fundamentally, almost inevitably, corrosive of the process of local political accommodation in great power–client state relationships. To effect local spheres of influence, the great powers establish local arms commitments and capabilities. These arms may in turn be variously used to the great powers' own ends vis-à-vis each other and other local parties, and to the ends of the local parties themselves vis-à-vis other local interests and parties. When great powers seek direct influence beyond the accustomed limits of their authority, arms to a client inevitably promise the quickest, easiest, cheapest, and most effective means available. And when free arms are available, conciliation, accommodation, and all the attendant activities that build effective political structures within countries and regions can wait forever upon one more round of violent exchange in pursuit of all or nothing.

Escalation and De-escalation

It will be recalled that escalation (E) and de-escalation (D) were defined as any intensification or moderation, respectively, of the scale or scope of ongoing hostilities that constitutes a fundamental change in the "rules of the game" governing their conduct. Only a quite fundamental change in the nature of the hostilities generated by these local conflicts may, then, be so defined. Moreover, since both of these stages of conflict may develop only within ongoing hostilities (P–III), the weighting device used to isolate the specific conditions of each type of escalation and de-escalation was the pseudotype applying at the threshold of the particular hostilities involved. The critical factor patterns isolated are thus the various sets of conditions that distinguish escalation (E) and de-escalation (D) from an existing level of ongoing hostilities (P–III). Accordingly, the composite scenario of each represents a summary statement of the individual factors that most vitally indicate the escalatory and de-escalatory potential of hostilities.

In the composite scenario of escalation (Table 6.5), we again find that great-power partiality, assistance, and involvement on *both* sides of the ongoing hostilities are critical in establishing the conditions of their escalation — even in the absence of an explicit promise of increased aid if escalation does occur.

Moreover, among these most critical conditions of escalation, we find that some third-party conciliatory activity has generally occurred by now, that, indeed, an international organization has made its "good offices" available to the antagonists for arbitration or negotiation of the dispute. This is not to suggest that such activity in itself preconditions escalation. Rather, the very fact of third-party accommodation activity reflects the extremely serious nature of the dispute and the degree of threat it poses to the peace of the larger international setting within which it is conducted. It is further apparent, however, that by the time these offices become available the positions of the antagonists have hardened to the point that both regimes no longer feel free to accept less than their stated demands, and both are pessimistic about their own futures if they achieve less than victory on their own terms. Mean-

Table 6.5
The Conditions of Escalation (E):
A Composite Scenario
("commitments too great to turn
back now")

Note: This composite factor pattern derives from an examination of eleven instances of escalation (E). It consists exclusively of item-response combinations found to define the higher-order classifications (genus or above) isolated by agreement analysis of the escalation patterns. It is therefore what may be termed a second level of abstraction from the real conflicts from which it proceeds.

The number sign (#) indicates those factors in the escalation patterns with which the Vietnam war (as of March 15, 1967, and in its maximal form) agreed precisely.

Item		Relationship Between Antagonists at Threshold of Escalation (E)	Previous Relationship (That Pertaining at Threshold of P–III in Which E Occurred)
5-22	Post–dispute expect'n of regim#	Pessimistic/Pessimistic	(Optimistic/Pessimistic)
5-30	Principal attempts at resol'n #	Military/Military	(Military/Political)
5-15	Conduct of conflict is limited#	No/No	(No/Yes)
7-14	Total manpower committed #	1/1	(1 or 2/0)
8-13	Overall military org'n balance#	Unfavorable/Favorable	(Favorable/Unfavorable)
5-18	Can accept les thn stated dmds#	No/No	(Yes/No)
6-30	Some 3Pty offered to arbitrate#	Yes/Yes	(No/No)
6-31	Intl orgn offered to arbitrate#	Yes/Yes	(No/No)
5-26	Treaty experience with adv. #	Unsatisf'ory/Unsatisf'ory	(NA/NA)
6-6	A GP is openly partial to ant.#	Yes/Yes	(No/No)
6-5	Is aided by GP hostile to adv.#	Yes/Yes	(No/No)
6-15	A G.P. is inv. on this side #	Yes/Yes	(No/No)
6-7	GP aid promised if esc. occurs	No/No	(No/Yes)

while, the likely inefficacy of a negotiated settlement has been demonstrated to them by their unsatisfactory experience with each other in previous matters of treaty arrangement.

A final point of interest in the composite preconditions of escalation is that while the total manpower committed by both sides is now relatively equal, a considerable shift in the overall military organization balance (in terms of training, morale, and efficiency) has lately occurred in favor of the antagonist who was originally disadvantaged in these terms.

Inspection of the composite scenario of de-escalation (Table 6.6) reveals that a recent change in the balance of overall military organization is also of central importance in establishing *its* preconditions. This factor is now accompanied by several further military considerations, however. Although both sides still have adequate logistic support to maintain operations at their current level, the antagonist against whom the military balance has recently shifted is seen also to be suffering considerably greater personnel losses than his adversary and to have grossly inadequate medical facilities for treatment of his casualties. (Both factors are generally considered reliable indicators of morale among military forces.) Moreover, the level of third-party troop support for the party in whose favor the military balance has shifted appears likely to increase in the near future. Conspicuous by their absence from the most critical preconditions of de-escalation, on

Table 6.6
The Conditions of De-escalation (D): A Composite Scenario ("retreat while one may for a better day")

Note: This composite factor pattern derives from an examination of seven instances of de-escalation (D). It consists exclusively of item-response combinations found to define the higher-order classifications (genus or above) isolated by agreement analysis of the de-escalation patterns. It is therefore what may be termed a second level of abstraction from the real conflicts from which it proceeds.

The number sign (#) indicates the factors in the de-escalation patterns with which the Vietnam war (as of March 15, 1967, and in its maximal form) agreed precisely.

Item		Relationship Between Antagonists at Threshold of De-escalation (D)	Previous Relationship (That Pertaining at Threshold of P–III in Which D Occurred)
8-14	Logis sup't adqt to maint opns#	Yes/Yes	(NA/NA)
7-13	3Pty troop aid seen likely to	Increase/Stay same	(Stay same/Stay same)
8-13	Overall military org'n balance#	Favorable/Unfavorable	(Unfavorable/Favorable)
9-5	Total cas'ties to own forces #	1/2	(1/1)
8-25	Treatment of own casualties	Good/Poor	(NA/NA)
9-3	Total no. civn population lost#	3/0	(1/1)
5-22	Post-dispute expect'n of regim#	Pessimistic/Pessimistic	(Pessimistic/Optimistic)
6-30	Some 3Pty offered to arbitrate	No/No	(Yes/Yes)

the other hand, are great-power partiality, assistance, and involvement in the conflict.

Thus two factors are common to the scenarios of both escalation and de-escalation: pessimism among the regimes of both antagonists concerning their prospects if victory is not achieved on their own terms, and a recent change in the overall military organization balance confronting them. These appear to be the most critical preconditions not specifically of either escalation or de-escalation but, rather, of the more inclusive concept of change in the rules of the game. When these conditions apply, the situation would seem ripe for a change in the rules; whether escalation or de-escalation results depends on the nature of other factors in the enabling pattern in which these operate. The most significant other factor in this regard appears to be the nature and degree of great-power involvement.

For once a great power undertakes to become actively and publicly involved in a partisan manner and so has committed its prestige to the outcome of a dispute, any shift in the military balance will prompt it to act (depending upon which side of the balance it finds itself on) to avert that trend or to expedite a favorable outcome. Either way, the dominant pressures operate to escalate the level of ongoing hostilities. In addition, if great powers are directly involved, the local antagonists may come to depend on them not only for support but also for fixing the limits to which that support may be employed in pursuit of their own local objectives. Without explicit and meaningful limits, the local antagonists may be encouraged by that support to escalate the level of hostilities indefinitely, confident that they will be bailed out of any real trouble by their great-power sponsors.

In the absence of great-power partiality and involvement, however, more sober considerations may prevail, and de-escalation may more readily be realized. For example, when neither side in strictly localized conflict has the political capital to sustain a military nonvictory, considerable and increasing pressure will exist toward its control and resolution before existing logistic capabilities—meaning military operations capability and, in turn, bargaining power—are expended by either side.

Finally, the composite scenarios of these two subphases of hostilities indicate the presence of a third-party offer of arbitration to both parties among the most critical conditions of escalation, and the absence of any such offer among those of de-escalation. This is not to say that the one is a sufficient condition of the other. Rather, it is felt that this curious situation reflects two facts. First, only in conflicts that are seen to contain within themselves the potential for escalation, that is, for getting out of control and involving additional segments of the international community, do the good offices of third parties (especially international organizations) tend to be offered to the combatants for arbitration or other peaceful disposition of the dispute. Such an offer is generally made only when escalation is imminent, if not a foregone conclusion, and too late to be effective. If no threat to the community of nations appears imminent, on the other hand, arbitration offers tend not to be made. It may well be that, once the conditions for the moderation of hostilities have been established, an opportunity for their more complete moderation — that is, their termination — is often missed for the want of these good offices; de-escalation takes place when termination might otherwise have occurred. In sum, then, it would seem that the good offices of third parties tend to be offered only in the cases in which they are least likely to be effective and only at the point when their effect is likely to be the least. Similarly, they tend not to be offered at all in the cases in which they are most likely to be effective and when their effect might be expected to be the greatest.

If we turn now to the various escalation types established (see Table 6.7), we may examine the specific configurations of factors found to precondition its development and within which the most critical individual factors operate. The most outstanding features are the following:

Type E1: characterized by the recent involvement of a nongreat power on one side of the conflict, where neither principal party anticipates great-power assistance in the event that hostilities are intensified. Here again is a vivid illustration of the fact that one factor may condition different results within various contexts. For, as will be seen, the absence of any prospect of increased great-power aid if escalation occurs equally conditions, in other circumstances, the advent of settlement (S). Moreover, as opposed to this most dominant type of escalation, the settlement type in question is preconditioned in part by the current absence of great-power involvement as well as the likely prospect of its continued absence.

Type E2: a particularly complex set of preconditions, including the failure of negotiation and arbitration attempts and the inability of either party to accept less than its public demands; a change in the perceived balance of will to persist accompanying a considerable increase in losses to one side; and recent centralization of the military commands on both sides with the involvement of an independent, subnational third-party military force on one. Involved here is the escalation of unconventional hostilities to a conventional level, as losses rise to the point where they can no longer be tolerated and where too much is now at stake to permit retreat.

Table 6.7
Escalation (E):
The Critical Factor Patterns

Note: Asterisk (*) indicates the factors found to define the higher-order classifications (genus or above) derived by agreement analysis of the escalation (E) patterns; the number of asterisks indicates the number of higher orders achieved by that particular item-response combination.

The number sign (#) indicates the factors in the escalation patterns with which the Vietnam war (as of March 15, 1967, and in its maximal form) agreed precisely.

Item		Relationship Between Antagonists at Threshold of Escalation (E)	Previous Relationship (That Pertaining at Threshold of P–III in Which E Occurred)

Type E1
("acting with the presumption of immunity")

The pattern derives from

Cyprus: independence (colonial government declares state of emergency — 11/55)

Cyprus: internal (first intervention threat by Turkey — 1/64)

Malayan insurgency (resumption of widespread terror campaign — 10/52)

Venezuelan insurgency (government changes from police to military response — 10/63)

Item		Rel.	Prev.
**6-7	GP aid promised if esc. occurs	No/No	(No/Yes)
6-16	A non-GP is inv. on this side	Yes/No	(No/No)
8-25	Treatment of own casualties	Poor/Good	(NA/NA)

Type E2
("diplomacy fails amid unacceptable losses")

The pattern derives from

Indonesia-Malaysia (Indonesian landings in Malaya — 8/64)

Kashmir (Pakistan commits regular troops — 5/48)

Item		Rel.	Prev.
1-9	Size of area at stake	Large	Small
9-3	Total No. civn population lost #	0/3	(1/1)
1-12	Dispute has been to int'l orgn	Yes	(No)
1-13	Introduced to int'l orgn by a	Antagonist	(NA)
6-11	Has asked an int'l. org'n. in	No/Yes	(No/No)
*6-31	Intl orgn offered to arbitrate #	Yes/Yes	(No/No)
6-41	Has honored recommends of I.O.	Gen'ly No/Gen'ly Yes	(NA/NA)
*5-26	Treaty experience with adv. #	Unsatisf'ory/Unsatisf'ory	(NA/NA)
5-28	Reliability of communications	High/High	(Low/Low)
5-34	Has sought a negot. settlement	Yes/Yes	(No/Yes)
5-35	Has offered bi-lateral negotns	Yes/Yes	(No/Yes)
5-18	Can accept les thn stated dmds #	No/No	(No/Yes)
5-20	Perceived balance of will	Even/Even	(Even/Unfavorable)
5-17	Rationalization of violence	Moralistic/Legal	(Moralistic/Expediency)
8-17	Centralization of mil. command #	Centralized/Centralized	(De-centr'zed/Centralized) or (Centralized/De-centr'zed)
8-20	Use of terror by this ant. is	Limited/Absent	(W'spr'd or Abt/Absent)
6-17	A aut org is inv. on this side	Yes/No	(No/No)
*7-14	Total manpower committed	1/1	(1 or 2/0)
7-16	Conventional manpwer committed	0/3	(1/1)
9-7	Total cas'ties to all forces #	2/1	(1/1)
9-10	Casualty rate for all forces #	2/1	(1/1)
9-13	Attrition rate for all forces	2/1	(1 or 3/1)

Type E3
("toward a foregone conclusion in proxy conflict")

The pattern derives from

Greek insurgency (guerrillas go conventional; Tito closes border — 7/49)

Spanish civil war (Italian ground troops intervene — 1/37)

Item		Rel.	Prev.
*5-18	Can accept les thn stated dmds #	No/No	(Yes/No)
*5-15	Conduct of conflict is limited #	No/No	(No/Yes or Yes/No)
5-14	Dispute is regarded as crusade #	Yes/Yes	(No/Yes)
5-13	Commitment to stated goals #	Total/Total	(Flexible/Total)
**5-22	Post-dispute expect'n of regim #	Pessimistic/Pessimistic	(Optimistic/Pessimistic)
*5-30	Principal attempts at resol'n #	Military/Military	(Military/Political)
5-21	Likely outcome is now obvious	No/Yes	(Yes/No)
8-14	Logis sup't adqt to maint opns	No/Yes	(Yes/Yes or No)
8-15	Logis sup't adqt to expand opn	No/Yes	(No/No or Yes/Yes)
8-4	Unity within military command	Factional/Unified	(Unified/Unified)
8-3	Rel'snip bet pol + mil leaders	Pol dominant/Mil dominant	(Pol dominant/Co-equal)
8-17	Centralization of mil. command #	Centralized/Centralized	(De-centr'zed/De-centr'zed)
4-34	Forn res are mainstay of regim	Yes/Yes	(No/Yes or No)
4-35	Regim appears maint by for res	Yes/Yes	(No/Yes or No)

Table 6.7 (*continued*)

Item		Relationship Between Antagonists at Threshold of Escalation (E)	Previous Relationship (That Pertaining at Threshold of P–III in Which E Occurred)
*6-6	A GP is openly partial to ant.#	Yes/Yes	(No/No)
*6-5	Is aided by GP hostile to adv.#	Yes/Yes	(No/No)
*6-15	A G.P. is inv. on this side #	Yes/Yes	(No/No)
*8-13	Overall military org'n balance#	Unfavorable/Favorable	(Favorable/Unfavorable)
7-14	Total manpower committed #	1/1	(2/0)
7-17	Guerrilla manpower committed	2/0	(1/1)
7-6	No. troops comm as pc tot frcs	1/1	(3/0 or 2/1)
7-47	Air armament supply likely to	Stay same/Stay same	(Increase/Stop)
9-5	Total cas'ties to own forces #	2/1	(3/0 or 1/1)
5-30	Principal attempts at resol'n #	Military/Military	(Delay/Delay)
5-21	Likely outcome is now obvious	Yes/Yes	(Yes/No)
7-6	No. troops comm as pc tot frcs	1/2	(2/1)
*6-30	Some 3Pty offered to arbitrate#	Yes/Yes	(No/No)
*6-31	Intl orgn offered to arbitrate#	Yes/Yes	(No/No)

The adjunct is

Ethiopian resistance (Britain declares war on Italy; supports insurgents—6/40)

Type E4
("reacting to the manifest: expedition and aversion")

The pattern derives from

Algeria-Morocco (Algeria accepts aid from UAR, USSR, Cuba—10/63)

Israel-Egypt (British bomb Egyptian airfields—11/56)

Type E3: the preconditions of escalation of a proxy conflict. The outcome is now apparent to a military regime that would expedite the matter, while the logistic capabilities of the other antagonist are rapidly vanishing and suggesting that, while it may, it make a concerted if desperate move toward victory.

Type E4: the likely outcome of hostilities is now obvious to both sides if their present levels of commitment are maintained. The possible reactions are to expedite that outcome or, alternatively, to act decisively to avert it.

On the other hand, turning to the various preconditions of de-escalation that were established (see Table 6.8), we find the following configurations of factors:

Type D1: one party undertakes strategic retreat in the face of mounting casualties, a shift of the military organization balance in its disfavor, and the likelihood of increased third-party troop support for its adversary; and does so even while it still has logistic support adequate to maintain its current level of military operations, though not indefinitely.

Type D2: disproportionate casualty and attrition rates beset one antagonist in intense hostilities, even while it faces an increase in third-party troop support to its adversary and an imposing buildup in the adversary's naval and air capabilities. Both here and in Type D3, moreover, we find that the dispute has recently been taken to the international organization by one of the antagonists, in the latter type on a complaint of aggression by the adversary. In two of the three sets of preconditions of de-escala-

Table 6.8
De-escalation (D):
The Critical Factor Patterns

Note: Asterisk (*) indicates the factors found to define the higher-order classifications (genus or above) derived by agreement analysis of the de-escalation (D) patterns; the number of asterisks indicates the number of higher orders achieved by that particular item-response combination.

The number sign (#) indicates the factors in the de-escalation patterns with which the Vietnam war (as of March 15, 1967, and in its maximal form) agreed precisely.

	Item	Relationship Between Antagonists at Threshold of De-escalation (D)	Previous Relationship (That Pertaining at Threshold of P–III in Which D Occurred)
Type D1 ("adjusting ambitions to reflect capabilities")	6-9 Has invoked avail sec'ty pacts	Yes/NA	(No/NA)
	6-21 A 3Pty is providing mil hdwre.#	Yes/Yes	(Yes/No)
	7-50 Overtness of 3Pty hardware aid#	Gen'ly overt/Gen'ly covert	(Gen'ly overt/High)
	7-30 No. bomber a/c available	2/0	(1/1)
	7-33 No. helicopters available	3/0	(1/1)
The pattern derives from	7-49 Transp. cap. supply likely to	Increase/NA	(Stay same/NA)
	7-51 Spare parts and ammunition aid	Adequate/Inadequate	(Adequate/NA)
Cyprus: independence (Makarios accepts no "enosis" – 9/58)	*7-13 3Pty troop aid seen likely to	Increase/Stay same	(Stay same/Stay same)
	***8-13 Overall military org'n balance#	Favorable/Unfavorable	(Unfavorable/Favorable)
	*8-14 Logis sup't adqt to maint opns#	Yes/Yes	(NA/NA)
Malayan insurgency (MCP shifts emphasis to political agitation – 10/51)	8-23 Tactics of forces on this side#	Tenacious/Yielding	(NA/NA)
	8-26 Larg-scal guer opn being waged	No/Yes	(NA/Yes)
	8-27 Stage of guerrilla operations	NA/Expansion	(NA/org + cons)
	8-20 Use of terror by this ant. is	Absent/Widespread	(Absent/Absent)
The adjunct is	**8-25 Treatment of own casualties	Good/Poor	(NA/NA)
	8-24 Treatment of enemy prisoners	Good/NA	(NA/NA)
	5-45 Legal status of adv. personnel	Com criminal/enemy agent	(Citizen/Citizen)
Cyprus: internal (agreement on U.N. peacekeeping force – 3/64)	5-46 Amnesty decl for adv personnel	No/No	(NA/NA)
	*9-3 Total no. civn population lost#	3/NA	(1/1)
	9-6 Total cas'ties to 3Pty forces	3/NA	(1/1)
	**9-5 Total cas'ties to own forces #	1/2	(1/1)
	4-25 Const'al status of pol. parties	Part compet./NA	(Competitive/NA)
Type D2 ("a gesture of conciliation in time saves nine")	1-10 Size of population at stake #	Very large	Small
	2-13 Popn under effective control	2/1	(3/0)
	2-17 Pc of involved area in control	1/2	(3/0 or 0/3)
	1-12 Dispute has been to int'l orgn	Yes	(No)
	1-13 Introduced to int'l orgn by a	Antagonist	(NA)
	**6-30 Some 3Pty offered to arbitrate	No/No	(Yes/Yes)
	5-28 Reliability of communications	High/High	(Low/Low)
The pattern derives from	5-26 Treaty experience with adv.	Unsatisf'ory/Unsatisf'ory	(NA/NA)
	7-1 No. of own active mil. troops #	1/1	(2/1)
Indonesia: independence (unsuccessful negotiations opened – 4/46)	7-4 Mobilization of reserves	Major/Major	(None/None)
	7-14 Total manpower committed #	1/1	(1/0)
	7-18 Naval manpower committed	1/3	(1/1)
Indonesia-Malaysia (Indonesian landings in Malaya cease – 5/65)	7-19 Air force manpower committed	1/2	(1/1)
	7-20 Medical personnel committed	1/2	(1/1)
	*7-13 3Pty troop aid seen likely to	Stay same/Increase	(Stay same/Stay same)
	8-21 Tactics of forces on this side#	Offensive/Offensive	(NA/NA)
	8-22 Tactics of forces on this side#	Mobile/Mobile	(NA/NA)
	8-23 Tactics of forces on this side#	Yielding/Tenacious	(NA/NA)
	8-26 Larg-scal guer opn being waged	No/No	(NA/NA)
	*8-25 Treatment of own casualties	Poor/Good	(NA/NA)
	*9-5 Total cas'ties to own forces #	2/1	(1/1)
	9-8 Casualty rate for own forces #	2/1	(1/1)
	9-11 Attrition rate for own forces	2/1	(1/1)
	9-13 Attrition rate for all forces	2/1	(1/1)
Type D3 ("recognizing a precarious cause for what it is")	*5-22 Post-dispute expect'n of regim#	Pessimistic/Pessimistic	(Optimistic/Pessimistic)
	5-14 Dispute is regarded as crusade#	Yes/Yes	(No/Yes)
	5-15 Conduct of conflict is limited#	No/No	(Yes/No)
	5-13 Commitment to stated goals #	Total/Total	(Flexible/Total)
	5-18 Can accept les thn stated dmds#	No/No	(Yes/No)
The pattern derives from	4-11 Recruitment to pol leadership	Elitist/Elitist	(Moderat./Elitist)
	4-20 Freedom of group opposition	Not toleratd/Not toleratd	(Full/Not toleratd)
Ethiopian resistance (new viceroy initiates conciliation policy – 1/38)	4-25 Const'al status of pol parties	Part compet./Non-compet.	Part compet./Part compet.)
	4-26 Effective pol. party system	One pty dom/One party	(Multi-party/Multi-party)
Spanish civil war (withdrawal of the International Brigade – 10/38)	6-6 A GP is openly partial to ant.#	Yes/Yes	(No/No)
	6-12 Some 3Pty is inv. on this side#	Yes/Yes	(No/Yes or No)
	6-15 A G.P. is inv. on this side #	Yes/Yes	(No/No)
	6-18 A 3Pty is providing pol. aid #	Yes/Yes	(No/No)
	6-20 A 3Pty is providing mil advice#	Yes/Yes	(No/No)
	6-22 A 3Pty is providing conv force	No/Yes	(No/No)
	6-24 Att. of 3Pty public to inv'mnt#	Favorable/Favorable	(NA/NA)
	6-24b Recent change in 3Pty governmt#	No/No	(NA/NA)

Table 6.8 (*continued*)

Item	Relationship Between Antagonists at Threshold of De-escalation (D)	Previous Relationship (That Pertaining at Threshold of P—III in Which D Occurred)
8-16 Overall mil. hardware balance #	Unfavorable/Favorable	(Favorable/Unfavorable)
8-22 Tactics of forces on this side#	Mobile/Mobile	(Static/Static)
8-14 Logis sup't adqt to maint opns	No/Yes	(Yes/Yes)
2-12 Area under effective control	1/1	(2/1)
5-32 Brought dispute to int'l orgn	Yes/No	(No/No)
1-12 Dispute has been to int'l orgn	Yes	(No)
1-13 Introduced to int'l orgn by a	Antagonist	(NA)
1-14 Basis of intro. to int'l orgn	Aggression	(NA)

tion of ongoing hostilities, then, the factor that might be termed world opinion is seen to play a moderating role. For, in general, any complaint of aggression is likely to reach the floor of the international organization only if there is considerable sympathy for it among the dominant member powers—that is, only if the great powers wish it there. And a party that once stands accused in that arena may ignore that sympathy and world opinion only at some considerable loss of its international standing, reputation, and influence.

Type D3: a total commitment by both antagonists to the fray, with high great-power involvement in the ongoing hostilities. A recent shift in the overall military hardware balance, however, is accompanied by exhaustion of the logistic support of the disadvantaged party. Under these conditions, de-escalation is effected despite the fact that neither side currently feels free to accept less than its stated demands.

This last factor, it will be recalled, is a very critical indicator under other circumstances of escalation, which reflects two facts. First, it is not only the principal parties involved in hostilities that may effect escalation or de-escalation; involved third parties may do so despite, and at times even because of, the local parties' inability to do so. Second, the local adversaries may themselves take specific action to de-escalate the level of hostilities, if overall strategic considerations dictate, without altering their stated objectives or determination to achieve them.

In summary, then, both escalation and de-escalation might best be viewed as alternative reactions to the considerable costs and enormous risks of hostilities. Escalation is an attempt on the one hand to expedite and on the other to avert what is rapidly becoming, if it has not already become, an obvious outcome of the conflict. De-escalation, alternatively, follows when at least one of the antagonists feels that he may, without irreversibly jeopardizing his position, alter his objectives, reduce the level of activity in pursuit of his continuing objectives, or broaden the political framework within which hostilities are conducted, for example, by introducing negotiations.

In both these subphases of local hostilities, the dominant influence of great-power activity or inactivity is observed. Again, it is ironic that while it is only through the uncontrollable effects of successive escalations of local conflicts that the great powers are likely ever to confront each other directly, the single most important factor involved in the escalation and de-escalation of local conflict is great-power involvement itself. The more partial, active, and substantial that involvement, the greater is the likelihood of escalation, and the greater is the likelihood of direct great-power confrontation; the less active that involvement, except as it may involve good offices for accommodation by the parties directly involved, the more likely is de-escalation.

Termination and Settlement

It will be recalled that each conflict from which the analysis derives eventuated in hostilities. At the conclusion of these hostilities, each also achieved some form of what we have called termination. And in a few of the conflicts a final disposition of the issue (as currently defined) was even effected between the antagonists, a settlement, as it were, of the dispute. Thus each instance of settlement (S) examined was specifically an instance of posthostilities settlement. Since most disputes do not result in hostilities, most settlements of disputes are not in fact of the posthostilities variety. Therefore, to be fully expressive of the various conditions of settlement, the analysis should be expanded to include prehostilities varieties. For the present, it need be borne in mind only that the conditions of settlement isolated here are those pertaining in disputes so intense as to have eventuated in hostilities.

In establishing the conditions of these two stages of conflict, the weighting device employed was the pseudotype applying at the threshold of the phase or subphase from which each instance proceeded. What results, then, is the various sets of specific preconditions that distinguish each type of termination and settlement from the conflict process or stage from which it emerged.

In the composite scenario of individual factors most important to the preconditions of termination (see Table 6.9), we find that one party no longer has adequate logistic support to maintain its ongoing level of military operations. This contrasts with the composite scenario of the lesser moderation of hostilities, de-escalation, where both sides retain adequate logistic support to continue operations at the ongoing level. In the termination scenario, this logistic factor is accompanied by other indications that things are indeed going badly for one side and that the processes of non-hostile accommodation are currently at work. Among these individual critical preconditions of termination, then, are a considerable imbalance in the troop strengths available to the antagonists and committed to their individual causes in the conflict; the expectation that third-party supplies of troops are likely to remain at present levels for both adversaries; an imbalance in

Table 6.9
The Conditions of Termination
(P–IV):
A Composite Scenario
("accommodating to the fact of a
stabilized imbalance")

Note: This composite factor pattern derives from an examination of sixteen instances of termination (P–IV). It consists exclusively of item-
response combinations found to define the higher-order classifications
(genus or above) isolated by agreement analysis of the termination patterns. It is therefore what may be termed a second level of abstraction
from the real conflicts from which it proceeds.

The number sign (#) indicates the factors in the termination patterns with
which the Vietnam war (as of March 15, 1967, and in its maximal form)
agreed precisely.

Item	Relationship Between Antagonists at Threshold of Termination (P–IV)	Previous Relationship (That Pertaining at Threshold of [Sub]phase III Preceding P–IV)
4-32 Recent leadership crisis	No/No	(No/Yes)
2-12 Area under effective control	3/0	(3/1)
2-13 Popn under effective control	3/0	(2/1)
2-17 Pc of involved area in control	3/0	(3/1)
2-18 Pc of involved popn in control	3/0	(3/1)
5-31 Offered to resolve const'ally #	No/No	(Yes/No)
5-34 Has sought a negot. settlement	Yes/Yes	(No/Yes)
5-36 Has attended bi-lat'l negot'ns	Yes/Yes	(No/No)
7-14 Total manpower committed	2/1	(1 or 0/1)
8-14 Logis sup't adqt to maint opns	Yes/No	(Yes/Yes)
7-13 3Pty troop aid seen likely to	Stay same/Stay same	(Increase/Stay same or Stay same/Decrease)
7-1 No. of own active mil. troops	2/1	(1/1)
7-5 No. of own troops committed #	2/1	(0/2)
7-15 Own trops as Pc of all commited#	1/1	(0/3)
8-25 Treatment of own casualties	Good/Poor	(Fair/Poor)
7-30 No. bomber a/c available	2/1	(1/1)
6-13 Int'l org is inv. on this side #	No/No	(No/Yes)

attack aircraft and medical facilities; and the control by one antagonist of all the land area and population directly involved in the
conflict, and the consequent elimination of the base support
area of the other. Another critical factor at this termination stage
is that the relatively new leadership of the party for whom things
are going badly has now solidly established its political position
and is prepared to deal with the opposition. In the context of
these conditions, both sides have now sought a negotiated settlement and have attended bilateral meetings to that end.

The prototypical conditions of termination of local conflict are
seemingly defined, then, by the situation in which things are going
very badly, militarily, for an antagonist that has only recently
undergone an internal crisis and change in leadership, perhaps
because of that very fact. The new regime is confronted with a
situation that appears most unlikely to improve, and, free as it is
from the commitments of the previous regime and desirous of
reinforcing its own political position, it is both able and willing to
effect an accommodation leading to termination of the hostilities.

Again the cause of moderation is served by the absence from this
scenario of the prospect of an increase in third-party involvement.
Notable in this connection is the fact that termination of conflict
is conditioned by the absence of partisan involvement by the

international organization, where once previously it had existed. It appears that, like partisan great-power involvement, such international organization activity is immoderating, or at least not moderating, in its effect upon conflict. Like the former, it is in itself an impediment to the establishment of local, and therefore possibly effective, accommodation of conflict.

Table 6.10
Termination (P–IV):
The Critical Factor Patterns

Note: Asterisk (*) indicates the factors found to define the higher-order classifications (genus or above) derived by agreement analysis of the termination (P–IV) patterns; the number of asterisks indicates the number of higher orders achieved by that particular item-response combination.

The number sign (#) indicates the factors in the termination patterns with which the Vietnam war (as of March 15, 1967, and in its maximal form) agreed precisely.

Item	Relationship Between Antagonists at Threshold of Termination (P–IV)	Previous Relationship (That Pertaining at Threshold of [Sub]phase III Preceding P–IV)
Type T1 ("depriving the rebels of their popular base")		
1-5 Effective nature of dispute #	Internal	(Colonial)
*2-13 Popn under effective control	0/3	(1/2)
4-1 Effective status of government#	Rebel orgn/Indep govt	(Rebel orgn/Colonial adm)
4-10 Regime came to power const'ly	NA/Yes	(NA/No)
4-7 Status of legislature	NA/Part effect.	(NA/Ineffective)
4-25 Const'al status of pol parties	NA/Part compet.	(NA/Competitive)
4-28 Pc of popn voting in elections#	NA/3	(NA/NA)
4-14 International policy of regime	Leftist/Moderate	(Leftist/None)
4-34 Forn res are mainstay of regim	No/No	(No/Yes)
5-30 Principal attempts at resol'n #	Military/Military	(Military/Judicial)
*5-31 Offered to resolve const'ally #	No/No	(No/Yes)
*7-1 No of own active mil. troops	1/2	(1/1)
*7-5 No.of own troops committed #	1/2	(2/0)
7-6 No. troops comm as Pc tot frcs#	2/1	(3/0)
5-16 Pc of avail mil frcs committed	70-100Pc/25-49Pc	(70-100Pc/0-10 or 50-69Pc)
*7-14 Total manpower committed	1/2	(1/1 or 0)
*7-15 Own trps as Pc of all commited#	1/1	(3/0)
8-11 Training fac for enlisted pers	Poor/Good	(Fair/Good)
7-22 No. auto. weapons available #	1/3	(1/2)
5-15 Conduct of conflict is limited	No/Yes	(Yes/Yes)
8-21 Tactics of forces on this side#	Offensive/Offensive	(Offensive/Defensive)
8-22 Tactics of forces on this side#	Mobile/Mobile	(Mobile/Static)
9-10 Casualty rate for all forces #	1/1	(2/1)
*8-14 Logis sup't adqt to maint opns	No/Yes	(Yes/Yes)
Type T2 ("accommodation follows foreclosure of arms aid")		
5-21 Likely outcome is now obvious	Yes/Yes	(No/Yes)
8-21 Tactics of forces on this side	Defensive/Offensive	(Offensive/Off. or Def.)
*5-34 Has sought a negot. settlement	Yes/Yes	(Yes/No)
5-35 Has offered bi-lateral negotns	Yes/Yes	(No/Yes)
*5-36 Has attended bi-lat'l negot'ns	Yes/Yes	(No/No)
5-18 Can accept les thn stated dmds	No/Yes	(No/No)
6-6 A GP is openly partial to ant.	No/No	(Yes/No)
6-21 A 3Pty is providing mil hdware	No/No	(Yes/Yes)
Type T3 ("guerrillas go conventional in absence of popular base")		
*2-12 Area under effective control	0/3	(1/3)
*2-13 Popn under effective control	0/3	(1/2)
*2-17 Pc of involved area in control	0/3	(1/3)
*2-18 Pc of involved popn in control	0/3	(1/3)
4-33 Recent change in leadership #	No/No	(Yes/No)
5-35 Has offered bi-lateral negotns#	No/No	(Yes/No
6-17 A aut org is inv. on this side#	No/No	(Yes/No)
6-5 Is aided by GP hostile to adv. #	Yes/Yes	(Yes/No)
6-24b Recent change in 3rd Pty govt.#	No/No	(Yes/Yes)

Text in left margin:

Type T1 ("depriving the rebels of their popular base")

The pattern derives from

Malayan insurgency (state of emergency declared terminated—7/60)

Venezuelan insurgency (insurgency slackens after successful elections—12/63)

The adjuncts are

Cuba: "little" war of 1906 (government declares unilateral cease-fire—9/06)

Cyprus: independence (London Agreement on Cypriot independence—2/59)

Type T2 ("accommodation follows foreclosure of arms aid")

The pattern derives from

Ethiopia-Somalia (cease-fire agreement—4/64)

Kashmir (proposed U.N. cease-fire accepted—9/65)

Type T3 ("guerrillas go conventional in absence of popular base")

The pattern derives from

Cuba: Bay of Pigs (defeat of invading exiles by government forces—4/61)

Table 6.10 (*continued*)

	Item	Relationship Between Antagonists at Threshold of Termination (P–IV)	Previous Relationship (That Pertaining at Threshold of [Sub]phase III Preceding P–IV)
Greek insurgency (Greek army victory — 12/49)	8-4 Unity within military command	Unified/Unified	(Factional/Unified)
	*7-1 No. of own active mil. troops	1/2	(1/1)
	7-4 Mobilization of reserves	NA/Total	(NA/Major)
	*7-14 Total manpower committed	1/2	(1/1)
	8-26 Larg-scal guer opn being waged	No/No	(Yes/No)
	8-28 Intell. among pop in conf area	Ineffective/Effective	(Effective/Occasional)
	*8-25 Treatment of own casualties	Poor/Good	(Poor/Fair)
	8-18 Sanctuary available to troops	Gen'ly not/Generally	(Generally/Gen'ly not)
	*8-14 Logis sup't adqt to maint opns	No/Yes	(Yes/Yes)
Type T4 ("interests not commensurate with the risk involved") The pattern derives from India-China (Chinese unilateral cease-fire — 11/62) USSR-Iran (Iranian forces gain control of all Iran — 12/46)	*4-32 Recent leadership crisis	No/No	(Yes/No)
	4-33 Recent change in leadership #	No/No	(Yes/No)
	4-37 Pop. support for regim's pols.	High/High	(Low/High)
	4-38 Att. of intellectuals to regim	Favorable/Favorable	(Unfavorable/Favorable)
	5-6 Interest involved-nat'l char.	Yes/No	(No/No)
	5-10 Interest involved-independence	Yes/No	(No/No)
	6-11 Has asked an int'l. orgn in #	No/No	(Yes/No)
	*6-13 Int'l org is inv. on this side #	No/No	(No/No)
	6-29 I.O. peace machinery is seen #	Irrelevant/Irrelevant	(Relevant/Irrelevant)
	7-16 Conventional manpwer committed	1/1	(1/2)
	6-20 A 3Pty is providing mil advice	Yes/No	(No/No)
	6-23 A 3Pty is providing guer force	No/No	(No/Yes)
	5-37 Esc likely bring GP aid to adv #	No/Yes	(No/No)
Type T5 ("keeping the thing within reason") The pattern derives from Algeria-Morocco (Bamoko agreement — 11/63) Israel-Egypt (U.N. cease-fire accepted — 11/56)	2-18 Pc of involved popn in control	3/0	(1/2)
	*7-30 No. bomber a/c available	2/1	(1/1)
	7-12 Overtess of 3Pty personnel aid	Gen'ly overt/NA	(Gen'ly covert/NA)
	5-37 Esc likely bring GP aid to adv	Yes/Yes	(No/Yes)
	5-13 Commitment to stated goals	Flexible/Flexible	(Total/Flexible)
	5-19 Present outlook wrt dispute	Moderate/Moderate	(Die-hard/Die-hard)
	5-30 Principal attempts at resol'n	Political/Political	(Military/Military)
Type T6 ("outside pressures conspire for decisive action") The pattern derives from Angolan insurgency (Portuguese suppress organized hostilities — 9/61) Indonesia: independence (cease-fire and Roem–Von Royen agreement — 10/49)	2-12 Area under effective control	3/1	(2/1)
	2-13 Popn under effective control	2/1	(1/1)
	2-18 Pc of involved popn in control	3/1	(1/3 or 2/1)
	4-14 International policy of regime	None/Moderate	(None/Leftist)
	4-15 Communist orient'n of regime	Anti-Com./Non-com.	(Anti-com./Soviet)
	5-30 Principal attempts at resol'n #	Military/Military	(Political/Political)
	5-15 Conduct of conflict is limited #	No/No	(Yes/No)
	5-46 Amnesty decl for adv personnel#	Yes/No	(No/No)
	8-22 Tactics of forces on this side	Static/Mobile	(Mobile/Mobile)
	8-23 Tactics of forces on this side#	Tenacious/Yielding	(Yielding/Yielding)
	5-21 Likely outcome is now obvious	Yes/No	(No/No)
	6-6 A GP is openly partial to ant.	No/Yes	(No/No)
	5-37 Esc likely bring GP aid to adv	Yes/No	(No/No)
	6-35 Intl orgn upheld ant's cause	No/Yes	(No/No)
	6-36 Intl orgn indicted ant's cause	Yes/No	(No/No)
Type T7 ("moderate faction prevails to confront reality") The pattern derives from Indonesia-Malaysia (hostilities end after Indonesian coup — 12/65) Spanish civil war (organized resistance ends after Casado coup in Madrid — 3/39)	1-6 Duration of dispute	Long	Short
	3-21 Industrial empl. as Pc of popn	1/2	(2/1)
	4-36 Pop. support for regime's obj. #	Low/High	(High/High)
	4-37 Pop. support for regime's pols.	Low/High	(High/High)
	4-32 Recent leadership crisis	Yes/No	(No/No)
	5-21 Likely outcome is now obvious	Yes/Yes	(No/Yes)
	5-19 Present outlook wrt dispute	Moderate/Die-hard	(Die-hard/Die-hard)
	8-16 Overall mil. hardware balance #	Unfavorable/Favorable	(Unfavorable/Unfavorable)
	8-4 Unity within military command	Factional/Unified	(Unified/Unified)
	9-11 Attrition rate for own forces	2/1	(1/1)
	*7-13 3Pty troop aid seen likely to	Stay same/Stay same	(Stay same/Increase or Decrease/Stay same)
	7-53 Pc total costs coming fm 3Pty	2/1	(1/1)
	5-29 Credibility of communications	High/High	(Low/Low)

If we turn directly to the specific configurations in which these individual factors operate to effect the preconditions of termination (see Table 6.10), we find the following:

Type T1: the effect of substituting an authentic, moderate government for alien domination and support of a puppet regime; with the issue of the regime's legitimacy thus resolved, the offer of a constitutional settlement of the conflict is withdrawn and superior force is applied to the point at which the insurgents lack both a popular base and adequate logistics to continue operations.

Type T2: the issue is a foregone conclusion, militarily, at the antagonists' present levels of capability; with the withdrawal of outside sources of military hardware from both antagonists, and the impartiality of the great powers between them, a negotiated peace is sought by both. Of interest in this pattern is the fact that one of the principals now feels that it may accept less than its former, publicly stated demands. It is in this case that the availability of good and impartial offices would seem to be critical if the new flexibility of one party is to be exploited to the end of moderating hostilities. The availability of such offices allows the opportunity to effect compromise and accommodation without the appearance of surrender and with the appearance of magnanimity.

Type T3: the complete elimination of the popular base, support area, and logistic capabilities of one party by the other. Although both antagonists have been aided by great powers in their efforts, the critical interests of the power supporting the loser are not sufficiently involved to risk further commitment.

Types T4, T5, and T6: each illustrates the efficacy, under certain additional conditions, of the threat of great-power involvement in establishing the preconditions of termination. In each of these patterns, at least one antagonist anticipates that (further) great-power involvement on behalf of the adversary will follow directly upon any escalatory or expansive action on its own part. Here we have identified something of a paradox or dilemma. The threat of great-power involvement in hostilities tends under certain circumstances to precondition their termination; but for this threat to be effective, it must be credible: the great power must be taken at its word. At the same time, if it is to be taken at its word, the great power must actually intervene when the threat is ignored. However, as we have seen, great-power involvement itself tends to escalate or intensify hostilities, to embroil the great power in an even more dangerous conflagration than had previously existed. Thus the threat may be counterproductive. The key to this seeming dilemma is that this threat is effective as a precondition of termination only as part of a configuration of other factors and only under certain other conditions. Under those conditions, as in Type T3, its effect will be inhibitive of hostilities. Under other, less auspicious conditions, the effect will be otherwise, possibly fanning the hostilities.

In Type T4 the key to the conditions under which this threat of intervention might be expected to lead to termination appears to be the relative disinterest in the conflict of the party perceiving the threat and his subsequent unwillingness to assume the extraordinary risks involved. Indeed, this party already confronts an antagonist with critical interests at stake and high popular support for its cause. In Type T5 the key to the effectiveness of this threat seems to be the flexibility enjoyed by both antagonists in the commitments to their publicly stated goals, and the moderation of both with respect to their pursuit of the stakes involved. This moderation makes the task of local accommodation and conciliation far simpler, even while it makes the prospect of a vastly expanded conflict and the loss of its local control to the great powers a most unpleasurable proposition. In Type T6 the great-power threat combines with the effect of strong, negative world opinion, as voiced in the international organization, upon the party perceiving the threat.

Thus the conditions that seem especially to sustain the efficacy of the threat of great-power intervention as an agent of termination of hostilities occur when (1) the involved interests of the party against whom intervention is directed are marginal or peripheral; (2) moderation and flexibility already prevail, especially among the party to whom the threat is directed and with respect to its commitment to its stated objectives; and (3) world opinion is clearly and vocally on the side that the great power would support. Under other conditions, such great-power intervention may be expected to have its established immoderating effects.

Also of note in Type T6 are the varying reactions, in the two conflicts from which the type derives, to censure by the international organization. In one case the conflict activity that followed censure accorded with the expressed wishes of the organization (accommodation), while in the other it was precisely the opposite (suppression). The common denominators of these actions were the swiftness of their implementation and their realization of the preconditions of termination. Indeed, inasmuch as this partisan international organization activity is part of a configuration of factors that produces termination, we find in Type T6 another exception to the usual immoderate consequence of partisan intervention. Here are the conditions of its effectiveness, if the objective of institutional intervention is termination at any cost—and possibly great human cost.

Type T7: the disintegration of the vanquished in a protracted conflict. A low level of popular support, an unfavorable military hardware balance, the prospect of no further outside support, a leader-

Table 6.11
The Conditions of Settlement (S):
A Composite Scenario
("being left alone to realize the
inevitable")

Note: This composite factor pattern derives from an examination of six instances of settlement (S). It consists exclusively of item-response combinations found to define the higher-order classifications (genus or above) isolated by agreement analysis of the settlement patterns. It is therefore what may be termed a second level of abstraction from the real conflicts from which it proceeds.

Item	Relationship Between Antagonists at Threshold of Settlement (S)	Previous Relationship (That Pertaining at Threshold of [Sub]phase Preceding S)
5-21 Likely outcome is now obvious	Yes/Yes	(No/No)
6-7 GP aid promised if esc. occurs	No/No	(No/Yes)

ship crisis in the face of an obvious outcome, factionalism among the military, and a new moderation in the political leadership yield the end of a painful struggle. Here, for the first time since our examination of the factors distinguishing mere conflict (P–II) from violent hostilities (P–III), we find high credibility of communications between the antagonists.

The composite scenario of posthostilities settlement (Table 6.11) is the briefest of the six scenarios. The two factors most critical in effecting the preconditions of settlement of local conflict are here found to be that (1) the likely outcome of the dispute, if present levels of commitment remain constant, is now apparent to both principal parties, and (2) there is now no expectation by either party that an increase in the level of conflict will bring any or further great-power support or involvement in its own behalf. In terms of our previous discussions of the effects of these two factors, I shall here let them speak for themselves.

At the same time, I would suggest that the three specific configurations of factors within which these two factors operate to yield the preconditions of settlement constitute three distinct and useful models of the settlement process (see Table 6.12):

Type S1: the "plebiscitarian" model, where settlement is achieved through the moderation of the conflict in the eyes of the antagonists, who see their continued existence as no longer at stake. Indeed, this is the first appearance of this perceptual factor since our examination of the conditions distinguishing prehostilities conflict from hostilities. The absence of any perceived threat to the continued existence of the parties to conflict is, then, critical both in averting open hostilities and, once they have occurred, in effecting a meaningful settlement. Herein lies the importance of the plebiscitarian model of effecting settlement through the

Table 6.12
Settlement (S):
The Critical Factor Patterns

Note: Asterisk (*) indicates the factors found to define the higher-order classifications (genus or above) derived by agreement analysis of the settlement (S) patterns; the number of asterisks indicates the number of higher orders achieved by that particular item-response combination.

The number sign (#) indicates the factors in the settlement patterns with which the Vietnam war (as of March 15, 1967, and in its maximal form) agreed precisely.

Item	Relationship Between Antagonists at Threshold of Settlement (S)	Previous Relationship (That Pertaining at Threshold of [Sub]phase Preceding S)
Type S1		
5-12 Interest involved-cont'd exis.	No/No	(Yes or No/Yes)
5-22 Post-dispute expect'n of regim	Pessimistic/Optimistic	(Pessimistic/Pessimistic)
8-3 Rel'snip be pol + mil leaders	Pol dominant/Pol dominant	(Co-equal/Pol dominant)
5-18 Can accept les thn stated dmds	Yes/Yes	(Yes/No)
5-15 Conduct of conflict is limited	Yes/Yes	(Yes or No/No)
8-20 Use of terror by this ant. is	Absent/Absent	(Widespread/Absent)
5-42 Martial law is in effect	NA/No	(NA/Yes)
5-16 Pc of avail mil frcs committed	0-10 Pc/0-10 Pc	(70-100 Pc/70-100 Pc)
9-8 Casualty rate for own forces	1/1	(2/1)
9-9 Casualty rate for 3Pty forces	1/1	(NA/2)
9-12 Attrition rate for 3Pty forces	1/1	(NA/2)
*6-7 GP aid promised if esc. occurs	No/No	(No/Yes)
6-29 I.O. peace machinery is seen #	Irrelevant/Irrelevant	(Relevant/Irrelevant)
6-11 Has asked an int'l. org'n. in #	No/No	(Yes/No)
4-13 Internal policies of regime	Moderate/Moderate	(Revol'ary/Trad. or Mod.)
4-20 Freedom of group opposition	NA/Full	(NA/L'td or out.pol)
4-25 Const'al status of pol parties	NA/Competitive	(NA/Part compet.)
4-28 Pc of popn voting in elections#	NA/3	(NA/NA)
4-21 Interest artic'n by anomic gps	NA/Infrequent	(NA/Frequent)
Type S2		
2-17 Pc of involved area in control #	2/1	(1/3)
5-7 Interest involved-prestige	No/No	(No/Yes)
5-18 Can accept les thn stated dmds	No/Yes	(No/No)
5-37 Esc likely to bring GP aid to adv	No/Yes	(Yes/No)
5-30 Principal attempts at resol'n	Political/Political	(Military/Military)
Type S3		
*5-21 Likely outcome is now obvious	Yes/Yes	(No/No)
5-31 Offered to resolve const'ally #	No/No	(Yes/No)
7-6 No. troops comm as Pc tot frcs	1/1	(0/3)
4-32 Recent leadership crisis	No/No	(Yes/No)
8-4 Unity within military command	Unified/Unified	(Factional/Unified)

Type S1
("plebiscitarian model: moderation prevails")

The pattern derives from

Cuba: "little" war of 1906 (U.S. peace commission leaves Cuba—10/06)

Cyprus: independence (Cypriot independence—8/60)

Type S2
("unilateral model: reality intrudes")

The pattern derives from

Ethiopian resistance (surrender of Italian forces in Ethiopia—11/41)

Indonesia: independence (formal transfer of sovereignty—12/49)

Type S3
("military model: a foregone conclusion enforced")

The pattern derives from

Spanish civil war (Franco forces occupy Spain unopposed—4/39)

USSR-Iran (Iranian parliament refuses to ratify Soviet oil agreement—10/47)

admission of the insurgents in internal conflict to meaningful, effective participation in the political system. Again, however, it is seen that this solution requires moderation and flexibility on both sides, a readiness to accept less than total victory, and an expectation that the political system accepted as the instrument of settlement will give effective expression to the legitimate grievances and demands of both sides.

Here also, in this settlement type, neither party expects great-power assistance to his cause if the level of the dispute is intensified: there is no prospect of total victory from an exogenous quarter. (It will be recalled that this same expectation, in other circumstances, constituted a precondition of escalation.) Finally, if the international organization had previously been looked to for assistance by the insurgent party, its activities are now seen to be irrelevant as the antagonists look to each other and demonstrate their own capacities for moderation, accommodation, and accord.

Type S2: the "unilateral" model, characterized by a marked shift in the control of the land area at stake, by the loser's perception that any significant intensification in the level of activities will bring (further) great-power support to its adversary and none to itself, and by the realization that its prestige is not now at stake in the conflict. The combined effect of these factors is to lead that antagonist to accept less than its previously stated demands, to yield to the overwhelming evidence of reality.

Type S3: the "military" model, where the consolidation of one party's power position after a change in its leadership, the establishment of unity in its previously factional military organization, and the withdrawal of its offer to pursue a constitutional resolution of the dispute precede the implementation of an outcome long since apparent to both principal parties.

From these various sets of preconditions, the termination of hostilities and the settlement of posthostilities disputes emerge as the culminations of complex political processes involving calculations among perceived and anticipated costs, interests, and advantages. As there is no one type of either termination or settlement in real life, there is no one set of analytic conditions under which they are effected. Rather, as in every significant stage in the conflict process, various sets of conditions yield the variously accommodated and enforced types of both termination and settlement.

Forecasting from the Factor Patterns

The preceding tables have presented the various dominant, configural sets of factors conditioning the origin, development, and termination of the eighteen instances of local conflict included in this analysis. We have briefly commented on the specific content of each set of conditions. But only the factor patterns can adequately speak for themselves as complete statements of the various analytic conditions of the several postulated stages of conflict.

If, however, these patterns are valid (if tentative) statements of the specific configurations of factors conditioning the development of each stage of conflict, their comparison to some conflict not included in their analysis should tell us something about its own likely course of development. This comparison should indicate in any conflict the dominance of the several types of each stage of conflict as well as the likely direction, in terms of the model, in which it is heading. Further, if it is known where a conflict presently stands within the model, it may be compared to the various types of preconditions of each of its possible subsequent paths. The statistical dominance of these analytic types in this conflict may then indicate its likely course both under present conditions and under other conditions that may be realized or hypothesized.

Before we proceed to an example, it may be worth recalling that the purpose of this study was experimental and that the various sets of conditions established are provisional and in need of the refinement that can come only from the addition of other real conflicts to the analysis. Within these constraints, the purpose of this example is, first, to illustrate the potential of the set of techniques developed here for establishing the dominant trends in real conflicts, for examining conditional statements concerning alternative outcomes, and for systematically simulating the conflict process itself. Only secondary is the purpose of examining the experimental results with reference to a specific, independent conflict to see if there is anything in those results that sheds light on the conflict, anything that is of specific relevance and applicability to it.

The example chosen was the Vietnam war as of March 15, 1967. This was the eve of the Guam conference, which was attended by the leaders of the Republic of South Vietnam, the United States government, and the United States and Allied military forces in South Vietnam. By this time, close to half a million American combat troops had been committed to the war, with no imminent sign of the military victory hoped for by President Johnson and envisioned by General Westmoreland, commander of the U.S. forces in Vietnam. Almost a year would pass from this date before the Tet offensive of January 1968 would demonstrate the continuing vitality and viability of the enemy forces, and the New Hampshire presidential primary would mark the beginning of the end of President Johnson's term of office.

This was to be the last conference before Ambassador Henry Cabot Lodge would be succeeded in Saigon by Ellsworth Bunker, a man of known ability as a negotiator and (at the time) of considerably less vocal and fixed personal opinions on the issues involved in the conflict. It was also the last such strategy meeting before the laying down of an air and ground bombardment that General Westmoreland is reported to have termed "the heaviest concentration of firepower in the history of warfare."[1] Its purpose, like so many other Allied operations in the war, was to interdict once and for all the continuing flow of troops and supplies to the enemy.

[1]*Boston Globe*, September 9, 1967.

These two postconference occurrences probably represent well the two dominant strains of thought and consideration at that conference: one political, one military; one conciliatory, one forceful; but both aimed equally, singly and in combination, at the objective of quickly terminating the hostilities on terms favorable to the participants in the conference. The decisions to take these actions also reflected certain assumptions on the part of the participants in the conference about the nature of conflict itself, about the manner in which this type of conflict might best be brought to a conclusion satisfactory to one's own interests, and about the very preconditions of what we have called the termination and settlement of this particular conflict.

Since the Vietnam war on March 15, 1967, was in the hostilities phase of the conflict model, four alternative paths of subsequent development were open to it: escalation, de-escalation, termination, and settlement. What, in terms of the various established types of each stage, did the Vietnam war look like at that time? To what extent did it resemble each type and so realize to that degree the particular preconditions of that stage of conflict? And what factors in any of those types did it not express, thereby lacking the specific preconditions of that developmental outcome?

The Vietnam war was coded as of March 15, 1967, in terms of the same conflict system of 300 variables within which were defined all the conflicts from which this analysis derives. The principal parties in this case were defined for coding purposes as the government of the Republic of South Vietnam and the National Liberation Front (NLF), the political extension of the Viet Cong. This represented a fundamental decision to regard and treat the conflict as an essentially internal phenomenon, a civil war. Some decision in this regard was necessitated by our assumption of the relationality of conflict and by the compound data format that follows from that assumption. As one alternative, the principal parties could have been defined as the South Vietnamese and North Vietnamese governments, and the war would thereby have been defined as interstate. The present decision, however, was prompted by the belief that the two principal antagonists in the central, core conflict taking place in Vietnam at the time were the government of South Vietnam and the National Liberation Front — with, of course, enormous and telling third-party support afforded both sides.

This belief was founded on the assumption that without outside assistance the government of South Vietnam would long since have fallen to the National Liberation Front, and the dispute would have been settled. On the other hand, the withdrawal of outside support was not seen as likely to eliminate either the National Liberation Front or the Viet Cong as effective insurgent forces. Their specific grievances, their reasons for being, their bases of indigenous support would survive in fact, if not wholly intact. While an enormously reduced level of military activity might follow such a withdrawal, no basic settlement of the dispute would be achieved except through the total extinction of the NLF forces in combat, and the South Vietnamese government had at no time demonstrated such a competence, even with the massive assistance of the United States. Therefore, the United States, North Vietnam, China, and the Soviet Union were coded as involved third parties to the conflict.

Having so coded the Vietnam war, the resulting individual factor pattern defined by the 300 item-compound response combinations was compared to each of the factor patterns deriving from the four relevant agreement analysis runs. Thus it was compared — in both its juxtapositions of principal parties — to each of the complete factor patterns, the critical factor patterns, and the composite scenarios deriving from the escalation, de-escalation, termination, and settlement runs. The results of these comparisons are presented in Figure 6.1. The percentiles indicate the extent to which the Vietnam war, as of March 15, 1967, maximally incorporated the entirety of each indicated factor pattern, there being one such figure for each juxtaposition of the principal parties. The specific factors on which Vietnam agreed with each of the complete factor patterns may be found in the relevant sections of Appendix D. In both the critical factor patterns and the composite scenario, these factors are indicated by a number sign (#) between each item and its compound response. The factors so indicated, then, are those on which the Vietnam war, as a configural pattern and in its maximal form, precisely matched the pattern in question on March 15, 1967.

Before we examine these scores in detail, it may be worthwhile to return briefly to some theoretical and methodological considerations. First, as noted, the same factor in a different context may effect a different result. If we take an individual conflict harboring the potential for four alternative courses of development and compare it to the actual preconditions of the four alternatives, we should expect it to manifest some degree of developmental potential for each alternative outcome. Thus, in comparing Vietnam to the established factor patterns, we should expect the comparison to demonstrate some degree of inclusiveness of all developmental paths potentially available to it. Second, the reader will observe that the farther to the right one proceeds among the established factor patterns in Figure 6.1, the closer one comes to the essential preconditions of that stage. This, it will be recalled, results from the manner of operation of the various analytic techniques employed: the complete factor patterns represented on the left are the unweighted statements of the several dominant states of the conflict system at each stage; the critical factor patterns effect their reduction to the various sets of specific preconditions of each stage; and the composite scenarios represented on the right are eclectic statements of the especially dominant individual factors involved in the preconditions of each stage.

Figure 6.1
Percentile Comparison of Vietnam
War (March 15, 1967) with the
Established Factor Patterns

Note: the percentiles (%) indicate the extent to which the Vietnam war, coded as of March 15, 1967, maximally incorporates the entirety of the indicated factor pattern. Each percentile was derived by dividing the number of item-response combinations with which Vietnam (in its maximal form) agreed precisely by the total number of factors in the indicated pattern. Included in this statement are all the "nonartificial" complete factor patterns derived by agreement analysis; these patterns, and the factors on which Vietnam was found to match each, are contained in Appendix D. The subtotal percentiles are summary statements of the total number of factors in all the relevant species patterns divided into the total number with which Vietnam agreed precisely (there being no factor in any higher-order pattern not contained in at least one species pattern). Similarly, the total percentiles are summary statements for all the patterns indicated.

Phase or Sub-phase	Complete Factor Patterns			Critical Factor Patterns			Composite Scenarios	
	(%)	Sub-total (%)	Total (%)		(%)	Total (%)		(%)
Escalation								
SP$_1$	0.57			Type E1	0.00		Escala-	
SP$_2$	0.35	0.44	0.49	Type E2	0.36	0.45	tion:	0.92
SP$_3$	0.55			Type E3	0.57			
SP$_4$	0.37			Type E4	0.60			
GP$_1$	0.80							
GP$_2$	0.57							
OP	1.00							
De-escalation								
SP$_1$	0.39			Type D1	0.32		De-esca-	
SP$_2$	0.42	0.44	0.45	Type D2	0.33	0.41	lation:	0.63
SP$_3$	0.56			Type De	0.56			
OP	0.78							
Termination								
SP$_1$	0.40			Type T1	0.46			
SP$_2$	0.29			Type T2	0.00			
SP$_3$	0.50			Type T3	0.28		Termina-	
SP$_4$	0.29	0.38	0.41	Type T4	0.39	0.28	tion:	0.24
SP$_5$	0.30			Type T5	0.00			
SP$_6$	0.39			Type T6	0.27			
SP$_7$	0.53			Type T7	0.15			
GP$_1$	0.71							
GP$_2$	0.61							
FP$_1$	0.63							
FP$_2$	1.00							
OP	1.00							
Settlement								
SP$_1$	0.35			Type S1	0.16		Settle-	
SP$_2$	0.41	0.39	0.40	Type S2	0.20	0.17	ment:	0.00
SP$_3$	0.46			Type S3	0.20			
FP	1.00							

SP = species pattern, corresponding to the types described earlier in this chapter; GP = genus pattern; FP = family pattern; and OP = order pattern.

An examination of the results of this comparison indicates that, in terms of the patterns established in the present study, Vietnam was clearly an escalatory type at the time of the convening of the Guam conference on March 15, 1967. Although the war also contained a great deal of the de-escalatory element, it is clear, as one moves farther away from the individual conflicts from which the analysis derives, that the dominance of the escalatory factors or components emerges even more fully. That the Vietnam war did indeed constitute such a dominant type in the early days of 1967 is perhaps best reflected in the fact that the total number of Americans killed in the conflict during that calendar year was officially reported at 9,353, more than the combined total of losses in the preceding six years.[2]

If we examine the specific escalation type (E4 in Table 6.7) with which Vietnam compared most closely at that time, it appears that the events immediately following the Guam conference increased the escalatory potential of the conflict still further. For, as increasing United States military force was applied, the likely outcome of the conflict became increasingly apparent to both sides if the level of their activities remained at their then current levels. With this added perception, the conflict compared even more markedly with this escalation type (E4) than before. It is interesting, moreover, to note that in both the conflicts from which this escalation type derives, the ensuing escalation was characterized by a drastic change in the nature of third-party involvement, one in the form of direct aid, the other in the form of direct intervention.

That continuing escalation of events in the war was not unlikely at the time is suggested in the other two escalation types characterizing the conflict. For it is clear that U.S. strategy in Vietnam at this time was to cut off the enemy's logistic supplies and supply routes through the use of massive air power, and to inflict losses upon him in ground engagements so severe as to force him to sue for peace. In Type E3, the one to which the war compared second best among the critical factor patterns, it is seen that escalation is preconditioned by the absence to one party of logistic support adequate to maintain its current level of operations. And in Type E4, escalation is effected amid considerable losses to one side despite the fact that both principals had actively sought a negotiated settlement and had even attended bilateral negotiations to that end.

It is also clear, however, that the Vietnam conflict on March 15, 1967, contained considerable elements of both de-escalation and termination, especially the former. From the de-escalation scenario (Table 6.8) it would seem clear that the key to effecting a de-escalation of the hostilities, even while the Viet Cong had ade-

[2] *New York Times*, January 3, 1968.

quate logistic supplies to maintain their operations, was to stem the flow of third-party troops to their aid. This prospect corresponds with our earlier argument about the basic nature of this conflict and the likely effect upon NLF activity of the withdrawal of its outside support. Moreover, in the D3 de-escalation with which Vietnam compared most favorably, two things stand out. First, it appears that the circumstances that, in combination with cutting off the logistic supplies of the Viet Cong, would have effected an imminent de-escalation were (1) that they cease to be provided with conventional troop support by a third party, and (2) that a more equal balance be achieved in the land area controlled than the approximate 3:2 ratio then existing. This is to suggest that if the United States and South Vietnamese forces were to gain control of approximately half the land area of South Vietnam, and if the flow of third-party conventional forces to the aid of the Viet Cong were terminated by some military or political means, the Viet Cong would soon be unable to maintain its own level of operations and would be forced to reduce that level significantly.

Second, it appears from this pattern (D3) that if the National Liberation Front could have successfully taken its case to the United Nations on a complaint of aggression the pressure of world opinion would have worked toward both de-escalation of U.S.–South Vietnamese activities and a considerable slackening of the military pressure then being exerted on their adversary.

If we turn to the termination patterns and the manner in which Vietnam compares to them, several points of interest emerge about the likely conditions of termination of the war. In the composite scenario (Table 6.9) we again find that cutting off the logistic supplies of one side is a critical condition of termination. In a guerrilla war, however, that means eliminating both the geographic base area of the insurgents and their popular base among the people. Thus we have the second set of critical conditions of termination in the scenario: complete military control of the area and population in question by one party. Such a condition was, in Vietnam in 1967, an impossibility. Lacking this condition, then, we turn to the final set of critical conditions of termination, the active quest by both antagonists for a negotiated settlement.

Although we have seen in the escalation types that accommodative activity carries with it no guarantees, the implication of the negotiation factor in the termination scenario would seem to be clear: to establish the most auspicious circumstances for termination of the hostilities in Vietnam, the South Vietnamese government had itself to declare, or to be made to declare, its willingness to seek and accept a negotiated settlement of the dispute with the National Liberation Front. The NLF might, accordingly, have been recognized as a viable actor and legitimate political entity, and so encouraged on its own to pursue some settlement involving less than total victory. Indeed, inasmuch as the Vietnam war retained strong escalatory elements even after the decisions of March 1967, the urgency of making such a declaration was all the greater if the ensuing campaign of intense military pressure on the National Liberation Front was to achieve its intended moderating effect. Instead, the result was the desperate Tet offensive and its awful evidence of the durability of the NLF forces.

In the termination type (T1 in Table 6.10) most closely resembled by the Vietnam war, it may be seen that considerable steps were taken subsequent to March 1967 to effect this set of preconditions of termination. Especially notable in this regard were the effects of the South Vietnamese Constituent Assembly and presidential elections of September 1967. Also curiously present in this termination pattern is the factor of moderation, rather than a doctrinaire position, in the international affairs of the government party. Given the peculiar international character of the Vietnam war, this would seem to indicate that the cause of termination would have been well served if the government of South Vietnam had effected (or had been made to effect) a moderate, or even neutralist, position in international affairs rather than a rabidly anticommunist one.

If we turn, finally, to the conditions of settlement, we can observe with respect to the composite scenario (Table 6.11) that, while the likely outcome of the conflict under existing commitments was in fact becoming increasingly apparent to both principal parties, at the time both also had considerable commitments of further assistance from the great powers. In terms of these critical conditions, then, the prospects for immediate settlement were dim. In terms of the particular settlement type (S2) that appears to have been most attainable, however, it may be seen that considerations of prestige by both sides constituted an essential impediment to some form of settlement in Vietnam. It appears that if the government of South Vietnam could have been persuaded to accept less than its stated total demands, and if some form of accommodation could have been devised that involved only modest loss of prestige to either party, the essential conditions of settlement might have been achieved. The best such accommodation, it would seem, might have been realized by holding genuinely free elections under international guarantees for a neutral coalition government in South Vietnam.

If we now leave aside altogether the question of whether the United States ever had any interest in South Vietnam that justified the level of its involvement there, we may say the following on the basis of the comparison of the Vietnam war to the dominant factor patterns established in this experimental analysis. First, it would appear that the essential decision reached at the Guam conference was to impose inexorable and increasing amounts of military pressure on the enemy's forces, under the assumption that in the face of unbearable losses and exhausted resources he would sue for peace. Second, if the overriding objective of the United States was thus to force an early termination of the hostilities, then it followed what would appear to be an appropriate course in attempting at once to stem the flow of troops and logistic support from the North and to extend Saigon's influence into new areas of South Vietnam (rather than to retreat to an "enclave" policy), thereby eliminating Viet Cong base areas and logistic sources.

It is also clear, however, that to be effective these policies should have been accompanied by less intransigence and greater policy flexibility on the part of the South Vietnamese government. Specifically, these military measures had to be accompanied by some declaration of that government's willingness to negotiate with the National Liberation Front a mutually acceptable compromise solution. Without the possibility of political accommodation, increased military pressure at this point promised almost surely to yield not its intent but the opposite: a further protraction of the conflict at an even more desperate and destructive level. The result was the devastating Tet offensive and its demonstration that neither side could "win" this heinous war within the terms of current capabilities and commitments.

While the preceding discussion is but a single example of the results proceeding from a comparison of real conflicts with the analytic types and factor patterns deriving from this experimental analysis, it is hoped that it does serve at least to illustrate the potential of the techniques developed in this study for two distinct but related areas. As we have argued, the addition of increasing numbers of cases to this analysis will increasingly refine the reliability and the sensitivity of the established factor patterns and the types they define. Comparisons of past or present, real or hypothetical conflicts may then be made with these patterns and types to determine, on the basis of their dominant configural characteristics, where these conflicts are tending and what may be done to achieve or induce alternative, preferred outcomes. For example, an ongoing conflict might be watched for evidence of the development of the preconditions of hostilities. Moreover, knowledge of the means by which settlement was effected in the various types of conflict characterized by this particular case would give an indication of the kinds of policy activity necessary to effect its settlement. And similarly with respect to cases in both the dispute and the hostilities phases.

For each stage in the conflict process contains within itself the potential for several alternative outcomes or paths of development. Having established the several dominant empirical types of each of these stages, as well as the configurations of factors that define their preconditions, we should now be in a position to ascertain the dominant developmental strains residing in any new or developing conflict and the specific factors that are likely to affect its various possible outcomes. Here, then, is the potential of this set of techniques as an early warning system of conflict.

Finally, it is apparent that this particular set of techniques provides a seemingly ideal basis for an experimental computer simulation of the conflict process. Indeed, the purpose of establishing such a simulation is to ask and examine the "what if" questions in a realm of variable outcomes. The techniques developed in this study operate specifically to establish the various dominant sets of nonunique conditions under which the several significant stages of conflict occur. The addition of further cases to the analysis and the subsequent refinement of those preconditions will enable the analyst to examine experimentally the several questions, under what conditions do what actions and events have what effects on conflicts at various stages of development? Such experimentation might then be carried out on past and present, real and hypothetical conflicts to examine the likely effects of various policy alternatives in specific instances, to determine what might or could be done to effect a desired outcome, and to illumine the likely effects of some specific turn of events. For answers to these and other such questions, the set of assumptions, concepts, and techniques established in this study seems to be especially well suited.

Afterword

To attempt a brief summary of the substantive results of this study would be a violation of our basic understanding both of the complex nature of events in general and of the conditions of conflict in particular. Suffice it to say that conflict has been found here to be a systematic phenomenon, and that the objectives established for this study in Chapter 1 proved to be attainable. These, it will be recalled, were (1) to explore and, if possible, establish the various configurations of factors that condition the origin, development, and termination of local conflict; (2) to determine the various empirical types of local conflict that occur at each significant stage of its development; and, hopefully, (3) to establish on the basis of these factors and types the foundations for an early warning system of conflict and a suggestive policy generator for its more effective control as an instrument of politics and human interaction.

To these ends, a set of concepts, assumptions, and techniques was developed and applied experimentally to eighteen conflicts. A static model of the conflict process was formulated, and its dynamics were established by the interaction of a set of original data manipulation techniques and a compound data base following from our assumptions about the nature of conflict itself. As we have seen, each case of conflict that is added to the present analysis may be expected to bring further precision and sensitivity to the dynamic rules governing movement from one stage of the conflict model to another.

On the basis of the experimental results of this study, the codebook defining the conflict system within which all conflicts are postulated to occur has been revised.[1] For, as understanding grew of the concepts and techniques developed in the analysis and of the conflict process itself, it became apparent that a number of the 300 items in Appendix B failed to discriminate satisfactorily between individual conflicts or conflict stages and did not contribute significant information. The reader will recognize those items as the ones regularly filtered out of the analysis by the weighting device described in Chapter 5. At the same time, more efficacious wordings of particular items emerged, and a number of new items suggested themselves for inclusion in the codebook. The result of all these considerations is a revised and refined codebook that reflects current understanding of these concepts and techniques, as well as the insights they have provided into the conflict process.

It should be further noted that the set of analytic techniques and the empirical data generated in the present study do not interact only in the fashions examined here. Further agreement analysis runs might profitably be made to determine the various sets of

[1] The revised codebook is included in the technical manual accompanying this volume.

conditions under which occur such things as successful and unsuccessful negotiations to avert or terminate hostilities, the collaboration of great powers to effect rigid control of a local conflict, the direct involvement in and disengagement from local conflict of great powers, accommodated versus enforced settlements, successful international organization activity of various sorts, and so on to the limits of the imagination and interest.

Moreover, to establish the various sets of conditions of each significant stage of conflict in the present study, only the entire set of 300 variables was employed to define each individual conflict at the threshold of each stage through which it passed. Thus each conflict submitted to each agreement analysis run consisted of a 300-item factor pattern comprising its unique definition of the conflict system at that point. It may be expected, however, that considerably different results will be forthcoming from analyses of specific subsets of the data. For example, it would seem most worthwhile to isolate the military hardware data and determine the various hardware configurations that apply at each significant stage of conflict. The classifications, types, and factor patterns effected by agreement analysis on such subsets would differ from those yielded by the entire data base and would thus provide more specific and precise insight into the operation of the hardware subsystem of the conflict system at each conflict stage.

These, then, would seem to be just a few of the many potential uses of these techniques, the present study being but the one to demonstrate their validity. It is my very fond wish that what is accomplished here may be the basis for further explorations by others with similar insterest in applying reason and rigor to the most portentous and intractable problems of these complex and frustrating but not unpromising and hardly hopeless times.

Appendixes

Analytic Contents of Appendixes

Appendix A:
The Course of the Conflicts

This appendix presents the characteristic definition of each conflict included in this analysis in terms of its own idiosyncratic path through the conflict model, together with the event and date marking the start of each phase and subphase involved (see Chapter 2). Since this study did not undertake to examine the various preconditions of dispute (P–I) and since it is often difficult, at best, to determine the precise moment of onset of the specific dispute leading to conflict, the date and event marking P–I are generally omitted. The exceptions are significant only in the ready availability and general credibility of the event marking the onset of the specific dispute at hand. In two conflicts (Ethiopia-Somalia and Israel-Egypt), the first phase listed is P–IV because only a partial cross section of each of these long-standing conflicts was coded for the present analysis.

Each of the eighteen conflicts was coded for each of its principal parties in terms of the situation, events, and conditions pertaining up to but not including the event marking the start of the second indicated phase and of each succeeding phase and subphase through which it passed (see Chapter 3).

1. Algeria-Morocco conflict, 1962–1963	P–I	. . .	. . .
	P–II	Algerian independence referendum	7/62
	P–III	Algerian attack on Tindouf	10/63
	E	Algeria accepts aid from UAR, USSR, Cuba	10/63
	P–IV	Bamoko agreement	11/63
2. Angolan insurgency, 1961 (Portuguese colonial administration versus African insurgents)	P–I	. . .	. . .
	P–II	Leopoldville riots in Congo; Portugal strengthens Angolan garrison	1/59
	P–III	African insurgents riot in Luanda	2/61
	P–IV	Portuguese suppress organized hostilities	9/61
3. Cuba: "little" war of August 1906 (Cuban government versus Liberal party insurgents)	P–I	Balanced cabinet dismissed by President Palma	5/05
	P–II	Liberal party withdraws from national elections	12/05
	P–III	First fire fight between insurgent and government forces	8/06
	P–IV	Government declares unilateral cease-fire	9/06
	S	U.S. peace commission leaves Cuba	10/06
4. Cuba: Bay of Pigs, 1961 (Cuban government versus Cuban exiles)	P–I	Castro prime minister of new provisional government	1/59
	P–II	U.S. president authorizes an exile organization	3/60
	P–III	Bay of Pigs invasion by Cuban exiles	4/61
	P–IV	Defeat of invading exiles by government forces	4/61
5. Cyprus: war of independence, 1952–1960 (U.K. colonial administration versus Enosists)	P–I	. . .	. . .
	P–II	Enosists establish a military planning committee	7/52
	P–III	Insurrection becomes widespread	4/55
	E	Colonial government declares state of emergency	11/55
	D	Makarios accepts no "enosis"	9/58
	P–IV	London Agreement on Cypriot independence	2/59
	S	Cypriot independence	8/60

6. Cyprus: internal conflict, 1959–1964 (Cypriot government versus Turkish Cypriots)	P–I	. . .	. . .
	P–II	London Agreement on Cypriot independence	2/59
	P–III	Fighting between Greek and Turkish Cypriots	12/63
	E	First intervention threat by Turkey	1/64
	D	Agreement on U.N. peacekeeping force	3/64
7. Ethiopian resistance, 1937–1941 (Italian colonial administration versus Ethiopian insurgents)	P–IV	Italians enter Addis Ababa, formally annex Ethiopia	5/36
	P–III	Attempted assassination of Italian viceroy	2/37
	D	New viceroy initiates conciliation policy	1/38
	E	Britain declares war on Italy; supports insurgents	6/40
	S	Surrender of Italian forces in Ethiopia	11/41
8. Ethiopia-Somalia conflict, 1960–1964	P–I	. . .	. . .
	P–II	Somali independence	7/60
	P–III	Ethiopia violates Somali borders	2/64
	P–IV	Cease-fire agreement	4/64
9. Greek insurgency, 1944–1949 (Greek government versus Greek insurgents)	P–I	. . .	. . .
	P–II	Formation of rival government in Greece	3/44
	P–III	Hostilities against returning Greek and British forces	12/44
	P–IV	Varkiza agreement	2/45
	P–III	Widespread guerrilla warfare resumed	1/46
	E	Guerrillas go conventional; Tito closes border	7/49
	P–IV	Greek army victory	12/49
10. India-China conflict, 1962	P–I	. . .	. . .
	P–II	Chinese violate Indian border	6/54
	P–III	Chinese attack Indian outposts	9/62
	P–IV	Chinese unilateral cease-fire	11/62
11. Indonesia: war of independence, 1945–1949 (Dutch colonial administration versus Indonesian insurgents)	P–I	. . .	. . .
	P–II	Both sides demonstrate a will to use force	8/45
	P–III	Armed youth attack Dutch patrols	10/45
	D(1)	End of large-scale fighting	12/45
	(2)	Unsuccessful negotiations opened	4/46
	P–IV	Cease-fire and Linggadjati agreements	10/46
	P–III	First Dutch attack	7/47
	D	Entry of United Nations into conflict	7/47
	P–IV	*Renville* agreement	1/48
	P–III	Second large-scale Dutch attack	12/48
	P–IV	Cease-fire and Roem–Von Royen agreement	10/49
	S	Formal transfer of sovereignty	12/49
12. Indonesia-Malaysia conflict, 1963–1965	P–I	. . .	. . .
	P–II	Brunei revolt; Indonesia arms "volunteers"	2/63
	P–III	Indonesian attack in Sarawak	4/63
	E	Indonesian landings in Malaya	8/64
	D	Indonesian landings in Malaya cease	5/65
	P–IV	Hostilities end after Indonesian coup	12/65
13. Israel-Egypt conflict, 1956	P–IV	Egyptian-Israeli armistice agreement	2/49
	P–II	Czech-Egyptian arms agreement	9/55
	P–III	Israeli attack in Sinai	10/56

	E(1)	British bomb Egyptian airfields	11/56
	(2)	Canal Zone invaded by British, French	11/56
	P–IV	U.N. cease-fire accepted	11/56
14. Kashmir conflict, 1947–1965 (India versus Pakistan)	P–I	British announcement of plan for partition of India	6/47
	P–II	Raiding tribesmen enter Kashmir from Pakistan	10/47
	P–III	India airlifts troops into Kashmir	10/47
	E	Pakistan commits regular troops	5/48
	P–IV	U.N. cease-fire accepted	1/49
	P–III	Pakistanis infiltrate Kashmir border	8/65
	E	Indian offensive into West Punjab	9/65
	P–IV	Proposed U.N. cease-fire accepted	9/65
15. Malayan insurgency, 1948–1960 (U.K.-Malay colonial administration and Malayan government versus Malayan Communist party)	P–I	Far East Communist International gains control of Malay Communist party	1930
	P–II	Calcutta conference—Fourth Plenum	2/48
	P–III	State of emergency declared by U.K.-Malay administration	6/48
	D	MCP shifts emphasis to political agitation	10/51
	E	Resumption of widespread terror campaign	10/52
	P–IV	State of emergency declared terminated	7/60
16. Spanish civil war, 1936–1939 (Republican government versus Nationalist insurgents)	P–I	Popular Front government elected	2/36
	P–II	Nationalist terror and political assassination	2/36
	P–III	Military rising in Morocco by senior officers	7/36
	E(1)	Soviet direct (covert) intervention	10/36
	(2)	Italian ground troops intervene	1/37
	D	Withdrawal of the International Brigade	10/38
	P–IV	Organized resistance ends after Casado coup in Madrid	3/39
	S	Franco forces occupy Spain unopposed	4/39
17. USSR-Iran conflict, 1941–1947	P–I	. . .	. . .
	P–II	USSR and Britain occupy Iran	8/41
	P–III	Soviet-aided rebels rise in Azerbaidzhan	11/45
	P–IV	Rebels proclaim Azerbaidzhan an autonomous republic	12/45
	P–III	Iranian military forces enter Azerbaidzhan	12/46
	P–IV	Iranian forces gain control of all Iran	12/46
	S	Iranian parliament refuses to ratify Soviet oil agreement	10/47
18. Venezuelan insurgency, 1959–1963 (Venezuelan government versus MIR/CPV and FLN/FALN)	P–I	. . .	. . .
	P–II	MIR/CPV formed	4/60
	P–III	Attempted "leftist" rebellion	6/61
	E(1)	Two major military uprisings by insurgents	6/62
	(2)	Government changes from police to military response	10/63
	P–IV	Insurgency slackens after successful elections	12/63

Appendix B:
The Conflict Codebook

Several noteworthy assumptions were made in structuring this test instrument or codebook for the collection of systematic data on conflict between parties capable of waging war upon one another.

First, it was assumed that any conflict may be defined in terms that permit the identification, at any given moment in its life cycle, of two principal antagonists or adversaries. All other participants—direct or indirect, partial or neutral—may then be regarded and defined as third parties to the dispute, regardless of their effect upon its eventual development or outcome. An antagonist was further assumed to comprise both the ruling regime (that is, government or effective elite) of each principal party plus whatever general population was in its political jurisdiction or effective control. In this regard a revolution, a rebellion, or an uprising against a colonial government represents a special or exceptional case. It was assumed in this instance that the colonial administration and the rebel or revolutionary organization could best be defined as the principal parties to the dispute, and the metropolitan country as an involved third party with which the colonial administration had formal security and economic alliances.

Second, it was assumed that conflict is essentially a relational phenomenon that may best be analyzed in terms of the relationship between the parties involved (along the dimensions measured by this instrument) rather than in terms of the absolute capabilities or isolated characteristics of each. Thus each item in the codebook was answered (or coded) for each of the two principal parties to each conflict examined. Moreover, in accordance with the requirements of the conflict model presented in Chapter 2, each item was coded for each principal party in terms of the situation, events, and conditions pertaining at each threshold of the conflict model through which the conflict passed. In this manner the data base for the present study was established.

Third, the agreement analysis technique of data manipulation and analysis employed in this study does not permit multiple responses to test items. Only one response alternative may therefore be applied to each item for each principal party to each dispute at each threshold. Similarly, agreement analysis at present has no generality beyond ordinal data; that is, its applicability is limited to qualitative data or quantitative data that have been assigned to ordered scalar intervals (see Chapter 4). Of the 300 items comprising this instrument, 210 were scaled (that is, their response alternatives were fixed) before the coding of the eighteen conflicts. The remaining 90 were scaled only subsequently, by means of either a simple quartile device (items 1–6, 1–9, and 1–10) or an original logarithmic scaling technique (see Chapter 3). Whenever either of these scaling techniques was employed, the item was designated OPEN to indicate that its possible response alternatives were not fixed prior to coding. The scale (that is, the scalar intervals) resulting from the application of that technique to the total data base generated for that item in this study is presented immediately below the item.

NA and DK were used throughout to indicate, respectively, ''Not applicable'' and ''Don't know,'' the latter subsuming instances in which the required data were known either not to exist or to be not readily available for any number of reasons.

Finally, the codebook was divided into nine substantive sections to facilitate its comprehension by the reader and its application by the user. The individual items follow in a sequence that promised in the early, trial applications of the codebook to ease the burden of the coder and to maximize the reliability of his effort. The careful reader will note that items 2–11, 3–24, and 5–40 are missing from the codebook. This is not a printer's omission. The codebook originally contained 303 items, and those three were subsequently dropped from the analysis because of their intercoder unreliability. By that time, however, the computer programs had been written, and renumbering the remaining 300 items could be done only at considerable cost. That cost was forgone.

The codebook proper is followed by an index that allows the reader rapidly to assess the scope and depth of this test instrument and to locate within it any specific item or subject matter of interest.

A list of the principal references and sources used in applying the codebook to the eighteen conflicts is given in Part 2 of the Selected Bibliography.

The Test Instrument

1.
Some characteristics of the Dispute

Note: This section contains only items characterizing the dispute itself, or the relations between the antagonists involved, rather than the antagonists.

1–1   Geographic locus of the dispute:
1. North America
2. Central or South America
3. Europe
4. Middle East or North Africa
5. Africa south of Sahara
6. Asia

1–2a   Predominant topographic environment of the conflict area:
1. Flat
2. Mountainous

    3. Mixed flat and mountainous

1–2b Predominant climatological environment of the conflict area:
    1. Dry (less than 15 inches of rain per year)
    2. Moderate (15–50 inches of rain per year)
    3. Wet (more than 50 inches of rain per year)

1–3 Characterize the nature of the prevailing political relationship between the antagonists within the past 20 years (previous to P–II):
    1. Cooperative
    2. Competitive
    3. Exploitive (e.g., colonial)

1–4 Characterize the nature of the prevailing military relationship between the antagonists within the past 20 years (previous to P–II):
    1. Peaceful
    2. Sporadic, random hostilities
    3. Prolonged, organized hostilities

1–5 Classify the predominant nature of this dispute for these antagonists:
    1. Colonial
    2. Interstate
    3. Internal
    4. Both interstate and internal

1–6 How long, in months, has this specific dispute (or this particular recurrence of this dispute) persisted since it went to Phase II? (OPEN)
    1.   0.1– 13.0
    2. 13.1– 29.0
    3. 32.0– 52.0
    4. 57.0–215.0
    8. 0 or NA
    9. DK

1–7 Do ideological differences exist between the antagonists (i.e., differences between their policy-relevant views of the world and of the desirable) at this point in the dispute?
    1. Extreme differences
    2. Mild differences
    3. None

1–8 Does the dispute at this point involve any specifiable piece of real estate (or the control of a piece of real estate)?
    1. Yes
    2. No

1–9 Size of the area involved (or at stake) in the dispute at this point, in thousands of square miles (indicate NA if no real estate involved): (OPEN)

1.   3.5– 50.0
2.   51.0– 77.0
3.   84.0–197.0
4. 340.0–480.0
8. 0 or NA
9. DK

1–10   Size of population in the area involved (or at stake) in the dispute at this point, in thousands (indicate NA if no real estate involved): (OPEN)

1.   10.0–   665.0
2.   1,000.0– 4,000.0
3.   5,000.0– 7,600.0
4. 10,000.0–76,000.0
8. 0 or NA
9. DK

1–11   Has this dispute ever been brought before any agency of a regional or supranational security organization (e.g., NATO, OAS, OAU)?

1. Yes
2. No

1–12   Has this dispute ever been brought before any agency of an international organization (League of Nations or United Nations)?

1. Yes
2. No

1–13   Who introduced this dispute to the international organization for its consideration?

1. One of the antagonists in the conflict
2. A neutral nation
3. A great power
4. Other party
8. NA (not before an international organization)

1–14   On the basis of what principal complaint was this dispute brought before the international organization?

1. Complaint of agression, intervention, occupation, or threats thereof
2. Demand for self-determination
3. Claim to territory or status
4. Denial of human rights
5. Claim of violation of other rights under international law or treaty
8. NA (not before an international organization)

2. Demographic Characteristics of the Antagonist

2–1   Characterize the single overriding ideal in the political culture of the present regime:

1. Nonresistance, or self-renunciation
2. Rationality, or instrumental self-seeking within constitutional limits
3. Aggressiveness, or struggle and competition without limitation of means

    4. Efficient administration, or the philosophy of "the bee is nothing, the hive is all"

2–2   Characterize the single preferred mode of conflict resolution in the political culture of the present regime:
1. Renunciatory (yield to opposition)
2. Conciliatory (compromise with opposition)
3. Dictatorial (dominate opposition)
4. Adjudicatory (submit controversy to group decision)

2–3   Major racial grouping to which this antagonist is generally considered to belong:
1. White
2. Brown
3. Black
4. Yellow
5. Mixed

2–4   Does the present regime belong to the same racial grouping as its general population?
1. Yes
2. No
8. NA (no general population)

2–5   Racial homogeneity (Caucasoid, Mongoloid, Negroid) of the general population:
1. Homogeneous (80%, or more, of one race)
2. Heterogeneous (less than 80% of one race)
8. NA (no general population)

2–6   Linguistic homogeneity of the general population:
1. Homogeneous (majority of 85% or more; no single significant minority)
2. Mildly heterogeneous (majority of 85% or more; significant minority of 15% or less)
3. Strongly heterogeneous (no group 85% or more)
8. NA (no general population)

2–7   Religious homogeneity of the general population:
1. Strongly homogeneous (90% or more of population of one religion)
2. Mildly homogeneous (70–90% of population of one religion)
3. Mildly heterogeneous (50–70% of population of one religion)
4. Heterogeneous (no single religious group with 50% of the population)
8. NA (no general population)

2–8   Dominant religious group: indicate the religion or religious tradition with greater following among the general population than any other:
1. Judeo-Christian
2. Hindu-Buddhist
3. Muslim

4. Confucian-Taoist
5. Other
8. NA (no general population)

2–9   Percentage of the general population able to read (i.e., literate) in at least one language:
1. High (80% or more)
2. Medium (40–79%)
3. Low (below 40%)
8. NA (no general population)

2–10   Daily newspaper circulation per 1,000 general population:
1. High (300 and over)
2. Medium (100–299)
3. Low (10–99)
4. Very low (below 10)
8. NA (no general population)

2–12   Size of area in the political jurisdiction or actual control of this regime, in thousands of square miles: (OPEN)
1.   1.0–   2.1
2.   2.7–   9.6
3.   13.7–500.0
8. 0 or NA
9. DK

2–13   Total population in the political jurisdiction or actual control of this regime, in thousands: (OPEN)
1.   1.0–   2.0
2.   3.2–   52.2
3.   499.0–65,000.0
8. 0 or NA
9. DK

2–14   If a piece of real estate is involved in this dispute, is it
1. Within the territorial boundaries claimed by this antagonist as its own?
2. Outside the territorial boundaries claimed by this antagonist as its own?
3. Both within and without the boundaries claimed by this antagonist as its own?
8. NA (no real estate involved)

2–15   If a piece of real estate is involved in this dispute, what percentage of this regime's total claimed land area does it represent? (Indicate NA if no real estate involved.) (OPEN)
1.   1.0–   1.0
2.   1.6–   6.7
3.   13.3–100.0
8. 0 or NA
9. DK

2–16 If a piece of real estate is involved in this dispute, what percentage of this regime's total claimed population does it represent? (Indicate NA if no real estate involved.) (OPEN)
1. 1.0– 1.0
2. 2.0– 13.0
3. 50.0–100.0
8. 0 or NA
9. DK

2–17 If a piece of real estate is involved in this dispute, what percentage of that specific area is actually controlled by this regime? (Indicate NA if no real estate involved.) (OPEN)
1. 1.0– 1.5
2. 1.9– 9.0
3. 24.0–100.0
8. 0 or NA
9. DK

2–18 If a piece of real estate is involved in this dispute, what percentage of the population in that specific area is actually controlled by this regime? (Indicate NA if no real estate involved.) (OPEN)
1. 1.0– 1.0
2. 1.6– 6.0
3. 9.0–100.0
8. 0 or NA
9. DK

2–19 Urbanization — percentage of the general population living in cities of more than 20,000 inhabitants:
1. High (more than 35%)
2. Medium (between 12 and 35%)
3. Low (less than 12%)
8. NA (no general population)

**3.
Economic and
Transportation Resources of
the Antagonist**

Note: In this section, GNP is used to indicate either gross national product or gross economic product, whichever is applicable; it refers to the annual economic product or resources available to the antagonist.

3–1 Economic development status of this antagonist:
1. Developed (self-sustaining; GNP per capita of $600)
2. Intermediate (near self-sustaining)
3. Underdeveloped (sustained growth in 10 years)
4. Very underdeveloped (no such prospect)
8. NA (no "economy" as such)

3–2 Gross national (or economic) product in U.S.$ millions per year (indicate NA if this regime commands no formal "economy" as such): (OPEN)
1. 1.0– 1.5
2. 2.2– 24.0

    3. 90.0–6,400.0
    8. 0 or NA
    9. DK

3–3   Growth rate of GNP – annual (indicate NA if no "economy" as such): (OPEN)
    1. 1.0– 1.0
    2. 1.3– 2.2
    3. 3.0–13.9
    8. 0 or NA
    9. DK

3–4   Rate of inflation in the economy over the preceding year (indicate NA if no "economy" as such): (OPEN)
    1. 0.2– 1.0
    2. 2.0– 10.0
    3. 20.0–1,300.0
    8. 0 or NA
    9. DK

3–5   Per capita GNP in U.S.$ per year (indicate NA if no "economy" as such): (OPEN)
    1. 1.0– 2.1
    2. 5.1– 60.0
    3. 115.0–855.0
    8. 0 or NA
    9. DK

3–6   Percentage of GNP originating in agriculture (indicate NA if no "economy" as such): (OPEN)
    1. 1.0– 2.0
    2. 2.7– 7.0
    3. 25.0–75.0
    8. 0 or NA
    9. DK

3–7   Percentage of GNP originating in durable goods and chemical industries (indicate NA if no "economy" as such): (OPEN)
    1. 1.0– 1.2
    2. 1.7– 4.0
    3. 11.0–45.0
    8. 0 or NA
    9. DK

3–8   Total production of steel in thousands of tons per year (indicate NA if no "economy" as such): (OPEN)
    1. 1.0– 1.0
    2. 4.0– 30.0
    3. 105.0–20,000.0
    8. 0 or NA
    9. DK

3–9   Percentage of this antagonist's GNP represented by its export
         trade (indicate NA if no "economy" as such): (OPEN)
         1. 1.0–   1.2
         2. 1.5–   4.2
         3. 22.0–1,000.0
         8. 0 or NA
         9. DK

3–10   Total foreign aid received (both military and economic, in U.S.$
         millions per year): (OPEN)
         1. 1.0–   1.0
         2. 1.3–   2.5
         3. 5.0–450.0
         8. 0 or NA
         9. DK

3–11   Total foreign economic aid received (in U.S.$ millions per year):
         (OPEN)
         1.   1.0–   1.0
         2.   1.8–   6.0
         3. 15.0–478.0
         8. 0 or NA
         9. DK

3–12   Foreign aid received as percentage of GNP plus foreign aid re-
         ceived (indicate NA if no "economy" as such): (OPEN)
         1. 0.01– 1.0
         2. 1.2 – 3.1
         3. 5.0 –30.0
         8. 0 or NA
         9. DK

3–13   Does this regime have what is generally considered a "progres-
         sive" tax structure?
         1. Yes
         2. No
         8. NA (no "tax structure" as such)

3–14   Revenue of regime as percentage of GNP (indicate NA if no
         "economy" as such): (OPEN)
         1. 1.0– 1.5
         2. 1.8– 6.0
         3. 10.0–50.0
         8. 0 or NA
         9. DK

3–15   Expenditures of regime as percentage of GNP (indicate NA if no
         "economy" as such): (OPEN)
         1. 1.1– 1.5
         2. 1.9– 2.3
         3. 6.0–50.0

8. 0 or NA
9. DK

3–16   Expenditures for social welfare services by this regime as a percentage of GNP (including health, education, public housing, and welfare benefits) (indicate NA if no "economy" as such): (OPEN)
1. 1.0– 1.3
2. 1.7– 5.0
3. 9.0–25.0
8. 0 or NA
9. DK

3–17   Total military defense budget in U.S.$ millions per year (indicate NA if no "economy" as such): (OPEN)
1.   1.0–   1.0
2.   1.4–   25.0
3. 136.0–4,500.0
8. 0 or NA
9. DK

3–18   Total military defense budget as percentage of GNP (indicate NA if no "economy" as such): (OPEN)
1.   0.3–   2.7
2.   5.0– 22.0
3. 37.0–200.0
8. 0 or NA
9. DK

3–19   Total military defense budget as percentage of GNP plus foreign aid received (indicate NA if no "economy" as such): (OPEN)
1.   0.3–   1.7
2.   2.3–   5.0
3. 13.0–200.0
8. 0 or NA
9. DK

3–20   Agricultural employment as percentage of the general population age 15–64 (indicate NA if no general population): (OPEN)
1.   1.0– 1.2
2.   1.6– 3.0
3. 13.0–70.0
8. 0 or NA
9. DK

3–21   Employment in industry as percentage of the general population age 15–64 (indicate NA if no general population): (OPEN)
1.   1.0– 1.1
2.   1.5– 5.0
3. 11.0–23.0

8. 0 or NA

9. DK

3–22   Unemployment as percentage of the general population age
15–64 (indicate NA if no general population): (OPEN)
1. 0.5– 1.0
2. 1.3– 2.0
3. 3.0–10.0
8. 0 or NA
9. DK

3–23   Unemployment or malemployment of local "intellectuals" in this
antagonist's general population — might this presently be considered a
1. Marked problem
2. Mild problem
3. Negligible problem
8. NA (no general population)

3–25   Number of miles of paved highway (in thousands) controlled by
or at the disposal of this regime in the conflict area(s) (indicate
NA if no real estate involved): (OPEN)
1.   0.05– 1.3
2.   1.8 – 20.0
3. 42.0 –500.0
8. 0 or NA
9. DK

3–26   Number of miles of railroad (in thousands) controlled by or at the
disposal of this regime in the conflict area(s) (indicate NA if no
real estate involved): (OPEN)
1.   0.02– 1.2
2.   1.5 – 11.3
3. 100.0 –1,000.0
8. 0 or NA
9. DK

3–27   Number of airports capable of handling heavy piston aircraft
(DC-3 or larger), which are controlled by or at the disposal of this
regime in the conflict area(s): (OPEN)
1.   1.0– 1.0
2.   1.5– 15.0
3. 26.0–181.0
8. 0 or NA
9. DK

3–28   Number of airports capable of handling jet transports, which are
controlled by or at the disposal of this regime in the conflict
area(s): (OPEN)
1. 1.0–1.0
2. 1.5–2.0
3. 3.0–4.0

8. 0 or NA
9. DK

3–29 Number of seaports (or comparable facilities) capable of handling ocean-going transport vessels, which are controlled by or at the disposal of this regime in the conflict area(s): (OPEN)
1. 1.0– 1.2
2. 1.6– 3.3
3. 6.0–45.0
8. 0 or NA
9. DK

4.
Political System and
Governmental Structure
of the Antagonist

4–1 Characterize the present regime:
1. Independent national government
2. Colonial administration
3. Internationally appointed trusteeship or interim government
4. Rebel or insurgent organization

4–2 Date of independence of this antagonist as a nation:
1. Before 1800
2. 1800–1913
3. 1914–1945
4. After 1945
8. NA (not an independent nation)

4–3 Modern colonial ruler (present or most recent) of this antagonist:
1. Britain
2. France
3. Spain, Portugal, or Italy
4. Netherlands or Belgium
5. None in modern times

4–4 Executive stability, i.e., number of chief executives or heads of government in previous ten years (indicate NA if rebel organization): (OPEN)
1. 1.0–1.0
2. 1.5–2.0
3. 3.0–9.0
8. 0 or NA
9. DK

4–5 Characterize the governmental or political structure of this regime:
1. Political democracy—autonomous executive, legislature, and courts, as well as interest groups, political parties, and mass media
2. Tutelary or modernizing oligarchy—structural forms of democracy may be present, but effective power is concentrated in hands of executive or military plus the bureaucracy; goal of modernization (especially economic) usually dominant
3. Totalitarian oligarchy—extreme concentration of power in political elite and penetration of society by the polity; goals may be nationalist and/or global revolutionary

4. Traditional oligarchy—usually monarchic or dynastic, based on custom rather than statute; goals are primarily maintenance goals

8. NA (no governmental structure as such)

4–6 Current status of executive, as opposed to other branches of government:
1. Dominant (throughout government establishment)
2. Strong (dominance limited to purely executive functions)
3. Weak (dominated by another branch of government, by political party, or by other group)
8. NA (rebel organization)

4–7 Current status of legislature, as opposed to other branches of government:
1. Fully effective (coequal branch of government)
2. Partially effective (virtually dominated by executive)
3. Wholly ineffective (rubber stamp)
4. None—no legislature
8. NA (rebel organization)

4–8 Current status of judiciary, as opposed to other branches of government:
1. Fully effective (coequal branch of government)
2. Partially effective (virtually dominated by executive)
3. Wholly ineffective (rubber stamp)
4. None—no judiciary
8. NA (rebel organization)

4–9 Character of bureaucracy or administrative organs:
1. Modern (generally rational and effective; recruitment based largely on achievement)
2. Semimodern (largely rational; limited efficiency)
3. Transitional (ex-colonial, largely rational, adapting to indigenous social institutions)
4. Traditional (largely nonrational; ascriptive recruitment dominates)
8. NA (rebel organization)

4–10 Did the present regime attain power by established constitutional procedure?
1. Yes
2. No (or none available)
8. NA (rebel organization)

4–11 Recruitment to political leadership: characterize the values dominant in recruitment of personnel into functional roles in the political system (beyond loyalty to the present regime or system):
1. Elitist—recruitment wholly according to ascriptive criteria (membership in a class, caste, political party, or other group)
2. Moderate—recruitment largely but not wholly according to ascriptive criteria
3. Nonelitist—achievement or ability criteria dominate recruitment process

4–12   Ideological orientation of regime:
    1. Left wing (communist, etc.)
    2. Moderate (democratic, socialist, etc.)
    3. Right wing (military, fascist, etc.)

4–13   Political orientation of regime toward domestic or internal affairs:
    1. Traditionalist or reactionary
    2. Moderate-pragmatic
    3. Revolutionary

4–14   Characterize the international policy of this regime:
    1. Doctrinaire-leftist
    2. Doctrinaire-rightist
    3. Moderate-pragmatic
    4. None

4–15   Communist orientation of this regime:
    1. Communist-Soviet oriented
    2. Communist-China oriented
    3. Communist-independent
    4. Noncommunist
    5. Avowed anticommunist
    8. NA (precommunist era)

4–16   Leadership charisma within regime:
    1. Pronounced
    2. Negligible or none

4–17   Mobilizational style of regime (efforts made by regime to mobilize general population to meet its established political goals):
    1. Fully mobilizational (all population)
    2. Limited mobilizational (specific segments of society)
    3. Nonmobilizational (opposes or suppresses popular participation in political process)
    8. NA (no general population)

4–18   Political integration of general population:
    1. High (integrated polity; no extreme opposition to political system or nonassimilated groups)
    2. Moderate (significant minority in opposition or nonassimilated)
    3. Low (nonintegrated or restrictive polity with majority in opposition or nonassimilated)
    8. NA (no general population)

4–19   Freedom of press allowed by this regime:
    1. Complete (no censorship)
    2. Intermittent (occasional or selective)
    3. Internally absent (domestic censorship, but none on news-gathering for foreign dissemination)

4. Internally and externally absent (strict domestic and foreign control)
8. NA (no press)

4-20   Freedom of group opposition allowed by this regime:
1. Autonomous groups free to enter politics and oppose government
2. Autonomous groups free to organize but limited in capacity to oppose government
3. Autonomous groups tolerated only outside politics
4. No autonomous groups tolerated
8. NA (no general population)

4-21   Interest articulation by anomic groups (e.g., mobs, demonstrators):
1. Frequent
2. Infrequent
3. None tolerated
8. NA (no general population)

4-22   Interest articulation by associational groups (i.e., specialized structures of specific interest articulation such as trade unions):
1. Significant politically
2. Insignificant politically
8. NA (no general population)

4-23   Interest articulation by institutional groups (i.e., institutions specifically performing other social functions, e.g., the church):
1. Significant politically
2. Insignificant politically
8. NA (no general population)

4-24   Interest articulation by political parties:
1. Significant politically
2. Insignificant politically
8. NA (no general population)

4-25   Constitutional status of political parties:
1. Competitive (no party ban at all)
2. Partially competitive (selective outlawry of parties)
3. Noncompetitive (no opposition parties allowed at all)
8. NA (no general population)

4-26   Effective party system:
1. One party (no opposition)
2. One party dominant or one and one-half party (no effective opposition able to win a majority)
3. Two party (reasonable expectation of party rotation)
4. Multiparty (coalition or minority party government normally mandatory)
8. NA (no general population)

4–27   Personalism within political parties (i.e., personality orientation):
1. Pronounced (all parties highly personalistic)
2. Moderate (some personalism)
3. Negligible (no significant personalism)
8. NA (no general population)

4–28   Percentage of voting age population voting in the most recent popular (or national) elections (indicate NA if no elections ever held, or no general population): (OPEN)
1. 1.0– 1.0
2. 1.2– 2.0
3. 9.5–95.0
8. 0 or NA
9. DK

4–29   Votes received by this regime in the most recent popular (or national) elections as a percentage of the total vote cast (indicate NA if no elections held during this regime's tenure, or no general population): (OPEN)
1. 1.2– 1.3
2. 1.7– 2.5
3. 7.8–100.0
8. 0 or NA
9. DK

4–30   How many votes, as a percentage of the total votes cast in the most recent popular (or national) elections, were received by all "left-wing" parties? (Indicate NA if no elections ever held, or no general population.) (OPEN)
1. 1.0– 1.0
2. 2.5– 6.7
3. 9.3–100.0
8. 0 or NA
9. DK

4–31   How many votes, as a percentage of the total votes cast in the most recent popular (or national) elections, were received by all "right-wing" parties? (Indicate NA if no elections ever held, or no general population.) (OPEN)
1. 1.0– 1.0
2. 2.5–10.0
3. 29.0–90.0
8. 0 or NA
9. DK

4–32   Has this antagonist experienced a leadership crisis during this phase?
1. Yes
2. No

4–33   Has a change occurred in the leadership of this regime, or a change in regime for this antagonist, during this phase?
1. Yes
2. No

4-34 Do outside manpower, motives, money, and other resources constitute the main capabilities of this regime (i.e., would it collapse without outside support)?
1. Yes
2. No

4-35 Do outside manpower, motives, money, and other resources appear publicly (i.e., to *its* own general public) to constitute the main capabilities of this regime?
1. Yes
2. No (i.e., it is seen as an autonomous entity or force)
8. NA (no general population)

4-36 What is the level of general popular support (among its own general population) for the regime's stated objectives in this dispute?
1. Generally high
2. Generally low
8. NA (no general population)

4-37 What is the level of general popular support for the regime's specific policies in this dispute?
1. Generally high
2. Generally low
8. NA (no general population)

4-38 Current attitude of the local intellectuals toward the present regime and its policies in this dispute:
1. Generally favorable
2. Generally unfavorable
8. NA (no general population)

4-39 Postdispute expectations of this antagonist's general population if "victory" is not achieved by this side:
1. Generally optimistic
2. Generally pessimistic
8. NA (no general population)

4-40 Effect of the dispute on the internal cohesion of the general population:
1. Greatly increased
2. Little or no change
3. Greatly decreased
8. NA (no general population)

5.
Perceptions and Policies
of the Antagonist with
Respect to the Dispute

5-1 Has this party been involved in organized violent conflict (i.e., hostilities) with any party other than the present adversary within the past twenty years?
1. Yes
2. No

5-2 Does this regime seek the overthrow or destruction of the regime (or leadership) of its adversary in this dispute?

1. Yes
2. No

5–3 Does this regime perceive the following interest as being at stake in this dispute: the spread of its ideology?
1. Yes
2. No

5–4 Does this regime perceive the following interest as being at stake in this dispute: observance of its commitment(s)?
1. Yes
2. No

5–5 Does this regime perceive the following interest as being at stake in this dispute: realization of an established and ongoing policy?
1. Yes
2. No

5–6 Does this regime perceive the following interest as being at stake in this dispute: preservation of national character?
1. Yes
2. No

5–7 Does this regime perceive the following interest as being at stake in this dispute: gaining or maintaining prestige?
1. Yes
2. No

5–8 Does this regime perceive the following interest as being at stake in this dispute: satisfaction of its pride?
1. Yes
2. No

5–9 Does this regime perceive the following interest as being at stake in this dispute: augmentation of its power?
1. Yes
2. No

5–10 Does this regime perceive the following interest as being at stake in this dispute: security of, or acquisition of, its independence?
1. Yes
2. No

5–11 Does this regime perceive the following interest as being at stake in this dispute: its territorial integrity?
1. Yes
2. No

5–12 Does this regime perceive the following interest as being at stake in this dispute: its continued existence?
1. Yes
2. No

5-13 How deeply is this regime personally and presently committed to the achievement of its broadest or overriding publicly stated goals in the dispute?
1. Totally (to the death)
2. Deeply, but flexible
3. Slightly
4. Not at all (purely expediential)

5-14 Does this regime regard this dispute as an ideological conflict, "holy war," or "crusade"?
1. Yes
2. No

5-15 Is this regime's conduct of the dispute limited? Is this, in terms of objective military capabilities, a limited conflict or war?
1. Yes
2. No
8. NA (no hostilities)

5-16 What portion of its available military manpower capabilities has this regime committed or allocated to this dispute at this point?
1. 0- 10%
2. 11- 24%
3. 25- 49%
4. 50- 69%
5. 70-100%

5-17 Characterize the principal or overriding terms in which the regime has rationalized whatever acts of violence have been perpetrated by its forces in this dispute:
1. Moralistic ("just")
2. Political or historical
3. Legal or judicial
4. Expediency ("necessary")
8. NA (no violence has occurred)

5-18 Does this regime feel free, given its public utterances, to accept lesser solutions than those publicly demanded of its adversary? (That is, does it feel it can accept lesser solutions without thereby causing itself grave internal consequences?)
1. Yes
2. No

5-19 Characterize the present outlook of the regime with respect to the dispute:
1. Die-hard (willing to suffer considerable losses to achieve its established objectives)
2. Realistic-moderate (willing to seek a negotiated settlement or compromise)
3. Conciliatory (willing to accept considerable compromise to end the dispute soon)

5-20 Overall balance of "will" (or determination to persist in the dispute) presently confronting this regime, compared to the adver-

sary (as adjudged by this regime):
1. Favorable
2. Even
3. Unfavorable

5–21   Is the likely outcome of the dispute, if the level of commitment remains constant, yet obvious to this regime or to any significant elements within this regime?
1. Yes
2. No

5–22   Postdispute expectations by this regime, if "victory" is not theirs:
1. Optimistic
2. Pessimistic

5–23   Distance in miles to the conflict area from the nearest border of this antagonist (if area is within, or on border of, antagonist's territory or claimed territory, indicate zero): (OPEN)
1.   1.0–   1.0
2.   4.0– 20.0
3. 100.0–600.0
8. 0 or NA
9. DK

5–24   If the conflict area is within or on the border of this antagonist's territory or claimed territory, indicate distance in miles to this area from this antagonist's capital, i.e., political and administrative headquarters (indicate NA if scene of conflict is outside these borders): (OPEN)
1.   1.0–   1.3
2.   1.7–   5.0
3. 10.0–300.0
8. 0 or NA
9. DK

5–25   Does it appear to this regime that its adversary in this present dispute is an
1. Agent or puppet of some other adversary or enemy of this regime
2. Autonomous or independent force operating primarily (if not wholly) on its own
3. Autonomous force maintained by support from another adversary or enemy of this regime

5–26   Characterize the general experience of this regime with formal treaty or other legal arrangements with the adversary in this dispute:
1. Generally satisfactory
2. Generally unsatisfactory
8. NA (no such experience with adversary)

5–27   Speed of communications with the adversary:
1. Rapid (a matter of hours)
2. Moderate (a matter of days)

3. Slow (a matter of weeks or months)

5–28   Reliability of communications with adversary:
    1. High (established and secure channels)
    2. Low (no established channels or security)

5–29   Credibility of communications with adversary:
    1. High or complete
    2. Low or none

5–30   Classify the regime's principal attempts at resolution of the dispute according to their primary character at this point:
    1. Delay (no action, wait for better conditions)
    2. Constitutional (e.g., elections)
    3. Judicial (i.e., adjudication by impartial application of law)
    4. Political (e.g., negotiation, compromise, bargaining)
    5. Military (i.e., dictation by violence or threats of violence)

5–31   Has this regime offered to resolve the dispute by constitutional means (such as elections or plebiscite)?
    1. Yes
    2. No

5–32   Has this regime brought this dispute before an agency of an international organization for its consideration?
    1. Yes
    2. No
    8. NA (none available)

5–33   Has this regime indicated to the adversary that the subject (or object) of this dispute is negotiable?
    1. Yes
    2. No

5–34   Has this regime made any attempt through diplomatic channels to negotiate a settlement of the dispute?
    1. Yes
    2. No

5–35   Has this regime offered the adversary bilateral negotiations (or a conference) aimed at settlement of the dispute?
    1. Yes
    2. No

5–36   Has this regime ever attended bilateral negotiations to resolve the dispute?
    1. Yes
    2. No
    8. NA (none held)

5–37   Does this regime presently perceive escalatory or expansive action on its part as likely to precipitate active (or further active) great-power support for its adversary in the dispute?

1. Yes
2. No

5–38   Characterize the general public opinion of this antagonist concerning the adversary's political institutions, existing or proposed:
1. Generally favorable
2. Generally unfavorable
8. NA (no general population)

5–39   Characterize the general public opinion concerning the adversary's social institutions:
1. Generally favorable
2. Generally unfavorable
8. NA (adversary has no such institutions, or no general population)

5–41   Characterize the general public opinion concerning the adversary's religious institutions:
1. Generally favorable
2. Generally unfavorable
8. NA (adversary has no such institutions, or no general population)

5–42   Has martial law been declared by this regime in the dispute?
1. Yes
2. No
8. NA (no power to declare it)

5–43   Has a state of war been declared by this regime?
1. Yes
2. No
8. NA (no power to declare it)

5–44   Does this regime generally apply the same legal standards and protections to jural persons (i.e., legal entities such as citizens or corporations) of its adversary as it does to its own?
1. Yes
2. No

5–45   What legal status is presently accorded the adversary's personnel by this regime?
1. Citizen of power not at war with this antagonist (with due rights)
2. Common criminal (subject to arrest and trial)
3. Traitor or rebel (subject to be shot)
4. Citizen of power at war with this antagonist (with conventions observed)
5. War criminal (subject to legal prosecution)

5–46   Has antagonist declared a general amnesty policy for adversary personnel?
1. Yes
2. No
8. NA (no hostilities)

6.
Foreign or External
Relations of the Antagonist
and Involvement by Third
Parties in the Dispute

Note: A "third party" to the dispute may be any of the following:
an international organization; a regional or supranational security
organization; an independent nation; an autonomous or independent rebel, insurgent, or guerrilla organization, or similar force.

The "colonial administration" (i.e., the regime in power in the colony itself) is, for purposes of this study, regarded as a principal
party to colonial disputes, having formal security and economic
alliances with its metropolitan country. The metropole itself is
a third party to the dispute and may or may not presently be considered a great power.

The "great powers" are, for these purposes, the overwhelmingly
dominant national powers during the historical era of the particular conflict.

Finally, an "active supportive role" is used here to indicate third-
party assistance—overt or covert, direct or indirect—that exceeds
the purely political or diplomatic, assuming some material form
in terms of goods, services, or resources that serve to support
the antagonist's cause in the dispute.

6–1   Does this antagonist have a formal security arrangement or alliance with any great power? (Note: if, in the case of a colonial administration, the metropolitan country is presently regarded as a
great power, the answer to this question is "yes"; otherwise, it is
"no.")
1. Yes
2. No

6–2   Does this antagonist have a formal security arrangement or alliance with any nation(s) other than the great powers?
1. Yes
2. No

6–3   Is this antagonist a formal ally of any great power that is openly
hostile or inimical to the adversary in this present dispute?
1. Yes
2. No

6–4   Is this antagonist a formal ally of any great power that is also allied
to the adversary in this present dispute?
1. Yes
2. No

6–5   Is this antagonist being supported or aided in this dispute by any
great power that is openly hostile or inimical to the adversary in
this present dispute?
1. Yes
2. No

6–6   Has any great power specifically expressed its partiality for this
antagonist (and its claim) in this dispute? (Note: if this antagonist

is a great power, has any other great power expressed partiality for it?)
1. Yes
2. No

6–7   Has any great power stated that any specific increase in the duration or intensity or scope of this dispute at this point would result in its (further) active intervention on behalf of this antagonist?
1. Yes
2. No

6–8   Are great-power defense facilities located within the established (de facto) jurisdiction of this antagonist?
1. Yes
2. No

6–9   Has any attempt been made by this regime to invoke any available bilateral or multilateral security arrangements on its behalf in this dispute?
1. Yes
2. No
8. NA (none available)

6–10   Has any regional or supranational security organization been consulted and asked by this regime to play an active role on its behalf in the dispute?
1. Yes
2. No
8. NA (none available)

6–11   Has an international organization been asked by this regime to play an active role in the dispute?
1. Yes
2. No
8. NA (none available)

6–12   Is (are) there any third-party (parties) involved in this dispute in an active supportive role on behalf of this antagonist?
1. Yes
2. No

6–13   Is an international organization involved in this dispute in an active supportive role on behalf of this antagonist?
1. Yes
2. No

6–14   Is any regional or supranational security organization involved in this dispute in an active supportive role on behalf of this antagonist?
1. Yes
2. No

6–15   Is any great power involved in this dispute in an active supportive role on behalf of this antagonist?

1. Yes
2. No

6–16   Is any non-great-power nation involved in this dispute in an active supportive role on behalf of this antagonist?
1. Yes
2. No

6–17   Is any autonomous or independent rebel, insurgent, or guerrilla force involved in this dispute in an active supportive role on behalf of this antagonist?
1. Yes
2. No

6–18   Is any third party providing political or diplomatic support on this antagonist's behalf in the dispute?
1. Yes
2. No

6–19   Is any third party providing economic (nonmilitary) support to this antagonist?
1. Yes
2. No

6–20   Is any third party supplying military advisory support to this antagonist?
1. Yes
2. No

6–21   Is any third party supplying arms or military hardware to this antagonist?
1. Yes
2. No

6–22   Is any third party supplying organized conventional forces (i.e., manpower) to this antagonist?
1. Yes
2. No

6–23   Is any third party supplying guerrilla or irregular troops to this antagonist?
1. Yes
2. No

6–24   If any national third party is involved in an active supportive role in this antagonist's behalf, indicate the support of that third party's general public for its involvement in this dispute. (Note: if more than one such national third party is involved, answer in terms of the major contributor.)
1. Generally in favor
2. Generally opposed
8. NA (no national third party involved)

6-24a   If any national third party is involved in an active supportive role in this antagonist's behalf, indicate the type of domestic government or political structure of that third party. (Note: if more than one such national third party is involved, answer in terms of the major contributor; see Item 4–5 for definitions of these categories).

1. Political democracy
2. Tutelary or modernizing oligarchy
3. Totalitarian oligarchy
4. Traditional oligarchy
8. NA (no national third party involved)

6–24b If any national third party is involved in an active supportive role in this antagonist's behalf, has a change occurred in the political leadership of this third party, or a change in its regime, during this phase? (Note: if more than one such national third party is so involved, answer in terms of the major contributor.)

1. Yes
2. No
8. NA (no national third party involved)

6–24c If any national third party is involved in an active supportive role in this antagonist's behalf, indicate the orientation of the present political leadership or ruling regime of that third party, in terms of its own current political system style. (Note: if more than one such national third party is so involved, answer in terms of the major contributor.)

1. Revolutionary
2. Liberal
3. Conservative
4. Traditionalist or reactionary
8. NA (no national third party involved)

6–25 If any national third party is involved in an active supportive role in this antagonist's behalf, is the cost of that support causing severe strains or dislocations in the economy of that third party? (Note: if more than one such national third party is involved, answer in terms of the major contributor.)

1. Yes
2. No
8. NA (no national third party involved)

6–26 If any national third party (or parties) is (are) involved in an active supportive role in this antagonist's behalf, what percentage of the total capital investment in this antagonist's economy represents holdings of this third party (parties)?

1. Less than 5%
2. 5–15%
3. 16–33%
4. 34–66%
5. More than 66%
8. NA (no third party involved, or antagonist has no economy or economic assets)

6–27 If any national third party (or parties) is (are) involved in an active supportive role in this antagonist's behalf, what percentage of the total exports of this antagonist's economy is consumed or claimed by this third party (parties)?

1. Less than 5%
2. 5–15%
3. 16–33%
4. 34–66%
5. More than 66%
8. NA (no third party involved, or antagonist has no exports)

6–28   Has this regime in the past been generally frustrated or gratified in making use of available international machinery for peaceful settlement of disputes?
1. Generally frustrated
2. Generally gratified
3. No experience with such
8. NA (no such machinery available)

6–29   Does this regime feel that available international machinery for peaceful settlement of disputes is applicable in this dispute?
1. Yes
2. No
8. NA (no such machinery available)

6–30   Has any third party offered its offices to this regime to arbitrate or adjudicate this dispute?
1. Yes
2. No

6–31   Has any international organization (or official representative thereof) offered its offices to this regime to arbitrate or adjudicate this dispute?
1. Yes
2. No

6–32   Has any regional or supranational organization (or official representative thereof) offered its offices to this regime to arbitrate or adjudicate this dispute?
1. Yes
2. No

6–33   Has any great power offered its offices to this regime to arbitrate or adjudicate this dispute?
1. Yes
2. No

6–34   Has this regime accepted or rejected any offer by any third party to arbitrate or adjudicate this dispute?
1. Accepted
2. Rejected
8. NA (no such offer made)

6–35   Has this antagonist's cause in this dispute ever been upheld by any resolution of an international organization?
1. Yes
2. No

6–36   Has this antagonist's cause in this dispute ever been repudiated or indicted by any resolution of an international organization?
1. Yes
2. No

6–37   Has an international organization formally recognized with respect to this dispute the violation by this antagonist of any of its obligations under international law?
1. Yes
2. No

6–38   Has this antagonist been cited by an international organization as having committed act(s) of aggression in this dispute?
1. Yes
2. No

6–39   Has this regime accepted or rejected any settlement recommended or proposed for this dispute by an international organization?
1. Accepted
2. Rejected
8. NA (no such settlement offered)

6–40   Has this regime declared its willingness to accept any cease-fire or armistice proposed for this dispute by an international organization?
1. Yes
2. No
8. NA (no such proposal made)

6–41   If an international organization has played any active role in this dispute, has this regime observed its recommendations and honored its decisions?
1. Generally yes
2. Generally no
8. NA (no active role by such)

6–42   Have sanctions of any kind been imposed by an international organization on this antagonist for its stand in this dispute?
1. Yes
2. No

6–43   Have any political or diplomatic sanctions been imposed by an international organization on this antagonist for its stand in this dispute?
1. Yes
2. No
8. NA (no sanctions by international organization)

6–44   Have any economic sanctions been imposed by an international organization on this antagonist for its stand in this dispute?
1. Yes
2. No
8. NA (no sanctions by international organization)

6-45 Have any military (or armament) sanctions been imposed by an international organization on this antagonist for its stand in this dispute?
1. Yes
2. No
8. NA (no sanctions by international organization)

6-46 If a regional or supranational organization of which this antagonist is a member has played any active role in this dispute, has this regime observed its recommendations and honored its decisions?
1. Generally yes
2. Generally no
8. NA (no active role by such)

6-47 Have sanctions of any kind been imposed by a regional or supranational organization on this antagonist for its stand in this dispute?
1. Yes
2. No

6-48 Have any political or diplomatic sanctions been imposed by a regional or supranational organization on this antagonist for its stand in this dispute?
1. Yes
2. No
8. NA (no sanctions by regional organization)

6-49 Have any economic sanctions been imposed by a regional or supranational organization on this antagonist for its stand in this dispute?
1. Yes
2. No
8. NA (no sanctions by regional organization)

6-50 Have any military sanctions been imposed by a regional or supranational organization on this antagonist for its stand in this dispute?
1. Yes
2. No
8. NA (no sanctions by regional organization)

**7.
Military Capabilities
of the Antagonist**

Note: in those items dealing with specific military hardware capabilities, 7-21 to 7-39, weaponry "available to the military forces committed to this side in the dispute" should include all weapons currently available to the antagonist's forces for use or deployment in this dispute (regardless of their source), plus all weapons with which any suppor ng third-party forces are equipped.

"Local procurement capability" is meant to indicate precisely that, and regardless of means — that is, procurement capability in the area of the dispute, whether by production, theft, appropriation, or other means.

7–1 Total number of active, full-time (nonreserve) military troops in this antagonist's own armed forces, in thousands: (OPEN)
  1. 0.02– 10.7
  2. 17.0 –213.7
  3. 330.0 –660.0
  8. 0 or NA
  9. DK

7–2 Total manpower in the antagonist's active armed forces as percentage of the total general population in its control or jurisdiction: (OPEN)
  1. 0.001– 1.0
  2. 1.3 – 174.0
  3. 666.7 –10,000.0
  8. 0 or NA
  9. DK

7–3 Number of nonmobilized reserve or paramilitary force manpower available to this antagonist, in thousands (includes organized military reserve forces, civilian militia forces, army-integrated police force, and other organized groups): (OPEN)
  1. 0.5– 1.4
  2. 1.8– 10.0
  3. 50.0–400.0
  8. 0 or NA
  9. DK

7–4 To what extent have the military reserve or paramilitary forces available to this antagonist been mobilized for this dispute:
  1. No mobilization at all
  2. Token mobilization (less than 10%)
  3. Slight mobilization (10–25%)
  4. Major mobilization (26–75%)
  5. Total mobilization (over 75%)
  8. NA (no such forces available)

7–5 Number of military troops in this antagonist's own armed forces (both active and reserve) actually committed or allocated to this dispute, in thousands: (OPEN)
  1. 0.02– 1.0
  2. 1.2 – 50.0
  3. 150.0 –540.0
  8. 0 or NA
  9. DK

7–6 Number of this antagonist's own armed forces committed or allocated to this dispute, as percentage of its own total available military manpower: (OPEN)
  1. 0.7– 1.0
  2. 1.2– 14.0
  3. 25.0–114.3
  8. 0 or NA
  9. DK

7–7 Percentage of this antagonist's general population mobilized for active military service in this dispute (indicate NA if no general population): (OPEN)
1. 0.001– 1.0
2. 1.5 – 9.0
3. 33.0 –500.0
8. 0 or NA
9. DK

7–8 Is there any internal threat to this regime from any adversary other than the present one that requires it to maintain any sizable portion of its normal military capabilities elsewhere than in the area(s) of immediate confrontation with present adversary?
1. Yes
2. No

7–9 Is there an external threat from any real (or potential) adversary other than the present one that requires this regime to maintain any sizable portion of its normal military capabilities elsewhere than in the area(s) of immediate confrontation with present adversary?
1. Yes
2. No

7–10 If any internal or external threat does exist, what percentage of this antagonist's total (or normal) military manpower capabilities is currently being allocated or committed to this other threat; i.e., what percentage of its total military manpower establishment is diverted from the present dispute thereby? (Indicate NA if no such threat exists.) (OPEN)
1. 1.0– 1.4
2. 2.0– 10.0
3. 25.0–100.0
8. 0 or NA
9. DK

7–11 Total number of military manpower supplied by third party (or parties) to this antagonist's cause in the dispute, in thousands: (OPEN)
1. 0.3– 1.0
2. 2.0– 3.0
3. 4.0–100.0
8. 0 or NA
9. DK

7–12 "Visibility" or overtness of personnel supplied by third party (or parties) to this antagonist's cause in the dispute (i.e., degree of secretiveness attempted and/or achieved in this arrangement between third party and antagonist):
1. Generally overt
2. Generally covert
8. NA (no such aid)

7–13 Does this antagonist expect the number of troops available to it from third-party sources to
1. Increase in the near future

2. Remain at its present level (whatever that may be, even zero)

3. Decrease in the near future

7–14   Total military manpower committed or allocated to this dispute by this side (i.e., total of this antagonist's own military forces committed, plus any military forces supplied by third parties), in thousands: (OPEN)
1.   0.02–   7.3
2.   9.7 – 55.0
3. 106.0 –600.0
8. 0 or NA
9. DK

7–15   What percentage of the total military manpower committed or allocated to this dispute (i.e., antagonist's own forces, plus any third-party forces) consists of this antagonist's own military forces? (Indicate NA if no troops committed to the dispute.) (OPEN)
1.   1.0–   1.5
2.   2.0– 50.0
3. 100.0–217.4
8. 0 or NA
9. DK

7–16   Total conventional army manpower committed or allocated to this dispute by this side (i.e., antagonist's own such forces committed, plus all third-party forces involved), in thousands: (OPEN)
1.   0.01–   3.0
2.   3.7 – 10.0
3. 15.0 –600.0
8. 0 or NA
9. DK

7–17   Total guerrilla or "irregular" manpower committed or allocated to this dispute by this side, in thousands: (OPEN)
1.   0.02–   1.0
2.   1.3 – 20.0
3. 36.0 –170.0
8. 0 or NA
9. DK

7–18   Total naval manpower committed or allocated to this dispute by this side, in thousands: (OPEN)
1. 0.5– 1.0
2. 1.0– 2.0
3. 5.0–20.0
8. 0 or NA
9. DK

7–19   Total air force manpower committed or allocated to this dispute by this side, in thousands: (OPEN)
1.   0.05–   1.0
2.   2.0 – 10.0

3. 20.0 −100.0
8. 0 or NA
9. DK

7–20 Trained medical personnel (doctors, nurses, corpsmen) in all military forces committed or allocated to this dispute by this side: (OPEN)
1.   1.0–   1.2
2.   2.0– 20.0
3. 100.0–500.0
8. 0 or NA
9. DK

7–21 Number of rifles available to the military forces (i.e., antagonist's own military forces, plus any third-party forces) committed to this side in the dispute, in thousands: (OPEN)
1.   0.05–   2.1
2.   3.0 – 85.7
3. 200.0 −1,000.0
8. 0 or NA
9. DK

7–22 Number of automatic weapons (including automatic rifles, submachine guns, and machine guns) available to the military forces committed to this side in the dispute, in thousands: (OPEN)
1. 1.0–   2.0
2. 2.7–   5.8
3. 10.0–1,000.0
8. 0 or NA
9. DK

7–23 Number of mortars (of any size) available to the military forces committed to this side in the dispute, in thousands: (OPEN)
1. 0.04–   1.0
2. 1.5 –   2.0
3. 4.0 −100.0
8. 0 or NA
9. DK

7–24 Number of antitank weapons (including recoilless rifles, rocket launchers or bazookas, and antitank missiles) available to the military forces committed to this side in the dispute, in thousands: (OPEN)
1. 0.01–   1.0
2. 1.3 –   2.1
3. 3.0 −100.0
8. 0 or NA
9. DK

7–25 Number of light cannon—cannon of caliber up to but not including 105 mm or 4.2 in., and not including mortars—available to the military forces committed to this side in the dispute: (OPEN)
1. 1.0–   1.0

2. 1.4–   20.0
3. 50.0–1,000.0
8. 0 or NA
9. DK

7–26   Number of medium cannon – cannon from 105 to 155 mm, or from 4.2 to 6 in., inclusive – available to the military forces committed to this side in the dispute: (OPEN)
1. 1.0–   1.0
2. 1.9– 10.0
3. 20.0–200.0
8. 0 or NA
9. DK

7–27   Number of heavy cannon – cannon of caliber over 155 mm or 6 in. – available to the military forces committed to this side in the dispute: (OPEN)
1. 1.0– 1.0
2. 2.8–50.0
3. 64.0–64.0
8. 0 or NA
9. DK

7–28   Number of tanks and other armored vehicles available to the military forces committed to this side in the dispute: (OPEN)
1. 1.0–   1.5
2. 3.0– 20.0
3. 35.0–370.0
8. 0 or NA
9. DK

7–29   Number of fighter aircraft, jet or prop-driven, available to the military forces committed to this side in the dispute: (OPEN)
1. 1.0–   1.3
2. 1.7– 30.0
3. 50.0–400.0
8. 0 or NA
9. DK

7–30   Number of bomber aircraft, jet or prop-driven, available to the military forces committed to this side in the dispute: (OPEN)
1. 1.0–   1.5
2. 2.0– 25.0
3. 66.0–500.0
8. 0 or NA
9. DK

7–31   Number of troop transport aircraft – DC-3 or larger – available to the military forces committed to this side in the dispute: (OPEN)
1. 1.0– 1.1
2. 1.5– 6.0

3. 10.0–60.0
8. 0 or NA
9. DK

7–32   Total number of jet aircraft available to the military forces committed to this side in the dispute: (OPEN)
1.   1.0– 1.1
2.   1.4– 7.5
3. 15.0–100.0
8. 0 or NA
9. DK

7–33   Number of helicopters available to the military forces committed
to this side in the dispute: (OPEN)
1.   1.0– 1.0
2.   6.7–10.0
3. 13.3–30.0
8. 0 or NA
9. DK

7–34   Number of surface-to-air missiles available to the military forces
committed to this side in the dispute: (OPEN)
1. 1.0– 1.0
2. 1.0– 1.0
3. 2.0–20.0
8. 0 or NA
9. DK

7–35   Number of surface-to-surface missiles available to the military
forces committed to this side in the dispute: (OPEN)
1. 1.0–1.0
2. 1.0–1.0
3. 1.0–1.0
8. 0 or NA
9. DK

7–36   Number of submarines available to the military forces committed
to this side in the dispute: (OPEN)
1. 1.0– 1.0
2. 2.0– 5.0
3. 6.0–12.0
8. 0 or NA
9. DK

7–37   Number of heavy naval vessels (i.e., destroyers or above) available to the military forces committed to this side in the dispute:
(OPEN)
1. 1.0– 1.0
2. 1.3– 3.0
3. 5.0–24.0
8. 0 or NA
9. DK

7-38   Number of troop landing craft available to the military forces committed to this side in the dispute: (OPEN)
1. 1.0– 1.1
2. 1.6– 5.0
3. 10.0–130.0
8. 0 or NA
9. DK

7-39   Number of motorized, shallow-draft torpedo or patrol boats available to the military forces committed to this side in the dispute: (OPEN)
1. 1.0– 1.2
2. 1.6– 3.0
3. 5.0–37.0
8. 0 or NA
9. DK

7-40   Does this antagonist have its own nuclear capability?
1. Yes
2. No, and not seeking to develop or acquire one
3. No, but seeking to develop or acquire one
8. NA (prenuclear era)

7-41   Does any third party involved in an active supportive role in this antagonist's behalf have a nuclear capability?
1. Yes
2. No
8. NA (prenuclear era)

7-42   To what extent is this antagonist currently dependent upon sources other than its own local procurement capabilities for battlefield armaments (i.e., infantry weapons, artillery, etc.)?
1. Exclusively dependent (almost all)
2. Highly dependent (more than half)
3. Somewhat dependent (less than half)
4. Not dependent at all (virtually none)

7-43   If this antagonist is at all dependent for battlefield armaments, does it perceive the immediate supply as likely to
1. Increase
2. Remain about the same
3. Decrease
4. Stop
8. NA (not so dependent)

7-44   To what extent is this antagonist currently dependent upon sources other than its own local procurement capabilities for naval armaments?
1. Exclusively dependent (almost all)
2. Highly dependent (more than half)
3. Somewhat dependent (less than half)
4. Not dependent at all (virtually none)
8. NA (it has none)

7–45   If this antagonist is at all dependent for naval armaments, does it perceive the immediate supply as likely to
1. Increase
2. Remain about the same
3. Decrease
4. Stop
8. NA (not so dependent)

7–46   To what extent is this antagonist currently dependent upon sources other than its own local procurement capabilities for air combat capabilities?
1. Exclusively dependent (almost all)
2. Highly dependent (more than half)
3. Somewhat dependent (less than half)
4. Not dependent at all (virtually none)
8. NA (it has none)

7–47   If this antagonist is at all dependent for air capabilities, does it perceive the immediate supply as likely to
1. Increase
2. Remain about the same
3. Decrease
4. Stop
8. NA (not so dependent)

7–48   To what extent is this antagonist currently dependent upon sources other than its own local procurement capabilities for mechanized transport capabilities?
1. Exclusively dependent (almost all)
2. Highly dependent (more than half)
3. Somewhat dependent (less than half)
4. Not dependent at all (virtually none)
8. NA (it has none)

7–49   If this antagonist is at all dependent for mechanized transport capabilities, does it perceive the immediate supply as likely to
1. Increase
2. Remain about the same
3. Decrease
4. Stop
8. NA (not so dependent)

7–50   "Visibility" or overtness of present military hardware aid by third party (or parties) to this antagonist's cause in the dispute (i.e., degree of secretiveness attempted and/or achieved in this aid relationship):
1. Generally overt
2. Generally covert
8. NA (no such aid)

7–51   Has the third party (parties) also supplied sufficient and adequate spare parts and ammunition for effective operation of the weapons provided?

1. Generally
2. Only selectively
3. Generally not
8. NA (no such aid from third-party sources)

7–52   Has the third party (parties) also provided that there be adequate training of this antagonist's own military forces for effective operation and use of these weapons?
1. Generally
2. Only selectively
3. Generally not
8. NA (no such aid from third-party sources)

7–53   What percentage of the total budget or expenditures for all military forces and armaments committed or allocated to this dispute is being supplied by or from third-party sources? (OPEN)
1. 1.0–   1.0
2. 1.2–   5.0
3. 8.0–100.0
8. 0 or NA
9. DK

8.
Status and Performance of the Antagonist's Military Capabilities

Note: The phrase "the military forces on this side in the dispute" is used here to designate the totality of all forces committed to this dispute by the antagonist and any supporting third parties.

8–1   Traditional political character of this antagonist's own military forces:
1. Interventive (political power oriented)
2. Supportive (parapolitical support role)
3. Neutral (apolitical, or of minor political importance)
8. NA (no such traditions)

8–2   Style of recruitment into this antagonist's own military officer corps (beyond loyalty to the present regime or political system):
1. Elitist (wholly ascriptive criteria such as class, caste, political party)
2. Moderate (largely, but not wholly ascriptive)
3. Nonelitist (nonascriptive criteria dominant, as achievement)

8–3   Characterize relationship between this antagonist's political and military leadership:
1. Political dominant
2. Military dominant
3. Coequal or identical

8–4   Characterize the unity within the officer corps of this antagonist's own armed forces with respect to goals and/or allegiances in the present dispute:
1. Unified—no politically significant dissension
2. Factionalist—politically significant feuding or dissension

8–5   If military manpower forces have been supplied by third-party

sources to this antagonist's cause in the dispute, has this antagonist effectively relinquished supreme command of the forces on this side?
1. Yes
2. No
8. NA (no third-party forces involved)

8–6 Recruitment rate into the military: rate at which this antagonist's own armed forces, active and/or reserve, are being added to, per month: (OPEN)
1. 1.0– 2.0
2. 3.0– 200.0
3. 500.0–20,000.0
8. 0 or NA
9. DK

8–7 Primary method of recruitment into this antagonist's own military forces:
1. Volunteers (voluntary)
2. Conscription (or draft)
3. Mercenaries (foreign or domestic)
4. Impressment, force, or threat

8–8 Primary method of recruitment employed by third-party military forces on this side (note: if more than one third party is involved, answer for the major contributor):
1. Volunteers (voluntary)
2. Conscription (or draft)
3. Mercenaries (foreign or domestic)
4. Impressment, force, or threat
8. NA (no third-party forces involved)

8–9 Training facilities for this antagonist's own military officers:
1. Generally good (at least 4 months, up-to-date program)
2. Generally fair (less than 4 months, ad hoc program)
3. Generally poor (little or no formal training)

8–10 Training facilities for third-party officers on this side in the dispute (note: if more than one third party is involved, answer for the major contributor):
1. Generally good (at least 4 months, up-to-date program)
2. Generally fair (less than 4 months, ad hoc program)
3. Generally poor (little or no formal training)
8. NA (no third-party forces involved)

8–11 Training facilities for this antagonist's own enlisted (i.e., non-officer) military personnel:
1. Generally good (at least 4 months, up-to-date program)
2. Generally fair (less than 4 months, ad hoc program)
3. Generally poor (little or no formal training)

8–12 Training facilities for third-party enlisted personnel on this side in the dispute (note: if more than one third party is involved, answer for the major contributor):

1. Generally good (at least 4 months, up-to-date program)
2. Generally fair (less than 4 months, ad hoc program)
3. Generally poor (little or no formal training)
8. NA (no third-party forces involved)

8–13   Overall balance presently confronting this antagonist, compared to its adversary, in terms of military training, morale, organization, and efficiency — regardless of the relative size of forces on each side (as perceived or adjudged by this regime):
1. Favorable
2. Even
3. Unfavorable

8–14   Do the military forces on this side in the dispute presently have adequate logistic support to maintain efficient operations at their current level?
1. Generally yes
2. Generally no
8. NA (no hostilities)

8–15   Do the military forces on this side in the dispute presently have adequate logistic support to expand their current operations, if they so wish?
1. Generally yes
2. Generally no
8. NA (no hostilities)

8–16   Overall military hardware balance presently confronting this antagonist, compared to its adversary (as perceived or adjudged by this regime):
1. Favorable
2. Even
3. Unfavorable

8–17   Characterize the military command of the forces on this side in the dispute:
1. Centralized (central direction of operations)
2. Decentralized (autonomous local control of operations with minimal central direction)

8–18   Is effective sanctuary (i.e., inviolable withdrawal areas) readily available in the conflict area(s) to the military forces engaged on this side?
1. Generally available to most forces
2. Available to some forces, some of the time
3. Generally not available to most forces
8. NA (no hostilities)

8–19   Is this side using aerial bombing as a tactical weapon against its adversary in this dispute?
1. Yes — daytime only
2. Yes — nighttime only
3. Yes — both night and day bombing
4. No

8. NA (no hostilities)

8–20   Use of terror tactics by the military forces on this side in the dispute:
1. Widespread
2. Limited
3. Absent

8–21   Characterize the military tactics employed by the forces on this side in the dispute:
1. Active or offensive
2. Passive or defensive
8. NA (no hostilities)

8–22   Characterize the military tactics employed by the forces on this side in the dispute:
1. Mobile or expansive
2. Static or stationary
8. NA (no hostilities)

8–23   Characterize the military tactics employed by the forces on this side in the dispute:
1. Tenacious
2. Yielding
8. NA (no hostilities)

8–24   Treatment of enemy prisoners by military forces on this side in the dispute:
1. Good (reasonable shelter, food, medical care)
2. Poor (no shelter, no medical care)
3. Brutal (regular killing, atrocities, etc.)
8. NA (none taken, or no hostilities)

8–25   Treatment of military casualties suffered by the forces on this side in the dispute:
1. Good (extensive use of corpsmen, hospitals)
2. Fair (corpsmen available, but no hospitals)
3. Poor (no corpsmen, no hospitals)
8. NA (no casualties, or no hostilities)

8–26   Is this side now waging a large-scale (i.e., in terms of its own manpower availability) guerrilla operation or war?
1. Yes
2. No
8. NA (no hostilities)

8–27   If large-scale guerrilla operations are being conducted by this side, specify stage or phase of guerrilla operations:
1. Organization and consolidation of regional base areas
2. Progressive expansion through sabotage, terror, direct action
3. Destruction of enemy in conventional battle (while terror and sabotage persist)
8. NA (no such operations waged by this side)

8–28   Intelligence organization and effectiveness of this antagonist among the civilian population in the conflict area(s):
1. Generally effective
2. Occasionally or frequently effective
3. Generally ineffective

8–29   Intelligence organization and effectiveness of this antagonist within the policy apparatus of the adversary in this dispute:
1. Generally effective
2. Occasionally or frequently effective
3. Generally ineffective

8–30   Extent or degree of sympathy between its general population and this antagonist's own military forces:
1. Generally sympathetic
2. Generally antagonistic
8. NA (no general population)

8–31   Extent or degree of sympathy between this antagonist's general population and third-party military forces involved on this side in the dispute:
1. Generally sympathetic
2. Generally antagonistic
8. NA (no third-party forces involved, or no general population)

8–32   Characterize the physical security of this antagonist's general population against conventional attack or raids by the adversary's regular military forces:
1. High — generally secure or invulnerable
2. Moderate — vulnerable only in certain specific and limited areas
3. Low — generally vulnerable
8. NA (no general population)

8–33   Characterize the physical security of this antagonist's general population against guerrilla attack or terror action by the adversary:
1. High — generally secure or invulnerable
2. Moderate — vulnerable only in certain specific and limited areas
3. Low — generally vulnerable
8. NA (no general population)

8–34   Characterize the physical security of this antagonist's general population against accidental or incidental attack by the armed forces on this side in the dispute:
1. High — generally secure or invulnerable
2. Moderate — vulnerable only in certain specific and limited areas
3. Low — generally vulnerable
8. NA (no general population)

8–35   Characterize the physical security of this antagonist's general population against intentional attack or abuse by the police or armed forces on this side in the dispute:
1. High — generally secure or invulnerable

2. Moderate—vulnerable only in certain specific and limited areas

3. Low—generally vulnerable

8. NA (no general population)

9.

Losses Due to the Dispute
for the Antagonist

9–1 What percentage of its total industrial capacity at the end of Phase I has to this point been lost by this antagonist due to the dispute (i.e., through destruction, sabotage, or capture by the adversary)? (Indicate NA if no industrial capacity at the end of P–I.) (OPEN)

1. 0.001– 1.0
2. 2.0 – 5.0
3. 10.0 –100.0
8. 0 or NA
9. DK

9–2 What percentage of the general population in its actual control or jurisdiction at the end of Phase 1 has to this point been lost by this antagonist (through casualties, capture, defection, or control by adversary) due to this dispute? (Indicate NA if no general population at the end of P–I.) (OPEN)

1. 0.003– 1.0
2. 2.0 – 5.0
3. 8.0 –100.0
8. 0 or NA
9. DK

9–3 Total number of this antagonist's general population at the end of Phase I that have been lost to this point due to this dispute, i.e., lost through casualties, capture, defection, or control by adversary (indicate NA if no general population at the end of P–I): (OPEN)

1. 1.0– 1.0
2. 5.0– 20.0
3. 50.0–59,000,000.0
8. 0 or NA
9. DK

9–4 Total attrition rate at this point for the general population, i.e., total number of civilians lost (through casualties, capture, defection, or control by adversary) per month at this point in the dispute (indicate NA if no general population at this point): (OPEN)

1. 0.5– 1.0
2. 1.7– 200.0
3. 1,200.0–2,000,000.0
8. 0 or NA
9. DK

9–5 Total number of casualties (i.e., killed) for this antagonist's own military forces at this point in the dispute: (OPEN)

1. 1.0– 1.2
2. 1.5– 20.0
3. 100.0–500.0
8. 0 or NA
9. DK

9–6   Total number of casualties (i.e., killed) for third-party military forces on this side at this point in the dispute (indicate NA if no third-party forces involved at this point) : (OPEN)
1. 1.0–   1.0
2. 1.6–   20.0
3. 75.0–1,925.0
8. 0 or NA
9. DK

9–7   Total number of casualties (i.e., killed) for all military forces on this side at this point in the dispute: (OPEN)
1. 1.0– 1.2
2. 1.3– 6.0
3. 8.2–500.0
8. 0 or NA
9. DK

9–8   Casualty rate at this point for this antagonist's own military forces: number of casualties (i.e., killed) per month at this point in the dispute: (OPEN)
1. 1.0– 2.0
2. 2.5– 5.0
3. 8.2–55.0
8. 0 or NA
9. DK

9–9   Casualty rate at this point for third-party military forces on this side in the dispute: number of casualties (i.e., killed) per month at this point in the dispute (indicate NA if no third-party forces involved at this point): (OPEN)
1. 0.1– 1.0
2. 1.7– 5.0
3. 8.0–500.0
8. 0 or NA
9. DK

9–10   Casualty rate at this point for all military forces on this side in the dispute: number of casualties (i.e., killed) per month at this point in the dispute: (OPEN)
1. 1.0– 2.0
2. 2.5– 5.0
3. 8.2–55.0
8. 0 or NA
9. DK

9–11   Total attrition rate at this point for this antagonist's own military forces: total number of troops lost through casualties, capture, surrender, defection, or desertion per month at this point in the dispute: (OPEN)
1. 1.0– 2.0
2. 2.5– 20.0
3. 55.0–125.0
8. 0 or NA
9. DK

9-12   Total attrition rate at this point for third-party forces on this side in the dispute: total number of troops lost through casualties, capture, surrender, defection, or desertion per month at this point in the dispute (indicate NA if no third-party forces involved at this point): (OPEN)
1. 0.1–   1.0
2. 1.7–   8.0
3. 55.0–2,000.0
8. 0 or NA
9. DK

9-13   Total attrition rate at this point for all military forces on this side in the dispute: total number of troops lost through casualties, capture, surrender, defection, or desertion per month at this point in the dispute: (OPEN)
1. 1.0– 2.0
2. 2.5– 8.0
3. 10.9–55.0
8. 0 or NA
9. DK

Index to the Conflict Codebook   This simple index is provided to allow the reader quickly to assess the scope and depth of this test instrument for conflict, and readily to locate within it any specific item or subject of interest.

The hyphenated numbers cited in the listings correspond to those employed in the codebook. Except for the items designed specifically to assess the nature of the dispute itself, the unit of response to all these items is the principal party or antagonist; that is, each item is answered for each antagonist, in terms of the situation and conditions applying to it, at each threshold of the conflict model. The combination of the responses to an item for the two principal parties at any given threshold of a dispute constitutes that item's compound response.

Appendix C:
Agreement Analysis Logical Flow Diagram

1. An individual pattern consists of the complete set of responses of an individual case (person, object, or event) to any specified test instrument or set of test items. A category pattern deriving from two or more such individual patterns consists of all the item-response combinations common to those individual patterns. Accordingly, any category pattern may be said to contain the individual (and category) patterns from which it derives.

2. An individual pattern is considered classified at any level of classification if it has either (a) been combined with another individual pattern or an existing tentative category pattern to form a new tentative category pattern, or (b) been designated an adjunct of a tentative category pattern. A tentative category pattern itself ceases to exist once any subsequent pattern in which it is contained is accepted as a new tentative category pattern; that is, it is superseded by any tentative category pattern deriving (in part) from itself.

3. Raw agreement score (RAS) = the number of items in the test instrument to which two patterns have exactly the same response (that is, agree in their responses).

Corrected agreement score (CAS) = RAS minus the number of items on which the two patterns agree by chance.

$$= n_{ij} - (r - n_{ij}) \left(\frac{\sum\limits_{Z,z} \dfrac{Z}{k_z^{\,p+q-1}}}{\sum\limits_{Z,z} \dfrac{Z(k_z^{\,p+q-1}-1)}{k_z^{\,p+q-1}}} \right)$$

for k variable; and

$$= n_{ij} - \frac{r - n_{ij}}{k^{p+q-1}-1}$$

for k constant, where

r = the total number of items in the test

i = any pattern at any level of classification

j = any other pattern at any level

p = the number of cases (or, at the first level, individual patterns) classified in the category that yields pattern i

q = the number of cases classified in the category that yields pattern j

k_z = the number of possible response alternatives to any item in the test

Z = the number of items in the test having k_z response alternatives

n_{ij} = the raw agreement score for patterns i and j.

4. In any selection among agreement scores, ties are resolved in favor of the pattern containing the least number of individual patterns. In the case of ties between individual patterns, either may be selected, the method itself ensuring that the final classification of each individual pattern is the best possible.

5. For the interested reader, a graphic illustration of the complete, integrated operation of the various steps in agreement analysis is presented in Figure C.1. The numbers employed in this illustration correspond to those entered in parentheses at the bottom of each step in the detailed diagram that follows (Figure C.2). A key is provided, including some of the more critical steps in the operation of the technique, to help the reader locate his stepwise progress within its overall flow.

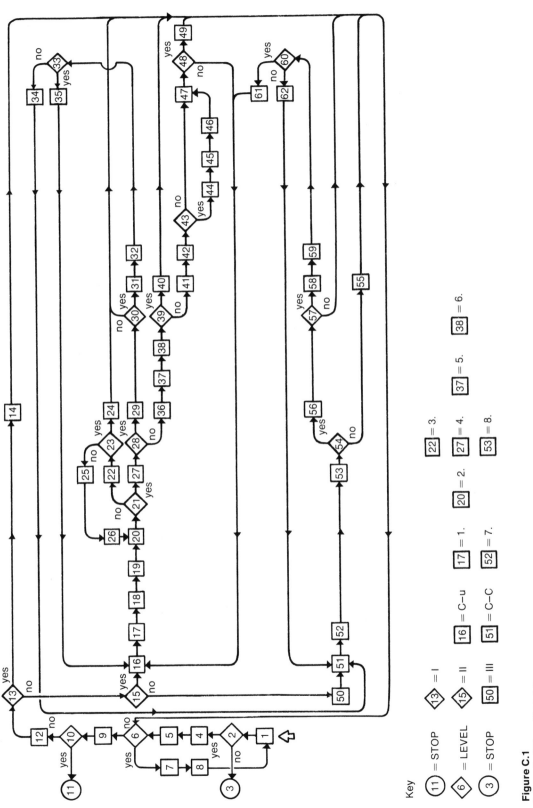

Key

⬡ 11 = STOP   ◇ 13 = I   ⬡ 17 = 1.   □ 22 = 3.

◇ 6 = LEVEL   ◇ 15 = II   □ 16 = C–u   □ 20 = 2.   □ 27 = 4.   □ 37 = 5.   □ 38 = 6.

⬡ 3 = STOP   □ 50 = III   □ 51 = C–C   □ 52 = 7.   □ 53 = 8.

Figure C.1
Integrated Flow Diagram
Note: The numbers employed in this illustration correspond to those entered in parentheses at the bottom of each step in the detailed flow diagram, Figure C.2.

Figure C.2
Detailed Flow Diagram

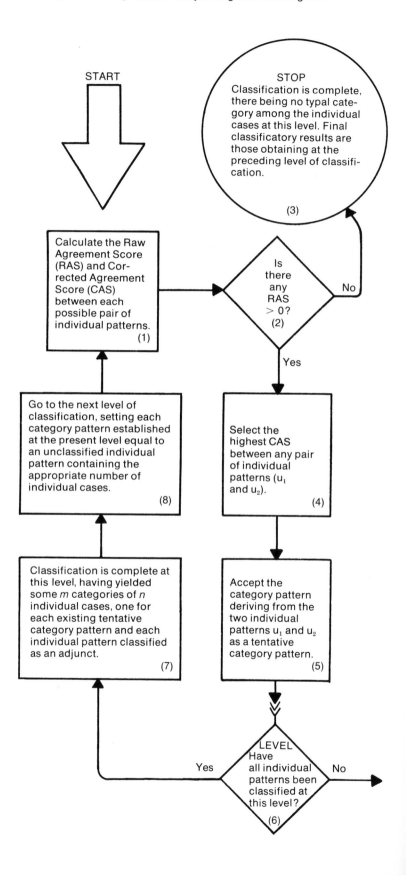

START

STOP
Classification is complete, there being no typal category among the individual cases at this level. Final classificatory results are those obtaining at the preceding level of classification.
(3)

Calculate the Raw Agreement Score (RAS) and Corrected Agreement Score (CAS) between each possible pair of individual patterns.
(1)

Is there any RAS > 0?
(2)

No

Yes

Go to the next level of classification, setting each category pattern established at the present level equal to an unclassified individual pattern containing the appropriate number of individual cases.
(8)

Select the highest CAS between any pair of individual patterns (u_1 and u_2).
(4)

Classification is complete at this level, having yielded some m categories of n individual cases, one for each existing tentative category pattern and each individual pattern classified as an adjunct.
(7)

Accept the category pattern deriving from the two individual patterns u_1 and u_2 as a tentative category pattern.
(5)

LEVEL
Have all individual patterns been classified at this level?
(6)

Yes

No

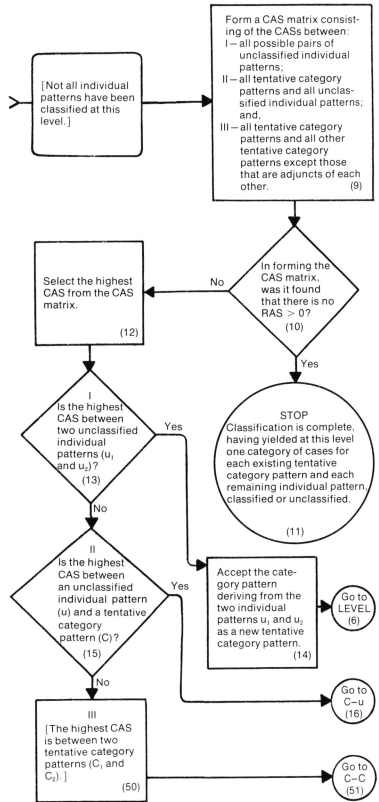

[Not all individual patterns have been classified at this level.]

Form a CAS matrix consisting of the CASs between:
I — all possible pairs of unclassified individual patterns;
II — all tentative category patterns and all unclassified individual patterns; and,
III — all tentative category patterns and all other tentative category patterns except those that are adjuncts of each other. (9)

In forming the CAS matrix, was it found that there is no RAS > 0? (10)

No

Select the highest CAS from the CAS matrix. (12)

Yes

STOP
Classification is complete, having yielded at this level one category of cases for each existing tentative category pattern and each remaining individual pattern, classified or unclassified. (11)

I
Is the highest CAS between two unclassified individual patterns (u_1 and u_2)? (13)

Yes

No

II
Is the highest CAS between an unclassified individual pattern (u) and a tentative category pattern (C)? (15)

Yes

Accept the category pattern deriving from the two individual patterns u_1 and u_2 as a new tentative category pattern. (14)

Go to LEVEL (6)

No

Go to C–u (16)

III
[The highest CAS is between two tentative category patterns (C_1 and C_2).] (50)

Go to C–C (51)

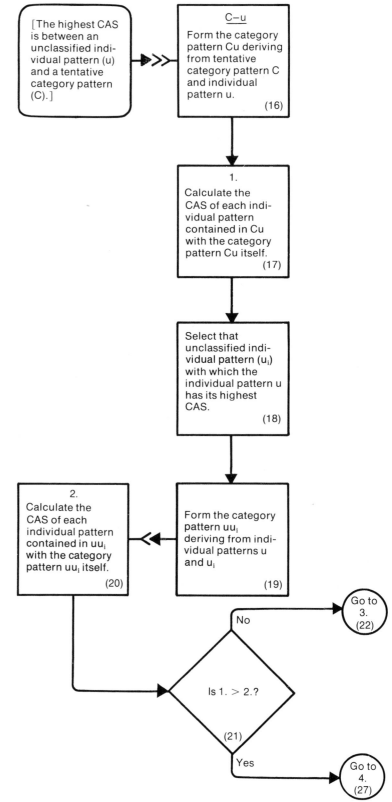

[The highest CAS is between an unclassified individual pattern (u) and a tentative category pattern (C).]

C–u
Form the category pattern Cu deriving from tentative category pattern C and individual pattern u.   (16)

1.
Calculate the CAS of each individual pattern contained in Cu with the category pattern Cu itself.   (17)

Select that unclassified individual pattern (u_i) with which the individual pattern u has its highest CAS.   (18)

2.
Calculate the CAS of each individual pattern contained in uu_i with the category pattern uu_i itself.   (20)

Form the category pattern uu_i deriving from individual patterns u and u_i (19)

Is 1. > 2.?   (21)

No → Go to 3. (22)

Yes → Go to 4. (27)

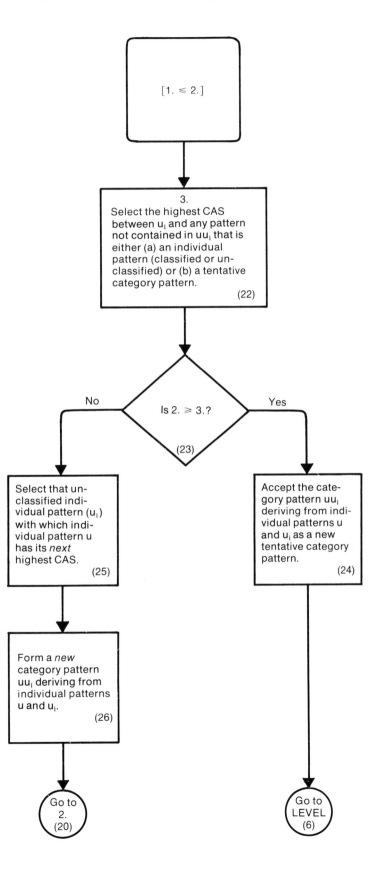

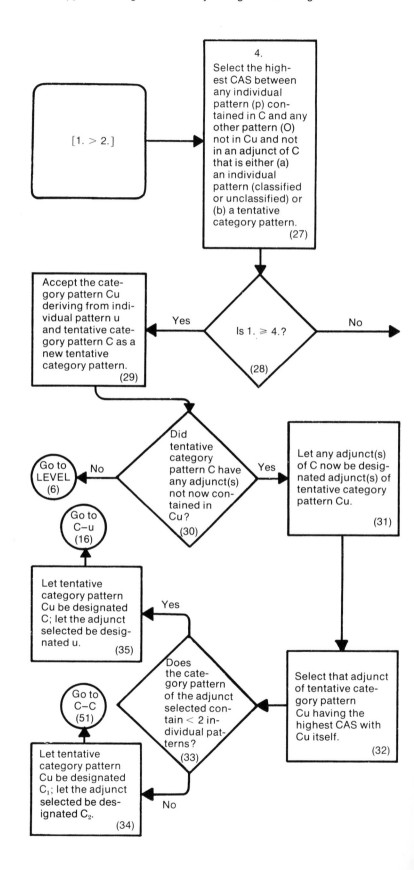

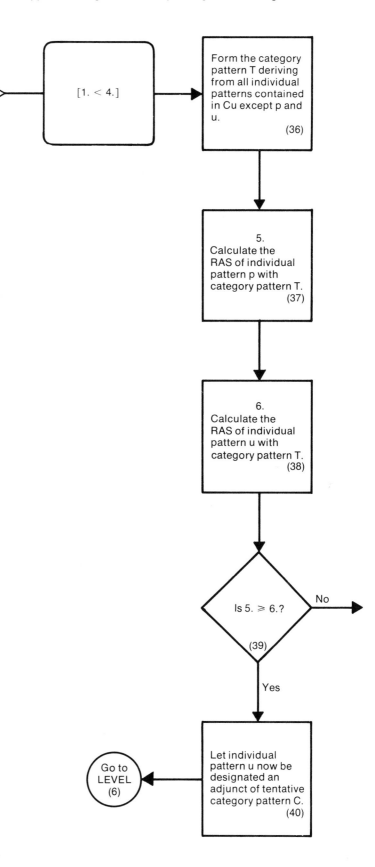

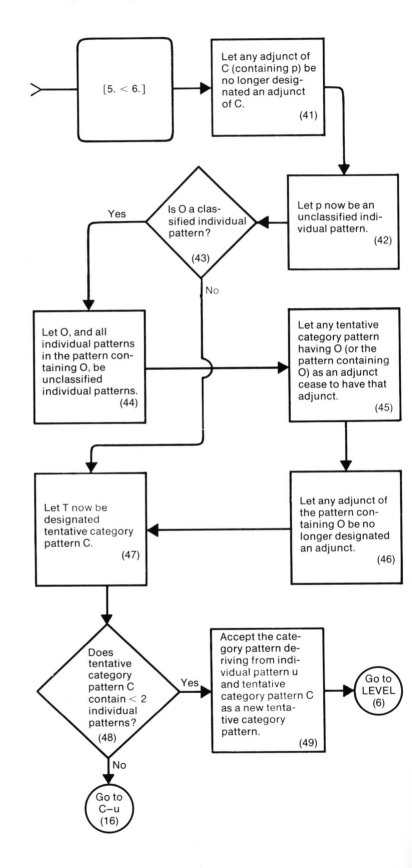

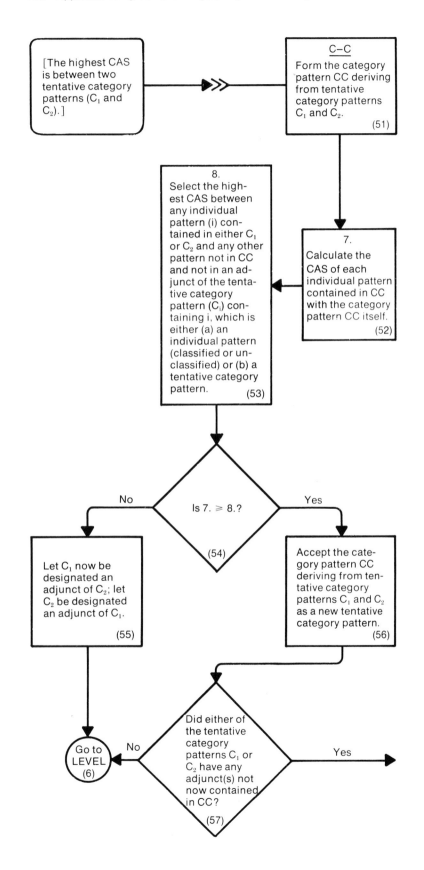

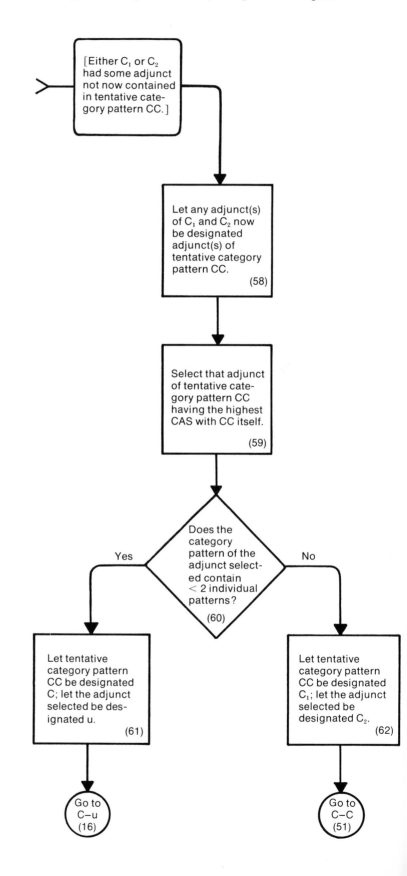

Appendix D:
The Complete Factor Patterns

This appendix presents the results of the application of compound agreement analysis to the conflicts as defined in terms of the conflict system at the thresholds of

P–II   Prehostilities conflict
P–III   Hostilities
  E   Escalation
  D   De-escalation
P–IV   Termination (or posthostilities)
S   Settlement

It contains six sections, one for each threshold examined, and each section is divided into five subsections as follows:

a. *Conflicts Included in the Analysis of the ~ Patterns,* a list of the conflicts yielding those patterns through the medium of agreement analysis, together with the date and event marking the start of the relevant stage of each conflict (the data input being that generated at the threshold immediately preceding the onset of each phase). These listings afford the reader easy access to the nature and kinds of events following directly upon the realization of the specified factor patterns.

b. *Derivation of the ~ Patterns,* a graphic illustration of the manner in which the individual conflicts combined under the aegis of agreement analysis to establish the several dominant typological categories (species, genera, and so on) resident among them. The factor pattern of each category comprises all the item-compound response combinations common to all the conflicts classified therein (see Chapter 4). As explained in Chapter 5, the significant conflict types isolated in this study are those obtaining at the species, or first, level of classificatory results. Those types are defined in full by the species patterns that proceed from the application of compound agreement analysis to the data base established at the threshold of each stage of the conflict model.

"Adj:" denotes the conflicts that were classified as adjuncts of the typal or category patterns in question. The species and other numbers designating these patterns at each level of classification indicate the order in which they were formed by agreement analysis and are thus an index of the statistical dominance of the patterns once all individual conflicts had been classified at that level.

c. *Percentile Distribution of the Conflicts across the ~ Patterns,* a percentile statement of the extent to which each conflict in the analysis incorporates each of the resulting category patterns. These scores were derived by comparing each conflict (or individual pattern) in both of its forms (that is, in both juxtapositions of the two principal parties) to each category pattern; counting the number of item-compound response combinations on which they agreed exactly; and taking the larger of these two numbers and dividing it by the total number of factors in the category pattern. The resulting percentile indicates the maximal extent to which each conflict itself incorporates each category pattern established (each incorporating, of course, all of the pattern of any category in which it was itself classified).

Similarly, although it was not involved in the determination of the category patterns, the Vietnam war (defined on March 15, 1967) was compared to each category pattern established at the threshold of escalation (E), de-escalation (D), termination (P–IV), and settlement (S). The extent to which it maximally incorporated each pattern at that time is indicated.

d. ~ : *Complete Factor Patterns,* a listing of the several sets of item-compound response combinations constituting the species patterns established at the threshold of each stage of conflict examined in the present study. In these computer printouts, both the items and their responses are abbreviated from their full form, which may be found in Appendix B (the codebook) by use of the item identification numbers. The conflicts from which each factor pattern derives are also shown, along with the antagonists (in parentheses) represented, respectively, in the two compound response columns of the printouts.

A number sign (#) between the item and its compound response marks each factor on which the Vietnam conflict (as of March 15, 1967, and in its maximal form) matched the factor pattern in question. Since the four alternatives open in the Vietnam war at that time were escalation, de-escalation, termination, and settlement, the sign will be found only in the factor patterns established at those thresholds. For the factors not so marked, the Vietnam conflict did not maximally match and to that extent was lacking the specific set of developmental preconditions.

e. ~ : *Higher-Order Factor Patterns,* presents the several higher-order factor patterns (genus or above) established at each of the conflict thresholds examined, as shown in subsection (b). The category patterns are arranged and presented in the same manner as in subsection (d). As noted in Chapter 5, too few factors remained in these patterns once the weighting device had been applied to use them as the basis for meaningful, significant conflict types. The addition of further cases to the analysis would be expected to alter this, however, and to produce more significant results at these higher levels of classification of increasing numbers of cases on the basis of fewer and fewer characteristics more widely shared.

At the highest level of classification at each threshold, then, the only item-compound responses remaining are those that are common to all the cases included in the analysis.

1.
The Conflict (P–II) Patterns

The data input for each conflict included in this analysis is that obtaining at the threshold of Phase II and is therefore a statement of the conditions pertaining when each was about to assume a military (though not yet violent) character. All but one of these conflicts passed into Phase II from Phase I, the premilitary phase. The remaining case, Israel-Egypt, passed from Phase IV (termination) to a new (or renewed) prehostilities phase (P–II).

a.
**Conflicts Included
in the Analysis
of the Conflict Patterns**

Conflict	Event Marking Conflict (P–II)	Date
Algeria-Morocco	Algerian independence referendum	7/62
Angolan insurgency	Leopoldville riots; Portugal strengthens Angolan garrison	1/59
Cuba: "little" war of 1906	Liberal party withdraws from national elections	12/05
Cuba: Bay of Pigs	U.S. President authorizes an exile organization	3/60
Cyprus: independence	Enosists establish a military committee	7/52
Cyprus: internal	London Agreement on Cypriot independence	2/59
Ethiopia-Somalia	Somali independence	7/60
Greek insurgency	Formation of rival government in Greece	3/44
India-China	Chinese violate Indian border	6/54
Indonesia: independence	Both sides demonstrate a will to use force	8/45
Indonesia-Malaysia	Brunei revolt; Indonesia arms "volunteers"	2/63
Israel-Egypt	Czech-Egyptian arms agreement	9/55
Kashmir	Raiding tribesmen enter Kashmir from Pakistan	10/47
Malayan insurgency	Calcutta conference—Fourth Plenum	2/48
Spanish civil war	Nationalist terror and political assassination	2/36
Venezuelan insurgency	MIR/CPV formed	4/60
USSR-Iran	USSR and Britain occupy Iran	8/41

b.

Derivation of the Conflict Patterns

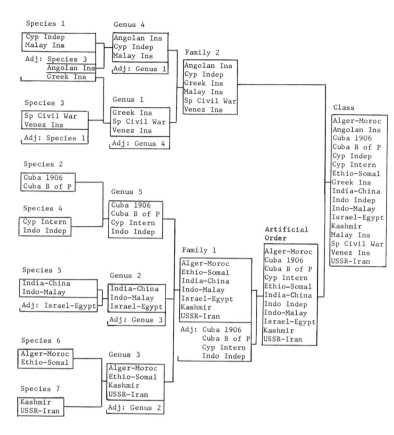

c.

Percentile Distribution of the Conflicts across the Conflict Patterns

	Species						
	C1	C2	C3	C4	C5	C6	C7
Algeria-Morocco	0.36	0.43	0.39	0.48	0.61	1.00	0.63
Angolan insurgency	0.43	0.43	0.44	0.48	0.33	0.49	0.38
Cuba: war of 1906	0.57	1.00	0.57	0.62	0.47	0.51	0.58
Cuba: Bay of Pigs	0.51	1.00	0.60	0.66	0.35	0.47	0.46
Cyprus: independence	1.00	0.55	0.60	0.74	0.48	0.50	0.47
Cyprus: internal	0.60	0.56	0.53	1.00	0.35	0.50	0.46
Ethiopia-Somalia	0.42	0.43	0.39	0.59	0.57	1.00	0.63
Greek insurgency	0.45	0.41	0.51	0.50	0.41	0.33	0.47
India-China	0.37	0.37	0.36	0.42	1.00	0.60	0.66
Indonesia: independence	0.49	0.51	0.46	1.00	0.42	0.43	0.46
Indonesia-Malaysia	0.50	0.37	0.34	0.52	1.00	0.55	0.61
Israel-Egypt	0.37	0.41	0.40	0.57	0.51	0.50	0.55
Kashmir	0.32	0.41	0.32	0.48	0.61	0.58	1.00
Malayan insurgency	1.00	0.52	0.64	0.66	0.51	0.47	0.42
Spanish civil war	0.51	0.65	1.00	0.62	0.37	0.58	0.54
Venezuelan insurgency	0.63	0.57	1.00	0.48	0.38	0.40	0.34
USSR-Iran	0.33	0.45	0.35	0.49	0.55	0.63	1.00

	Genus					Family		Arti-ficial Order	Class
	1	2	3	4	5	1	2		
Algeria-Morocco	0.49	0.76	1.00	0.56	0.65	1.00	0.64	1.00	1.00
Angolan insurgency	0.58	0.39	0.58	1.00	0.63	0.60	1.00	~	1.00
Cuba: war of 1906	0.67	0.59	0.71	0.65	1.00	0.72	0.80	1.00	1.00
Cuba: Bay of Pigs	0.70	0.48	0.62	0.67	1.00	0.68	0.84	1.00	1.00
Cyprus: independence	0.75	0.56	0.53	1.00	0.86	0.64	1.00	~	1.00
Cyprus: internal	0.72	0.48	0.64	0.68	1.00	0.68	0.80	1.00	1.00
Ethiopia-Somalia	0.53	0.74	1.00	0.56	0.72	1.00	0.60	1.00	1.00
Greek insurgency	1.00	0.54	0.51	0.61	0.60	0.68	1.00	~	1.00
India-China	0.58	1.00	0.84	0.49	0.53	1.00	0.72	1.00	1.00
Indonesia: independence	0.63	0.56	0.60	0.60	1.00	0.64	0.84	1.00	1.00
Indonesia-Malaysia	0.53	1.00	0.71	0.56	0.65	1.00	0.64	1.00	1.00
Israel-Egypt	0.58	1.00	0.67	0.40	0.67	1.00	0.64	1.00	1.00
Kashmir	0.51	0.80	1.00	0.37	0.65	1.00	0.52	1.00	1.00
Malayan insurgency	0.68	0.61	0.49	1.00	0.79	0.68	1.00	~	1.00
Spanish civil war	1.00	0.57	0.78	0.72	0.84	0.80	1.00	~	1.00
Venezuelan insurgency	1.00	0.54	0.47	0.68	0.63	0.64	1.00	~	1.00
USSR-Iran	0.54	0.80	1.00	0.49	0.65	1.00	0.68	1.00	1.00

d.

Conflict:
Complete Factor Patterns

Species Type C1
("an insurgent order in search of a sponsor")

The factor pattern derives from

Cyprus: independence (U.K. colonial administration vs. Enosists)

Malayan insurgency (U.K.-Malay colonial administration and Malayan government vs. Malayan Communist party)

The adjuncts are

Angolan insurgency

Greek insurgency

Item				Compound Response	
1-2A	TOPOGRAPHY OF CONFLICT AREA	1.	FLAT	1.	FLAT
1-4	PAST MIL. REL'SHIP BETW PARTYS	1.	PEACEFUL	1.	PEACEFUL
1-5	EFFECTIVE NATURE OF DISPUTE	1.	COLONIAL	1.	COLONIAL
1-8	CONTROL OF REAL ESTATE INVOLVD	1.	YES	1.	YES
1-11	DISPUTE HAS BEEN TO REG'L ORGN	2.	NO	2.	NO
1-12	DISPUTE HAS BEEN TO INT'L ORGN	2.	NO	2.	NO
2-6	LINGUISTIC HOMOGENEITY OF POPN	3.	VERY HETERO	1.	HOMOGENEOUS
2-13	POPN UNDER EFFECTIVE CONTROL	3.	499.0-65TH	8.	0 OR N/A
2-14	REAL ESTATE INVOLVED IS	1.	IN CLMD BDY	1.	IN CLMD BDY
2-15	PC OF ANT'S CLMD AREA INVOLVED	1.	1.0-1.0	1.	1.0-1.0
2-16	PC OF ANT'S CLMD POPN INVOLVED	1.	1.0-1.0	1.	1.0-1.0
2-17	PC OF INVOLVED AREA IN CONTROL	3.	24.0-100.0	8.	0 OR N/A
2-18	PC OF INVOLVED POPN IN CONTROL	3.	9.0-100.0	8.	0 OR N/A
2-19	URBANIZATION	2.	MEDIUM	8.	0 OR N/A
3-2	GROSS NAT'L. OR ECON. PRODUCT	3.	90.0-6.4TH	8.	0 OR N/A
3-3	GROWTH RATE OF ECONOMY	3.	3.0-13.9	8.	0 OR N/A
3-4	RATE OF INFLATION IN ECONOMY	2.	2.0-10.0	8.	0 OR N/A
3-5	PER CAPITA INCOME	3.	115.0-855.0	8.	0 OR N/A
3-6	PC OF GNP IN AGRICULTURE	3.	25.0-75.0	8.	0 OR N/A
3-8	PRODUCTION OF STEEL	1.	1.0-1.0	1.	1.0-1.0
3-9	PC OF GNP IN EXPORTS	3.	22.0-1.0TH	8.	0 OR N/A
3-13	PROGRESSIVE TAX STRUCTURE	1.	YES	8.	0 OR N/A

Item		Compound Response			
3-14	GOVERNMENT INCOME AS PC OF GNP	3.	10.0-50.0	8.	0 OR N/A
3-15	GOVT. SPENDING AS PC OF GNP	3.	6.0-50.0	8.	0 OR N/A
3-20	AGRIC EMPLOYMENT AS PC OF POPN	3.	13.0-70.0	8.	0 OR N/A
3-21	INDUSTRIAL EMPL. AS PC OF POPN	3.	11.0-23.0	8.	0 OR N/A
3-29	NO. SEAPORTS CONTROLLED	2.	1.6-3.3	8.	0 OR N/A
4-1	EFFECTIVE STATUS OF GOVERNMENT	2.	COLONIAL ADM	4.	REBEL ORGN
4-3	MODERN COLONIAL RULER	5.	NONE	1.	BRITAIN
4-4	EXECUTIVE STABILITY	3.	3.0-9.0	8.	0 OR N/A
4-5	TYPE OF GOVERNMENT	2.	TUT/MOD OLIG	8.	0 OR N/A
4-6	STATUS OF EXECUTIVE	1.	DOMINANT	8.	0 OR N/A
4-10	REGIME CAME TO POWER CONST'LY	2.	NO	8.	0 OR N/A
4-13	INTERNAL POLICIES OF REGIME	2.	MODERATE	3.	REVOL'ARY
4-17	MOBILIZATIONAL STYLE OF REGIME	2.	LIMITED	8.	0 OR N/A
4-18	POL. INTEGRATION OF GENL POPN	2.	MODERATE	8.	0 OR N/A
4-22	INTEREST ARTIC'N BY ASSOC'L GP	1.	POL SIGNIF	8.	0 OR N/A
4-23	INTEREST ARTIC'N BY INST'L GPS	1.	POL SIGNIF	8.	0 OR N/A
4-24	INTEREST ARTIC'N BY POL PARTYS	1.	POL SIGNIF	8.	0 OR N/A
4-25	CONST'AL STATUS OF POL PARTIES	1.	COMPETITIVE	8.	0 OR N/A
4-27	PERSONALISM IN POL. PARTIES	2.	MODERATE	8.	0 OR N/A
4-32	RECENT LEADERSHIP CRISIS	2.	NO	2.	NO
4-34	FORN RES ARE MAINSTAY OF REGIM	1.	YES	2.	NO
4-35	REGIM APPEARS MAINT BY FOR RES	1.	YES	8.	0 OR N/A
4-40	EFFECT ON POPULAR COHESION	2.	LITTLE CHANGE	8.	0 OR N/A
5-2	REGIME SEEKS OVERTHROW OF ADV.	2.	NO	1.	YES
5-7	INTEREST INVOLVED-PRESTIGE	2.	NO	1.	YES
5-9	INTEREST INVOLVED-POWER	2.	NO	1.	YES
5-10	INTEREST INVOLVED-INDEPENDENCE	2.	NO	1.	YES
5-13	COMMITMENT TO STATED GOALS	2.	FLEXIBLE	2.	FLEXIBLE
5-22	POST-DISPUTE EXPECT'N OF REGIM	2.	PESSIMISTIC	2.	PESSIMISTIC
5-23	DIST FM BORDER TO CONFL AREA	1.	1.0-1.0	1.	1.0-1.0
5-24	DIST FM CAPITAL TO CONFL AREA	1.	1.0-1.3	1.	1.0-1.3
5-25	ADVERSARY APPEARS TO ANT TO BE	1.	AUT + INDEP.	1.	A PUPPET
5-27	SPEED OF COMMUNICATIONS	1.	RAPID	1.	RAPID
5-28	RELIABILITY OF COMMUNICATIONS	1.	HIGH	1.	HIGH
5-32	BROUGHT DISPUTE TO INT'L ORGN	2.	NO	2.	NO
5-33	INDICATED DISPUT IS NEGOT.ABLE	2.	NO	2.	NO
5-34	HAS SOUGHT A NEGOT. SETTLEMENT	2.	NO	2.	NO
5-35	HAS OFFERED BI-LATERAL NEGOTNS	2.	NO	2.	NO
5-37	ESC LIKELY BRING GP AID TO ADV	2.	NO	2.	NO
5-42	MARTIAL LAW IS IN EFFECT	2.	NO	8.	0 OR N/A
5-43	STATE OF WAR HAS BEEN DECLARED	2.	NO	8.	0 OR N/A
5-45	LEGAL STATUS OF ADV. PERSONNEL	1.	CITIZEN	1.	CITIZEN
6-1	IS SEC'TY ALLY OF GREAT POWER	1.	YES	2.	NO
6-2	IS SEC'TY ALLY OF NON-G.P.	2.	NO	2.	NO
6-3	IS ALLY OF G.P. HOSTILE TO ADV	1.	YES	2.	NO
6-4	IS ALLY OF G.P. ALLIED TO ADV.	2.	NO	2.	NO
6-5	IS AIDED BY GP HOSTILE TO ADV.	1.	YES	2.	NO
6-8	GP DEF. FAC'TIES IN ANT'S AREA	1.	YES	2.	NO
6-9	HAS INVOKED AVAIL SEC'TY PACTS	2.	NO	8.	0 OR N/A
6-12	SOME 3PTY IS INV. ON THIS SIDE	1.	YES	1.	YES
6-13	INT'L ORG IS INV. ON THIS SIDE	2.	NO	2.	NO
6-14	REG'L ORG IS INV. ON THIS SIDE	2.	NO	2.	NO
6-15	A G.P. IS INV. ON THIS SIDE	1.	YES	2.	NO
6-16	A NON-GP IS INV. ON THIS SIDE	2.	NO	1.	YES
6-17	A AUT ORG IS INV. ON THIS SIDE	2.	NO	2.	NO
6-18	A 3PTY IS PROVIDING POL. AID	1.	YES	1.	YES
6-20	A 3PTY IS PROVIDING MIL ADVICE	1.	YES	2.	NO
6-21	A 3PTY IS PROVIDING MIL HDWRE.	1.	YES	2.	NO
6-23	A 3PTY IS PROVIDING GUER FORCE	2.	NO	2.	NO
6-24	ATT. OF 3PTY PUBLIC TO INV'MNT	1.	FAVORABLE	1.	FAVORABLE
6-27	PC ANT'S EXPORTS CONS. BY 3PTY	3.	16-33 PC	8.	0 OR N/A
6-28	EXPERIENCE WITH IO PEACE MACH	2.	GRATIFYING	3.	NONE
6-30	SOME 3PTY OFFERED TO ARBITRATE	2.	NO	2.	NO
6-31	INTL ORGN OFFERED TO ARBITRATE	2.	NO	2.	NO
6-32	REGL ORGN OFFERED TO ARBITRATE	2.	NO	2.	NO
6-33	A G.P. OFFERED TO ARBITRATE	2.	NO	2.	NO
6-35	INT'L ORG'N UPHELD ANT'S CAUSE	2.	NO	2.	NO
6-36	INTL ORGN INDICTED ANT'S CAUSE	2.	NO	2.	NO
6-37	CITED IN VIOLATION OF INT'L LAW	2.	NO	2.	NO
6-38	CITED BY I.O. FOR AGGRESSION	2.	NO	2.	NO
6-40	ACCEPTED IO'S PROP. CEASEFIRE	2.	NO	2.	NO
6-42	I.O. HAS IMPOSED SANCTIONS	2.	NO	2.	NO
6-47	REG ORGN HAS IMPOSED SANCTIONS	2.	NO	2.	NO
7-4	MOBILIZATION OF RESERVES	1.	NONE	1.	NONE
7-5	NO. TROOPS COMMITTED TO CONFL.	1.	0.02-1.0	1.	0.02-1.0
7-6	NO. TROOPS COMM AS PC TOT FRCS	8.	0 OR N/A	3.	25.0-114.3
7-7	PC POPN MOB'ZED FOR ACTIV DUTY	1.	0.001-1.0	1.	0.001-1.0
7-8	OTHER SIGNIF INTERNAL THREAT	2.	NO	2.	NO
7-9	OTHER SIGNIF EXTERNAL THREAT	2.	NO	2.	NO
7-12	OVERTNES OF 3PTY PERSONNEL AID	1.	GEN'LY OVERT	8.	0 OR N/A
7-13	3PTY TROOP AID SEEN LIKELY TO	2.	STAY SAME	2.	STAY SAME
7-17	GUERRILLA MANPOWER COMMITTED	1.	0.02-1.0	1.	0.02-1.0
7-18	NAVAL MANPOWER COMMITTED	1.	0.5-1.0	1.	0.5-1.0
7-19	AIR FORCE MANPOWER COMMITTED	1.	0.05-1.0	1.	0.05-1.0
7-21	NO. RIFLES AVAILABLE	1.	0.05-2.1	1.	0.05-2.1
7-22	NO. AUTO. WEAPONS AVAILABLE	1.	1.0-2.0	1.	1.0-2.0
7-27	NO. HVY. CANNON AVAILABLE	1.	1.0-1.0	1.	1.0-1.0
7-32	NO. JET AIRCRAFT AVAILABLE	1.	1.0-1.1	1.	1.0-1.1
7-33	NO. HELICOPTERS AVAILABLE	1.	1.0-1.0	1.	1.0-1.0
7-34	NO. SAM'S AVAILABLE	1.	1.0-1.0	1.	1.0-1.0
7-35	NO. SSM'S AVAILABLE	1.	1.0-1.0	1.	1.0-1.0
7-36	NO. SUBMARINES AVAILABLE	1.	1.0-1.0	1.	1.0-1.0

Item		Compound Response		
7-40	HAS A NUCLEAR CAPABILITY	2. NO	2. NO
7-48	DEP FOR TRANSPORT CAPABILITIES	1. EXCLUSIVE	8. 0 OR N/A
7-49	TRANSP. CAP. SUPPLY LIKELY TO	2. STAY SAME	8. 0 OR N/A
8-3	REL'SHIP BET POL + MIL LEADERS	1. POL DOMINANT	1. POL DOMINANT
8-4	UNITY WITHIN MILITARY COMMAND	1. UNIFIED	1. UNIFIED
8-7	METHOD OF MILITARY RECRUITMENT	1. VOLUNTARY	1. VOLUNTARY
8-17	CENTRALIZATION OF MIL. COMMAND	1. CENTRALIZED	2. DE-CENTR'ZED
8-26	LARG-SCAL GUER OPN BEING WAGED	8. 0 OR N/A	1. YES
8-27	STAGE OF GUERRILLA OPERATIONS	8. 0 OR N/A	1. ORG + CONS
8-33	CIVN SECURITY V. GUERR ATTACK	3. LOW	8. 0 OR N/A
9-1	PC OF INDUSTRIAL CAPACITY LOST	1. 0.001-1.0	1. 0.001-1.0
9-2	PC OF CIVILIAN POPULATION LOST	1. 0.003-1.0	1. 0.003-1.0
9-3	TOTAL NO. CIVN POPULATION LOST	1. 1.0-1.0	1. 1.0-1.0
9-4	ATTRITION RATE FOR CIV'N POPN	1. 0.5-1.0	1. 0.5-1.0
9-5	TOTAL CAS'TIES TO OWN FORCES	1. 1.0-1.2	1. 1.0-1.2
9-7	TOTAL CAS'TIES TO ALL FORCES	1. 1.0-1.2	1. 1.0-1.2
9-8	CASUALTY RATE FOR OWN FORCES	1. 1.0-2.0	1. 1.0-2.0
9-10	CASUALTY RATE FOR ALL FORCES	1. 1.0-2.0	1. 1.0-2.0
9-11	ATTRITION RATE FOR OWN FORCES	1. 1.0-2.0	1. 1.0-2.0
9-13	ATTRITION RATE FOR ALL FORCES	1. 1.0-2.0	1. 1.0-2.0

Species Type C2
("great-power interests do not yet prevail")

The factor pattern derives from

Cuba: "little" war of 1906 (Liberal party insurgents vs. Cuban government)

Cuba: Bay of Pigs (Cuban exiles vs. Cuban government)

Item		Compound Response	
1-1	GEOGRAPHIC LOCUS OF DISPUTE	2. SO. AMERICA	2. SO. AMERICA
1-2A	TOPOGRAPHY OF CONFLICT AREA	1. FLAT	1. FLAT
1-2B	CLIMATE IN THE CONFLICT AREA	3. WET	3. WET
1-3	PAST POL. REL'SHIP BETW PARTYS	1. COOPERATIVE	1. COOPERATIVE
1-4	PAST MIL. REL'SHIP BETW PARTYS	1. PEACEFUL	1. PEACEFUL
1-5	EFFECTIVE NATURE OF DISPUTE	3. INTERNAL	3. INTERNAL
2-1	OVERRIDING CULTURAL IDEAL	3. AGGRESSIVE	3. AGGRESSIVE
2-2	PREFERRED MODE OF CONFL RESOLN	3. DICTATORIAL	3. DICTATORIAL
2-3	RACIAL GROUPING OF ANTAGONIST	1. WHITE	1. WHITE
2-4	REGIM + GENL POPN OF SAME RACE	1. YES	1. YES
2-6	LINGUISTIC HOMOGENEITY OF POPN	1. HOMOGENEOUS	1. HOMOGENEOUS
2-7	RELIGIOUS HOMOGENEITY OF POPN	1. VERY HOMO	1. VERY HOMO
2-8	DOMINANT RELIGION AMONG POPN	1. JUD-XIAN	1. JUD-XIAN
2-10	NEWSPAPER CIRCULATION IN POPN	8. 0 OR N/A	3. LOW
2-12	AREA UNDER EFFECTIVE CONTROL	8. 0 OR N/A	3. 13.7-500.0
2-13	POPN UNDER EFFECTIVE CONTROL	8. 0 OR N/A	3. 499.0-65TH
3-2	GROSS NAT'L. OR ECON. PRODUCT	8. 0 OR N/A	3. 90.0-6.4TH
3-4	RATE OF INFLATION IN ECONOMY	1. 0.2-1.0	1. 0.2-1.0
3-5	PER CAPITA INCOME	8. 0 OR N/A	3. 115.0-855.0
3-9	PC OF GNP IN EXPORTS	8. 0 OR N/A	3. 22.0-1.0TH
3-13	PROGRESSIVE TAX STRUCTURE	8. 0 OR N/A	2. NO
3-14	GOVERNMENT INCOME AS PC OF GNP	8. 0 OR N/A	3. 10.0-50.0
3-15	GOVT. SPENDING AS PC OF GNP	8. 0 OR N/A	3. 6.0-50.0
3-18	DEFENSE BUDGET AS PC OF GNP	8. 0 OR N/A	2. 5.0-22.0
3-20	AGRIC EMPLOYMENT AS PC OF POPN	8. 0 OR N/A	3. 13.0-70.0
3-29	NO. SEAPORTS CONTROLLED	8. 0 OR N/A	3. 6.0-45.0
4-1	EFFECTIVE STATUS OF GOVERNMENT	4. REBEL ORGN	1. INDEP GOVT
4-2	DATE OF INDEPENDENCE	8. 0 OR N/A	2. 1800-1913
4-3	MODERN COLONIAL RULER	3. SP/PORT/IT	3. SP/PORT/IT
4-4	EXECUTIVE STABILITY	8. 0 OR N/A	3. 3.0-9.0
4-8	STATUS OF JUDICIARY	8. 0 OR N/A	2. PART EFFECT.
4-9	CHARACTER OF BUREAUCRACY	8. 0 OR N/A	3. TRANSITIONAL
4-11	RECRUITMENT TO POL LEADERSHIP	2. MODERATE	2. MODERATE
4-14	INTERNATIONAL POLICY OF REGIME	4. NONE	3. MODERATE
4-16	LEADERSHIP CHARISMA	1. PRONOUNCED	1. PRONOUNCED
4-23	INTEREST ARTIC'N BY INST'L GPS	8. 0 OR N/A	1. POL SIGNIF
4-25	CONST'AL STATUS OF POL PARTIES	8. 0 OR N/A	1. COMPETITIVE
4-26	EFFECTIVE POL. PARTY SYSTEM	8. 0 OR N/A	2. ONE PTY DOM
4-27	PERSONALISM IN POL. PARTIES	8. 0 OR N/A	1. PRONOUNCED
4-32	RECENT LEADERSHIP CRISIS	2. NO	2. NO
4-33	RECENT CHANGE IN LEADERSHIP	2. NO	2. NO
4-35	REGIM APPEARS MAINT BY FOR RES	8. 0 OR N/A	2. NO
4-37	POP. SUPPORT FOR REGIM'S POLS.	8. 0 OR N/A	1. HIGH
4-40	EFFECT ON POPULAR COHESION	8. 0 OR N/A	2. LITTLE CHANGE
5-6	INTEREST INVOLVED-NAT'L CHAR.	1. YES	2. NO
5-9	INTEREST INVOLVED-POWER	1. YES	1. YES
5-10	INTEREST INVOLVED-INDEPENDENCE	2. NO	2. NO
5-13	COMMITMENT TO STATED GOALS	2. FLEXIBLE	1. TOTAL
5-21	LIKELY OUTCOME IS NOW OBVIOUS	2. NO	2. NO
5-22	POST-DISPUTE EXPECT'N OF REGIM	2. PESSIMISTIC	2. PESSIMISTIC
5-25	ADVERSARY APPEARS TO ANT TO BE	2. AUT + INDEP.	2. AUT + INDEP.
5-32	BROUGHT DISPUTE TO INT'L ORGN	2. NO	2. NO
5-33	INDICATED DISPUT IS NEGOTIABLE	1. YES	2. NO
5-37	ESC LIKELY BRING GP AID TO ADV	2. NO	2. NO
5-43	STATE OF WAR HAS BEEN DECLARED	8. 0 OR N/A	2. NO
5-44	APPLIES OWN LEGAL STDS TO ADV.	1. YES	2. NO
5-45	LEGAL STATUS OF ADV. PERSONNEL	1. CITIZEN	3. TRAITOR
6-2	IS SEC'TY ALLY OF NON-G.P.	2. NO	2. NO
6-3	IS ALLY OF G.P. HOSTILE TO ADV	2. NO	2. NO
6-4	IS ALLY OF G.P. ALLIED TO ADV.	2. NO	2. NO
6-5	IS AIDED BY GP HOSTILE TO ADV.	2. NO	2. NO
6-6	A GP IS OPENLY PARTIAL TO ANT.	2. NO	2. NO
6-7	GP AID PROMISED IF ESC. OCCURS	2. NO	2. NO
6-9	HAS INVOKED AVAIL SEC'TY PACTS	8. 0 OR N/A	2. NO
6-11	HAS ASKED AN INT'L. ORG'N. IN	2. NO	2. NO
6-12	SOME 3PTY IS INV. ON THIS SIDE	2. NO	2. NO
6-13	INT'L ORG IS INV. ON THIS SIDE	2. NO	2. NO

Item		Compound Response		
6-14	REG'L ORG IS INV. ON THIS SIDE	2. NO	2. NO
6-15	A G.P. IS INV. ON THIS SIDE	2. NO	2. NO
6-16	A NON-GP IS INV. ON THIS SIDE	2. NO	2. NO
6-20	A 3PTY IS PROVIDING MIL ADVICE	2. NO	2. NO
6-21	A 3PTY IS PROVIDING MIL HDWRE.	2. NO	2. NO
6-22	A 3PTY IS PROVIDING CONV FORCE	2. NO	2. NO
6-23	A 3PTY IS PROVIDING GUER FORCE	2. NO	2. NO
6-28	EXPERIENCE WITH IO PEACE MACH	3. NONE	3. NONE
6-29	I.O. PEACE MACHUNERY IS SEEN	2. IRRELEVANT	2. IRRELEVANT
6-30	SOME 3PTY OFFERED TO ARBITRATE	2. NO	2. NO
6-31	INTL ORGN OFFERED TO ARBITRATE	2. NO	2. NO
6-32	REGL ORGN OFFERED TO ARBITRATE	2. NO	2. NO
6-33	A G.P. OFFERED TO ARBITRATE	2. NO	2. NO
6-35	INT'L ORG'N UPHELD ANT'S CAUSE	2. NO	2. NO
6-36	INTL ORGN INDICTED ANT'S CAUSE	2. NO	2. NO
6-37	CITED IN VIOLATION OF INTL LAW	2. NO	2. NO
6-38	CITED BY I.O. FOR AGGRESSION	2. NO	2. NO
6-40	ACCEPTED IO'S PROP. CEASEFIRE	2. NO	2. NO
6-42	I.O. HAS IMPOSED SANCTIONS	2. NO	2. NO
6-47	REG ORGN HAS IMPOSED SANCTIONS	2. NO	2. NO
7-17	GUERRILLA MANPOWER COMMITTED	1. 0.02-1.0	1. 0.02-1.0
7-18	NAVAL MANPOWER COMMITTED	1. 0.5-1.0	1. 0.5-1.0
7-24	NO. ANTI-TANK WPNS. AVAILABLE	1. 0.01-1.0	1. 0.01-1.0
7-25	NO. LT. CANNON AVAILABLE	1. 1.0-1.0	1. 1.0-1.0
7-26	NO. MED. CANNON AVAILABLE	1. 1.0-1.0	1. 1.0-1.0
7-27	NO. HVY. CANNON AVAILABLE	1. 1.0-1.0	1. 1.0-1.0
7-36	NO. SUBMARINES AVAILABLE	1. 1.0-1.0	1. 1.0-1.0
7-37	NO. HEAVY VESSELS AVAILABLE	1. 1.0-1.0	1. 1.0-1.0
7-38	NO. LANDING CRAFT AVAILABLE	1. 1.0-1.1	1. 1.0-1.1
7-53	PC TOTAL COSTS COMING FM 3PTY	1. 1.0-1.0	1. 1.0-1.0
8-1	POLITICAL CHARACTER OF MILTARY	8. 0 OR N/A	1. INTERVENTIVE
8-13	OVERALL MILITARY ORG'N BALANCE	3. UNFAVORABLE	1. FAVORABLE
8-16	OVERALL MIL. HARDWARE BALANCE	3. UNFAVORABLE	1. FAVORABLE
8-34	CIVN SEC V AC ATK BY OWN FRCES	8. 0 OR N/A	1. HIGH
8-35	CIVN SEC V ABUSE BY OWN FORCES	8. 0 OR N/A	1. HIGH
9-1	PC OF INDUSTRIAL CAPACITY LOST	1. 0.001-1.0	1. 0.001-1.0
9-2	PC OF CIVILIAN POPULATION LOST	1. 0.003-1.0	1. 0.003-1.0
9-3	TOTAL NO. CIVN POPULATION LOST	1. 1.0-1.0	1. 1.0-1.0
9-5	TOTAL CAS'TIES TO OWN FORCES	1. 1.0-1.2	1. 1.0-1.2
9-7	TOTAL CAS'TIES TO ALL FORCES	1. 1.0-1.2	1. 1.0-1.2
9-8	CASUALTY RATE FOR OWN FORCES	1. 1.0-2.0	1. 1.0-2.0
9-10	CASUALTY RATE FOR ALL FORCES	1. 1.0-2.0	1. 1.0-2.0

Species Type C3

("moderation prevails till accommodation fails")

The factor pattern derives from

Spanish civil war (Republican government vs. Nationalist insurgents)

Venezuelan insurgency (Venezuelan government vs. MIR/CPV and FLN/FALN)

1-2A	TOPOGRAPHY OF CONFLICT AREA	2. MOUNTAINOUS	2. MOUNTAINOUS
1-2B	CLIMATE IN THE CONFLICT AREA	2. MODERATE	2. MODERATE
1-5	EFFECTIVE NATURE OF DISPUTE	3. INTERNAL	3. INTERNAL
1-8	CONTROL OF REAL ESTATE INVOLVD	1. YES	1. YES
1-11	DISPUTE HAS BEEN TO REG'L ORGN	2. NO	2. NO
1-12	DISPUTE HAS BEEN TO INT'L ORGN	2. NO	2. NO
2-2	PREFERRED MODE OF CONFL RESOLN	2. CONCILIATORY	3. DICTATORIAL
2-4	REGIM + GENL POPN OF SAME RACE	1. YES	1. YES
2-7	RELIGIOUS HOMOGENEITY OF POPN	1. VERY HOMO	1. VERY HOMO
2-8	DOMINANT RELIGION AMONG POPN	1. JUD-X'IAN	1. JUD-X'IAN
2-9	LITERACY RATE AMONG GENL POPN	2. MEDIUM	8. 0 OR N/A
2-12	AREA UNDER EFFECTIVE CONTROL	3. 13.7-500.0	8. 0 OR N/A
2-13	POPN UNDER EFFECTIVE CONTROL	3. 499.0-65TH	8. 0 OR N/A
2-14	REAL ESTATE INVOLVED IS	1. IN CLMD BDY	1. IN CLMD BDY
2-15	PC OF ANT'S CLMD AREA INVOLVED	1. 1.0-1.0	1. 1.0-1.0
2-16	PC OF ANT'S CLMD POPN INVOLVED	1. 1.0-1.0	1. 1.0-1.0
2-17	PC OF INVOLVED AREA IN CONTROL	3. 24.0-100.0	8. 0 OR N/A
2-18	PC OF INVOLVED POPN IN CONTROL	3. 9.0-100.0	8. 0 OR N/A
3-2	GROSS NAT'L. OR ECON. PRODUCT	3. 90.0-6.4TH	8. 0 OR N/A
3-5	PER CAPITA INCOME	3. 115.0-855.0	8. 0 OR N/A
3-7	PC OF GNP IN DURABLE GOODS	3. 11.0-45.0	8. 0 OR N/A
3-8	PRODUCTION OF STEEL	3. 105.0-20TH	8. 0 OR N/A
3-14	GOVERNMENT INCOME AS PC OF GNP	3. 10.0-50.0	8. 0 OR N/A
3-15	GOVT. SPENDING AS PC OF GNP	3. 6.0-50.0	8. 0 OR N/A
3-18	DEFENSE BUDGET AS PC OF GNP	1. 0.3-2.7	9. 0 OR N/A
3-20	AGRIC EMPLOYMENT AS PC OF POPN	3. 13.0-70.0	8. 0 OR N/A
3-21	INDUSTRIAL EMPL. AS PC OF POPN	3. 11.0-23.0	8. 0 OR N/A
3-22	UNEMPLOYED AS PC OF GENL POPN	3. 3.0-13.0	8. 0 OR N/A
3-27	NO. AIRPORTS CONTROLLED	3. 26.0-181.0	9. 0 OR N/A
3-29	NO. SEAPORTS CONTROLLED	3. 6.0-45.0	8. 0 OR N/A
4-1	EFFECTIVE STATUS OF GOVERNMENT	1. INDEP GOVT	4. REBEL ORGN
4-4	EXECUTIVE STABILITY	3. 3.0-9.0	8. 0 OR N/A
4-5	TYPE OF GOVERNMENT	1. POL DEMOC	8. 0 OR N/A
4-8	STATUS OF JUDICIARY	2. PART EFFECT.	8. 0 OR N/A
4-9	CHARACTER OF BUREAUCRACY	2. SEMI-MODERN	8. 0 OR N/A
4-10	REGIME CAME TO POWER CONST'LY	1. YES	8. 0 OR N/A
4-18	POL. INTEGRATION OF GENL POPN	2. MODERATE	8. 0 OR N/A
4-22	INTEREST ARTIC'N BY ASSOC'L GP	1. POL SIGNIF	8. 0 OR N/A
4-23	INTEREST ARTIC'N BY INST'L GPS	1. POL SIGNIF	9. 0 OR N/A
4-24	INTEREST ARTIC'N BY POL PARTYS	1. POL SIGNIF	8. 0 OR N/A
4-25	CONST'AL STATUS OF POL PARTIES	1. COMPETITIVE	8. 0 OR N/A
4-26	EFFECTIVE POL. PARTY SYSTEM	4. MULTI-PARTY	8. 0 OR N/A
4-33	RECENT CHANGE IN LEADERSHIP	2. NO	2. NO
4-34	FORN RES ARE MAINSTAY OF REGIM	2. NO	2. NO
4-35	REGIM APPEARS MAIN'T BY FOR RES	2. NO	2. NO
4-40	EFFECT ON POPULAR COHESION	2. LITTLE CHANGE	8. 0 OR N/A

Item		Compound Response		
5-2	REGIME SEEKS OVERTHROW OF ADV.	2.	NO	1.	YES
5-3	INTEREST INVOLVED-IDEOLOGY	1.	YES	1.	YES
5-4	INTEREST INVOLVED-COMMITMENTS	1.	YES	1.	YES
5-7	INTEREST INVOLVED-PRESTIGE	1.	YES	1.	YES
5-8	INTEREST INVOLVED-PRIDE	1.	YES	1.	YES
5-9	INTEREST INVOLVED-POWER	1.	YES	1.	YES
5-11	INTEREST INVOLVED-TERR. INTEG.	2.	NO	2.	NO
5-13	COMMITMENT TO STATED GOALS	2.	FLEXIBLE	2.	FLEXIBLE
5-14	DISPUTE IS REGARDED AS CRUSADE	2.	NO	1.	YES
5-16	PC OF AVAIL MIL FRCS COMMITTED	1.	0 -10 PC	1.	0 -10 PC
5-19	PRESENT OUTLOOK WRT DISPUTE	2.	MODERATE	2.	MODERATE
5-23	DIST FM BORDER TO CONFL AREA	1.	1.0-1.0	1.	1.0-1.0
5-24	DIST FM CAPITAL TO CONFL AREA	1.	1.0-1.3	1.	1.0-1.3
5-27	SPEED OF COMMUNICATIONS	2.	MODERATE	2.	MODERATE
5-31	OFFERED TO RESOLVE CONST'ALLY	1.	YES	2.	NO
5-32	BROUGHT DISPUTE TO INT'L ORGN	2.	NO	2.	NO
5-34	HAS SOUGHT A NEGOT. SETTLEMENT	2.	NO	2.	NO
5-35	HAS OFFERED BI-LATERAL NEGOTNS	2.	NO	2.	NO
5-38	P.O. RE ADV'S POL. INST'NS.	2.	UNFAVORABLE	8.	0 OR N/A
5-42	MARTIAL LAW IS IN EFFECT	2.	NO	8.	0 OR N/A
5-43	STATE OF WAR HAS BEEN DECLARED	2.	NO	8.	0 OR N/A
6-4	IS ALLY OF G.P. ALLIED TO ADV.	2.	NO	2.	NO
6-7	GP AID PROMISED IF ESC. OCCURS	2.	NO	2.	NO
6-8	GP DEF. FAC'TIES IN ANT'S AREA	2.	NO	2.	NO
6-13	INT'L ORG IS INV. ON THIS SIDE	2.	NO	2.	NO
6-14	REG'L ORG IS INV. ON THIS SIDE	2.	NO	2.	NO
6-16	A NON-GP IS INV. ON THIS SIDE	2.	NO	2.	NO
6-22	A 3PTY IS PROVIDING CONV FORCE	2.	NO	2.	NO
6-23	A 3PTY IS PROVIDING GUER FORCE	2.	NO	2.	NO
6-28	EXPERIENCE WITH IO PEACE MACH	3.	NONE	3.	NONE
6-30	SOME 3PTY OFFERED TO ARBITRATE	2.	NO	2.	NO
6-31	INTL ORGN OFFERED TO ARBITRATE	2.	NO	2.	NO
6-32	REGL ORGN OFFERED TO ARBITRATE	2.	NO	2.	NO
6-33	A G.P. OFFERED TO ARBITRATE	2.	NO	2.	NO
6-35	INT'L ORG'N UPHELD ANT'S CAUSE	2.	NO	2.	NO
6-36	INTL ORGN INDICTED ANT'S CAUSE	2.	NO	2.	NO
6-37	CITED IN VIOLATION OF INTL LAW	2.	NO	2.	NO
6-38	CITED BY I.O. FOR AGGRESSION	2.	NO	2.	NO
6-40	ACCEPTED IO'S PROP. CEASEFIRE	2.	NO	2.	NO
6-42	I.O. HAS IMPOSED SANCTIONS	2.	NO	2.	NO
6-47	REG ORGN HAS IMPOSED SANCTIONS	2.	NO	2.	NO
7-2	NO. ACTIV TROOPS AS PC OF POPN	1.	0.001-1.0	8.	0 OR N/A
7-3	NO. RESERVE TROOPS AVAILABLE	1.	0.5-1.4	1.	0.5-1.4
7-8	OTHER SIGNIF INTERNAL THREAT	2.	NO	2.	NO
7-9	OTHER SIGNIF EXTERNAL THREAT	2.	NO	2.	NO
7-11	TOTAL TROOPS GIVEN BY 3RD PTY	1.	0.3-1.0	1.	0.3-1.0
7-13	3PTY TROOP AID SEEN LIKELY TO	2.	STAY SAME	2.	STAY SAME
7-23	NO. MORTARS AVAILABLE	1.	0.04-1.0	8.	0 OR N/A
7-25	NO. LT. CANNON AVAILABLE	3.	50.0-1.0TH	8.	0 OR N/A
7-26	NO. MED. CANNON AVAILABLE	3.	20.0-200.0	8.	0 OR N/A
7-30	NO. BOMBER A/C AVAILABLE	2.	2.0-25.0	8.	0 OR N/A
7-37	NO. HEAVY VESSELS AVAILABLE	3.	5.0-24.0	8.	0 OR N/A
7-39	NO. PATROL BOATS AVAILABLE	3.	5.0-37.0	8.	0 OR N/A
7-46	DEP. FOR AIR COMBAT ARMAMENTS	1.	EXCLUSIVE	8.	0 OR N/A
7-47	AIR ARMAMENT SUPPLY LIKELY TO	2.	STAY SAME	8.	0 OR N/A
8-7	METHOD OF MILITARY RECRUITMENT	2.	CONSCRIPTIVE	1.	VOLUNTARY
8-20	USE OF TERROR BY THIS ANT. IS	3.	ABSENT	2.	LIMITED
8-30	SYMPATHY BETW POPN + OWN MIL.	1.	SYMPATHETIC	2.	ANTAGONISTIC
8-34	CIV. SEC V AC ATK BY OWN FRCES	1.	HIGH	8.	0 OR N/A
9-1	PC OF INDUSTRIAL CAPACITY LOST	1.	0.001-1.0	1.	0.001-1.0
9-3	TOTAL NO. CIVN POPULATION LOST	1.	1.0-1.0	1.	1.0-1.0
9-8	CASUALTY RATE FOR OWN FORCES	1.	1.0-2.0	1.	1.0-2.0
9-10	CASUALTY RATE FOR ALL FORCES	1.	1.0-2.0	1.	1.0-2.0
9-11	ATTRITION RATE FOR OWN FORCES	1.	1.0-2.0	1.	1.0-2.0
9-13	ATTRITION RATE FOR ALL FORCES	1.	1.0-2.0	1.	1.0-2.0

Species Type C4
("the prospect of compromise not yet foreclosed")

The factor pattern derives from

Cyprus: internal (Cypriot government vs. Turkish Cypriots)

Indonesia: independence (Indonesian insurgents vs. Dutch colonial administration)

Item		Compound Response		
1-2A	TOPOGRAPHY OF CONFLICT AREA	1.	FLAT	1.	FLAT
1-11	DISPUTE HAS BEEN TO REG'L ORGN	2.	NO	2.	NO
2-5	RACIAL HOMOGENEITY OF GENL POP	1.	HOMOGENEOUS	1.	HOMOGENEOUS
2-13	POPN UNDER EFFECTIVE CONTROL	3.	499.0-65TH	8.	0 OR N/A
3-2	GROSS NAT'L. OR ECON. PRODUCT	3.	90.0-6.4TH	8.	0 OR N/A
3-6	PC OF GNP IN AGRICULTURE	3.	25.0-75.0	8.	0 OR N/A
3-8	PRODUCTION OF STEEL	1.	1.0-1.0	1.	1.0-1.0
3-14	GOVERNMENT INCOME AS PC OF GNP	3.	10.0-50.0	8.	0 OR N/A
3-15	GOVT. SPENDING AS PC OF GNP	3.	6.0-50.0	8.	0 OR N/A
3-16	SOC WELFARE SPENDING AS PC GNP	3.	1.7-5.0	8.	0 OR N/A
3-20	AGRIC EMPLOYMENT AS PC OF POPN	3.	13.0-70.0	8.	0 OR N/A
5-3	INTEREST INVOLVED-IDEOLOGY	2.	NO	2.	NO
5-7	INTEREST INVOLVED-PRESTIGE	2.	NO	2.	NO
5-9	INTEREST INVOLVED-POWER	1.	YES	2.	NO
5-13	COMMITMENT TO STATED GOALS	2.	FLEXIBLE	1.	TOTAL
5-14	DISPUTE IS REGARDED AS CRUSADE	2.	NO	2.	NO
5-18	CAN ACCEPT LES THN STATED DMDS	1.	YES	1.	YES
5-22	POST-DISPUTE EXPECT'N OF REGIM	2.	PESSIMISTIC	2.	PESSIMISTIC
5-23	DIST FM BORDER TO CONFL AREA	1.	1.0-1.0	1.	1.0-1.0
5-24	DIST FM CAPITAL TO CONFL AREA	1.	1.0-1.3	1.	1.0-1.3
5-28	RELIABILITY OF COMMUNICATIONS	2.	LOW	2.	LOW

Item		Compound Response			
5-29	CREDIBILITY OF COMMUNICATIONS	2.	LOW	2.	LOW
5-31	OFFERED TO RESOLVE CONST'ALLY	2.	NO	2.	NO
5-32	BROUGHT DISPUTE TO INT'L ORGN	2.	NO	2.	NO
5-34	HAS SOUGHT A NEGOT. SETTLEMENT	2.	NO	2.	NO
5-35	HAS OFFERED BI-LATERAL NEGOTNS	2.	NO	2.	NO
5-37	ESC LIKELY BRING GP AID TO ADV	2.	NO	2.	NO
5-44	APPLIES OWN LEGAL STDS TO ADV.	1.	YES	2.	NO
6-1	IS SEC'TY ALLY OF GREAT POWER	2.	NO	2.	NO
6-3	IS ALLY OF G.P. HOSTILE TO ADV	2.	NO	2.	NO
6-4	IS ALLY OF G.P. ALLIED TO ADV.	2.	NO	2.	NO
6-5	IS AIDED BY GP HOSTILE TO ADV.	2.	NO	2.	NO
6-6	A GP IS OPENLY PARTIAL TO ANT.	2.	NO	2.	NO
6-7	GP AID PROMISED IF ESC. OCCURS	2.	NO	2.	NO
6-11	HAS ASKED AN INT'L. ORG'N. IN	2.	NO	2.	NO
6-13	INT'L ORG IS INV. ON THIS SIDE	2.	NO	2.	NO
6-14	REG'L ORG IS INV. ON THIS SIDE	2.	NO	2.	NO
6-15	A G.P. IS INV. ON THIS SIDE	2.	NO	2.	NO
6-16	A NON-GP IS INV. ON THIS SIDE	2.	NO	1.	YES
6-17	A AUT ORG IS INV. ON THIS SIDE	2.	NO	2.	NO
6-20	A 3PTY IS PROVIDING MIL ADVICE	2.	NO	1.	YES
6-21	A 3PTY IS PROVIDING MIL HDWRE.	2.	NO	1.	YES
6-23	A 3PTY IS PROVIDING GUER FORCE	2.	NO	2.	NO
6-30	SOME 3PTY OFFERED TO ARBITRATE	2.	NO	2.	NO
6-31	INTL ORGN OFFERED TO ARBITRATE	2.	NO	2.	NO
6-32	REGL ORGN OFFERED TO ARBITRATE	2.	NO	2.	NO
6-33	A G.P. OFFERED TO ARBITRATE	2.	NO	2.	NO
6-35	INT'L ORG'N UPHELD ANT'S CAUSE	2.	NO	2.	NO
6-36	INTL ORGN INDICTED ANT'S CAUSE	2.	NO	2.	NO
6-37	CITED IN VIOLATION OF INTL LAW	2.	NO	2.	NO
6-38	CITED BY I.O. FOR AGGRESSION	2.	NO	2.	NO
6-40	ACCEPTED IO'S PROP. CEASEFIRE	2.	NO	2.	NO
6-42	I.O. HAS IMPOSED SANCTIONS	2.	NO	2.	NO
6-47	REG ORGN HAS IMPOSED SANCTIONS	2.	NO	2.	NO
7-1	NO. OF OWN ACTIVE MIL. TROOPS	1.	0.02-10.7	1.	0.02-10.7
7-6	NO. TROOPS COMM AS PC TOT FRCS	1.	0.7-1.0	1.	0.7-1.0
7-7	PC POPN MOB'ZED FOR ACTIV DUTY	1.	0.001-1.0	8.	0 OR N/A
7-8	OTHER SIGNIF INTERNAL THREAT	2.	NO	2.	NO
7-9	OTHER SIGNIF EXTERNAL THREAT	2.	NO	2.	NO
7-15	OWN TRPS AS PC OF ALL COMMITED	1.	1.0-1.5	1.	1.0-1.5
7-26	NO. MED. CANNON AVAILABLE	1.	1.0-1.0	1.	1.0-1.0
7-27	NO. HVY. CANNON AVAILABLE	1.	1.0-1.0	1.	1.0-1.0
7-30	NO. BOMBER A/C AVAILABLE	1.	1.0-1.5	1.	1.0-1.5
7-31	NO. TRANSPORT A/C AVAILABLE	1.	1.0-1.1	1.	1.0-1.1
7-32	NO. JET AIRCRAFT AVAILABLE	1.	1.0-1.1	1.	1.0-1.1
7-33	NO. HELICOPTERS AVAILABLE	1.	1.0-1.0	1.	1.0-1.0
7-34	NO. SAM'S AVAILABLE	1.	1.0-1.0	1.	1.0-1.0
7-35	NO. SSM'S AVAILABLE	1.	1.0-1.0	1.	1.0-1.0
7-36	NO. SUBMARINES AVAILABLE	1.	1.0-1.0	1.	1.0-1.0
7-37	NO. HEAVY VESSELS AVAILABLE	1.	1.0-1.0	1.	1.0-1.0
7-38	NO. LANDING CRAFT AVAILABLE	1.	1.0-1.1	1.	1.0-1.1
7-39	NO. PATROL BOATS AVAILABLE	3.	5.0-37.0	8.	0 OR N/A
7-42	DEP. FOR BATTLEFIELD ARMAMENTS	4.	NONE	1.	EXCLUSIVE
7-51	SPARE PARTS AND AMMUNITION AID	8.	0 OR N/A	1.	ADEQ'IATE
7-53	PC TOTAL COSTS COMING FM 3PTY	8.	0 OR N/A	3.	8.0-100.0
8-7	METHOD OF MILITARY RECRUITMENT	1.	VOLUNTARY	1.	VOLUNTARY
8-16	OVERALL MIL. HARDWARE BALANCE	3.	UNFAVORABLE	1.	FAVORABLE
9-1	PC OF INDUSTRIAL CAPACITY LOST	1.	0.001-1.0	1.	0.001-1.0
9-2	PC OF CIVILIAN POPULATION LOST	1.	0.003-1.0	1.	0.003-1.0
9-3	TOTAL NO. CIVN POPULATION LOST	1.	1.0-1.0	1.	1.0-1.0
9-5	TOTAL CAS'TIES TO OWN FORCES	1.	1.0-1.2	1.	1.0-1.2
9-7	TOTAL CAS'TIES TO ALL FORCES	1.	1.0-1.2	1.	1.0-1.2
9-8	CASUALTY RATE FOR OWN FORCES	1.	1.0-2.0	1.	1.0-2.0
9-10	CASUALTY RATE FOR ALL FORCES	1.	1.0-2.0	1.	1.0-2.0
9-11	ATTRITION RATE FOR OWN FORCES	1.	1.0-2.0	1.	1.0-2.0
9-13	ATTRITION RATE FOR ALL FORCES	1.	1.0-2.0	1.	1.0-2.0

Species Type C5
("present commitments bid fair an acceptable outcome")

The factor pattern derives from

India-China (India vs. China)

Indonesia-Malaysia (Malaysia vs. Indonesia)

The adjunct is

Israel-Egypt

1-1	GEOGRAPHIC LOCUS OF DISPUTE	6.	ASIA	6.	ASIA
1-3	PAST POL. REL'SHIP BETW PARTYS	2.	COMPETITIVE	2.	COMPETITIVE
1-4	PAST MIL. REL'SHIP BETW PARTYS	1.	PEACEFUL	1.	PEACEFUL
1-5	EFFECTIVE NATURE OF DISPUTE	2.	INTERSTATE	2.	INTERSTATE
1-8	CONTROL OF REAL ESTATE INVOLVD	1.	YES	1.	YES
1-11	DISPUTE HAS BEEN TO REG'L ORGN	2.	NO	2.	NO
1-12	DISPUTE HAS BEEN TO INT'L ORGN	2.	NO	2.	NO
2-4	REGIM + GENL POPN OF SAME RACE	1.	YES	1.	YES
2-12	AREA UNDER EFFECTIVE CONTROL	1.	1.0-2.1	2.	2.7-9.6
2-15	PC OF ANT'S CLMD AREA INVOLVED	2.	1.6-6.7	1.	1.0-1.0
2-19	URBANIZATION	2.	MEDIUM	2.	MEDIUM
3-5	PER CAPITA INCOME	1.	1.0-2.1	1.	1.0-2.1
3-6	PC OF GNP IN AGRICULTURE	1.	1.0-2.0	1.	1.0-2.0
3-20	AGRIC EMPLOYMENT AS PC OF POPN	1.	1.0-1.2	1.	1.0-1.2
3-21	INDUSTRIAL EMPL. AS PC OF POPN	2.	1.5-5.0	1.	1.0-1.1
3-27	NO. AIRPORTS CONTROLLED	2.	1.5-15.0	8.	0 OR N/A
3-28	NO. JETPORTS CONTROLLED	1.	1.0-1.0	1.	1.0-1.0

Item		Compound Response	
4-1	EFFECTIVE STATUS OF GOVERNMENT	1. INDEP GOVT	1. INDEP GOVT
4-6	STATUS OF EXECUTIVE	2. STRONG	1. DOMINANT
4-10	REGIME CAME TO POWER CONST'LY	1. YES	2. NO
4-11	RECRUITMENT TO POL LEADERSHIP	3. NON-ELITIST	2. MODERATE
4-12	IDEOL. ORIENTATION OF REGIME	2. MODERATE	1. LEFT-WING
4-13	INTERNAL POLICIES OF REGIME	2. MODERATE	3. REVOL'ARY
4-14	INTERNATIONAL POLICY OF REGIME	3. MODERATE	1. LEFTIST
4-17	MOBILIZATIONAL STYLE OF REGIME	1. FULL	1. FULL
4-21	INTEREST ARTIC'N BY ANOMIC GPS	1. FREQUENT	3. NOT TOLERATD
4-28	PC OF POPN VOTING IN ELECTIONS	1. 1.0-1.0	2. 1.2-2.0
4-30	PC VOTE RECD BY LT WING PTIES	1. 1.0-1.0	2. 2.5-6.7
4-32	RECENT LEADERSHIP CRISIS	2. NO	2. NO
4-33	RECENT CHANGE IN LEADERSHIP	2. NO	2. NO
4-34	FORN RES ARE MAINSTAY OF REGIM	2. NO	2. NO
4-35	REGIM APPEARS MAINT BY FOR RES	2. NO	2. NO
4-36	POP. SUPPORT FOR REGIME'S OBJ.	1. HIGH	1. HIGH
4-37	POP. SUPPORT FOR REGIM'S POLS.	1. HIGH	1. HIGH
4-38	ATT. OF INTELLECTUALS TO REGIM	1. FAVORABLE	1. FAVORABLE
5-1	RECENTLY INVOLVED IN OTHER WAR	1. YES	1. YES
5-3	INTEREST INVOLVED-IDEOLOGY	2. NO	2. NO
5-4	INTEREST INVOLVED-COMMITMENTS	2. NO	2. NC
5-7	INTEREST INVOLVED-PRESTIGE	2. NO	1. YES
5-9	INTEREST INVOLVED-POWER	2. NO	1. YES
5-12	INTEREST INVOLVED-CONT'D EXIS.	2. NO	2. NO
5-15	CONDUCT OF CONFLICT IS LIMITED	1. YES	1. YES
5-16	PC OF AVAIL MIL FRCS COMMITTED	1. 0 -10 PC	1. 0 -10 PC
5-21	LIKELY OUTCOME IS NOW OBVIOUS	2. NO	2. NO
5-23	DIST FM BORDER TO CONFL AREA	1. 1.0-1.0	1. 1.0-1.0
5-28	RELIABILITY OF COMMUNICATIONS	1. HIGH	1. HIGH
5-30	PRINCIPAL ATTEMPTS AT RESOL'N	4. POLITICAL	4. POLITICAL
5-32	BROUGHT DISPUTE TO INT'L ORGN	2. NO	2. NO
5-37	ESC LIKELY BRING GP AID TO ADV	2. NO	2. NO
5-38	P.O. RE ADV'S POL. INST'NS.	2. UNFAVORABLE	2. UNFAVORABLE
5-39	P.O. RE ADV'S SOCIAL INST'NS.	2. UNFAVORABLE	2. UNFAVORABLE
5-43	STATE OF WAR HAS BEEN DECLARED	2. NO	2. NO
6-3	IS ALLY OF G.P. HOSTILE TO ADV	1. YES	2. NO
6-4	IS ALLY OF G.P. ALLIED TO ADV.	2. NO	2. NO
6-11	HAS ASKED AN INT'L. ORG'N. IN	2. NO	2. NO
6-13	INT'L ORG IS INV. ON THIS SIDE	2. NO	2. NO
6-14	REG'L ORG IS INV. ON THIS SIDE	2. NO	2. NO
6-17	A AUT ORG IS INV. ON THIS SIDE	2. NO	2. NO
6-19	A 3PTY IS PROVIDING ECON. AID	1. YES	1. YES
6-21	A 3PTY IS PROVIDING MIL HDWRE.	1. YES	1. YES
6-23	A 3PTY IS PROVIDING GUER FORCE	2. NO	2. NO
6-24	ATT. OF 3PTY PUBLIC TO INV'MNT	1. FAVORABLE	1. FAVORABLE
6-24A	TYPE OF GOVERNMENT OF 3RD PTY.	1. POL. DEMOC.	3. TOTAL OLIG
6-24C	INTERNAL POLICIES OF 3PTY GOVT	3. CONSERVATIVE	3. CONSERVATIVE
6-25	AID TO ANT. HURTS 3PTY ECONOMY	2. NO	2. NO
6-27	PC ANT'S EXPORTS CONS. BY 3PTY	3. 16-33 PC	1. 0 - 4 PC
6-29	I.O. PEACE MACHINERY IS SEEN	2. IRRELEVANT	2. IRRELEVANT
6-30	SOME 3PTY OFFERED TO ARBITRATE	2. NO	2. NO
6-31	INTL ORGN OFFERED TO ARBITRATE	2. NO	2. NO
6-32	REGL ORGN OFFERED TO ARBITRATE	2. NO	2. NO
6-33	A G.P. OFFERED TO ARBITRATE	2. NO	2. NO
6-35	INT'L ORG'N UPHELD ANT'S CAUSE	2. NO	2. NO
6-36	INTL ORGN INDICTED ANT'S CAUSE	2. NO	2. NO
6-37	CITED IN VIOLATION OF INTL LAW	2. NO	2. NO
6-38	CITED BY I.O. FOR AGGRESSION	2. NO	2. NO
6-40	ACCEPTED IO'S PROP. CEASEFIRE	2. NO	2. NC
6-42	I.O. HAS IMPOSED SANCTIONS	2. NO	2. NC
6-47	REG ORGN HAS IMPOSED SANCTIONS	2. NO	2. NO
7-2	NO. ACTIV TROOPS AS PC OF POPN	1. 0.001-1.0	2. 1.3-174.0
7-4	MOBILIZATION OF RESERVES	1. NONE	1. NONE
7-6	NO. TROOPS COMM AS PC TOT FRCS	1. 0.7-1.0	1. 0.7-1.0
7-7	PC POPN MOB'ZED FOR ACTIV DUTY	1. 0.001-1.0	1. 0.001-1.0
7-13	3PTY TROOP AID SEEN LIKELY TO	2. STAY SAME	2. STAY SAME
7-14	TOTAL MANPOWER COMMITTED	1. 0.02-7.3	1. 0.02-7.3
7-17	GUERRILLA MANPOWER COMMITTED	1. 0.02-1.0	1. 0.02-1.0
7-18	NAVAL MANPOWER COMMITTED	1. 0.5-1.0	1. 0.5-1.0
7-19	AIR FORCE MANPOWER COMMITTED	1. 0.05-1.0	1. 0.05-1.0
7-21	NO. RIFLES AVAILABLE	1. 0.05-2.1	2. 3.0-85.7
7-40	HAS A NUCLEAR CAPABILITY	2. NO	3. IN DEV'MENT
7-43	BATTLE ARMS SUPPLY LIKELY TO	2. STAY SAME	2. STAY SAME
7-44	DEPENDENCE FOR NAVAL ARMAMENTS	1. EXCLUSIVE	1. EXCLUSIVE
7-45	NAVAL ARMS SUPPLY LIKELY TO	2. STAY SAME	2. STAY SAME
7-49	TRANSP. CAP. SUPPLY LIKELY TO	2. STAY SAME	2. STAY SAME
7-50	OVERTNESS OF 3PTY HARDWARE AID	1. GEN'LY OVERT	1. GEN'LY OVERT
7-51	SPARE PARTS AND AMMUNITION AID	1. ADEQUATE	1. ADEQUATE
8-3	REL'SHIP BET POL + MIL LEADERS	1. POL DOMINANT	1. POL DOMINANT
8-7	METHOD OF MILITARY RECRUITMENT	1. VOLUNTARY	1. VOLUNTARY
8-9	TRAINING FACILITY FOR OFFICERS	1. GOOD	1. GOOD
8-11	TRAINING FAC FOR ENLISTED PERS	1. GOOD	2. FAIR
8-20	USE OF TERROR BY THIS ANT. IS	3. ABSENT	3. ABSENT
8-28	INTELL. AMONG POP IN CONF AREA	1. EFFECTIVE	2. OCCASIONAL
8-30	SYMPATHY BETW POPN + OWN MIL.	1. SYMPATHETIC	1. SYMPATHETIC
9-1	PC OF INDUSTRIAL CAPACITY LOST	1. 0.001-1.0	1. 0.001-1.0
9-2	PC OF CIVILIAN POPULATION LOST	1. 0.003-1.0	1. 0.003-1.0
9-3	TOTAL NO. CIVN POPULATION LOST	1. 1.0-1.0	1. 1.0-1.0
9-4	ATTRITION RATE FOR CIV'N POPN	1. 0.5-1.0	1. 0.5-1.0

Species Type C6
("reason and stability precede the
intrusion of ideology")

The factor pattern derives from

Algeria-Morocco (Morocco vs.
Algeria)

Ethiopia-Somalia (Somalia vs.
Ethiopia)

Item		Compound Response		
1-1	GEOGRAPHIC LOCUS OF DISPUTE	4.	MIDDLE EAST	4. MIDDLE EAST
1-2A	TOPOGRAPHY OF CONFLICT AREA	1.	FLAT	1. FLAT
1-2B	CLIMATE IN THE CONFLICT AREA	1.	DRY	1. DRY
1-7	IDEOLOGICAL DIFF. BETW PARTIES	2.	MILD	2. MILD
1-8	CONTROL OF REAL ESTATE INVOLVD	1.	YES	1. YES
1-11	DISPUTE HAS BEEN TO REG'L ORGN	2.	NO	2. NO
2-4	REGIM + GENL POPN OF SAME RACE	1.	YES	1. YES
2-9	LITERACY RATE AMONG GENL POPN	3.	LOW	3. LOW
2-15	PC OF ANT'S CLMD AREA INVOLVED	2.	1.6-6.7	1. 1.0-1.0
2-17	PC OF INVOLVED AREA IN CONTROL	8.	0 GR N/A	3. 24.0-100.0
2-18	PC OF INVOLVED POPN IN CONTROL	8.	0 GR N/A	3. 9.0-100.0
3-5	PER CAPITA INCOME	1.	1.0-2.1	1. 1.0-2.1
3-7	PC OF GNP IN DURABLE GOODS	1.	1.0-1.2	1. 1.0-1.2
3-8	PRODUCTION OF STEEL	1.	1.0-1.0	1. 1.0-1.0
3-27	NO. AIRPORTS CONTROLLED	1.	1.0-1.0	2. 1.5-15.0
4-1	EFFECTIVE STATUS OF GOVERNMENT	1.	INDEP GOVT	1. INDEP GOVT
4-23	INTEREST ARTIC'N BY INST'L GPS	1.	POL SIGNIF	1. POL SIGNIF
4-24	INTEREST ARTIC'N BY POL PARTYS	1.	POL SIGNIF	2. POL INSIGNIF
4-34	FORN RES ARE MAINSTAY OF REGIM	2.	NO	2. NO
4-35	REGIM APPEARS MAINT BY FOR RES	2.	NO	2. NO
4-36	POP. SUPPORT FOR REGIME'S OBJ.	1.	HIGH	1. HIGH
4-37	POP. SUPPORT FOR REGIM'S POLS.	1.	HIGH	1. HIGH
4-38	ATT. OF INTELLECTUALS TO REGIM	1.	FAVORABLE	1. FAVORABLE
4-39	POST-DISPUTE EXPECT'N OF POPN	2.	PESSIMISTIC	2. PESSIMISTIC
5-2	REGIME SEEKS OVERTHROW OF ADV.	2.	NO	2. NO
5-4	INTEREST INVOLVED-COMMITMENTS	1.	YES	1. YES
5-5	INTEREST INVOLVED-EST. POLICY	1.	YES	1. YES
5-9	INTEREST INVOLVED-POWER	1.	YES	2. NO
5-12	INTEREST INVOLVED-CONT'D EXIS.	2.	NO	2. NO
5-13	COMMITMENT TO STATED GOALS	2.	FLEXIBLE	2. FLEXIBLE
5-15	CONDUCT OF CONFLICT IS LIMITED	1.	YES	1. YES
5-16	PC OF AVAIL MIL FRCS COMMITTED	1.	0 -10 PC	1. 0 -10 PC
5-19	PRESENT OUTLOOK WRT DISPUTE	2.	MODERATE	2. MODERATE
5-23	DIST FM BORDER TO CONFL AREA	1.	1.0-1.0	1. 1.0-1.0
5-25	ADVERSARY APPEARS TO ANT TO BE	2.	AUT + INDEP.	2. AUT + INDEP.
5-28	RELIABILITY OF COMMUNICATIONS	1.	HIGH	1. HIGH
5-29	CREDIBILITY OF COMMUNICATIONS	1.	HIGH	1. HIGH
5-37	ESC LIKELY BRING GP AID TO ADV	2.	NO	2. NO
5-42	MARTIAL LAW IS IN EFFECT	2.	NO	2. NO
5-43	STATE OF WAR HAS BEEN DECLARED	2.	NO	2. NO
5-45	LEGAL STATUS OF ADV. PERSONNEL	1.	CITIZEN	1. CITIZEN
6-1	IS SEC'TY ALLY OF GREAT POWER	2.	NO	2. NO
6-3	IS ALLY OF G.P. HOSTILE TO ADV	2.	NO	2. NO
6-4	IS ALLY OF G.P. ALLIED TO ADV.	2.	NO	2. NO
6-5	IS AIDED BY GP HOSTILE TO ADV.	2.	NO	2. NO
6-6	A GP IS OPENLY PARTIAL TO ANT.	2.	NO	2. NO
6-7	GP AID PROMISED IF ESC. OCCURS	2.	NO	2. NO
6-10	HAS ASKED A REGIONAL ORG'N IN	2.	NO	2. NO
6-11	HAS ASKED AN INT'L. ORG'N. IN	2.	NO	2. NO
6-12	SOME 3PTY IS INV. ON THIS SIDE	2.	NO	2. NO
6-13	INT'L ORG IS INV. ON THIS SIDE	2.	NO	2. NO
6-14	REG'L ORG IS INV. ON THIS SIDE	2.	NO	2. NO
6-15	A G.P. IS INV. ON THIS SIDE	2.	NO	2. NO
6-16	A NON-GP IS INV. ON THIS SIDE	2.	NO	2. NO
6-17	A AUT ORG IS INV. ON THIS SIDE	2.	NO	2. NO
6-18	A 3PTY IS PROVIDING POL. AID	2.	NO	2. NO
6-19	A 3PTY IS PROVIDING ECON. AID	2.	NO	2. NO
6-20	A 3PTY IS PROVIDING MIL ADVICE	2.	NO	2. NO
6-21	A 3PTY IS PROVIDING MIL HDWRE.	2.	NO	2. NO
6-22	A 3PTY IS PROVIDING CONV FORCE	2.	NO	2. NO
6-23	A 3PTY IS PROVIDING GUER FORCE	2.	NO	2. NO
6-30	SOME 3PTY OFFERED TO ARBITRATE	1.	YES	1. YES
6-32	REGL ORGN OFFERED TO ARBITRATE	2.	NO	2. NO
6-33	A G.P. OFFERED TO ARBITRATE	2.	NO	2. NO
6-35	INT'L ORG'N UPHELD ANT'S CAUSE	2.	NO	2. NO
6-36	INT'L ORGN INDICTED ANT'S CAUSE	2.	NO	2. NO
6-37	CITED IN VIOLATION OF INT'L LAW	2.	NO	2. NO
6-38	CITED BY I.O. FOR AGGRESSION	2.	NO	2. NO
6-40	ACCEPTED IO'S PROP. CEASEFIRE	2.	NO	2. NO
6-42	I.O. HAS IMPOSED SANCTIONS	2.	NO	2. NO
6-47	REG ORGN HAS IMPOSED SANCTIONS	2.	NO	2. NO
7-2	NO. ACTIV TROOPS AS PC OF POPN	1.	0.001-1.0	2. 1.3-174.0
7-7	PC POPN MOB'ZED FOR ACTIV DUTY	1.	0.001-1.0	1. 0.001-1.0
7-9	OTHER SIGNIF EXTERNAL THREAT	2.	NO	2. NO
7-11	TOTAL TROOPS GIVEN BY 3RD PTY	1.	0.3-1.0	1. 0.3-1.0
7-13	3PTY TROOP AID SEEN LIKELY TO	2.	STAY SAME	2. STAY SAME
7-17	GUERRILLA MANPOWER COMMITTED	1.	0.02-1.0	1. 0.02-1.0
7-18	NAVAL MANPOWER COMMITTED	1.	0.5-1.0	1. 0.5-1.0
7-32	NO. JET AIRCRAFT AVAILABLE	1.	1.0-1.1	2. 1.4-7.5
7-34	NO. SAM'S AVAILABLE	1.	1.0-1.0	1. 1.0-1.0
7-35	NO. SSM'S AVAILABLE	1.	1.0-1.0	1. 1.0-1.0
7-36	NO. SUBMARINES AVAILABLE	1.	1.0-1.0	1. 1.0-1.0
7-40	HAS A NUCLEAR CAPABILITY	2.	NO	2. NO
7-41	AIDING 3PTY HAS NUCLEAR CAP'TY	2.	NO	2. NO
7-43	BATTLE ARMS SUPPLY LIKELY TO	2.	STAY SAME	2. STAY SAME
7-46	DEP. FOR AIR COMBAT ARMAMENTS	1.	EXCLUSIVE	1. EXCLUSIVE
7-47	AIR ARMAMENT SUPPLY LIKELY TO	2.	STAY SAME	2. STAY SAME
7-49	TRANSP. CAP. SUPPLY LIKELY TO	2.	STAY SAME	2. STAY SAME

Item		Compound Response			
8-1	POLITICAL CHARACTER OF MILTARY	2.	SUPPORTIVE	1.	INTERVENTIVE
8-4	UNITY WITHIN MILITARY COMMAND	1.	UNIFIED	2.	FACTIONAL
8-7	METHOD OF MILITARY RECRUITMENT	1.	VOLUNTARY	1.	VOLUNTARY
8-9	TRAINING FACILITY FOR OFFICERS	1.	GOOD	1.	GOOD
8-13	OVERALL MILITARY ORG'N BALANCE	2.	EVEN	2.	EVEN
8-29	INTELL. IN ADV'S POLICY ORGANS	3.	INEFFECTIVE	3.	INEFFECTIVE
8-30	SYMPATHY BETW POPN + OWN MIL.	1.	SYMPATHETIC	1.	SYMPATHETIC
8-32	CIVN SECURITY V. CONV. ATTACK	1.	HIGH	1.	HIGH
8-34	CIVN SEC V AC ATK BY OWN FRCES	1.	HIGH	1.	HIGH
9-1	PC OF INDUSTRIAL CAPACITY LOST	1.	0.001-1.0	1.	0.001-1.0
9-2	PC OF CIVILIAN POPULATION LOST	1.	0.003-1.0	1.	0.003-1.0
9-3	TOTAL NO. CIVN POPULATION LOST	1.	1.0-1.0	1.	1.0-1.0
9-4	ATTRITION RATE FOR CIV'N POPN	1.	0.5-1.0	1.	0.5-1.0

Species Type C7
("no threat to survival is yet discerned")

The factor pattern derives from
Kashmir (Pakistan vs. India)
USSR-Iran (Iran vs. USSR)

Item					
1-2A	TOPOGRAPHY OF CONFLICT AREA	2.	MOUNTAINOUS	2.	MOUNTAINOUS
1-3	PAST POL. REL'SHIP BETW PARTYS	2.	COMPETITIVE	2.	COMPETITIVE
1-4	PAST MIL. REL'SHIP BETW PARTYS	2.	RANDOM HOST.	2.	RANDOM HOST.
1-7	IDEOLOGICAL DIFF. BETW PARTIES	1.	EXTREME	1.	EXTREME
1-8	CONTROL OF REAL ESTATE INVOLVD	1.	YES	1.	YES
1-10	SIZE OF POPN AT STAKE (THOUS.)	2.	1.0TH-4.0TH	2.	1.0TH-4.0TH
1-11	DISPUTE HAS BEEN TO REG'L ORGN	2.	NO	2.	NO
1-12	DISPUTE HAS BEEN TO INT'L ORGN	2.	NO	2.	NO
2-3	RACIAL GROUPING OF ANTAGONIST	1.	WHITE	1.	WHITE
2-4	REGIM + GENL POPN OF SAME RACE	1.	YES	1.	YES
2-13	POPN UNDER EFFECTIVE CONTROL	1.	1.0-2.0	2.	3.2-52.2
2-16	PC OF ANT'S CLMD POPN INVOLVED	2.	2.0-13.0	1.	1.0-1.0
3-2	GROSS NAT'L. OR ECON. PRODUCT	1.	1.0-1.5	2.	2.2-24.0
3-5	PER CAPITA INCOME	1.	1.0-2.1	1.	1.0-2.1
3-6	PC OF GNP IN AGRICULTURE	1.	1.0-2.0	1.	1.0-2.0
3-7	PC OF GNP IN DURABLE GOODS	1.	1.0-1.2	2.	1.7-4.0
3-10	TOTAL FOREIGN AID RECEIVED	1.	1.0-1.0	1.	1.0-1.0
3-11	FOREIGN ECONOMIC AID RECEIVED	1.	1.0-1.0	1.	1.0-1.0
3-12	FOR AID AS PC OF GNP + FOR AID	1.	0.01-1.0	1.	0.01-1.0
3-13	PROGRESSIVE TAX STRUCTURE	2.	NO	2.	NO
4-1	EFFECTIVE STATUS OF GOVERNMENT	1.	INDEP GOVT	1.	INDEP GOVT
4-14	INTERNATIONAL POLICY OF REGIME	3.	MODERATE	1.	LEFTIST
4-16	LEADERSHIP CHARISMA	1.	PRONOUNCED	1.	PRONOUNCED
4-18	POL. INTEGRATION OF GENL POPN	2.	MODERATE	2.	MODERATE
4-32	RECENT LEADERSHIP CRISIS	2.	NO	2.	NO
4-33	RECENT CHANGE IN LEADERSHIP	2.	NO	2.	NO
4-34	FORN RES ARE MAINSTAY OF REGIM	2.	NO	2.	NO
4-35	REGIM APPEARS MAINT BY FOR RES	2.	NO	2.	NO
4-36	POP. SUPPORT FOR REGIME'S OBJ.	1.	HIGH	1.	HIGH
4-37	POP. SUPPORT FOR REGIM'S POLS.	1.	HIGH	1.	HIGH
4-38	ATT. OF INTELLECTUALS TO REGIM	1.	FAVORABLE	1.	FAVORABLE
5-2	REGIME SEEKS OVERTHROW OF ADV.	2.	NO	2.	NO
5-4	INTEREST INVOLVED-COMMITMENTS	2.	NO	2.	NO
5-6	INTEREST INVOLVED-NAT'L CHAR.	1.	YES	2.	NO
5-10	INTEREST INVOLVED-INDEPENDENCE	1.	YES	2.	NO
5-11	INTEREST INVOLVED-TERR. INTEG.	1.	YES	2.	NO
5-12	INTEREST INVOLVED-CONT'D EXIS.	2.	NO	2.	NO
5-13	COMMITMENT TO STATED GOALS	2.	FLEXIBLE	3.	SLIGHT
5-15	CONDUCT OF CONFLICT IS LIMITED	1.	YES	1.	YES
5-25	ADVERSARY APPEARS TO ANT TO BE	2.	AUT + INDEP.	2.	AUT + INDEP.
5-27	SPEED OF COMMUNICATIONS	1.	RAPID	1.	RAPID
5-29	CREDIBILITY OF COMMUNICATIONS	1.	HIGH	1.	HIGH
5-32	BROUGHT DISPUTE TO INT'L ORGN	2.	NO	2.	NO
5-37	ESC LIKELY BRING GP AID TO ADV	2.	NO	2.	NO
5-38	P.O. RE ADV'S POL. INST'NS.	2.	UNFAVORABLE	2.	UNFAVORABLE
5-39	P.O. RE ADV'S SOCIAL INST'NS.	2.	UNFAVORABLE	2.	UNFAVORABLE
5-41	P.O. RE ADV'S REL. INST'NS.	2.	UNFAVORABLE	2.	UNFAVORABLE
5-43	STATE OF WAR HAS BEEN DECLARED	2.	NO	2.	NO
5-45	LEGAL STATUS OF ADV. PERSONNEL	1.	CITIZEN	1.	CITIZEN
6-1	IS SEC'TY ALLY OF GREAT POWER	2.	NO	2.	NO
6-2	IS SEC'TY ALLY OF NON-G.P.	2.	NO	2.	NO
6-3	IS ALLY OF G.P. HOSTILE TO ADV	2.	NO	2.	NO
6-4	IS ALLY OF G.P. ALLIED TO ADV.	2.	NO	2.	NO
6-5	IS AIDED BY GP HOSTILE TO ADV.	2.	NO	2.	NO
6-6	A GP IS OPENLY PARTIAL TO ANT.	2.	NO	2.	NO
6-7	GP AID PROMISED IF ESC. OCCURS	2.	NO	2.	NO
6-11	HAS ASKED AN INT'L. ORG'N. IN	2.	NO	2.	NO
6-13	INT'L ORG IS INV. ON THIS SIDE	2.	NO	2.	NO
6-14	REG'L ORG IS INV. ON THIS SIDE	2.	NO	2.	NO
6-15	A G.P. IS INV. ON THIS SIDE	2.	NO	2.	NO
6-16	A NON-GP IS INV. ON THIS SIDE	2.	NO	2.	NO
6-18	A 3PTY IS PROVIDING POL. AID	2.	NO	2.	NO
6-29	I.O. PEACE MACHINERY IS SEEN	2.	IRRELEVANT	2.	IRRELEVANT
6-31	INTL ORGN OFFERED TO ARBITRATE	2.	NO	2.	NO
6-32	REGL ORGN OFFERED TO ARBITRATE	2.	NO	2.	NO
6-33	A G.P. OFFERED TO ARBITRATE	2.	NO	2.	NO
6-35	INT'L ORG'N UPHELD ANT'S CAUSE	2.	NO	2.	NO
6-36	INTL ORGN INDICTED ANT'S CAUSE	2.	NO	2.	NO
6-37	CITED IN VIOLATION OF INTL LAW	2.	NO	2.	NO
6-38	CITED BY I.O. FOR AGGRESSION	2.	NO	2.	YES
6-40	ACCEPTED IO'S PROP. CEASEFIRE	2.	NO	2.	NO
6-42	I.O. HAS IMPOSED SANCTIONS	2.	NO	2.	NO
6-47	REG ORGN HAS IMPOSED SANCTIONS	2.	NO	2.	NO

Item		Compound Response			
7-10	PC OF TRPS ALLOC TO OTHER THRT	1.	1.0-1.4	2.	2.0-10.0
7-14	TOTAL MANPOWER COMMITTED	1.	0.02-7.3	1.	0.02-7.3
7-15	OWN TRPS AS PC OF ALL COMMITED	1.	1.0-1.5	1.	1.0-1.5
7-16	CONVENTIONAL MANPWER COMMITTED	1.	0.01-3.0	1.	0.01-3.0
7-17	GUERRILLA MANPOWER COMMITTED	1.	0.02-1.0	1.	0.02-1.0
7-18	NAVAL MANPOWER COMMITTED	1.	0.5-1.0	1.	0.5-1.0
8-4	UNITY WITHIN MILITARY COMMAND	1.	UNIFIED	1.	UNIFIED
8-11	TRAINING FAC FOR ENLISTED PERS	2.	FAIR	1.	GOOD
8-13	OVERALL MILITARY ORG'N BALANCE	3.	UNFAVORABLE	1.	FAVORABLE
8-16	OVERALL MIL. HARDWARE BALANCE	3.	UNFAVORABLE	1.	FAVORABLE
8-20	USF OF TERROR BY THIS ANT. IS	3.	ABSENT	3.	ABSENT
8-28	INTELL. AMONG PCP IN CONF AREA	2.	OCCASIONAL	3.	INEFFECTIVE
8-29	INTELL. IN ADV'S POLICY ORGANS	3.	INEFFECTIVE	3.	INEFFECTIVE
8-30	SYMPATHY BETW POPN + OWN MIL.	1.	SYMPATHETIC	1.	SYMPATHETIC
8-32	CIVN SECURITY V. CONV. ATTACK	3.	LOW	1.	HIGH
8-34	CIVN SEC V AC ATK BY OWN FRCES	3.	LOW	2.	MODERATE
9-1	PC OF INDUSTRIAL CAPACITY LOST	1.	0.001-1.0	1.	0.001-1.0
9-2	PC OF CIVILIAN POPULATION LOST	1.	0.003-1.0	1.	0.003-1.0
9-7	TOTAL CAS'TIES TO ALL FORCES	1.	1.0-1.2	1.	1.0-1.2

e.

Conflict:

Higher-Order Factor Patterns

Genus 1

The factor pattern derives from

Greek insurgency (Greek government vs. Greek insurgents)

Spanish civil war (Republican government vs. Nationalist insurgents)

Venezuelan insurgency (Venezuelan government vs. MIR/CPV and FLN/FALN)

Item		Compound Response			
1-2A	TOPOGRAPHY OF CONFLICT AREA	2.	MOUNTAINOUS	2.	MOUNTAINOUS
1-2B	CLIMATE IN THE CONFLICT AREA	2.	MODERATE	2.	MODERATE
1-5	EFFECTIVE NATURE OF DISPUTE	3.	INTERNAL	3.	INTERNAL
1-8	CONTROL OF REAL ESTATE INVOLVD	1.	YES	1.	YES
1-11	DISPUTE HAS BEEN TO REG'L ORGN	2.	NO	2.	NO
1-12	DISPUTE HAS BEEN TO INT'L ORGN	2.	NO	2.	NO
2-2	PREFERRED MODE OF CONFL RESOLN	2.	CONCILIATORY	3.	DICTATORIAL
2-4	REGIM + GENL POPN OF SAME PACE	1.	YES	1.	YES
2-8	DOMINANT RELIGION AMONG POPN	1.	JUD-XIAN	1.	JUD-XIAN
2-14	REAL ESTATE INVOLVED IS	1.	IN CLMD BDY	1.	IN CLMD BDY
2-15	PC OF ANT'S CLMD AREA INVOLVED	1.	1.0-1.0	1.	1.0-1.0
2-16	PC OF ANT'S CLMD POPN INVOLVED	1.	1.0-1.0	1.	1.0-1.0
4-1	EFFECTIVE STATUS OF GOVERNMENT	1.	INDEP GOVT	4.	REBEL ORGN
4-4	EXECUTIVE STABILITY	3.	3.0-9.0	8.	0 OR N/A
4-18	POL. INTEGRATION OF GENL POPN	2.	MODERATE	8.	0 OR N/A
4-33	RECENT CHANGE IN LEADERSHIP	2.	NO	2.	NO
5-7	INTEREST INVOLVED-PRESTIGE	1.	YES	1.	YES
5-8	INTEREST INVOLVED-PRIDE	1.	YES	1.	YES
5-9	INTEREST INVOLVED-POWER	1.	YES	1.	YES
5-23	DIST FM BORDER TO CONFL AREA	1.	1.0-1.0	1.	1.0-1.0
5-24	DIST FM CAPITAL TO CONFL AREA	1.	1.0-1.3	1.	1.0-1.3
5-27	SPEED OF COMMUNICATIONS	2.	MODERATE	2.	MODERATE
5-31	OFFERED TO RESOLVE CONST'ALLY	1.	YES	2.	NO
5-32	BROUGHT DISPUTE TO INT'L ORGN	2.	NO	2.	NO
5-34	HAS SOUGHT A NEGOT. SETTLEMENT	2.	NO	2.	NO
5-35	HAS OFFERED BI-LATERAL NEGOTNS	2.	NO	2.	NO
5-38	P.O. RE ADV'S POL. INST'NS.	2.	UNFAVORABLE	8.	0 OR N/A
5-42	MARTIAL LAW IS IN EFFECT	2.	NO	8.	0 OR N/A
5-43	STATE OF WAR HAS BEEN DECLARED	2.	NO	8.	0 OR N/A
6-4	IS ALLY OF G.P. ALLIED TO ADV.	2.	NO	2.	NO
6-7	GP AID PROMISED IF ESC. OCCURS	2.	NO	2.	NO
6-8	GP DEF. FAC'TIES IN ANT'S AREA	2.	NO	2.	NO
6-13	INT'L ORG IS INV. ON THIS SIDE	2.	NO	2.	NO
6-14	REG'L ORG IS INV. ON THIS SIDE	2.	NO	2.	NO
6-22	A 3PTY IS PROVIDING CONV FORCE	2.	NO	2.	NO
6-23	A 3PTY IS PROVIDING GUER FORCE	2.	NO	2.	NO
6-28	EXPERIENCE WITH IO PEACE MACH	3.	NONE	3.	NONE
6-30	SOME 3PTY OFFERED TO ARBITRATE	2.	NO	2.	NO
6-31	INTL ORGN OFFERED TO ARBITRATE	2.	NO	2.	NO
6-32	REGL ORGN OFFERED TO ARBITRATE	2.	NO	2.	NO
6-33	A G.P. OFFERED TO ARBITRATE	2.	NO	2.	NO
6-35	INT'L ORG'N UPHELD ANT'S CAUSE	2.	NO	2.	NO
6-36	INTL ORGN INDICTED ANT'S CAUSE	2.	NO	2.	NO
6-37	CITED IN VIOLATION OF INTL LAW	2.	NO	2.	NO
6-38	CITED BY I.O. FOR AGGRESSION	2.	NO	2.	NO
6-40	ACCEPTED IO'S PROP. CEASEFIRE	2.	NO	2.	NO
6-42	I.O. HAS IMPOSED SANCTIONS	2.	NO	2.	NO
6-47	REG ORGN HAS IMPOSED SANCTIONS	2.	NO	2.	NO
7-3	NO. RESERVE TROOPS AVAILABLE	1.	0.5-1.4	1.	0.5-1.4
7-8	OTHER SIGNIF INTERNAL THREAT	2.	NO	2.	NO
7-11	TOTAL TROOPS GIVEN BY 3RD PTY	1.	0.5-1.0	1.	0.5-1.0
7-46	DEP. FOR AIR COMBAT ARMAMENTS	1.	EXCLUSIVE	8.	0 OR N/A
9-1	PC OF INDUSTRIAL CAPACITY LOST	1.	0.001-1.0	1.	0.001-1.0
9-8	CASUALTY RATE FOR OWN FORCES	1.	1.0-2.0	1.	1.0-2.0
9-10	CASUALTY RATE FOR ALL FORCES	1.	1.0-2.0	1.	1.0-2.0
9-11	ATTRITION RATE FOR OWN FORCES	1.	1.0-2.0	1.	1.0-2.0
9-13	ATTRITION RATE FOR ALL FORCES	1.	1.0-2.0	1.	1.0-2.0

	Item		Compound Response	

Genus 2

The factor pattern derives from

India-China (India vs. China)

Indonesia-Malaysia (Malaysia vs. Indonesia)

Israel-Egypt (Israel vs. Egypt)

Item		Compound Response	
1-3	PAST POL. REL'SHIP BETW PARTYS	2. COMPETITIVE	2. COMPETITIVE
1-5	EFFECTIVE NATURE OF DISPUTE	2. INTERSTATE	2. INTERSTATE
1-8	CONTROL OF REAL ESTATE INVOLVD	1. YES	1. YES
1-12	DISPUTE HAS BEEN TO INT'L ORGN	2. NO	2. NO
2-4	REGIM + GENL POPN OF SAME RACE	1. YES	1. YES
3-21	INDUSTRIAL EMPL. AS PC OF POPN	2. 1.5-5.0	1. 1.0-1.1
4-1	EFFECTIVE STATUS OF GOVERNMENT	1. INDEP GOVT	1. INDEP GOVT
4-6	STATUS OF EXECUTIVE	2. STRONG	1. DOMINANT
4-10	REGIME CAME TO POWER CONST'LY	1. YES	2. NO
4-13	INTERNAL POLICIES OF REGIME	2. MODERATE	3. REVOL'ARY
4-32	RECENT LEADERSHIP CRISIS	2. NO	2. NO
4-34	FORN RES ARE MAINSTAY OF REGIM	2. NO	2. NO
4-35	REGIM APPEARS MAINT BY FOR RES	2. NO	2. NO
4-36	POP. SUPPORT FOR REGIME'S OBJ.	1. HIGH	1. HIGH
4-37	POP. SUPPORT FOR REGIM'S POLS.	1. HIGH	1. HIGH
4-38	ATT. OF INTELLECTUALS TO REGIM	1. FAVORABLE	1. FAVORABLE
5-15	CONDUCT OF CONFLICT IS LIMITED	1. YES	1. YES
5-16	PC OF AVAIL MIL FRCS COMMITTED	1. 0 -10 PC	1. 0 -10 PC
5-21	LIKELY OUTCOME IS NOW OBVIOUS	2. NO	2. NO
5-23	DIST FM BORDER TO CONFL AREA	1. 1.0-1.0	1. 1.0-1.0
5-32	BROUGHT DISPUTE TO INT'L ORGN	2. NO	2. NO
5-38	P.O. RE ADV'S POL. INST'NS.	2. UNFAVORABLE	2. UNFAVORABLE
5-39	P.O. RE ADV'S SOCIAL INST'NS.	2. UNFAVORABLE	2. UNFAVORABLE
6-4	IS ALLY OF G.P. ALLIED TO ADV.	2. NO	2. NO
6-11	HAS ASKED AN INT'L. ORG'N. IN	2. NO	2. NO
6-13	INT'L ORG IS INV. ON THIS SIDE	2. NO	2. NO
6-14	REG'L ORG IS INV. ON THIS SIDE	2. NO	2. NO
6-17	A AUT ORG IS INV. ON THIS SIDE	2. NO	2. NO
6-19	A 3PTY IS PROVIDING ECON. AID	1. YES	1. YES
6-23	A 3PTY IS PROVIDING GUER FORCE	2. NO	2. NO
6-29	I.O. PEACE MACHINERY IS SEEN	2. IRRELEVANT	2. IRRELEVANT
6-30	SOME 3PTY OFFERED TO ARBITRATE	2. NO	2. NO
6-31	INTL ORGN OFFERED TO ARBITRATE	2. NO	2. NO
6-32	REGL ORGN OFFERED TO ARBITRATE	2. NO	2. NO
6-33	A G.P. OFFERED TO ARBITRATE	2. NO	2. NO
6-35	INT'L ORG'N UPHELD ANT'S CAUSE	2. NO	2. NO
6-36	INTL ORGN INDICTED ANT'S CAUSE	2. NO	2. NO
6-37	CITED IN VIOLATION OF INTL LAW	2. NO	2. NO
6-38	CITED BY I.O. FOR AGGRESSION	2. NO	2. NO
6-40	ACCEPTED IO'S PROP. CEASEFIRE	2. NO	2. NO
6-42	I.O. HAS IMPOSED SANCTIONS	2. NO	2. NO
7-17	GUERRILLA MANPOWER COMMITTED	1. 0.02-1.0	1. 0.02-1.0
8-30	SYMPATHY BETW POPN + OWN MIL.	1. SYMPATHETIC	1. SYMPATHETIC
9-1	PC OF INDUSTRIAL CAPACITY LOST	1. 0.001-1.0	1. 0.001-1.0
9-2	PC OF CIVILIAN POPULATION LOST	1. 0.003-1.0	1. 0.003-1.0

Genus 3

The factor pattern derives from

Algeria-Morocco (Morocco vs. Algeria)

Ethiopia-Somalia (Somalia vs. Ethiopia)

Kashmir (Pakistan vs. India)

USSR-Iran (Iran vs. USSR)

Item		Compound Response	
1-8	CONTROL OF REAL ESTATE INVOLVD	1. YES	1. YES
1-11	DISPUTE HAS BEEN TO REG'L ORGN	2. NO	2. NO
2-4	REGIM + GENL POPN OF SAME RACE	1. YES	1. YES
3-5	PER CAPITA INCOME	1. 1.0-2.1	1. 1.0-2.1
4-1	EFFECTIVE STATUS OF GOVERNMENT	1. INDEP GOVT	1. INDEP GOVT
4-34	FORN RES ARE MAINSTAY OF REGIM	2. NO	2. NO
4-35	REGIM APPEARS MAINT BY FOR RES	2. NO	2. NO
4-36	POP. SUPPORT FOR REGIME'S OBJ.	1. HIGH	1. HIGH
4-37	POP. SUPPORT FOR REGIM'S POLS.	1. HIGH	1. HIGH
4-38	ATT. OF INTELLECTUALS TO REGIM	1. FAVORABLE	1. FAVORABLE
5-2	REGIME SEEKS OVERTHROW OF ADV.	2. NO	2. NO
5-12	INTEREST INVOLVED-CONT'D EXIS.	2. NO	2. NO
5-15	CONDUCT OF CONFLICT IS LIMITED	1. YES	1. YES
5-25	ADVERSARY APPEARS TO ANT TO BE	2. AUT + INDEP.	2. AUT + INDEP.
5-29	CREDIBILITY OF COMMUNICATIONS	1. HIGH	1. HIGH
5-37	ESC LIKELY BRING GP AID TO ADV	2. NO	2. NO
5-43	STATE OF WAR HAS BEEN DECLARED	2. NO	2. NO
5-45	LEGAL STATUS OF ADV. PERSONNEL	1. CITIZEN	1. CITIZEN
6-1	IS SEC'TY ALLY OF GREAT POWER	2. NO	2. NO
6-3	IS ALLY OF G.P. HOSTILE TO ADV	2. NO	2. NO
6-4	IS ALLY OF G.P. ALLIED TO ADV.	2. NO	2. NO
6-5	IS AIDED BY GP HOSTILE TO ADV.	2. NO	2. NO
6-6	A GP IS OPENLY PARTIAL TO ANT.	2. NO	2. NO
6-7	GP AID PROMISED IF ESC. OCCURS	2. NO	2. NO
6-11	HAS ASKED AN INT'L. ORG'N. IN	2. NO	2. NO
6-13	INT'L ORG IS INV. ON THIS SIDE	2. NO	2. NO
6-14	REG'L ORG IS INV. ON THIS SIDE	2. NO	2. NO
6-15	A G.P. IS INV. ON THIS SIDE	2. NO	2. NO
6-16	A NON-GP IS INV. ON THIS SIDE	2. NO	2. NO
6-18	A 3PTY IS PROVIDING POL. AID	2. NO	2. NO
6-32	REGL ORGN OFFERED TO ARBITRATE	2. NO	2. NO
6-33	A G.P. OFFERED TO ARBITRATE	2. NO	2. NO
6-35	INT'L ORG'N UPHELD ANT'S CAUSE	2. NO	2. NO
6-36	INTL ORGN INDICTED ANT'S CAUSE	2. NO	2. NO

Item		Compound Response	

6-37	CITED IN VIOLATION OF INTL LAW	2.	NO	2.	NO
6-38	CITED BY I.O. FOR AGGRESSION	2.	NO	2.	NO
6-40	ACCEPTED IO'S PROP. CEASEFIRE	2.	NO	2.	NO
6-42	I.O. HAS IMPOSED SANCTIONS	2.	NO	2.	NO
6-47	REG ORGN HAS IMPOSED SANCTIONS	2.	NO	2.	NO
7-17	GUERRILLA MANPOWER COMMITTED	1.	0.02-1.0	1.	0.02-1.0
7-18	NAVAL MANPOWER COMMITTED	1.	0.5-1.0	1.	0.5-1.0
8-29	INTELL. IN ADV'S POLICY ORGANS	3.	INEFFECTIVE	3.	INEFFECTIVE
8-30	SYMPATHY BETW POPN + OWN MIL.	1.	SYMPATHETIC	1.	SYMPATHETIC
9-1	PC OF INDUSTRIAL CAPACITY LOST	1.	0.001-1.0	1.	0.001-1.0
9-2	PC OF CIVILIAN POPULATION LOST	1.	0.003-1.0	1.	0.003-1.0

Genus 4

The factor pattern derives from

Angolan insurgency (Portuguese colonial administration vs. African insurgents)

Cyprus: independence (U.K. colonial administration vs. Eno-sists)

Malayan insurgency (U.K.-Malay colonial administration and Malayan government vs. Malayan Communist party)

1-5	EFFECTIVE NATURE OF DISPUTE	1.	COLONIAL	1.	COLONIAL
1-8	CONTROL OF REAL ESTATE INVOLVD	1.	YES	1.	YES
2-13	POPN UNDER EFFECTIVE CONTROL	3.	499.0-65TH	8.	0 OR N/A
2-14	REAL ESTATE INVOLVED IS	1.	IN CLMD BDY	1.	IN CLMD BDY
2-15	PC OF ANT'S CLMD AREA INVOLVED	1.	1.0-1.0	1.	1.0-1.0
2-16	PC OF ANT'S CLMD POPN INVOLVED	1.	1.0-1.0	1.	1.0-1.0
2-17	PC OF INVOLVED AREA IN CONTROL	3.	24.0-100.0	8.	0 OR N/A
2-18	PC OF INVOLVED POPN IN CONTROL	3.	9.0-100.0	8.	0 OR N/A
3-2	GROSS NAT'L. OR ECON. PRODUCT	3.	90.0-6.4TH	8.	0 OR N/A
3-8	PRODUCTION OF STEEL	1.	1.0-1.0	1.	1.0-1.0
3-29	NO. SEAPORTS CONTROLLED	2.	1.6-3.3	8.	0 OR N/A
4-1	EFFECTIVE STATUS OF GOVERNMENT	2.	COLONIAL ADM	4.	REBEL ORGN
4-4	EXECUTIVE STABILITY	3.	3.0-9.0	8.	0 OR N/A
4-5	TYPE OF GOVERNMENT	2.	TUT/MOD OLIG	8.	0 OR N/A
4-6	STATUS OF EXECUTIVE	1.	DOMINANT	8.	0 OR N/A
4-10	REGIME CAME TO POWER CONST'LY	2.	NO	8.	0 OR N/A
4-17	MOBILIZATIONAL STYLE OF REGIME	2.	LIMITED	8.	0 OR N/A
4-18	FOL. INTEGRATION OF GENL POPN	2.	MODERATE	8.	0 OR N/A
4-22	INTEREST ARTIC'N BY ASSOC'L GP	1.	POL SIGNIF	8.	0 OR N/A
4-23	INTEREST ARTIC'N BY INST'L GPS	1.	POL SIGNIF	8.	0 OR N/A
4-34	FORN RES ARE MAINSTAY OF REGIM	1.	YES	2.	NO
5-7	INTEREST INVOLVED-PRESTIGE	2.	NO	1.	YES
5-9	INTEREST INVOLVED-POWER	2.	NO	1.	YES
5-13	COMMITMENT TO STATED GOALS	2.	FLEXIBLE	2.	FLEXIBLE
5-22	POST-DISPUTE EXPECT'N OF REGIM	2.	PESSIMISTIC	2.	PESSIMISTIC
5-23	DIST FM BORDER TO CONFL AREA	1.	1.0-1.0	1.	1.0-1.0
5-25	ADVERSARY APPEARS TO ANT TO BE	2.	AUT + INDEP.	1.	A PUPPET
5-28	RELIABILITY OF COMMUNICATIONS	1.	HIGH	1.	HIGH
5-35	HAS OFFERED BI-LATERAL NEGOTNS	2.	NO	2.	NO
5-37	ESC LIKELY BRING GP AID TO ADV	2.	NO	2.	NO
5-42	MARTIAL LAW IS IN EFFECT	2.	NO	8.	0 OR N/A
5-43	STATE OF WAR HAS BEEN DECLARED	2.	NO	8.	0 OR N/A
6-4	IS ALLY OF G.P. ALLIED TO ADV.	2.	NO	2.	NO
6-13	INT'L ORG IS INV. ON THIS SIDE	2.	NO	2.	NO
6-14	REG'L ORG IS INV. ON THIS SIDE	2.	NO	2.	NO
6-17	A AUT ORG IS INV. ON THIS SIDE	2.	NO	2.	NO
6-23	A 3PTY IS PROVIDING GUER FORCE	2.	NO	2.	NO
6-30	SOME 3PTY OFFERED TO ARBITRATE	2.	NO	2.	NO
6-31	INTL ORGN OFFERED TO ARBITRATE	2.	NO	2.	NO
6-32	REGL ORGN OFFERED TO ARBITRATE	2.	NO	2.	NO
6-33	A G.P. OFFERED TO ARBITRATE	2.	NO	2.	NO
6-35	INT'L ORG'N UPHELD ANT'S CAUSE	2.	NO	2.	NO
6-38	CITED BY I.O. FOR AGGRESSION	2.	NO	2.	NO
6-40	ACCEPTED IO'S PROP. CEASEFIRE	2.	NO	2.	NO
6-42	I.O. HAS IMPOSED SANCTIONS	2.	NO	2.	NO
6-47	REG ORGN HAS IMPOSED SANCTIONS	2.	NO	2.	NO
7-5	NO. TROOPS COMMITTED TO CONFL.	1.	0.02-1.0	1.	0.02-1.0
7-8	OTHER SIGNIF INTERNAL THREAT	2.	NO	2.	NO
7-9	OTHER SIGNIF EXTERNAL THREAT	2.	NO	2.	NO
7-17	GUERRILLA MANPOWER COMMITTED	1.	0.02-1.0	1.	0.02-1.0
7-18	NAVAL MANPOWER COMMITTED	1.	0.5-1.0	1.	0.5-1.0
7-40	HAS A NUCLEAR CAPABILITY	2.	NO	2.	NO
7-49	TRANSP. CAP. SUPPLY LIKELY TO	2.	STAY SAME	8.	0 OR N/A
9-1	PC OF INDUSTRIAL CAPACITY LOST	1.	0.001-1.0	1.	0.001-1.0
9-2	PC OF CIVILIAN POPULATION LOST	1.	0.003-1.0	1.	0.003-1.0
9-3	TOTAL NO. CIVN POPULATION LOST	1.	1.0-1.0	1.	1.0-1.0
9-4	ATTRITION RATE FOR CIV'N POPN	1.	0.5-1.0	1.	0.5-1.0

Genus 5

The factor pattern derives from

Cuba: "little" war of 1906 (Liberal party insurgents vs. Cuban government)

1-2A	TOPOGRAPHY OF CONFLICT AREA	1.	FLAT	1.	FLAT
2-13	POPN UNDER EFFECTIVE CONTROL	8.	0 OR N/A	3.	499.0-65TH
3-2	GROSS NAT'L. OR ECON. PRODUCT	8.	0 OR N/A	3.	90.0-6.4TH
3-14	GOVERNMENT INCOME AS PC OF GNP	8.	0 OR N/A	3.	10.0-50.0
3-15	GOVT. SPENDING AS PC OF GNP	8.	0 OR N/A	3.	6.0-50.0
3-20	AGRIC EMPLOYMENT AS PC OF POPN	8.	0 OR N/A	3.	13.0-70.0

	Item		Compound Response		

Cuba: Bay of Pigs (Cuban exiles vs. Cuban government)

Cyprus: internal (Turkish Cypriots vs. Cypriot government)

Indonesia: independence (Indonesian insurgents vs. Dutch colonial administration)

Item	Description	Col A		Col B	
5-22	POST-DISPUTE EXPECT'N OF REGIM	2.	PESSIMISTIC	2.	PESSIMISTIC
5-32	BROUGHT DISPUTE TO INT'L ORGN	2.	NO	2.	NO
5-37	ESC LIKELY BRING GP AID TO ADV	2.	NO	2.	NO
6-3	IS ALLY OF G.P. HOSTILE TO ADV	2.	NO	2.	NO
6-4	IS ALLY OF G.P. ALLIED TO ADV.	2.	NO	2.	NO
6-5	IS AIDED BY GP HOSTILE TO ADV.	2.	NO	2.	NO
6-6	A GP IS OPENLY PARTIAL TO ANT.	2.	NO	2.	NO
6-7	GP AID PROMISED IF ESC. OCCURS	2.	NO	2.	NO
6-11	HAS ASKED AN INT'L. ORG'N. IN	2.	NO	2.	NO
6-13	INT'L ORG IS INV. ON THIS SIDE	2.	NO	2.	NO
6-14	REG'L ORG IS INV. ON THIS SIDE	2.	NO	2.	NO
6-15	A G.P. IS INV. ON THIS SIDE	2.	NO	2.	NO
6-23	A 3PTY IS PROVIDING GUER FORCE	2.	NO	2.	NO
6-30	SOME 3PTY OFFERED TO ARBITRATE	2.	NO	2.	NO
6-31	INTL ORGN OFFERED TO ARBITRATE	2.	NO	2.	NO
6-32	REGL ORGN OFFERED TO ARBITRATE	2.	NO	2.	NO
6-33	A G.P. OFFERED TO ARBITRATE	2.	NO	2.	NO
6-35	INT'L ORG'N UPHELD ANT'S CAUSE	2.	NO	2.	NO
6-36	INTL ORGN INDICTED ANT'S CAUSE	2.	NO	2.	NO
6-37	CITED IN VIOLATION OF INTL LAW	2.	NO	2.	NO
6-38	CITED BY I.O. FOR AGGRESSION	2.	NO	2.	NO
6-40	ACCEPTED IO'S PROP. CEASEFIRE	2.	NO	2.	NO
6-42	I.O. HAS IMPOSED SANCTIONS	2.	NO	2.	NO
6-47	REG ORGN HAS IMPOSED SANCTIONS	2.	NO	2.	NO
7-6	NO. TROOPS COMM AS PC TOT FRCS	1.	0.7-1.0	1.	0.7-1.0
7-26	NO. MED. CANNON AVAILABLE	1.	1.0-1.0	1.	1.0-1.0
7-27	NO. HVY. CANNON AVAILABLE	1.	1.0-1.0	1.	1.0-1.0
7-36	NO. SUBMARINES AVAILABLE	1.	1.0-1.0	1.	1.0-1.0
7-37	NO. HEAVY VESSELS AVAILABLE	1.	1.0-1.0	1.	1.0-1.0
7-38	NO. LANDING CRAFT AVAILABLE	1.	1.0-1.1	1.	1.0-1.1
9-1	PC OF INDUSTRIAL CAPACITY LOST	1.	0.001-1.0	1.	0.001-1.0
9-2	PC OF CIVILIAN POPULATION LOST	1.	0.003-1.0	1.	0.003-1.0
9-3	TOTAL NO. CIVN POPULATION LOST	1.	1.0-1.0	1.	1.0-1.0
9-5	TOTAL CAS'TIES TO OWN FORCES	1.	1.0-1.2	1.	1.0-1.2
9-7	TOTAL CAS'TIES TO ALL FORCES	1.	1.0-1.2	1.	1.0-1.2
9-8	CASUALTY RATE FOR OWN FORCES	1.	1.0-2.0	1.	1.0-2.0
9-10	CASUALTY RATE FOR ALL FORCES	1.	1.0-2.0	1.	1.0-2.0

Family 1

The factor pattern derives from

Algeria-Morocco (Morocco vs. Algeria)

Ethiopia-Somalia (Somalia vs. Ethiopia)

India-China (India vs. China)

Indonesia-Malaysia (Malaysia vs. Indonesia)

Israel-Egypt (Israel vs. Egypt)

Kashmir (Pakistan vs. India)

USSR-Iran (Iran vs. USSR)

The adjuncts are

Cuba: "little" war of 1906

Cuba: Bay of Pigs

Cyprus: internal

Indonesia: independence

Item	Description	Col A		Col B	
1-8	CONTROL OF REAL ESTATE INVOLVD	1.	YES	1.	YES
2-4	REGIM + GENL POPN OF SAME RACE	1.	YES	1.	YES
4-1	EFFECTIVE STATUS OF GOVERNMENT	1.	INDEP GOVT	1.	INDEP GOVT
4-34	FORN RES ARE MAINSTAY OF REGIM	2.	NO	2.	NO
4-35	REGIM APPEARS MAINT BY FOR RES	2.	NO	2.	NO
4-36	POP. SUPPORT FOR REGIME'S OBJ.	1.	HIGH	1.	HIGH
4-37	POP. SUPPORT FOR REGIM'S POLS.	1.	HIGH	1.	HIGH
4-38	ATT. OF INTELLECTUALS TO REGIM	1.	FAVORABLE	1.	FAVORABLE
5-15	CONDUCT OF CONFLICT IS LIMITED	1.	YES	1.	YES
6-4	IS ALLY OF G.P. ALLIED TO ADV.	2.	NO	2.	NO
6-11	HAS ASKED AN INT'L. ORG'N. IN	2.	NO	2.	NO
6-13	INT'L ORG IS INV. ON THIS SIDE	2.	NO	2.	NO
6-14	REG'L ORG IS INV. ON THIS SIDE	2.	NO	2.	NO
6-32	REGL ORGN OFFERED TO ARBITRATE	2.	NO	2.	NO
6-33	A G.P. OFFERED TO ARBITRATE	2.	NO	2.	NO
6-35	INT'L ORG'N UPHELD ANT'S CAUSE	2.	NO	2.	NO
6-36	INTL ORGN INDICTED ANT'S CAUSE	2.	NO	2.	NO
6-37	CITED IN VIOLATION OF INTL LAW	2.	NO	2.	NO
6-38	CITED BY I.O. FOR AGGRESSION	2.	NO	2.	NO
6-40	ACCEPTED IO'S PROP. CEASEFIRE	2.	NO	2.	NO
6-42	I.O. HAS IMPOSED SANCTIONS	2.	NO	2.	NO
7-2	NO. ACTIV TROOPS AS PC OF POPN	1.	0.001-1.0	2.	1.3-174.0
7-4	MOBILIZATION OF RESERVES	1.	NONE	1.	NONE
7-13	3PTY TROOP AID SEEN LIKELY TO	2.	STAY SAME	2.	STAY SAME
7-14	TOTAL MANPOWER COMMITTED	1.	0.02-7.3	1.	0.02-7.3
7-17	GUERRILLA MANPOWER COMMITTED	1.	0.02-1.0	1.	0.02-1.0
7-19	AIR FORCE MANPOWER COMMITTED	1.	0.05-1.0	1.	0.05-1.0
7-44	DEPENDENCE FOR NAVAL ARMAMENTS	1.	EXCLUSIVE	1.	EXCLUSIVE
7-45	NAVAL ARMS SUPPLY LIKELY TO	2.	STAY SAME	2.	STAY SAME
8-11	TRAINING FAC FOR ENLISTED PERS	1.	GOOD	2.	FAIR
8-20	USE OF TERROR BY THIS ANT. IS	3.	ABSENT	3.	ABSENT
8-30	SYMPATHY BETW POPN + OWN MIL.	1.	SYMPATHETIC	1.	SYMPATHETIC
9-1	PC OF INDUSTRIAL CAPACITY LOST	1.	0.001-1.0	1.	0.001-1.0
9-2	PC OF CIVILIAN POPULATION LOST	1.	0.003-1.0	1.	0.003-1.0

Family 2

The factor pattern derives from

Angolan insurgency (Portuguese colonial administration vs. African insurgents)

Item	Description	Col A		Col B	
1-8	CONTROL OF REAL ESTATE INVOLVD	1.	YES	1.	YES
2-14	REAL ESTATE INVOLVED IS	1.	IN CLMD BDY	1.	IN CLMD BDY
2-15	PC OF ANT'S CLMD AREA INVOLVED	1.	1.0-1.0	1.	1.0-1.0
2-16	PC OF ANT'S CLMD POPN INVOLVED	1.	1.0-1.0	1.	1.0-1.0
4-4	EXECUTIVE STABILITY	3.	3.0-9.0	8.	0 OR N/A
4-18	POL. INTEGRATION OF GENL POPN	2.	MODERATE	8.	0 OR N/A

Item			Compound Response		

Cyprus: independence (U.K. colonial administration vs. Enosists)

Greek insurgency (Greek government vs. Greek insurgents)

Malayan insurgency (U.K.-Malay colonial administration and Malayan government vs. Malayan Communist party)

Spanish civil war (Republican government vs. Nationalist insurgents)

Venezuelan insurgency (Venezuelan government vs. MIR/CPV and FLN/FALN)

5-23	DIST FM BORDER TO CONFL AREA	1.	1.C-1.0	1.	1.0-1.0
5-35	HAS OFFERED BI-LATERAL NEGOTNS	2.	NO	2.	NO
5-42	MARTIAL LAW IS IN EFFECT	2.	NO	8.	C OR N/A
5-43	STATE OF WAR HAS BEEN DECLARED	2.	NO	8.	O OR N/A
6-4	IS ALLY OF G.P. ALLIED TO ADV.	2.	NO	2.	NO
6-13	INT'L ORG IS INV. ON THIS SIDE	2.	NO	2.	NO
6-14	REG'L ORG IS INV. ON THIS SIDE	2.	NO	2.	NO
6-23	A 3PTY IS PROVIDING GUER FORCE	2.	NO	2.	NO
6-30	SOME 3PTY OFFERED TO ARBITRATE	2.	NO	2.	NO
6-31	INTL ORGN OFFERED TO ARBITRATE	2.	NO	2.	NO
6-32	REGL ORGN OFFERED TO ARBITRATE	2.	NO	2.	NO
6-33	A G.P. OFFERED TO ARBITRATE	2.	NO	2.	NO
6-35	INT'L ORG'N UPHELD ANT'S CAUSE	2.	NO	2.	NO
6-38	CITED BY I.O. FOR AGGRESSION	2.	NO	2.	NO
6-40	ACCEPTED IO'S PROP. CEASEFIRE	2.	NO	2.	NO
6-42	I.O. HAS IMPOSED SANCTIONS	2.	NO	2.	NO
6-47	REG ORGN HAS IMPOSED SANCTIONS	2.	NO	2.	NO
7-8	OTHER SIGNIF INTERNAL THREAT	2.	NO	2.	NO
9-1	PC OF INDUSTRIAL CAPACITY LOST	1.	0.001-1.0	1.	0.001-1.0

Artificial Order

The factor pattern derives from

Algeria-Morocco (Morocco vs. Algeria)

Cuba: "little" war of 1906 (Liberal party insurgents vs. Cuban government)

Cuba: Bay of Pigs (Cuban exiles vs. Cuban government)

Cyprus: internal (Cypriot government vs. Turkish Cypriots)

Ethiopia-Somalia (Somalia vs. Ethiopia)

India-China (India vs. China)

Indonesia: independence (Indonesian insurgents vs. Dutch colonial administration)

Indonesia-Malaysia (Malaysia vs. Indonesia)

Israel-Egypt (Israel vs. Egypt)

Kashmir (India vs. Pakistan)

USSR-Iran (Iran vs. USSR)

6-4	IS ALLY OF G.P. ALLIED TO ADV.	2.	NO	2.	NO
6-11	HAS ASKED AN INT'L. ORG'N. IN	2.	NO	2.	NO
6-13	INT'L ORG IS INV. ON THIS SIDE	2.	NO	2.	NO
6-14	REG'L ORG IS INV. ON THIS SIDE	2.	NO	2.	NO
6-32	REGL ORGN OFFERED TO ARBITRATE	2.	NO	2.	NO
6-33	A G.P. OFFERED TO ARBITRATE	2.	NO	2.	NO
6-35	INT'L ORG'N UPHELD ANT'S CAUSE	2.	NO	2.	NO
6-36	INTL ORGN INDICTED ANT'S CAUSE	2.	NO	2.	NO
6-37	CITED IN VIOLATION OF INTL LAW	2.	NO	2.	NO
6-38	CITED BY I.O. FOR AGGRESSION	2.	NO	2.	NO
6-40	ACCEPTED IO'S PROP. CEASEFIRE	2.	NO	2.	NO
6-42	I.O. HAS IMPOSED SANCTIONS	2.	NO	2.	NO
9-1	PC OF INDUSTRIAL CAPACITY LOST	1.	0.001-1.0	1.	0.001-1.0
9-2	PC OF CIVILIAN POPULATION LOST	1.	0.003-1.0	1.	0.003-1.0

Class

The factor pattern derives from all seventeen instances of prehostilities conflict included in the analysis.

6-4	IS ALLY OF G.P. ALLIED TO ADV.	2.	NO	2.	NO
6-13	INT'L ORG IS INV. ON THIS SIDE	2.	NO	2.	NO
6-14	REG'L ORG IS INV. ON THIS SIDE	2.	NO	2.	NO
6-32	REGL ORGN OFFERED TO ARBITRATE	2.	NO	2.	NO
6-33	A G.P. OFFERED TO ARBITRATE	2.	NO	2.	NO
6-35	INT'L ORG'N UPHELD ANT'S CAUSE	2.	NO	2.	NO
6-38	CITED BY I.O. FOR AGGRESSION	2.	NO	2.	NO
6-40	ACCEPTED IO'S PROP. CEASEFIRE	2.	NO	2.	NO
6-42	I.O. HAS IMPOSED SANCTIONS	2.	NO	2.	NO
9-1	PC OF INDUSTRIAL CAPACITY LOST	1.	0.001-1.0	1.	0.001-1.0

2.
The Hostilities (P–III) Patterns

The data input for each conflict included in this analysis is that obtaining at the threshold of Phase III and is therefore a statement of the conditions pertaining when each was about to erupt into organized and purposeful violence. In the four conflicts (Greek insurgency, Indonesia: independence, Kashmir, and USSR-Iran) in which two outbreaks of hostilities occurred, the later instance was included in this analysis so that the resulting factor patterns might be equally expressive of the conditions of renewed, as well as initial, hostilities.

a.
Conflicts Included
in the Analysis
of the Hostilities Patterns

Conflict	Event Marking Hostilities (P–III)	Date
Algeria-Morocco	Algerian attack on Tindouf	10/63
Angolan insurgency	African insurgents riot in Luanda	2/61
Cuba: "little" war of 1906	First fire fight between insurgents and government forces	8/06
Cuba: Bay of Pigs	Bay of Pigs invasion by Cuban exiles	4/61
Cyprus: independence	Insurrection becomes widespread	4/55
Cyprus: internal	Fighting between Greek and Turkish Cypriots	12/63
Ethiopian resistance	Attempted assassination of Italian viceroy	2/37
Ethiopia-Somalia	Ethiopia violates Somali borders	2/64
Greek insurgency	Widespread guerrilla warfare resumed	1/46
India-China	Chinese attack Indian outposts	9/62
Indonesia: independence	Second large-scale Dutch attack	12/48
Indonesia-Malaysia	Indonesian attack in Sarawak	4/63
Israel-Egypt	Israeli attack in Sinai	10/56
Kashmir	Pakistanis infiltrate Kashmir border	8/65
Malayan insurgency	State of emergency declared by U.K.-Malay administration	6/48
Spanish civil war	Military rising in Morocco by senior officers	7/36
Venezuelan insurgency	Attempted "leftist" rebellion	6/61
USSR-Iran	Iranian military forces enter Azerbaidzhan	12/46

b.

Derivation of the Hostilities
Patterns

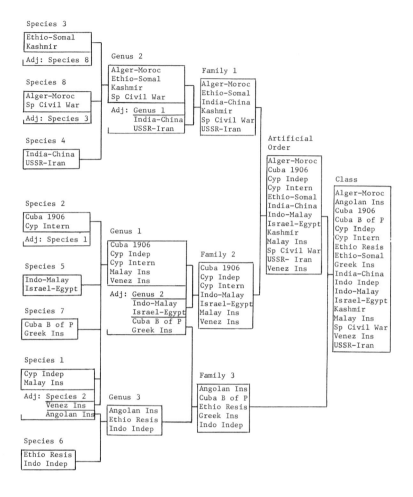

c.

Percentile Distribution of the
Conflicts across the
Hostilities Patterns

	Species							
	H1	H2	H3	H4	H5	H6	H7	H8
Algeria-Morocco	0.30	0.39	0.51	0.44	0.52	0.51	0.38	1.00
Angolan insurgency	0.25	0.21	0.23	0.18	0.20	0.55	0.37	0.35
Cuba: war of 1906	0.54	1.00	0.38	0.32	0.34	0.39	0.37	0.49
Cuba: Bay of Pigs	0.45	0.42	0.33	0.24	0.39	0.39	1.00	0.33
Cyprus: independence	1.00	0.68	0.35	0.36	0.46	0.59	0.49	0.31
Cyprus: internal	0.60	1.00	0.42	0.37	0.38	0.47	0.45	0.41
Ethiopian resistance	0.34	0.22	0.26	0.31	0.27	1.00	0.55	0.36
Ethiopia-Somalia	0.41	0.43	1.00	0.51	0.46	0.49	0.45	0.67
Greek insurgency	0.41	0.38	0.32	0.38	0.40	0.63	1.00	0.36
India-China	0.36	0.38	0.58	1.00	0.47	0.51	0.35	0.59
Indonesia: independence	0.45	0.39	0.40	0.35	0.33	1.00	0.45	0.40
Indonesia-Malaysia	0.47	0.39	0.50	0.48	1.00	0.51	0.48	0.45
Israel-Egypt	0.34	0.37	0.51	0.37	1.00	0.45	0.49	0.50
Kashmir	0.28	0.38	1.00	0.53	0.49	0.41	0.42	0.51
Malayan insurgency	1.00	0.61	0.36	0.39	0.53	0.61	0.52	0.35

	Species							
	H1	H2	H3	H4	H5	H6	H7	H8
Spanish civil war	0.31	0.43	0.50	0.43	0.33	0.47	0.49	1.00
Venezuelan insurgency	0.61	0.50	0.35	0.37	0.42	0.51	0.54	0.41
USSR-Iran	0.24	0.27	0.46	1.00	0.33	0.39	0.37	0.41

	Genus			Family			Arti-ficial Order	Class
	1	2	3	1	2	3		
Algeria-Morocco	0.45	1.00	0.61	1.00	0.84	0.64	1.00	1.00
Angolan insurgency	0.21	0.28	1.00	0.26	0.21	1.00	~	1.00
Cuba: war of 1906	1.00	0.62	0.39	0.61	1.00	0.27	~	1.00
Cuba: Bay of Pigs	0.67	0.44	0.43	0.52	0.74	1.00	1.00	1.00
Cyprus: independence	1.00	0.44	0.64	0.48	1.00	0.64	1.00	1.00
Cyprus: internal	1.00	0.54	0.46	0.57	1.00	0.36	1.00	1.00
Ethiopian resistance	0.40	0.38	1.00	0.43	0.58	1.00	~	1.00
Ethiopia-Somalia	0.52	1.00	0.46	1.00	0.84	0.27	1.00	1.00
Greek insurgency	0.60	0.44	0.68	0.48	0.63	1.00	~	1.00
India-China	0.50	0.87	0.39	1.00	0.95	0.45	1.00	1.00
Indonesia: independence	0.55	0.51	1.00	0.57	0.79	1.00	~	1.00
Indonesia-Malaysia	0.60	0.64	0.46	0.74	1.00	0.45	1.00	1.00
Israel-Egypt	0.50	0.72	0.54	0.78	1.00	0.73	1.00	1.00
Kashmir	0.43	1.00	0.36	1.00	0.68	0.36	1.00	1.00
Malayan insurgency	1.00	0.46	0.64	0.52	1.00	0.73	1.00	1.00
Spanish civil war	0.50	1.00	0.50	1.00	0.68	0.73	1.00	1.00
Venezuelan insurgency	1.00	0.56	0.46	0.65	1.00	0.73	1.00	1.00
USSR-Iran	0.38	0.62	0.36	1.00	0.58	0.36	1.00	1.00

d. Hostilities: Complete Factor Patterns

Species Type H1
("commitment hardens as accommodation fails")

The factor pattern derives from
Cyprus: independence (U.K. colonial administration vs. Enosists)
Malayan insurgency (U.K.-Malay colonial administration and Malayan government vs. Malayan Communist party)

The adjuncts are
Angolan insurgency
Venuzuelan insurgency

Item		Compound Response		
1-2A	TOPOGRAPHY OF CONFLICT AREA	1.	FLAT	1. FLAT
1-4	PAST MIL. REL'SHIP BETW PARTYS	1.	PEACEFUL	1. PEACEFUL
1-5	EFFECTIVE NATURE OF DISPUTE	1.	COLONIAL	1. COLONIAL
1-8	CONTROL OF REAL ESTATE INVOLVD	1.	YES	1. YES
1-11	DISPUTE HAS BEEN TO REG'L ORGN	2.	NO	2. NC
2-6	LINGUISTIC HOMOGENEITY OF POPN	3.	VERY HETERO	1. HOMOGENEOUS
2-14	REAL ESTATE INVOLVED IS	1.	IN CLMD BDY	1. IN CLMD BDY
2-15	PC OF ANT'S CLMD AREA INVOLVED	1.	1.0-1.0	1. 1.0-1.0
2-16	PC OF ANT'S CLMC POPN INVOLVED	1.	1.0-1.0	1. 1.0-1.0
2-17	PC OF INVOLVED AREA IN CONTROL	3.	24.0-100.0	8. 0 OR N/A
2-18	PC OF INVOLVED POPN IN CONTROL	3.	9.0-100.0	8. 0 OR N/A
2-19	URBANIZATION	2.	MEDIUM	8. 0 OR N/A
3-2	GROSS NAT'L. OR ECON. PRODUCT	3.	90.0-6.4TH	8. 0 OR N/A
3-3	GROWTH RATE OF ECONOMY	3.	3.0-13.9	8. 0 OR N/A
3-4	RATE OF INFLATION IN ECONOMY	2.	2.0-10.0	8. 0 OR N/A
3-5	PER CAPITA INCOME	3.	115.0-855.0	8. 0 OR N/A
3-6	PC OF GNP IN AGRICULTURE	3.	25.0-75.0	8. 0 OR N/A
3-8	PRODUCTION OF STEEL	1.	1.0-1.0	1. 1.0-1.0
3-9	PC OF GNP IN EXPORTS	3.	22.0-1.0TH	8. 0 OR N/A
3-13	PROGRESSIVE TAX STRUCTURE	1.	YES	8. 0 OR N/A
3-14	GOVERNMENT INCOME AS PC OF GNP	3.	10.0-50.0	8. 0 OR N/A
3-15	GOVT. SPENDING AS PC OF GNP	3.	6.0-50.0	8. 0 OR N/A
3-20	AGRIC EMPLOYMENT AS PC OF POPN	3.	13.0-70.0	8. 0 OR N/A
3-21	INDUSTRIAL EMPL. AS PC OF POPN	3.	11.0-23.0	8. 0 OR N/A
3-29	NO. SEAPORTS CONTROLLED	2.	1.6-3.3	8. 0 OR N/A

Item		Compound Response			
4-1	EFFECTIVE STATUS OF GOVERNMENT	2.	COLONIAL ADM	4.	REBEL ORGN
4-3	MODERN COLONIAL RULER	5.	NONE	1.	BRITAIN
4-4	EXECUTIVE STABILITY	3.	3.0-9.0	8.	0 OR N/A
4-5	TYPE OF GOVERNMENT	2.	TUT/MOD OLIG	8.	0 OR N/A
4-6	STATUS OF EXECUTIVE	1.	DOMINANT	8.	0 OR N/A
4-10	REGIME CAME TO POWER CONST'LY	2.	NO	8.	0 OR N/A
4-13	INTERNAL POLICIES OF REGIME	2.	MODERATE	3.	REVOL'ARY
4-17	MOBILIZATIONAL STYLE OF REGIME	2.	LIMITED	8.	0 OR N/A
4-18	POL. INTEGRATION OF GENL POPN	2.	MODERATE	8.	0 OR N/A
4-19	FREEDOM OF THE PRESS ALLOWED	2.	INTERMITTENT	8.	0 OR N/A
4-22	INTEREST ARTIC'N BY ASSOC'L GP	1.	POL SIGNIF	8.	0 OR N/A
4-23	INTEREST ARTIC'N BY INST'L GPS	1.	POL SIGNIF	8.	0 OR N/A
4-24	INTEREST ARTIC'N BY POL PARTYS	1.	POL SIGNIF	8.	0 OR N/A
4-25	CONST'AL STATUS OF POL PARTIES	1.	COMPETITIVE	8.	0 OR N/A
4-27	PERSONALISM IN POL. PARTIES	2.	MODERATE	8.	0 OR N/A
4-32	RECENT LEADERSHIP CRISIS	2.	NO	2.	NO
4-33	RECENT CHANGE IN LEADERSHIP	2.	NO	2.	NO
4-34	FORN RES ARE MAINSTAY OF REGIM	1.	YES	2.	NO
4-35	REGIM APPEARS MAINT BY FOR RES	1.	YES	8.	0 OR N/A
4-40	EFFECT ON POPULAR COHESION	2.	LITTLE CHANGE	8.	0 OR N/A
5-2	REGIME SEEKS OVERTHROW OF ADV.	2.	NO	1.	YES
5-7	INTEREST INVOLVED-PRESTIGE	2.	NO	1.	YES
5-9	INTEREST INVOLVED-POWER	2.	NO	1.	YES
5-10	INTEREST INVOLVED-INDEPENDENCE	2.	NO	1.	YES
5-13	COMMITMENT TO STATED GOALS	2.	FLEXIBLE	2.	FLEXIBLE
5-19	PRESENT OUTLOOK WRT DISPUTE	2.	MODERATE	1.	DIE-HARD
5-22	POST-DISPUTE EXPECT'N OF REGIM	2.	PESSIMISTIC	2.	PESSIMISTIC
5-23	DIST FM BORDER TO CONFL AREA	1.	1.0-1.0	1.	1.0-1.0
5-24	DIST FM CAPITAL TO CONFL AREA	1.	1.0-1.3	1.	1.0-1.3
5-25	ADVERSARY APPEARS TO ANT TO BE	2.	AUT + INDEP.	1.	A PUPPET
5-27	SPEED OF COMMUNICATIONS	1.	RAPID	1.	RAPID
5-28	RELIABILITY OF COMMUNICATIONS	1.	HIGH	1.	HIGH
5-32	BROUGHT DISPUTE TO INT'L ORGN	2.	NO	2.	NO
5-33	INDICATED DISPUT IS NEGOTIABLE	2.	NO	2.	NO
5-34	HAS SOUGHT A NEGOT. SETTLEMENT	2.	NO	2.	NO
5-35	HAS OFFERED BI-LATERAL NEGOTNS	2.	NO	2.	NO
5-37	ESC LIKELY BRING GP AID TO ADV	2.	NO	2.	NO
5-42	MARTIAL LAW IS IN EFFECT	2.	NO	8.	0 OR N/A
5-43	STATE OF WAR HAS BEEN DECLARED	2.	NO	8.	0 OR N/A
5-45	LEGAL STATUS OF ADV. PERSONNEL	1.	CITIZEN	1.	CITIZEN
6-1	IS SEC'TY ALLY OF GREAT POWER	1.	YES	2.	NO
6-2	IS SEC'TY ALLY OF NON-G.P.	2.	NO	2.	NO
6-3	IS ALLY OF G.P. HOSTILE TO ADV	1.	YES	2.	NO
6-4	IS ALLY OF G.P. ALLIED TO ADV.	2.	NO	2.	NO
6-5	IS AIDED BY GP HOSTILE TO ADV.	1.	YES	2.	NO
6-8	GP DEF. FAC'TIES IN ANT'S AREA	1.	YES	2.	NO
6-9	HAS INVOKED AVAIL SEC'TY PACTS	2.	NO	8.	0 OR N/A
6-12	SOME 3PTY IS INV. ON THIS SIDE	1.	YES	1.	YES
6-13	INT'L ORG IS INV. ON THIS SIDE	2.	NO	2.	NO
6-14	REG'L ORG IS INV. ON THIS SIDE	2.	NO	2.	NO
6-15	A G.P. IS INV. ON THIS SIDE	1.	YES	2.	NO
6-16	A NON-GP IS INV. ON THIS SIDE	2.	NO	1.	YES
6-17	A AUT ORG IS INV. ON THIS SIDE	2.	NO	2.	NO
6-18	A 3PTY IS PROVIDING POL. AID	1.	YES	1.	YES
6-20	A 3PTY IS PROVIDING MIL ADVICE	1.	YES	2.	NO
6-23	A 3PTY IS PROVIDING GUER FORCE	2.	NO	2.	NO
6-24	ATT. OF 3PTY PUBLIC TO INV'MNT	1.	FAVORABLE	1.	FAVORABLE
6-27	PC ANT'S EXPORTS CONS. BY 3PTY	3.	16-33 PC	8.	0 OR N/A
6-28	EXPERIENCE WITH IO PEACE MACH	2.	GRATIFYING	3.	NONE
6-30	SOME 3PTY OFFERED TO ARBITRATE	2.	NO	2.	NO
6-31	INTL ORG OFFERED TO ARBITRATE	2.	NO	2.	NO
6-32	REGL ORG OFFERED TO ARBITRATE	2.	NO	2.	NO
6-33	A G.P. OFFERED TO ARBITRATE	2.	NO	2.	NO
6-35	INT'L ORG'N UPHELD ANT'S CAUSE	2.	NO	2.	NO
6-36	INTL ORGN INDICTED ANT'S CAUSE	2.	NO	2.	NO
6-37	CITED IN VIOLATION OF INTL LAW	2.	NO	2.	NO
6-38	CITED BY I.O. FOR AGGRESSION	2.	NO	2.	NO
6-40	ACCEPTED IO'S PROP. CEASEFIRE	2.	NO	2.	NO
6-42	I.O. HAS IMPOSED SANCTIONS	2.	NO	2.	NO
6-47	REG ORGN HAS IMPOSED SANCTIONS	2.	NO	2.	NO
7-6	NO. TROOPS COMM AS PC TOT FRCS	8.	0 OR N/A	3.	25.0-114.3
7-7	PC POPN MOB'ZED FOR ACTIV DUTY	1.	0.001-1.0	1.	0.001-1.0
7-8	OTHER SIGNIF INTERNAL THREAT	2.	NO	2.	NO
7-9	OTHER SIGNIF EXTERNAL THREAT	2.	NO	2.	NO
7-12	OVERTNES OF 3PTY PERSONNEL AID	1.	GEN'LY OVERT	8.	0 OR N/A
7-18	NAVAL MANPOWER COMMITTED	1.	0.5-1.0	1.	0.5-1.0
7-19	AIR FORCE MANPOWER COMMITTED	1.	0.05-1.0	1.	0.05-1.0
7-22	NO. AUTO. WEAPONS AVAILABLE	1.	1.0-2.0	1.	1.0-2.0
7-27	NO. HVY. CANNON AVAILABLE	1.	1.0-1.0	1.	1.0-1.0
7-32	NO. JET AIRCRAFT AVAILABLE	1.	1.0-1.1	1.	1.0-1.1
7-33	NO. HELICOPTERS AVAILABLE	1.	1.0-1.0	1.	1.0-1.0
7-34	NO. SAM'S AVAILABLE	1.	1.0-1.0	1.	1.0-1.0
7-35	NO. SSM'S AVAILABLE	1.	1.0-1.0	1.	1.0-1.0
7-36	NO. SUBMARINES AVAILABLE	1.	1.0-1.0	1.	1.0-1.0
7-40	HAS A NUCLEAR CAPABILITY	2.	NO	2.	NO
7-48	DEP FOR TRANSPORT CAPABILITIES	1.	EXCLUSIVE	8.	0 OR N/A
7-49	TRANSP. CAP. SUPPLY LIKELY TO	2.	STAY SAME	8.	0 OR N/A
8-3	REL'SHIP BET POL + MIL LEADERS	1.	POL DOMINANT	1.	POL DOMINANT
8-4	UNITY WITHIN MILITARY COMMAND	1.	UNIFIED	1.	UNIFIED
8-7	METHOD OF MILITARY RECRUITMENT	1.	VOLUNTARY	1.	VOLUNTARY

Item		Compound Response			

8-17	CENTRALIZATION OF MIL. COMMAND	1.	CENTRALIZED	2.	DE-CENTR'ZED
8-26	LARG-SCAL GUER OPN BEING WAGED	8.	0 OR N/A	1.	YES
8-27	STAGE OF GUERRILLA OPERATIONS	8.	0 OR N/A	1.	ORG + CONS
8-33	CIVN SECURITY V. GUERR ATTACK	3.	LOW	8.	0 OR N/A
9-1	PC OF INDUSTRIAL CAPACITY LOST	1.	0.001-1.0	1.	0.001-1.0
9-2	PC OF CIVILIAN POPULATION LOST	1.	0.003-1.0	1.	0.003-1.0
9-3	TOTAL NO. CIVN POPULATION LOST	1.	1.0-1.0	1.	1.0-1.0
9-4	ATTRITION RATE FOR CIV'N POPN	1.	0.5-1.0	1.	0.5-1.0
9-5	TOTAL CAS'TIES TO OWN FORCES	1.	1.0-1.2	1.	1.0-1.2
9-7	TOTAL CAS'TIES TO ALL FORCES	1.	1.0-1.2	1.	1.0-1.2
9-8	CASUALTY RATE FOR OWN FORCES	1.	1.0-2.0	1.	1.0-2.0
9-10	CASUALTY RATE FOR ALL FORCES	1.	1.0-2.0	1.	1.0-2.0
9-11	ATTRITION RATE FOR OWN FORCES	1.	1.0-2.0	1.	1.0-2.0
9-13	ATTRITION RATE FOR ALL FORCES	1.	1.0-2.0	1.	1.0-2.0

Species Type H2

("revolt of the dispossessed in a 'moderate' system")

The factor pattern derives from

Cuba: "little" war of 1906 (Liberal party insurgents vs. Cuban government)

Cyprus: internal (Turkish Cypriots vs. Cypriot government)

1-2A	TOPOGRAPHY OF CONFLICT AREA	1.	FLAT	1.	FLAT
1-3	PAST POL. REL'SHIP BETW PARTYS	1.	COOPERATIVE	1.	COOPERATIVE
1-5	EFFECTIVE NATURE OF DISPUTE	3.	INTERNAL	3.	INTERNAL
1-7	IDEOLOGICAL DIFF. BETW PARTIES	3.	NONE	3.	NONE
1-8	CONTROL OF REAL ESTATE INVOLVD	2.	NO	2.	NO
1-11	DISPUTE HAS BEEN TO REG'L ORGN	2.	NO	2.	NO
2-3	RACIAL GROUPING OF ANTAGONIST	1.	WHITE	1.	WHITE
2-4	REGIM + GENL POPN OF SAME RACE	1.	YES	1.	YES
2-13	POPN UNDER EFFECTIVE CONTROL	8.	0 OR N/A	3.	499.0-65TH
2-19	URBANIZATION	8.	0 OR N/A	2.	MEDIUM
3-2	CROSS NAT'L. OR ECON. PRODUCT	8.	0 OR N/A	3.	90.0-6.4TH
3-3	GROWTH RATE OF ECONOMY	8.	0 OR N/A	3.	3.0-13.9
3-5	PER CAPITA INCOME	8.	0 OR N/A	3.	115.0-855.0
3-6	PC OF GNP IN AGRICULTURE	8.	0 OR N/A	3.	25.0-75.0
3-8	PRODUCTION OF STEEL	1.	1.0-1.0	1.	1.0-1.0
3-9	PC OF GNP IN EXPORTS	8.	0 OR N/A	3.	22.0-1.0TH
3-14	GOVERNMENT INCOME AS PC OF GNP	8.	0 OR N/A	3.	10.0-50.0
3-15	GOVT. SPENDING AS PC OF GNP	8.	0 OR N/A	3.	6.0-50.0
3-20	AGRIC EMPLOYMENT AS PC OF POPN	8.	0 OR N/A	3.	13.0-70.0
3-21	INDUSTRIAL EMPL. AS PC OF POPN	8.	0 OR N/A	3.	11.0-23.0
3-23	UNEMPLOYMENT OF INTELLECTUALS	8.	0 OR N/A	3.	NONE
4-1	EFFECTIVE STATUS OF GOVERNMENT	4.	REBEL ORGN	1.	INDEP GOVT
4-4	EXECUTIVE STABILITY	8.	0 OR N/A	3.	3.0-9.0
4-6	STATUS OF EXECUTIVE	8.	0 OR N/A	2.	STRONG
4-7	STATUS OF LEGISLATURE	8.	0 OR N/A	1.	FULL EFFECT.
4-10	REGIME CAME TO POWER CONST'LY	8.	0 OR N/A	1.	YES
4-11	RECRUITMENT TO POL LEADERSHIP	2.	MODERATE	2.	MODERATE
4-12	IDEOL. ORIENTATION OF REGIME	2.	MODERATE	2.	MODERATE
4-14	INTERNATIONAL POLICY OF REGIME	4.	NONE	3.	MODERATE
4-18	POL. INTEGRATION OF GENL POPN	8.	0 OR N/A	2.	MODERATE
4-19	FREEDOM OF THE PRESS ALLOWED	8.	0 OR N/A	1.	COMPLETE
4-23	INTEREST ARTIC'N BY INST'L GPS	8.	0 OR N/A	1.	POL SIGNIF
4-24	INTEREST ARTIC'N BY POL PARTYS	8.	0 OR N/A	1.	POL SIGNIF
4-25	CONST'AL STATUS OF POL PARTIES	8.	0 OR N/A	1.	COMPETITIVE
4-26	EFFECTIVE POL. PARTY SYSTEM	8.	0 OR N/A	2.	ONE PTY DOM
4-28	PC OF POPN VOTING IN ELECTIONS	8.	0 OR N/A	3.	9.5-95.0
4-29	PC OF VOTE REC'D BY THIS REGIM	8.	0 OR N/A	3.	7.8-100.0
4-32	RECENT LEADERSHIP CRISIS	2.	NO	2.	NO
4-33	RECENT CHANGE IN LEADERSHIP	2.	NO	2.	NO
4-35	REGIM APPEARS MAINT BY FOR RES	8.	0 OR N/A	2.	NO
5-2	REGIME SEEKS OVERTHROW OF ADV.	2.	NO	2.	NO
5-3	INTEREST INVOLVED-IDEOLOGY	2.	NO	2.	NO
5-4	INTEREST INVOLVED-COMMITMENTS	2.	NO	2.	NO
5-10	INTEREST INVOLVED-INDEPENDENCE	2.	NO	2.	NO
5-11	INTEREST INVOLVED-TERR. INTEG.	2.	NO	2.	NO
5-12	INTEREST INVOLVED-CONT'D EXIS.	1.	YES	2.	NO
5-14	DISPUTE IS REGARDED AS CRUSADE	2.	NO	2.	NO
5-15	CONDUCT OF CONFLICT IS LIMITED	1.	YES	1.	YES
5-17	RATIONALIZATION OF VIOLENCE	4.	EXPEDIENCY	8.	0 OR N/A
5-21	LIKELY OUTCOME IS NOW OBVIOUS	2.	NO	2.	NO
5-22	POST-DISPUTE EXPECT'N OF REGIM	2.	PESSIMISTIC	2.	PESSIMISTIC
5-23	DIST FM BORDER TO CONFL AREA	1.	1.0-1.0	1.	1.0-1.0
5-27	SPEED OF COMMUNICATIONS	1.	RAPID	1.	RAPID
5-32	BROUGHT DISPUTE TO INT'L ORGN	2.	NO	2.	NO
5-37	ESC LIKELY BRING GP AID TO ADV	2.	NO	2.	NO
5-42	MARTIAL LAW IS IN EFFECT	8.	0 OR N/A	2.	NO
5-43	STATE OF WAR HAS BEEN DECLARED	8.	0 OR N/A	2.	NO
6-2	IS SEC'TY ALLY OF NON-G.P.	2.	NO	2.	NO
6-3	IS ALLY OF G.P. HOSTILE TO ADV	2.	NO	2.	NO
6-4	IS ALLY OF G.P. ALLIED TO ADV.	2.	NO	2.	NO
6-5	IS AIDED BY GP HOSTILE TO ADV.	2.	NO	2.	NO
6-6	A GP IS OPENLY PARTIAL TO ANT.	2.	NO	2.	NO
6-7	GP AID PROMISED IF ESC. OCCURS	2.	NO	2.	NO
6-8	GP DEF. FAC'TIES IN ANT'S AREA	2.	NO	2.	NO
6-11	HAS ASKED AN INT'L. ORG'N. IN	2.	NO	2.	NO
6-13	INT'L ORG IS INV. ON THIS SIDE	2.	NO	2.	NO
6-14	REG'L ORG IS INV. ON THIS SIDE	2.	NO	2.	NO
6-15	A G.P. IS INV. ON THIS SIDE	2.	NO	2.	NO
6-17	A AUT ORG IS INV. ON THIS SIDE	2.	NO	2.	NO
6-18	A 3PTY IS PROVIDING POL. AID	2.	NO	2.	NO

Item		Compound Response			

6-19	A 3PTY IS PROVIDING ECON. AID	2.	NO	2.	NO
6-22	A 3PTY IS PROVIDING CONV FORCE	2.	NO	2.	NO
6-23	A 3PTY IS PROVIDING GUER FORCE	2.	NO	2.	NO
6-28	EXPERIENCE WITH IO PEACE MACH	3.	NONE	3.	NONE
6-29	I.O. PEACE MACHINERY IS SEEN	2.	IRRELEVANT	2.	IRRELEVANT
6-30	SOME 3PTY OFFERED TO ARBITRATE	2.	NO	2.	NO
6-31	INTL ORGN OFFERED TO ARBITRATE	2.	NO	2.	NO
6-32	REGL ORGN OFFERED TO ARBITRATE	2.	NO	2.	NO
6-33	A G.P. OFFERED TO ARBITRATE	2.	NO	2.	NO
6-35	INT'L ORG'N UPHELD ANT'S CAUSE	2.	NO	2.	NO
6-36	INTL ORGN INDICTED ANT'S CAUSE	2.	NO	2.	NO
6-37	CITED IN VIOLATION OF INTL LAW	2.	NO	2.	NO
6-38	CITED BY I.O. FOR AGGRESSION	2.	NO	2.	NO
6-40	ACCEPTED IO'S PROP. CEASEFIRE	2.	NO	2.	NO
6-42	I.O. HAS IMPOSED SANCTIONS	2.	NO	2.	NO
6-47	REG ORGN HAS IMPOSED SANCTIONS	2.	NO	2.	NO
7-6	NO. TROOPS COMM AS PC TOT FRCS	1.	0.7-1.0	1.	0.7-1.0
7-8	OTHER SIGNIF INTERNAL THREAT	2.	NO	2.	NO
7-9	OTHER SIGNIF EXTERNAL THREAT	2.	NO	2.	NO
7-11	TOTAL TROOPS GIVEN BY 3RD PTY	1.	0.3-1.0	1.	0.3-1.0
7-14	TOTAL MANPOWER COMMITTED	1.	0.02-7.3	1.	0.02-7.3
7-18	NAVAL MANPOWER COMMITTED	1.	0.5-1.0	1.	0.5-1.0
7-19	AIR FORCE MANPOWER COMMITTED	1.	0.05-1.0	1.	0.05-1.0
7-21	NO. RIFLES AVAILABLE	1.	0.05-2.1	1.	0.05-2.1
7-25	NO. LT. CANNON AVAILABLE	1.	1.0-1.0	1.	1.0-1.0
7-26	NO. MED. CANNON AVAILABLE	1.	1.0-1.0	1.	1.0-1.0
7-27	NO. HVY. CANNON AVAILABLE	1.	1.0-1.0	1.	1.0-1.0
7-28	NO. ARMORED VEH. AVAILABLE	1.	1.0-1.5	1.	1.0-1.5
7-36	NO. SUBMARINES AVAILABLE	1.	1.0-1.0	1.	1.0-1.0
7-37	NO. HEAVY VESSELS AVAILABLE	1.	1.0-1.0	1.	1.0-1.0
7-38	NO. LANDING CRAFT AVAILABLE	1.	1.0-1.1	1.	1.0-1.1
7-39	NO. PATROL BOATS AVAILABLE	1.	1.0-1.2	1.	1.0-1.2
8-4	UNITY WITHIN MILITARY COMMAND	1.	UNIFIED	1.	UNIFIED
8-7	METHOD OF MILITARY RECRUITMENT	1.	VOLUNTARY	1.	VOLUNTARY
8-9	TRAINING FACILITY FOR OFFICERS	3.	POOR	1.	GOOD
8-11	TRAINING FAC FOR ENLISTED PERS	3.	POOR	1.	GOOD
8-13	OVERALL MILITARY ORG'N BALANCE	3.	UNFAVORABLE	1.	FAVORABLE
8-17	CENTRALIZATION OF MIL. COMMAND	2.	DE-CENTR'ZED	1.	CENTRALIZED
8-20	USE OF TERROR BY THIS ANT. IS	3.	ABSENT	3.	ABSENT
9-1	PC OF INDUSTRIAL CAPACITY LOST	1.	0.001-1.0	1.	0.001-1.0
9-2	PC OF CIVILIAN POPULATION LOST	1.	0.003-1.0	1.	0.003-1.0
9-3	TOTAL NO. CIVN POPULATION LOST	1.	1.0-1.0	1.	1.0-1.0
9-4	ATTRITION RATE FOR CIV'N POPN	1.	0.5-1.0	1.	0.5-1.0
9-5	TOTAL CAS'TIES TO OWN FORCES	1.	1.0-1.2	1.	1.0-1.2
9-7	TOTAL CAS'TIES TO ALL FORCES	1.	1.0-1.2	1.	1.0-1.2
9-8	CASUALTY RATE FOR OWN FORCES	1.	1.0-2.0	1.	1.0-2.0
9-10	CASUALTY RATE FOR ALL FORCES	1.	1.0-2.0	1.	1.0-2.0

Species Type H3
("taking advantage of the moment")

The factor pattern derives from
Ethiopia-Somalia (Ethiopia vs.
Somalia)

Kashmir (Pakistan vs. India)

1-3	PAST POL. REL'SHIP BETW PARTYS	2.	COMPETITIVE	2.	COMPETITIVE
1-4	PAST MIL. REL'SHIP BETW PARTYS	2.	RANDOM HOST.	2.	RANDOM HOST.
1-8	CONTROL OF REAL ESTATE INVOLVD	1.	YES	1.	YES
1-9	SIZE OF AREA AT STAKE(TH SQ M)	3.	84.0-197.0	3.	84.0-197.0
1-10	SIZE OF POPN AT STAKE (THOUS.)	2.	1.0TH-4.0TH	2.	1.0TH-4.0TH
1-11	DISPUTE HAS BEEN TO REG'L ORGN	1.	YES	1.	YES
1-12	DISPUTE HAS BEEN TO INT'L ORGN	1.	YES	1.	YES
1-13	INTRODUCED TO INT'L ORGN BY A	1.	ANTAGONIST	1.	ANTAGONIST
1-14	BASIS OF INTRO. TO INT'L ORGN	1.	AGGRESSION	1.	AGGRESSION
2-4	REGIM + GENL POPN OF SAME RACE	1.	YES	1.	YES
2-5	RACIAL HOMOGENEITY OF GENL POP	2.	HETERO	1.	HOMOGENEOUS
2-9	LITERACY RATE AMONG GENL POPN	3.	LOW	3.	LOW
2-10	NEWSPAPER CIRCULATION IN POPN	4.	VERY LOW	4.	VERY LOW
3-5	PER CAPITA INCOME	1.	1.0-2.1	1.	1.0-2.1
3-14	GOVERNMENT INCOME AS PC OF GNP	1.	1.0-1.5	2.	1.8-6.0
3-18	DEFENSE BUDGET AS PC OF GNP	1.	0.3-2.7	1.	0.3-2.7
4-1	EFFECTIVE STATUS OF GOVERNMENT	1.	INDEP GOVT	1.	INDEP GOVT
4-6	STATUS OF EXECUTIVE	1.	DOMINANT	2.	STRONG
4-10	REGIME CAME TO POWER CONST'LY	2.	NO	1.	YES
4-14	INTERNATIONAL POLICY OF REGIME	3.	MODERATE	3.	MODERATE
4-15	COMMUNIST ORIENT'N OF REGIME	4.	NON-COM.	4.	NON-COM.
4-17	MOBILIZATIONAL STYLE OF REGIME	2.	LIMITED	1.	FULL
4-18	POL. INTEGRATION OF GENL POPN	2.	MODERATE	1.	HIGH
4-20	FREEDOM OF GROUP OPPOSITION	2.	LIMITED	1.	FULL
4-22	INTEREST ARTIC'N BY ASSOC'L GP	2.	POL INSIGNIF	1.	POL SIGNIF
4-23	INTEREST ARTIC'N BY INST'L GPS	1.	POL SIGNIF	1.	POL SIGNIF
4-24	INTEREST ARTIC'N BY POL PARTYS	2.	POL INSIGNIF	1.	POL SIGNIF
4-25	CONST'AL STATUS OF POL PARTIES	2.	PART COMPET.	1.	COMPETITIVE
4-34	FOR. RES ARE MAINSTAY OF REGIM	2.	NO	2.	NO
4-35	REGIM APPEARS MAINT BY FOR RES	2.	NO	2.	NO
4-36	POP. SUPPORT FOR REGIME'S OBJ.	1.	HIGH	1.	HIGH
4-37	POP. SUPPORT FOR REGIM'S POLS.	1.	HIGH	1.	HIGH
4-38	ATT. OF INTELLECTUALS TO REGIM	1.	FAVORABLE	1.	FAVORABLE
5-2	REGIME SEEKS OVERTHROW OF ADV.	2.	NO	2.	NO
5-3	INTEREST INVOLVED-IDEOLOGY	2.	NO	2.	NO

Item		Compound Response			

Item					
5-4	INTEREST INVOLVED-COMMITMENTS	1.	YES	1.	YES
5-10	INTEREST INVOLVED-INDEPENDENCE	2.	NO	2.	NO
5-12	INTEREST INVOLVED-CONT'D EXIS.	2.	NO	2.	NO
5-13	COMMITMENT TO STATED GOALS	2.	FLEXIBLE	2.	FLEXIBLE
5-15	CONDUCT OF CONFLICT IS LIMITED	1.	YES	1.	YES
5-19	PRESENT OUTLOOK WRT DISPUTE	2.	MODERATE	2.	MODERATE
5-20	PERCEIVED BALANCE OF WILL	2.	EVEN	2.	EVEN
5-25	ADVERSARY APPEARS TO ANT TO BE	2.	AUT + INDEP.	2.	AUT + INDEP.
5-28	RELIABILITY OF COMMUNICATIONS	1.	HIGH	1.	HIGH
5-29	CREDIBILITY OF COMMUNICATIONS	1.	HIGH	1.	HIGH
5-33	INDICATED DISPUT IS NEGOTIABLE	1.	YES	2.	NO
5-38	P.O. RE ADV'S POL. INST'NS.	2.	UNFAVORABLE	2.	UNFAVORABLE
5-39	P.O. RE ADV'S SOCIAL INST'NS.	2.	UNFAVORABLE	2.	UNFAVORABLE
5-41	P.O. RE ADV'S REL. INST'NS.	2.	UNFAVORABLE	2.	UNFAVORABLE
5-43	STATE OF WAR HAS BEEN DECLARED	2.	NO	2.	NO
5-45	LEGAL STATUS OF ADV. PERSONNEL	1.	CITIZEN	1.	CITIZEN
5-46	AMNESTY DECL FOR ADV PERSONNEL	2.	NO	2.	NO
6-2	IS SEC'TY ALLY OF NON-G.P.	1.	YES	2.	NO
6-3	IS ALLY OF G.P. HOSTILE TO ADV	2.	NO	2.	NO
6-4	IS ALLY OF G.P. ALLIED TO ADV.	2.	NO	2.	NO
6-5	IS AIDED BY GP HOSTILE TO ADV.	2.	NO	2.	NO
6-7	GP AID PROMISED IF ESC. OCCURS	2.	NO	2.	NO
6-13	INT'L ORG IS INV. ON THIS SIDE	2.	NO	2.	NO
6-14	REG'L ORG IS INV. ON THIS SIDE	2.	NO	2.	NO
6-16	A NON-GP IS INV. ON THIS SIDE	2.	NO	2.	NO
6-18	A 3PTY IS PROVIDING POL. AID	1.	YES	2.	NO
6-24	ATT. OF 3PTY PUBLIC TO INV'MNT	1.	FAVORABLE	8.	0 OR N/A
6-25	AID TO ANT. HURTS 3PTY ECONOMY	2.	NO	8.	0 OR N/A
6-26	PC ANT'S ECONOMY OWNED BY 3PTY	1.	0 - 4 PC	8.	0 OR N/A
6-27	PC ANT'S EXPORTS CONS. BY 3PTY	1.	0 - 4 PC	8.	0 OR N/A
6-28	EXPERIENCE WITH IO PEACE MACH	1.	FRUSTRATING	1.	FRUSTRATING
6-30	SOME 3PTY OFFERED TO ARBITRATE	2.	NO	2.	NO
6-31	INTL ORGN OFFERED TO ARBITRATE	2.	NO	2.	NO
6-32	REGL ORGN OFFERED TO ARBITRATE	2.	NO	2.	NO
6-33	A G.P. OFFERED TO ARBITRATE	2.	NO	2.	NO
6-35	INT'L ORG'N UPHELD ANT'S CAUSE	2.	NO	2.	NO
6-36	INTL ORGN INDICTED ANT'S CAUSE	2.	NO	2.	NO
6-37	CITED IN VIOLATION OF INTL LAW	2.	NO	2.	NO
6-38	CITED BY I.O. FOR AGGRESSION	2.	NO	2.	NO
6-40	ACCEPTED IO'S PROP. CEASEFIRE	2.	NO	2.	NO
6-42	I.O. HAS IMPOSED SANCTIONS	2.	NO	2.	NO
6-47	REG ORGN HAS IMPOSED SANCTIONS	2.	NO	2.	NO
7-1	NO. OF OWN ACTIVE MIL. TROOPS	1.	0.02-10.7	1.	0.02-10.7
7-4	MOBILIZATION OF RESERVES	1.	NONE	1.	NONE
7-5	NO. TROOPS COMMITTED TO CONFL.	1.	0.02-1.0	2.	1.2-50.0
7-8	OTHER SIGNIF INTERNAL THREAT	2.	NO	2.	NO
7-11	TOTAL TROOPS GIVEN BY 3RD PTY	1.	0.3-1.0	1.	0.3-1.0
7-13	3PTY TROOP AID SEEN LIKELY TO	2.	STAY SAME	2.	STAY SAME
7-14	TOTAL MANPOWER COMMITTED	1.	0.02-7.3	1.	0.02-7.3
7-15	OWN TRPS AS PC OF ALL COMMITED	1.	1.0-1.5	1.	1.0-1.5
7-16	CONVENTIONAL MANPOWER COMMITTED	1.	0.01-3.0	1.	0.01-3.0
7-17	GUERRILLA MANPOWER COMMITTED	1.	0.02-1.0	1.	0.02-1.0
7-18	NAVAL MANPOWER COMMITTED	1.	0.5-1.0	1.	0.5-1.0
7-40	HAS A NUCLEAR CAPABILITY	2.	NO	2.	NO
7-50	OVERTNESS OF 3PTY HARDWARE AID	1.	GEN'LY OVERT	1.	GEN'LY OVERT
7-51	SPARE PARTS AND AMMUNITION AID	1.	ADEQUATE	1.	ADEQUATE
8-7	METHOD OF MILITARY RECRUITMENT	1.	VOLUNTARY	1.	VOLUNTARY
8-9	TRAINING FACILITY FOR OFFICERS	1.	GOOD	1.	GOOD
8-16	OVERALL MIL. HARDWARE BALANCE	1.	FAVORABLE	3.	UNFAVORABLE
8-17	CENTRALIZATION OF MIL. COMMAND	1.	CENTRALIZED	1.	CENTRALIZED
8-30	SYMPATHY BETW POPN + OWN MIL.	1.	SYMPATHETIC	1.	SYMPATHETIC
8-33	CIVN SECURITY V. GUERR ATTACK	2.	MODERATE	2.	MODERATE
8-34	CIV.I SEC V AC ATK BY OWN FRCES	1.	HIGH	1.	HIGH
8-35	CIVN SEC V ABUSE BY OWN FORCES	1.	HIGH	1.	HIGH
9-1	PC OF INDUSTRIAL CAPACITY LOST	1.	0.001-1.0	1.	0.001-1.0
9-2	PC OF CIVILIAN POPULATION LOST	1.	0.003-1.0	1.	0.003-1.0
9-4	ATTRITION RATE FOR CIV'N POPN	1.	0.5-1.0	1.	0.5-1.0
9-8	CASUALTY RATE FOR OWN FORCES	1.	1.0-2.0	1.	1.0-2.0
9-10	CASUALTY RATE FOR ALL FORCES	1.	1.0-2.0	1.	1.0-2.0
9-11	ATTRITION RATE FOR OWN FORCES	1.	1.0-2.0	1.	1.0-2.0
9-13	ATTRITION RATE FOR ALL FORCES	1.	1.0-2.0	1.	1.0-2.0

Species Type H4
("exploratory probe in a continuing confrontation")

The factor pattern derives from

India-China (India vs. China)

USSR-Iran (Iran vs. USSR)

Item					
1-2A	TOPOGRAPHY OF CONFLICT AREA	2.	MOUNTAINOUS	2.	MOUNTAINOUS
1-2B	CLIMATE IN THE CONFLICT AREA	2.	MODERATE	2.	MODERATE
1-3	PAST POL. REL'SHIP BETW PARTYS	2.	COMPETITIVE	2.	COMPETITIVE
1-6	DURATION OF DISPUTE (IN MOS.)	4.	57.0-215.0	4.	57.0-215.0
1-7	IDEOLOGICAL DIFF. BETW PARTIES	1.	EXTREME	1.	EXTREME
1-8	CONTROL OF REAL ESTATE INVOLVD	1.	YES	1.	YES
1-11	DISPUTE HAS BEEN TO REG'L ORGN	2.	NO	2.	NO
2-4	REGIM + GENL POPN OF SAME RACE	1.	YES	1.	YES
2-5	RACIAL HOMOGENEITY OF GENL POP	1.	HOMOGENEOUS	1.	HOMOGENEOUS
2-17	PC OF INVOLVED AREA IN CONTROL	1.	1.0-1.5	1.	1.0-1.5
2-19	URBANIZATION	2.	MEDIUM	2.	MEDIUM
3-3	GROWTH RATE OF ECONOMY	1.	1.0-1.0	3.	3.0-13.9

Item		Compound Response			
3-5	PER CAPITA INCOME	1.	1.0-2.1	1.	1.0-2.1
3-6	PC OF GNP IN AGRICULTURE	1.	1.0-2.0	1.	1.0-2.0
4-1	EFFECTIVE STATUS OF GOVERNMENT	1.	INDEP GOVT	1.	INDEP GOVT
4-3	MODERN COLONIAL RULER	1.	BRITAIN	5.	NONE
4-4	EXECUTIVE STABILITY	1.	1.0-1.0	1.	1.0-1.0
4-6	STATUS OF EXECUTIVE	2.	STRONG	1.	DOMINANT
4-10	REGIME CAME TO POWER CONST'LY	1.	YES	2.	NO
4-12	IDEOL. ORIENTATION OF REGIME	2.	MODERATE	1.	LEFT-WING
4-13	INTERNAL POLICIES OF REGIME	2.	MODERATE	3.	REVOL'ARY
4-14	INTERNATIONAL POLICY OF REGIME	3.	MODERATE	1.	LEFTIST
4-19	FREEDOM OF THE PRESS ALLOWED	2.	INTERMITTENT	4.	FULLY ABSENT
4-20	FREEDOM OF GROUP OPPOSITION	1.	FULL	4.	NOT TOLERATD
4-21	INTEREST ARTIC'N BY ANOMIC GPS	1.	FREQUENT	3.	NOT TOLERATD
4-23	INTEREST ARTIC'N BY INST'L GPS	1.	POL SIGNIF	2.	POL INSIGNIF
4-25	CONST'AL STATUS OF POL PARTIES	1.	COMPETITIVE	3.	NON-COMPET.
4-29	PC OF VOTE REC'D BY THIS REGIM	1.	1.2-1.3	2.	1.7-2.5
4-30	PC VOTE RECD BY LT WING PTIES	1.	1.0-1.0	2.	2.5-6.7
4-34	FORN RES ARE MAINSTAY OF REGIM	2.	NO	2.	NO
4-35	REGIM APPEARS MAINT BY FOR RES	2.	NO	2.	NO
4-36	POP. SUPPORT FOR REGIME'S OBJ.	1.	HIGH	1.	HIGH
4-39	POST-DISPUTE EXPECT'N OF POPN	2.	PESSIMISTIC	1.	OPTIMISTIC
5-4	INTEREST INVOLVED-COMMITMENTS	2.	NO	2.	NO
5-7	INTEREST INVOLVED-PRESTIGE	2.	NO	1.	YES
5-8	INTEREST INVOLVED-PRIDE	2.	NO	2.	NO
5-9	INTEREST INVOLVED-POWER	2.	NO	1.	YES
5-13	COMMITMENT TO STATED GOALS	2.	FLEXIBLE	3.	SLIGHT
5-14	DISPUTE IS REGARDED AS CRUSADE	2.	NO	2.	NO
5-15	CONDUCT OF CONFLICT IS LIMITED	1.	YES	1.	YES
5-19	PRESENT OUTLOOK WRT DISPUTE	2.	MODERATE	1.	MODERATE
5-22	POST-DISPUTE EXPECT'N OF REGIM	2.	PESSIMISTIC	1.	OPTIMISTIC
5-23	DIST FM BORDER TO CONFL AREA	1.	1.0-1.0	1.	1.0-1.0
5-24	DIST FM CAPITAL TO CONFL AREA	1.	1.0-1.3	2.	1.7-5.0
5-26	TREATY EXPERIENCE WITH ADV.	2.	UNSATISF'ORY	1.	SATISFACTORY
5-28	RELIABILITY OF COMMUNICATIONS	1.	HIGH	1.	HIGH
5-34	HAS SOUGHT A NEGOT. SETTLEMENT	1.	YES	1.	YES
5-35	HAS OFFERED BI-LATERAL NEGOTNS	1.	YES	1.	YES
5-36	HAS ATTENDED BI-LAT'L NEGOT'NS	1.	YES	1.	YES
5-38	P.O. RE ADV'S POL. INST'NS.	2.	UNFAVORABLE	2.	UNFAVORABLE
5-39	P.O. RE ADV'S SOCIAL INST'NS.	2.	UNFAVORABLE	2.	UNFAVORABLE
5-41	P.O. RE ADV'S REL. INST'NS.	2.	UNFAVORABLE	2.	UNFAVORABLE
5-43	STATE OF WAR HAS BEEN DECLARED	2.	NO	2.	NO
5-45	LEGAL STATUS OF ADV. PERSONNEL	1.	CITIZEN	1.	CITIZEN
6-2	IS SEC'TY ALLY OF NON-G.P.	2.	NO	2.	NO
6-4	IS ALLY OF G.P. ALLIED TO ADV.	2.	NO	2.	NO
6-5	IS AIDED BY GP HOSTILE TO ADV.	1.	YES	2.	NO
6-6	A GP IS OPENLY PARTIAL TO ANT.	1.	YES	2.	NO
6-7	GP AID PROMISED IF ESC. OCCURS	2.	NO	2.	NO
6-8	GP DEF. FAC'TIES IN ANT'S AREA	2.	NO	2.	NO
6-14	REG'L ORG IS INV. ON THIS SIDE	2.	NO	2.	NO
6-15	A G.P. IS INV. ON THIS SIDE	1.	YES	2.	NO
6-16	A NON-GP IS INV. ON THIS SIDE	2.	NO	2.	NO
6-18	A 3PTY IS PROVIDING POL. AID	1.	YES	2.	NO
6-22	A 3PTY IS PROVIDING CONV FORCE	2.	NO	2.	NO
6-24	ATT. OF 3PTY PUBLIC TO INV'MNT	1.	FAVORABLE	8.	0 OR N/A
6-24A	TYPE OF GOVERNMENT OF 3RD PTY.	1.	POL. DEMOC.	8.	0 OR N/A
6-26	PC ANT'S ECONOMY OWNED BY 3PTY	2.	5 -15 PC	8.	0 OR N/A
6-30	SOME 3PTY OFFERED TO ARBITRATE	2.	NO	2.	NO
6-31	INTL ORGN OFFERED TO ARBITRATE	2.	NO	2.	NO
6-32	REGL ORGN OFFERED TO ARBITRATE	2.	NO	2.	NO
6-33	A G.P. OFFERED TO ARBITRATE	2.	NO	2.	NO
6-37	CITED IN VIOLATION OF INTL LAW	2.	NO	2.	NO
6-38	CITED BY I.O. FOR AGGRESSION	2.	NO	2.	NO
6-40	ACCEPTED IO'S PROP. CEASEFIRE	2.	NO	2.	NO
6-42	I.O. HAS IMPOSED SANCTIONS	2.	NO	2.	NO
6-47	REG ORGN HAS IMPOSED SANCTIONS	2.	NO	2.	NO
7-2	NO. ACTIV TROOPS AS PC OF POPN	1.	0.001-1.0	2.	1.3-174.0
7-5	NO. TROOPS COMMITTED TO CONFL.	1.	0.02-1.0	2.	1.2-50.0
7-8	OTHER SIGNIF INTERNAL THREAT	1.	YES	2.	NO
7-13	3PTY TROOP AID SEEN LIKELY TO	2.	STAY SAME	2.	STAY SAME
7-14	TOTAL MANPOWER COMMITTED	1.	0.02-7.3	1.	0.02-7.3
7-15	OWN TRPS AS PC OF ALL COMMITED	1.	1.0-1.5	1.	1.0-1.5
7-18	NAVAL MANPOWER COMMITTED	1.	0.5-1.0	1.	0.5-1.0
7-40	HAS A NUCLEAR CAPABILITY	2.	NO	3.	IN DEV'MENT
7-41	AIDING 3PTY HAS NUCLEAR CAP'TY	1.	YES	2.	NO
7-50	OVERTNESS OF 3PTY HARDWARE AID	1.	GEN'LY OVERT	8.	0 OR N/A
8-3	REL'SHIP BET POL + MIL LEADERS	1.	POL DOMINANT	1.	POL DOMINANT
8-4	UNITY WITHIN MILITARY COMMAND	1.	UNIFIED	1.	UNIFIED
8-16	OVERALL MIL. HARDWARE BALANCE	3.	UNFAVORABLE	1.	FAVORABLE
8-17	CENTRALIZATION OF MIL. COMMAND	1.	CENTRALIZED	1.	CENTRALIZED
8-29	INTELL. IN ADV'S POLICY ORGANS	3.	INEFFECTIVE	2.	OCCASIONAL
8-30	SYMPATHY BETW POPN + OWN MIL.	1.	SYMPATHETIC	1.	SYMPATHETIC
8-33	CIVN SECURITY V. GUERR ATTACK	2.	MODERATE	1.	HIGH

Species Type H5
("my big brother can lick yours; or, what are guns for, anyway?")

Item		Compound Response			
1-2A	TOPOGRAPHY OF CONFLICT AREA	1.	FLAT	1.	FLAT
1-3	PAST POL. REL'SHIP BETW PARTYS	2.	COMPETITIVE	2.	COMPETITIVE
1-5	EFFECTIVE NATURE OF DISPUTE	2.	INTERSTATE	2.	INTERSTATE
1-6	DURATION OF DISPUTE (IN MOS.)	1.	0.1-13.0	1.	0.1-13.0
1-8	CONTROL OF REAL ESTATE INVOLVD	1.	YES	1.	YES
1-10	SIZE OF POPN AT STAKE (THOUS.)	2.	1.0TH-4.0TH	2.	1.0TH-4.0TH

The factor pattern derives from

Indonesia-Malaysia (Malaysia vs. Indonesia)

Israel-Egypt (Israel vs. Egypt)

Item		Compound Response			
2-1	OVERRIDING CULTURAL IDEAL	2.	RATIONALITY	3.	AGGRESSIVE
2-4	REGIM + GENL POPN OF SAME RACE	1.	YES	1.	YES
2-5	RACIAL HOMOGENEITY OF GENL POP	2.	HETERO	1.	HOMOGENEOUS
2-13	POPN UNDER EFFECTIVE CONTROL	1.	1.0-2.0	2.	3.2-52.2
3-17	MILITARY DEFENSE BUDGET	1.	1.0-1.0	2.	1.4-25.0
3-21	INDUSTRIAL EMPL. AS PC OF POPN	2.	1.5-5.0	1.	1.0-1.1
3-22	UNEMPLOYED AS PC OF GENL POPN	1.	0.5-1.0	1.	0.5-1.0
4-1	EFFECTIVE STATUS OF GOVERNMENT	1.	INDEP GOVT	1.	INDEP GOVT
4-5	TYPE OF GOVERNMENT	1.	POL DEMOC	2.	TUT/MOD OLIG
4-6	STATUS OF EXECUTIVE	2.	STRONG	1.	DOMINANT
4-10	REGIME CAME TO POWER CONST'LY	1.	YES	2.	NO
4-13	INTERNAL POLICIES OF REGIME	2.	MODERATE	3.	REVOL'ARY
4-19	FREEDOM OF THE PRESS ALLOWED	2.	INTERMITTENT	3.	DOM. ABSENCE
4-28	PC OF POPN VOTING IN ELECTIONS	1.	1.0-1.0	2.	1.2-2.0
4-32	RECENT LEADERSHIP CRISIS	2.	NO	2.	NO
4-33	RECENT CHANGE IN LEADERSHIP	2.	NO	2.	NO
4-35	REGIM APPEARS MAINT BY FOR RES	2.	NO	2.	NO
4-37	POP. SUPPORT FOR REGIM'S POLS.	1.	HIGH	1.	HIGH
4-38	ATT. OF INTELLECTUALS TO REGIM	1.	FAVORABLE	1.	FAVORABLE
5-14	DISPUTE IS REGARDED AS CRUSADE	2.	NO	1.	YES
5-22	POST-DISPUTE EXPECT'N OF REGIM	2.	PESSIMISTIC	2.	PESSIMISTIC
5-23	DIST FM BORDER TO CONFL AREA	1.	1.0-1.0	1.	1.0-1.0
5-29	CREDIBILITY OF COMMUNICATIONS	2.	LOW	2.	LOW
5-32	BROUGHT DISPUTE TO INT'L ORGN	2.	NO	2.	NO
5-33	INDICATED DISPUT IS NEGOTIABLE	2.	NO	2.	NO
5-38	P.O. RE ADV'S POL. INST'NS.	2.	UNFAVORABLE	2.	UNFAVORABLE
5-39	P.O. RE ADV'S SOCIAL INST'NS.	2.	UNFAVORABLE	2.	UNFAVORABLE
5-45	LEGAL STATUS OF ADV. PERSONNEL	4.	ENEMY AGENT	4.	ENEMY AGENT
6-1	IS SEC'TY ALLY OF GREAT POWER	1.	YES	2.	NO
6-4	IS ALLY OF G.P. ALLIED TO ADV.	2.	NO	2.	NO
6-5	IS AIDED BY GP HOSTILE TO ADV.	1.	YES	1.	YES
6-6	A GP IS OPENLY PARTIAL TO ANT.	1.	YES	1.	YES
6-11	HAS ASKED AN INT'L ORG'N. IN	2.	NO	2.	NO
6-12	SOME 3PTY IS INV. ON THIS SIDE	1.	YES	1.	YES
6-13	INT'L ORG IS INV. ON THIS SIDE	2.	NO	2.	NO
6-14	REG'L ORG IS INV. ON THIS SIDE	2.	NO	2.	NO
6-15	A G.P. IS INV. ON THIS SIDE	1.	YES	1.	YES
6-17	A AUT ORG IS INV. ON THIS SIDE	2.	NO	2.	NO
6-18	A 3PTY IS PROVIDING POL. AID	1.	YES	1.	YES
6-19	A 3PTY IS PROVIDING ECON. AID	1.	YES	1.	YES
6-21	A 3PTY IS PROVIDING MIL HDWRE.	1.	YES	1.	YES
6-23	A 3PTY IS PROVIDING GUER FORCE	2.	NO	2.	NO
6-24	ATT. OF 3PTY PUBLIC TO INV'MNT	1.	FAVORABLE	1.	FAVORABLE
6-24A	TYPE OF GOVERNMENT OF 3RD PTY.	1.	POL. DEMOC.	3.	TOTAL OLIG
6-24B	RECENT CHANGE IN 3RD PTY GOVT.	2.	NO	2.	NO
6-25	AID TO ANT. HURTS 3PTY ECONOMY	2.	NO	2.	NO
6-29	I.O. PEACE MACHINERY IS SEEN	2.	IRRELEVANT	2.	IRRELEVANT
6-31	INTL ORGN OFFERED TO ARBITRATE	2.	NO	2.	NO
6-32	REGL ORGN OFFERED TO ARBITRATE	2.	NO	2.	NO
6-33	A G.P. OFFERED TO ARBITRATE	2.	NO	2.	NO
6-35	INT'L ORG'N UPHELD ANT'S CAUSE	2.	NO	2.	NO
6-36	INTL ORGN INDICTED ANT'S CAUSE	2.	NO	2.	NO
6-37	CITED IN VIOLATION OF INTL LAW	2.	NO	2.	NO
6-38	CITED BY I.O. FOR AGGRESSION	2.	NO	2.	NO
6-40	ACCEPTED IO'S PROP. CEASEFIRE	2.	NO	2.	NO
6-42	I.O. HAS IMPOSED SANCTIONS	2.	NO	2.	NO
7-3	NO. RESERVE TROOPS AVAILABLE	1.	0.5-1.4	1.	0.5-1.4
7-8	OTHER SIGNIF INTERNAL THREAT	2.	NO	1.	YES
7-16	CONVENTIONAL MANPWER COMMITTED	1.	0.01-3.0	1.	0.01-3.0
7-18	NAVAL MANPOWER COMMITTED	1.	0.5-1.0	1.	0.5-1.0
7-35	NO. SSM'S AVAILABLE	1.	1.0-1.0	1.	1.0-1.0
7-41	AIDING 3PTY HAS NUCLEAR CAP'TY	1.	YES	1.	YES
7-43	BATTLE ARMS SUPPLY LIKELY TO	2.	STAY SAME	2.	STAY SAME
7-44	DEPENDENCE FOR NAVAL ARMAMENTS	1.	EXCLUSIVE	1.	EXCLUSIVE
7-45	NAVAL ARMS SUPPLY LIKELY TO	2.	STAY SAME	2.	STAY SAME
7-49	TRANSP. CAP. SUPPLY LIKELY TO	2.	STAY SAME	2.	STAY SAME
7-52	TRAINING FOR WEAPONS IN AID	1.	ADEQUATE	2.	SELECTIVE
7-53	PC TOTAL COSTS COMING FM 3PTY	8.	0 OR N/A	3.	8.0-100.0
8-1	POLITICAL CHARACTER OF MILTARY	3.	NEUTRAL	1.	INTERVENTIVE
8-11	TRAINING FAC FOR ENLISTED PERS	1.	GOOD	2.	FAIR
8-13	OVERALL MILITARY ORG'N BALANCE	1.	FAVORABLE	3.	UNFAVORABLE
8-20	USE OF TERROR BY THIS ANT. IS	3.	ABSENT	3.	ABSENT
8-30	SYMPATHY BETW POPN + OWN MIL.	1.	SYMPATHETIC	1.	SYMPATHETIC
8-31	SYMPATHY BETW POPN + 3PTY MIL.	1.	SYMPATHETIC	8.	0 OR N/A
8-34	CIVN SEC V AC ATK BY OWN FRCES	1.	HIGH	1.	HIGH
9-2	PC OF CIVILIAN POPULATION LOST	1.	0.003-1.0	1.	0.003-1.0
9-6	TOTAL CAS'TIES TO 3PTY FORCES	1.	1.0-1.0	1.	1.0-1.0
9-9	CASUALTY RATE FOR 3PTY FORCES	1.	0.1-1.0	1.	0.1-1.0
9-12	ATTRITION RATE FOR 3PTY FORCES	1.	0.1-1.0	1.	0.1-1.0

Species Type H6

("a new conductor, a new arrangement")

The factor pattern derives from

Item		Compound Response			
1-3	PAST POL. REL'SHIP BETW PARTYS	3.	EXPLOITIVE	3.	EXPLOITIVE
1-5	EFFECTIVE NATURE OF DISPUTE	1.	COLONIAL	1.	COLONIAL
1-7	IDEOLOGICAL DIFF. BETW PARTIES	1.	EXTREME	1.	EXTREME
1-8	CONTROL OF REAL ESTATE INVOLVD	1.	YES	1.	YES
1-9	SIZE OF AREA AT STAKE(TH SQ M)	4.	340.0-480.0	4.	340.0-480.0
1-10	SIZE OF POPN AT STAKE (THOUS.)	4.	101H-76TH	4.	10TH-76TH
1-11	DISPUTE HAS BEEN TO REG'L ORGN	2.	NO	2.	NO

	Item		Compound Response	

Ethiopian resistance (Ethiopian insurgents vs. Italian colonial administration)

Indonesia: independence (Dutch colonial administration vs. Indonesian insurgents)

Item		Compound Response	
1-12	DISPUTE HAS BEEN TO INT'L ORGN	1. YES	1. YES
1-14	BASIS OF INTRO. TO INT'L ORGN	1. AGGRESSION	1. AGGRESSION
2-5	RACIAL HOMOGENEITY OF GENL POP	1. HOMOGENEOUS	1. HOMOGENEOUS
2-14	REAL ESTATE INVOLVED IS	1. IN CLMD BDY	1. IN CLMD BDY
2-15	PC OF ANT'S CLMD AREA INVOLVED	1. 1.0-1.0	1. 1.0-1.0
2-16	PC OF ANT'S CLMD POPN INVOLVED	1. 1.0-1.0	1. 1.0-1.0
2-17	PC OF INVOLVED AREA IN CONTROL	2. 1.9-9.0	1. 1.0-1.5
2-19	URBANIZATION	3. LOW	3. LOW
3-5	PER CAPITA INCOME	1. 1.0-2.1	1. 1.0-2.1
3-6	PC OF GNP IN AGRICULTURE	1. 1.0-2.0	1. 1.0-2.0
3-7	PC OF GNP IN DURABLE GOODS	1. 1.0-1.2	1. 1.0-1.2
3-8	PRODUCTION OF STEEL	1. 1.0-1.0	1. 1.0-1.0
4-24	INTEREST ARTIC'N BY POL PARTYS	2. POL INSIGNIF	1. POL SIGNIF
4-32	RECENT LEADERSHIP CRISIS	2. NO	2. NO
4-33	RECENT CHANGE IN LEADERSHIP	2. NO	2. NO
5-2	REGIME SEEKS OVERTHROW OF ADV.	1. YES	1. YES
5-9	INTEREST INVOLVED-POWER	2. NO	1. YES
5-11	INTEREST INVOLVED-TERR. INTEG.	1. YES	1. YES
5-12	INTEREST INVOLVED-CONT'D EXIS.	1. YES	1. YES
5-21	LIKELY OUTCOME IS NOW OBVIOUS	2. NO	2. NO
5-22	POST-DISPUTE EXPECT'N OF REGIM	2. PESSIMISTIC	2. PESSIMISTIC
5-23	DIST FM BORDER TO CONFL AREA	1. 1.0-1.0	1. 1.0-1.0
5-24	DIST FM CAPITAL TO CONFL AREA	1. 1.0-1.3	1. 1.0-1.3
5-26	TREATY EXPERIENCE WITH ADV.	2. UNSATISF'ORY	2. UNSATISF'ORY
5-29	CREDIBILITY OF COMMUNICATIONS	2. LOW	2. LOW
5-43	STATE OF WAR HAS BEEN DECLARED	2. NO	2. NO
6-4	IS ALLY OF G.P. ALLIED TO ADV.	2. NO	2. NO
6-7	GP AID PROMISED IF ESC. OCCURS	2. NO	2. NO
6-12	SOME 3PTY IS INV. ON THIS SIDE	2. NO	1. YES
6-14	REG'L ORG IS INV. ON THIS SIDE	2. NO	2. NO
6-17	A AUT ORG IS INV. ON THIS SIDE	2. NO	2. NO
6-18	A 3PTY IS PROVIDING POL. AID	1. YES	1. YES
6-23	A 3PTY IS PROVIDING GUER FORCE	2. NO	2. NO
6-24	ATT. OF 3PTY PUBLIC TO INV'MNT	1. FAVORABLE	1. FAVORABLE
6-24B	RECENT CHANGE IN 3RD PTY GOVT.	1. YES	2. NO
6-30	SOME 3PTY OFFERED TO ARBITRATE	2. NO	2. NO
6-32	REGL ORGN OFFERED TO ARBITRATE	2. NO	2. NO
6-33	A G.P. OFFERED TO ARBITRATE	2. NO	2. NO
6-47	REG ORGN HAS IMPOSED SANCTIONS	2. NO	2. NO
7-4	MOBILIZATION OF RESERVES	5. TOTAL	5. TOTAL
7-8	OTHER SIGNIF INTERNAL THREAT	2. NO	2. NO
7-9	OTHER SIGNIF EXTERNAL THREAT	2. NO	2. NO
8-3	REL'SHIP BET POL + MIL LEADERS	1. POL DOMINANT	1. POL DOMINANT
8-7	METHOD OF MILITARY RECRUITMENT	1. VOLUNTARY	1. VOLUNTARY

Species Type H7
("grist for the great-power mill")

The factor pattern derives from

Cuba: Bay of Pigs (Cuban government vs. Cuban exiles)

Greek insurgency (Greek insurgents vs. Greek government)

Item		Compound Response	
1-5	EFFECTIVE NATURE OF DISPUTE	3. INTERNAL	3. INTERNAL
1-7	IDEOLOGICAL DIFF. BETW PARTIES	1. EXTREME	1. EXTREME
1-8	CONTROL OF REAL ESTATE INVOLVD	1. YES	1. YES
1-10	SIZE OF POPN AT STAKE (THOUS.)	3. 5.0TH-7.6TH	3. 5.0TH-7.6TH
1-14	BASIS OF INTRO. TO INT'L ORGN	1. AGGRESSION	1. AGGRESSION
2-3	RACIAL GROUPING OF ANTAGONIST	1. WHITE	1. WHITE
2-4	REGIM + GENL POPN OF SAME RACE	1. YES	1. YES
2-6	LINGUISTIC HOMOGENEITY OF POPN	1. HOMOGENEOUS	1. HOMOGENEOUS
2-8	DOMINANT RELIGION AMONG POPN	1. JUD-XIAN	1. JUD-XIAN
2-14	REAL ESTATE INVOLVED IS	1. IN CLMD BDY	1. IN CLMD BDY
2-15	PC OF ANT'S CLMD AREA INVOLVED	1. 1.0-1.0	1. 1.0-1.0
2-16	PC OF ANT'S CLMD POPN INVOLVED	1. 1.0-1.0	1. 1.0-1.0
3-3	GROWTH RATE OF ECONOMY	1. 1.0-1.0	1. 1.0-1.0
4-12	IDEOL. ORIENTATION OF REGIME	1. LEFT-WING	2. MODERATE
4-15	COMMUNIST ORIENT'N OF REGIME	1. SOVIET	5. ANTI-COM.
4-33	RECENT CHANGE IN LEADERSHIP	2. NO	2. NO
4-34	FORN RES ARE MAINSTAY OF REGIM	1. YES	1. YES
5-2	REGIME SEEKS OVERTHROW OF ADV.	1. YES	1. YES
5-3	INTEREST INVOLVED-IDEOLOGY	1. YES	2. NO
5-4	INTEREST INVOLVED-COMMITMENTS	2. NO	1. YES
5-6	INTEREST INVOLVED-NAT'L CHAR.	2. NO	1. YES
5-9	INTEREST INVOLVED-POWER	1. YES	1. YES
5-12	INTEREST INVOLVED-CONT'D EXIS.	1. YES	1. YES
5-13	COMMITMENT TO STATED GOALS	1. TOTAL	1. TOTAL
5-18	CAN ACCEPT LES THN STATED DMDS	2. NO	2. NO
5-19	PRESENT OUTLOOK WRT DISPUTE	1. DIE-HARD	1. DIE-HARD
5-22	POST-DISPUTE EXPECT'N OF REGIM	2. PESSIMISTIC	2. PESSIMISTIC
5-28	RELIABILITY OF COMMUNICATIONS	2. LOW	2. LOW
5-29	CREDIBILITY OF COMMUNICATIONS	2. LOW	2. LOW
5-31	OFFERED TO RESOLVE CONST'ALLY	2. NO	2. NO
5-33	INDICATED DISPUT IS NEGOTIABLE	2. NO	2. NO
5-34	HAS SOUGHT A NEGOT. SETTLEMENT	2. NO	2. NO
5-35	HAS OFFERED BI-LATERAL NEGOTNS	2. NO	2. NO
5-44	APPLIES OWN LEGAL STDS TO ADV.	2. NO	1. YES

Item	Compound Response		
6-3 IS ALLY OF G.P. HOSTILE TO ADV	2.	NO	2. NO
6-4 IS ALLY OF G.P. ALLIED TO ADV.	2.	NO	2. NO
6-6 A GP IS OPENLY PARTIAL TO ANT.	1.	YES	1. YES
6-7 GP AID PROMISED IF ESC. OCCURS	2.	NO	2. NO
6-12 SOME 3PTY IS INV. ON THIS SIDE	1.	YES	1. YES
6-14 REG'L ORG IS INV. ON THIS SIDE	2.	NO	2. NO
6-15 A G.P. IS INV. ON THIS SIDE	1.	YES	1. YES
6-20 A 3PTY IS PROVIDING MIL ADVICE	1.	YES	1. YES
6-21 A 3PTY IS PROVIDING MIL HDWRE.	1.	YES	1. YES
6-22 A 3PTY IS PROVIDING CONV FORCE	2.	NO	2. NO
6-23 A 3PTY IS PROVIDING GUER FORCE	2.	NO	2. NO
6-24 ATT. OF 3PTY PUBLIC TO INV'MNT	1.	FAVORABLE	1. FAVORABLE
6-24A TYPE OF GOVERNMENT OF 3RD PTY.	3.	TOTAL OLIG	1. POL. DEMOC.
6-32 REGL ORGN OFFERED TO ARBITRATE	2.	NO	2. NO
6-40 ACCEPTED IO'S PROP. CEASEFIRE	2.	NO	2. NO
6-42 I.O. HAS IMPOSED SANCTIONS	2.	NO	2. NO
6-47 REG ORGN HAS IMPOSED SANCTIONS	2.	NO	2. NO
7-11 TOTAL TROOPS GIVEN BY 3RD PTY	1.	0.3-1.0	1. 0.3-1.0
7-15 OWN TRPS AS PC OF ALL COMMITED	1.	1.0-1.5	1. 1.0-1.5
7-40 HAS A NUCLEAR CAPABILITY	2.	NO	2. NO
7-42 DEP. FOR BATTLEFIELD ARMAMENTS	1.	EXCLUSIVE	1. EXCLUSIVE
8-17 CENTRALIZATION OF MIL. COMMAND	1.	CENTRALIZED	1. CENTRALIZED
8-20 USE OF TERROR BY THIS ANT. IS	2.	LIMITED	3. ABSENT
8-28 INTELL. AMONG POP IN CONF AREA	1.	EFFECTIVE	3. INEFFECTIVE
8-29 INTELL. IN ADV'S POLICY ORGANS	2.	OCCASIONAL	3. INEFFECTIVE
8-30 SYMPATHY BETW POPN + OWN MIL.	1.	SYMPATHETIC	1. SYMPATHETIC
9-1 PC OF INDUSTRIAL CAPACITY LOST	1.	0.001-1.0	1. 0.001-1.0
9-8 CASUALTY RATE FOR OWN FORCES	1.	1.0-2.0	1. 1.0-2.0
9-10 CASUALTY RATE FOR ALL FORCES	1.	1.0-2.0	1. 1.0-2.0
9-11 ATTRITION RATE FOR OWN FORCES	1.	1.0-2.0	1. 1.0-2.0
9-13 ATTRITION RATE FOR ALL FORCES	1.	1.0-2.0	1. 1.0-2.0

Species Type H8
("the injection of ideology")

The factor pattern derives from

Algeria-Morocco (Morocco vs. Algeria)

Spanish civil war (Republican government vs. Nationalist insurgents)

Item	Compound Response		
1-7 IDEOLOGICAL DIFF. BETW PARTIES	1.	EXTREME	1. EXTREME
1-8 CONTROL OF REAL ESTATE INVOLVD	1.	YES	1. YES
1-12 DISPUTE HAS BEEN TO INT'L ORGN	2.	NO	2. NO
2-3 RACIAL GROUPING OF ANTAGONIST	1.	WHITE	1. WHITE
2-4 REGIM + GENL POPN OF SAME RACE	1.	YES	1. YES
2-5 RACIAL HOMOGENEITY OF GENL POP	1.	HOMOGENEOUS	1. HOMOGENEOUS
2-7 RELIGIOUS HOMOGENEITY OF POPN	1.	VERY HOMO	1. VERY HOMO
2-14 REAL ESTATE INVOLVED IS	1.	IN CLMD BDY	1. IN CLMD BDY
3-5 PER CAPITA INCOME	1.	1.0-2.1	1. 1.0-2.1
3-6 PC OF GNP IN AGRICULTURE	1.	1.0-2.0	1. 1.0-2.0
3-21 INDUSTRIAL EMPL. AS PC OF POPN	1.	1.0-1.1	1. 1.0-1.1
3-22 UNEMPLOYED AS PC OF GENL POPN	1.	0.5-1.0	1. 0.5-1.0
3-25 MILES PAVED HIGHWAY CONTROLLED	2.	1.6-20.0	1. 0.05-1.3
3-29 NO. SEAPORTS CONTROLLED	2.	1.6-3.3	1. 1.0-1.2
4-19 FREEDOM OF THE PRESS ALLOWED	4.	FULLY ABSENT	4. FULLY ABSENT
4-22 INTEREST ARTIC'N BY ASSOC'L GP	1.	POL SIGNIF	1. POL SIGNIF
4-24 INTEREST ARTIC'N BY POL PARTYS	1.	POL SIGNIF	2. POL INSIGNIF
4-31 PC VOTE RECD BY RT WING PTIES	1.	1.0-1.0	1. 1.0-1.0
4-34 FORN RES ARE MAINSTAY OF REGIM	2.	NO	2. NO
4-35 REGIM APPEARS MAINT BY FOR RES	2.	NO	2. NO
4-36 POP. SUPPORT FOR REGIME'S OBJ.	1.	HIGH	1. HIGH
4-39 POST-DISPUTE EXPECT'N OF POPN	2.	PESSIMISTIC	2. PESSIMISTIC
5-3 INTEREST INVOLVED-IDEOLOGY	1.	YES	1. YES
5-4 INTEREST INVOLVED-COMMITMENTS	1.	YES	1. YES
5-5 INTEREST INVOLVED-EST. POLICY	1.	YES	1. YES
5-7 INTEREST INVOLVED-PRESTIGE	1.	YES	1. YES
5-8 INTEREST INVOLVED-PRIDE	1.	YES	1. YES
5-13 COMMITMENT TO STATED GOALS	2.	FLEXIBLE	1. TOTAL
5-23 DIST FM BORDER TO CONFL AREA	1.	1.0-1.0	1. 1.0-1.0
5-25 ADVERSARY APPEARS TO ANT TO BE	2.	AUT + INDEP.	2. AUT + INDEP.
5-30 PRINCIPAL ATTEMPTS AT RESOL'N	5.	MILITARY	5. MILITARY
5-32 BROUGHT DISPUTE TO INT'L ORGN	2.	NO	2. NO
5-33 INDICATED DISPUT IS NEGOTIABLE	1.	YES	2. NO
5-38 P.O. RE ADV'S POL. INST'NS.	2.	UNFAVORABLE	2. UNFAVORABLE
5-39 P.O. RE ADV'S SOCIAL INST'NS.	2.	UNFAVORABLE	2. UNFAVORABLE
5-41 P.O. RE ADV'S REL. INST'NS.	2.	UNFAVORABLE	2. UNFAVORABLE
5-42 MARTIAL LAW IS IN EFFECT	2.	NO	1. YES
5-44 APPLIES OWN LEGAL STDS TO ADV.	2.	NO	2. NO
5-46 AMNESTY DECL FOR ADV PERSONNEL	2.	NO	2. NO
6-1 IS SEC'TY ALLY OF GREAT POWER	2.	NO	2. NO
6-3 IS ALLY OF G.P. HOSTILE TO ADV	2.	NO	2. NO
6-4 IS ALLY OF G.P. ALLIED TO ADV.	2.	NO	2. NO
6-5 IS AIDED BY GP HOSTILE TO ADV.	2.	NO	2. NO
6-6 A GP IS OPENLY PARTIAL TO ANT.	2.	NO	2. NO
6-7 GP AID PROMISED IF ESC. OCCURS	2.	NO	2. NO
6-11 HAS ASKED AN INT'L. ORG'N. IN	2.	NO	2. NO
6-12 SOME 3PTY IS INV. ON THIS SIDE	2.	NO	2. NO
6-13 INT'L ORG IS INV. ON THIS SIDE	2.	NO	2. NO
6-14 REG'L ORG IS INV. ON THIS SIDE	2.	NO	2. NO
6-15 A G.P. IS INV. ON THIS SIDE	2.	NO	2. NO

Item		Compound Response		
6-16	A NON-GP IS INV. ON THIS SIDE	2.	NO	2.	NO
6-17	A AUT ORG IS INV. ON THIS SIDE	2.	NO	2.	NO
6-19	A 3PTY IS PROVIDING ECON. AID	2.	NO	2.	NO
6-20	A 3PTY IS PROVIDING MIL ADVICE	2.	NO	2.	NO
6-21	A 3PTY IS PROVIDING MIL HDWRE.	2.	NO	2.	NO
6-22	A 3PTY IS PROVIDING CONV FORCE	2.	NO	2.	NO
6-23	A 3PTY IS PROVIDING GUER FORCE	2.	NO	2.	NC
6-33	A G.P. OFFERED TO ARBITRATE	2.	NO	2.	NC
6-35	INT'L ORG'N UPHELD ANT'S CAUSE	2.	NO	2.	NO
6-36	INTL ORGN INDICTED ANT'S CAUSE	2.	NO	2.	NO
6-37	CITED IN VIOLATION OF INTL LAW	2.	NO	2.	NO
6-38	CITED BY I.O. FOR AGGRESSION	2.	NO	2.	NO
6-40	ACCEPTED IO'S PROP. CEASEFIRE	2.	NO	2.	NO
6-42	I.O. HAS IMPOSED SANCTIONS	2.	NO	2.	NO
6-47	REG ORGN HAS IMPOSED SANCTIONS	2.	NO	2.	NO
7-1	NO. OF OWN ACTIVE MIL. TROOPS	1.	0.02-10.7	1.	0.02-10.7
7-2	NO. ACTIV TROOPS AS PC OF POPN	1.	0.001-1.0	2.	1.3-174.0
7-4	MOBILIZATION OF RESERVES	4.	MAJOR	5.	TOTAL
7-5	NO. TROOPS COMMITTED TO CONFL.	1.	0.02-1.0	2.	1.2-50.0
7-9	OTHER SIGNIF EXTERNAL THREAT	2.	NO	2.	NO
7-11	TOTAL TROOPS GIVEN BY 3RD PTY	1.	0.3-1.0	1.	0.3-1.0
7-13	3PTY TROOP AID SEEN LIKELY TO	2.	STAY SAME	2.	STAY SAME
7-14	TOTAL MANPOWER COMMITTED	1.	0.02-7.3	1.	0.02-7.3
7-15	OWN TRPS AS PC OF ALL COMMITED	1.	1.0-1.5	1.	1.0-1.5
7-16	CONVENTIONAL MANPWER COMMITTED	1.	0.01-3.0	1.	0.01-3.0
7-17	GUERRILLA MANPOWER COMMITTED	1.	0.02-1.0	1.	0.02-1.0
7-46	DEP. FOR AIR COMBAT ARMAMENTS	1.	EXCLUSIVE	1.	EXCLUSIVE
8-7	METHOD OF MILITARY RECRUITMENT	1.	VOLUNTARY	1.	VOLUNTARY
8-9	TRAINING FACILITY FOR OFFICERS	1.	GOOD	1.	GOOD
8-11	TRAINING FAC FOR ENLISTED PERS	1.	GOOD	1.	GOOD
8-14	LOGIS SUP'T ADQT TO MAINT OPNS	1.	YES	1.	YES
8-15	LOGIS SUP'T ADQT TO EXPAND OPN	1.	YES	1.	YES
8-21	TACTICS OF FORCES ON THIS SIDE	2.	DEFENSIVE	1.	OFFENSIVE
8-24	TREATMENT OF ENEMY PRISONERS	3.	BRUTAL	3.	BRUTAL
8-29	INTELL. IN ADV'S POLICY ORGANS	3.	INEFFECTIVE	3.	INEFFECTIVE
8-34	CIVN SEC V AC ATK BY OWN FRCES	1.	HIGH	1.	HIGH

e.

Hostilities:

Higher-Order Factor Patterns

Genus 1

The factor pattern derives from

Cuba: "little" war of 1906 (Cuban government vs. Liberal party insurgents)

Cyprus: independence (U.K. colonial administration vs. Enosists)

Cyprus: internal (Cypriot government vs. Turkish Cypriots)

Malayan insurgency (U.K.-Malay colonial administration and Malayan government vs. Malayan Communist party)

Venezuelan insurgency (Venezuelan government vs. MIR/CPV and FLN/FALN)

The adjuncts are

Indonesia-Malaysia
Israel-Egypt

Cuba: Bay of Pigs
Greek insurgency

Item		Compound Response		
1-11	DISPUTE HAS BEEN TO REG'L ORGN	2.	NO	2.	NO
3-2	GROSS NAT'L. OR ECON. PRODUCT	3.	90.0-6.4TH	8.	0 OR N/A
3-5	PER CAPITA INCOME	3.	115.0-855.0	8.	0 OR N/A
3-9	PC OF GNP IN EXPORTS	3.	22.0-1.0TH	8.	0 OR N/A
3-14	GOVERNMENT INCOME AS PC OF GNP	3.	10.0-50.0	8.	0 OR N/A
3-15	GOVT. SPENDING AS PC OF GNP	3.	6.0-50.0	8.	0 OR N/A
3-20	AGRIC EMPLOYMENT AS PC OF POPN	3.	13.0-70.0	8.	0 OR N/A
3-21	INDUSTRIAL EMPL. AS PC OF POPN	3.	11.0-23.0	8.	0 OR N/A
4-4	EXECUTIVE STABILITY	3.	3.0-9.0	8.	0 OR N/A
4-18	POL. INTEGRATION OF GENL POPN	2.	MODERATE	8.	0 OR N/A
4-23	INTEREST ARTIC'N BY INST'L GPS	1.	POL SIGNIF	8.	0 OR N/A
4-24	INTEREST ARTIC'N BY POL PARTYS	1.	POL SIGNIF	8.	0 OR N/A
4-25	CONST'AL STATUS OF POL PARTIES	1.	COMPETITIVE	8.	0 OR N/A
4-32	RECENT LEADERSHIP CRISIS	2.	NO	2.	NO
4-33	RECENT CHANGE IN LEADERSHIP	2.	NO	2.	NO
5-22	POST-DISPUTE EXPECT'N OF REGIM	2.	PESSIMISTIC	2.	PESSIMISTIC
5-23	DIST FM BORDER TO CONFL AREA	1.	1.0-1.0	1.	1.0-1.0
5-32	BROUGHT DISPUTE TO INT'L ORGN	2.	NO	2.	NO
5-42	MARTIAL LAW IS IN EFFECT	2.	NO	8.	0 OR N/A
5-43	STATE OF WAR HAS BEEN DECLARED	2.	NO	8.	0 OR N/A
6-4	IS ALLY OF G.P. ALLIED TO ADV.	2.	NO	2.	NO
6-13	INT'L ORG IS INV. ON THIS SIDE	2.		2.	NO
6-14	REG'L ORG IS INV. ON THIS SIDE	2.		2.	NO
6-23	A 3PTY IS PROVIDING GUER FORCE	2.		2.	NO
6-30	SOME 3PTY OFFERED TO ARBITRATE	2.			NO
6-31	INTL ORGN OFFERED TO ARBITRATE	2.			NO
6-32	REGL ORGN OFFERED TO ARBITRATE	2.			NO
6-33	A G.P. OFFERED TO ARBITRATE	2.	NO		
6-35	INT'L ORG'N UPHELD ANT'S CAUSE	2.	NO		
6-36	INTL ORGN INDICTED ANT'S CAUSE	2.	NO		
6-37	CITED IN VIOLATION OF INTL LAW	2.	NO		
6-38	CITED BY I.O. FOR AGGRESSION	2.	NO		
6-40	ACCEPTED IO'S PROP. CEASEFIRE	2.	NO		
6-42	I.O. HAS IMPOSED SANCTIONS	2.	NO		
6-47	REG ORGN HAS IMPOSED SANCTIONS	2.	NO		
7-8	OTHER SIGNIF INTERNAL THREAT	2.	NO	2.	
7-9	OTHER SIGNIF EXTERNAL THREAT	2.	NO	2.	N.
7-18	NAVAL MANPOWER COMMITTED	1.	0.5-1.0	1.	0.5-
7-19	AIR FORCE MANPOWER COMMITTED	1.	0.05-1.0	1.	0.05-1.

Item		Compound Response		

8-17	CENTRALIZATION OF MIL. COMMAND	1.	CENTRALIZED	2.	DE-CENTR'ZED
9-8	CASUALTY RATE FOR OWN FORCES	1.	1.0-2.0	1.	1.0-2.0
9-10	CASUALTY RATE FOR ALL FORCES	1.	1.0-2.0	1.	1.0-2.0

Genus 2

The factor pattern derives from

Algeria-Morocco (Morocco vs. Algeria)

Ethiopia-Somalia (Ethiopia vs. Somalia)

Kashmir (Pakistan vs. India)

Spanish civil war (Republican government vs. Nationalist insurgents)

The adjuncts are

India-China
USSR-Iran

1-8	CONTROL OF REAL ESTATE INVOLVD	1.	YES	1.	YES
2-4	REGIM + GENL POPN OF SAME RACE	1.	YES	1.	YES
4-34	FORN RES ARE MAINSTAY OF REGIM	2.	NO	2.	NO
4-35	REGIM APPEARS MAINT BY FOR RES	2.	NO	2.	NO
4-36	POP. SUPPORT FOR REGIME'S OBJ.	1.	HIGH	1.	HIGH
5-4	INTEREST INVOLVED-COMMITMENTS	1.	YES	1.	YES
5-25	ADVERSARY APPEARS TO ANT TO BE	2.	AUT + INDEP.	2.	AUT + INDEP.
5-33	INDICATED DISPUT IS NEGOTIABLE	1.	YES	2.	NO
5-38	P.O. RE ADV'S POL. INST'NS.	2.	UNFAVORABLE	2.	UNFAVORABLE
5-39	P.O. RE ADV'S SOCIAL INST'NS.	2.	UNFAVORABLE	2.	UNFAVORABLE
5-41	P.O. RE ADV'S REL. INST'NS.	2.	UNFAVORABLE	2.	UNFAVORABLE
5-46	AMNESTY DECL FOR ADV PERSONNEL	2.	NO	2.	NO
6-3	IS ALLY OF G.P. HOSTILE TO ADV.	2.	NO	2.	NO
6-4	IS ALLY OF G.P. ALLIED TO ADV.	2.	NO	2.	NO
6-5	IS AIDED BY GP HOSTILE TO ADV.	2.	NO	2.	NO
6-7	GP AID PROMISED IF ESC. OCCURS	2.	NO	2.	NO
6-13	INT'L ORG IS INV. ON THIS SIDE	2.	NO	2.	NO
6-14	REG'L ORG IS INV. ON THIS SIDE	2.	NO	2.	NO
6-16	A NON-GP IS INV. ON THIS SIDE	2.	NO	2.	NO
6-33	A G.P. OFFERED TO ARBITRATE	2.	NO	2.	NO
6-35	INT'L ORG'N UPHELD ANT'S CAUSE	2.	NO	2.	NO
6-36	INTL ORGN INDICTED ANT'S CAUSE	2.	NO	2.	NO
6-37	CITED IN VIOLATION OF INTL LAW	2.	NO	2.	NO
6-38	CITED BY I.O. FOR AGGRESSION	2.	NO	2.	NO
6-40	ACCEPTED IO'S PROP. CEASEFIRE	2.	NO	2.	NO
6-42	I.O. HAS IMPOSED SANCTIONS	2.	NO	2.	NO
7-11	TOTAL TROOPS GIVEN BY 3RD PTY	1.	0.3-1.0	1.	0.3-1.0
8-9	TRAINING FACILITY FOR OFFICERS	1.	GOOD	1.	GOOD

Genus 3

The factor pattern derives from

Angolan insurgency (African insurgents vs. Portuguese colonial administration)

Ethiopian resistance (Ethiopian insurgents vs. Italian colonial administration)

Indonesia: independence (Indonesian insurgents vs. Dutch colonial administration)

1-3	PAST POL. REL'SHIP BETW PARTYS	3.	EXPLOITIVE	3.	EXPLOITIVE
1-5	EFFECTIVE NATURE OF DISPUTE	1.	COLONIAL	1.	COLONIAL
1-7	IDEOLOGICAL DIFF. BETW PARTIES	1.	EXTREME	1.	EXTREME
1-8	CONTROL OF REAL ESTATE INVOLVD	1.	YES	1.	YES
1-12	DISPUTE HAS BEEN TO INT'L ORGN	1.	YES	1.	YES
2-5	RACIAL HOMOGENEITY OF GENL POP	1.	HOMOGENEOUS	1.	HOMOGENEOUS
2-14	REAL ESTATE INVOLVED IS	1.	IN CLMD BDY	1.	IN CLMD BDY
2-15	PC OF ANT'S CLMD AREA INVOLVED	1.	1.0-1.0	1.	1.0-1.0
2-19	URBANIZATION	3.	LOW	3.	LOW
3-7	PC OF GNP IN DURABLE GOODS	1.	1.0-1.2	1.	1.0-1.2
3-8	PRODUCTION OF STEEL	1.	1.0-1.0	1.	1.0-1.0
4-24	INTEREST ARTIC'N BY POL PARTYS	2.	POL INSIGNIF	1.	POL SIGNIF
5-2	REGIME SEEKS OVERTHROW OF ADV.	1.	YES	1.	YES
5-9	INTEREST INVOLVED-POWER	2.	NO	1.	YES
5-11	INTEREST INVOLVED-TERR. INTEG.	1.	YES	1.	YES
5-12	INTEREST INVOLVED-CONT'D EXIS.	1.	YES	1.	YES
5-21	LIKELY OUTCOME IS NOW OBVIOUS	2.	NO	2.	NO
5-22	POST-DISPUTE EXPECT'N C= REGIM	2.	PESSIMISTIC	2.	PESSIMISTIC
5-23	DIST FM BORDER TO CONFL AREA	1.	1.0-1.0	1.	1.0-1.0
5-29	CREDIBILITY OF COMMUNICATIONS	2.	LOW	2.	LOW
6-4	IS ALLY OF G.P. ALLIED TO ADV.	2.	NO	2.	NO
6-7	GP AID PROMISED IF ESC. OCCURS	2.	NO	2.	NO
6-17	A AUT ORG IS INV. ON THIS SIDE	2.	NO	2.	NO
6-18	A 3PTY IS PROVIDING POL. AID	1.	YES	1.	YES
6-24	ATT. OF 3PTY PUBLIC TO INV'MNT	1.	FAVORABLE	1.	FAVORABLE
6-33	A G.P. OFFERED TO ARBITRATE	2.	NO	2.	NO
7-8	OTHER SIGNIF INTERNAL THREAT	2.	NO	2.	NO
7-9	OTHER SIGNIF EXTERNAL THREAT	2.	NO	2.	NO

Far

...s from

...rocco vs.

...omalia (Ethiopia vs.
...ia)

1-8	CONTROL OF REAL ESTATE INVOLVD	1.	YES	1.	YES
2-4	REGIM + GENL POPN OF SAME RACE	1.	YES	1.	YES
3-5	PER CAPITA INCOME	1.	1.0-2.1	1.	1.0-2.1
4-34	FORN RES ARE MAINSTAY OF REGIM	2.	NO	2.	NO
4-35	REGIM APPEARS MAINT BY FOR RES	2.	NO	2.	NO
4-36	POP. SUPPORT FOR REGIME'S OBJ.	1.	HIGH	1.	HIGH

Item		Compound Response	

India-China (India vs. China)
Kashmir (Pakistan vs. India)
Spanish civil war (Nationalist insurgents vs. Republican government)
USSR-Iran (Iran vs. USSR)

5-38	P.O. RE ADV'S POL. INST'NS.	2. UNFAVORABLE	2. UNFAVORABLE
5-39	P.O. RE ADV'S SOCIAL INST'NS.	2. UNFAVORABLE	2. UNFAVORABLE
5-41	P.O. RE ADV'S REL. INST'NS.	2. UNFAVORABLE	2. UNFAVORABLE
6-4	IS ALLY OF G.P. ALLIED TO ADV.	2. NO	2. NO
6-7	GP AID PROMISED IF ESC. OCCURS	2. NO	2. NO
6-14	REG'L ORG IS INV. ON THIS SIDE	2. NO	2. NO
6-16	A NON-GP IS INV. ON THIS SIDE	2. NO	2. NO
6-33	A G.P. OFFERED TO ARBITRATE	2. NO	2. NO
6-37	CITED IN VIOLATION OF INT. LAW	2. NO	2. NO
6-38	CITED BY I.O. FOR AGGRESSION	2. NO	2. NO
6-40	ACCEPTED IO'S PROP. CEASEFIRE	2. NO	2. NO
6-42	I.O. HAS IMPOSED SANCTIONS	2. NO	2. NO
6-47	REG ORGN HAS IMPOSED SANCTIONS	2. NO	2. NO
7-5	NO. TROOPS COMMITTED TO CONFL.	1. 0.02-1.0	2. 1.2-50.0
7-13	3PT/ TROOP AID SEEN LIKELY TO	2. STAY SAME	2. STAY SAME
7-14	TOTAL MANPOWER COMMITTED	1. 0.02-7.3	1. 0.02-7.3
7-15	OWN TRPS AS PC OF ALL COMMITED	1. 1.0-1.5	1. 1.0-1.5

Family 2

The factor pattern derives from

Cuba: "little" war of 1906 (Liberal party insurgents vs. Cuban government)
Cyprus: independence (U.K. colonial administration vs. Enosists)
Cyprus: internal (Turkish Cypriots vs. Cypriot government)
Indonesia-Malaysia (Indonesia vs. Malaysia)
Israel-Egypt (Israel vs. Egypt)
Malayan insurgency (Malayan Communist party vs. U.K.-Malay colonial administration and Malayan government)
Venezuelan insurgency (Venezuelan government vs. MIR/CPV and FLN/FALN)

4-32	RECENT LEADERSHIP CRISIS	2. NO	2. NO
4-33	RECENT CHANGE IN LEADERSHIP	2. NO	2. NO
5-22	POST-DISPUTE EXPECT'N OF REGIM	2. PESSIMISTIC	2. PESSIMISTIC
5-23	DIST FM BORDER TO CONFL AREA	1. 1.0-1.0	1. 1.0-1.0
5-32	BROUGHT DISPUTE TO INT'L ORGN	2. NO	2. NO
6-4	IS ALLY OF G.P. ALLIED TO ADV.	2. NO	2. NO
6-13	INT'L ORG IS INV. ON THIS SIDE	2. NO	2. NO
6-14	REG'L ORG IS INV. ON THIS SIDE	2. NO	2. NO
6-23	A 3PTY IS PROVIDING GUER FORCE	2. NO	2. NO
6-31	INTL ORGN OFFERED TO ARBITRATE	2. NO	2. NO
6-32	REGL ORGN OFFERED TO ARBITRATE	2. NO	2. NO
6-33	A G.P. OFFERED TO ARBITRATE	2. NO	2. NO
6-35	INT'L ORG'N UPHELD ANT'S CAUSE	2. NO	2. NO
6-36	INTL ORGN INDICTED ANT'S CAUSE	2. NO	2. NO
6-37	CITED IN VIOLATION OF INTL LAW	2. NO	2. NO
6-38	CITED BY I.O. FOR AGGRESSION	2. NO	2. NO
6-40	ACCEPTED IO'S PROP. CEASEFIRE	2. NO	2. NO
6-42	I.O. HAS IMPOSED SANCTIONS	2. NO	2. NO
7-18	NAVAL MANPOWER COMMITTED	1. 0.5-1.0	1. 0.5-1.0

Family 3

The factor pattern derives from

Angolan insurgency (Portuguese colonial administration vs. African insurgents)
Cuba: Bay of Pigs (Cuban exiles vs. Cuban government)
Ethiopian resistance (Ethiopian insurgents vs. Italian colonial administration)
Greek insurgency (Greek insurgents vs. Greek government)
Indonesia: independence (Indonesian insurgents vs. Dutch colonial administration)

1-7	IDEOLOGICAL DIFF. BETW PARTIES	1. EXTREME	1. EXTREME
1-8	CONTROL OF REAL ESTATE INVOLVD	1. YES	1. YES
2-14	REAL ESTATE INVOLVED IS	1. IN CLMD BDY	1. IN CLMD BDY
2-15	PC OF ANT'S CLMD AREA INVOLVED	1. 1.0-1.0	1. 1.0-1.0
5-2	REGIME SEEKS OVERTHROW OF ADV.	1. YES	1. YES
5-12	INTEREST INVOLVED-CONT'D EXIS.	1. YES	1. YES
5-22	POST-DISPUTE EXPECT'N OF REGIM	2. PESSIMISTIC	2. PESSIMISTIC
5-29	CREDIBILITY OF COMMUNICATIONS	2. LOW	2. LOW
6-4	IS ALLY OF G.P. ALLIED TO ADV.	2. NO	2. NO
6-7	GP AID PROMISED IF ESC. OCCURS	2. NO	2. NO
6-24	ATT. OF 3PTY PUBLIC TO INV'MNT	1. FAVORABLE	1. FAVORABLE

Artificial Order

The factor pattern derives from

Algeria-Morocco (Morocco vs. Algeria)

6-4	IS ALLY OF G.P. ALLIED TO ADV.	2. NO	2. NO
6-14	REG'L ORG IS INV. ON THIS SIDE	2. NO	2. NO
6-33	A G.P. OFFERED TO ARBITRATE	2. NO	2. NO
6-37	CITED IN VIOLATION OF INTL LAW	2. NO	2. NO
6-38	CITED BY I.O. FOR AGGRESSION	2. NO	2. NO
6-40	ACCEPTED IO'S PROP. CEASEFIRE	2. NO	2. NO
6-42	I.O. HAS IMPOSED SANCTIONS	2. NO	2. NO

Item	Compound Response

Cuba: "little" war of 1906 (Liberal party insurgents vs. Cuban government)

Cyprus: independence (U.K. colonial administration vs. Enosists)

Cyprus: internal (Turkish Cypriots vs. Cypriot government)

Ethiopia-Somalia (Ethiopia vs. Somalia)

India-China (India vs. China)

Indonesia-Malaysia (Indonesia vs. Malaysia)

Israel-Egypt (Israel vs. Egypt)

Kashmir (India vs. Pakistan)

Malayan insurgency (U.K.-Malay colonial administration and Malayan government vs. Malayan Communist party)

Spanish civil war (Nationalist insurgents vs. Republican government)

Venezuelan insurgency (Venezuelan government vs. MIR/CPV and FLN/FALN)

USSR-Iran (Iran vs. USSR)

Class

The factor pattern derives from all eighteen instances of hostilities included in the analysis.

```
6-4    IS ALLY OF G.P. ALLIED TO ADV.    2.  NO        2.  NO
```

3.
The Escalation (E) Patterns

The data input for each conflict included in this analysis is that obtaining at the threshold of subphase E and is therefore a statement of the conditions pertaining when the ongoing hostilities in each case were about to escalate, that is, when the rules governing the conduct of hostilities in each case were about to undergo a change that would effect an intensification in the scale or the scope of the hostilities. In the conflicts in which more than one instance of escalation occurred, that representing the better, more definitive example of its kind was included in this analysis.

a.
Conflicts Included
in the Analysis
of the Escalation Patterns

Conflict	Event Marking Escalation (E)	Date
Algeria-Morocco	Algeria accepts aid from UAR, USSR, Cuba	10/63
Cyprus: independence	Colonial government declares state of emergency	11/55
Cyprus: internal	First intervention threat by Turkey	1/64

Conflict	Event Marking Escalation (E)	Date
Ethiopian resistance	Britain declares war on Italy; supports insurgents	6/40
Greek insurgency	Guerrillas go conventional; Tito closes border	7/49
Indonesia-Malaysia	Indonesian landings in Malaya	8/64
Israel-Egypt	British bomb Egyptian airfields	11/56
Kashmir	Pakistan commits regular troops	5/48
Malayan insurgency	Resumption of widespread terror campaign	10/52
Spanish civil war	Italian ground troops intervene	1/37
Venezuelan insurgency	Government changes from police to military action	10/63

b.

Derivation of the Escalation
Patterns

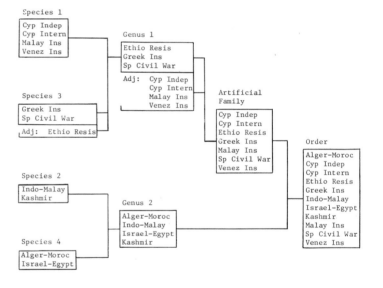

c.

Percentile Distribution of the
Conflicts across the
Escalation Patterns

	Species				Genus		Arti-ficial Family	Order
	E1	E2	E3	E4	1	2		
Algeria-Morocco	0.45	0.49	0.33	<u>1.00</u>	0.40	<u>1.00</u>	~	1.00
Cyprus: independence	<u>1.00</u>	0.31	0.42	0.26	0.63	0.30	<u>1.00</u>	1.00
Cyprus: internal	<u>1.00</u>	0.30	0.38	0.33	0.40	0.35	<u>1.00</u>	1.00
Ethiopian resistance	0.39	0.27	0.45	0.28	<u>1.00</u>	0.30	<u>1.00</u>	1.00
Greek insurgency	0.52	0.27	<u>1.00</u>	0.31	<u>1.00</u>	0.35	<u>1.00</u>	1.00
Indonesia-Malaysia	0.36	<u>1.00</u>	0.29	0.40	0.31	<u>1.00</u>	~	1.00
Israel-Egypt	0.32	0.39	0.41	<u>1.00</u>	0.54	<u>1.00</u>	~	1.00
Kashmir	0.36	<u>1.00</u>	0.36	0.45	0.37	<u>1.00</u>	~	1.00
Malayan insurgency	<u>1.00</u>	0.38	0.45	0.34	0.69	0.35	<u>1.00</u>	1.00

	Species				Genus		Arti-ficial Family	Order
	E1	E2	E3	E4	1	2		
Spanish civil war	0.50	0.41	<u>1.00</u>	0.51	<u>1.00</u>	0.57	<u>1.00</u>	1.00
Venezuelan insurgency	<u>1.00</u>	0.27	0.51	0.33	0.63	0.39	<u>1.00</u>	1.00
Vietnam 3/67	0.57	0.35	0.55	0.37	0.80	0.57	0.57	1.00

d.
Escalation:
Complete Factor Patterns

Species Type E1
("acting with the presumption of immunity")

The factor pattern derives from

Cyprus: independence (Enosists vs. U.K. colonial administration)

Cyprus: internal (Turkish Cypriots vs. Cypriot government)

Malayan insurgency (Malayan Communist party vs. U.K.-Malay colonial administration and Malayan government)

Venezuelan insurgency (MIR/CPV and FLN/FALN vs. Venezuelan government)

Item			Compound Response		
1-11	DISPUTE HAS BEEN TO REG'L ORGN	# 2.	NO	2.	NO
3-2	GROSS NAT'L. OR ECON. PRODUCT	# 8.	0 OR N/A	3.	90.0-6.4TH
3-3	GROWTH RATE OF ECONOMY	8.	0 OR N/A	3.	3.0-13.9
3-5	PER CAPITA INCOME	# 8.	0 CR N/A	3.	115.0-855.0
3-9	PC OF GNP IN EXPORTS	8.	0 OR N/A	3.	22.0-1.0TH
3-13	PROGRESSIVE TAX STRUCTURE	8.	0 OR N/A	1.	YES
3-14	GOVERNMENT INCOME AS PC OF GNP	# 8.	0 CR N/A	3.	10.0-50.0
3-15	GOVT. SPENDING AS PC OF GNP	# 8.	0 CR N/A	3.	6.0-50.0
3-20	AGRIC EMPLOYMENT AS PC OF POPN	8.	0 OR N/A	3.	13.0-70.0
3-21	INDUSTRIAL EMPL. AS PC OF POPN	8.	0 OR N/A	3.	11.0-23.0
4-4	EXECUTIVE STABILITY	# 8.	0 CR N/A	3.	3.0-9.0
4-18	POL. INTEGRATION OF GENL POPN	8.	0 OR N/A	2.	MODERATE
4-22	INTEREST ARTIC'N BY ASSOC'L GP	8.	0 CR N/A	1.	POL SIGNIF
4-23	INTEREST ARTIC'N BY INST'L GPS	8.	0 CR N/A	1.	POL SIGNIF
4-24	INTEREST ARTIC'N BY POL PARTYS	8.	0 OR N/A	1.	POL SIGNIF
4-32	RECENT LEADERSHIP CRISIS	2.	NO	2.	NO
4-33	RECENT CHANGE IN LEADERSHIP	# 2.	NO	2.	NO
5-22	POST-DISPUTE EXPECT'N OF REGIM	# 2.	PESSIMISTIC	2.	PESSIMISTIC
5-23	DIST FM BORDER TO CONFL AREA	# 1.	1.0-1.0	1.	1.0-1.0
5-24	DIST FM CAPITAL TO CONFL AREA	# 1.	1.0-1.3	1.	1.0-1.3
5-32	BROUGHT DISPUTE TO INT'L ORGN	# 2.	NO	2.	NO
5-35	HAS OFFERED BI-LATERAL NEGOTNS	# 2.	NO	2.	NO
5-43	STATE OF WAR HAS BEEN DECLARED	8.	0 CR N/A	2.	NO
6-4	IS ALLY OF G.P. ALLIED TO ADV.	# 2.	NO	2.	NO
6-7	GP AID PROMISED IF ESC. OCCURS	2.	NO	2.	NO
6-13	INT'L ORG IS INV. ON THIS SIDE	# 2.	NO	2.	NO
6-14	REG'L ORG IS INV. ON THIS SIDE	# 2.	NO	2.	NO
6-16	A NON-GP IS INV. ON THIS SIDE	1.	YES	2.	NO
6-30	SOME 3PTY OFFERED TO ARBITRATE	2.	NO	2.	NO
6-31	INTL ORGN OFFERED TO ARBITRATE	2.	NO	2.	NO
6-32	REGL ORGN OFFERED TO ARBITRATE	# 2.	NO	2.	NO
6-33	A G.P. OFFERED TO ARBITRATE	2.	NO	2.	NO
6-35	INT'L ORG'N UPHELD ANT'S CAUSE	# 2.	NO	2.	NO
6-36	INTL ORGN INDICTED ANT'S CAUSE	# 2.	NO	2.	NO
6-37	CITED IN VIOLATION OF INTL LAW	# 2.	NO	2.	NO
6-38	CITED BY I.O. FOR AGGRESSION	# 2.	NO	2.	NO
6-42	I.O. HAS IMPOSED SANCTIONS	# 2.	NO	2.	NO
7-8	OTHER SIGNIF INTERNAL THREAT	# 2.	NO	2.	NO
7-9	OTHER SIGNIF EXTERNAL THREAT	# 2.	NO	2.	NO
7-34	NO. SAM'S AVAILABLE	1.	1.0-1.0	1.	1.0-1.0
7-35	NO. SSM'S AVAILABLE	# 1.	1.0-1.0	1.	1.0-1.0
7-40	HAS A NUCLEAR CAPABILITY	# 2.	NO	2.	NO
8-17	CENTRALIZATION OF MIL. COMMAND	2.	DE-CENTR'ZED	1.	CENTRALIZED
8-25	TREATMENT OF OWN CASUALTIES	3.	POOR	1.	GOOD

Species Type E2
("diplomacy fails amid unacceptable losses")

The factor pattern derives from

Indonesia-Malaysia (Indonesia vs. Malaysia)

Kashmir (Pakistan vs. India)

Item			Compound Response		
1-1	GEOGRAPHIC LOCUS OF DISPUTE	6.	ASIA	6.	ASIA
1-2B	CLIMATE IN THE CONFLICT AREA	# 3.	WET	3.	WET
1-3	PAST POL. REL'SHIP BETW PARTYS	# 2.	COMPETITIVE	2.	COMPETITIVE
1-5	EFFECTIVE NATURE OF DISPUTE	2.	INTERSTATE	2.	INTERSTATE
1-8	CONTROL OF REAL ESTATE INVOLVD	# 1.	YES	1.	YES
1-9	SIZE OF AREA AT STAKE(TH SQ M)	3.	84.0-197.0	3.	84.0-197.0
1-11	DISPUTE HAS BEEN TO REG'L ORGN	# 2.	NO	2.	NO
1-13	INTRODUCED TO INT'L ORGN BY A	1.	ANTAGONIST	1.	ANTAGONIST
2-4	REGIM + GENL POPN OF SAME RACE	# 1.	YES	1.	YES
3-2	GROSS NAT'L. OR ECON. PRODUCT	1.	1.0-1.5	2.	2.2-24.0
3-5	PER CAPITA INCOME	1.	1.0-2.1	1.	1.0-2.1
3-6	FC OF GNP IN AGRICULTURE	1.	1.0-2.0	1.	1.0-2.0
3-20	AGRIC EMPLOYMENT AS PC OF POPN	1.	1.0-1.2	1.	1.0-1.2
3-27	NO. AIRPORTS CONTROLLED	8.	0 CR N/A	2.	1.5-15.0
3-28	NO. JETPORTS CONTROLLED	1.	1.0-1.0	1.	1.0-1.0

Item			Compound Response			

4-1	EFFECTIVE STATUS OF GOVERNMENT		1.	INDEP GOVT	1.	INDEP GOVT
4-2	DATE OF INDEPENDENCE		4.	AFTER 1945	4.	AFTER 1945
4-5	TYPE OF GOVERNMENT		2.	TUT/MOD OLIG	1.	POL DEMOC
4-6	STATUS OF EXECUTIVE		1.	DOMINANT	2.	STRONG
4-8	STATUS OF JUDICIARY		2.	PART EFFECT.	1.	FULL EFFECT.
4-11	RECRUITMENT TO POL LEADERSHIP		2.	MODERATE	3.	NON-ELITIST
4-18	POL. INTEGRATION OF GENL POPN		2.	MODERATE	2.	MODERATE
4-23	INTEREST ARTIC'N BY INST'L GPS		1.	POL SIGNIF	1.	POL SIGNIF
4-24	INTEREST ARTIC'N BY POL PARTYS		1.	POL SIGNIF	1.	POL SIGNIF
4-25	CONST'AL STATUS OF POL PARTIES		2.	PART COMPET.	1.	COMPETITIVE
4-27	PERSONALISM IN POL. PARTIES		2.	MODERATE	2.	MODERATE
4-32	RECENT LEADERSHIP CRISIS		2.	NO	2.	NO
4-33	RECENT CHANGE IN LEADERSHIP	#	2.	NO	2.	NO
4-34	FORN RES ARE MAINSTAY OF REGIM		2.	NO	2.	NO
4-35	REGIM APPEARS MAINT BY FOR RES		2.	NO	2.	NO
4-36	POP. SUPPORT FOR REGIME'S OBJ.		1.	HIGH	1.	HIGH
4-37	POP. SUPPORT FOR REGIM'S POLS.		1.	HIGH	1.	HIGH
4-38	ATT. OF INTELLECTUALS TO REGIM		1.	FAVORABLE	1.	FAVORABLE
4-40	EFFECT ON POPULAR COHESION		2.	LITTLE CHANGE	2.	LITTLE CHANGE

5-3	INTEREST INVOLVED-IDEOLOGY		2.	NO	2.	NO
5-9	INTEREST INVOLVED-POWER		1.	YES	2.	NO
5-12	INTEREST INVOLVED-CONT'D EXIS.		2.	NO	2.	NO
5-14	DISPUTE IS REGARDED AS CRUSADE		1.	YES	2.	NO
5-15	CONDUCT OF CONFLICT IS LIMITED		1.	YES	1.	YES
5-17	RATIONALIZATION OF VIOLENCE		1.	MORALISTIC	3.	LEGAL/JUD.
5-18	CAN ACCEPT LES THN STATED DMDS	#	2.	NO	2.	NO
5-20	PERCEIVED BALANCE OF WILL		2.	EVEN	2.	EVEN
5-26	TREATY EXPERIENCE WITH ADV.		2.	UNSATISF'ORY	2.	UNSATISF'ORY
5-27	SPEED OF COMMUNICATIONS		1.	RAPID	1.	RAPID
5-28	RELIABILITY OF COMMUNICATIONS		1.	HIGH	1.	HIGH
5-31	OFFERED TO RESOLVE CONST'ALLY		1.	YES	1.	YES
5-34	HAS SOUGHT A NEGOT. SETTLEMENT		1.	YES	1.	YES
5-35	HAS OFFERED BI-LATERAL NEGOTNS		1.	YES	1.	YES
5-36	HAS ATTENDED BI-LAT'L NEGOT'NS		1.	YES	1.	YES
5-38	P.O. RE ADV'S POL. INST'NS.	#	2.	UNFAVORABLE	2.	UNFAVORABLE
5-39	P.O. RE ADV'S SOCIAL INST'NS.		2.	UNFAVORABLE	2.	UNFAVORABLE
5-43	STATE OF WAR HAS BEEN DECLARED	#	2.	NO	2.	NO
5-46	AMNESTY DECL FOR ADV PERSONNEL		2.	NO	2.	NO

6-4	IS ALLY OF G.P. ALLIED TO ADV.	#	2.	NO	2.	NO
6-11	HAS ASKED AN INT'L. ORG'N. IN		2.	NO	1.	YES
6-12	SOME 3PTY IS INV. ON THIS SIDE	#	1.	YES	1.	YES
6-13	INT'L ORG IS INV. ON THIS SIDE	#	2.	NO	2.	NO
6-14	REG'L ORG IS INV. ON THIS SIDE	#	2.	NO	2.	NO
6-17	A AUT ORG IS INV. ON THIS SIDE		1.	YES	2.	NO
6-18	A 3PTY IS PROVIDING POL. AID		2.	NO	1.	YES
6-20	A 3PTY IS PROVIDING MIL ADVICE	#	1.	YES	1.	YES
6-21	A 3PTY IS PROVIDING MIL HDWRE.	#	1.	YES	1.	YES
6-30	SOME 3PTY OFFERED TO ARBITRATE	#	1.	YES	1.	YES
6-31	INTL ORGN OFFERED TO ARBITRATE	#	1.	YES	1.	YES
6-37	CITED IN VIOLATION OF INTL LAW	#	2.	NO	2.	NO
6-38	CITED BY I.O. FOR AGGRESSION	#	2.	NO	2.	NO
6-40	ACCEPTED IO'S PROP. CEASEFIRE	#	2.	NO	2.	NO
6-41	HAS HONORED RECOMMENDS OF I.O.		2.	GEN'LY NO	1.	GEN'LY YES
6-42	I.O. HAS IMPOSED SANCTIONS	#	2.	NO	2.	NO
6-47	REG ORGN HAS IMPOSED SANCTIONS	#	2.	NO	2.	NO

7-2	NO. ACTIV TROOPS AS PC OF POPN		2.	1.3-174.0	1.	0.001-1.0
7-9	OTHER SIGNIF EXTERNAL THREAT	#	2.	NO	2.	NO
7-14	TOTAL MANPOWER COMMITTED	#	2.	0.02-7.3	1.	0.02-7.3
7-16	CONVENTIONAL MANPWER COMMITTED		8.	0 OR N/A	3.	15.0-600.0
7-44	DEPENDENCE FOR NAVAL ARMAMENTS	#	1.	EXCLUSIVE	1.	EXCLUSIVE
7-50	OVERTNESS OF 3PTY HARDWARE AID		1.	GEN'LY OVERT	1.	GEN'LY OVERT
7-53	PC TOTAL COSTS COMING FM 3PTY		2.	1.2-5.0	1.	1.0-1.0

8-2	RECRUITMENT TO OFFICER CORPS		3.	NON-ELITIST	3.	NON-ELITIST
8-3	FEL'SHIP BET POL + MIL LEADERS		1.	POL DOMINANT	1.	POL DOMINANT
8-7	METHOD OF MILITARY RECRUITMENT		1.	VOLUNTARY	1.	VOLUNTARY
8-9	TRAINING FACILITY FOR OFFICERS		1.	GOOD	1.	GOOD
8-11	TRAINING FAC FOR ENLISTED PERS	#	2.	FAIR	1.	GOOD
8-13	OVERALL MILITARY ORG'N BALANCE	#	3.	UNFAVORABLE	1.	FAVORABLE
8-17	CENTRALIZATION OF MIL. COMMAND	#	1.	CENTRALIZED	1.	CENTRALIZED
8-20	USE OF TERROR BY THIS ANT. IS		2.	LIMITED	3.	ABSENT
8-30	SYMPATHY BETW POPN + OWN MIL.	#	1.	SYMPATHETIC	1.	SYMPATHETIC

9-1	PC OF INDUSTRIAL CAPACITY LOST		1.	0.001-1.0	1.	0.001-1.0
9-2	PC OF CIVILIAN POPULATION LOST		1.	0.003-1.0	1.	0.003-1.0
9-3	TOTAL NO. CIVN POPULATION LOST	#	8.	0 OR N/A	3.	50.0-59MIL
9-4	ATTRITION RATE FOR CIV'N POPN		8.	0 OR N/A	2.	1.7-200.0
9-7	TOTAL CAS'TIES TO ALL FORCES	#	2.	1.3-6.0	1.	1.0-1.2
9-10	CASUALTY RATE FOR ALL FORCES	#	2.	2.5-5.0	1.	1.0-2.0
9-13	ATTRITION RATE FOR ALL FORCES		2.	2.5-8.0	1.	1.0-2.0

Species Type E3
("toward a foregone conclusion in proxy conflict")

The factor pattern derives from

1-1	GEOGRAPHIC LOCUS OF DISPUTE		3.	EUROPE	3.	EUROPE
1-2A	TOPOGRAPHY OF CONFLICT AREA	#	2.	MOUNTAINOUS	2.	MOUNTAINOUS
1-2B	CLIMATE IN THE CONFLICT AREA		2.	MODERATE	2.	MODERATE
1-3	PAST POL. REL'SHIP BETW PARTYS	#	2.	COMPETITIVE	2.	COMPETITIVE
1-4	PAST MIL. REL'SHIP BETW PARTYS	#	2.	RANDOM HOST.	2.	RANDOM HOST.
1-5	EFFECTIVE NATURE OF DISPUTE	#	3.	INTERNAL	3.	INTERNAL
1-7	IDEOLOGICAL DIFF. BETW PARTIES	#	1.	EXTREME	1.	EXTREME
1-8	CONTROL OF REAL ESTATE INVOLVD	#	1.	YES	1.	YES

	Item		Compound Response		

Greek insurgency (Greek insurgents vs. Greek government)

Spanish civil war (Republican government vs. Nationalist insurgents)

The adjunct is

Ethiopian resistance

	Item		Compound Response	
2-3	RACIAL GROUPING OF ANTAGONIST	1. WHITE	1. WHITE	
2-4	REGIM + GENL POPN OF SAME RACE #	1. YES	1. YES	
2-5	RACIAL HOMOGENEITY OF GENL POP #	1. HOMOGENEOUS	1. HOMOGENEOUS	
2-6	LINGUISTIC HOMOGENEITY OF POPN	2. MILD HETERO	1. HOMOGENEOUS	
2-8	DOMINANT RELIGICN AMONG POPN	1. JUD-XIAN	1. JUD-XIAN	
2-14	REAL ESTATE INVOLVED IS #	1. IN CLMD BDY	1. IN CLMD BDY	
2-15	PC OF ANT'S CLMD AREA INVOLVED #	1. 1.0-1.0	1. 1.0-1.0	
2-16	PC OF ANT'S CLMD POPN INVOLVED #	1. 1.0-1.0	1. 1.0-1.0	
2-19	URBANIZATION	2. MEDIUM	2. MEDIUM	
3-3	GROWTH RATE OF ECONOMY	1. 1.0-1.0	1. 1.0-1.0	
4-3	MODERN COLONIAL RULER	5. NONE	5. NONE	
4-23	INTEREST ARTIC'N BY INST'L GPS #	2. POL INSIGNIF	1. POL SIGNIF	
4-34	FORN RES ARE MAINSTAY OF REGIM	1. YES	1. YES	
4-35	REGIM APPEARS MAINT BY FOR RES	1. YES	1. YES	
4-39	POST-DISPUTE EXPECT'N OF POPN	2. PESSIMISTIC	2. PESSIMISTIC	
5-1	RECENTLY INVOLVED IN OTHER WAR	2. NO	1. YES	
5-2	REGIME SEEKS OVERTHROW OF ADV. #	1. YES	1. YES	
5-6	INTEREST INVOLVED-NAT'L CHAR.	2. NO	1. YES	
5-7	INTEREST INVOLVED-PRESTIGE #	1. YES	1. YES	
5-8	INTEREST INVOLVED-PRIDE #	1. YES	1. YES	
5-9	INTEREST INVOLVED-POWER #	1. YES	1. YES	
5-12	INTEREST INVOLVED-CONT'D EXIS. #	1. YES	1. YES	
5-13	COMMITMENT TO STATED GOALS #	1. TOTAL	1. TOTAL	
5-14	DISPUTE IS REGARDED AS CRUSADE #	1. YES	1. YES	
5-15	CONDUCT OF CONFLICT IS LIMITED #	2. NO	2. NO	
5-18	CAN ACCEPT LES THN STATED DMDS #	2. NO	2. NO	
5-21	LIKELY OUTCOME IS NOW OBVIOUS	2. NO	1. YES	
5-22	POST-DISPUTE EXPECT'N OF REGIM #	2. PESSIMISTIC	2. PESSIMISTIC	
5-23	DIST FM BORDER TO CONFL AREA #	1. 1.0-1.0	1. 1.0-1.0	
5-27	SPEED OF COMMUNICATIONS #	2. MODERATE	2. MODERATE	
5-30	PRINCIPAL ATTEMPTS AT RESOL'N #	5. MILITARY	5. MILITARY	
5-31	OFFERED TO RESOLVE CONST'ALLY #	2. NO	2. NO	
5-34	HAS SOUGHT A NEGOT. SETTLEMENT #	2. NO	2. NO	
5-46	AMNESTY DECL FOR ADV PERSONNEL	2. NO	2. NO	
6-1	IS SEC'TY ALLY CF GREAT POWER	2. NO	2. NO	
6-2	IS SEC'TY ALLY OF NON-G.P.	2. NO	2. NO	
6-3	IS ALLY OF G.P. HOSTILE TO ADV	2. NO	2. NO	
6-4	IS ALLY OF G.P. ALLIED TO ADV. #	2. NO	2. NO	
6-5	IS AIDED BY GP HOSTILE TO ADV. #	1. YES	1. YES	
6-6	A GP IS OPENLY PARTIAL TO ANT. #	1. YES	1. YES	
6-7	GP AID PROMISED IF ESC. OCCURS	2. NO	2. NO	
6-8	GP DEF. FAC'TIES IN ANT'S AREA	2. NO	2. NO	
6-15	A G.P. IS INV. ON THIS SIDE #	1. YES	1. YES	
6-18	A 3PTY IS PROVIDING POL. AID #	1. YES	1. YES	
6-24B	RECENT CHANGE IN 3RD PTY GOVT. #	2. NO	2. NO	
6-30	SOME 3PTY OFFERED TO ARBITRATE	2. NO	2. NO	
6-31	INTL ORGN OFFERED TO ARBITRATE	2. NO	2. NO	
6-32	REGL ORGN OFFERED TO ARBITRATE #	2. NO	2. NO	
6-33	A G.P. OFFERED TO ARBITRATE	2. NO	2. NO	
6-40	ACCEPTED IO'S PROP. CEASEFIRE #	2. NO	2. NO	
6-42	I.O. HAS IMPOSED SANCTIONS #	2. NO	2. NO	
7-1	NO. OF OWN ACTIVE MIL. TROOPS #	1. 0.02-10.7	1. 0.02-10.7	
7-6	NO. TROOPS COMM AS PC TOT FRCS	1. 0.7-1.0	1. 0.7-1.0	
7-9	OTHER SIGNIF EXTERNAL THREAT #	2. NO	2. NO	
7-11	TOTAL TROOPS GIVEN BY 3RD PTY	1. 0.3-1.0	1. 0.3-1.0	
7-14	TOTAL MANPOWER COMMITTED #	1. 0.02-7.3	1. 0.02-7.3	
7-15	OWN TRPS AS PC OF ALL COMMITED #	1. 1.0-1.5	1. 1.0-1.5	
7-17	GUERRILLA MANPOWER COMMITTED	2. 1.3-20.0	8. 0 OR N/A	
7-22	NO. AUTO. WEAPONS AVAILABLE	1. 1.0-2.0	1. 1.0-2.0	
7-47	AIR ARMAMENT SUPPLY LIKELY TO	2. STAY SAME	2. STAY SAME	
8-3	REL'SHIP BET POL + MIL LEADERS	1. POL DOMINANT	2. MIL DOMINANT	
8-4	UNITY WITHIN MILITARY COMMAND	2. FACTIONAL	1. UNIFIED	
8-13	CVERALL MILITARY ORG'N BALANCE #	3. UNFAVORABLE	1. FAVORABLE	
8-14	LOGIS SUP'T ADQT TO MAINT OPNS	2. NO	1. YES	
8-15	LOGIS SUP'T ADQT TO EXPAND OPN	2. NO	1. YES	
8-17	CENTRALIZATION OF MIL. COMMAND #	1. CENTRALIZED	1. CENTRALIZED	
9-5	TOTAL CAS'TIES TO OWN FORCES #	2. 1.5-20.0	1. 1.0-1.2	
9-8	CASUALTY RATE FOR OWN FORCES	1. 1.0-2.0	1. 1.0-2.0	
9-11	ATTRITION RATE FOR OWN FORCES	1. 1.0-2.0	1. 1.0-2.0	
9-13	ATTRITION RATE FOR ALL FORCES	1. 1.0-2.0	1. 1.0-2.0	

Species Type E4

("reacting to the manifest: expedition and aversion")

The factor pattern derives from

Algeria-Morocco (Morocco vs. Algeria)

Israel-Egypt (Israel vs. Egypt)

	Item		Compound Response	
1-1	GEOGRAPHIC LOCUS OF DISPUTE	4. MIDDLE EAST	4. MIDDLE EAST	
1-2A	TOPOGRAPHY OF CONFLICT AREA	1. FLAT	1. FLAT	
1-2B	CLIMATE IN THE CONFLICT AREA	1. DRY	1. DRY	
1-5	EFFECTIVE NATURE OF DISPUTE	2. INTERSTATE	2. INTERSTATE	
1-6	DURATION OF DISFJTE (IN MOS.)	2. 13.1-29.0	2. 13.1-29.0	
1-7	IDEOLOGICAL DIFF. BETW PARTIES #	1. EXTREME	1. EXTREME	
1-8	CONTROL OF REAL ESTATE INVOLVD	1. YES	1. YES	
1-11	DISPUTE HAS BEEN TO REG'L ORGN	1. YES	1. YES	
2-1	OVERRIDING CULTURAL IDEAL	2. RATIONALITY	3. AGGRESSIVE	
2-4	REGIM + GENL POPN OF SAME RACE #	1. YES	1. YES	
2-7	RELIGIOUS HOMOGENEITY OF POPN	1. VERY HOMO	1. VERY HOMO	
2-19	URBANIZATION	1. HIGH	1. HIGH	

Item		Compound Response		
3-14	GOVERNMENT INCOME AS PC OF GNP	1.	1.0-1.5	1. 1.0-1.5
3-15	GOVT. SPENDING AS PC OF GNP	1.	1.1-1.5	1. 1.1-1.5
3-18	DEFENSE BUDGET AS PC OF GNP	1.	0.3-2.7	1. 0.3-2.7
3-22	UNEMPLOYED AS PC OF GENL POPN	1.	0.5-1.0	1. 0.5-1.0
3-23	UNEMPLOYMENT OF INTELLECTUALS #	3.	NONE	2. MILD
3-27	NO. AIRPORTS CONTROLLED	1.	1.0-1.0	2. 1.5-15.0
3-29	NO. SEAPORTS CONTROLLED	2.	1.6-3.3	1. 1.0-1.2
4-1	EFFECTIVE STATUS OF GOVERNMENT	1.	INDEP GOVT	1. INDEP GOVT
4-13	INTERNAL POLICIES OF REGIME	2.	MODERATE	3. REVOL'ARY
4-16	LEADERSHIP CHARISMA	1.	PRONOUNCED	1. PRONOUNCED
4-24	INTEREST ARTIC'N BY POL PARTYS	1.	POL SIGNIF	2. POL INSIGNIF
4-26	EFFECTIVE POL. PARTY SYSTEM	2.	ONE PTY DOM	1. ONE PARTY
4-29	PC OF VOTE REC'D BY THIS REGIM	1.	1.2-1.3	2. 1.7-2.5
4-30	PC VOTE RECD BY LT WING PTIES	3.	9.5-100.0	8. 0 OR N/A
4-33	RECENT CHANGE IN LEADERSHIP #	2.	NO	2. NO
4-34	FORN RES ARE MAINSTAY OF REGIM	2.	NO	2. NO
4-35	REGIM APPEARS MAINT BY FOR RES	2.	NO	2. NO
4-36	POP. SUPPORT FOR REGIME'S OBJ.	1.	HIGH	1. HIGH
4-37	POP. SUPPORT FOR REGIM'S POLS.	1.	HIGH	1. HIGH
4-38	ATT. OF INTELLECTUALS TO REGIM	1.	FAVORABLE	1. FAVORABLE
4-39	POST-DISPUTE EXPECT'N OF POPN	2.	PESSIMISTIC	2. PESSIMISTIC
4-40	EFFECT ON POPULAR COHESION	1.	GRT INCREASE	1. GRT INCREASE
5-5	INTEREST INVOLVED-EST. POLICY #	1.	YES	1. YES
5-6	INTEREST INVOLVED-NAT'L CHAR.	1.	YES	1. YES
5-7	INTEREST INVOLVED-PRESTIGE #	1.	YES	1. YES
5-8	INTEREST INVOLVED-PRIDE #	1.	YES	1. YES
5-11	INTEREST INVOLVED-TERR. INTEG. #	1.	YES	1. YES
5-21	LIKELY OUTCOME IS NOW OBVIOUS	1.	YES	1. YES
5-22	POST-DISPUTE EXPECT'N OF REGIM #	2.	PESSIMISTIC	2. PESSIMISTIC
5-25	ADVERSARY APPEARS TO ANT TO BE	2.	AUT + INDEP.	2. AUT + INDEP.
5-26	TREATY EXPERIENCE WITH ADV.	2.	UNSATISF'ORY	2. UNSATISF'ORY
5-28	RELIABILITY OF COMMUNICATIONS #	2.	LOW	2. LOW
5-29	CREDIBILITY OF COMMUNICATIONS #	2.	LOW	2. LOW
5-30	PRINCIPAL ATTEMPTS AT RESOL'N #	5.	MILITARY	5. MILITARY
5-32	BROUGHT DISPUTE TO INT'L ORGN #	2.	NO	2. NO
5-38	P.O. RE ADV'S POL. INST'NS. #	2.	UNFAVORABLE	2. UNFAVORABLE
5-39	P.O. RE ADV'S SOCIAL INST'NS.	2.	UNFAVORABLE	2. UNFAVORABLE
5-41	P.O. RE ADV'S REL. INST'NS.	2.	UNFAVORABLE	2. UNFAVORABLE
5-44	APPLIES OWN LEGAL STDS TO ADV. #	2.	NO	2. NO
5-45	LEGAL STATUS OF ADV. PERSONNEL	4.	ENEMY AGENT	4. ENEMY AGENT
6-3	IS ALLY OF G.P. HOSTILE TO ADV	2.	NO	2. NO
6-4	IS ALLY OF G.P. ALLIED TO ADV. #	2.	NO	2. NO
6-11	HAS ASKED AN INT'L. ORG'N. IN #	2.	NO	2. NO
6-14	REG'L ORG IS INV. ON THIS SIDE #	2.	NO	2. NO
6-17	A AUT ORG IS INV. ON THIS SIDE #	2.	NO	2. NO
6-23	A 3PTY IS PROVIDING GUER FORCE	2.	NO	2. NO
6-29	I.O. PEACE MACHINERY IS SEEN #	2.	IRRELEVANT	2. IRRELEVANT
6-30	SOME 3PTY OFFERED TO ARBITRATE #	1.	YES	1. YES
6-31	INTL ORGN OFFERED TO ARBITRATE #	1.	YES	1. YES
6-33	A G.P. OFFERED TO ARBITRATE	2.	NO	2. NO
6-40	ACCEPTED IO'S PROP. CEASEFIRE #	2.	NO	2. NO
6-42	I.O. HAS IMPOSED SANCTIONS #	2.	NO	2. NO
7-1	NO. OF OWN ACTIVE MIL. TROOPS #	1.	0.02-10.7	1. 0.02-10.7
7-6	NO. TROOPS COMM AS PC TOT FRCS	1.	0.7-1.0	2. 1.2-14.0
7-14	TOTAL MANPOWER COMMITTED #	1.	0.02-7.3	1. 0.02-7.3
7-15	OWN TRPS AS PC OF ALL COMMITED #	1.	1.0-1.5	1. 1.0-1.5
7-16	CONVENTIONAL MANPWER COMMITTED	1.	0.01-3.0	1. 0.01-3.0
7-17	GUERRILLA MANPOWER COMMITTED	1.	0.02-1.0	1. 0.02-1.0
7-30	NO. BOMBER A/C AVAILABLE #	1.	1.0-1.0	2. 2.0-25.0
7-34	NO. SAM'S AVAILABLE	1.	1.0-1.0	1. 1.0-1.0
7-35	NO. SSM'S AVAILABLE #	1.	1.0-1.0	1. 1.0-1.0
7-36	NO. SUBMARINES AVAILABLE	1.	1.0-1.0	1. 1.0-1.0
7-43	BATTLE ARMS SUPPLY LIKELY TO	2.	STAY SAME	2. STAY SAME
7-44	DEPENDENCE FOR NAVAL ARMAMENTS #	1.	EXCLUSIVE	1. EXCLUSIVE
7-45	NAVAL ARMS SUPPLY LIKELY TO	2.	STAY SAME	2. STAY SAME
7-48	DEP FOR TRANSPORT CAPABILITIES	2.	HIGH	2. HIGH
8-20	USE OF TERROR BY THIS ANT. IS	3.	ABSENT	3. ABSENT
8-23	TACTICS OF FORCES ON THIS SIDE	1.	TENACIOUS	1. TENACIOUS
8-26	LARG-SCAL GUER OPN BEING WAGED	2.	NO	2. NO
8-30	SYMPATHY BETW POPN + OWN MIL. #	1.	SYMPATHETIC	1. SYMPATHETIC
8-34	CIVN SEC V AC ATK BY OWN FRCES	1.	HIGH	1. HIGH
9-2	PC OF CIVILIAN POPULATION LOST	1.	0.003-1.0	1. 0.003-1.0
9-9	CASUALTY RATE FOR 3PTY FORCES	1.	0.1-1.0	1. 0.1-1.0
9-12	ATTRITION RATE FOR 3PTY FORCES	1.	0.1-1.0	1. 0.1-1.0

e.
Escalation:
Higher-Order Factor Patterns

Genus 1

Item			Compound Response	
1-2A	TOPOGRAPHY OF CONFLICT AREA	#	2. MOUNTAINOUS	2. MOUNTAINOUS

	Item			Compound Response		

The factor pattern derives from

Ethiopian resistance (Italian colonial administration vs. Ethiopian insurgents)

Greek insurgency (Greek insurgents vs. Greek government)

Spanish civil war (Republican government vs. Nationalist insurgents)

The adjuncts are

Cyprus: independence
Cyprus: internal
Malayan insurgency
Venezuelan insurgency

Item	Description			Resp 1		Resp 2
1-2B	CLIMATE IN THE CONFLICT AREA		2.	MODERATE	2.	MODERATE
1-4	PAST MIL. REL'SHIP BETW PARTYS	#	2.	RANDOM HOST.	2.	RANDOM HOST.
1-7	IDFOLOGICAL DIFF. BETW PARTIES	#	1.	EXTREME	1.	EXTREME
1-8	CONTROL OF REAL ESTATE INVOLVD	#	1.	YES	1.	YES
2-5	RACIAL HOMOGENEITY OF GENL POP	#	1.	HOMOGENEOUS	1.	HOMOGENEOUS
2-8	DOMINANT RELIGION AMONG POPN		1.	JUD-XIAN	1.	JUD-XIAN
2-14	REAL ESTATE INVOLVED IS		1.	IN CLMD BDY	1.	IN CLMD BDY
2-15	PC OF ANT'S CLMD AREA INVOLVED	#	1.	1.0-1.0	1.	1.0-1.0
2-16	PC OF ANT'S CLMD POPN INVOLVED	#	1.	1.0-1.0	1.	1.0-1.0
4-23	INTEREST ARTIC'N BY INST'L GPS	#	2.	POL INSIGNIF	1.	POL SIGNIF
5-2	REGIME SEEKS OVERTHROW OF ADV.	#	1.	YES	1.	YES
5-6	INTEREST INVOLVED-NAT'L CHAR.		2.	NO	1.	YES
5-8	INTEREST INVOLVED-PRIDE	#	1.	YES	1.	YES
5-12	INTEREST INVOLVED-CONT'D EXIS.	#	1.	YES	1.	YES
5-15	CONDUCT OF CONFLICT IS LIMITED	#	2.	NO	2.	NO
5-18	CAN ACCEPT LES THN STATED DMDS	#	2.	NO	2.	NO
5-22	POST-DISPUTE EXPECT'N CF REGIM	#	2.	PESSIMISTIC	2.	PESSIMISTIC
5-23	DIST FM BORDER TO CONFL AREA	#	1.	1.0-1.0	1.	1.0-1.0
5-30	PRINCIPAL ATTEMPTS AT RESOL'N	#	5.	MILITARY	5.	MILITARY
5-31	CFFERED TO RESOLVE CONST'ALLY	#	2.	NO	2.	NO
5-34	HAS SOUGHT A NEGOT. SETTLEMENT	#	2.	NO	2.	NO
6-2	IS SEC'TY ALLY OF NON-G.P.		2.	NO	2.	NO
6-4	IS ALLY OF G.P. ALLIED TO ADV.	#	2.	NO	2.	NC
6-5	IS AIDED BY GP HOSTILE TO ADV.	#	1.	YES	1.	YES
6-6	A GP IS OPENLY PARTIAL TO ANT.	#	1.	YES	1.	YES
6-7	GP AID PROMISED IF ESC. OCCURS		2.	NO	2.	NO
6-15	A G.P. IS INV. ON THIS SIDE	#	1.	YES	1.	YES
6-18	A 3PTY IS PROVICING POL. AID	#	1.	YES	1.	YES
6-30	SOME 3PTY OFFERED TO ARBITRATE		2.	NO	2.	NO
6-32	REGL ORGN OFFERED TO ARBITRATE	#	2.	NO	2.	NO
6-33	A G.P. OFFERED TO ARBITRATE		2.	NO	2.	NO
6-40	ACCEPTED IO'S PROP. CEASEFIRE	#	2.	NO	2.	NO
7-15	OWN TRPS AS PC CF ALL COMMITED	#	1.	1.0-1.5	1.	1.0-1.5
8-13	OVERALL MILITARY ORG'N BALANCE	#	3.	UNFAVORABLE	1.	FAVORABLE

Genus 2

The factor pattern derives from

Algeria-Morocco (Morocco vs. Algeria)

Indonesia-Malaysia (Indonesia vs. Malaysia)

Israel-Egypt (Israel vs. Egypt)

Kashmir (Pakistan vs. India)

Item	Description			Resp 1		Resp 2
1-5	EFFECTIVE NATURE OF DISPUTE		2.	INTERSTATE	2.	INTERSTATE
1-8	CONTROL OF REAL ESTATE INVOLVD	#	1.	YES	1.	YES
2-4	REGIM + GENL POPN OF SAME RACE	#	1.	YES	1.	YES
4-1	EFFECTIVE STATUS OF GOVERNMENT		1.	INDEP GOVT	1.	INDEP GOVT
4-33	RECENT CHANGE IN LEADERSHIP	#	2.	NO	2.	NO
4-34	FORN RES ARE MAINSTAY CF REGIM		2.	NO	2.	NO
4-35	REGIM APPEARS MAINT BY FOR RES		2.	NO	2.	NO
4-36	POP. SUPPORT FOR REGIME'S OBJ.		1.	HIGH	1.	HIGH
4-37	POP. SUPPORT FOR REGIM'S POLS.		1.	HIGH	1.	HIGH
4-38	ATT. OF INTELLECTUALS TO REGIM		1.	FAVORABLE	1.	FAVORABLE
5-26	TREATY EXPERIENCE WITH ADV.		2.	UNSATISF'ORY	2.	UNSATISF'ORY
5-38	F.O. RE ADV'S POL. INST'NS.	#	2.	UNFAVORABLE	2.	UNFAVORABLE
5-39	P.O. RE ADV'S SOCIAL INST'NS.		2.	UNFAVORABLE	2.	UNFAVORABLE
6-4	IS ALLY OF G.P. ALLIED TO ADV.	#	2.	NO	2.	NO
6-14	REG'L ORG IS INV. ON THIS SIDE	#	2.	NO	2.	NC
6-30	SOME 3PTY OFFERED TO ARBITRATE	#	1.	YES	1.	YES
6-31	INTL ORGN OFFERED TO ARBITRATE	#	1.	YES	1.	YES
6-40	ACCEPTED IO'S PROP. CEASEFIRE	#	2.	NO	2.	NO
6-42	I.O. HAS IMPOSED SANCTIONS	#	2.	NO	2.	NO
7-14	TOTAL MANPOWER COMMITTED	#	1.	0.02-7.3	1.	0.02-7.3
7-44	DEPENDENCE FOR NAVAL ARMAMENTS	#	1.	EXCLUSIVE	1.	EXCLUSIVE
8-30	SYMPATHY BETW POPN + OWN MIL.	#	1.	SYMPATHETIC	1.	SYMPATHETIC
9-2	PC OF CIVILIAN POPULATION LOST		1.	0.003-1.0	1.	0.003-1.0

Artificial Family

The factor pattern derives from

Cyprus: independence (U.K. colonial administration vs. Enosists)

Cyprus: internal (Cypriot government vs. Turkish Cypriots)

Ethiopian resistance (Ethiopian insurgents vs. Italian colonial administration)

Greek insurgency (Greek insur-

Item	Description			Resp 1		Resp 2
5-22	POST-DISPUTE EXPECT'N OF REGIM	#	2.	PESSIMISTIC	2.	PESSIMISTIC
5-23	DIST FM BORDER TO CONFL AREA	#	1.	1.0-1.0	1.	1.0-1.0
6-4	IS ALLY OF G.P. ALLIED TO ADV.	#	2.	NO	2.	NO
6-7	GP AID PROMISED IF ESC. OCCURS		2.	NO	2.	I.O
6-30	SOME 3PTY OFFERED TO ARBITRATE		2.	NO	2.	NO
6-32	REGL ORGN OFFERED TO ARBITRATE	#	2.	NO	2.	NO
6-33	A G.P. OFFERED TO ARBITRATE		2.	NO	2.	NO

Item	Compound Response

gents vs. Greek government)

Malayan insurgency (Malayan Communist party vs. U.K.-Malay colonial administration and Malayan government)

Spanish civil war (Republican government vs. Nationalist insurgents)

Venezuelan insurgency (MIR/CPV and FLN/FALN vs. Venezuelan government.

Order

6-4 IS ALLY OF G.P. ALLIED TO ADV. # 2. NO	2. NO

The factor pattern derives from all eleven instances of escalation included in the analysis.

4.
The De-escalation (D) Patterns

The data input for each conflict included in this analysis is that obtaining at the threshold of subphase D and is therefore a statement of the conditions pertaining when the ongoing hostilities in each case were about to de-escalate, that is, when the rules governing the conduct of hostilities in each case were about to undergo a change that would effect a diminution in the scale or the scope of the hostilities. In the conflict (Indonesia: independence) in which more than one instance of de-escalation occurred, that representing the better, more definitive example of its kind was included in this analysis.

a.
Conflicts Included in the Analysis of the De-escalation Patterns

Conflict	Event Marking De-escalation (D)	Date
Cyprus: independence	Makarios accepts no "enosis"	9/58
Cyprus: internal	Agreement on U.N. peacekeeping force	3/64
Ethiopian resistance	New viceroy initiates conciliation policy	1/38
Indonesia: independence	Unsuccessful negotiations opened	4/46
Indonesia-Malaysia	Indonesian landings in Malaya cease	5/65
Malayan insurgency	MCP shifts emphasis to political agitation	10/51
Spanish civil war	Withdrawal of the International Brigade	10/38

b.

Derivation of the De-escalation
Patterns

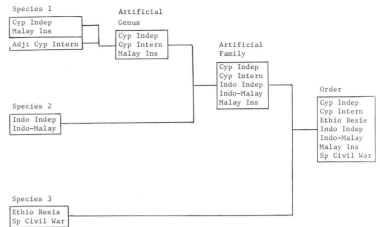

c.

Percentile Distribution of the
Conflicts across the
De-escalation patterns

	Species			Artificial Genus	Artificial Family	Order
	D1	D2	D3			
Cyprus: independence	1.00	0.51	0.37	1.00	1.00	1.00
Cyprus: internal	0.50	0.40	0.27	1.00	1.00	1.00
Ethiopian resistance	0.31	0.38	1.00	~	~	1.00
Indonesia: independence	0.47	1.00	0.41	~	1.00	1.00
Indonesia–Malaysia	0.39	1.00	0.43	~	1.00	1.00
Malayan insurgency	1.00	0.51	0.39	1.00 ،	1.00	1.00
Spanish civil war	0.29	0.40	1.00	~	~	1.00
Vietnam 3/67	0.39	0.42	0.56	0.52	0.76	0.78

d.

De-escalation:
Complete Factor Patterns

Species Type D1
("adjusting ambitions to reflect
capabilities")

The factor pattern derives from

Cyprus: independence (U.K. colonial administration vs. Enosists)

Malayan insurgency (U.K.-Malay
colonial administration and Malayan government vs. Malayan Communist party)

The adjunct is

Cyprus: internal

Item		Compound Response	
1-2A TOPOGRAPHY OF CONFLICT AREA	1. FLAT	1. FLAT
1-4 PAST MIL. REL'SHIP BETW PARTYS	1. PEACEFUL	1. PEACEFUL
1-5 EFFECTIVE NATURE OF DISPUTE	1. COLONIAL	1. COLONIAL
1-8 CONTROL OF REAL ESTATE INVOLVD #	1. YES	1. YES
1-11 DISPUTE HAS BEEN TO REG'L ORGN #	2. NO	2. NO
2-6 LINGUISTIC HOMOGENEITY OF POPN	3. VERY HETERO	1. HOMOGENEOUS
2-14 REAL ESTATE INVOLVED IS #	1. IN CLMD BDY	1. IN CLMD BDY
2-15 PC OF ANT'S CLMD AREA INVOLVED #	1. 1.0-1.0	1. 1.0-1.0
2-16 PC OF ANT'S CLMD POPN INVOLVED #	1. 1.0-1.0	1. 1.0-1.0
2-19 URBANIZATION	2. MEDIUM	8. 0 OR N/A
3-2 GROSS NAT'L. OR ECON. PRODUCT #	3. 90.0-6.4TH	8. 0 OR N/A
3-3 GROWTH RATE OF ECONOMY	3. 3.0-13.9	8. 0 OR N/A
3-4 FATE OF INFLATION IN ECONOMY	2. 2.0-10.0	8. 0 OR N/A
3-5 PER CAPITA INCOME #	3. 115.0-855.0	8. 0 OR N/A
3-6 PC OF GNP IN AGRICULTURE #	3. 25.0-75.0	8. 0 OR N/A
3-8 PRODUCTION OF STEEL #	1. 1.0-1.0	1. 1.0-1.0
3-9 PC OF GNP IN EXPORTS	3. 22.0-1.0TH	8. 0 OR N/A
3-12 FOR AID AS PC OF GNP + FOR AID #	3. 5.0-30.0	8. 0 OR N/A
3-13 PROGRESSIVE TAX STRUCTURE	1. YES	8. 0 OR N/A
3-14 GOVERNMENT INCOME AS PC OF GNP #	3. 10.0-50.0	8. 0 OR N/A
3-15 GOVT. SPENDING AS PC OF GNP #	3. 6.0-50.0	8. 0 OR N/A
3-17 MILITARY DEFENSE BUDGET	2. 1.4-25.0	8. 0 OR N/A

Item			Compound Response		
3-18	DEFENSE BUDGET AS PC OF GNP		1. 0.3-2.7	8.	0 OR N/A
3-20	AGRIC EMPLOYMENT AS PC OF POPN		3. 13.0-70.0	8.	0 OR N/A
3-21	INDUSTRIAL EMPL. AS PC OF POPN		3. 11.0-23.0	8.	0 OR N/A
3-29	NO. SEAPORTS CONTROLLED		2. 1.6-3.3	8.	0 OR N/A
4-1	EFFECTIVE STATUS OF GOVERNMENT		2. COLONIAL ADM	4.	REBEL ORGN
4-3	MODERN COLONIAL RULER		5. NONE	1.	BRITAIN
4-4	EXECUTIVE STABILITY	#	3. 3.0-9.0	8.	0 OR N/A
4-5	TYPE OF GOVERNMENT		2. TUT/MOD OLIG	8.	0 OR N/A
4-6	STATUS OF EXECUTIVE		1. DOMINANT	8.	0 OR N/A
4-10	REGIME CAME TO POWER CONST'LY	#	2. NO	8.	0 OR N/A
4-13	INTERNAL POLICIES OF REGIME		2. MODERATE	3.	REVOL'ARY
4-17	MOBILIZATIONAL STYLE OF REGIME		2. LIMITED	8.	0 OR N/A
4-19	FREEDOM OF THE PRESS ALLOWED		2. INTERMITTENT	8.	0 OR N/A
4-22	INTEREST ARTIC'N BY ASSOC'L GP		1. POL SIGNIF	8.	0 OR N/A
4-23	INTEREST ARTIC'N BY INST'L GPS		1. POL SIGNIF	8.	0 OR N/A
4-24	INTEREST ARTIC'N BY POL PARTYS		1. POL SIGNIF	8.	0 OR N/A
4-25	CONST'AL STATUS OF POL PARTIES		2. PART COMPET.	8.	0 OR N/A
4-27	PERSONALISM IN POL. PARTIES		2. MODERATE	8.	0 OR N/A
4-32	RECENT LEADERSHIP CRISIS		2. NO	2.	NO
4-34	FORN RES ARE MAINSTAY OF REGIM	#	1. YES	2.	NO
4-35	REGIM APPEARS MAINT BY FOR RES		1. YES	8.	0 OR N/A
5-7	INTEREST INVOLVED-PRESTIGE		2. NO	1.	YES
5-9	INTEREST INVOLVED-POWER		2. NO	1.	YES
5-10	INTEREST INVOLVED-INDEPENDENCE		2. NO	1.	YES
5-12	INTEREST INVOLVED-CONT'D EXIS.		1. YES	2.	NO
5-13	COMMITMENT TO STATED GOALS		2. FLEXIBLE	2.	FLEXIBLE
5-20	PERCEIVED BALANCE OF WILL		2. EVEN	2.	EVEN
5-22	POST-DISPUTE EXPECT'N OF REGIM	#	2. PESSIMISTIC	2.	PESSIMISTIC
5-23	DIST FM BORDER TO CONFL AREA	#	1. 1.0-1.0	1.	1.0-1.0
5-24	DIST FM CAPITAL TO CONFL AREA	#	1. 1.0-1.3	1.	1.0-1.3
5-25	ADVERSARY APPEARS TO ANT TO BE		2. AUT + INDEP.	1.	A PUPPET
5-32	BROUGHT DISPUTE TO INT'L ORGN	#	2. NO	2.	NO
5-37	ESC LIKELY BRING GP AID TO ADV		2. NO	2.	NO
5-43	STATE OF WAR HAS BEEN DECLARED		2. NO	8.	0 OR N/A
5-45	LEGAL STATUS OF ADV. PERSONNEL		2. COM CRIMINAL	4.	ENEMY AGENT
5-46	AMNESTY DECL FOR ADV PERSONNEL		2. NO	2.	NO
6-1	IS SEC'TY ALLY OF GREAT POWER	#	1. YES	2.	NO
6-2	IS SEC'TY ALLY OF NON-G.P.		2. NO	2.	NO
6-3	IS ALLY OF G.P. HOSTILE TO ADV	#	1. YES	2.	NO
6-4	IS ALLY OF G.P. ALLIED TO ADV.	#	2. NO	2.	NO
6-8	GP DEF. FAC'TIES IN ANT'S AREA	#	1. YES	2.	NO
6-9	HAS INVOKED AVAIL SEC'TY PACTS		1. YES	8.	0 OR N/A
6-12	SOME 3PTY IS INV. ON THIS SIDE	#	1. YES	1.	YES
6-13	INT'L ORG IS INV. ON THIS SIDE	#	2. NO	2.	NO
6-14	REG'L ORG IS INV. ON THIS SIDE	#	2. NO	2.	NO
6-15	A G.P. IS INV. ON THIS SIDE		1. YES	2.	NO
6-16	A NON-GP IS INV. ON THIS SIDE		2. NO	1.	YES
6-17	A AUT ORG IS INV. ON THIS SIDE	#	2. NO	2.	NO
6-18	A 3PTY IS PROVIDING POL. AID	#	1. YES	1.	YES
6-21	A 3PTY IS PROVIDING MIL HDWRE.	#	1. YES	1.	YES
6-27	PC ANT'S EXPORTS CONS. BY 3PTY		3. 16-33 PC	8.	0 OR N/A
6-28	EXPERIENCE WITH IO PEACE MACH		2. GRATIFYING	3.	NONE
6-30	SOME 3PTY OFFERED TO ARBITRATE		2. NO	2.	NO
6-31	INTL ORGN OFFERED TO ARBITRATE		2. NO	2.	NO
6-32	REGL ORGN OFFERED TO ARBITRATE	#	2. NO	2.	NO
6-33	A G.P. OFFERED TO ARBITRATE		2. NO	2.	NO
6-35	INT'L ORG'N UPHELD ANT'S CAUSE	#	2. NO	2.	NO
6-36	INTL ORGN INDICTED ANT'S CAUSE	#	2. NO	2.	NO
6-37	CITED IN VIOLATION OF INTL LAW	#	2. NO	2.	NO
6-38	CITED BY I.O. FOR AGGRESSION	#	2. NO	2.	NO
6-42	I.O. HAS IMPOSED SANCTIONS	#	2. NO	2.	NO
6-47	REG ORGN HAS IMPOSED SANCTIONS	#	2. NO	2.	NO
7-2	NO. ACTIV TROOPS AS PC OF POPN		1. 0.001-1.0	1.	0.001-1.0
7-6	NO. TROOPS COMM AS PC TOT FRCS		1. 0.7-1.0	1.	0.7-1.0
7-9	OTHER SIGNIF EXTERNAL THREAT	#	2. NO	2.	NO
7-13	3PTY TROOP AID SEEN LIKELY TO		1. INCREASE	2.	STAY SAME
7-27	NO. HVY. CANNON AVAILABLE		1. 1.0-1.0	1.	1.0-1.0
7-28	NO. ARMORED VEH. AVAILABLE	#	3. 35.0-370.0	8.	0 OR N/A
7-30	NO. BOMBER A/C AVAILABLE		2. 2.0-25.0	8.	0 OR N/A
7-33	NO. HELICOPTERS AVAILABLE		3. 13.3-30.0	8.	0 OR N/A
7-34	NO. SAM'S AVAILABLE		1. 1.0-1.0	1.	1.0-1.0
7-35	NO. SSM'S AVAILABLE	#	1. 1.0-1.0	1.	1.0-1.0
7-36	NO. SUBMARINES AVAILABLE		1. 1.0-1.0	1.	1.0-1.0
7-39	NO. PATROL BOATS AVAILABLE		3. 5.0-37.0	8.	0 OR N/A
7-40	HAS A NUCLEAR CAPABILITY	#	2. NO	2.	NO
7-41	AIDING 3PTY HAS NUCLEAR CAP'TY		1. YES	2.	NO
7-48	DEP FOR TRANSPORT CAPABILITIES		1. EXCLUSIVE	8.	0 OR N/A
7-49	TRANSP. CAP. SUPPLY LIKELY TO		1. INCREASE	8.	0 OR N/A
7-50	OVERTNESS OF 3PTY HARDWARE AID	#	1. GEN'LY OVERT	2.	GEN'LY COVERT
7-51	SPARE PARTS AND AMMUNITION AID		1. ADEQUATE	3.	INADEQUATE
8-3	REL'SHIP BET POL + MIL LEADERS		1. POL DOMINANT	1.	POL DOMINANT
8-4	UNITY WITHIN MILITARY COMMAND		1. UNIFIED	1.	UNIFIED
8-7	METHOD OF MILITARY RECRUITMENT		1. VOLUNTARY	1.	VOLUNTARY
8-13	OVERALL MILITARY ORG'N BALANCE	#	1. FAVORABLE	3.	UNFAVORABLE
8-14	LOGIS SUP'T ADQT TO MAINT OPNS	#	1. YES	1.	YES
8-17	CENTRALIZATION OF MIL. COMMAND		1. CENTRALIZED	2.	DE-CENTR'IZED
8-20	USE OF TERROR BY THIS ANT. IS		3. ABSENT	1.	WIDESPREAD
8-23	TACTICS OF FORCES ON THIS SIDE	#	1. TENACIOUS	2.	YIELDING
8-24	TREATMENT OF ENEMY PRISONERS		1. GOOD	8.	0 OR N/A

Item			Compound Response		
8-25	TREATMENT OF OWN CASUALTIES		1. GOOD	3.	POOR
8-26	LARG-SCAL GUER OPN BEING WAGED		2. NO	1.	YES
8-27	STAGE OF GUERRILLA OPERATIONS		8. 0 OR N/A	2.	EXPANSION
8-33	CIVN SECURITY V. GUERR ATTACK		3. LOW	8.	0 OR N/A
9-3	TOTAL NO. CIVN POPULATION LOST	#	3. 50.0-59MIL	8.	0 OR N/A
9-5	TOTAL CAS'TIES TO OWN FORCES	#	1. 1.0-1.2	2.	1.5-20.0
9-6	TOTAL CAS'TIES TO 3PTY FORCES		3. 75.0-1.9TH	8.	0 OR N/A
9-8	CASUALTY RATE FOR OWN FORCES		1. 1.0-2.0	1.	1.0-2.0

Species Type D2
("a gesture of conciliation in time saves nine")

The factor pattern derives from

Indonesia: independence (Indonesian insurgents vs. Dutch colonial administration)

Indonesia-Malaysia (Indonesia vs. Malaysia)

Item			Compound Response		
1-1	GEOGRAPHIC LOCUS OF DISPUTE	#	6. ASIA	6.	ASIA
1-2A	TOPOGRAPHY OF CONFLICT AREA		1. FLAT	1.	FLAT
1-2B	CLIMATE IN THE CONFLICT AREA	#	3. WET	3.	WET
1-4	PAST MIL. REL'SHIP BETW PARTYS		1. PEACEFUL	1.	PEACEFUL
1-8	CONTROL OF REAL ESTATE INVOLVD	#	1. YES	1.	YES
1-10	SIZE OF POPN AT STAKE (THOUS.)	#	4. 10TH-76TH	4.	10TH-76TH
1-11	DISPUTE HAS BEEN TO REG'L ORGN	#	2. NO	2.	NO
1-12	DISPUTE HAS BEEN TO INT'L ORGN		1. YES	1.	YES
1-13	INTRODUCED TO INT'L ORGN BY A		1. ANTAGONIST	1.	ANTAGONIST
2-9	LITERACY RATE AMONG GENL POPN		2. MEDIUM	2.	MEDIUM
2-13	POPN UNDER EFFECTIVE CONTROL		2. 3.2-52.2	1.	1.0-2.0
2-17	PC OF INVOLVED AREA IN CONTROL		1. 1.0-1.5	2.	1.9-9.0
3-5	PER CAPITA INCOME		1. 1.0-2.1	1.	1.0-2.1
3-6	PC OF GNP IN AGRICULTURE		1. 1.0-2.0	1.	1.0-2.0
3-8	PRODUCTION OF STEEL	#	1. 1.0-1.0	1.	1.0-1.0
3-13	PROGRESSIVE TAX STRUCTURE		1. YES	1.	YES
3-17	MILITARY DEFENSE BUDGET		2. 1.4-25.0	1.	1.0-1.0
3-20	AGRIC EMPLOYMENT AS PC OF POPN		1. 1.0-1.2	1.	1.0-1.2
3-21	INDUSTRIAL EMPL. AS PC OF POPN		1. 1.0-1.1	2.	1.5-5.0
4-4	EXECUTIVE STABILITY		1. 1.0-1.0	2.	1.5-2.0
4-6	STATUS OF EXECUTIVE		1. DOMINANT	2.	STRONG
4-8	STATUS OF JUDICIARY		2. PART EFFECT.	1.	FULL EFFECT.
4-9	CHARACTER OF BUREAUCRACY		3. TRANSITIONAL	1.	MODERN
4-12	IDEOL. ORIENTATION OF REGIME		1. LEFT-WING	2.	MODERATE
4-13	INTERNAL POLICIES OF REGIME		3. REVOL'ARY	2.	MODERATE
4-16	LEADERSHIP CHARISMA	#	1. PRONOUNCED	2.	NEGLIGIBLE
4-32	RECENT LEADERSHIP CRISIS		2. NO	2.	NO
4-33	RECENT CHANGE IN LEADERSHIP	#	2. NO	2.	NO
4-40	EFFECT ON POPULAR COHESION		2. LITTLE CHANGE	2.	LITTLE CHANGE
5-2	REGIME SEEKS OVERTHROW OF ADV.	#	1. YES	1.	YES
5-3	INTEREST INVOLVED-IDEOLOGY		2. NO	2.	NO
5-9	INTEREST INVOLVED-POWER		1. YES	2.	NO
5-20	PERCEIVED BALANCE OF WILL		2. EVEN	2.	EVEN
5-22	POST-DISPUTE EXPECT'N OF REGIM	#	2. PESSIMISTIC	2.	PESSIMISTIC
5-23	DIST FM BORDER TO CONFL AREA	#	1. 1.0-1.0	1.	1.0-1.0
5-24	DIST FM CAPITAL TO CONFL AREA	#	1. 1.0-1.3	1.	1.0-1.3
5-26	TREATY EXPERIENCE WITH ADV.		2. UNSATISF'ORY	2.	UNSATISF'ORY
5-27	SPEED OF COMMUNICATIONS		1. RAPID	1.	RAPID
5-28	RELIABILITY OF COMMUNICATIONS		1. HIGH	1.	HIGH
5-29	CREDIBILITY OF COMMUNICATIONS	#	2. LOW	2.	LOW
5-41	P.O. RE ADV'S REL. INST'NS.		1. FAVORABLE	1.	FAVORABLE
5-43	STATE OF WAR HAS BEEN DECLARED	#	2. NO	2.	NO
6-2	IS SEC'TY ALLY OF NON-G.P.		2. NO	1.	YES
6-4	IS ALLY OF G.P. ALLIED TO ADV.		2. NO	2.	NO
6-13	INT'L ORG IS INV. ON THIS SIDE	#	2. NO	2.	NO
6-14	REG'L ORG IS INV. ON THIS SIDE	#	2. NO	2.	NO
6-16	A NON-GP IS INV. ON THIS SIDE		2. NO	1.	YES
6-18	A 3PTY IS PROVIDING POL. AID		2. NO	1.	YES
6-22	A 3PTY IS PROVIDING CONV FORCE		2. NO	1.	YES
6-30	SOME 3PTY OFFERED TO ARBITRATE		2. NO	2.	NO
6-31	INTL ORGN OFFERED TO ARBITRATE		2. NO	2.	NO
6-32	REGL ORGN OFFERED TO ARBITRATE	#	2. NO	2.	NO
6-33	A G.P. OFFERED TO ARBITRATE		2. NO	2.	NO
6-35	INT'L ORG'N UPHELD ANT'S CAUSE	#	2. NO	2.	NO
6-36	INTL ORGN INDICTED ANT'S CAUSE	#	2. NO	2.	NO
6-37	CITED IN VIOLATION OF INTL LAW	#	2. NO	2.	NO
6-38	CITED BY I.O. FOR AGGRESSION	#	2. NO	2.	NO
6-40	ACCEPTED IO'S PROP. CEASEFIRE	#	2. NO	2.	NO
6-42	I.O. HAS IMPOSED SANCTIONS	#	2. NO	2.	NO
6-47	REG ORGN HAS IMPOSED SANCTIONS	*	2. NO	2.	NO
7-1	NO. OF OWN ACTIVE MIL. TROOPS	#	1. 0.02-10.7	1.	0.02-10.7
7-4	MOBILIZATION OF RESERVES		4. MAJOR	4.	MAJOR
7-9	OTHER SIGNIF EXTERNAL THREAT		2. NO	2.	NO
7-13	3PTY TROOP AID SEEN LIKELY TO		2. STAY SAME	1.	INCREASE
8-3	REL'SHIP BET POL + MIL LEADERS		1. POL DOMINANT	1.	POL DOMINANT
8-5	3PTY HAS ASSUMED MIL. COMMAND		8. 0 OR N/A	1.	YES
8-8	METHOD OF RECRUIT TO 3PTY MIL.		8. 0 OR N/A	1.	VOLUNTARY
8-10	TRAINING FAC FOR 3PTY OFFICERS		8. 0 OR N/A	1.	GOOD
7-11	TOTAL TROOPS GIVEN BY 3RD PTY		8. 0 OR N/A	3.	4.0-100.0
8-12	TRAINING FAC FOR 3PTY ENLISTED		8. 0 OR N/A	1.	GOOD
7-14	TOTAL MANPOWER COMMITTED	#	1. 0.02-7.3	1.	0.02-7.3
7-18	NAVAL MANPOWER COMMITTED	#	1. 0.5-1.0	3.	5.0-20.0
7-19	AIR FORCE MANPOWER COMMITTED		1. 0.05-1.0	2.	2.0-10.0
7-20	MEDICAL PERSONNEL COMMITTED		1. 1.0-1.2	2.	2.0-20.0
7-21	NO. RIFLES AVAILABLE		2. 3.0-85.7	1.	0.05-2.1
7-35	NO. SSM'S AVAILABLE	#	1. 1.0-1.0	1.	1.0-1.0
7-39	NO. PATROL BOATS AVAILABLE		1. 1.0-1.2	2.	1.6-3.0

Item			Compound Response		
8-6	RECRUITMENT RATE INTO MILITARY		2.	3.0-200.0	1.	1.0-2.0
8-13	OVERALL MILITARY ORG'N BALANCE	#	3.	UNFAVORABLE	1.	FAVORABLE
8-19	AERIAL BOMBING USED V. ADV.		4.	NO	4.	NO
8-21	TACTICS OF FORCES ON THIS SIDE	#	1.	OFFENSIVE	1.	OFFENSIVE
8-22	TACTICS OF FORCES ON THIS SIDE	#	1.	MOBILE	1.	MOBILE
8-23	TACTICS OF FORCES ON THIS SIDE	#	2.	YIELDING	1.	TENACIOUS
8-25	TREATMENT OF OWN CASUALTIES		3.	POOR	1.	GOOD
8-26	LARG-SCAL GUER OPN BEING WAGED		2.	NO	2.	NO
9-5	TOTAL CAS'TIES TO OWN FORCES	#	2.	1.5-20.0	1.	1.0-1.2
9-8	CASUALTY RATE FOR OWN FORCES	#	2.	2.5-5.0	1.	1.0-2.0
9-11	ATTRITION RATE FOR OWN FORCES		2.	2.5-20.0	1.	1.0-1.0
9-13	ATTRITION RATE FOR ALL FORCES		2.	2.5-8.0	1.	1.0 2.0
1-2A	TOPOGRAPHY OF CONFLICT AREA	#	2.	MOUNTAINOUS	2.	MOUNTAINOUS
1-2B	CLIMATE IN THE CONFLICT AREA		2.	MODERATE	2.	MODERATE
1-4	PAST MIL. REL'SHIP BETW PARTYS	#	2.	RANDOM HOST.	2.	RANDOM HOST.
1-7	IDEOLOGICAL DIFF. BETW PARTIES	#	1.	EXTREME	1.	EXTREME
1-8	CONTROL OF REAL ESTATE INVOLVD	#	1.	YES	1.	YES
1-10	SIZE OF POPN AT STAKE (THOUS.)	#	4.	10TH-76TH	4.	10TH-76TH
1-13	INTRODUCED TO INT'L ORGN BY A		1.	ANTAGONIST	1.	ANTAGONIST
1-14	BASIS OF INTRO. TO INT'L ORGN		1.	AGGRESSION	1.	AGGRESSION
2-2	PREFERRED MODE OF CONFL RESOLN		2.	CONCILIATORY	3.	DICTATORIAL
2-5	RACIAL HOMOGENEITY OF GENL POP	#	1.	HOMOGENEOUS	1.	HOMOGENEOUS
2-8	DOMINANT RELIGION AMONG POPN		1.	JUD-XIAN	1.	JUD-XIAN
2-12	AREA UNDER EFFECTIVE CONTROL		1.	1.0-2.1	1.	1.0-2.1
2-14	REAL ESTATE INVOLVED IS	#	1.	IN CLMD BDY	1.	IN CLMD BDY
2-15	PC OF ANT'S CLMD AREA INVOLVED	#	1.	1.0-1.0	1.	1.0-1.0
2-16	PC OF ANT'S CLMD POPN INVOLVED	#	1.	1.0-1.0	1.	1.0-1.0
3-5	PER CAPITA INCOME		1.	1.0-2.1	1.	1.0-2.1
3-6	PC OF GNP IN AGRICULTURE		1.	1.0-2.0	1.	1.0-2.0
3-7	PC OF GNP IN DURABLE GOODS		1.	1.0-1.2	1.	1.0-1.2
3-23	UNEMPLOYMENT OF INTELLECTUALS		3.	NONE	3.	NONE
4-11	RECRUITMENT TO POL LEADERSHIP		1.	ELITIST	1.	ELITIST
4-12	IDEOL. ORIENTATION OF REGIME		2.	MODERATE	3.	RIGHT WING
4-13	INTERNAL POLICIES OF REGIME		2.	MODERATE	2.	TRADITIONAL
4-14	INTERNATIONAL POLICY OF REGIME		3.	MODERATE	2.	RIGHTIST
4-20	FREEDOM OF GROUP OPPOSITION		4.	NOT TOLERATD	4.	NOT TOLERATD
4-22	INTEREST ARTIC'N BY ASSOC'L GP		2.	POL INSIGNIF	2.	POL INSIGNIF
4-25	CONST'AL STATUS OF POL PARTIES		2.	PART COMPET.	3.	NON-COMPET.
4-26	EFFECTIVE POL. PARTY SYSTEM		2.	ONE PTY DOM	1.	ONE PARTY
4-38	ATT. OF INTELLECTUALS TO REGIM	#	1.	FAVORABLE	2.	UNFAVORABLE
5-1	RECENTLY INVOLVED IN OTHER WAR		2.	NO	1.	YES
5-2	REGIME SEEKS OVERTHROW OF ADV.	#	1.	YES	1.	YES
5-4	INTEREST INVOLVED-COMMITMENTS	#	1.	YES	1.	YES
5-8	INTEREST INVOLVED-PRIDE	#	1.	YES	1.	YES
5-12	INTEREST INVOLVED-CONT'D EXIS.	#	1.	YES	1.	YES
5-13	COMMITMENT TO STATED GOALS	#	1.	TOTAL	1.	TOTAL
5-14	DISPUTE IS REGARDED AS CRUSADE	#	1.	YES	1.	YES
5-15	CONDUCT OF CONFLICT IS LIMITED	#	2.	NO	2.	NO
5-16	PC OF AVAIL MIL FRCS COMMITTED		5.	70-100PC	5.	70-100PC
5-18	CAN ACCEPT LES THN STATED DMDS	#	2.	NO	2.	NO
5-22	POST-DISPUTE EXPECT'N OF REGIM	#	2.	PESSIMISTIC	2.	PESSIMISTIC
5-23	DIST FM BORDER TO CONFL AREA	#	1.	1.0-1.0	1.	1.0-1.0
5-30	PRINCIPAL ATTEMPTS AT RESOL'N	#	5.	MILITARY	5.	MILITARY
5-31	OFFERED TO RESOLVE CONST'ALLY	#	2.	NO	2.	NO
5-32	BROUGHT DISPUTE TO INT'L ORGN		1.	YES	2.	NO
5-34	HAS SOUGHT A NEGOT. SETTLEMENT	#	2.	NO	2.	NO
5-35	HAS OFFERED BI-LATERAL NEGOTNS	#	2.	NO	2.	NO
5-43	STATE OF WAR HAS BEEN DECLARED	#	2.	NO	2.	NO
5-44	APPLIES OWN LEGAL STDS TO ADV.	#	2.	NO	2.	NO
6-2	IS SEC'TY ALLY OF NON-G.P.		2.	NO	2.	NO
6-4	IS ALLY OF G.P. ALLIED TO ADV.	#	2.	NO	2.	NO
6-6	A GP IS OPENLY PARTIAL TO ANT.	#	1.	YES	1.	YES
6-7	GP AID PROMISED IF ESC. OCCURS		2.	NO	2.	NO
6-10	HAS ASKED A REGIONAL ORG'N IN		2.	NO	2.	NO
6-12	SOME 3PTY IS INV. ON THIS SIDE	#	1.	YES	1.	YES
6-13	INT'L ORG IS INV. ON THIS SIDE	#	2.	NO	2.	NO
6-15	A G.P. IS INV. ON THIS SIDE	#	1.	YES	1.	YES
6-18	A 3PTY IS PROVIDING POL. AID	#	1.	YES	1.	YES
6-20	A 3PTY IS PROVIDING MIL ADVICE	#	1.	YES	1.	YES
6-22	A 3PTY IS PROVIDING CONV FORCE		2.	NO	1.	YES
6-24	ATT. OF 3PTY PUBLIC TO INV'MNT	#	1.	FAVORABLE	1.	FAVORABLE
6-24B	RECENT CHANGE IN 3RD PTY GOVT.		2.	NO	2.	NO
6-29	I.O. PEACE MACHINERY IS SEEN		1.	RELEVANT	2.	IRRELEVANT
6-30	SOME 3PTY OFFERED TO ARBITRATE		2.	NO	2.	NO
6-32	REGL ORGN OFFERED TO ARBITRATE	#	2.	NO	2.	NO
6-33	A G.P. OFFERED TO ARBITRATE		2.	NO	2.	NO
6-40	ACCEPTED IO'S PROP. CEASEFIRE	#	2.	NO	2.	NO
7-4	MOBILIZATION OF RESERVES		5.	TOTAL	5.	TOTAL
7-9	OTHER SIGNIF EXTERNAL THREAT	#	2.	NO	2.	NO
7-11	TOTAL TROOPS GIVEN BY 3RD PTY		8.	0 OR N/A	3.	4.0-100.0
7-13	3PTY TROOP AID SEEN LIKELY TO		3.	DECREASE	2.	STAY SAME
7-15	OWN TRPS AS PC OF ALL COMMITED	#	1.	1.0-1.5	1.	1.0-1.5
7-46	DEP. FOR AIR COMBAT ARMAMENTS	#	1.	EXCLUSIVE	1.	EXCLUSIVE

Species Type D3
("recognizing a precarious cause for what it is")

The factor pattern derives from

Ethiopian resistance (Ethiopian insurgents vs. Italian colonial administration)

Spanish civil war (Republican government vs. Nationalist insurgents)

Item			Compound Response		
8-2	RECRUITMENT TO OFFICER CORPS		1. ELITIST	1. ELITIST
8-10	TRAINING FAC FOR 3PTY OFFICERS	#	1. GOOD	1. GOOD
8-13	OVERALL MILITARY ORG'N BALANCE	#	3. UNFAVORABLE	1. FAVORABLE
8-14	LOGIS SUP'T ADQT TO MAINT OPNS		2. NO	1. YES
8-16	OVERALL MIL. HARDWARE BALANCE	#	3. UNFAVORABLE	1. FAVORABLE
8-21	TACTICS OF FORCES ON THIS SIDE		2. DEFENSIVE	1. OFFENSIVE
8-22	TACTICS OF FORCES ON THIS SIDE	#	1. MOBILE	1. MOBILE
8-24	TREATMENT OF ENEMY PRISONERS		3. BRUTAL	3. BRUTAL

e.

**De-escalation:
Higher-Order Factor Patterns**

Artificial Genus

The factor pattern derives from

Cyprus: independence (U.K. colonial administration vs. Enosists)

Cyprus internal (Cypriot government vs. Turkish Cypriots)

Malayan insurgency (U.K.-Malay colonial administration and Malayan government vs. Malayan Communist party)

Item			Compound Response		
1-2A	TOPOGRAPHY OF CONFLICT AREA		1. FLAT	1. FLAT
1-11	DISPUTE HAS BEEN TO REG'L ORGN	#	2. NO	2. NO
2-6	LINGUISTIC HOMOGENEITY OF POPN		3. VERY HETERO	1. HOMOGENEOUS
2-19	URBANIZATION		2. MEDIUM	8. 0 OR N/A
3-2	GROSS NAT'L. OR ECON. PRODUCT	#	3. 90.0-6.4TH	8. 0 OR N/A
3-3	GROWTH RATE OF ECONOMY		3. 3.0-13.9	8. 0 OR N/A
3-5	PER CAPITA INCOME	#	3. 115.0-855.0	8. 0 OR N/A
3-6	PC OF GNP IN AGRICULTURE	#	3. 25.0-75.0	8. 0 OR N/A
3-8	PRODUCTION OF STEEL	#	1. 1.0-1.0	1. 1.0-1.0
3-9	PC OF GNP IN EXPORTS		3. 22.0-1.0TH	8. 0 OR N/A
3-12	FOP AID AS PC OF GNP + FOR AID	#	3. 5.0-30.0	8. 0 OR N/A
3-13	PROGRESSIVE TAX STRUCTURE		1. YES	8. 0 OR N/A
3-14	GOVERNMENT INCOME AS PC OF GNP	#	3. 10.0-50.0	8. 0 OR N/A
3-15	GOVT. SPENDING AS PC OF GNP	#	3. 6.0-50.0	8. 0 OR N/A
3-20	AGRIC EMPLOYMENT AS PC OF POPN		3. 13.0-70.0	8. 0 OR N/A
3-21	INDUSTRIAL EMPL. AS PC OF POPN		3. 11.0-23.0	8. 0 OR N/A
3-29	NO. SEAPORTS CONTROLLED		2. 1.6-3.3	8. 0 OR N/A
4-4	EXECUTIVE STABILITY	#	3. 3.0-9.0	8. 0 OR N/A
4-22	INTEREST ARTIC'N BY ASSOC'L GP		1. POL SIGNIF	8. 0 OR N/A
4-23	INTEREST ARTIC'N BY INST'L GPS		1. POL SIGNIF	8. 0 OR N/A
4-24	INTEREST ARTIC'N BY POL PARTYS		1. POL SIGNIF	8. 0 OR N/A
4-27	PERSONALISM IN POL. PARTIES		2. MODERATE	8. 0 OR N/A
4-32	RECENT LEADERSHIP CRISIS		2. NO	2. NO
5-22	POST-DISPUTE EXPECT'N OF REGIM	#	2. PESSIMISTIC	2. PESSIMISTIC
5-23	DIST FM BORDER TO CONFL AREA	#	1. 1.0-1.0	1. 1.0-1.0
5-24	DIST FM CAPITAL TO CONFL AREA	#	1. 1.0-1.3	1. 1.0-1.3
5-32	BROUGHT DISPUTE TO INT'L ORGN	#	2. NO	2. NO
5-43	STATE OF WAR HAS BEEN DECLARED		2. NO	2. NO
6-2	IS SEC'TY ALLY OF NON-G.P.		2. NO	2. NO
6-4	IS ALLY OF G.P. ALLIED TO ADV.	#	2. NO	2. NO
6-13	INT'L ORG IS INV. ON THIS SIDE	#	2. NO	2. NO
6-14	REG'L ORG IS INV. ON THIS SIDE	#	2. NO	2. NC
6-16	A NON-GP IS INV. ON THIS SIDE		2. NO	1. YES
6-17	A AUT ORG IS INV. ON THIS SIDE	#	2. NO	2. NO
6-30	SOME 3PTY OFFERED TO ARBITRATE		2. NO	2. NO
6-31	INTL ORGN OFFERED TO ARBITRATE		2. NO	2. NO
6-32	REGL ORGN OFFERED TO ARBITRATE	#	2. NO	2. NO
6-33	A G.P. OFFERED TO ARBITRATE		2. NO	2. NO
6-35	INT'L ORG'N UPHELD ANT'S CAUSE	#	2. NO	2. NO
6-36	INTL ORGN INDICTED ANT'S CAUSE	#	2. NO	2. NO
6-37	CITED IN VIOLATION OF INTL LAW	#	2. NO	2. NO
6-38	CITED BY I.O. FOR AGGRESSION	#	2. NO	2. NO
6-42	I.O. HAS IMPOSED SANCTIONS	#	2. NO	2. NO
6-47	REG ORGN HAS IMPOSED SANCTIONS	#	2. NO	2. I,O
7-6	NO. TROOPS COMM AS PC TOT FRCS		1. 0.7-1.0	1. 0.7-1.0
7-9	OTHER SIGNIF EXTERNAL THREAT	#	2. NO	2. NO
7-27	NO. HVY. CANNON AVAILABLE		1. 1.0-1.0	1. 1.0-1.0
7-34	NO. SAM'S AVAILABLE		1. 1.0-1.0	1. 1.0-1.0
7-35	NO. SSM'S AVAILABLE	#	1. 1.0-1.0	1. 1.0-1.0
7-36	NO. SUBMARINES AVAILABLE		1. 1.0-1.0	1. 1.0-1.0
7-40	HAS A NUCLEAR CAPABILITY	#	2. NO	2. NO
8-4	UNITY WITHIN MILITARY COMMAND		1. UNIFIED	1. UNIFIED
8-7	METHOD OF MILITARY RECRUITMENT		1. VOLUNTARY	1. VOLUNTARY
8-13	OVERALL MILITARY ORG'N BALANCE	#	1. FAVORABLE	3. UNFAVORABLE
8-14	LOGIS SUP'T ADQT TO MAINT OPNS	#	1. YES	1. YES
8-17	CENTRALIZATION OF MIL. COMMAND		1. CENTRALIZED	2. DE-CENTR'ZED
8-25	TREATMENT OF OWN CASUALTIES		1. GOOD	3. POOR
9-3	TOTAL NO. CIVN POPULATION LOST	#	3. 50.0-59MIL	8. 0 OR N/A
9-5	TOTAL CAS'TIES TO OWN FORCES	#	1. 1.0-1.2	2. 1.5-20.0
9-8	CASUALTY RATE FOR OWN FORCES		1. 1.0-2.0	1. 1.0-2.0

Artificial Family

1-2A	TOPOGRAPHY OF CONFLICT AREA	1. FLAT	1. FLAT

Item			Compound Response		
1-11	DISPUTE HAS BEEN TO REG'L ORGN	# 2.	NO	2.	NO
3-8	PRODUCTION OF STEEL	# 1.	1.0-1.0	1.	1.0-1.0
4-32	RECENT LEADERSHIP CRISIS	2.	NO	2.	NO
5-22	POST-DISPUTE EXPECT'N OF REGIM	# 2.	PESSIMISTIC	2.	PESSIMISTIC
5-23	DIST FM BORDER TO CONFL AREA	# 1.	1.0-1.0	1.	1.0-1.0
5-24	DIST FM CAPITAL TO CONFL AREA	# 1.	1.0-1.3	1.	1.0-1.3
6-4	IS ALLY OF G.P. ALLIED TO ADV.	# 2.	NO	2.	NO
6-13	INT'L ORG IS INV. ON THIS SIDE	# 2.	NO	2.	NO
6-14	REG'L ORG IS INV. ON THIS SIDE	# 2.	NO	2.	NO
6-30	SOME 3PTY OFFERED TO ARBITRATE	2.	NO	2.	NO
6-31	INTL ORGN OFFERED TO ARBITRATE	# 2.	NO	2.	NO
6-32	REGL ORGN OFFERED TO ARBITRATE	# 2.	NO	2.	NO
6-33	A G.P. OFFERED TO ARBITRATE	2.	NO	2.	NO
6-35	INT'L ORG'N UPHELD ANT'S CAUSE	# 2.	NO	2.	NO
6-36	INTL ORGN INDICTED ANT'S CAUSE	# 2.	NO	2.	NO
6-37	CITED IN VIOLATION OF INTL LAW	# 2.	NO	2.	NO
6-38	CITED BY I.O. FOR AGGRESSION	# 2.	NO	2.	NO
6-42	I.O. HAS IMPOSED SANCTIONS	# 2.	NO	2.	NO
6-47	REG ORGN HAS IMPOSED SANCTIONS	# 2.	NO	2.	NC
7-9	OTHER SIGNIF EXTERNAL THREAT	# 2.	NO	2.	NO
7-35	NO. SSM'S AVAILABLE	# 1.	1.0-1.0	1.	1.0-1.0
8-13	OVERALL MILITARY ORG'N BALANCE	# 1.	FAVORABLE	3.	UNFAVORABLE
8-25	TREATMENT OF OWN CASUALTIES	1.	GOOD	3.	POOR
9-5	TOTAL CAS'TIES TO OWN FORCES	# 1.	1.0-1.2	2.	1.5-20.0

The factor pattern derives from

Cyprus: independence (U.K. colonial administration vs. Enosists)

Cyprus: internal (Cypriot government vs. Turkish Cypriots)

Indonesia-Malaysia (Malaysia vs. Indonesia)

Indonesia: independence (Dutch colonial administration vs. Indonesian insurgents)

Malayan insurgency (U.K.-Malay colonial administration and Malayan government vs. Malayan Communist party)

Order

The factor pattern derives from all seven instances of de-escalation included in the analysis.

5-22	POST-DISPUTE EXPECT'N OF REGIM	# 2.	PESSIMISTIC	2.	PESSIMISTIC
5-23	DIST FM BORDER TO CONFL AREA	# 1.	1.0-1.0	1.	1.0-1.0
6-4	IS ALLY OF G.P. ALLIED TO ADV.	# 2.	NO	2.	NO
6-13	INT'L ORG IS INV. ON THIS SIDE	# 2.	NO	2.	NO
6-30	SOME 3PTY OFFERED TO ARBITRATE	2.	NO	2.	NO
6-32	REGL ORGN OFFERED TO ARBITRATE	# 2.	NO	2.	NO
6-33	A G.P. OFFERED TO ARBITRATE	2.	NO	2.	NO
7-9	OTHER SIGNIF EXTERNAL THREAT	# 2.	NO	2.	NO
8-13	OVERALL MILITARY ORG'N BALANCE	# 1.	FAVORABLE	3.	UNFAVORABLE

5.
The Termination (P–IV) Patterns

The data input for each conflict included in this analysis is that obtaining at the threshold of Phase IV and is therefore a statement of the conditions pertaining when the ongoing hostilities in each case were about to terminate. In those conflicts in which more than one instance of hostilities occurred, the termination constituting the more definitive, conclusive, or final example of its kind was included in the analysis.

a.
Conflicts Included in the Analysis of the Termination Patterns

Conflict	Event Marking Termination (P–IV)	Date
Algeria-Morocco	Bamoko agreement	11/63
Angolan insurgency	Portuguese suppress organized hostilities	9/61
Cuba: "little" war of 1906	Government declares unilateral cease-fire	9/06
Cuba: Bay of Pigs	Defeat of invading exiles by government forces	4/61
Cyprus: independence	London Agreement on Cypriot independence	2/59
Ethiopia-Somalia	Cease-fire agreement	4/64

Conflict	Event Marking Termination (P–IV)	Date
Greek insurgency	Greek army victory	12/49
India-China	Chinese unilateral cease-fire	11/62
Indonesia: independence	Cease-fire and Roem–Von Royen agreement	10/49
Indonesia-Malaysia	Hostilities end after Indonesian coup	12/65
Israel-Egypt	U.N. cease-fire accepted	11/56
Kashmir	Proposed U.N. cease-fire accepted	9/65
Malayan insurgency	State of emergency declared terminated	7/60
Spanish civil war	Organized resistance ends after Casado coup	3/39
Venezuelan insurgency	Insurgency slackens after successful elections	12/63
USSR-Iran	Iranian forces gain control of all Iran	12/46

b.
Derivation of the Termination
Patterns

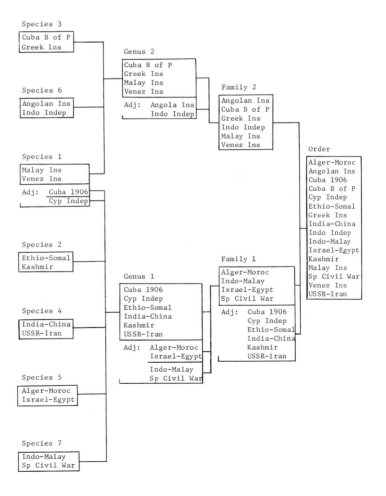

c.
Percentile Distribution of the
Conflicts across the
Termination Patterns

	Species						
	T1	T2	T3	T4	T5	T6	T7
Algeria-Morocco	0.22	0.58	0.23	0.52	1.00	0.30	0.44
Angolan insurgency	0.23	0.21	0.30	0.19	0.25	1.00	0.24
Cuba: "little" war of 1906	0.34	0.40	0.38	0.36	0.33	0.27	0.34
Cuba: Bay of Pigs	0.50	0.30	1.00	0.26	0.28	0.22	0.42
Cyprus: independence	0.55	0.29	0.41	0.37	0.30	0.33	0.39
Ethiopia-Somalia	0.25	1.00	0.32	0.55	0.50	0.33	0.51
Greek insurgency	0.52	0.26	1.00	0.38	0.22	0.40	0.40
India-China	0.25	0.53	0.32	1.00	0.49	0.27	0.42
Indonesia: independence	0.38	0.37	0.34	0.37	0.34	1.00	0.39
Indonesia-Malaysia	0.32	0.49	0.34	0.46	0.39	0.20	1.00
Israel-Egypt	0.27	0.44	0.35	0.38	1.00	0.28	0.46
Kashmir	0.21	1.00	0.28	0.53	0.53	0.22	0.54
Malayan insurgency	1.00	0.29	0.58	0.39	0.32	0.35	0.38
Spanish civil war	0.29	0.43	0.45	0.38	0.39	0.39	1.00
Venezuelan insurgency	1.00	0.30	0.65	0.36	0.30	0.26	0.47
USSR-Iran	0.24	0.50	0.32	1.00	0.38	0.30	0.45
Vietnam 3/67	0.40	0.29	0.50	0.29	0.30	0.39	0.52

	Genus		Family		
	1	2	1	2	Order
Algeria-Morocco	0.86	0.24	1.00	0.33	1.00
Angolan insurgency	0.21	0.37	0.38	1.00	1.00
Cuba: "little" war of 1906	1.00	0.34	0.38	0.33	1.00
Cuba: Bay of Pigs	0.71	1.00	0.38	1.00	1.00
Cyprus: independence	1.00	0.46	0.38	0.56	1.00
Ethiopia-Somalia	1.00	0.34	0.75	0.33	1.00
Greek insurgency	0.50	1.00	0.38	1.00	1.00
India-China	1.00	0.41	0.69	0.56	1.00
Indonesia: independence	0.79	0.34	0.50	1.00	1.00
Indonesia-Malaysia	0.79	0.37	1.00	0.33	1.00
Israel-Egypt	0.43	0.39	1.00	0.67	1.00
Kashmir	1.00	0.22	0.75	0.33	1.00
Malayan insurgency	0.79	1.00	0.31	1.00	1.00
Spanish civil war	0.64	0.44	1.00	0.78	1.00
Venezuelan insurgency	0.71	1.00	0.38	1.00	1.00
USSR-Iran	1.00	0.32	0.63	0.44	1.00
Vietnam 3/67	0.71	0.61	0.63	1.00	1.00

d.

Termination:
Complete Factor Patterns

Species Type T1
("depriving the rebels of their popular base")

The factor pattern derives from

Malayan insurgency (Malayan Communist party vs. U.K.-Malay colonial administration and Malayan government)

Venezuelan insurgency (MIR/CPV and FLN/FALN vs. Venezuelan government)

The adjuncts are

Cuba: "little" war of 1906

Cyprus: independence

Item			Compound Response			
1-4	PAST MIL. REL'SHIP BETW PARTYS		1.	PEACEFUL	1.	PEACEFUL
1-5	EFFECTIVE NATURE OF DISPUTE	#	3.	INTERNAL	3.	INTERNAL
1-7	IDEOLOGICAL DIFF. BETW PARTIES	#	1.	EXTREME	1.	EXTREME
1-8	CONTROL OF REAL ESTATE INVOLVD	#	1.	YES	1.	YES
1-10	SIZE OF POPN AT STAKE (THOUS.)		3.	5.0TH-7.6TH	3.	5.0TH-7.6TH
1-12	DISPUTE HAS BEEN TO INT'L ORGN		2.	NO	2.	NO
2-1	OVERRIDING CULTURAL IDEAL		3.	AGGRESSIVE	2.	RATIONALITY
2-2	PREFERRED MODE OF CONFL RESOLN		3.	DICTATORIAL	2.	CONCILIATORY
2-12	AREA UNDER EFFECTIVE CONTROL		8.	0 OR N/A	3.	13.7-500.0
2-13	POPN UNDER EFFECTIVE CONTROL		8.	0 OR N/A	3.	499.0-65TH
2-14	REAL ESTATE INVOLVED IS	#	1.	IN CLMD BDY	1.	IN CLMD BDY
2-15	PC OF ANT'S CLMD AREA INVOLVED	#	1.	1.0-1.0	1.	1.0-1.0
2-16	PC OF ANT'S CLMD POPN INVOLVED	#	1.	1.0-1.0	1.	1.0-1.0
2-17	PC OF INVOLVED AREA IN CONTROL		8.	0 OR N/A	3.	24.0-100.0
2-18	PC OF INVOLVED POPN IN CONTROL		8.	0 OR N/A	3.	9.0-100.0
3-2	GROSS NAT'L. OR ECON. PRODUCT	#	8.	0 OR N/A	3.	90.0-6.4TH
3-3	GROWTH RATE OF ECONOMY		8.	0 OR N/A	3.	3.0-13.9
3-4	RATE OF INFLATION IN ECONOMY		8.	0 OR N/A	2.	2.0-10.0
3-5	PER CAPITA INCOME	#	8.	0 OR N/A	3.	115.0-855.0
3-9	PC OF GNP IN EXPORTS		8.	0 OR N/A	3.	22.0-1.0TH
3-11	FOREIGN ECONOMIC AID RECEIVED		8.	0 OR N/A	3.	15.0-478.0
3-13	PROGRESSIVE TAX STRUCTURE		8.	0 OR N/A	1.	YES
3-14	GOVERNMENT INCOME AS PC OF GNP	#	8.	0 OR N/A	3.	10.0-50.0
3-15	GOVT. SPENDING AS PC OF GNP	#	8.	0 OR N/A	3.	6.0-50.0
3-16	SOC WELFARE SPENDING AS PC GNP		8.	0 OR N/A	3.	9.0-25.0
3-17	MILITARY DEFENSE BUDGET		8.	0 OR N/A	2.	1.4-25.0
3-18	DEFENSE BUDGET AS PC OF GNP		8.	0 OR N/A	1.	0.3-2.7
3-20	AGRIC EMPLOYMENT AS PC OF POPN		8.	0 OR N/A	3.	13.0-70.0
3-21	INDUSTRIAL EMPL. AS PC OF POPN		8.	0 OR N/A	3.	11.0-23.0
3-22	UNEMPLOYED AS PC OF GENL POPN		8.	0 OR N/A	3.	0.0-10.0
4-1	EFFECTIVE STATUS OF GOVERNMENT	#	4.	REBEL ORGN	1.	INDEP GOVT
4-4	EXECUTIVE STABILITY	#	8.	0 OR N/A	3.	3.0-9.0
4-6	STATUS OF EXECUTIVE		8.	0 OR N/A	1.	DOMINANT
4-7	STATUS OF LEGISLATURE		8.	0 OR N/A	2.	PART EFFECT.
4-10	REGIME CAME TO POWER CONST'LY		8.	0 OR N/A	1.	YES
4-12	IDEOL. ORIENTATION OF REGIME		1.	LEFT-WING	2.	MODERATE
4-13	INTERNAL POLICIES OF REGIME		3.	REVOL'ARY	2.	MODERATE
4-14	INTERNATIONAL POLICY OF REGIME		1.	LEFTIST	3.	MODERATE
4-17	MOBILIZATION STYLE OF REGIME		8.	0 OR N/A	1.	FULL
4-18	POL. INTEGRATION OF GENL POPN		8.	0 OR N/A	2.	MODERATE
4-19	FREEDOM OF THE PRESS ALLOWED		8.	0 OR N/A	2.	INTERMITTENT
4-22	INTEREST ARTIC'N BY ASSOC'L GP		8.	0 OR N/A	1.	POL SIGNIF
4-23	INTEREST ARTIC'N BY INST'L GPS		8.	0 OR N/A	1.	POL SIGNIF
4-24	INTEREST ARTIC'N BY POL PARTYS		8.	0 OR N/A	1.	POL SIGNIF
4-25	CONST'AL STATUS OF POL PARTIES		8.	0 OR N/A	2.	PART COMPET.
4-28	PC OF POPN VOTING IN ELECTIONS	#	8.	0 OR N/A	3.	9.5-95.0
4-32	RECENT LEADERSHIP CRISIS		2.	NO	2.	NO
4-34	FORN RES ARE MAINSTAY OF REGIM		2.	NO	2.	NO
4-37	POP. SUPPORT FOR REGIM'S POLS.		8.	0 OR N/A	1.	HIGH
4-38	ATT. OF INTELLECTUALS TO REGIM		8.	0 OR N/A	1.	FAVORABLE
4-40	EFFECT ON POPULAR COHESION		8.	0 OR N/A	2.	LITTLE CHANGE
5-6	INTEREST INVOLVED-NAT'L CHAR.		1.	YES	1.	YES
5-11	INTEREST INVOLVED-TERR. INTEG.		2.	NO	2.	NO
5-13	COMMITMENT TO STATED GOALS		2.	FLEXIBLE	2.	FLEXIBLE
5-14	DISPUTE IS REGARDED AS CRUSADE		1.	YES	2.	NO
5-15	CONDUCT OF CONFLICT IS LIMITED		2.	NO	1.	YES
5-16	PC OF AVAIL MIL FRCS COMMITTED		5.	70-100PC	3.	<5-49 PC
5-22	POST-DISPUTE EXPECT'N OF REGIM	#	2.	PESSIMISTIC	2.	PESSIMISTIC
5-23	DIST FM BORDER TO CONFL AREA	#	1.	1.0-1.0	1.	1.0-1.0
5-24	DIST FM CAPITAL TO CONFL AREA	#	1.	1.0-1.3	1.	1.0-1.3
5-26	TREATY EXPERIENCE WITH ADV.		2.	UNSATISF'ORY	2.	UNSATISF'ORY
5-28	RELIABILITY OF COMMUNICATIONS	#	2.	LOW	2.	LOW
5-29	CREDIBILITY OF COMMUNICATIONS	#	2.	LOW	2.	LOW
5-30	PRINCIPAL ATTEMPTS AT RESOL'N	#	5.	MILITARY	5.	MILITARY
5-31	OFFERED TO RESOLVE CONST'ALLY	#	2.	NO	2.	NO
5-32	BROUGHT DISPUTE TO INT'L ORGN	#	2.	NO	2.	NO
5-33	INDICATED DISPUT IS NEGOTIABLE		2.	NO	2.	NO
5-34	HAS SOUGHT A NEGOT. SETTLEMENT	#	2.	NO	2.	NO
5-38	P.O. RE ADV'S POL. INST'NS.		8.	0 OR N/A	2.	UNFAVORABLE
5-42	MARTIAL LAW IS IN EFFECT		8.	0 OR N/A	2.	NO
5-43	STATE OF WAR HAS BEEN DECLARED		8.	0 OR N/A	2.	NO
6-1	IS SEC'TY ALLY OF GREAT POWER	#	2.	NO	1.	YES
6-3	IS ALLY OF G.P. HOSTILE TO ADV	#	2.	NO	1.	YES
6-4	IS ALLY OF G.P. ALLIED TO ADV	#	2.	NO	2.	NO
6-5	IS AIDED BY GP HOSTILE TO ADV.		2.	NO	1.	YES
6-6	A GP IS OPENLY PARTIAL TO ANT.	#	1.	YES	1.	YES
6-7	GP AID PROMISED IF ESC. OCCURS		2.	NO	2.	NO
6-12	SOME 3PTY IS INV. ON THIS SIDE	#	1.	YES	1.	YES
6-13	INT'L ORG IS INV. ON THIS SIDE	#	2.	NO	2.	NO
6-14	REG'L ORG IS INV. ON THIS SIDE	#	2.	NO	2.	NO
6-15	A G.P. IS INV. ON THIS SIDE		2.	NO	1.	YES
6-16	A NON-GP IS INV. ON THIS SIDE		1.	YES	2.	NO
6-18	A 3PTY IS PROVIDING POL. AID	#	1.	YES	1.	YES
6-22	A 3PTY IS PROVIDING CONV FORCE		2.	NO	2.	NO
6-24	ATT. OF 3PTY PUBLIC TO INV'MNT	#	1.	FAVORABLE	1.	FAVORABLE

Item			Compound Response		
6-30	SOME 3PTY OFFERED TO ARBITRATE		2. NO	2.	NO
6-31	INTL ORGN OFFERED TO ARBITRATE		2. NO	2.	NO
6-32	REGL ORGN OFFERED TO ARBITRATE	#	2. NO	2.	NO
6-33	A G.P. OFFERED TO ARBITRATE		2. NO	2.	NO
6-35	INT'L ORG'N UPHELD ANT'S CAUSE	#	2. NO	2.	I.O
6-36	INTL ORGN INDICTED ANT'S CAUSE	#	2. NO	2.	NO
6-37	CITED IN VIOLATION OF INTL LAW	#	2. NC	2.	NO
6-38	CITED BY I.O. FOR AGGRESSION	#	2. NO	2.	NO
6-40	ACCEPTED IO'S PROP. CEASEFIRE	#	2. NO	2.	NO
6-42	I.O. HAS IMPOSED SANCTIONS	#	2. NO	2.	NO
7-1	NO. OF OWN ACTIVE MIL. TROOPS		1. 0.02-10.7	2.	17.0-213.7
7-2	NO. ACTIV TROOPS AS PC OF POPN		8. 0 OR N/A	1.	0.001-1.0
7-5	NO. TROOPS COMMITTED TO CONFL.	#	1. 0.C2-1.0	2.	1.2-50.0
7-6	NO. TROOPS COMM AS PC TOT FRCS	#	2. 1.2-14.0	1.	0.7-1.0
7-7	PC POPN MOB'ZED FOR ACTIV DUTY		8. 0 OR N/A	1.	0.001-1.0
7-8	OTHER SIGNIF INTERNAL THREAT	#	2. NO	2.	I.0
7-9	OTHER SIGNIF EXTERNAL THREAT		2. NO	2.	NO
7-13	3PTY TROOP AID SEEN LIKELY TO		2. STAY SAME	2.	STAY SAME
7-14	TOTAL MANPOWER COMMITTED		1. 0.02-7.3	2.	9.7-55.0
7-15	OWN TRPS AS PC OF ALL COMMITED	#	1. 1.0-1.5	1.	1.0-1.5
7-21	NO. RIFLES AVAILABLE		1. 0.C5-2.1	2.	3.0-85.7
7-22	NO. AUTO. WEAPONS AVAILABLE	#	1. 1.0-2.0	3.	10.0-1.0TH
7-26	NO. MED. CANNON AVAILABLE		8. 0 CR N/A	3.	20.0-200.0
7-28	NO. ARMORED VEH. AVAILABLE	#	8. 0 CR N/A	3.	35.0-370.0
7-29	NO. FIGHTER A/C AVAILABLE		8. 0 OR N/A	3.	50.0-400.0
7-30	NO. BOMBER A/C AVAILABLE		8. 0 OR N/A	2.	2.0-25.0
7-31	NO. TRANSPORT A/C AVAILABLE		8. 0 CR N/A	3.	10.0-60.0
7-32	NO. JET AIRCRAFT AVAILABLE		8. 0 OR N/A	3.	15.0-100.0
7-33	NO. HELICOPTERS AVAILABLE		8. 0 CR N/A	3.	13.3-30.0
7-34	NO. SAM'S AVAILABLE		1. 1.0-1.0	1.	1.0-1.0
7-35	NO. SSM'S AVAILABLE		1. 1.0-1.0	1.	1.0-1.0
7-37	NO. HEAVY VESSELS AVAILABLE	#	8. 0 OR N/A	3.	5.0-24.0
7-39	NO. PATROL BOATS AVAILABLE		8. 0 CR N/A	3.	5.0-57.0
7-41	AIDING 3PTY HAS NUCLEAR CAP'TY		2. NO	1.	YES
7-44	DEPENDENCE FOR NAVAL ARMAMENTS		8. 0 OR N/A	1.	EXCLUSIVE
7-46	DEP. FOR AIR COMBAT ARMAMENTS		8. 0 OR N/A	1.	EXCLUSIVE
7-47	AIR ARMAMENT SUPPLY LIKELY TO		8. 0 OR N/A	2.	STAY SAME
7-48	DEP FOR TRANSPORT CAPABILITIES		8. 0 OR N/A	1.	EXCLUSIVE
8-9	TRAINING FACILITY FOR OFFICERS	#	2. FAIR	1.	GOOD
8-11	TRAINING FAC FOR ENLISTED PERS		3. POOR	1.	GOOD
8-13	OVERALL MILITARY ORG'N BALANCE	#	2. UNFAVORABLE	1.	FAVORABLE
8-14	LOGIS SUP'T ADQT TO MAINT OPNS		2. NO	1.	YES
8-15	LOGIS SUP'T ADQT TO EXPAND OPN		2. NO	1.	YES
8-16	OVERALL MIL. HARDWARE BALANCE	#	3. UNFAVORABLE	1.	FAVORABLE
8-17	CENTRALIZATION OF MIL. COMMAND		2. DE-CENTR'ZED	1.	CENTRALIZED
8-20	USE OF TERROR BY THIS ANT. IS		1. WIDESPREAD	3.	ABSENT
8-21	TACTICS OF FORCES ON THIS SIDE	#	1. OFFENSIVE	1.	OFFENSIVE
8-22	TACTICS OF FORCES ON THIS SIDE	#	1. MOBILE	1.	MOBILE
8-25	TREATMENT OF OWN CASUALTIES		3. POOR	1.	GOOD
8-26	LARG-SCAL GUER OPN BEING WAGED		1. YES	2.	NO
8-27	STAGE OF GUERRILLA OPERATIONS		2. EXPANSION	8.	0 OR N/A
8-30	SYMPATHY BETW POPN + OWN MIL.		2. ANTAGONISTIC	1.	SYMPATHETIC
8-32	CIVN SECURITY V. CONV. ATTACK		8. 0 CR N/A	1.	HIGH
8-34	CIVN SEC V AC ATK BY OWN FRCES		8. 0 OR N/A	1.	HIGH
9-3	TOTAL NO. CIVN POPULATION LOST	#	8. 0 OR N/A	3.	50.0-59MIL
9-5	TOTAL CAS'TIES TO OWN FORCES	#	2. 1.5-20.0	1.	1.0-1.2
9-7	TOTAL CAS'TIES TO ALL FORCES	#	2. 1.3-6.0	1.	1.0-1.2
9-10	CASUALTY RATE FOR ALL FORCES		1. 1.0-2.0	1.	1.0-2.0

Species Type T2
("accommodation follows fore-closure of arms aid")

The factor pattern derives from

Ethiopia-Somalia (Ethiopia vs. Somalia)

Kashmir (Pakistan vs. India)

Item			Compound Response		
1-3	PAST POL. REL'SHIP BETW PARTYS	#	2. COMPETITIVE	2.	COMPETITIVE
1-4	PAST MIL. REL'SHIP BETW PARTYS	#	2. RANDOM HOST.	2.	RANDOM HOST.
1-8	CONTROL OF REAL ESTATE INVOLVD		1. YES	1.	YES
1-9	SIZE OF AREA AT STAKE(TH SQ M)		3. 84.0-197.0	3.	84.0-197.0
1-10	SIZE OF POPN AT STAKE (THOUS.)		2. 1.0TH-4.0TH	2.	1.0TH-4.0TH
1-11	DISPUTE HAS BEEN TO REG'L ORGN		1. YES	1.	YES
1-12	DISPUTE HAS BEEN TO INT'L ORGN		1. YES	1.	YES
1-13	INTRODUCED TO INT'L ORGN BY A		1. ANTAGONIST	1.	ANTAGONIST
1-14	BASIS OF INTRO. TO INT'L ORGN		1. AGGRESSION	1.	AGGRESSION
2-4	REGIM + GENL POPN OF SAME RACE	#	1. YES	1.	YES
2-5	RACIAL HOMOGENEITY OF GENL POP		2. HETERO	1.	HOMOGENEOUS
2-9	LITERACY RATE AMONG GENL POPN	#	3. LOW	3.	LOW
2-10	NEWSPAPER CIRCULATION IN POPN		4. VERY LOW	4.	VERY LOW
3-5	PER CAPITA INCOME		1. 1.0-2.1	1.	1.0-2.1
3-14	GOVERNMENT INCOME AS PC OF GNP		1. 1.0-1.5	2.	1.8-6.0
3-18	DEFENSE BUDGET AS PC OF GNP		1. 0.3-2.7	1.	0.3-2.7
4-1	EFFECTIVE STATUS OF GOVERNMENT		1. INDEP GOVT	1.	INDEP GOVT
4-6	STATUS OF EXECUTIVE		1. DOMINANT	2.	STRONG
4-10	REGIME CAME TO POWER CONST'LY		2. NO	1.	YES
4-14	INTERNATIONAL POLICY OF REGIME		3. MODERATE	3.	MODERATE
4-15	COMMUNIST ORIENT'N OF REGIME		4. NON-COM.	4.	NON-COM.
4-17	MOBILIZATIONAL STYLE OF REGIME	#	2. LIMITED	1.	FULL
4-18	POL. INTEGRATION OF GENL POPN		2. MODERATE	1.	HIGH
4-20	FREEDOM OF GROUP OPPOSITION		2. LIMITED	1.	FULL
4-22	INTEREST ARTIC'N BY ASSOC'L GP		2. POL INSIGNIF	1.	POL SIGNIF
4-23	INTEREST ARTIC'N BY INST'L GPS		1. POL SIGNIF	1.	POL SIGNIF
4-24	INTEREST ARTIC'N BY POL PARTYS		2. POL INSIGNIF	1.	POL SIGNIF
4-25	CONST'AL STATUS OF POL PARTIES		2. PART COMPET.	1.	COMPETITIVE

Item		Compound Response			
4-32	RECENT LEADERSHIP CRISIS		2.	NO	2.	NO
4-34	FORN RES ARE MAINSTAY OF REGIM		2.	NO	2.	NO
4-35	REGIM APPEARS MAINT BY FOR RES		2.	NO	2.	NO
4-36	FOP. SUPPORT FOR REGIME'S OBJ.		1.	HIGH	1.	HIGH
4-37	POP. SUPPORT FOR REGIM'S POLS.		1.	HIGH	1.	HIGH
4-38	ATT. OF INTELLECTUALS TO REGIM		1.	FAVORABLE	1.	FAVORABLE
5-2	REGIME SEEKS OVERTHROW OF ADV.		2.	NO	2.	NO
5-3	INTEREST INVOLVED-IDEOLOGY		2.	NO	2.	NO
5-4	INTEREST INVOLVED-COMMITMENTS	#	1.	YES	1.	YES
5-10	INTEREST INVOLVED-INDEPENDENCE		2.	NO	2.	NO
5-12	INTEREST INVOLVED-CONT'D EXIS.		2.	NO	2.	NO
5-13	COMMITMENT TO STATED GOALS		2.	FLEXIBLE	2.	FLEXIBLE
5-15	CONDUCT OF CONFLICT IS LIMITED		2.	YES	1.	YES
5-18	CAN ACCEPT LES THN STATED DMDS		2.	NO	1.	YES
5-19	PRESENT OUTLOOK WRT DISPUTE		2.	MODERATE	2.	MODERATE
5-20	PERCEIVED BALANCE OF WILL		2.	EVEN	2.	EVEN
5-21	LIKELY OUTCOME IS NOW OBVIOUS		1.	YES	1.	YES
5-23	DIST FM BORDER TO CONFL AREA	#	1.	1.0-1.0	1.	1.0-1.0
5-25	ADVERSARY APPEARS TO ANT TO BE		2.	AUT + INDEP.	2.	AUT + INDEP.
5-28	RELIABILITY OF COMMUNICATIONS		1.	HIGH	1.	HIGH
5-29	CREDIBILITY OF COMMUNICATIONS		1.	HIGH	1.	HIGH
5-34	HAS SOUGHT A NEGOT. SETTLEMENT		1.	YES	1.	YES
5-35	HAS OFFERED BI-LATERAL NEGOTNS		1.	YES	1.	YES
5-36	HAS ATTENDED BI-LAT'L NEGOT'NS		1.	YES	1.	YES
5-38	P.O. RE ADV'S POL. INST'NS.	#	2.	UNFAVORABLE	2.	UNFAVORABLE
5-39	P.O. RE ADV'S SOCIAL INST'NS.		2.	UNFAVORABLE	2.	UNFAVORABLE
5-43	STATE OF WAR HAS BEEN DECLARED	#	2.	NO	2.	NO
5-45	LEGAL STATUS OF ADV. PERSONNEL		1.	CITIZEN	1.	CITIZEN
5-46	AMNESTY DECL FOR ADV PERSONNEL		2.	NO	2.	NO
6-2	IS SEC'TY ALLY OF NON-G.P.		1.	YES	2.	NO
6-3	IS ALLY OF G.P. HOSTILE TO ADV		2.	NO	2.	NO
6-4	IS ALLY OF G.P. ALLIED TO ADV.	#	2.	NO	2.	NO
6-5	IS AIDED BY GP HOSTILE TO ADV.		2.	NO	2.	NO
6-6	A GP IS OPENLY PARTIAL TO ANT.		2.	NO	2.	NO
6-7	CP AID PROMISED IF ESC. OCCURS		2.	NO	2.	NO
6-13	INT'L ORG IS INV. ON THIS SIDE	#	2.	NO	2.	NO
6-14	REG'L ORG IS INV. ON THIS SIDE	#	2.	NO	2.	NO
6-16	A NON-GP IS INV. ON THIS SIDE		2.	NO	2.	NO
6-18	A 3PTY IS PROVIDING POL. AID		1.	YES	2.	NC
6-21	A 3PTY IS PROVIDING MIL HDWRE.		2.	NO	2.	NO
6-24	ATT. OF 3PTY PUBLIC TO INV'MNT		1.	FAVORABLE	8.	0 OR N/A
6-24B	RECENT CHANGE IN 3RD PTY GOVT.		2.	NO	8.	0 OR N/A
6-25	AID TO ANT. HURTS 3PTY ECONOMY		2.	NO	8.	0 OR N/A
6-26	PC ANT'S ECONOMY OWNED BY 3PTY	#	1.	0 - 4 PC	8.	0 OR N/A
6-27	PC ANT'S EXPORTS CONS. BY 3PTY	#	1.	0 - 4 PC	8.	0 OR N/A
6-28	EXPERIENCE WITH IO PEACE MACH	#	1.	FRUSTRATING	1.	FRUSTRATING
6-32	REGL ORGN OFFERED TO ARBITRATE	#	2.	NO	2.	NO
6-35	INT'L ORG'N UPHELD ANT'S CAUSE	#	2.	NO	2.	NO
6-36	INTL ORGN INDICTED ANT'S CAUSE	#	2.	NO	2.	NO
6-37	CITED IN VIOLATION OF INTL LAW	#	2.	NO	2.	NO
6-38	CITED BY I.O. FOR AGGRESSION	#	2.	NO	2.	NO
6-42	I.O. HAS IMPOSED SANCTIONS	#	2.	NO	2.	NO
6-47	REG ORGN HAS IMPOSED SANCTIONS	#	2.	NO	2.	NO
7-1	NO. OF OWN ACTIVE MIL. TROOPS	#	1.	0.02-10.7	1.	0.02-10.7
7-5	NO. TROOPS COMMITTED TO CONFL.		1.	0.02-1.0	2.	1.2-50.0
7-8	OTHER SIGNIF INTERNAL THREAT	#	2.	NO	2.	NO
7-13	3PTY TROOP AID SEEN LIKELY TO		2.	STAY SAME	2.	STAY SAME
7-14	TOTAL MANPOWER COMMITTED	#	1.	0.02-7.3	1.	0.02-7.3
7-15	OWN TRPS AS PC OF ALL COMMITED	#	1.	1.0-1.5	1.	1.0-1.5
7-16	CONVENTIONAL MANPWER COMMITTED		1.	0.01-3.0	1.	0.01-3.0
7-18	NAVAL MANPOWER COMMITTED		1.	0.5-1.0	1.	0.5-1.0
7-40	HAS A NUCLEAR CAPABILITY	#	2.	NO	2.	NO
7-50	OVERTNESS OF 3PTY HARDWARE AID		1.	GEN'LY OVERT	1.	GEN'LY OVERT
8-7	METHOD OF MILITARY RECRUITMENT		1.	VOLUNTARY	1.	VOLUNTARY
8-9	TRAINING FACILITY FOR OFFICERS		1.	GOOD	1.	GOOD
8-17	CENTRALIZATION OF MIL. COMMAND	#	1.	CENTRALIZED	1.	CENTRALIZED
8-21	TACTICS OF FORCES ON THIS SIDE		2.	DEFENSIVE	1.	OFFENSIVE
8-26	LARG-SCAL GUER OPN BEING WAGED		2.	NO	2.	NO
8-30	SYMPATHY BETW POPN + OWN MIL.	#	1.	SYMPATHETIC	1.	SYMPATHETIC
8-33	CIVN SECURITY V. GUERR ATTACK		2.	MODERATE	2.	MODERATE
8-34	CIVN SEC V AC ATK BY OWN FRCES		1.	HIGH	1.	HIGH
8-35	CIVN SEC V ABUSE BY OWN FORCES		1.	HIGH	1.	HIGH
9-1	PC OF INDUSTRIAL CAPACITY LOST		1.	0.001-1.0	1.	0.001-1.0
9-8	CASUALY RATE FOR OWN FORCES		1.	1.0-2.0	1.	1.0-2.0
9-10	CASUALY RATE FOR ALL FORCES		1.	1.0-2.0	1.	1.0-2.0
9-11	ATTRITION RATE FOR OWN FORCES		1.	1.0-2.0	1.	1.0-2.0
9-13	ATTRITION RATE FOR ALL FORCES		1.	1.0-2.0	1.	1.0-2.0
1-5	EFFECTIVE NATURE OF DISPUTE	#	3.	INTERNAL	3.	INTERNAL
1-7	IDEOLOGICAL DIFF. BETW PARTIES	#	1.	EXTREME	1.	EXTREME
1-8	CONTROL OF REAL ESTATE INVOLVD	#	1.	YES	1.	YES
1-10	SIZE OF POPN AT STAKE (THOUS.)		3.	5.0TH-7.6TH	3.	5.0TH-7.6TH
1-13	INTRODUCED TO INT'L ORGN BY A		1.	ANTAGONIST	1.	ANTAGONIST
1-14	BASIS OF INTRO. TO INT'L ORGN		1.	AGGRESSION	1.	AGGRESSION
2-3	RACIAL GROUPING OF ANTAGONIST		1.	WHITE	1.	WHITE
2-4	REGIM + GENL POPN OF SAME RACE	#	1.	YES	1.	YES
2-8	DOMINANT RELIGION AMONG POPN		1.	JUD-XIAN	1.	JUD-XIAN
2-12	AREA UNDER EFFECTIVE CONTROL		8.	0 OR N/A	3.	13.7-500.0

Species Type T3
("guerrillas go conventional in absence of popular base")

The factor pattern derives from

Cuba: Bay of Pigs (Cuban exiles vs. Cuban government)

Greek insurgency (Greek insurgents vs. Greek government)

Item			Compound Response	
2-13	POPN UNDER EFFECTIVE CONTROL		8. 0 OR N/A	3. 499.0-65TH
2-14	REAL ESTATE INVOLVED IS	#	1. IN CLMD BDY	1. IN CLMD BDY
2-15	PC OF ANT'S CLMD AREA INVOLVED	#	1. 1.0-1.0	1. 1.0-1.0
2-16	PC OF ANT'S CLMD POPN INVOLVED	#	1. 1.0-1.0	1. 1.0-1.0
2-17	PC OF INVOLVED AREA IN CONTROL		8. 0 OR N/A	3. 24.0-100.0
2-18	PC OF INVOLVED POPN IN CONTROL		8. 0 OR N/A	3. 9.0-100.0
3-2	GROSS NAT'L. OR ECON. PRODUCT	#	8. 0 OR N/A	3. 90.0-6.4TH
3-5	PER CAPITA INCOME	#	8. 0 OR N/A	3. 115.0-855.0
3-20	AGRIC EMPLOYMENT AS PC OF POPN		8. 0 OR N/A	3. 13.0-70.0
3-29	NO. SEAPORTS CONTROLLED	#	8. 0 OR N/A	3. 6.0-45.0
4-1	EFFECTIVE STATUS OF GOVERNMENT	#	4. REBEL ORGN	1. INDEP GOVT
4-2	DATE OF INDEPENDENCE		8. 0 OR N/A	2. 1800-1913
4-4	EXECUTIVE STABILITY	#	8. 0 OR N/A	3. 3.0-9.0
4-18	POL. INTEGRATION OF GENL POPN		8. 0 OR N/A	2. MODERATE
4-33	RECENT CHANGE IN LEADERSHIP	#	2. NO	2. NO
4-34	FORN RES ARE MAINSTAY OF REGIM		1. YES	1. YES
5-1	RECENTLY INVOLVED IN OTHER WAR		2. NO	1. YES
5-2	REGIME SEEKS OVERTHROW OF ADV.	#	1. YES	1. YES
5-9	INTEREST INVOLVED-POWER	#	1. YES	1. YES
5-11	INTEREST INVOLVED-TERR. INTEG.		2. NO	1. YES
5-12	INTEREST INVOLVED-CONT'D EXIS.	#	1. YES	1. YES
5-13	COMMITMENT TO STATED GOALS	#	1. TOTAL	1. TOTAL
5-15	CONDUCT OF CONFLICT IS LIMITED	#	2. NO	2. NO
5-18	CAN ACCEPT LES THN STATED DMDS	#	2. NO	2. NO
5-19	PRESENT OUTLOOK WRT DISPUTE	#	1. DIE-HARD	1. DIE-HARD
5-22	POST-DISPUTE EXPECT'N OF REGIM	#	2. PESSIMISTIC	2. PESSIMISTIC
5-24	DIST FM CAPITAL TO CONFL AREA		8. 0 OR N/A	3. 10.0-300.0
5-25	ADVERSARY APPEARS TO ANT TO BE		3. AUT BUT DEP.	1. A PUPPET
5-28	RELIABILITY OF COMMUNICATIONS	#	2. LOW	2. LOW
5-29	CREDIBILITY OF COMMUNICATIONS	#	2. LOW	2. LOW
5-31	OFFERED TO RESOLVE CONST'ALLY	#	2. NO	2. NO
5-32	BROUGHT DISPUTE TO INT'L ORGN		2. NO	1. YES
5-33	INDICATED DISPUT IS NEGOTIABLE		2. NO	2. NO
5-34	HAS SOUGHT A NEGOT. SETTLEMENT	#	2. NO	2. NO
5-35	HAS OFFERED BI-LATERAL NEGOTNS	#	2. NO	2. NO
5-42	MARTIAL LAW IS IN EFFECT		8. 0 OR N/A	1. YES
6-4	IS ALLY OF G.P. ALLIED TO ADV.	#	2. NO	2. NO
6-5	IS AIDED BY GP HOSTILE TO ADV.	#	1. YES	1. YES
6-6	A GP IS OPENLY PARTIAL TO ANT.	#	1. YES	1. YES
6-9	HAS INVOKED AVAIL SEC'TY PACTS		8. 0 OR N/A	1. YES
6-11	HAS ASKED AN INT'L. ORG'N. IN		2. NO	1. YES
6-14	REG'L ORG IS INV. ON THIS SIDE	#	2. NO	2. NO
6-15	A G.P. IS INV. ON THIS SIDE	#	1. YES	1. YES
6-17	A AUT ORG IS INV. ON THIS SIDE	#	2. NO	2. NO
6-19	A 3PTY IS PROVIDING ECON. AID		2. NO	1. YES
6-22	A 3PTY IS PROVIDING CONV FORCE		2. NO	2. NO
6-23	A 3PTY IS PROVIDING GUER FORCE		2. NO	2. NO
6-24B	RECENT CHANGE IN 3RD PTY GOVT.	#	2. NO	2. NO
6-25	AID TO ANT. HURTS 3PTY ECONOMY		2. NO	2. NO
6-26	PC ANT'S ECONOMY OWNED BY 3PTY		8. 0 OR N/A	1. 0 - 4 PC
6-32	REGL ORGN OFFERED TO ARBITRATE	#	2. NO	2. NO
6-40	ACCEPTED IO'S PROP. CEASEFIRE	#	2. NO	2. NO
6-42	I.O. HAS IMPOSED SANCTIONS	#	2. NO	2. NO
6-47	REG ORGN HAS IMPOSED SANCTIONS	#	2. NO	2. NO
7-1	NO. OF OWN ACTIVE MIL. TROOPS		1. 0.02-10.7	2. 17.0-213.7
7-4	MOBILIZATION OF RESERVES		8. 0 OR N/A	5. TOTAL
7-5	NO. TROOPS COMMITTED TO CONFL.	#	1. 0.02-1.0	2. 1.2-50.0
7-7	PC POPN MOB'ZED FOR ACTIV DUTY		8. 0 OR N/A	2. 1.5-9.0
7-11	TOTAL TROOPS GIVEN BY 3RD PTY		1. 0.3-1.0	1. 0.3-1.0
7-14	TOTAL MANPOWER COMMITTED		1. 0.02-7.3	2. 9.0-55.0
7-15	OWN TRPS AS PC OF ALL COMMITED	#	1. 1.0-1.5	1. 1.0-1.5
7-21	NO. RIFLES AVAILABLE	#	1. 0.05-2.1	2. 3.0-85.7
7-39	NO. PATROL BOATS AVAILABLE		8. 0 OR N/A	3. 5.0-37.0
7-40	HAS A NUCLEAR CAPABILITY	#	2. NO	2. NO
8-4	UNITY WITHIN MILITARY COMMAND		1. UNIFIED	1. UNIFIED
8-14	LOGIS SUP'T ADQT TO MAINT OPNS		2. NO	1. YES
8-15	LOGIS SUP'T ADQT TO EXPAND OPN		2. NO	1. YES
8-16	OVERALL MIL. HARDWARE BALANCE	#	3. UNFAVORABLE	1. FAVORABLE
8-17	CENTRALIZATION OF MIL. COMMAND	#	1. CENTRALIZED	1. CENTRALIZED
8-18	SANCTUARY AVAILABLE TO TROOPS		3. GEN'LY NOT	1. GENERALLY
8-25	TREATMENT OF OWN CASUALTIES		3. POOR	1. GOOD
8-26	LARG-SCAL GUER OPN BEING WAGED		2. NO	2. NO
8-28	INTELL. AMONG POP IN CONF AREA		3. INEFFECTIVE	1. EFFECTIVE
8-32	CIVN SECURITY V. CONV. ATTACK		8. 0 OR N/A	1. HIGH
8-34	CIVN SEC V AC ATK BY OWN FRCES		8. 0 OR N/A	2. MODERATE
9-1	PC OF INDUSTRIAL CAPACITY LOST		1. 0.001-1.0	1. 0.001-1.0
9-11	ATTRITION RATE FOR OWN FORCES		1. 1.0-2.0	1. 1.0-2.0
9-13	ATTRITION RATE FOR ALL FORCES		1. 1.0-2.0	1. 1.0-2.0

Species Type T4
("interests not commensurate with the risk involved")

The factor pattern derives from

Item			Compound Response	
1-2A	TOPOGRAPHY OF CONFLICT AREA	#	2. MOUNTAINOUS	2. MOUNTAINOUS
1-2B	CLIMATE IN THE CONFLICT AREA		2. MODERATE	2. MODERATE
1-3	PAST POL. REL'SHIP BETW PARTYS	#	2. COMPETITIVE	2. COMPETITIVE
1-6	DURATION OF DISPUTE (IN MOS.)	#	4. 57.0-215.0	4. 57.0-215.0
1-7	IDEOLOGICAL DIFF. BETW PARTIES	#	1. EXTREME	1. EXTREME
1-8	CONTROL OF REAL ESTATE INVOLVD	#	1. YES	1. YES
1-11	DISPUTE HAS BEEN TO REG'L ORGN	#	2. NO	2. NO

India-China (India vs. China)
USSR-Iran (Iran vs. USSR)

Item			Compound Response			
2-4	REGIM + GENL POPN OF SAME RACE	#	1.	YES	1.	YES
2-5	RACIAL HOMOGENEITY OF GENL POP	#	1.	HOMOGENEOUS	1.	HOMOGENEOUS
2-19	URBANIZATION		2.	MEDIUM	2.	MEDIUM
3-3	GROWTH RATE OF ECONOMY		1.	1.0-1.0	3.	3.0-13.9
3-5	PER CAPITA INCOME		1.	1.0-2.1	1.	1.0-2.1
3-6	PC OF GNP IN AGRICULTURE		1.	1.0-2.0	1.	1.0-2.0
4-1	EFFECTIVE STATUS OF GOVERNMENT		1.	INDEP GOVT	1.	INDEP GOVT
4-3	MODERN COLONIAL RULER		1.	BRITAIN	5.	NONE
4-4	EXECUTIVE STABILITY		1.	1.0-1.0	1.	1.0-1.0
4-6	STATUS OF EXECUTIVE		2.	STRONG	1.	DOMINANT
4-10	REGIME CAME TO POWER CONST'LY		1.	YES	2.	NC
4-12	IDEOL. ORIENTATION OF REGIME		2.	MODERATE	1.	LEFT-WING
4-13	INTERNAL POLICIES OF REGIME		2.	MODERATE	3.	REVOL'ARY
4-14	INTERNATIONAL POLICY OF REGIME		3.	MODERATE	1.	LEFTIST
4-19	FREEDOM OF THE PRESS ALLOWED		2.	INTERMITTENT	4.	FULLY ABSENT
4-20	FREEDOM OF GROUP OPPOSITION		1.	FULL	4.	NOT TOLERATD
4-21	INTEREST ARTIC'N BY ANOMIC GPS		1.	FREQUENT	3.	NOT TOLERATD
4-23	INTEREST ARTIC'N BY INST'L GPS	#	1.	POL SIGNIF	2.	POL INSIGNIF
4-25	CONST'AL STATUS OF POL PARTIES		1.	COMPETITIVE	3.	NON-COMPET.
4-29	PC OF VOTE REC'D BY THIS REGIM		1.	1.2-1.3	2.	1.7-2.5
4-30	PC VOTE RECD BY LT WING PTIES		1.	1.0-1.0	2.	2.5-6.7
4-32	RECENT LEADERSHIP CRISIS		2.	NO	2.	NO
4-33	RECENT CHANGE IN LEADERSHIP	#	2.	NO	2.	NO
4-34	FORN RES ARE MAINSTAY OF REGIM		2.	NO	2.	NO
4-35	REGIM APPEARS MAINT BY FOR RES		2.	NO	2.	NO
4-36	POP. SUPPORT FOR REGIME'S OBJ.		1.	HIGH	1.	HIGH
4-37	POP. SUPPORT FOR REGIM'S POLS.		1.	HIGH	1.	HIGH
4-38	ATT. OF INTELLECTUALS TO REGIM		1.	FAVORABLE	1.	FAVORABLE
4-39	POST-DISPUTE EXPECT'N OF POPN	#	2.	PESSIMISTIC	1.	OPTIMISTIC
5-4	INTEREST INVOLVED-COMMITMENTS		2.	NO	2.	NO
5-6	INTEREST INVOLVED-NAT'L CHAR.		1.	YES	2.	NO
5-7	INTEREST INVOLVED-PRESTIGE		2.	NO	1.	YES
5-9	INTEREST INVOLVED-POWER		2.	NO	1.	YES
5-10	INTEREST INVOLVED-INDEPENDENCE		1.	YES	2.	NO
5-13	COMMITMENT TO STATED GOALS		2.	FLEXIBLE	3.	SLIGHT
5-14	DISPUTE IS REGARDED AS CRUSADE		2.	NO	2.	NO
5-19	PRESENT OUTLOOK WRT DISPUTE		2.	MODERATE	2.	MODERATE
5-22	POST-DISPUTE EXPECT'N OF REGIM		2.	PESSIMISTIC	1.	OPTIMISTIC
5-23	DIST FM BORDER TO CONFL AREA	#	1.	1.0-1.0	1.	1.0-1.0
5-24	DIST FM CAPITAL TO CONFL AREA		1.	1.0-1.3	2.	1.7-5.0
5-28	RELIABILITY OF COMMUNICATIONS		1.	HIGH	1.	HIGH
5-34	HAS SOUGHT A NEGOT. SETTLEMENT		1.	YES	1.	YES
5-36	HAS ATTENDED BI-LAT'L NEGOT'NS		1.	YES	1.	YES
5-37	ESC LIKELY BRING GP AID TO ADV	#	2.	NO	1.	YES
5-38	P.O. RE ADV'S POL. INST'NS.	#	2.	UNFAVORABLE	2.	UNFAVORABLE
5-39	P.O. RE ADV'S SOCIAL INST'NS.		2.	UNFAVORABLE	2.	UNFAVORABLE
5-41	P.O. RE ADV'S REL. INST'NS.		2.	UNFAVORABLE	2.	UNFAVORABLE
5-43	STATE OF WAR HAS BEEN DECLARED	#	2.	NO	2.	NO
5-46	AMNESTY DECL FOR ADV PERSONNEL		2.	NO	2.	NO
6-2	IS SEC'TY ALLY OF NON-G.P.		2.	NO	2.	NO
6-4	IS ALLY OF G.P. ALLIED TO ADV.	#	2.	NO	2.	NO
6-5	IS AIDED BY GP HOSTILE TO ADV.		1.	YES	2.	NO
6-6	A GP IS OPENLY PARTIAL TO ANT.		1.	YES	2.	NO
6-8	GP DEF. FAC'TIES IN ANT'S AREA		2.	NO	2.	NO
6-11	HAS ASKED AN INT'L. ORG'N. IN	#	2.	NO	2.	NO
6-13	INT'L ORG IS INV. ON THIS SIDE	#	2.	NO	2.	NO
6-14	REG'L ORG IS INV. ON THIS SIDE	#	2.	NO	2.	NO
6-15	A G.P. IS INV. ON THIS SIDE		1.	YES	2.	NO
6-16	A NON-GP IS INV. ON THIS SIDE		2.	NO	2.	NO
6-18	A 3PTY IS PROVIDING POL. AID		1.	YES	2.	NO
6-20	A 3PTY IS PROVIDING MIL ADVICE		1.	YES	2.	NO
6-22	A 3PTY IS PROVIDING CONV FORCE		2.	NO	2.	NO
6-23	A 3PTY IS PROVIDING GUER FORCE		2.	NO	2.	NO
6-24	ATT. OF 3PTY PUBLIC TO INV'MNT		1.	FAVORABLE	8.	0 OR N/A
6-24A	TYPE OF GOVERNMENT OF 3RD PTY.		1.	POL. DEMOC.	8.	0 OR N/A
6-26	PC ANT'S ECONOMY OWNED BY 3PTY		2.	5 -15 PC	8.	0 OR N/A
6-29	I.O. PEACE MACHINERY IS SEEN	#	2.	IRRELEVANT	2.	IRRELEVANT
6-31	INTL ORGN OFFERED TO ARBITRATE		2.	NO	2.	NO
6-32	REGL ORGN OFFERED TO ARBITRATE	#	2.	NO	2.	NO
6-33	A G.P. OFFERED TO ARBITRATE		2.	NO	2.	NO
6-37	CITED IN VIOLATION OF INTL LAW	#	2.	NO	2.	NO
6-38	CITED BY I.O. FOR AGGRESSION	#	2.	NO	2.	NO
6-40	ACCEPTED IO'S PROP. CEASEFIRE	#	2.	NO	2.	NO
6-42	I.O. HAS IMPOSED SANCTIONS	#	2.	NO	2.	NO
6-47	REG ORGN HAS IMPOSED SANCTIONS	#	2.	NO	2.	NO
7-2	NO. ACTIV TROOPS AS PC OF POPN		1.	0.001-1.0	2.	1.3-174.0
7-8	OTHER SIGNIF INTERNAL THREAT		1.	YES	2.	NO
7-13	3PTY TROOP AID SEEN LIKELY TO		2.	STAY SAME	2.	STAY SAME
7-14	TOTAL MANPOWER COMMITTED	#	1.	0.02-7.3	1.	0.02-7.3
7-16	CONVENTIONAL MANPWER COMMITTED		1.	0.01-3.0	1.	0.01-3.0
7-18	NAVAL MANPOWER COMMITTED		1.	0.5-1.0	1.	0.5-1.0
7-40	HAS A NUCLEAR CAPABILITY		2.	NO	3.	IN DEV'MENT
7-41	AIDING 3PTY HAS NUCLEAR CAP'TY		1.	YES	2.	NO
7-50	OVERTNESS OF 3PTY HARDWARE AID		1.	GEN'LY OVERT	8.	0 OR N/A
8-3	REL'SHIP BET POL + MIL LEADERS		1.	POL DOMINANT	1.	POL DOMINANT
8-4	UNITY WITHIN MILITARY COMMAND		1.	UNIFIED	1.	UNIFIED
8-16	OVERALL MIL. HARDWARE BALANCE		3.	UNFAVORABLE	1.	FAVORABLE
8-17	CENTRALIZATION OF MIL. COMMAND	#	1.	CENTRALIZED	1.	CENTRALIZED
8-19	AERIAL BOMBING USED V. ADV.		4.	NO	4.	NO

Item		Compound Response	

8-26	LARG-SCAL GUER OPN BEING WAGED	2. NO	2. NO
8-30	SYMPATHY BETW POPN + OWN MIL. #	1. SYMPATHETIC	1. SYMPATHETIC
8-33	CIVN SECURITY V. GUERR ATTACK	2. MODERATE	1. HIGH

Species Type T5
("keeping the thing within reason")

The factor pattern derives from

Algeria-Morocco (Algeria vs. Morocco)

Israel-Egypt (Israel vs. Egypt)

1-1	GEOGRAPHIC LOCUS OF DISPUTE	4. MIDDLE EAST	4. MIDDLE EAST
1-2A	TOPOGRAPHY OF CONFLICT AREA	1. FLAT	1. FLAT
1-2B	CLIMATE IN THE CONFLICT AREA	1. DRY	1. DRY
1-5	EFFECTIVE NATURE OF DISPUTE	2. INTERSTATE	2. INTERSTATE
1-6	DURATION OF DISPUTE (IN MOS.)	2. 13.1-29.0	2. 13.1-29.0
1-8	CONTROL OF REAL ESTATE INVOLVD #	1. YES	1. YES
1-11	DISPUTE HAS BEEN TO REG'L ORGN	1. YES	1. YES
2-4	REGIM + GENL POPN OF SAME RACE #	1. YES	1. YES
2-7	RELIGIOUS HOMOGENEITY OF POPN	1. VERY HOMO	1. VERY HOMO
2-17	PC OF INVOLVED AREA IN CONTROL	3. 24.0-100.0	8. 0 OR N/A
2-18	PC OF INVOLVED POPN IN CONTROL	3. 9.0-100.0	8. 0 OR N/A
2-19	URBANIZATION	1. HIGH	1. HIGH
3-14	GOVERNMENT INCOME AS PC OF GNP	1. 1.0-1.5	1. 1.0-1.5
3-15	GOVT. SPENDING AS PC OF GNP	1. 1.1-1.5	1. 1.1-1.5
3-17	MILITARY DEFENSE BUDGET	1. 1.0-1.0	2. 1.4-25.0
3-18	DEFENSE BUDGET AS PC OF GNP	1. 0.3-2.7	1. 0.3-2.7
3-22	UNEMPLOYED AS PC OF GENL POPN	1. 0.5-1.0	1. 0.5-1.0
3-27	NO. AIRPORTS CONTROLLED	2. 1.5-15.0	1. 1.0-1.0
4-1	EFFECTIVE STATUS OF GOVERNMENT	1. INDEP GOVT	1. INDEP GOVT
4-16	LEADERSHIP CHARISMA	1. PRONOUNCED	1. PRONOUNCED
4-17	MOBILIZATIONAL STYLE OF REGIME #	1. FULL	2. LIMITED
4-33	PECENT CHANGE IN LEADERSHIP #	2. NO	2. NO
4-34	FORN RES ARE MAINSTAY OF REGIM	2. NO	2. NO
4-35	REGIM APPEARS MAINT BY FOR RES	2. NO	2. NO
4-36	POP. SUPPORT FOR REGIME'S OBJ.	1. HIGH	1. HIGH
4-37	POP. SUPPORT FOR REGIM'S POLS.	1. HIGH	1. HIGH
4-38	ATT. OF INTELLECTUALS TO REGIM	1. FAVORABLE	1. FAVORABLE
4-39	POST-DISPUTE EXPECT'N OF POPN	2. PESSIMISTIC	2. PESSIMISTIC
5-5	INTEREST INVOLVED-EST. POLICY #	1. YES	1. YES
5-6	INTEREST INVOLVED-NAT'L CHAR.	1. YES	1. YES
5-7	INTEREST INVOLVED-PRESTIGE #	1. YES	1. YES
5-8	INTEREST INVOLVED-PRIDE #	1. YES	1. YES
5-11	INTEREST INVOLVED-TERR. INTEG. #	1. YES	1. YES
5-13	COMMITMENT TO STATED GOALS	2. FLEXIBLE	2. FLEXIBLE
5-19	PRESENT OUTLOOK WRT DISPUTE	2. MODERATE	2. MODERATE
5-25	ADVERSARY APPEARS TO ANT TO BE	2. AUT + INDEP.	2. AUT + INDEP.
5-26	TREATY EXPERIENCE WITH ADV.	2. UNSATISF'ORY	2. UNSATISF'ORY
5-30	PRINCIPAL ATTEMPTS AT RESOL'N	4. POLITICAL	4. POLITICAL
5-32	BROUGHT DISPUTE TO INT'L ORGN #	2. NO	2. NO
5-37	ESC LIKELY BRING GP AID TO ADV	1. YES	1. YES
5-38	P.O. RE ADV'S POL. INST'NS. #	2. UNFAVORABLE	2. UNFAVORABLE
5-39	P.O. RE ADV'S SOCIAL INST'NS.	2. UNFAVORABLE	2. UNFAVORABLE
5-41	P.O. RE ADV'S REL. INST'NS.	2. UNFAVORABLE	2. UNFAVORABLE
6-3	IS ALLY OF G.P. HOSTILE TO ADV	2. NO	2. NO
6-4	IS ALLY OF G.P. ALLIED TO ADV. #	2. NO	2. NO
6-11	HAS ASKED AN INT'L. ORG'N. IN #	2. NO	2. NO
6-14	REG'L ORG IS INV. ON THIS SIDE #	2. NO	2. NO
6-17	A AUT ORG IS INV. ON THIS SIDE #	2. NO	2. NO
6-22	A 3PTY IS PROVIDING CONV FORCE	1. YES	2. NO
6-23	A 3PTY IS PROVIDING GUER FORCE	2. NO	2. NO
6-30	SOME 3PTY OFFERED TO ARBITRATE #	1. YES	1. YES
6-31	INTL ORGN OFFERED TO ARBITRATE #	1. YES	1. YES
6-33	A G.P. OFFERED TO ARBITRATE	2. NO	2. NO
6-42	I.O. HAS IMPOSED SANCTIONS #	2. NO	2. NO
7-1	NO. OF OWN ACTIVE MIL. TROOPS #	1. 0.02-10.7	1. 0.02-10.7
7-2	NO. ACTIV TROOPS AS PC OF POPN	2. 1.3-174.0	1. 0.001-1.0
7-12	OVERTNES OF 3PTY PERSONNEL AID	1. GEN'LY OVERT	8. 0 OR N/A
7-13	3PTY TROOP AID SEEN LIKELY TO	2. STAY SAME	2. STAY SAME
7-14	TOTAL MANPOWER COMMITTED #	1. 0.02-7.3	1. 0.02-7.3
7-16	CONVENTIONAL MANPWER COMMITTED	1. 0.01-3.0	1. 0.01-3.0
7-30	NO. BOMBER A/C AVAILABLE	2. 2.0-25.0	1. 1.0-1.5
7-34	NO. SAM'S AVAILABLE	1. 1.0-1.0	1. 1.0-1.0
7-35	NO. SSM'S AVAILABLE #	1. 1.0-1.0	1. 1.0-1.0
7-36	NO. SUBMARINES AVAILABLE	1. 1.0-1.0	1. 1.0-1.0
7-43	BATTLE ARMS SUPPLY LIKELY TO	1. STAY SAME	2. STAY SAME
7-44	DEPENDENCE FOR NAVAL ARMAMENTS #	1. EXCLUSIVE	1. EXCLUSIVE
7-45	NAVAL ARMS SUPPLY LIKELY TO	2. STAY SAME	2. STAY SAME
7-48	DEP FOR TRANSPORT CAPABILITIES	1. HIGH	2. HIGH
8-2	RECRUITMENT TO OFFICER CORPS #	3. NON-ELITIST	2. MODERATE
8-8	METHOD OF RECRUIT TO 3PTY MIL.	1. VOLUNTARY	8. 0 OR N/A
8-10	TRAINING FAC FOR 3PTY OFFICERS	1. GOOD	8. 0 OR N/A
8-12	TRAINING FAC FOR 3PTY ENLISTED	1. GOOD	8. 0 OR N/A
8-17	CENTRALIZATION OF MIL. COMMAND	2. DE-CENTR'ZED	1. CENTRALIZED
8-22	USE OF TERROR BY THIS ANT. IS	3. ABSENT	3. ABSENT
8-30	SYMPATHY BETW POPN + OWN MIL. #	1. SYMPATHETIC	1. SYMPATHETIC
8-34	CIVN SEC V AC ATK BY OWN FPCES	1. HIGH	1. HIGH

Species Type T6

| 1-3 | PAST POL. REL'SHIP BETW PARTYS | 3. EXPLOITIVE | 3. EXPLOITIVE |
| 1-5 | EFFECTIVE NATURE OF DISPUTE | 1. COLONIAL | 1. COLONIAL |

("outside pressures conspire for decisive action")

The factor pattern derives from

Angolan insurgency (Portuguese colonial administration vs. African insurgents)

Indonesia: independence (Dutch colonial administration vs. Indonesian insurgents)

Item		Compound Response		
1-7	IDEOLOGICAL DIFF. BETW PARTIES	#	1. EXTREME	1. EXTREME
1-8	CONTROL OF REAL ESTATE INVOLVD	#	1. YES	1. YES
1-12	DISPUTE HAS BEEN TO INT'L ORGN		1. YES	1. YES
1-13	INTRODUCED TO INT'L ORGN BY A		2. NEUTRAL	2. NEUTRAL
2-4	REGIM + GENL POPN OF SAME RACE		2. NO	1. YES
2-5	RACIAL HOMOGENEITY OF GENL POP	#	1. HOMOGENEOUS	1. HOMOGENEOUS
2-12	AREA UNDER EFFECTIVE CONTROL		3. 13.7-500.0	1. 1.0-2.1
2-13	POPN UNDER EFFECTIVE CONTROL		2. 3.2-52.2	1. 1.0-2.0
2-14	REAL ESTATE INVOLVED IS	#	1. IN CLMD BDY	1. IN CLMD BDY
2-15	PC OF ANT'S CLMD AREA INVOLVED	#	1. 1.0-1.0	1. 1.0-1.0
2-18	PC OF INVOLVED POPN IN CONTROL		3. 9.0-100.0	1. 1.0-1.0
2-19	URBANIZATION		3. LOW	3. LOW
3-2	GROSS NAT'L. OR ECON. PRODUCT	#	3. 90.0-6.4TH	8. 0 OR N/A
3-7	PC OF GNP IN DURABLE GOODS		1. 1.0-1.2	1. 1.0-1.2
3-8	PRODUCTION OF STEEL	#	1. 1.0-1.0	1. 1.0-1.0
3-20	AGRIC EMPLOYMENT AS PC OF POPN		1. 1.0-1.2	1. 1.0-1.2
3-26	MILES RAILROAD CONTROLLED		2. 1.5-11.3	8. 0 OR N/A
4-1	EFFECTIVE STATUS OF GOVERNMENT		2. COLONIAL ADM	4. REBEL ORGN
4-11	RECRUITMENT TO POL LEADERSHIP		1. ELITIST	2. MODERATE
4-14	INTERNATIONAL POLICY OF REGIME		4. NONE	3. MODERATE
4-15	COMMUNIST ORIENT'N OF REGIME		5. ANTI-COM.	4. NON-COM.
4-16	LEADERSHIP CHARISMA	#	2. NEGLIGIBLE	1. PRONOUNCED
4-17	MOBILIZATIONAL STYLE OF REGIME	#	2. LIMITED	1. FULL
4-18	POL. INTEGRATION OF GENL POPN		3. LOW	3. LOW
4-21	INTEREST ARTIC'N BY ANOMIC GPS		3. NOT TOLERATD	1. FREQUENT
4-24	INTEREST ARTIC'N BY POL PARTYS		2. POL INSIGNIF	1. POL SIGNIF
4-35	REGIM APPEARS MAINT BY FOR RES	#	1. YES	2. NO
4-36	POP. SUPPORT FOR REGIME'S OBJ.		2. LOW	1. HIGH
4-39	POST-DISPUTE EXPECT'N OF POPN		1. OPTIMISTIC	2. PESSIMISTIC
5-2	REGIME SEEKS OVERTHROW OF ADV.	#	1. YES	1. YES
5-9	INTEREST INVOLVED-POWER		2. NO	1. YES
5-10	INTEREST INVOLVED-INDEPENDENCE		2. NO	1. YES
5-11	INTEREST INVOLVED-TERR. INTEG.	#	1. YES	1. YES
5-12	INTEREST INVOLVED-CONT'D EXIS.	#	1. YES	1. YES
5-15	CONDUCT OF CONFLICT IS LIMITED	#	2. NO	2. NO
5-17	RATIONALIZATION OF VIOLENCE		1. MORALISTIC	1. MORALISTIC
5-21	LIKELY OUTCOME IS NOW OBVIOUS		1. YES	2. NO
5-22	POST-DISPUTE EXPECT'N OF REGIM	#	2. PESSIMISTIC	2. PESSIMISTIC
5-23	DIST FM BORDER TO CONFL AREA	#	1. 1.0-1.0	1. 1.0-1.0
5-29	CREDIBILITY OF COMMUNICATIONS	#	2. LOW	2. LOW
5-30	PRINCIPAL ATTEMPTS AT RESOL'N	#	5. MILITARY	5. MILITARY
5-32	BROUGHT DISPUTE TO INT'L ORGN		2. NO	1. YES
5-37	ESC LIKELY BRING GP AID TO ADV		1. YES	2. NC
5-38	P.O. RE ADV'S POL. INST'NS.		1. FAVORABLE	2. UNFAVORABLE
5-39	P.O. RE ADV'S SOCIAL INST'NS.		1. FAVORABLE	2. UNFAVORABLE
5-41	P.O. RE ADV'S REL. INST'NS.	#	1. FAVORABLE	1. FAVORABLE
5-45	LEGAL STATUS OF ADV. PERSONNEL		3. TRAITOR	4. ENEMY AGENT
5-46	AMNESTY DECL FOR ADV PERSONNEL	#	1. YES	2. NO
6-1	IS SEC'TY ALLY OF GREAT POWER		2. NO	2. NO
6-3	IS ALLY OF G.P. HOSTILE TO ADV		2. NO	2. NO
6-4	IS ALLY OF G.P. ALLIED TO ADV.	#	2. NO	2. NO
6-5	IS AIDED BY GP HOSTILE TO ADV.		2. NO	2. NO
6-6	A GP IS OPENLY PARTIAL TO ANT.		2. NO	1. YES
6-7	GP AID PROMISED IF ESC. OCCURS		2. NO	2. NO
6-8	GP DEF. FAC'TIES IN ANT'S AREA		2. NO	2. NO
6-11	HAS ASKED AN INT'L. ORG'N. IN		2. NO	1. YES
6-13	INT'L ORG IS INV. ON THIS SIDE		2. NO	1. YES
6-16	A NON-GP IS INV. ON THIS SIDE	#	1. YES	1. YES
6-17	A AUT ORG IS INV. ON THIS SIDE	#	2. NO	2. NO
6-18	A 3PTY IS PROVIDING POL. AID	#	1. YES	1. YES
6-22	A 3PTY IS PROVIDING CONV FORCE		1. YES	2. NO
6-24	ATT. OF 3PTY PUBLIC TO INV'MNT	#	1. FAVORABLE	1. FAVORABLE
6-29	I.O. PEACE MACHINERY IS SEEN		2. IRRELEVANT	1. RELEVANT
6-33	A G.P. OFFERED TO ARBITRATE		2. NO	2. NO
6-35	INT'L ORG'N UPHELD ANT'S CAUSE		2. NO	1. YES
6-36	INTL ORG'N INDICTED ANT'S CAUSE		1. YES	2. NO
7-1	NO. OF OWN ACTIVE MIL. TROOPS	#	1. 0.02-10.7	1. 0.02-10.7
7-3	NO. RESERVE TROOPS AVAILABLE		1. 0.5-1.4	2. 1.8-10.0
7-8	OTHER SIGNIF INTERNAL THREAT	#	2. NO	2. NO
7-9	OTHER SIGNIF EXTERNAL THREAT	#	2. NO	2. NO
7-14	TOTAL MANPOWER COMMITTED	#	1. 0.02-7.3	1. 0.02-7.3
7-40	HAS A NUCLEAR CAPABILITY	#	2. NO	2. NO
7-41	AIDING 3PTY HAS NUCLEAR CAP'TY		2. NO	2. NO
7-53	PC TOTAL COSTS COMING FM 3PTY		1. 1.0-1.0	1. 1.0-1.0
8-2	RECRUITMENT TO OFFICER CORPS	#	2. MODERATE	3. NON-ELITIST
8-4	UNITY WITHIN MILITARY COMMAND		2. FACTIONAL	2. FACTIONAL
8-9	TRAINING FACILITY FOR OFFICERS		1. GOOD	3. POOR
8-11	TRAINING FAC FOR ENLISTED PERS		1. GOOD	3. POOR
8-13	OVERALL MILITARY ORG'N BALANCE	#	1. FAVORABLE	3. UNFAVORABLE
8-16	OVERALL MIL. HARDWARE BALANCE	#	1. FAVORABLE	3. UNFAVORABLE
8-17	CENTRALIZATION OF MIL. COMMAND		1. CENTRALIZED	2. DE-CENTR'ZED
8-19	AERIAL BOMBING USED V. ADV.		1. DAYTIME	4. NO
8-22	TACTICS OF FORCES ON THIS SIDE		2. STATIC	1. MOBILE
8-23	TACTICS OF FORCES ON THIS SIDE	#	1. TENACIOUS	2. YIELDING
8-29	INTELL. IN ADV'S POLICY ORGANS		3. INEFFECTIVE	3. INEFFECTIVE
8-35	CIVN SEC V ABUSE BY OWN FORCES		2. MODERATE	2. MODERATE

Species Type T7
("moderate faction prevails to confront reality")

The factor pattern derives from

Indonesia-Malaysia (Indonesia vs. Malaysia)

Spanish civil war (Republican government vs. Nationalist insurgents)

Item			Compound Response		
1-3	PAST POL. REL'SHIP BETW PARTYS	#	2. COMPETITIVE	2.	COMPETITIVE
1-6	DURATION OF DISPUTE (IN MOS.)		3. 32.0-52.0	3.	32.0-52.0
1-8	CONTROL OF REAL ESTATE INVOLVD	#	1. YES	1.	YES
1-9	SIZE OF AREA AT STAKE(TH SQ M)		3. 84.0-197.0	3.	84.0-197.0
1-10	SIZE OF POPN AT STAKE (THOUS.)	#	4. 10TH-76TH	4.	10TH-76TH
1-13	INTRODUCED TO INT'L ORGN BY A		1. ANTAGONIST	1.	ANTAGONIST
1-14	BASIS OF INTRO. TO INT'L ORGN		1. AGGRESSION	1.	AGGRESSION
2-4	REGIM + GENL POPN OF SAME RACE	#	1. YES	1.	YES
2-17	PC OF INVOLVED AREA IN CONTROL		1. 1.0-1.5	2.	1.9-9.0
3-5	PER CAPITA INCOME		1. 1.0-2.1	1.	1.0-2.1
3-6	PC OF GNP IN AGRICULTURE		1. 1.0-2.0	1.	1.0-2.0
3-20	AGRIC EMPLOYMENT AS PC OF POPN		1. 1.0-1.2	1.	1.0-1.2
3-21	INDUSTRIAL EMPL. AS PC OF POPN		1. 1.0-1.1	2.	1.5-5.0
3-22	UNEMPLOYED AS PC OF GENL POPN		1. 0.5-1.0	1.	0.5-1.0
4-17	MOBILIZATIONAL STYLE OF REGIME		1. FULL	1.	FULL
4-29	PC OF VOTE REC'D BY THIS REGIM		1. 1.2-1.3	1.	1.2-1.3
4-32	RECENT LEADERSHIP CRISIS		1. YES	2.	NO
4-36	POP. SUPPORT FOR REGIME'S OBJ.	#	2. LOW	1.	HIGH
4-37	POP. SUPPORT FOR REGIM'S POLS.		2. LOW	1.	HIGH
5-19	PRESENT OUTLOOK WRT DISPUTE		2. MODERATE	1.	DIE-HARD
5-21	LIKELY OUTCOME IS NOW OBVIOUS		1. YES	1.	YES
5-23	DIST FM BORDER TO CONFL AREA	#	1. 1.0-1.0	1.	1.0-1.0
5-28	RELIABILITY OF COMMUNICATIONS		1. HIGH	1.	HIGH
5-29	CREDIBILITY OF COMMUNICATIONS		1. HIGH	1.	HIGH
5-31	OFFERED TO RESOLVE CONST'ALLY	#	2. NO	2.	NO
5-34	HAS SOUGHT A NEGOT. SETTLEMENT	#	2. NO	2.	NO
5-35	HAS OFFERED BI-LATERAL NEGOTNS	#	2. NO	2.	NO
5-38	P.O. RE ADV'S POL. INST'NS.	#	2. UNFAVORABLE	2.	UNFAVORABLE
5-39	P.O. RE ADV'S SOCIAL INST'NS.		2. UNFAVORABLE	2.	UNFAVORABLE
5-43	STATE OF WAR HAS BEEN DECLARED	#	2. NO	2.	NO
5-46	AMNESTY DECL FOR ADV PERSONNEL		2. NO	2.	NO
6-4	IS ALLY OF G.P. ALLIED TO ADV.	#	2. NO	2.	NO
6-5	IS AIDED BY GP HOSTILE TO ADV.	#	1. YES	1.	YES
6-6	A GP IS OPENLY PARTIAL TO ANT.	#	1. YES	1.	YES
6-10	HAS ASKED A REGIONAL ORG'N IN		2. NO	2.	NO
6-12	SOME 3PTY IS INV. ON THIS SIDE	#	1. YES	1.	YES
6-13	INT'L ORG IS INV. ON THIS SIDE	#	2. NO	1.	YES
6-15	A G.P. IS INV. ON THIS SIDE	#	1. YES	1.	YES
6-16	A NON-GP IS INV. ON THIS SIDE		2. NO	1.	YES
6-17	A AUT ORG IS INV. ON THIS SIDE		1. YES	2.	NO
6-19	A 3PTY IS PROVIDING ECON. AID	#	1. YES	1.	YES
6-20	A 3PTY IS PROVIDING MIL ADVICE	#	1. YES	1.	YES
6-21	A 3PTY IS PROVIDING MIL HDWRE.	#	1. YES	1.	YES
6-22	A 3PTY IS PROVIDING CONV FORCE		2. NO	1.	YES
6-24	ATT. OF 3PTY PUBLIC TO INV'MNT	#	1. FAVORABLE	1.	FAVORABLE
6-25	AID TO ANT. HURTS 3PTY ECONOMY		2. NO	2.	NO
6-30	SOME 3PTY OFFERED TO ARBITRATE		2. NO	2.	NO
6-31	INTL ORGN OFFERED TO ARBITRATE		2. NO	2.	NO
6-32	REGL ORGN OFFERED TO ARBITRATE	#	2. NO	2.	NO
6-33	A G.P. OFFERED TO ARBITRATE		2. NO	2.	NO
6-35	INT'L ORG'N UPHELD ANT'S CAUSE	#	2. NO	2.	NO
6-36	INTL ORGN INDICTED ANT'S CAUSE	#	2. NO	2.	NO
6-37	CITED IN VIOLATION OF INTL LAW	#	2. NO	2.	NO
6-38	CITED BY I.O. FOR AGGRESSION	#	2. NO	2.	NO
6-40	ACCEPTED IO'S PROP. CEASEFIRE	#	2. NO	2.	NO
6-42	I.O. HAS IMPOSED SANCTIONS	#	2. NO	2.	NO
7-1	NO. OF OWN ACTIVE MIL. TROOPS	#	1. 0.02-10.7	1.	0.02-10.7
7-3	NO. RESERVE TROOPS AVAILABLE		1. 0.5-1.4	1.	0.5-1.4
7-5	NO. TROOPS COMMITTED TO CONFL.	#	1. 0.02-1.0	2.	1.2-50.0
7-9	OTHER SIGNIF EXTERNAL THREAT	#	2. NO	2.	NO
7-11	TOTAL TROOPS GIVEN BY 3RD PTY		8. 0 OR N/A	3.	4.0-100.0
7-13	3PTY TROOP AID SEEN LIKELY TO		2. STAY SAME	2.	STAY SAME
7-14	TOTAL MANPOWER COMMITTED	#	1. 0.02-7.3	1.	0.02-7.3
7-15	OWN TRPS AS PC OF ALL COMMITED	#	1. 1.0-1.5	1.	1.0-1.5
7-29	NO. FIGHTER A/C AVAILABLE	#	1. 1.0-1.5	2.	1.7-30.0
7-30	NO. BOMBER A/C AVAILABLE	#	1. 1.0-1.5	2.	2.0-25.0
7-44	DEPENDENCE FOR NAVAL ARMAMENTS	#	1. EXCLUSIVE	1.	EXCLUSIVE
7-52	TRAINING FOR WEAPONS IN AID		2. SELECTIVE	1.	ADEQUATE
7-53	PC TOTAL COSTS COMING FM 3PTY		2. 1.2-5.0	1.	1.0-1.0
8-4	UNITY WITHIN MILITARY COMMAND		2. FACTIONAL	1.	UNIFIED
8-11	TRAINING FAC FOR ENLISTED PERS	#	2. FAIR	1.	GOOD
8-13	OVERALL MILITARY ORG'N BALANCE	#	3. UNFAVORABLE	1.	FAVORABLE
8-16	OVERALL MIL. HARDWARE BALANCE	#	3. UNFAVORABLE	1.	FAVORABLE
8-17	CENTRALIZATION OF MIL. COMMAND	#	1. CENTRALIZED	1.	CENTRALIZED
8-22	TACTICS OF FORCES ON THIS SIDE	#	1. MOBILE	1.	MOBILE
8-26	LARG-SCAL GUER OPN BEING WAGED		2. NO	2.	NO
8-30	SYMPATHY BETW POPN + OWN MIL.	#	1. SYMPATHETIC	1.	SYMPATHETIC
8-34	CIVN SEC V AC ATK BY OWN FRCES		1. HIGH	1.	HIGH
9-10	CASUALTY RATE FOR ALL FORCES		1. 1.0-2.0	1.	1.0-2.0
9-11	ATTRITION RATE FOR OWN FORCES		2. 2.5-20.0	1.	1.0-2.0

	Item	Compound Response	

e.
Termination:
Higher-Order Factor Patterns

Genus 1

The factor pattern derives from

Cuba: "little" war of 1906 (Liberal party insurgents vs. Cuban government)

Cyprus: independence (U.K. colonial administration vs. Enosists)

Ethiopia-Somalia (Ethiopia vs. Somalia)

India-China (India vs. China)

Kashmir (Pakistan vs. India)

USSR-Iran (Iran vs. USSR)

The adjuncts are

Indonesia-Malaysia
Spanish civil war

Algeria-Morocco
Israel-Egypt

Item	Description	Resp A	Resp B
2-4	REGIM + GENL POPN OF SAME RACE #	1. YES	1. YES
4-32	RECENT LEADERSHIP CRISIS	2. NO	2. NO
5-23	DIST FM BORDER TO CONFL AREA #	1. 1.0-1.0	1. 1.0-1.0
5-28	RELIABILITY OF COMMUNICATIONS	1. HIGH	1. HIGH
5-34	HAS SOUGHT A NEGOT. SETTLEMENT	1. YES	1. YES
5-36	HAS ATTENDED BI-LAT'L NEGOT'NS	1. YES	1. YES
6-4	IS ALLY OF G.P. ALLIED TO ADV. #	2. NO	2. NO
6-13	INT'L ORG IS INV. ON THIS SIDE #	2. NO	2. NO
6-14	REG'L ORG IS INV. ON THIS SIDE #	2. NO	2. NO
6-32	REGL ORGN OFFERED TO ARBITRATE #	2. NO	2. NO
6-37	CITED IN VIOLATION OF INTL LAW #	2. NO	2. NC
6-38	CITED BY I.O. FOR AGGRESSION #	2. NO	2. NO
6-42	I.O. HAS IMPOSED SANCTIONS #	2. NO	2. NO
6-47	REG ORGN HAS IMPOSED SANCTIONS #	2. NO	2. NO

Genus 2

The factor pattern derives from

Cuba: Bay of Pigs (Cuban exiles vs. Cuban government)

Greek insurgency (Greek insurgents vs. Greek government)

Malayan insurgency (Malayan Communist party vs. U.K.-Malay colonial administration and Malayan government)

Venezuelan insurgency (MIR/CPV and FLN/FALN vs. Venezuelan government)

The adjuncts are

Angolan insurgency
Indonesia: independence

Item	Description	Resp A	Resp B
1-5	EFFECTIVE NATURE OF DISPUTE #	3. INTERNAL	3. INTERNAL
1-7	IDEOLOGICAL DIFF. BETW PARTIES #	1. EXTREME	1. EXTREME
1-8	CONTROL OF REAL ESTATE INVOLVD #	1. YES	1. YES
1-10	SIZE OF POPN AT STAKE (THOUS.)	3. 5.0TH-7.6TH	3. 5.0TH-7.6TH
2-12	AREA UNDER EFFECTIVE CONTROL	8. 0 OR N/A	3. 13.7-500.0
2-13	POPN UNDER EFFECTIVE CONTROL	8. 0 OR N/A	3. 499.0-65TH
2-14	REAL ESTATE INVOLVED IS #	1. IN CLMD BDY	1. IN CLMD BDY
2-15	PC OF ANT'S CLMD AREA INVOLVED #	1. 1.0-1.0	1. 1.0-1.0
2-16	PC OF ANT'S CLMD POPN INVOLVED #	1. 1.0-1.0	1. 1.0-1.0
2-17	PC OF INVOLVED AREA IN CONTROL	8. 0 OR N/A	3. 24.0-100.0
2-18	PC OF INVOLVED POPN IN CONTROL	8. 0 OR N/A	3. 5.0-100.0
3-2	GROSS NAT'L. OR ECON. PRODUCT #	8. 0 OR N/A	3. 90.0-6.4TH
3-5	PER CAPITA INCOME #	8. 0 OR N/A	3. 115.0-855.0
3-20	AGRIC EMPLOYMENT AS PC OF POPN	8. 0 OR N/A	3. 13.0-70.0
4-1	EFFECTIVE STATUS OF GOVERNMENT #	4. REBEL ORGN	1. INDEP GOVT
4-4	EXECUTIVE STABILITY #	8. 0 OR N/A	3. 3.0-9.0
4-18	POL. INTEGRATION OF GENL POPN	8. 0 OR N/A	2. MODERATE
5-22	POST-DISPUTE EXPECT'N OF REGIM #	2. PESSIMISTIC	2. PESSIMISTIC
5-28	RELIABILITY OF COMMUNICATIONS #	2. LOW	2. LOW
5-29	CREDIBILITY OF COMMUNICATIONS #	2. LOW	2. LOW
5-31	OFFERED TO RESOLVE CONST'ALLY #	2. NO	2. NO
5-33	INDICATED DISPUT IS NEGOTIABLE	2. NO	2. NO
5-34	HAS SOUGHT A NEGOT. SETTLEMENT #	2. NO	2. NO
6-4	IS ALLY OF G.P. ALLIED TO ADV. #	2. NO	2. NO
6-6	A GP IS OPENLY PARTIAL TO ANT. #	1. YES	1. YES
6-14	REG'L ORG IS INV. ON THIS SIDE #	2. NO	2. NO
6-22	A 3PTY IS PROVIDING CONV FORCE #	2. NO	2. NO
6-32	REGL ORGN OFFERED TO ARBITRATE #	2. NO	2. NO
6-40	ACCEPTED IO'S PROP. CEASEFIRE #	2. NO	2. NC
6-42	I.O. HAS IMPOSED SANCTIONS #	2. NO	2. NC
7-1	NO. OF OWN ACTIVE MIL. TROOPS	1. 0.02-10.7	2. 17.0-213.7
7-5	NO. TROOPS COMMITTED TO CONFL. #	1. 0.02-1.0	2. 1.2-50.0
7-14	TOTAL MANPOWER COMMITTED	1. 0.02-7.3	2. 9.7-55.0
7-15	OWN TRPS AS PC OF ALL COMMITED #	1. 1.0-1.5	1. 1.0-1.5
7-21	NO. RIFLES AVAILABLE #	1. 0.05-2.1	2. 3.0-85.7
7-39	NO. PATROL BOATS AVAILABLE	8. 0 OR N/A	3. 5.0-37.0
8-14	LOGIS SUP'T ADQT TO MAINT OPNS	2. NO	1. YES
8-15	LOGIS SUP'T ADQT TO EXPAND OPN	2. NO	1. YES
8-16	OVERALL MIL. HARDWARE BALANCE #	3. UNFAVORABLE	1. FAVORABLE
8-25	TREATMENT OF OWN CASUALTIES	3. POOR	1. GOOD
8-32	CIVN SECURITY V. CONV. ATTACK	8. 0 OR N/A	1. HIGH

Family 1

Item	Description	Resp A	Resp B
1-8	CONTROL OF REAL ESTATE INVOLVD #	1. YES	1. YES

The factor pattern derives from

Algeria-Morocco (Algeria vs. Morocco)

Indonesia-Malaysia (Malaysia vs. Indonesia)

Israel-Egypt (Israel vs. Egypt)

Spanish civil war (Nationalist insurgents vs. Republican government)

The adjuncts are

Cuba: "little" war of 1906
Cyprus: independence
Ethiopia-Somalia
India-China
Kashmir
USSR-Iran

Item		Compound Response	
2-4	REGIM + GENL POPN OF SAME RACE # 1.	YES	1. YES
3-22	UNEMPLOYED AS PC OF GENL POPN 1.	0.5-1.0	1. 0.5-1.0
5-38	P.O. RE ADV'S POL. INST'NS. # 2.	UNFAVORABLE	2. UNFAVORABLE
5-39	P.O. RE ADV'S SOCIAL INST'NS. 2.	UNFAVORABLE	2. UNFAVORABLE
6-4	IS ALLY OF G.P. ALLIED TO ADV. # 2.	NO	2. NO
6-22	A 3PTY IS PROVIDING CONV FORCE 1.	YES	2. NO
6-33	A G.P. OFFERED TO ARBITRATE 2.	NO	2. NO
6-42	I.O. HAS IMPOSED SANCTIONS # 2.	NO	2. NO
7-1	NO. OF OWN ACTIVE MIL. TROOPS # 1.	0.02-10.7	1. 0.02-10.7
7-13	3PTY TROOP AID SEEN LIKELY TO 2.	STAY SAME	2. STAY SAME
7-14	TOTAL MANPOWER COMMITTED # 1.	0.02-7.3	1. 0.02-7.3
7-30	NO. BOMBER A/C AVAILABLE # 2.	2.0-25.0	1. 1.0-1.5
7-44	DEPENDENCE FOR NAVAL ARMAMENTS # 1.	EXCLUSIVE	1. EXCLUSIVE
8-30	SYMPATHY BETW POPN + OWN MIL. # 1.	SYMPATHETIC	1. SYMPATHETIC
8-34	CIVN SEC V AC ATK BY OWN FRCES 1.	HIGH	1. HIGH

Family 2

The factor pattern derives from

Angolan insurgency (African insurgents vs. Portuguese colonial administration)

Cuba: Bay of Pigs (Cuban exiles vs. Cuban government)

Greek insurgency (Greek insurgents vs. Greek government)

Indonesia: independence (Indonesian insurgents vs. Dutch colonial administration)

Malayan insurgency (Malayan Communist party vs. U.K.-Malay colonial administration and Malayan government)

Venezuelan insurgency (MIR/CPV and FLN/FALN vs. Venezuelan government)

1-7	IDEOLOGICAL DIFF. BETW PARTIES # 1.	EXTREME	1. EXTREME
1-8	CONTROL OF REAL ESTATE INVOLVD # 1.	YES	1. YES
2-14	REAL ESTATE INVOLVED IS # 1.	IN CLMD BDY	1. IN CLMD BDY
2-15	PC OF ANT'S CLMD AREA INVOLVED # 1.	1.0-1.0	1. 1.0-1.0
3-2	CROSS NAT'L. OR ECON. PRODUCT # 8.	0 OR N/A	3. 90.0-6.4TH
5-22	POST-DISPUTE EXPECT'N OF REGIM # 2.	PESSIMISTIC	2. PESSIMISTIC
5-29	CREDIBILITY OF COMMUNICATIONS # 2.	LOW	2. LOW
6-4	IS ALLY OF G.P. ALLIED TO ADV. # 2.	NO	2. NO
8-16	OVERALL MIL. HARDWARE BALANCE # 3.	UNFAVORABLE	1. FAVORABLE

Order

The factor pattern derives from all sixteen instances of termination included in the analysis.

6-4	IS ALLY OF G.P. ALLIED TO ADV. # 2.	NO	2. NO

6.
The Settlement (S) Patterns

The data input for each conflict included in this analysis is that obtaining at the threshold of S and is therefore a statement of the conditions pertaining when the dispute at the heart of each was about to realize its particular form of settlement. All but one of these conflicts passed into S from P–IV, the posthostilities phase. In the Ethiopian resistance, this passage was effected directly from P–III (hostilities) by final, decisive military action.

a.
Conflicts Included
in the Analysis
of the Settlement Patterns

Conflict	Event Marking Settlement (S)	Date
Cuba: "little" war of 1906	U.S. peace commission leaves Cuba	10/06
Cyprus: independence	Cypriot independence	8/60
Ethiopian resistance	Surrender of Italian forces in Ethiopia	11/41
Indonesia: independence	Formal transfer of sovereignty	12/49
Spanish civil war	Franco forces occupy Spain unopposed	4/39
USSR-Iran	Iranian parliament refuses to ratify Soviet oil agreement	10/47

b.
Derivation of the Settlement
Patterns

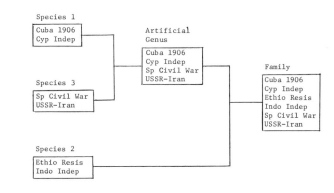

c.
Percentile Distribution of the
Conflicts across the Settlement
Patterns

	Species			Genus	Family
	S1	S2	S3		
Cuba: "little" war of 1906	1.00	0.23	0.38	1.00	1.00
Cyprus: independence	1.00	0.46	0.44	1.00	1.00
Ethiopian resistance	0.21	1.00	0.48	~	1.00
Indonesia: independence	0.32	1.00	0.48	~	1.00
Spanish civil war	0.32	0.35	1.00	1.00	1.00
USSR-Iran	0.35	0.44	1.00	1.00	1.00
Vietnam 3/67	0.35	0.41	0.46	0.53	1.00

d.
Settlement:
Complete Factor Patterns

Species Type S1
("plebiscitarian model: moderation
prevails")

Item		Compound Response	
1-2A	TOPOGRAPHY OF CONFLICT AREA	1. FLAT	1. FLAT
1-4	PAST MIL. REL'SHIP BETW PARTYS	1. PEACEFUL	1. PEACEFUL
1-7	IDEOLOGICAL DIFF. BETW PARTIES	3. NONE	3. NONE
1-11	DISPUTE HAS BEEN TO REG'L ORGN #	2. NO	2. NO
1-12	DISPUTE HAS BEEN TO INT'L ORGN #	2. NO	2. NO

The factor pattern derives from

Cuba: "little" war of 1906 (Liberal party insurgents vs. Cuban government)

Cyprus: independence (Enosists vs. U.K. colonial administration)

Item		Compound Response		
2-3	RACIAL GROUPING OF ANTAGONIST	1. WHITE	1. WHITE
2-4	REGIM + GENL POPN OF SAME RACE #	1. YES	1. YES
2-8	DOMINANT RELIGION AMONG POPN	1. JUD-XIAN	1. JUD-XIAN
2-19	URBANIZATION	8. 0 OR N/A	2. MEDIUM
3-2	GROSS NAT'L. OR ECON. PRODUCT #	8. 0 OR N/A	3. 90.0-6.4TH
3-3	GROWTH RATE OF ECONOMY	8. 0 OR N/A	3. 3.0-13.9
3-5	PER CAPITA INCOME #	8. 0 OR N/A	3. .15.0-855.0
3-6	PC OF GNP IN AGRICULTURE #	8. 0 OR N/A	3. 25.0-75.0
3-8	PRODUCTION OF STEEL #	1. 1.0-1.0	1. 1.0-1.0
3-9	PC OF GNP IN EXPORTS	8. 0 OR N/A	3. 22.0-1.0TH
3-11	FOREIGN ECONOMIC AID RECEIVED	1. 1.0-1.0	1. 1.0-1.0
3-14	GOVERNMENT INCOME AS PC OF GNP #	8. 0 OR N/A	3. 10.0-50.0
3-15	GOVT. SPENDING AS PC OF GNP #	8. 0 OR N/A	3. 6.0-50.0
3-20	AGRIC EMPLOYMENT AS PC OF POPN	8. 0 OR N/A	3. 13.0-70.0
3-21	INDUSTRIAL EMPL. AS PC OF POPN	8. 0 OR N/A	3. 11.0-23.0
3-22	UNEMPLOYED AS PC OF GENL POPN	8. 0 OR N/A	3. 3.0-10.0
4-4	EXECUTIVE STABILITY #	8. 0 OR N/A	3. 3.0-9.0
4-5	TYPE OF GOVERNMENT	8. 0 OR N/A	2. TUT/MOD OLIG
4-8	STATUS OF JUDICIARY	8. 0 OR N/A	2. PART EFFECT.
4-10	REGIME CAME TO POWER CONST'LY #	8. 0 OR N/A	2. NO
4-12	IDEOL. ORIENTATION OF REGIME	2. MODERATE	2. MODERATE
4-13	INTERNAL POLICIES OF REGIME	2. MODERATE	2. MODERATE
4-20	FREEDOM OF GROUP OPPOSITION	8. 0 OR N/A	1. FULL
4-21	INTEREST ARTIC'N BY ANOMIC GPS	8. 0 OR N/A	2. INFREQUENT
4-23	INTEREST ARTIC'N BY INST'L GPS	8. 0 OR N/A	1. POL SIGNIF
4-24	INTEREST ARTIC'N BY POL PARTYS	8. 0 OR N/A	1. POL SIGNIF
4-25	CONST'AL STATUS OF POL PARTIES	8. 0 OR N/A	1. COMPETITIVE
4-28	PC OF POPN VOTING IN ELECTIONS #	8. 0 OR N/A	3. 9.5-95.0
4-36	POP. SUPPORT FOR REGIME'S OBJ.	8. 0 OR N/A	2. LOW
4-37	POP. SUPPORT FOR REGIM'S POLS.	8. 0 OR N/A	2. LOW
4-38	ATT. OF INTELLECTUALS TO REGIM	8. 0 OR N/A	2. UNFAVORABLE
4-39	POST-DISPUTE EXPECT'N OF POPN	8. 0 OR N/A	1. OPTIMISTIC
5-3	INTEREST INVOLVED-IDEOLOGY	2. NO	2. NO
5-5	INTEREST INVOLVED-EST. POLICY	2. NO	1. YES
5-12	INTEREST INVOLVED-CONT'D EXIS.	2. NO	2. NO
5-14	DISPUTE IS REGARDED AS CRUSADE	2. NO	2. NO
5-15	CONDUCT OF CONFLICT IS LIMITED	1. YES	1. YES
5-16	PC OF AVAIL MIL FRCS COMMITTED	1. 0 -10 PC	1. 0 -10 PC
5-18	CAN ACCEPT LES THN STATED DMDS	1. YES	1. YES
5-21	LIKELY OUTCOME IS NOW OBVIOUS	1. YES	1. YES
5-22	POST-DISPUTE EXPECT'N OF REGIM	2. PESSIMISTIC	1. OPTIMISTIC
5-23	DIST FM BORDER TO CONFL AREA #	1. 1.0-1.0	1. 1.0-1.0
5-24	DIST FM CAPITAL TO CONFL AREA #	1. 1.0-1.3	1. 1.0-1.3
5-27	SPEED OF COMMUNICATIONS	1. RAPID	1. RAPID
5-28	RELIABILITY OF COMMUNICATIONS	1. HIGH	1. HIGH
5-29	CREDIBILITY OF COMMUNICATIONS	1. HIGH	1. HIGH
5-31	OFFERED TO RESOLVE CONST'ALLY	1. YES	2. NO
5-32	BROUGHT DISPUTE TO INT'L ORGN #	2. NO	2. NO
5-33	INDICATED DISPUT IS NEGOTIABLE	1. YES	1. YES
5-42	MARTIAL LAW IS IN EFFECT	8. 0 OR N/A	2. NO
6-1	IS SEC'TY ALLY OF GREAT POWER #	2. NO	1. YES
6-2	IS SEC'TY ALLY OF NON-G.P.	2. NO	2. NO
6-7	GP AID PROMISED IF ESC. OCCURS	2. NO	2. NO
6-11	HAS ASKED AN INT'L. ORG'N. IN #	2. NO	2. NO
6-13	INT'L ORG IS INV. ON THIS SIDE #	2. NO	2. NO
6-14	REG'L ORG IS INV. ON THIS SIDE #	2. NO	2. NO
6-17	A AUT ORG IS INV. ON THIS SIDE #	2. NO	2. NO
6-23	A 3PTY IS PROVIDING GUER FORCE	2. NO	2. NO
6-29	I.O. PEACE MACHINERY IS SEEN #	2. IRRELEVANT	2. IRRELEVANT
6-31	INTL ORGN OFFERED TO ARBITRATE #	2. NO	2. NO
6-32	REGL ORGN OFFERED TO ARBITRATE #	2. NO	2. NO
6-35	INTL ORG'N UPHELD ANT'S CAUSE #	2. NO	2. NO
6-36	INTL ORGN INDICTED ANT'S CAUSE #	2. NO	2. NO
6-37	CITED IN VIOLATION OF INTL LAW #	2. NO	2. NO
6-38	CITED BY I.O. FOR AGGRESSION #	2. NO	2. NO
6-40	ACCEPTED IO'S PROP. CEASEFIRE #	2. NO	2. NO
6-42	I.O. HAS IMPOSED SANCTIONS #	2. NO	2. NO
6-47	REG ORGN HAS IMPOSED SANCTIONS #	2. NO	2. NO
7-2	NO. ACTIV TROOPS AS PC OF POPN	1. 0.001-1.0	1. 0.001-1.0
7-7	PC POPN MOB'ZED FOR ACTIV DUTY	1. 0.001-1.0	1. 0.001-1.0
7-8	OTHER SIGNIF INTERNAL THREAT #	2. NO	2. NO
7-9	OTHER SIGNIF EXTERNAL THREAT #	2. NO	2. NO
7-23	NO. MORTARS AVAILABLE #	1. 0.04-1.0	1. 0.04-1.0
7-24	NO. ANTI-TANK WPNS. AVAILABLE	1. 0.01-1.0	1. 0.01-1.0
7-27	NO. HVY. CANNON AVAILABLE	1. 1.0-1.0	1. 1.0-1.0
7-36	NO. SUBMARINES AVAILABLE	1. 1.0-1.0	1. 1.0-1.0
7-38	NO. LANDING CRAFT AVAILABLE	1. 1.0-1.1	1. 1.0-1.1
8-3	REL'SHIP BET POL + MIL LEADERS	1. POL DOMINANT	1. POL DOMINANT
8-6	RECRUITMENT RATE INTO MILITARY	1. 1.0-2.0	1. 1.0-2.0
8-20	USE OF TERROR BY THIS ANT. IS	3. ABSENT	3. ABSENT
8-32	CIVN SECURITY V. CONV. ATTACK	8. 0 OR N/A	3. LOW
8-33	CIVN SECURITY V. GUERR ATTACK	8. 0 OR N/A	3. LOW
9-1	PC OF INDUSTRIAL CAPACITY LOST	1. 0.001-1.0	1. 0.001-1.0
9-3	TOTAL NO. CIVN POPULATION LOST #	8. 0 OR N/A	3. 50.0-59MIL
9-7	TOTAL CAS'TIES TO ALL FORCES	1. 1.0-1.2	2. 1.3-6.0
9-8	CASUALTY RATE FOR OWN FORCES	1. 1.0-2.0	1. 1.0-2.0
9-9	CASUALTY RATE FOR 3PTY FORCES	1. 0.1-1.0	1. 0.1-1.0
9-10	CASUALTY RATE FOR ALL FORCES	1. 1.0-2.0	1. 1.0-2.0
9-12	ATTRITION RATE FOR 3PTY FORCES	1. 0.1-1.0	1. 0.1-1.0

Item		Compound Response			

Species Type S2
("unilateral model: reality intrudes")

The factor pattern derives from

Ethiopian resistance (Ethiopian insurgents vs. Italian colonial administration)

Indonesia: independence (Indonesian insurgents vs. Dutch colonial administration)

Item	Description				
1-3	PAST POL. REL'SHIP BETW PARTYS		3. EXPLOITIVE		3. EXPLOITIVE
1-5	EFFECTIVE NATURE OF DISPUTE		1. COLONIAL		1. COLONIAL
1-7	IDEOLOGICAL DIFF. BETW PARTIES	# 1. EXTREME			1. EXTREME
1-8	CONTROL OF REAL ESTATE INVOLVD		1. YES		1. YES
1-9	SIZE OF AREA AT STAKE(TH SQ M)		4. 340.0-480.0		4. 340.0-480.0
1-10	SIZE OF POPN AT STAKE (THOUS.)	# 4. 10TH-76TH			4. 10TH-76TH
1-11	DISPUTE HAS BEEN TO REG'L ORGN	# 2. NO			2. NO
1-12	DISPUTE HAS BEEN TO INT'L ORGN		1. YES		1. YES
1-14	BASIS OF INTRO. TO INT'L ORGN		1. AGGRESSION		1. AGGRESSION
2-4	REGIM + GENL POPN OF SAME RACE		1. YES		2. NO
2-5	RACIAL HOMOGENEITY OF GENL POP	# 1. HOMOGENEOUS			1. HOMOGENEOUS
2-14	REAL ESTATE INVOLVED IS	# 1. IN CLMD BDY			1. IN CLMD BDY
2-15	PC OF ANT'S CLMD AREA INVOLVED	# 1. 1.0-1.0			1. 1.0-1.0
2-16	PC OF ANT'S CLMD POPN INVOLVED	# 1. 1.0-1.0			1. 1.0-1.0
2-17	PC OF INVOLVED AREA IN CONTROL	# 2. 1.5-9.0			1. 1.0-1.5
2-19	URBANIZATION		3. LOW		3. LOW
3-5	PER CAPITA INCOME		1. 1.0-2.1		1. 1.0-2.1
3-6	PC OF GNP IN AGRICULTURE		1. 1.0-2.0		1. 1.0-2.0
3-7	PC OF GNP IN DURABLE GOODS		1. 1.0-1.2		1. 1.0-1.2
3-8	PRODUCTION OF STEEL	# 1. 1.0-1.0			1. 1.0-1.0
4-1	EFFECTIVE STATUS OF GOVERNMENT		4. REBEL ORGN		2. COLONIAL ADM
4-4	EXECUTIVE STABILITY		1. 1.0-1.0		2. 1.5-2.0
4-6	STATUS OF EXECUTIVE		1. DOMINANT		2. STRONG
4-16	LEADERSHIP CHARISMA	# 1. PRONOUNCED			2. NEGLIGIBLE
4-23	INTEREST ARTIC'N BY INST'L GPS		1. POL SIGNIF		2. POL INSIGNIF
4-32	RECENT LEADERSHIP CRISIS		2. NO		2. NO
4-33	RECENT CHANGE IN LEADERSHIP	# 2. NO			2. NO
4-34	FORM RES ARE MAINSTAY OF REGIM	# 2. NO			1. YES
4-35	REGIM APPEARS MAINT BY FOR RES	# 2. NO			1. YES
4-36	POP. SUPPORT FOR REGIME'S OBJ.		1. HIGH		2. LOW
4-37	POP. SUPPORT FOR REGIM'S POLS.		1. HIGH		2. LOW
4-38	ATT. OF INTELLECTUALS TO REGIM	# 1. FAVORABLE			2. UNFAVORABLE
4-39	POST-DISPUTE EXPECT'N OF POPN		2. PESSIMISTIC		1. OPTIMISTIC
5-1	RECENTLY INVOLVED IN OTHER WAR		2. NO		1. YES
5-2	REGIME SEEKS OVERTHROW OF ADV.	# 1. YES			1. YES
5-3	INTEREST INVOLVED-IDEOLOGY		2. NO		2. NO
5-5	INTEREST INVOLVED-EST. POLICY		2. NO		1. YES
5-6	INTEREST INVOLVED-NAT'L CHAR.		1. YES		2. NO
5-7	INTEREST INVOLVED-PRESTIGE		2. NO		2. NO
5-10	INTEREST INVOLVED-INDEPENDENCE		1. YES		2. NO
5-12	INTEREST INVOLVED-CONT'D EXIS.	# 1. YES			1. YES
5-18	CAN ACCEPT LES THN STATED DMDS		2. NO		1. YES
5-20	PERCEIVED BALANCE OF WILL		1. FAVORABLE		3. UNFAVORABLE
5-23	DIST FM BORDER TO CONFL AREA	# 1. 1.0-1.0			1. 1.0-1.0
5-24	DIST FM CAPITAL TO CONFL AREA	# 1. 1.0-1.3			1. 1.0-1.3
5-26	TREATY EXPERIENCE WITH ADV.		2. UNSATISF'ORY		2. UNSATISF'ORY
5-29	CREDIBILITY OF COMMUNICATIONS	# 2. LOW			2. LOW
5-30	PRINCIPAL ATTEMPTS AT RESOL'N		4. POLITICAL		4. POLITICAL
5-32	BROUGHT DISPUTE TO INT'L ORGN		1. YES		2. NO
5-37	ESC LIKELY BRING GP AID TO ADV		2. NO		1. YES
5-38	P.O. RE ADV'S POL. INST'NS.		2. UNFAVORABLE		1. FAVORABLE
5-39	P.O. RE ADV'S SOCIAL INST'NS.		2. UNFAVORABLE		1. FAVORABLE
5-43	STATE OF WAR HAS BEEN DECLARED	# 2. NO			2. NO
6-4	IS ALLY OF G.P. ALLIED TO ADV.	# 2. NO			2. NO
6-14	REG'L ORG IS INV. ON THIS SIDE	# 2. NO			2. NO
6-17	A AUT ORG IS INV. ON THIS SIDE	# 2. NO			2. NO
6-18	A 3PTY IS PROVIDING POL. AID	# 1. YES			1. YES
6-24	ATT. OF 3PTY PUBLIC TO INV'MNT	# 1. FAVORABLE			1. FAVORABLE
6-25	AID TO ANT. HURTS 3PTY ECONOMY		2. NO		1. YES
6-30	SOME 3PTY OFFERED TO ARBITRATE		2. NO		2. NO
6-32	REGL ORGN OFFERED TO ARBITRATE	# 2. NO			2. NO
6-33	A G.P. OFFERED TO ARBITRATE		2. NO		2. NO
6-35	INT'L ORG'N UPHELD ANT'S CAUSE		1. YES		2. NO
6-36	INTL ORGN INDICTED ANT'S CAUSE		2. NO		1. YES
6-47	REG ORGN HAS IMPOSED SANCTIONS	# 2. NO			2. NO
7-4	MOBILIZATION OF RESERVES		5. TOTAL		5. TOTAL
7-8	OTHER SIGNIF INTERNAL THREAT	# 2. NO			2. NO
7-52	TRAINING FOR WEAPONS IN AID		8. 0 GR N/A		1. ADEQUATE
8-3	REL'SHIP BET POL + MIL LEADERS		1. POL DOMINANT		1. POL DOMINANT
8-17	CENTRALIZATION OF MIL. COMMAND		2. DE-CENTR'ZED		1. CENTRALIZED
8-30	SYMPATHY BETW POPN + OWN MIL.		1. SYMPATHETIC		2. ANTAGONISTIC

Species Type S3
("military model: a foregone conclusion enforced")

The factor pattern derives from

Spanish civil war (Republican government vs. Nationalist insurgents)

USSR-Iran (USSR vs. Iran)

Item	Description				
1-2A	TOPOGRAPHY OF CONFLICT AREA	# 2. MOUNTAINOUS			2. MOUNTAINOUS
1-2B	CLIMATE IN THE CONFLICT AREA		2. MODERATE		2. MODERATE
1-3	PAST POL. REL'SHIP BETW PARTYS	# 2. COMPETITIVE			2. COMPETITIVE
1-4	PAST MIL. REL'SHIP BETW PARTYS	# 2. RANDOM HOST.			2. RANDOM HOST.
1-7	IDEOLOGICAL DIFF. BETW PARTIES	# 1. EXTREME			1. EXTRCME
1-13	INTRODUCED TO INT'L ORGN BY A		1. ANTAGONIST		1. ANTAGONIST
1-14	BASIS OF INTRO. TO INT'L ORGN		1. AGGRESSION		1. AGGRESSION
2-3	RACIAL GROUPING OF ANTAGONIST		1. WHITE		1. WHITE
2-4	REGIM + GENL POPN OF SAME RACE	# 1. YES			1. YES
2-5	RACIAL HOMOGENEITY OF GENL POP	# 1. HOMOGENEOUS			1. HOMOGENEOUS
3-6	PC OF GNP IN AGRICULTURE		1. 1.0-2.0		1. 1.0-2.0
3-13	PROGRESSIVE TAX STRUCTURE	# 2. NO			2. NO

Item			Compound Response		

4-21	INTEREST ARTIC'N BY ANOMIC GPS		3.	NOT TOLERATD	1.	FREQUENT
4-22	INTEREST ARTIC'N BY ASSOC'L GP		2.	POL INSIGNIF	2.	POL INSIGNIF
4-23	INTEREST ARTIC'N BY INST'L GPS	#	2.	POL INSIGNIF	1.	POL SIGNIF
4-32	RECENT LEADERSHIP CRISIS		2.	NO	2.	NO
4-33	RECENT CHANGE IN LEADERSHIP	#	2.	NO	2.	NO

5-5	INTEREST INVOLVED-EST. POLICY	#	1.	YES	1.	YES
5-21	LIKELY OUTCOME IS NOW OBVIOUS		1.	YES	1.	YES
5-23	DIST FM BORDER TO CONFL AREA	#	1.	1.0-1.0	1.	1.0-1.0
5-28	RELIABILITY OF COMMUNICATIONS		1.	HIGH	1.	HIGH
5-29	CREDIBILITY OF COMMUNICATIONS		1.	HIGH	1.	HIGH
5-31	OFFERED TO RESOLVE CONST'ALLY	#	2.	NO	2.	LO
5-35	HAS OFFERED BI-LATERAL NEGOTNS	#	2.	NO	2.	NO
5-38	P.O. RE ADV'S POL. INST'NS.		2.	UNFAVORABLE	2.	UNFAVORABLE
5-39	P.O. RE ADV'S SOCIAL INST'NS.		2.	UNFAVORABLE	2.	UNFAVORABLE
5-41	P.O. RE ADV'S REL. INST'NS.		2.	UNFAVORABLE	2.	UNFAVORABLE
5-43	STATE OF WAR HAS BEEN DECLARED	#	2.	NO	2.	NO
5-46	AMNESTY DECL FOR ADV PERSONNEL		2.	NO	2.	NO

6-1	IS SEC'TY ALLY OF GREAT POWER		2.	NO	2.	NO
6-2	IS SEC'TY ALLY OF NON-G.P.		2.	NO	2.	NO
6-3	IS ALLY OF G.P. HOSTILE TO ADV		2.	NO	2.	NO
6-4	IS ALLY OF G.P. ALLIED TO ADV.	#	2.	NO	2.	NO
6-7	GP AID PROMISED IF ESC. OCCURS		2.	NO	2.	NO
6-8	GP DEF. FAC'TIES IN ANT'S AREA		2.	NO	2.	NO
6-13	INT'L ORG IS INV. ON THIS SIDE	#	2.	NO	2.	NO
6-30	SOME 3PTY OFFERED TO ARBITRATE		2.	NO	2.	NO
6-31	INTL ORGN OFFERED TO ARBITRATE		2.	NO	2.	NO
6-32	REGL ORGN OFFERED TO ARBITRATE	#	2.	NO	2.	NO
6-33	A G.P. OFFERED TO ARBITRATE		2.	NO	2.	NO
6-37	CITED IN VIOLATION OF INTL LAW	#	2.	NO	2.	NO
6-38	CITED BY I.O. FOR AGGRESSION	#	2.	NO	2.	NO
6-40	ACCEPTED IO'S PROP. CEASEFIRE	#	2.	NO	2.	NO
6-42	I.O. HAS IMPOSED SANCTIONS	#	2.	NO	2.	LO

| 7-6 | NO. TROOPS COMM AS PC TOT FRCS | | 1. | 0.7-1.0 | 1. | 0.7-1.0 |
| 7-13 | 3PTY TROOP AID SEEN LIKELY TO | | 2. | STAY SAME | 2. | STAY SAME |

8-4	UNITY WITHIN MILITARY COMMAND		1.	UNIFIED	1.	UNIFIED
8-7	METHOD OF MILITARY RECRUITMENT		2.	CONSCRIPTIVE	2.	CONSCRIPTIVE
8-17	CENTRALIZATION OF MIL. COMMAND	#	1.	CENTRALIZED	1.	CENTRALIZED
8-29	INTELL. IN ADV'S POLICY ORGANS		3.	INEFFECTIVE	3.	INEFFECTIVE
8-30	SYMPATHY BETW POPN + OWN MIL.	#	1.	SYMPATHETIC	1.	SYMPATHETIC

| 9-7 | TOTAL CAS'TIES TO ALL FORCES | | 1. | 1.0-1.2 | 1. | 1.0-1.2 |

---

e.
Settlement:
Higher-Order Factor Patterns

Artificial Genus

The factor pattern derives from

Cuba: "little" war of 1906 (Liberal party insurgents vs. Cuban government)

Cyprus: independence (Enosists vs. U.K. colonial administration)

Spanish civil war (Republican government vs. Nationalist insurgents)

USSR-Iran (USSR vs. Iran)

Family

The factor pattern derives from all six instances of settlement included in the analysis.

Item			Compound Response		

| 2-3 | RACIAL GROUPING OF ANTAGONIST | | 1. | WHITE | 1. | WHITE |
| 2-4 | REGIM + GENL POPN OF SAME RACE | # | 1. | YES | 1. | YES |

5-21	LIKELY OUTCOME IS NOW OBVIOUS		1.	YES	1.	YES
5-23	DIST FM BORDER TO CONFL AREA	#	1.	1.0-1.0	1.	1.0-1.0
5-28	RELIABILITY OF COMMUNICATIONS		1.	HIGH	1.	HIGH
5-29	CREDIBILITY OF COMMUNICATIONS		1.	HIGH	1.	HIGH

6-2	IS SEC'TY ALLY OF NON-G.P.		2.	NO	2.	NO
6-7	GP AID PROMISED IF ESC. OCCURS		2.	NO	2.	NO
6-13	INT'L ORG IS INV. ON THIS SIDE	#	2.	NO	2.	NO
6-31	INTL ORGN OFFERED TO ARBITRATE		2.	NO	2.	LO
6-32	REGL ORGN OFFERED TO ARBITRATE	#	2.	NO	2.	NO
6-37	CITED IN VIOLATION OF INTL LAW	#	2.	NO	2.	LO
6-38	CITED BY I.O. FOR AGGRESSION	#	2.	NO	2.	NO
6-40	ACCEPTED IO'S PROP. CEASEFIRE	#	2.	NO	2.	NO
6-42	I.O. HAS IMPOSED SANCTIONS	#	2.	NO	2.	NO

| 5-23 | DIST FM BORDER TO CONFL AREA | # | 1. | 1.0-1.0 | 1. | 1.0-1.0 |
| 6-32 | REGL ORGN OFFERED TO ARBITRATE | # | 2. | NO | 2. | NO |

Selected Bibliography

Part 1.
Substantive and
Methodological Sources

Abt, Clark C. "The Termination of General War." Ph.D. dissertation, Massachusetts Institute of Technology, Department of Political Science, 1965.

Almond, Gabriel A., and James S. Coleman, eds. *The Politics of the Developing Areas.* Princeton: Princeton University Press, 1960.

Angell, Robert C. "Discovering Paths to Peace." Chapter 4 in International Sociological Association, *The Nature of Conflict.* Tensions and Technology Series. Paris: UNESCO, 1957.

Banks, Arthur S., and Robert B. Textor. *A Cross-Polity Survey.* Cambridge, Mass.: The M.I.T. Press, 1963.

Bloomfield, Lincoln P., and Amelia C. Leiss. *Controlling Small Wars: A Strategy for the Seventies.* New York: Alfred A. Knopf, 1969.

Brinton, Crane. *The Anatomy of Revolution.* Rev. ed. Englewood Cliffs, N.J.: Prentice-Hall, 1952.

Cattell, Raymond B. *Factor Analysis.* New York: Harper & Brothers, 1952.

Claude, Inis L., Jr. *Power and International Relations.* New York: Random House, 1962.

————. "United Nations Use of Military Force." *Journal of Conflict Resolution*, vol. 7, no. 2 (June 1963).

Clausewitz, Karl von. *On War.* Translated by O. J. Matthijs Jolles. Washington, D.C.: Infantry Journal Press, 1950.

Coleman, James S. *Community Conflict.* New York: Free Press, 1957.

Conroe, Wallace W. "A Cross-National Analysis of the Impact of Modernization upon Political Stability." Master's thesis, San Diego State College, 1965.

Crozier, Brian. *The Rebels.* Boston: Beacon Press, 1960.

Cutwright, Phillips. "National Political Development: Measurement and Analysis." *American Sociological Review*, vol. 28, no. 2 (April 1963).

Davies, James C. "Toward a Theory of Revolution." *American Sociological Review*, vol. 27, no. 1 (February 1962).

Deitchman, Seymour J. *Limited War and American Defense Policy.* Cambridge, Mass.: The M.I.T. Press, 1964.

Denton, F. H. *Some Regularities in International Conflict, 1820–1949.* Santa Monica, Calif.: RAND Corporation, September 1965.

Deutsch, Karl. "External Involvement in Internal War." In *Internal War*, edited by Harry Eckstein. New York: Free Press, 1964.

————. *Nationalism and Social Communication.* Cambridge, Mass.: The M.I.T. Press, 1953.

_____, et al. "Political Community and the North Atlantic Area." In *International Political Communities: An Anthology.* Garden City, N.Y.: Anchor Books, 1966.

————. "Toward an Inventory of Basic Trends and Patterns in Comparative Government and International Politics." *American Political Science Review*, vol. 54, no. 1 (March 1960).

Deutsch, Morton. "Conflict and Its Resolution." Paper presented at meeting of the American Psychological Association, September 1965.

Eckstein, Harry. "Internal War: The Problem of Anticipation." Report submitted to the Research Group in Psychology and the Social Sciences, Smithsonian Institution, Washington, D.C., January 1962.

————. "Introduction: Toward the Theoretical Study of Internal War." In *Internal War*, edited by Harry Eckstein. New York: Free Press, 1964.

Edwards, L. P. *Natural History of Revolution*. Chicago: University of Chicago Press, 1927.

Feierabend, Ivo K., and Rosalind L. Feierabend. "Aggressive Behavior within Polities, 1948–62: A Cross-National Study." *Journal of Conflict Resolution*, vol. 10, no. 3 (September 1966).

Fruchter, Benjamin. *Introduction to Factor Analysis*. New York: D. Van Nostrand Company, 1954.

Furniss, Edgar, S., Jr. "Memorandum on Interstate Conflicts." Paper prepared for the Carnegie Endowment for International Peace, New York, December 1955.

Gregg, Philip M., and Arthur S. Banks. "Dimensions of Political Systems: Factor Analysis of *A Cross-Polity Survey*." *American Political Science Review*, vol. 59, no. 3 (September 1965).

Grivas, George. *General Grivas on Guerrilla Warfare*. Translated by A. A. Pallis. New York: Frederick A. Praeger, 1965.

Gross, Felix. *The Seizure of Political Power in a Century of Revolutions*. New York: Philosophical Library, 1958.

Guevara, Ernesto Che. *Guerrilla Warfare*. New York: Monthly Review Press, 1961.

Gurr, Ted. "The Genesis of Violence: A Multivariate Theory of the Preconditions of Civil Strife." Ph.D. dissertation, New York University, 1965.

Haas, Michael. "Social Change and National Aggressiveness, 1900–1960." In *Quantitative International Politics: Insights and Evidence*, edited by J. David Singer. New York: Free Press, 1968.

Halperin, Morton H. *Limited War in the Nuclear Age*. New York: John Wiley & Sons, 1963.

Hemingway, Peter W. "Multiple Agreement Analysis." Ph.D. dissertation, Michigan State University, Department of Psychology, 1961.

Hoffmann, Stanley. *The State of War*. New York: Frederick A. Praeger, 1965.

Holsti, K. J. "Resolving International Conflicts: A Taxonomy of Behavior and Some Figures on Procedures." *Journal of Conflict Resolution*, vol. 10, no. 3 (September 1966).

———. "The Use of Objective Criteria for the Measurement of International Tension Levels." *Background*, vol. 7, no. 2 (August 1963).

Holsti, Ole, Robert C. North, and Richard A. Brody. "Perception and Action in the 1914 Crisis." In *Quantitative International Politics: Insights and Evidence*, edited by J. David Singer. New York: Free Press, 1968.

Huntington, Samuel P. *Instability at the Non-Strategic Level of Conflict.* Institute for Defense Analyses, Special Studies Group, Study Memorandum no. 2. Washington, D.C., 1961.

Janos, A. C. "Unconventional Warfare: Framework and Analysis." *World Politics,* vol. 15, no. 4 (July 1963).

Johnson, Chalmers. *Revolution and the Social System.* Hoover Institution Study 3. Stanford, Calif.: Stanford University Press, 1964.

Kahn, Herman. *On Escalation: Metaphors and Scenarios.* New York: Hudson Institute, 1965.

Katz, Daniel. "Group Process and Social Integration: A System Analysis of Two Movements of Social Protest." *Journal of Social Issues,* vol. 23, no. 1 (January 1967).

Kelly, E. Lowell, and James C. Lingoes. "Data Processing in Psychological Research." In *Computer Applications in the Behavioral Sciences*, edited by Harold Borko. Englewood Cliffs, N.J.: Prentice-Hall, 1962.

Knorr, Klaus. *The War Potential of Nations.* Princeton: Princeton University Press, 1956.

———, and Thornton Read, eds. *Limited Strategic War.* New York: Frederick A. Praeger, 1962.

Landhear, B., ed. *Some Sociological Aspects of the Phenomenon "War" and Their Possible Interpretations.* The Hague: Research Center for International Peace, 1965.

Lasswell, Harold D., Daniel Lerner, and Ithiel de Sola Pool. *The Comparative Study of Symbols.* Stanford, Calif.: Stanford University Press, 1952.

Lerner, Daniel. *The Passing of Traditional Society: Modernizing the Middle East.* Glencoe, Ill.: Free Press, 1958.

Machiavelli, Niccolo. "*The Art of War.*" In *Chief Works and Others.* Translated by Allan Gilbert. Durham, N.C.: Duke University Press, 1965.

Mack, Raymond W., and Richard C. Snyder, "The Analysis of Social Conflict — Toward an Overview and Synthesis." *Journal of Conflict Resolution*, vol. 1, no. 1 (March 1957).

Mao Tse-tung. *Guerrilla Warfare.* Translated by Samuel B. Griffith. New York: Frederick A. Praeger, 1961.

Marshall, Charles Burton. "Foresight and Blindness in Foreign Policy." In *Conflict and Cooperation among Nations*, edited by Ivo. D. Duchacek. New York: Holt, Rinehart, and Winston, 1960.

McClelland, Charles. "Action Structures and Communication in Two International Crises: Quemoy and Berlin." *Background*, vol. 7, no. 4 (February 1964).

McQuitty, Louis L. "Agreement Analysis: Classifying Persons by Predominant Patterns of Responses." *British Journal of Statistical Psychology*, vol. 9, no. 1 (May 1956).

—————. "A Mutual Development of Some Typological Theories and Pattern-Analytic Methods." *Educational and Psychological Measurement*, vol. 27, no. 1 (Spring 1967), pp. 21–46.

Meehl, P. E. "Configural Scoring." *Journal of Consulting Psychology*, vol. 14, no. 3 (June 1950).

Merritt, Richard L., and Stein Rokkan, eds. *Comparing Nations: The Uses of Quantitative Data in Cross-National Research*. New Haven: Yale University Press, 1966.

Morgenthau, Hans J. "American and Soviet Alliance Policies." In *Conflict and Cooperation among Nations*, edited by Ivo D. Duchacek. New York: Holt, Rinehart, and Winston, 1960.

—————. *Politics among Nations*. 3rd ed. New York: Alfred A. Knopf, 1962.

Moses, Lincoln E., et al. "Scaling Data on Inter-Nation Action." *Science*, vol. 156 (May 26, 1967).

North, Robert C. "Perception and Action in the 1914 Crisis." *Journal of International Affairs*, vol. 21, no. 1 (1967).

—————. "When Deterrence Fails." Paper presented at meeting of the American Political Science Association, September 1963.

Osgood, Robert E. *Limited War: The Challenge to American Strategy*. Chicago: University of Chicago Press, 1957.

Phelps, John, et al. *Studies on Accidental War*. Institute for Defense Analyses, Economic and Political Studies Division, Research Paper P–6. Washington, D.C., 1963.

Pool, Ithiel de Sola. "Memorandum on Interstate Conflicts." Paper prepared for the Carnegie Endowment for International Peace, New York, February 1956.

Pye, Lucian W. *Guerrilla Communism in Malaya*. Princeton: Princeton University Press, 1956.

—————. "The Roots of Insurgency and the Commencement of Rebellions." In *Internal War*, edited by Harry Eckstein. New York: Free Press, 1964.

Richardson, Lewis F. *Arms and Insecurity: A Mathematical Study of the Causes and Origins of War*. Edited by N. Rashevsky and E. Trucco. Pittsburgh, Pa.: Boxwood Press, 1960.

—————. *Statistics of Deadly Quarrels*. Edited by Quincy Wright and C. C. Lienau. Pittsburgh, Pa.: Boxwood Press, 1960.

Rogers, Everett M. *Diffusion of Innovations*. New York: Free Press, 1962.

Rummel, Rudolph J. "Dimensions of Conflict Behavior within Nations, 1946–59." *Journal of Conflict Resolution*, vol. 10, no. 1 (March 1966).

—————. "The Relationship Between National Attributes and Foreign Conflict Behavior." In *Quantitative International Politics: Insights and Evidence*, edited by J. David Singer. New York: Free Press, 1968.

————. "A Social Field Theory of Foreign Conflict Behavior." *Peace Research Society (International), Papers,* no. 6, (1966).

————, et al. *Dimensions of Nations.* Evanston, Ill.: Northwestern University Press, 1967.

Russett, Bruce. "Calculus of Deterrence." *Journal of Conflict Resolution,* vol. 7, no. 2 (June 1963).

————, et al. *World Handbook of Political and Social Indicators.* New Haven: Yale University Press, 1964.

Schelling, Thomas C. *The Strategy of Conflict.* Cambridge, Mass.: Harvard University Press, 1963.

Singer, J. David. *Deterrence, Arms Control, and Disarmament: Toward a Synthesis in National Security Policy.* Cleveland: Ohio State University Press, 1962.

Singer, J. David, and Melvin Small. "Alliance Aggregation and the Onset of War, 1815–1945." In *Quantitative International Politics: Insights and Evidence*, edited by J. David Singer. New York: Free Press, 1968.

————. *The Wages of War.* New York: John Wiley & Sons, forthcoming.

Smoker, Paul. "Nation State Escalation and International Integration." *Journal of Peace Research*, vol. 1 (1967).

Sorensen, John L., and David K. Pack. "Applied Analysis of Unconventional Warfare." NOTS TP 3458. China Lake, Calif.: U.S. Naval Ordnance Test Station, 1964.

Sorokin, Pitrim A. *Man and Society in Calamity.* New York: E. P. Dutton & Company, 1942.

————. *The Sociology of Revolution.* Philadelphia, Pa.: J. P. Lippincott, 1925.

Stone, Julius. "Memorandum on Interstate Conflicts." Paper prepared for the Carnegie Endowment for International Peace, New York, April 1956.

Stone, Lawrence. "Theories of Revolution." *World Politics*, vol. 18, no. 2 (January 1966).

Taylor, A. J. P. "Causes of International Conflict." Paper prepared for the Carnegie Endowment for International Peace, New York, February 1956.

————. *The Origins of the Second World War.* New York: Atheneum, 1961.

Tanter, Raymond. "Dimensions of Conflict Behavior within and between Nations, 1958–60." *Journal of Conflict Resolution*, vol. 10, no. 1 (March 1966).

Thucydides. *The History of the Peloponnesian Wars.* Translated by Richard Crawley. London: J. M. Dent, 1910.

Thurstone, L. L. *Multiple Factor Analysis.* Chicago: University of Chicago Press, 1947.

Trinquier, Roger. *Modern Warfare: A French View of Counterinsurgency.* New York: Frederick A. Praeger, 1963.

Williams, Robin M., Jr. *The Reduction of Intergroup Tensions.* New York: Social Science Research Council, 1947.

Wright, Quincy. *The Causes of War and the Conditions of Peace.* Graduate Institute of International Studies, Geneva, Publication no. 14. New York: Longmans, Green & Co., 1935.

————. "Criteria for Judging the Relevance of Researches on the Problems of Peace." In *Research for Peace*, by Quincy Wright et al. Oslo: Institute for Social Research, 1954.

————. "The Escalation of International Conflicts." *Journal of Conflict Resolution*, vol. 9, no. 4 (December 1965).

————. "Memorandum on Interstate Conflicts." Paper prepared for the Carnegie Endowment for International Peace, New York, December 1955.

————. *The Study of International Relations.* New York: Appleton-Century-Crofts, 1955.

————. *A Study of War.* 2nd ed. Chicago: University of Chicago Press, 1964.

Wrigley, Charles. "The University Computing Center." In *Computer Applications in the Behavioral Sciences*, edited by Harold Borko. Englewood Cliffs, N.J.: Prentice-Hall, 1962.

Zinnes, Dina, Robert C. North, and Howard E. Koch, Jr. "Capability, Threat, and the Outbreak of War." In *International Politics and Foreign Policy*, edited by James Rosenau. New York: Free Press, 1961.

Zubin, J., "A Technique for Measuring Like-Mindedness." *Journal of Abnormal and Social Psychology*, vol. 33, no. 4 (October 1938).

Part 2.
Selected Data Sources
General References

Banks, Arthur S., and Robert B. Textor. *A Cross-Polity Survey.* Cambridge, Mass.: The M.I.T. Press, 1963.

Coward, H. Roberts. "Military Technology in Developing Areas." Cambridge, Mass.: M.I.T., Center for International Studies, 1964.

Economist. London.

Encyclopaedia Britannica. Various editions.

Encyclopaedia Britannica Book of the Year. Annual. 1913+.

Ewing, Laurence L., and Robert C. Sellers, eds. *Reference Handbook of the Armed Forces of the World.* Annual. Washington, D.C.: Robert C. Sellers and Associates, 1966+.

Green, William, and J. Fricker. *The Air Forces of the World.* New York: Hanover House, 1958.

Green, William, and Dennis Punnett. *The MacDonald World Air Power Guide.* New York: Doubleday & Company, 1963.

Hovey, Harold A. *United States Military Assistance.* New York: Frederick A. Praeger, 1965.

Institute for Strategic Studies, London. *Adelphi Papers.*

————. *The Military Balance.* Annual. 1959–60+.

Institute of Electoral Research. *Parliaments and Electoral Systems: A World Handbook.* London, 1962.

————. *A Review of Elections.* Annual. London, 1954 +.

International Monetary Fund. *International Financial Statistics.* Annual. Washington, D.C., 1948 +.

Jane's All the World's Aircraft. Annual. London: Sampson, Low, Marston & Co., 1909 +.

Jane's Fighting Ships. Annual. London: Sampson, Low, Marston & Co., 1898 +.

Johnson, George, and Hans Bert Lockhoven. *International Armament.* 2 vols. Cologne: International Small Arms Publishers, 1965.

Keesing's Contemporary Archives. London: Keesing's Ltd., July 1, 1931 +.

League of Nations. Secretariat. *Statistical Yearbook of the League of Nations.* Geneva, 1926 +.

————. *Armaments Year-book: General and Statistical Information.* Geneva, 1924 +.

New York Times.

Organization for Economic Cooperation and Development. *Statistics of National Accounts, 1950–1961.* Paris, 1964.

Russett, Bruce, et al. *World Handbook of Political and Social Indicators.* New Haven: Yale University Press, 1964.

Statesman's Yearbook. Annual. London, 1864 +.

Statistical Abstracts and *Statistical Yearbooks*, by countries.

Times (London).

United Nations. Educational, Scientific, and Cultural Organization. *Basic Facts and Figures: International Statistics Relating to Education, Culture, and Mass Communications.* Annual. Paris, 1950–1962.

————. *Statistical Yearbook.* Paris, 1963 +.

United Nations. Food and Agricultural Organization. *Production Yearbook.* New York, 1947 +.

————. *Trade Yearbook.* New York, 1947 +.

United Nations, Statistical Office. *Demographic Yearbook.* New York, 1948 +.

————. *Statistical Yearbook.* New York, 1948 +.

U.S. Bureau of the Census. *Statistical Abstract of the United States.* Washington, D.C., 1878 +.

U.S. Department of Defense. Director of Military Assistance. *Military Assistance Programs: Programs and Deliveries, FY 1950– FY 1961.* Washington, D. C., May 1961.

"The World Today." *Chatham House Review.* Monthly. London: Royal Institute of International Affairs, July 1945 +.

Wright, Quincy. *A Study of War.* 2nd ed. Chicago: University of Chicago Press, 1964. Appendixes.

Algeria-Morocco Conflict, 1962–1963

Ashford, Douglas E. "The Irredentist Appeal in Morocco and Mauritania." *Western Political Quarterly*, vol. 15, no. 4 (December 1962).

————. *Political Change in Morocco.* Princeton: Princeton University Press, 1961.

————. "Politics and Violence in Morocco." *Middle East Journal*, vol. 13, no. 1 (Winter 1959).

Brace, Richard M. *Morocco, Algeria, Tunisia.* Englewood Cliffs, N.J.: Prentice-Hall, 1964.

Husson, Philippe. *La question des frontières terrestres du Maroc.* Paris: Institut d'Etudes Politiques, 1960.

Kitchen, Helen, ed. *A Handbook of African Affairs.* New York: Frederick A. Praeger, 1964.

Louis, William H. "Rural Administration in Morocco." *Middle East Journal*, vol. 14, no. 1 (Winter 1960).

Mikesell, Marvin W. *Northern Morocco: A Cultural Geography.* Berkeley and Los Angeles: University of California Press, 1961.

Revue du Ministre des Affaires Etranges (Rabat, Morocco), no. 10 (November 1963).

Wild, Patricia Berko. "The Organization of African Unity and the Algerian-Moroccan Border Conflict: A Study of New Machinery for Peacekeeping and for the Peaceful Settlement of Disputes among African States." *International Organization*, vol. 20, no. 1 (Winter 1966).

Zartman, I. William. "The Organization of African Unity and Territorial Disputes." Mimeographed. 1966.

Angolan Insurgency, 1961

Davidson, Basil. "Phase Two in Angola." *West Africa*, no. 2382 (January 26, 1963).

Duffy, James. *Portuguese Africa.* Cambridge, Mass.: Harvard University Press, 1959.

Ehnmark, Anders, and Per Wastburg. *Angola and Mozambique: The Case Against Portugal.* London: Pall Mall Press, 1963.

Institute of Race Relations. *Angola: A Symposium.* London: Oxford University Press, 1962.

Kitchen, Helen, ed. *A Handbook of African Affairs.* New York: Frederick A. Praeger, 1964.

Larcier, Henri. "The Union of Angolese Populations (UPA)." *Présence Africaine*, vol. 14/15, no. 42/43 (third quarter 1962).

Marcum, John. "The Angola Rebellion: Status Report." *Africa Report*, vol. 9, no. 2 (February 1964).

Okuma, Thomas. *Angola in Ferment: The Background and Prospects of Angolan Nationalism.* Boston: Beacon Press, 1962.

Tam-Tam. "Dossier sur Angola." *Revue des Etudiants Catholiques Africains*, no. 304 (1961).

United Nations. General Assembly. *Report of the United Nations High Commission on Refugees.* A/5511/Rev. 1. New York, 1963.

United Nations Review, vols. 7–11 (1960–1964) passim.

Westwood, Andrew. "The Politics of Revolt in Angola." *African Report*, vol. 7, no. 10 (November 1962).

Wohlgemuth, Patricia. "The Portuguese Territories and the United Nations." *International Conciliation*, no. 545 (November 1963).

Cuba: "Little" War of August 1906

Chapman, Charles E. *A History of the Cuban Republic: A Study in Hispanic American Politics.* New York: Charles Scribner's Sons, 1927.

Collazo, Enrique. *Cuba: Intervenida.* Havana: C. Martínez y Ca., 1910.

————. *La revolución de agosto de 1906.* Havana: C. Martínez y Ca., 1907.

Fitzgibbon, Russell H. *Cuba and the U.S.: 1900–1935.* Menasha, Wis.: George Banta Publishing Co., 1936.

Lieuwen, Edwin. *Arms and Politics in Latin America.* New York: Frederick A. Praeger, 1960.

Lockmiller, David A. *Magoon in Cuba: A History of the Second Intervention, 1906–1909.* Chapel Hill: University of North Carolina Press, 1938.

Magoon, Charles E. *Report of the Provincial Administration from October 13, 1906, to December 1, 1908.* 2 vols. Havana: Rambla y Bouza, 1908.

Marrero, Levi. *Elementos de geografía de Cuba.* Havana: Minerva, 1946.

Martínez Ortiz, Rafael. *Cuba: los primeros años de independencia.* 3rd ed. Vols. 1 and 6. Paris: Le Livre Libre, 1924.

Mecham, J. Lloyd. *A Survey of U.S.–Latin American Relations.* Boston: Houghton Mifflin Co., 1965.

Olmsted, Victor H., and Henry Gannett, eds. *Cuba: Population, History and Resources, 1907.* Washington, D.C.: U.S. Bureau of the Census, 1909.

Puri, Manual C., ed. *La revolución de agosto: historia de un corresponsal por Arturo F. Sainz de la Peña.* Havana: Imprenta La Prueba, 1909.

Roig de Leuchsenring, Emilio. "La enmienda Platt." In *La sociedad cubana de derecho Internacional.* Annual. Havana, 1922+.

Root, Elihu. *The Military and Colonial Policy of the U.S.* Cambridge, Mass.: Harvard University Press, 1916.

Sainz de la Peña, Arturo F., *La revolución de agosto: historia de un corresponsal.* Havana: Imprenta La Prueba, 1909.

Taft, William H., and Robert Bacon. "Cuban Pacification." Excerpt from the Report of the Secretary of War, 1906. Washington, D.C.: Government Printing Office, 1907.

U.S. Department of War. *Report of Major General Wood, Governor of Cuba*. Washington, D.C., 1903.

Varela Zequeira, Eduardo. *La política en 1905: o episodios de una lucha electoral*. Havana: Rambla y Bouza, 1905.

Cuba: Bay of Pigs, 1961

Draper, Theodore. *Castro's Revolution: Myths and Realities*. New York: Frederick A. Praeger, 1962.

Institute for Strategic Studies. *The Communist Bloc and the Western Alliances: The Military Balance, 1962–1963*. London, November 1962.

Johnson, Haynes. *The Bay of Pigs: The Leaders' Story of Brigade 2506*. New York: W. W. Norton, 1964.

Light, Robert E., and Carl Marzani. *Cuba vs. the C.I.A.* New York: Marzani and Munsell, 1961.

Murphy, Charles J. V. "Cuba: The Record Set Straight." *Fortune*, September 1961.

Phillips, R. Hart. *The Cuban Dilemma*. New York: Ivan Oblensky, 1962.

A Press Digest on U.S.-Cuba Relations, 1957–1961. Cambridge, Mass.: Press Digest, 1961.

Schlesinger, Arthur M., Jr. *A Thousand Days: John F. Kennedy in the White House*. Boston: Houghton Mifflin Co., 1965.

Smith, Earl E. T. *The Fourth Floor*. New York: Random House, 1962.

Smith, Jean Edward. "The Unanswered Questions. . . ." *Nation*, April 13, 1964.

Smith, Robert F. *What Happened in Cuba?* New York: Twayne, 1963.

Sorensen, Theodore C. *Kennedy*. New York: Harper & Row, 1965.

Szulc, Tad, and Karl Ernest Meyer. *The Cuban Invasion: Chronicle of a Disaster*. New York: Ballantine Books, 1962.

Wohlstetter, Albert, and Roberta Wohlstetter. "Controlling the Risks in Cuba." *Adelphi Paper*, no. 17. London: Institute for Strategic Studies, 1964.

Cyprus: War of Independence, 1952–1960, and Cyprus: Internal Conflict, 1959–1964

Adams, T., and A. Cottrell. "The Cyprus Conflict." *Orbis*, vol. 8, no. 1 (Spring 1964).

Boyd, James M. "Cyprus: Episode in Peacekeeping," *International Organization*, vol. 20, no. 1 (Winter 1966).

Crawshaw, Nancy. "Cyprus: The Closed Issue." *World Today*, vol. 10, no. 9 (September 1954).

———. "Cyprus: Collapse of the Zurich Agreement." *World Today*, vol. 10, no. 8 (August 1954).

———. "Cyprus: Conflict and Resolution." *World Today*, vol. 15, no. 4 (April 1959).

———. "The Cyprus Deadlock." *World Today*, vol. 13, no. 4 (April 1957).

———. "The Republic of Cyprus: From the Zurich Agreement to Independence." *World Today*, vol. 16, no. 12 (December 1960).

———. "Restoring Order in Cyprus." *World Today*, vol. 12, no. 4 (April 1956).

———. "Some Wider Aspects of the Cyprus Problem." *World Today*, vol. 11, no. 10 (October 1955).

———. "The Uneasy Truce in Cyprus." *World Today,* vol. 13, no. 10 (October 1957).

Durrell, Lawrence. *Bitter Lemons*. New York: E. P. Dutton & Company, 1957.

Foley, Charles. *Legacy of Strife: Cyprus from Rebellion to Civil War*. Baltimore: Penguin Books, 1964.

Great Britain. Colonial Office. *Cyprus Report for the Year 1955*. London, 1956.

Grivas, George. *The Memoirs of General Grivas*. Edited by Charles Foley. London: Longmans, Green & Co., 1964.

———. *General Grivas on Guerrilla Warfare*. New York: Frederick A. Praeger, 1965.

Mayes, Stanley. *Cyprus and Makarios*. London: Putnam, 1960.

Royal Institute of International Affairs. "Cyprus: The Dispute and the Settlement." *Chatham House Memoranda*. London, 1959.

Stephens, Robert. *Cyprus: A Place of Arms*. London: Pall Mall Press, 1966.

U.S. Department of the Army. *U.S. Army Area Handbook for Cyprus*. Washington, D.C., 1964.

Windsor, Philip. "NATO and the Cyprus Crisis." *Adelphi Paper*, no. 14. London: Institute for Strategic Studies, November 1964.

Xydis, Stephen G. "Toward 'Toil and Moil' in Cyprus." *Middle East Journal*, vol. 20, no. 1 (Winter 1966).

Ethiopian Resistance, 1937–1941

Allen, W. E. D. *Guerrilla War in Abyssinia*. Middlesex: Penguin Books, 1943.

Badoglio, Pietro. *The War in Abyssinia.* London: Methuen, 1937.

Great Britain. War Office. *The Abyssinian Campaigns.* London: H. M. Stationery Office, 1942.

Marcus, Harold. "Ethiopia (1937–1941)." Task NUMISMATICS. Washington, D.C.: American University, Special Operations Research Office, 1966.

Renaud, J. F. "Ambush in Ethiopia." *Living Age*, vol. 355, no. 4464 (September 1938).

Steer, George L. *Caesar in Abyssinia*. London: Hodden & Stoughton, 1936.

———. *Sealed and Delivered*. London: Hodden & Stoughton, 1942.

Ethiopia-Somalia Conflict, 1960–1964

Bell, M. J. V. "Military Assistance to Independent African States." *Adelphi Paper*, no. 15. London: Institute for Strategic Studies, December 1964.

Brown, Neville, and W. F. Gutteridge. "The African Military Balance." *Adelphi Paper*, no. 12. London: Institute for Strategic Studies, August 1964.

Castagno, Alphonso A., Jr. "Conflicts in the Horn of Africa." *Orbis*, vol. 4, no. 2 (Summer 1960).

_____ "Somalia." *International Conciliation,* no. 522 (March 1959).

———. "The Somali-Kenyan Controversy: Implications for the Future." *Journal of Modern African Studies*, vol. 2, no. 2 (July 1964).

Drysdale, John. *The Somali Dispute.* New York: Frederick A. Praeger, 1964.

Greenfield, Richard. *Ethiopia: A New Political History.* London: Pall Mall Press, 1965.

Gurr, Ted. "Tensions in the Horn of Africa." Appendix 3 in *World Politics and Tension Areas*, edited by Felix Green. New York: New York University Press, 1966.

Lewis, I. M. *The Modern History of Somaliland, from Nation to State.* London: Weidenfeld and Nicolson, 1965.

———. "Pan-Africanism and Pan-Somalism," *Journal of Modern African Studies,* vol. 1, no. 2 (June 1963).

Lipsky, George A., et al. *U.S. Army Handbook for Ethiopia.* Washington, D.C.: U.S. Department of the Army, 1964.

Mariam, Mesfin Wolde. "The Background of the Ethio-Somalian Boundary Dispute." *Journal of Modern African Studies*, vol. 2, no. 2 (July 1964).

Reyner, Anthony S. "Somalia: The Problems of Independence." *Middle East Journal*, vol. 14, no. 3 (Summer 1960).

Somalia. Information Service. *The Somali Peninsula: A New Light on Imperial Motives.* London, 1962.

Greek Insurgency, 1944–1949

Barker, Elizabeth. *Macedonia: Its Place in Balkan Power Politics.* London: Royal Institute of International Affairs, 1950.

Burks, R. V. *The Dynamics of Communism in Eastern Europe.* Princeton: Princeton University Press, 1961.

Chamberlin, W. C., and J. D. Iams. "The Rise and Fall of the Greek Communist Party." Typescript. Washington, D.C.: U.S. Department of State, Foreign Service Institute, June 1963.

Condit, D. M. "Case Study in Guerrilla War: Greece during World War II." Washington, D.C.: The American University, Special Operations Research Office, 1961.

Djilas, Milovan. *Conversations with Stalin.* New York: Harcourt, Brace & World, 1962.

Howard, Harry N. *Greece and the United Nations, 1946–1949: A Summary Record. Report of the U.N. Special Committee on the*

Balkans: A Chronology. Pub. 3645, International Organization and Conference Series III, 40. Washington, D.C.: U.S. Department of State, 1949.

Kousoulas, D. George. *Revolution and Defeat: The Story of the Greek Communist Party.* London: Oxford University Press, 1965.

McNeill, William H. *Greece: American Aid in Action, 1947–56.* New York: Twentieth Century Fund, 1957.

Murray, J. C. "The Anti-Bandit War." *Marine Corps Gazette*, no. 38 (January–May 1954).

Papagos, Alexander. "Guerrilla Warfare." *Foreign Affairs*, vol. 30, no. 2 (January 1952).

United Nations. General Assembly. *Report of the United Nations Special Committee on the Balkans.* Official Records: Sixth Session, supplement no. 11–A/1857. New York, 1951.

United Nations. Security Council. *Report of the Commission of Investigation Concerning Greek Frontier Incidents to the Security Council.* S/360, May 27, 1947. Vols. 1–3. New York, 1947.

U.S. Department of State. *Assistance to Greece and Turkey.* Eighth Report to Congress, period ending June 30, 1949. Pub. no. 3674. Washington, D.C., 1949.

Zacharakis, E. E. "Lessons Learned from Anti-Guerrilla War in Greece (1946–1949)." *General Military Review* (London), July 1960.

India-China Conflict, 1962

Bains, J. S. *India's International Disputes.* New York: Asia Publishing House, 1962.

Chakravarti, P. C. *India's China Policy.* Bloomington: Indiana University Press, 1962.

Dutt, Vidya Prakash. *China and the World.* New York: Frederick A. Praeger, 1964.

Ginsburgs, George, and Michael Mathos. *Communist China and Tibet.* The Hague: Martinus Nijhoff, 1964.

India. Ministry of Information and Broadcasting. *India 1963.* Delhi, 1963.

Palmer, Norman D. *South Asia and United States Policy.* Boston: Houghton Mifflin Co., 1966.

Satyapalan, C. N. "The Sino-Indian Border Conflict." *Orbis*, vol. 8 (1964), no. 2.

Tinker, Hugh. *India and Pakistan: A Political Analysis.* New York: Frederick A. Praeger, 1962.

Van Eekelen, W. F. *Indian Foreign Policy and the Border Dispute with China.* The Hague: Martinus Nijhoff, 1964.

Varma, Shanti Prasad. *Struggle for the Himalayas.* Jullundur: University Publishers, 1965.

Wilcox, Wayne A. *India, Pakistan and the Rise of China.* New York: Walker, 1964.

Indonesia: War of
Independence, 1945–1949

Brackman, Arnold C. *Indonesian Communism*. New York: Frederick A. Praeger, 1963.

Crockett, Frederick E. "How the Trouble Began in Java." *Harper's Magazine*, April 1946.

Djajadiningrat, Idurs N. "The Beginnings of the Indonesian-Dutch Negotiations and the Hoge Veluwe Talks." Ithaca, N.Y.: Cornell University, Modern Indonesia Project, 1958.

Emerson, Rupert. "Reflections on the Indonesian Case." *World Politics*, vol. 1, no. 1 (October 1948).

Feith, Herbert. *The Decline of Constitutional Democracy in Indonesia*. Ithaca, N.Y.: Cornell University Press, 1962.

Fischer, Louis. *The Story of Indonesia*. New York: Harper, 1959.

Jureidini, P., et al. *Casebook on Insurgency and Revolutionary Warfare: 23 Summary Accounts*. Section I: "Southeast Asia." Washington, D.C.: The American University, Special Operations Research Office, 1962.

Kahin, George. "Indonesia." In *Major Governments of Asia*, edited by George Kahin. Ithaca, N.Y.: Cornell University, 1963.

Nasution, Abdul H. *Fundamentals of Guerrilla Warfare*. New York: Frederick A. Praeger, 1965.

Taylor, Alastair M. *Indonesian Independence and the United Nations*. Ithaca, N.Y.: Cornell University Press, 1960.

United Nations. Security Council. *First Interim Report of the United Nations Commission for Indonesia to the Security Council*. S/1373/Rev. 1. New York, 1951.

———. *Fourth Interim Report of the Committee of Good Offices on the Indonesian Question to the Security Council*. S/1085. New York, 1950.

———. *Report by the Consular Commission at Batavia to the Security Council*. S/586/Rev. 1. New York, 1949.

Van der Kroef, Justus M. "The Indonesian Revolution in Retrospect." *World Politics*, vol. 3, no. 3 (April 1951).

Wehl, David. *The Birth of Indonesia*. London: George Allen & Unwin, 1948.

Wolf, Charles, Jr. *The Indonesian Story*. New York: John Day, 1948.

Indonesia-Malaysia Conflict,
1963–1965

Brackman, Arnold. *Southeast Asia's Second Front*. New York: Frederick A. Praeger, 1966.

Françillon, Jacques. "Sukarno's War Against Malaysia." *New Republic*, April 19, 1965.

Gordon, Bernard K. *The Dimensions of Conflict in Southeast Asia*. Englewood Cliffs, N.J.: Prentice-Hall, 1966.

———. "The Potential for Indonesian Expansionism." *Pacific Affairs,* vol. 36, no. 4 (Winter 1963).

Gourley, B. I. S. "Struggle in Sarawak." *Marine Corps Gazette*, December 1965.

Hanna, Willard A. *The Formation of Malaysia*. New York: American Universities Field Staff, 1964.

Kahin, George. "Malaysia and Indonesia." *Pacific Affairs*, vol. 37, no. 3 (Fall 1964).

Means, Gordon P. "Malaysia—A New Federation in Southeast Asia." *Pacific Affairs*, vol. 36, no. 2 (Summer 1963).

Palmier, Leslie. *Indonesia*. New York: Walker, 1966.

Pluvier, Jan M. *Confrontations: A Study in Indonesian Politics*. Kuala Lumpur: Oxford University Press, 1965.

Van der Kroef, Justus. "Indonesian Communism and the Changing Balance of Power." *Pacific Affairs*, vol. 37, no. 4 (Winter 1964).

Israel-Egypt Conflict, 1956

Barker, Alan. *Suez: The Seven Day War*. New York: Frederick A. Praeger, 1964.

Berger, Earl. *The Covenant and the Sword: Arab-Israeli Relations, 1948–56*. London: Routledge & Kegan Paul, 1965.

Bromberger, Merry, and Serge Bromberger. *Secrets of Suez*. London: Sidgwick and Jackson, 1957.

Burns, E. L. M. *Between Arab and Israel*. New York: Ivan Oblensky, 1962.

Campbell, John C. *Defense of the Middle East*. Rev. ed. New York: Harper, 1960.

Childers, Erskine B. *The Road to Suez*. London: MacGibbon & Kee, 1962.

Dayan, Moshe. *Diary of the Suez Campaign*. New York: Harper, 1966.

Eden, Anthony. *Full Circle: The Memoirs of Sir Anthony Eden*. Boston: Houghton Mifflin Co., 1960.

Finer, Herman. *Dulles over Suez*. Chicago: Quadrangle Books, 1964.

Heiman, Leo. "Moscow's Export Arsenal: The Soviet Bloc and the Middle Eastern Arms Race." *East Europe*, vol. 13, no. 5 (May 1964).

Marshall, S. L. A. *Sinai Victory*. New York: William Morrow, 1958.

O'Ballance, Edgar. *The Sinai Campaign, 1956*. London: Faber and Faber, 1959.

———. "The Egyptian Army." *Royal United Service Institution Journal*, February 1958.

Robertson, Terrence. *Crisis: The Inside Story of the Suez Conspiracy*. New York: Atheneum, 1965.

Royal Institute of International Affairs. *British Interests in the Mediterranean and Middle East*. London: Oxford University Press, 1958.

Kashmir Conflict, 1947–1965

Auchinleck, Claude. "The Final Phase of the British-Indian Army." *Great Britain and the East* (London), October 1948.

Birdwood, Lord. *India and Pakistan: A Continent Decides*. New York: Frederick A. Praeger, 1954.

Brecher, Michael. *The Struggle for Kashmir*. New York: Oxford University Press, 1953.

Cooke, Noel. "The Tribesmen in Kashmir." *Eastern World*, vol. 2, nos. 6–7 (June–July 1948).

Das Gupta, Jyoti Bhusan, *Indo-Pakistan Relations, 1947–1955*. Amsterdam: Djambatan, 1958.

Goddard, E. N. "Indian Review." *Army Quarterly* (London), vol. 57, no. 1 (October 1948).

Harrison, Selig. *India: The Most Dangerous Decades*. Princeton: Princeton University Press, 1960.

Hartwell, J. R. "The Kashmir Deadlock." *Eastern World*, vol. 2, no. 3 (March 1948).

———. "Whither the New Dominions." *Eastern World*, vol. 1, no. 6 (October 1947).

Heiman, Leo. "Lessons from the War in Kashmir." *Military Review*, February 1966.

Irwin, S. F. "The Indian Army in Partition." *Army Quarterly* (London), vol. 56, no. 2 (July 1948).

Korbel, Josef. *Danger in Kashmir*. Princeton: Princeton University Press, 1966.

Maurele, C. "Le conflit indo-pakistanais." *Revue de Défense Nationale*, no. 22 (janvier 1966).

Menon, V. P. *The Story of the Integration of the Indian States*. New York: Macmillan Co., 1956.

Messervy, Frank. "Kashmir." *Asiatic Review*, vol. 45, no. 161 (January 1949).

Mountbatten, Earl. "Lord Mountbatten on His Viceroyalty." *Asiatic Review*, vol. 44, no. 160 (October 1948).

Palmer, Norman D. *South Asia and United States Policy*. Boston: Houghton Mifflin Co., 1966.

Price, M. Philips. "Impressions of Pakistan, Kashmir and the North-West Frontier." *Asiatic Review*, vol. 45, no. 162 (April 1949).

Rowlands, Archibald. "The Financial and Economic Prospects of Pakistan." *Journal of the Royal Central Asian Society*, vol. 35, nos. 3–4 (July–August 1948).

Thorner, Alice. "The Kashmir Conflict." *Middle East Journal*, vol. 3, nos. 1–2 (January and April 1949).

"Some Strategical Aspects of Pakistan." *Army Quarterly* (London), vol. 57, no. 1 (October 1948).

Spate, Oscar. "The Resources of Pakistan." *Eastern World*, vol. 1, no. 7 (November 1947).

Strettell, Dashwood. "The Indian Army before and after 1947." *Journal of the Royal Central Asian Society*, vol. 35, no. 2 (April 1948).

Wilcox, Wayne A. *Pakistan: The Consolidation of a Nation*. New York: Columbia University Press, 1963.

Malayan Insurgency,
1948–1960

Benham, Frederic. *The National Income of Malaya, 1947–49 (with a Note on 1950)*. Singapore: Government Printing Office, 1951.

Brimmell, J. H. *A Short History of the Malayan Communist Party*. Singapore: Donald Moore, MacDarald House, 1956.

Clutterbuck, Richard L. *The Long, Long War*. New York: Frederick A. Praeger, 1966.

Douglas, William O. *North from Malaya: Adventure on Five Points*. New York: Doubleday & Company, 1953.

Federation of Malaya. *Official Year Book, 1962*. Vol. 2. Kuala Lumpur: Government Press, 1962.

Hanna, Willard A. *Sequel to Colonialism: The 1957–1960 Foundations for Malaysia*. New York: American Universities Field Staff, 1965.

Hanrahan, Gene Z. *The Communist Struggle in Malaya*. New York: Institute of Pacific Relations, 1954.

International Bank for Reconstruction and Development. *The Economic Development of Malaya*. Baltimore: Johns Hopkins Press, 1955.

Maday, Bela C., et al. *Area Handbook for Malaysia and Singapore*. Washington, D.C.: U.S. Government Printing Office, July 1965.

Malaysia Official Year Book, 1963. Vol. 3. Kuala Lumpur: Government Press, 1964.

McLane, Charles B. *Soviet Strategies in Southeast Asia: An Exploration of Eastern Policy under Lenin and Stalin*. Princeton: Princeton University Press, 1966.

Miller, Harry. *The Communist Menace in Malaya*. New York: Frederick A. Praeger, 1954.

Mills, Lennox A. *Southeast Asia: Illusion and Reality in Politics and Economics*. Minneapolis: University of Minnesota Press, 1964.

Peterson, A. H., G. C. Reinhardt, and E. E. Conger, eds. "Symposium on the Role of Airpower in Counterinsurgency and Unconventional Warfare: The Malayan Emergency." Santa Monica, Calif.: RAND Corporation, 1963.

Purcell, Victor. *The Chinese in Southeast Asia*. London: Oxford University Press, 1965.

Pye, Lucian W. *Guerrilla Communism in Malaya*. Princeton: Princeton University Press, 1956.

Ratnam, K. J. *Communalism and the Political Process in Malaya*. Kuala Lumpur: University of Malaya Press for the University of Singapore, 1965.

Seth, D. R. "The Employment of Air Power in Malaya." *India Quarterly*, vol. 11, no. 2 (April–June 1955).

Silcock, T. H., and E. K. Fisk, eds. *The Political Economy of Independent Malaya: A Case Study in Development*. Berkeley and Los Angeles: University of California Press, 1963.

Tregonning, K. G. *A History of Modern Malaya.* London: Eastern University Press, 1964.

Wang, Gungwu, ed. *Malaysia: A Survey.* New York: Frederick A. Praeger, 1964.

Spanish Civil War, 1936–1939

Aznar, Manuel. *Historia militar de la guerra de España (1936–1939).* 3rd ed. 3 vols. Madrid: Editora Nacional, 1958–1963.

Bolloten, Burnett. *The Grand Camouflage.* New York: Frederick A. Praeger, 1961.

Brenan, Gerald. *The Spanish Labyrinth.* 2nd ed. New York: Macmillan Co., 1950.

Broué, Pierre, and Emile Témime. *La révolution et la guerre d'Espagne.* Paris: Editions du Minuit, 1961; and (in translation) Cambridge, Mass.: The M.I.T. Press, 1970.

Carr, Raymond. *Spain: 1808–1939.* Oxford: Clarendon Press, 1966.

Cattell, David T. *Soviet Diplomacy and the Spanish Civil War.* Berkeley and Los Angeles: University of California Press, 1957.

———. *Communism and the Spanish Civil War.* Berkeley and Los Angeles: University of California Press, 1955.

Davis, William H. "The Naval Side of the Spanish Civil War, 1936–1939." *U.S. Naval InstituteProceedings,* vol. 66, no. 6 (June 1940).

Padelford, Norman J. *International Law and Diplomacy in the Spanish Civil Strife.* New York: Macmillan Co., 1939.

Thomas, Hugh. *The Spanish Civil War.* New York: Harper, 1961.

Van der Esch, P. A. M. *Prelude to War: The International Repercussions of the Spanish Civil War (1936–1939).* The Hague: Martinus Nijhoff, 1951.

Whaley, Barton. "Guerrillas in the Spanish Civil War." Cambridge, Mass.: M.I.T., Center for International Studies, 1967.

USSR-Iran Conflict, 1941–1947

Arfa, Hassan. *Under Five Shahs.* London: John Murray, 1964.

Cottam, Richard W. *Nationalism in Iran.* Pittsburgh, Pa.: University of Pittsburgh Press, 1964.

Fatemi, Nasrollan Saifpour. *Oil Diplomacy: Powderkeg in Iran.* New York: Whittier Books, 1954.

Hamzavi, A. H. *Persia and the Powers: An Account of Diplomatic Relations, 1941–1946.* London: Hutchinson, 1946.

Lenczowski, George. *Russia and the West in Iran, 1918–1948: A Study in Big-Power Rivalry.* Ithaca, N.Y.: Cornell University Press, 1949.

Pahlavi, Mohammed Reza Shah, Shahinshah of Iran. *Mission for My Country.* New York: McGraw-Hill, 1961.

Roosevelt, Archie, Jr. "The Kurdish Republic of Mahabad." *Middle East Journal,* vol. 1, no. 3 (July 1947).

Rossow, Robert, Jr. "The Battle of Azerbaijan, 1946." *Middle East Journal,* vol. 10, no. 1 (Winter 1946).

Shawdran, Benjamin. *The Middle East, Oil and the Great Powers.* 2nd ed., rev. New York: Council for Middle Eastern Affairs, 1949.

U.S. Department of the Army. *U.S. Army Handbook for Iran.* Washington, D.C., 1963.

Van Wagenen, Richard W., in consultation with T. Cuyler Young. "The Iranian Case: 1946." New York: Carnegie Endowment for International Peace, 1952.

Whaley, Barton. "Soviet Covert Arms Aid." Cambridge, Mass.: M.I.T., Center for International Studies, 1965.

Venezuelan Insurgency, 1959–1963

Alexander, Robert J. *The Venezuelan Democratic Revolution.* New Brunswick, N.J.: Rutgers University Press, 1964.

American University. Special Operations Research Office. *U.S. Army Area Handbook for Venezuela.* Washington, D.C.: Government Printing Office, 1964.

Atlantic Research Corporation. "Castro-Communist Insurgency in Venezuela: A Study of Insurgency and Counterinsurgency Operations and Techniques in Venezuela, 1960–64." Submitted to the Advanced Research Projects Agency, U.S. Department of Defense, Washington, D.C., December 1964.

Friedmann, John. *Venezuela: From Doctrine to Dialogue.* Syracuse, N.Y.: Syracuse University Press, 1965.

Gall, Norman. "Venezuela's Guerrillas." *New Statesman*, April 16, 1965.

International Bank for Reconstruction and Development. *The Economic Development of Venezuela.* Baltimore: The Johns Hopkins Press, 1961.

Listov, V. "Venezuelan Guerrillas." *International Affairs* (Moscow), December 1963.

Martínez Suárez, Félix. *Tres años de Castro comunismo: Venezuela ante la agresión totalitaria.* Caracas, 1964.

Martz, John D. "The Venezuelan Elections of December 1, 1963." 3 vols. Washington, D.C.: Institute for the Comparative Study of Political Systems, 1964.

Pan American Union. General Secretariat. Organization of American States. *Applications of the Inter-American Treaty of Reciprocal Assistance, Vol. II, 1960–64: Examination of the Acts Denounced by the Government of Venezuela.* Washington, D.C.: Pan American Union, Department of Legal Affairs, 1964.

Sorensen, John L. "Venezuelan Society and Unconventional Warfare." China Lake, Calif.: U.S. Naval Ordnance Test Station, 1966.

U.S. Congress. House of Representatives. Subcommittee on Inter-American Affairs. *Hearings: Castro-Communist Subversion in the Western Hemisphere.* 88th Congress, 1st session. Washington, D.C., 1963.

U.S. Congress. Senate. Committee on the Judiciary. Subcommittee to Investigate the Administration of the Internal Security Act and Other Internal Security Laws. *Hearings: Red Chinese Infiltration into Latin America.* 89th Congress, 1st session. Washington, D.C., 1965.

Venezuela. Ministry of Interior Relations. *Memoria y Cuenta.* Annual. Caracas, Imprenta Nacional.

Index